# Handbook of
# Governmental
# Accounting

# PUBLIC ADMINISTRATION AND PUBLIC POLICY

## A Comprehensive Publication Program

EDITOR-IN-CHIEF

### EVAN M. BERMAN

*Distinguished University Professor*
*J. William Fulbright Distinguished Scholar*
*National Chengchi University*
*Taipei, Taiwan*

*Founding Editor*

### JACK RABIN

1. *Public Administration as a Developing Discipline,* Robert T. Golembiewski
2. *Comparative National Policies on Health Care,* Milton I. Roemer, M.D.
3. *Exclusionary Injustice: The Problem of Illegally Obtained Evidence,* Steven R. Schlesinger
5. *Organization Development in Public Administration,* edited by Robert T. Golembiewski and William B. Eddy
7. *Approaches to Planned Change,* Robert T. Golembiewski
8. *Program Evaluation at HEW,* edited by James G. Abert
9. *The States and the Metropolis,* Patricia S. Florestano and Vincent L. Marando
11. *Changing Bureaucracies: Understanding the Organization before Selecting the Approach,* William A. Medina
12. *Handbook on Public Budgeting and Financial Management,* edited by Jack Rabin and Thomas D. Lynch
15. *Handbook on Public Personnel Administration and Labor Relations,* edited by Jack Rabin, Thomas Vocino, W. Bartley Hildreth, and Gerald J. Miller
19. *Handbook of Organization Management,* edited by William B. Eddy
22. *Politics and Administration: Woodrow Wilson and American Public Administration,* edited by Jack Rabin and James S. Bowman
23. *Making and Managing Policy: Formulation, Analysis, Evaluation,* edited by G. Ronald Gilbert
25. *Decision Making in the Public Sector,* edited by Lloyd G. Nigro
26. *Managing Administration,* edited by Jack Rabin, Samuel Humes, and Brian S. Morgan
27. *Public Personnel Update,* edited by Michael Cohen and Robert T. Golembiewski
28. *State and Local Government Administration,* edited by Jack Rabin and Don Dodd
29. *Public Administration: A Bibliographic Guide to the Literature,* Howard E. McCurdy

31. *Handbook of Information Resource Management,* edited by Jack Rabin and Edward M. Jackowski

32. *Public Administration in Developed Democracies: A Comparative Study,* edited by Donald C. Rowat

33. *The Politics of Terrorism: Third Edition,* edited by Michael Stohl

34. *Handbook on Human Services Administration,* edited by Jack Rabin and Marcia B. Steinhauer

36. *Ethics for Bureaucrats: An Essay on Law and Values, Second Edition,* John A. Rohr

37. *The Guide to the Foundations of Public Administration,* Daniel W. Martin

39. *Terrorism and Emergency Management: Policy and Administration,* William L. Waugh, Jr.

40. *Organizational Behavior and Public Management: Second Edition,* Michael L. Vasu, Debra W. Stewart, and G. David Garson

43. *Government Financial Management Theory,* Gerald J. Miller

46. *Handbook of Public Budgeting,* edited by Jack Rabin

49. *Handbook of Court Administration and Management,* edited by Steven W. Hays and Cole Blease Graham, Jr.

50. *Handbook of Comparative Public Budgeting and Financial Management,* edited by Thomas D. Lynch and Lawrence L. Martin

53. *Encyclopedia of Policy Studies: Second Edition,* edited by Stuart S. Nagel

54. *Handbook of Regulation and Administrative Law,* edited by David H. Rosenbloom and Richard D. Schwartz

55. *Handbook of Bureaucracy,* edited by Ali Farazmand

56. *Handbook of Public Sector Labor Relations,* edited by Jack Rabin, Thomas Vocino, W. Bartley Hildreth, and Gerald J. Miller

57. *Practical Public Management,* Robert T. Golembiewski

58. *Handbook of Public Personnel Administration,* edited by Jack Rabin, Thomas Vocino, W. Bartley Hildreth, and Gerald J. Miller

60. *Handbook of Debt Management,* edited by Gerald J. Miller

61. *Public Administration and Law: Second Edition,* David H. Rosenbloom and Rosemary O'Leary

62. *Handbook of Local Government Administration,* edited by John J. Gargan

63. *Handbook of Administrative Communication,* edited by James L. Garnett and Alexander Kouzmin

64. *Public Budgeting and Finance: Fourth Edition,* edited by Robert T. Golembiewski and Jack Rabin

67. *Handbook of Public Finance,* edited by Fred Thompson and Mark T. Green

68. *Organizational Behavior and Public Management: Third Edition,* Michael L. Vasu, Debra W. Stewart, and G. David Garson

69. *Handbook of Economic Development,* edited by Kuotsai Tom Liou

70. *Handbook of Health Administration and Policy,* edited by Anne Osborne Kilpatrick and James A. Johnson

72. *Handbook on Taxation,* edited by W. Bartley Hildreth and James A. Richardson

73. *Handbook of Comparative Public Administration in the Asia-Pacific Basin,* edited by Hoi-kwok Wong and Hon S. Chan

74. *Handbook of Global Environmental Policy and Administration,* edited by Dennis L. Soden and Brent S. Steel

75. *Handbook of State Government Administration,* edited by John J. Gargan

76. *Handbook of Global Legal Policy,* edited by Stuart S. Nagel

78. *Handbook of Global Economic Policy,* edited by Stuart S. Nagel

79. *Handbook of Strategic Management: Second Edition,* edited by Jack Rabin, Gerald J. Miller, and W. Bartley Hildreth

80. *Handbook of Global International Policy,* edited by Stuart S. Nagel

81. *Handbook of Organizational Consultation: Second Edition,* edited by Robert T. Golembiewski

82. *Handbook of Global Political Policy,* edited by Stuart S. Nagel

83. *Handbook of Global Technology Policy,* edited by Stuart S. Nagel

84. *Handbook of Criminal Justice Administration,* edited by M. A. DuPont-Morales, Michael K. Hooper, and Judy H. Schmidt

85. *Labor Relations in the Public Sector: Third Edition,* edited by Richard C. Kearney

86. *Handbook of Administrative Ethics: Second Edition,* edited by Terry L. Cooper

87. *Handbook of Organizational Behavior: Second Edition,* edited by Robert T. Golembiewski

88. *Handbook of Global Social Policy,* edited by Stuart S. Nagel and Amy Robb

89. *Public Administration: A Comparative Perspective, Sixth Edition,* Ferrel Heady

90. *Handbook of Public Quality Management,* edited by Ronald J. Stupak and Peter M. Leitner

91. *Handbook of Public Management Practice and Reform,* edited by Kuotsai Tom Liou

93. *Handbook of Crisis and Emergency Management,* edited by Ali Farazmand

94. *Handbook of Comparative and Development Public Administration: Second Edition,* edited by Ali Farazmand

95. *Financial Planning and Management in Public Organizations,* Alan Walter Steiss and Emeka O. Cyprian Nwagwu

96. *Handbook of International Health Care Systems,* edited by Khi V. Thai, Edward T. Wimberley, and Sharon M. McManus

97. *Handbook of Monetary Policy,* edited by Jack Rabin and Glenn L. Stevens

98. *Handbook of Fiscal Policy,* edited by Jack Rabin and Glenn L. Stevens

99. *Public Administration: An Interdisciplinary Critical Analysis,* edited by Eran Vigoda

100. *Ironies in Organizational Development: Second Edition, Revised and Expanded,* edited by Robert T. Golembiewski

101. *Science and Technology of Terrorism and Counterterrorism,* edited by Tushar K. Ghosh, Mark A. Prelas, Dabir S. Viswanath, and Sudarshan K. Loyalka

102. *Strategic Management for Public and Nonprofit Organizations,* Alan Walter Steiss

103. *Case Studies in Public Budgeting and Financial Management: Second Edition,* edited by Aman Khan and W. Bartley Hildreth

104. *Handbook of Conflict Management,* edited by William J. Pammer, Jr. and Jerri Killian

105. *Chaos Organization and Disaster Management,* Alan Kirschenbaum

106. *Handbook of Gay, Lesbian, Bisexual, and Transgender Administration and Policy,* edited by Wallace Swan

107. *Public Productivity Handbook: Second Edition,* edited by Marc Holzer

108. *Handbook of Developmental Policy Studies,* edited by Gedeon M. Mudacumura, Desta Mebratu and M. Shamsul Haque

109. *Bioterrorism in Medical and Healthcare Administration,* Laure Paquette

110. *International Public Policy and Management: Policy Learning Beyond Regional, Cultural, and Political Boundaries,* edited by David Levi-Faur and Eran Vigoda-Gadot

111. *Handbook of Public Information Systems, Second Edition,* edited by G. David Garson

112. *Handbook of Public Sector Economics,* edited by Donijo Robbins

113. *Handbook of Public Administration and Policy in the European Union,* edited by M. Peter van der Hoek

114. *Nonproliferation Issues for Weapons of Mass Destruction,* Mark A. Prelas and Michael S. Peck

115. *Common Ground, Common Future: Moral Agency in Public Administration, Professions, and Citizenship,* Charles Garofalo and Dean Geuras

116. *Handbook of Organization Theory and Management: The Philosophical Approach, Second Edition,* edited by Thomas D. Lynch and Peter L. Cruise

117. *International Development Governance,* edited by Ahmed Shafiqul Huque and Habib Zafarullah

118. *Sustainable Development Policy and Administration,* edited by Gedeon M. Mudacumura, Desta Mebratu, and M. Shamsul Haque

119. *Public Financial Management,* edited by Howard A. Frank

120. *Handbook of Juvenile Justice: Theory and Practice,* edited by Barbara Sims and Pamela Preston

121. *Emerging Infectious Diseases and the Threat to Occupational Health in the U.S. and Canada,* edited by William Charney

122. *Handbook of Technology Management in Public Administration,* edited by David Greisler and Ronald J. Stupak

123. *Handbook of Decision Making,* edited by Göktuğ Morçöl

124. *Handbook of Public Administration, Third Edition,* edited by Jack Rabin, W. Bartley Hildreth, and Gerald J. Miller

125. *Handbook of Public Policy Analysis,* edited by Frank Fischer, Gerald J. Miller, and Mara S. Sidney

126. *Elements of Effective Governance: Measurement, Accountability and Participation,* edited by Kathe Callahan

127. *American Public Service: Radical Reform and the Merit System,* edited by James S. Bowman and Jonathan P. West

128. *Handbook of Transportation Policy and Administration,* edited by Jeremy Plant

129. *The Art and Practice of Court Administration,* Alexander B. Aikman

130. *Handbook of Globalization, Governance, and Public Administration,* edited by Ali Farazmand and Jack Pinkowski

131. *Handbook of Globalization and the Environment,* edited by Khi V. Thai, Dianne Rahm, and Jerrell D. Coggburn

132. *Personnel Management in Government: Politics and Process, Sixth Edition,* Norma M. Riccucci and Katherine C. Naff

133. *Handbook of Police Administration,* edited by Jim Ruiz and Don Hummer

134. *Handbook of Research Methods in Public Administration, Second Edition,* edited by Kaifeng Yang and Gerald J. Miller

135. *Social and Economic Control of Alcohol: The 21st Amendment in the 21st Century,* edited by Carole L. Jurkiewicz and Murphy J. Painter

136. *Government Public Relations: A Reader,* edited by Mordecai Lee

137. *Handbook of Military Administration,* edited by Jeffrey A. Weber and Johan Eliasson

138. *Disaster Management Handbook,* edited by Jack Pinkowski

139. *Homeland Security Handbook,* edited by Jack Pinkowski

140. *Health Capital and Sustainable Socioeconomic Development,* edited by Patricia A. Cholewka and Mitra M. Motlagh

141. *Handbook of Administrative Reform: An International Perspective,* edited by Jerri Killian and Niklas Eklund

142. *Government Budget Forecasting: Theory and Practice,* edited by Jinping Sun and Thomas D. Lynch

143. *Handbook of Long-Term Care Administration and Policy,* edited by Cynthia Massie Mara and Laura Katz Olson

144. *Handbook of Employee Benefits and Administration,* edited by Christopher G. Reddick and Jerrell D. Coggburn

145. *Business Improvement Districts: Research, Theories, and Controversies,* edited by Göktuğ Morçöl, Lorlene Hoyt, Jack W. Meek, and Ulf Zimmermann

146. *International Handbook of Public Procurement,* edited by Khi V. Thai

147. *State and Local Pension Fund Management,* Jun Peng

148. *Contracting for Services in State and Local Government Agencies,* William Sims Curry

149. *Understanding Research Methods: A Guide for the Public and Nonprofit Manager,* Donijo Robbins

150. *Labor Relations in the Public Sector, Fourth Edition,* Richard Kearney

151. *Performance-Based Management Systems: Effective Implementation and Maintenance,* Patria de Lancer Julnes

152. *Handbook of Governmental Accounting,* edited by Frederic B. Bogui

*Available Electronically*

*Principles and Practices of Public Administration,* edited by
Jack Rabin, Robert F. Munzenrider, and Sherrie M. Bartell

PublicADMINISTRATION*netBASE*

# Handbook of Governmental Accounting

Frederic B. Bogui

CRC Press
Taylor & Francis Group
Boca Raton   London   New York

CRC Press is an imprint of the
Taylor & Francis Group, an **informa** business

CRC Press
Taylor & Francis Group
6000 Broken Sound Parkway NW, Suite 300
Boca Raton, FL 33487-2742

© 2009 by Taylor & Francis Group, LLC
CRC Press is an imprint of Taylor & Francis Group, an Informa business

No claim to original U.S. Government works
Printed in the United States of America on acid-free paper
10 9 8 7 6 5 4 3 2 1

International Standard Book Number-13: 978-1-57444-758-3 (Hardcover)

### Library of Congress Cataloging-in-Publication Data

Handbook of governmental accounting / editors, Frederic Bogui.
    p. cm. -- (Public administration and public policy ; 152)
    Includes bibliographical references and index.
    ISBN 978-1-57444-758-3 (alk. paper)
    1. Finance, Public--United States--States--Accounting. 2. Local finance--United States--Accounting. 3. Finance, Public--United States--Accounting. 4. Budget--United States. 5. Finance, Public--Accounting. I. Bogui, Frederic. II. Title. III. Series.

HJ9816.H36 2009
657'.83500973--dc22
                                      2008030230

**Visit the Taylor & Francis Web site at**
**http://www.taylorandfrancis.com**

**and the CRC Press Web site at**
**http://www.crcpress.com**

To My Dearest Dr. Victoire M. Bogui

# Contents

Preface...................................................................................................xv

Acknowledgments ................................................................................xvii

About the Editor...................................................................................xix

Contributors.........................................................................................xxi

1   The Growth of GAAP ...........................................................1
    G. ROBERT SMITH, JR.

2   Progressive Government Budgeting.......................................71
    GERALD J. MILLER AND DONIJO ROBBINS

3   Expenditures and Revenues in U.S. Governments .............129
    ZHIRONG ZHAO

4   Fund Accounting.................................................................149
    FREDERIC B. BOGUI

5   The General Fund................................................................161
    ROBERT S. KRAVCHUK

6   Debt Service Funds.............................................................191
    DWAYNE N. McSWAIN

7   Capital Projects Funds .......................................................215
    BARBARA CHANEY

8   Proprietary Funds ..............................................................249
    JOHN D. WONG, CARL D. EKSTROM, STEPHEN COBERLEY, AND
    VINCENT MILLER

9   Fiduciary Funds.................................................................317
    JUN PENG

**10** Governmental Financial Reporting......................................................339
RANDALL L. KINNERSLEY

**11** Government-Wide Financial Benchmarks for State Governments.....389
CRAIG L. JOHNSON

**12** Auditing Governmental Entities .........................................................409
SUZANNE LOWENSOHN AND KRISTEN REILLY

**13** Federal Accounting and Financial Reporting ....................................439
RICHARD FONTENROSE

**14** International Public Sector Accounting Standards...........................491
JESSE HUGHES

Index .................................................................................................519

# Preface

It is in compliance with the earnest requests of colleagues and friends that I have embarked on the task of editing a handbook of governmental accounting. Practitioners in the private sector, public administrators, and students in colleges and universities will find this handbook a useful reference. We hope our readers from a diverse range of fields will use it to gain understanding and familiarity with government accounting concepts.

Drawing on the expertise of a distinguished group of contributors, the handbook begins with in-depth discussions of the growth of Generally Accepted Accounting Principles (GAAP), budgeting, revenues, and expenditures in U.S. governments that highlight greater levels of accountability in government finance. The book covers governmental funds, proprietary funds, fiduciary funds, financial reporting, and the latest developments in auditing requirements for governmental entities. While the majority of the chapters relate to state and local governments in the United States, the book also provides insight into federal accounting and international public sector accounting standards to introduce readers to the broader scope of government accounting. This handbook is a complete manual to a wide range of governmental accounting topics that fall under the Governmental Accounting Standards Board (GASB) Statement 34 reporting model, and subsequent Statements, which have significantly changed governmental financial statements presentation.

The chief objective of this handbook is to contribute to the readers' appreciation and understanding of governmental accounting. The handbook's contents reflect the increasing complexities in this dynamic field.

The contributing authors made it possible to bring this handbook to fruition. As the editor, I have been enriched by their scholarship and technical skills, and to each of the contributors I tender my great and sincere appreciation.

**Frederic B. Bogui**

# Acknowledgments

I am especially grateful to Terry Patton at Midwestern State University who provided many leads to find a number of contributors for this handbook.

I am also grateful to Prof. Gerald J. Miller at Arizona State University. Jerry is a mentor and a supporter of this project.

I extend my thanks to Prof. Marc Holzer at Rutgers University. Dr. Holzer is the dean of the School of Public Affairs and Administration at Rutgers University–Newark.

And I would like to remember the late Dr. Jack Rabin, founding editor of the Public Administration and Public Policy series.

# About the Editor

**Frederic B. Bogui** is a senior university lecturer of accounting and finance at New Jersey Institute of Technology. His doctoral work at Rutgers University–Newark focused on public finance. A management consultant, Dr. Bogui is a certified public accountant (CPA) and a member of the American Institute of Certified Public Accountants (AICPA) and the New Jersey Society of CPAs (NJSCPA).

# Contributors

**Frederic B. Bogui, Ph.D., CPA**
School of Management
New Jersey Institute of Technology
Newark, New Jersey

**Barbara Chaney, Ph.D., CPA**
School of Business Administration
University of Montana
Missoula, Montana

**Stephen Coberley, MPA**
Certified Public Finance Officer
(CPFO)
City of Wichita
Wichita, Kansas

**Carl D. Ekstrom, Ph.D.**
School of Public Administration
University of Nebraska at Omaha
Omaha, Nebraska

**Richard Fontenrose, CPA, CGFM**
Federal Accounting Standards
Advisory Board
Washington, DC

**Jesse Hughes, Ph.D., CPA, CIA, CGFM**
Professor Emeritus of Accounting
Old Dominion University
Norfolk, Virginia

**Craig L. Johnson, Ph.D.**
School of Public and Environmental
Affairs
Indiana University
Bloomington, Indiana

**Randall L. Kinnersley, Ph.D., CPA, CGFM**
Department of Accounting
Gordon Ford College of Business
Western Kentucky University
Bowling Green, Kentucky

**Robert S. Kravchuk, Ph.D., CMA**
Department of Political Science
University of North
Carolina–Charlotte
Charlotte, North Carolina

**Suzanne Lowensohn, Ph.D., CPA**
College of Business
Colorado State University
Fort Collins, Colorado

**Dwayne N. McSwain, Ph.D., CPA**
Department of Accounting
Jennings A. Jones College of Business
Middle Tennessee State University
Murfreesboro, Tennessee

**Gerald J. Miller, Ph.D.**
School of Public Affairs
Arizona State University
Phoenix, Arizona

**Vincent Miller, MPA**
Office of Institutional Research
Wichita State University
Wichita, Kansas

**Jun Peng, Ph.D.**
School of Public Administration
and Policy
University of Arizona
Tucson, Arizona

**Kristen Reilly, CPA**
College of Business
Colorado State University
Fort Collins, Colorado

**Donijo Robbins, Ph.D.**
School of Public and Nonprofit
Administration
Grand Valley State University
Grand Rapids, Michigan

**G. Robert Smith, Jr., Ph.D., CPA,
CGFM**
Department of Accounting
Jennings A. Jones College of Business
Middle Tennessee State University
Murfreesboro, Tennessee

**John D. Wong, J.D., Ph.D.**
Hugo Wall School of Urban and
Public Affairs
Wichita State University
Wichita, Kansas

**Zhirong Zhao, Ph.D.**
Hubert H. Humphrey Institute of
Public Affairs
University of Minnesota
Minneapolis, Minnesota

# Chapter 1

# The Growth of GAAP

## G. Robert Smith, Jr.

*Middle Tennessee State University, Jennings A. Jones College of Business, Department of Accounting*

## Contents

1.1  GAAP: The Early Years ........................................................................2
1.2  The Growth of GAAP: The Middle Years........................................3
1.3  The Growth of GAAP: The GASB ..................................................7
    1.3.1  The First Board ........................................................................10
    1.3.2  The GASB Gets Rolling............................................................11
1.4  The 5-Year Review...........................................................................22
1.5  The Original Board's "Last Stand" ................................................24
1.6  New Board, New Issues, New Standards.......................................27
1.7  A New Board—and a Whole New Ball Game ...............................42
    1.7.1  Changing of the Guard............................................................42
    1.7.2  The Preliminary to the Big Show .............................................43
    1.7.3  The New Reporting Model ......................................................44
    1.7.4  Impact on the Funds Statements.............................................49
    1.7.5  The Change in Focus ...............................................................52
    1.7.6  The Government-Wide Financial Statements ...........................54
    1.7.7  Notes to the Financial Statements...........................................57
    1.7.8  MD&A and Other RSI ...........................................................58
1.8  More Recent GASB Standards .......................................................60
1.9  Conclusion ......................................................................................64

## 1.1 GAAP: The Early Years

Seventy-five years ago, there were no generally accepted accounting principles (GAAP)—at least as we know them today—in the United States. Some might say the lack of GAAP was at least a contributing factor in the stock market crash of 1929. With the ensuing Great Depression and America's attempts to recover from it, some felt that it was time to get the accounting house in order.

Among the many efforts of the Franklin Delano Roosevelt administration to help get the country on the road to recovery was designating a federal agency to have the authority and responsibility to set GAAP. In the 1933 Securities Act, this agency was the Federal Trade Commission. Having been around since 1914, this agency seemed to be a natural for this designation. However, it was soon realized that another organization with broader powers was necessary. In the 1934 Securities Act, Congress created just such an organization: the Securities and Exchange Commission (SEC).

Interestingly, the SEC did not immediately act on setting accounting standards. Instead, the agency adopted an approach of giving the authority to set these standards (while retaining the responsibility) to the private sector. In existence at this time was an organization known as the American Institute of Accountants (AIA). This organization was already administering the certified public accountants examination as well as attempting to set auditing standards for the United States. The SEC felt the AIA would be a natural organization for this new authority for setting accounting standards. As a result, it fell to the AIA to get the ball rolling on GAAP.

The history of GAAP can be summarized as shown in Figure 1.1. As you can see, there were two sectors of the economy that required GAAP: the private sector (made up of publicly traded companies and other business entities) and the public sector (consisting of state and local governments, or SLGs). As discussed previously, the AIA assumed the authority for the private sector. It established the Committee on Accounting Procedure (CAP) to establish GAAP. At the same time, a government organization in Chicago, the Municipal Finance Officers Association (MFOA), assumed the authority for the public sector. The MFOA created the National Committee on Municipal Accounting (NCMA).

Rarely, if ever, did these two organizations—the CAP and NCMA—interact. In theory, the CAP could have set accounting standards that applied to the public sector, but it did not seem to do so. Also, the NCMA could have adopted the CAP standards for the public sector, but the limited information available indicates that this did not happen. Unfortunately, much of what the NCMA did has been lost (for reasons that will be explained shortly). However, we do have a good record of some of the organization's bulletins that established early guidelines of the principles of municipal accounting.

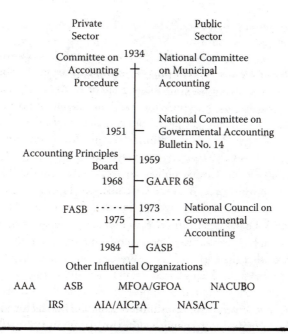

| Private Sector | | Public Sector |
|---|---|---|
| Committee on Accounting Procedure | 1934 | National Committee on Municipal Accounting |
| | 1951 | National Committee on Governmental Accounting Bulletin No. 14 |
| Accounting Principles Board | 1959 | |
| 1968 | | GAAFR 68 |
| FASB | 1973 | National Council on Governmental Accounting |
| 1975 | | |
| 1984 | | GASB |

Other Influential Organizations

AAA        ASB        MFOA/GFOA        NACUBO
IRS        AIA/AICPA        NASACT

**Figure 1.1   Development of governmental and financial accounting standards.**

## 1.2  The Growth of GAAP: The Middle Years

The CAP was in existence for 25 years. It eventually issued 51 accounting research bulletins for the private sector. In 1959, some interesting name changes occurred in the private sector accounting standard-setting process. The old AIA became the American Institute of Certified Public Accountants (AICPA). The AICPA then reconstituted the CAP as the Accounting Principles Board (APB).

A similar name change had occurred in the public sector 8 years earlier. In an apparent effort to broaden the perspective of the NCMA, the MFOA changed its name to the National Committee on Governmental Accounting (NCGA). Other than changing "municipal" to "governmental," little else seems to have changed. The two organizations—APB and NCGA—went about setting their accounting standards pretty much the same way as the CAP and NCMA had done previously.

A very significant event occurred in the public sector in 1968: the MFOA published the first edition of *Governmental Accounting, Auditing, and Financial Reporting*. This volume, known both as the GAAFR and as the "Blue Book" (because of its color), represented a milestone in GAAP process in the public sector. As stated in the foreword, the GAAFR was

> ... the eighteenth publication of the National Committee on
> Governmental Accounting (NCGA), combines and revises the fol-
> lowing publications: *Municipal Accounting and Auditing* (1951), and
> *A Standard Classification of Municipal Accounts* (1953).... There is now
> presented in one volume most of the NCGA's releases over the many
> years of its existence, modified to meet the current needs. [GAAFR,
> 1968, iii]

Indeed, this "one volume" provided a compilation of GAAP for the public sector,
much as ARB #43 provided a restatement of all previously issued accounting research
bulletins (ARBs) of the CAP. In 14 chapters and 5 appendices, the GAAFR

- ■ Established the basic principles of governmental accounting
- ■ Outlined on how to use the various fund types and account groups
- ■ Described what the annual financial report should look like
- ■ Discussed how to audit governments

Just how broadly accepted this first edition of the Blue Book was can be seen in the
foreword of the second edition (published by the MFOA in 1980). It states that over
40,000 copies were printed and distributed in a 12-year period. The foreword also
notes that, "Unlike 1968 GAAFR, this text neither establishes nor authoritatively
interprets GAAP for governments." This is a somewhat indirect way of indicating
that the 1968 edition was authoritative GAAP.

However, this authoritative level didn't last long. In 1973, the MFOA made a
name change very similar to the one in 1954. The NCGA was reorganized, this
time changing only one word in its name—"Committee" to "Council."

The first action of the newly renamed standard-setter was to issue NCGA
Interpretation No. 1, *GAAFR and the AICPA Audit Guide*. This interpretation was
necessitated by a challenge to the 1968 GAAFR by the AICPA Audit Guide, *Audits
of State and Local Governmental Units* (ASLGU), issued by the AICPA in 1974. In
this Audit Guide, the legal compliance principle of governmental accounting stated
the following:

> A governmental accounting system should incorporate such account-
> ing information in its records as necessary to make it possible to both
> (a) show compliance with all legal provisions and (b) present fairly the
> financial position and results of operations of the respective funds and
> financial position of the self-balancing account groups of the govern-
> mental unit in conformity with generally accepted accounting prin-
> ciples. Where these two objectives are in conflict, *generally accepted
> accounting principles take precedence in financial reporting*. [ASLGU,
> 1974, pp. 12–13, emphasis added]

This position was in direct conflict with the Accounting Principles and Legal Provisions laid out in the 1968 GAAFR: "If there is a conflict between legal provisions and generally accepted accounting principles applicable to governmental units, *legal provisions must take precedence*" [GAAFR, 1968, p. 4, emphasis added]. NCGA Interpretation 1 (NCGAI 1) resolved this conflict by establishing a balance between the 1968 GAAFR and the 1974 ASLGU. It restated the principle to read

> A governmental accounting system must make it possible *both* (a) to present fairly and with full disclosure the financial position and results of operations of the funds and account groups of the governmental unit in conformity with generally accepted accounting principles; *and* (b) to determine and demonstrate compliance with finance-related legal and contractual provisions. [Adapted from NCGA Statement 1, emphasis added]

Thus was resolved the first—but not the last—conflict between accounting standard-setters and audit standard-setters.

Obviously, the NCGA didn't stop with Interpretation 1. NCGA Statement 1, *Governmental Accounting and Financial Reporting Principles* (NCGAS 1), followed a few years later (issued in March 1979 and effective for fiscal years ending after June 30, 1980). This first standard restated the principles in the 1968 GAAFR and replaced all the predecessor governmental accounting standards issued in the public sector, including NCGAI 1. It is the reason why copies of many of these previous standards have been lost. No one saw the need to keep standards that were no longer in effect. In fact, when the Governmental Accounting Standards Board (GASB) issued its first *Original Pronouncements* volume (in 1991, after the GASB had been in existence for 7 years), the oldest standard in it was NCGAS 1. In a conversation with a GASB staff member, I asked where the "old stuff" was—the things that came before NCGAS 1. The staff member responded that since NCGAS 1 replaced all that came before, no one would care except an academic. To which, with arms outstretched, I responded, "So?" With a chuckle, the staff member just shook his head and walked away.

Another contribution of NCGAS 1 was the *Financial Reporting Pyramid*, shown in Figure 1.2. This pyramid graphically demonstrated what an annual report of a government should look like. It also showed how detailed the information would be. The most detailed information is at bottom of the pyramid—the accounting system. From this starting point, as we head up the pyramid, the information gets more and more summarized, but all of it comes from the accounting system. The next level is the schedules. Government annual reports may contain many schedules, depending on the type of report being prepared. The next level is the individual fund and account group statements. These statements were essential to prepare the statements found on the upper levels, but governments rarely included the individual fund statements in their annual reports as they provided no more information

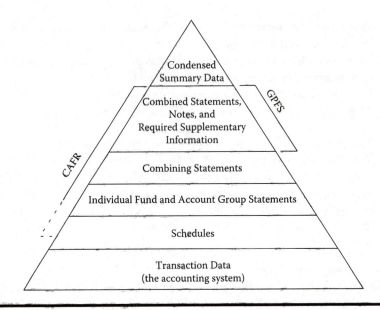

**Figure 1.2 The Financial Reporting Pyramid. (Used with permission of the Financial Accounting Foundation.)**

than what was found in the combining statements. Combining statements were necessary any time a government had more than one fund of any fund type (special revenue funds, capital projects funds, debt service funds, enterprise funds, internal service funds, pension trust funds, nonexpendable trust funds, expendable trust funds, and agency funds). Only the General Fund would not have a combining statement since only one General Fund is allowed per government. The next step up the pyramid was the General Purpose Financial Statements (GPFS). The GPFS presented the combined statements (in which each fund type made up a column in the report), the notes to the financial statements, and required supplementary information. Finally, the top of the pyramid was to contain condensed summary data, but this portion of the pyramid was never defined by the NCGA or, later, by the GASB. The GPFS represented the minimum financial statements a government could prepare for external use. However, governments were encouraged to prepare a Comprehensive Annual Financial Report (CAFR). The CAFR included the GPFS and went as far down the pyramid as was necessary for full disclosure. Normally, the CAFR would include the GPFS, combining statements, account group statements, and some schedules.

Statement 1 was followed by six more standards and 10 additional interpretations. The standards addressed a variety of issues, including the following:

■ Grant, entitlement, and shared revenue accounting (Statement 2)
■ Defining the governmental reporting entity (Statement 3)

- Accounting and reporting for claims and judgments and compensated absences (Statement 4)
- Accounting and reporting for leases (Statement 5)
- Accounting and reporting for pensions (Statement 6)
- Accounting and reporting for component units (Statement 7)

By the very of definition of the documents, these same issues were addressed in the interpretations, only in greater detail. Of the 10 interpretations issued by the NCGA, five affected NCGAS 1, one affected Statement 3, one affected Statement 4, and two affected Statement 6. Only one interpretation (#5) did not directly address an existing standard. Rather, it made the examples in the 1968 GAAFR illustrations of the principles in NCGAS 1 as long as the examples were consistent with this standard.

The NCGA went out of business in 1984, when the Governmental Accounting Standards Board (GASB) was created. Fortunately, most of its standards and interpretations are still available to us in the *Original Pronouncements* volume published annually by the GASB. As can be seen by the shading in this volume, most of these GAAP documents have been affected or superceded by newer GASB pronouncements. These documents are the topic of the last big section in this chapter.

## 1.3 The Growth of GAAP: The GASB

The year 1984 was a banner year for two reasons. First, the successor organization to the NCGA—the GASB—was established. Of lesser importance, but still interesting from a timing perspective, the MFOA became the GFOA: the Governmental Finance Officers Association of the United States and Canada. Clearly, the former event was more important than the latter, but it was still an interesting year.

When it was established, the GASB was substantially different from its FASB counterpart in the private sector. Keep in mind that the FASB had been established in 1973, so the Financial Accounting Foundation (FAF) had a good model to use in setting up the GASB. Still, the differences are remarkable. These differences are summarized in Figure 1.3.

In addition to these differences, the GASB members were paid substantially less than their FASB counterparts. This difference was due in no small part to where the members came from: the public sector versus the private sector. The staffs of the two boards were quite different. The FASB has more than 50 staff members, whereas the GASB staff at the time was less than 15.

To better understand the operation of the GASB, I highly encourage you to visit their Web site, www.gasb.org. This Web site provides much information about the Board, its publications, calendar, and other important activities of the GASB. Of interest may be a document called *Facts about GASB*, which can be found at

|  | GASB | FASB |
|---|---|---|
| Number of members | 5 | 7 |
| Status of members (full-time/part-time) | 2/3 | 7/0 |
| Full-time chairman | Yes | Yes |
| Full-time vice-chairman | No | Yes |
| Full-time director of research | No | Yes |

**Figure 1.3   Differences in organization of the GASB and FASB.**

www.gasb.org/facts/index.html. This document provides information on the GASB's mission, the Board's structure, and the current members of the Board.

This chapter is devoted to the development of GAAP in the public sector. As such, we will only discuss the final pronouncements of the GASB. However, it is important to understand the GASB's process for developing a new accounting standard.

A project starts by getting on the GASB agenda. Depending on the complexity of the issue, one or more documents may be issued by the Board before the final standard is issued. If an issue is sufficiently complex, the Board may appoint a task force to study the issue before any documents are published. Once the task force completes its work, the GASB may ask for a greater variety of opinions by issuing a discussion memorandum (DM). Other documents may include an Invitation to Comment (ITC) or a Preliminary Views (PV) document or both. Once sufficient discussion has been launched, the Board may hold one or more public hearings on the topic. The GASB staff analyzes the oral and written comments and makes one or more recommendations to the Board. Several meetings may take place as the Board reviews the comments and papers written by the staff. Eventually, an exposure draft (ED) will be issued that shows where the Board intends to go on the issue, but many changes can still take place. The staff and Board have further meetings to analyze comments on the ED, and then the final document is prepared.

That final document can take several forms. It may be a Statement of Governmental Accounting Standards (referred to here as GASBS). A statement provides the actual accounting standard and the vote of the Board on that standard. If members of the Board vote against the standard, the dissenting opinions are also included in the statement.

The document could also become a Statement of Governmental Accounting Concepts. To date, the Board has issued four concept statements:

- No. 1, *Objectives of Financial Reporting*
- No. 2, *Service Efforts and Accomplishments Reporting*

- No. 3, *Communication Methods in General Purpose External Financial Reports That Contain Basic Financial Statements*
- No. 4, *Elements of Financial Statements*

The third form of document is an interpretation. These documents provide additional practical information about a particular standard. The GASB has issued only six of these in the 20 years of its existence. Similar to a standard, interpretations provide information on the standard, effective date, and the vote of the Board.

Two other documents that may be issued are Technical Bulletins (TBs) and Question-and-Answer Reports (Q&A; also known as *Implementation Guides*). These publications are staff documents in that they do not require a vote of the Board before they are issued. However, as a practical matter, the Board reviews all documents before they are issued to the public. These two do not contain a vote count of the Board or dissenting opinions.

Naturally, no standard-setting body can exist on its own. It must have supporters—financially and conceptually—in order to exist. Without financial support, the Board simply cannot exist. And, if organizations do not agree to implement GASB standards (remember, these standards are not law and cannot be enforced that way), there would be little point in having the GASB. The same organizations that supported the GFOA continued to support the GASB. Some of these organizations are the following:

- GFOA: The predecessor organizations of the GASB were established by the GFOA.
- National Association of State Auditors, Controllers, and Treasurers (NASACT): This organization has been very influential with the GASB. It is interesting that all the GASB chairmen have been affiliated with state audit organizations prior to taking the chairman position.
- American Institute of Certified Public Accountants (AICPA): After all, the members of this organization—the certified public accountants (CPAs)—are predominantly the ones that do the audits of SLGs. The AICPA has a significant interest in the types of standards issued by the GASB.
- Auditing Standards Board (ASB): Although now replaced in the private sector by the Public Company Accounting Oversight Board, the ASB has played a significant role in influencing accounting standard-setting.
- National Association of College and University Business Officers (NACUBO): The FASB, GASB, and predecessor organizations have focused primarily on businesses or SLGs. NACUBO took up the slack to assist colleges and universities in developing their own unique set of financial statements. While the GASB and FASB have the final say, NACUBO has had a major impact on the development of accounting standards for higher education.
- American Accounting Association (AAA): Made up largely of academics, members of this organization have done much in the way of research for the

GASB, although the GASB now has its own research staff. Still, members contribute ideas to the GASB and serve on various task forces and committees.

- Internal Revenue Service (IRS): While its influence has been stronger in the private sector, one need look no further than the accounting rules for inventory to see the impact of the IRS on accounting standards.

Of course, there are many other organizations that support the GASB that are not mentioned here. Any professional organization that represents constituents of the GASB would have an interest in the Board's activities.

## 1.3.1 The First Board

The first five men appointed to the GASB were the following:

- Chairman, James F. Antonio, former Missouri State Auditor.
- Vice Chairman and Director of Research, Martin Ives, who had served on the NCGA. Mr. Ives had worked with the State of New York for many years as the First Deputy Comptroller for New York City from 1976 to 1983, when he helped reestablish the city's accounting systems after its financial troubles of the 1970s and early 1980s.
- Philip L. Defliese, the former national governmental partner for Coopers & Lybrand.
- W. Gary Harmer, who, similar to Ives, had served on the NCGA and was the former Chief Financial Officer of the Salt Lake City Independent School District.
- Elmer B. Staats, who served for 15 years as the Comptroller General of the United States.

None of these names were new to governmental accounting. As you can see, all five men had accounting or auditing experience at various levels of government. Now that public sector standard-setting was finally independent of its governments, some interesting things would likely develop. Also, it is interesting to note that only Mr. Antonio and Mr. Ives were to work at the Board full time. The other three gentlemen were to be part-time members.

When the GASB was organized under the auspices of the FAF, an interesting relationship developed between this new board and the FASB, which had already been in existence for 11 years. When looking at the organization chart in Figure 1.4, it would appear that the two boards are equal. However, in the differences pointed out earlier (see Figure 1.3), this equality was not there. Still, the AICPA in setting the GAAP hierarchy placed the pronouncements of the GASB at level one and the pronouncements of the FASB at level two. This linking of the two boards would cause some confusion later.

I have always thought it interesting to compare the first standards issued by each board. When the FASB was first created in 1973, its first standard was titled *Disclosure of Foreign Currency Translation Information*. On the other hand, the

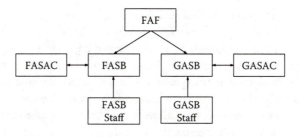

**Figure 1.4    Organization of the Financial Accounting Foundation.**

GASB's first standard was titled *Authoritative Status of NCGA Pronouncements and AICPA Audit Guide*. Unlike the FASB, the GASB formally adopted its predecessors' standards. The FASB didn't do this. Instead, the FASB left it to the AICPA in its professional standards to establish a hierarchy of GAAP—just one for the private sector rather than the public sector hierarchy mentioned previously. This hierarchy left in place the pronouncements of the earlier standard-setting boards: the Committee on Accounting Procedure and the Accounting Principles Board.

As you might expect, over time, much of what was in GASB Statement No. 1 (GASBS 1) has been amended or superceded. Four of the seven NCGA standards have been superceded entirely, as have five of the ten interpretations still in force when the GASB was created. For the AICPA pronouncements, three of its four SOPs have been superceded, and the Industry Audit Guide that was in effect at the time has long since been abandoned (the 1974 edition was in effect at the time). Of the remaining standards and interpretations, all have been heavily amended by later GASB pronouncements.

## 1.3.2  The GASB Gets Rolling

In the same year that the Board issued GASBS 1, it also issued its first Technical Bulletin (TB). TB 94-1 was very similar to GASBS 1: *Purpose and Scope of GASB Technical Bulletins and Procedures for Issuance*. Clearly, all this bulletin did is explain why the GASB would issue a TB and what procedures would be followed to issue one. It would be 3 years before another TB would be issued.

The next official pronouncement of the Board was not another standard, but its first interpretation of an earlier standard or interpretation. Interpretation documents have a unique mission. They are used to explain particular points in previous pronouncements. They cannot be used to amend previous pronouncements; an amendment requires the issuance of a new standard. After this interpretation, it would be almost 11 years before the GASB would issue its next one.

GASB Interpretation No. 1 (GASBI 1) was titled *Demand Bonds Issued by State and Local Governmental Entities*, and was an interpretation of NCGA Statement No. 1 and NCGA Interpretation No. 9. Think of a demand bond as being the opposite of a callable bond. Recall that a callable bond is one in which an issuer can instruct bondholders to redeem their bonds, usually with a premium involved. With a demand bond, the bondholder can demand payment from the issuer. The aforementioned interpretation provided guidance on how demand bonds should be classified in the financial statements of the issuer: either as current liabilities or long-term debt. Naturally, the government would prefer to classify the bonds as long-term debt. To do so, all the following conditions have to be met for an event in which the bondholder has (or may) demand payment:

- Before the financial statements are issued, the issuer must have an agreement to convert the bonds into some other form of long-term obligation, if not resold.
- The agreement does not expire within one year of the balance sheet date.
- The agreement cannot be canceled by a third party during the year.
- The third party is financially capable of honoring the agreement.

Failure to meet all these requirements would result in the demand bonds being reported as a current (or fund) liability.

More than a year would pass before the GASB would issue its next official document. In fact, 1985 was the only year of the GASB's existence in which it did not issue at least one pronouncement of any type: Standard, Interpretation, Technical Bulletin, or Concept Statement. However, that does not mean the Board was inactive. Much of 1985 was consumed with work on the GASB's most far-reaching project addressing perceived problems with the overall governmental reporting model. In 1985, the first discussion memorandum (DM) dealing with issue was published. This document would later develop into GASBS 11 (to be discussed shortly).

GASBS 2, *Financial Reporting of Deferred Compensation Plans Adopted Under the Provisions of Internal Revenue Code Section 457*, was the next standard issued by the Board. This standard laid out the requirements for accounting and reporting of deferred compensation plans. It made very clear that the assets of the plan remained the property of the government until paid to the participants. Thus, the assets were subject to the claims of the general creditors of the government. No one thought much about this issue until the bankruptcy of Orange County, California, in the early 1990s. When this government was forced to declare bankruptcy, many of its creditors were worried if they would be paid. Then, it was noticed that the so-called 457 Plans had substantial assets, which could be used to settle these claims. Obviously, such a settlement would cause considerable unrest among the participants of the plan, retirees who stood to lose a substantial part of their retirement assets. So much unrest was caused that the federal government changed the law concerning these plans, which required the GASB to issue another standard (GASBS 32, issued in 1997) to reflect the new federal law. The change in the law required that the assets be held in trust for the participants and their beneficiaries.

All plans had to adopt this new format by January 1, 1999. GASBS 32 rescinded GASBS 2, and provided new accounting and reporting guidance for these plans. Whereas GASBS 2 had the plans reported as an agency fund, GASBS 43 required reporting as an expendable trust fund (the same as a private purpose trust fund under GASBS 34) if the government continued to have a fiduciary relationship with the fund. As a result of the new federal law, however, many governments transferred the fiduciary responsibility to a third party, thus eliminating the plan from its annual report.*

The first GASB pronouncement issued as a result of a fiscal crisis was GASBS 3, *Deposits with Financial Institutions, Investments (including Repurchase Agreements), and Reverse Repurchase Agreements*, issued in 1986. This standard was a direct result of several investment failures in the early 1980s, including the failure of ESM Government Securities, Inc., in March 1985. In that failure, SLGs lost money because of improper securities transactions by brokerage firms. GASBS 3 sought to help alleviate such problems in the future by requiring certain deposit and investment disclosures.

Much of GASBS 3 had been amended by either GASBS 31, *Accounting and Reporting for Certain Investments and for External Investment Pools*, issued by the Board in 1997 (as part of the reaction to the problems in Orange County), or by GASBS 40, *Deposit and Investment Risk Disclosures*, issued by the Board in 2003. Because of the close relationship between these three standards, many of the provisions are discussed in this section (other provisions of GASBS 31 will be discussed in Section 1.6).

GASBS 3 largely dealt with custodial issues related to deposits and investments. The standard contained guidance on how to report such deposits and investments in one of three categories of custodial risk—from the most secure to the least secure. The categories were based on who held the collateral for the deposits and investments and in whose name the collateral was carried. These categories are summarized is Figure 1.5.

Since categories one and two were considered quite secure and most governments reported the greatest majority of their deposits and investments in one of these two categories, GASBS 40 amended GASBS 3 by requiring governments to report only those deposits and investments held in the third category at the end of the fiscal year.†

Other disclosures required by GASBS 3—and not eliminated by GASBS 40—include the following:

---

* No retiree lost money in the Orange County bankruptcy. The law was still changed to avoid the problem in the future. The bankruptcy also caused the GASB to issue other pronouncements (discussed later) addressing investment issues of SLGs.
† There was some discussion about reporting categories of investments and deposits during the year, but this idea was not adopted by the Board.

| Category | Deposits | Investments |
|---|---|---|
| 1 | Insured or collateralized with securities held by the entity or by its agent in the entity's name. | Insured or registered, or securities held by the entity or its agent in the entity's name. |
| 2 | Collateralized with securities held by the pledging financial institution's trust department or agent in the entity's name. | Uninsured or unregistered, with securities held by the counterparty's trust department or agent in the entity's name. |
| 3 | Uncollateralized, including balances collateralized with securities held by the pledging financial institution, its trust department, or its agent, but not in the entity's name. | Uninsured or unregistered, with securities held by the counterparty, its trust department, or agent, but not in the entity's name. |

**Figure 1.5    Categories of deposits and investments.**

- Brief description of the types of investments the government is allowed to purchase
- Significant violations during the period of legal and contractual provisions for deposits and investments
- Types of investments held during the period but not held at year-end
- Certain reverse repurchase agreement disclosures

Also, GASBS 3 required reporting the carrying value and market value of deposits and investments. GASBS 31, *Accounting and Financial Reporting for Certain Investments and for External Investment Pools,* issued in 1997 (and discussed later in Section 1.6), dropped the requirement to report carrying value and changed market value to fair value. New disclosures required by GASBS 40 include the credit risk—bond ratings—of certain investments; concentration of investments when the amount in one issue exceeds 5% of the value of the portfolio; not aggregating dissimilar investments (such as Treasury bonds and strips); focusing the disclosure of risk on the primary government unless the governmental activities, business-type activities, individual major funds, nonmajor funds in the aggregate, or fiduciary fund types have greater exposure to risk; reporting interest rate risk by any one of five methods; disclosing investments that are highly susceptible to changes in interest rates; and reporting foreign currency risks.

The next standard issued by the GASB was not so much a declaration of new accounting and reporting policies, but one that directed SLGs to not follow a recent

FASB standard. Recall that the GAAP hierarchy in force at this time required SLGs to first follow GASB standards and then apply FASB standards if the GASB had not yet ruled on a topic. In late 1985, the FASB had issued its Statement No. 87, *Employers' Accounting for Pensions*, and made it applicable to all employers including SLGs. GASBS 4, *Applicability of FASB Statement No. 87, "Employers' Accounting for Pensions," to State and Local Government Employers*, issued in 1986, reversed this requirement directing SLGs to wait until it published its own guidance on the topic. Thus, GASBS 4 became the first of the so-called "negative standards" in that it instructed SLGs to ignore a standard issued by the FASB.* GASBS 5, *Disclosure of Pension Information by Public Employee Retirement Systems and State and Local Government Employers*, issued 2 months after GASBS 4, provided the guidance mentioned in that standard. It has since been superceded by a number of GASB standards and thus is no longer in effect.

There is one other interesting point about GASBS 5 that makes it different from the previous four standards: there was a dissenting vote. It was cast by the chairman, James Antonio. He believed that the measurement focus of the standard was different from the measurement focus of governmental accounting and should reflect the approach used by governments for funding purposes. This would not be the last time a member of the Board dissented on a standard.

GASBS 6, *Accounting and Financial Reporting for Special Assessments*, issued in early 1987, was the first accounting standard to do away with a fund: special assessment fund. These funds had been in use for a number of years (they were included in the 1968 edition of GAAFR). The standard eliminated the fund from external financial reporting, although governments could continue to use them for internal purposes. However, special assessments continue to be an important part of government operations. Those related to capital projects are accounted for in a capital projects fund during the construction phase. If debt is issued to finance the project, collection of the appropriate special assessments will occur in a debt service fund, unless the government is not obligated on the debt in any manner; in that case, an agency fund may be used. When no debt is involved or for a service special assessment, the transaction is accounted for in the General Fund or in a special revenue fund.

However, this standard went further than just changing financial reporting for special assessments. As noted earlier, if the government is not obligated in any manner on a debt, the debt need not be included in the notes to the financial statements. So, what determines whether a government is obligated in any manner on a debt issue? GASBS 6 provides this guidance in paragraph 16:

---

* One should remember that GASB and FASB have been colocated in the same building throughout their joint history. As a result, you would think they could talk to one another and avoid problems such as this one.

- The government is obligated to honor deficiencies to the extent that lien fore-closure proceeds are insufficient.
- The government is required to establish a reserve, guarantee, or sinking fund with other resources.
- The government is required to cover delinquencies with other resources until foreclosure proceeds are received.
- The government must purchase all properties ("sold" for delinquent assessments) that were not sold at a public auction.
- The government is authorized to establish a reserve, guarantee, or sinking fund, and it establishes such a fund. (If a fund is not established, the considerations in subparagraphs g and h may nevertheless provide evidence that the government is obligated in some manner.)
- The government may establish a separate fund with other resources for the purpose of purchasing or redeeming special assessment debt, and it establishes such a fund. (If a fund is not established, the considerations in subparagraphs g and h may nevertheless provide evidence that the government is obligated in some manner.)
- The government explicitly indicates by contract (such as the bond agreement or offering statement) that in the event of default, it may cover delinquencies, although it has no legal obligation to do so.
- Legal decisions within the state or previous actions by the government related to defaults on other special assessment projects make it probable that the government will assume responsibility for the debt in the event of default.

This information has proved invaluable when trying to determine whether a government needs to include a debt issue in its annual report. About the same time GASBS 6 was published, the GASB staff issued only its second TB, TB 87-1, *Applying Paragraph 68 of GASB Statement 3*. Obviously, this TB addressed a very specific issue—one particular paragraph in an earlier GASB standard. The questions posed in the document addressed clarification provided on the categories of risk for financial reporting.

The next standard issued by the original Board was GASBS 7, *Advance Refunding Resulting in Defeasance of Debt*, also issued in 1987. This standard addressed many of the same issues raised in FASB Statement No. 76, *Extinguishment of Debt*, issued four years earlier. Although the GASB statement didn't adopt the FASB rule as its own, there is a definite influence of the older Board's standard in this one.

Essentially, the GASB realized that SLGs were taking advantage of lower interest rates in the mid-1980s to refinance old higher interest rate debt with lower interest rate debt. The accounting for these activities varied widely, so the statement standardized the process. GASBS 7 allows for two types of defeasances, or early refunding, in which the old bond issue does not allow for an immediate call (if the call provision was in the bond covenant, there would be no need for a defeasance). The two types were legal defeasance and in-substance defeasance. The difference is that if the covenant of the old bond issue allows for a refunding, then the refunding is a legal defeasance. If the old bond covenant is silent on the issue, then the refunding is an in-substance defeasance.

There is no accounting difference in the two types of refunding. In either case, when a new bond issue is to be used to finance the defeasance, the issue is recorded as an other financing source (and the new debt is recorded in the General Long-Term Liability list). Then, when the proceeds are used to pay the escrow agent, the payment is recorded as an other financing use (and the old debt is removed from the General Long-Term Liability list). Should the government use its own resources in the refunding, that payment would be recorded as a debt service expenditure.

Once the payments are made to the escrow agent, the agent is restricted on the types of investments that may be made with the money:

■ Direct obligations of the U.S. government
■ Obligations backed by the U.S. government
■ Securities backed by U.S. government obligations

For, you see, only the U.S. government issues bonds that are considered risk free. In fact, a further restriction is placed on the bonds that they cannot be callable, as that would not guarantee the interest flow from the investment. If the escrow agent were to make the wrong investments, then a defeasance would not occur, and a whole host of other problems would be initiated.

What then is the difference between a legal defeasance and an in-substance one? The answer lies in the required disclosures. For both types of defeasances, there are three basic disclosures:

■ A general description of the transaction including the debt issues involved and why the refunding was undertaken
■ The difference between cash flows required to service the old debt and the new debt issued to finance the refunding
■ The economic gain or loss from the transaction

An economic gain occurs when the present value of the cash flows of the new debt is less than the present value of the cash flows required for the old debt. An economic loss occurs if the opposite conditions are true. If done properly, a defeasance should always result in an economic gain.

The difference in the disclosures for the two defeasances lies in the fourth disclosure required only for an in-substance defeasance. Since the old bond issue did not specifically allow for a refunding, the amount of old debt still outstanding at the end of the accounting period must be disclosed. This disclosure continues until the old issue is completely retired.

In late 1987, the FASB issued another of its all-encompassing standards—one that effected both the private and public sectors. This time, it was Statement No. 93, *Recognition of Depreciation by Not-for-Profit Organizations*. This statement required that certain organizations, including nonprofit organizations and colleges and universities, begin to recognize depreciation on capital assets where no requirement had existed previously. As was the case with the pension issue, the GASB disagreed with the FASB's position and instructed the nonprofit organizations that used its accounting model to not implement FASB Statement No. 93. GASBS 8 has since been superceded by GASBS 35, which is discussed later in this chapter.

It wasn't too long until a similar event occurred again. This time the issue was funds flow reporting. Also in 1987, the FASB had issued its Statement No. 95, *The Statement of Cash Flows*, which replaced the Statement of Changes in Financial Position as the funds flow statement for private sector entities. This latter statement had been adopted in NCGA Statement 1, and was still applicable to certain public sector entities. Hence, these governmental entities were confused as to whether they should prepare the new Statement of Cash Flows (SCF) or the old Statement of Changes in Financial Position.

The position of the GASB was not immediately apparent. In its bimonthly newsletter, *The Action Report* (now called *The GASB Report*), the Board reported that it intended to come out with its own standard for funds flow reporting. Two months later in the next publication, the Board announced that it would allow governments to use either the FASB format of the SCF or the old Statement of Changes in Financial Position provided all the disclosures required by the older statement are still met. Then, in the next publication of *The Action Report,* the Board announced its final position: it would be issuing its own standard.

That standard became GASBS 9, *Reporting Cash Flows of Proprietary and Nonexpendable Trust Funds and Governmental Entities that Use Proprietary Fund Accounting,* issued by the Board in late 1989. We will not discuss the preparation of this statement here as it is accomplished in the proprietary funds chapter. However, we do want to point out some similarities and differences between the FASB cash flow model and the one adopted by the GASB.

Figure 1.6 summarizes the formats required for the SCF for the GASB and FASB, respectively. What is not apparent from the exhibit is a more subtle similarity. When the FASB was debating the format of the SCF, the Board considered requiring the direct method of preparing the Operating Activities section. Due to strong opposition during the exposure draft phase of the standard-development process, the FASB opted to allow the use of either the direct method or the indirect method. However, it should be pointed out that, in the standard, the FASB still indicated that the direct method was the preferred format. Unfortunately, very few private sector entities use the direct method. In one study done several years ago, researchers found that only 4 of the top 600 companies in the United States used the direct method. Since the FASB elected to allow either method, the GASB took a similar position.

From Figure 1.6, a few other similarities are apparent. Both formats have an Operating Activities section and an Investing Section. However, as will become apparent in a moment, these sections are similar in title only. When preparing the

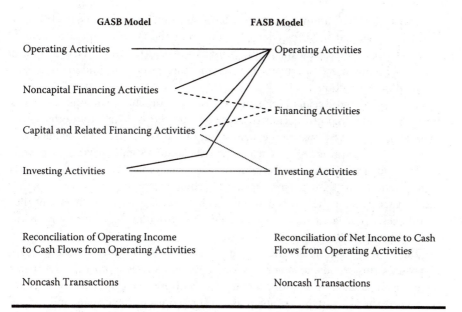

**Figure 1.6  Comparison of Statement of Cash Flow formats.**

statement using the direct method, both formats require a separate reconciliation of income to cash flows from operating activities. Finally, both formats require the presentation of noncash transactions. Despite these apparent similarities, there are many underlying differences between the formats.

The most obvious difference in the two formats is the number of sections: the GASB model has four sections, while the FASB model has three sections. As pointed out here, some of these sections have the same name, but not the same content. Both formats have an Operating Activities section. When prepared using the direct method, both report gross cash receipts from customers and other sources, and cash payments to employees and suppliers. However, the FASB model includes cash received from interest and dividends and cash paid for interest in this section. The GASB requires that cash received from interest and dividends be reported in the Investing Activities section (where the investments that generated these cash flows are reported). Also, the GASB requires that cash paid for interest be reported as either in Noncapital Financing Activities section or Capital and Related Financing Activities section, depending on the nature of the borrowing.

The FASB model uses a single Financing Activities section for all debt and equity financing of the entity. Obviously, equity financing (issuing and retiring stock) is not an issue for governments, but the GASB felt it was important to have two financing sections in its format. These two sections are used to highlight the different purposes of financing in its business-type activities that prepare the SCF. The Noncapital Financing Activities section is used for the receipt or repayment of debt and other financing sources and uses (such as taxes or transfers from or to other funds) that are not related to the acquisition of capital assets. This type of financing should be infrequent in a fund, but the GASB wanted it reported separately from the capital financing transactions reported in the next section in the format. Any interest payments on these debt issues or interfund loans are also recorded in this section.

The Capital and Related Financing Activities section has two important parts. First, this section reports receipts of debt and transfers or loans from other funds that are to be used to finance the acquisition of capital assets. Also included here will be the subsequent repayment of this debt and, possibly, payments to other funds for loans, including appropriate interest payments. The second part of the section reports the cash payments for the acquisition of capital assets and then the cash receipts for the subsequent sale of these assets at or near the end of their useful lives. These latter transactions would be reported in the Investing Activities section of the FASB model.

The final section of each SCF model is the Investing Activities section. The FASB uses this section to report all long-term investments, whether the investments be for capital assets or for debt and equity investments of the entity. As noted previously, the GASB reports capital asset transactions in the Capital and Related Financing Activities section, leaving this section for only its debt and equity investment transactions. This section would also include cash receipts for interest and dividends earned on these investments.

When preparing the SCF using the direct method, both the GASB and FASB models require a presentation of reconciling income to cash flows from operating activities. If the indirect method is used, these schedules become the Operating Activities section of the report. Note, however, that the GASB uses operating income, whereas the FASB uses net income when preparing this section. By using operating income, the GASB excludes automatically cash receipts and payments of interest. The format also avoids deducting gains and adding losses from the sales of capital assets and other investments required in the FASB model.

The final section required in both formats is the reporting of noncash transactions, or the investing and financing transactions that do not require the use of cash. For example, issuing debt to acquire a capital asset or signing a capital lease would be reported in this section. The FASB allows the information to be reported either on the face of the SCF or in the notes to financial statements. The GASB felt that the information was too important to be relegated to the notes; hence, GASBS requires that the information be reported on the face of the statement.*

Scarcely 2 months after Statement No. 9 was issued, the GASB followed it up with #10. This standard was different from the others. Generally, standards go

---

* Interestingly, GASBS 9 does not require placing the noncash transactions on the face of the SCF. However, it is apparent from the Basis for Conclusions in the back of the standard that such placement was the GASB's intent. This intention was put into practice with the Q&A that was issued for this standard.

into effect a few months to one year after issuance. Of standards 2 through 9, the longest period until implementation was 11 months; the shortest period was upon issuance. Statement No. 10 went into effect in two different time periods. For public entity risk pools, the standard went into effect within 8 months; for all other entities, the standard would not go into effect for over **4 years!** The reason for the delay had to do with Statement No. 11, which we will review shortly.

The purpose of GASBS 10, *Accounting and Financial Reporting for Risk Financing and Related Insurance Issues*, was to address what had fairly recently become a very hot topic in governmental accounting and reporting: self-insurance. In earlier years, governments insured virtually all risks of loss with commercial insurance. Then, the United States became a much more litigious society, thus driving up the cost of commercial insurance. Many governments began to finance all losses up to a certain point, and then bought commercial insurance to cover only catastrophic losses. This self-financing became known as *self-insurance*, or to some as "no insurance." In fact, that is what it was. Governments had no insurance until the catastrophic insurance policies kicked in (think of a policy with a $1 to $5 million deductible).

But why two implementation dates? The answer lies with another statement the GASB was planning on issuing soon. That statement, which became No. 11, was going to make some radical changes in the way governmental funds reported expenditures. Since much of GASBS 10 addresses expenditures and the simultaneous recognition of liabilities, the GASBS 10 needed to go into effect at near the same time as GASBS 11 and some other standards the GASB would be issuing. However, public entity risk pools use proprietary fund accounting. Therefore, waiting for GASBS 11 was not essential to insurance accounting in these entities, and the standard could be implemented immediately.

What did GASBS 10 bring to the GAAP table? First, it reaffirmed the use of FASB Statement No. 5, *Accounting for Contingencies*, in accounting for insurance claims: if the claim is reasonably probable and the amount can be reasonably estimated, the claim—and related expense or expenditures and liability—should be recognized. Second, it provided rules on how to account for self-insured risk management transactions. Third, it provided guidance on how to account for risk management. The standard gives governments the option of accounting for risk management in individual funds or consolidating the accounting into a single fund. If a government elects to consolidate the accounting into a single fund, it must be either the General Fund or an Internal Service Fund (ISF). If the General Fund is used, only expenditures for claims paid for from current financial resources are recognized in it. Other claims were to be recorded in what was then the General Long-Term Debt Account Group (under GASBS 34, discussed in Section 1.7.3, this account group becomes merely the General Long-Term Liability list). If an ISF is used, all claims are recognized as expenses of the fund. However, the fund is allowed to build reserves for large self-insurance losses, an option not available if the General Fund is used. For this reason, many recommended using an ISF over the General Fund when accounting for risk management.

This standard has been modified twice. GASB Statement No. 30, *Risk Financing Omnibus*, made some slight changes to the standard.* It provides some additional note disclosures and required supplementary information for public entity risk pools and some additional disclosure requirements for entities other than pools. GASB Interpretation No. 4, *Accounting and Financial Reporting for Capitalization Contributions to Public Entity Risk Pools*, requires that contributions made to provide initial capitalization for public entity risk pools should be treated as prepaid insurance in the fund making the payment and amortized over the period that the pool will provide insurance coverage.

## 1.4 The 5-Year Review

It was decided when the GASB was established in 1984 that, after 5 years, there would be a review of its operations to determine if the Board was a success. If so, recommendations were to be made for its continuance. The review board made a total of 35 recommendations on the structure and operation of the GASB in its final report (issued on November 30, 1989). Although a complete copy of this review was unavailable at the time this chapter was written, the more significant aspects of it are well known and are reviewed here.

You may remember that in 1989, the FASB consisted of seven, full-time Board members who were quite well compensated for their work (the actual amount isn't known, but it is believed to have been in the $300,000 range). Meanwhile, over at the GASB, the Board had only two full time members—the Chairman (Mr. Antonio) and Vice Chairman/Director of Research (Mr. Ives)—and three part-time members. One recommendation of the review panel was to make all five members full time. However, because of the cost involved, it was decided that the financial supporters of the GASB (at this time, all funding came from CPA firms, state and local governments [SLGs], and other organizations that relied on governmental accounting standards) could not, or would not, support such an organization. But, a realignment was made. The position of Vice Chairman/Director of Research was divided into two positions. The Board member position of Vice Chairman became a part-time appointment (although Mr. Ives continued to serve as a full-time Vice Chairman until he left the Board in June 1994). The newly created position of Director of Research became a full-time staff position. The first person to fill that position was David R. Bean, who continues to serve 18 years after his appointment in the fall of 1990.

Another recommendation of the review board dealt with compensation for the Board members. The full-time members were not paid nearly as well as their FASB

---

* It is interesting to note that every time a GASB pronouncement contains the word "ominbus," it means that the pronouncement is fixing errors in an earlier standard.

counterparts, and the part-time members' salaries were, obviously, even less. The review board recommended that the full-time compensation be raised to the same level as the FASB. However, just as the organizations that support the GASB would not agree to a full-time Board, they would not support paying the Board members at the same rate as their FASB counterparts. Many in government felt that the Board members' pay should be consistent with large government salaries for financial personnel, not private sector financial personnel.

The third recommendation was to establish an Emerging Issues Task Force (EITF), similar to the one the FASB has, to handle hot topic issues. The GASB briefly considered such a plan, but no action was ever taken. Currently, the GASB has no plans to establish an EITF.

The fourth recommendation was to have a conceptual framework for SLG accounting and reporting, similar to the one in the private sector. By 1989, the GASB had issued only one concepts statement, *Objectives of Financial Reporting*, in 1987. Five years after the review board's recommendations, another entitled *Service Efforts and Accomplishments* was issued (in 1994), which examines the possibility of nonfinancial reporting. To date, no accounting standards have been issued based on this concepts statement.

The fifth recommendation of the review board, and one that was immediately acted upon, was regarding the apparent inability of the FASB and GASB to coordinate some of their standards. The review board felt, as did many others, that the GASB issuing standards directing its constituents not to follow certain FASB standards did not look very professional. Of course, the problem was caused by some colleges and universities, hospitals, and nonprofit organizations following GASB standards, and others following FASB standards. In the opinion of the review board, there was a simple solution: put all these organizations under the same standard-setting body—the FASB. The FAF put this resolution to a vote. At the time, the FAF consisted of 15 members: 12 from the private sector and 3 from the public sector. As you might suspect, that was the result of the vote—12 to 3 in favor of moving the entities under the FASB.

Reaction to this vote by the public sector was immediate. Many of the supporters of the GASB met to discuss this action. The result of this meeting was a strongly worded letter to the FAF indicating the displeasure of these organizations to the vote. There is some speculation that the letter included a threat to reestablish the NCGA and not follow GASB or FASB standards. Regardless of the actual content of the letter, the FAF did reconsider its position and voted to reverse its original position.*

---

* In the years since the review board's recommendations, there have been other suggestions on how to improve accounting and reporting for hospitals and colleges and universities. One suggestion was to put all colleges and universities under the GASB and all hospitals under the FASB. However, no action has ever been taken on this proposal or other similar ones.

What, then, was the result of the 5-year review? The Board's make-up was substantially altered to one full-time member (the Chairman) and four part-time members. A full-time Director of Research position was established and separated from a Board member's responsibility. This change made the staff a little more independent from the Board. Finally, the necessity of the GASB was recognized, and the review board recommended that it continue to set accounting standards for the public sector.

However, there was still one sticking point from the 5-year review: how to more appropriately handle conflicts between the GASB and FASB on certain accounting issues and avoid the GASB having to issue negative standards. Clearly, the problem lay in the GAAP hierarchy that placed the FASB second to the GASB in issuing standards for the public sector. In what became known as the *jurisdictional agreement,* the hierarchy was changed to remove the FASB from the GASB GAAP hierarchy. The change in hierarchy was made formal by the Auditing Standards Board (ASB) in its Statement on Auditing Standards No. 69, *The Meaning of "Present Fairly" in the Auditor's Report* (issued in January 1992). A comparison of the old and new hierarchies of GAAP is shown in Figure 1.7.

Clearly, the most significant change in the hierarchy is at the second level. The FASB statements and interpretations have been dropped from the hierarchy unless they are formally adopted by the GASB in one of its publications. This change solved the problem of negative standards.

## 1.5 The Original Board's "Last Stand"

The implementation of the review board's recommendations had little impact on the ongoing actions of the GASB. However, the five members of the Board had been originally appointed for 5-year terms. Those terms expired in 1989, but with the ongoing review, were extended another year. Thus, the standard issued in late 1989 (GASBS 10) and the three issued in early 1990 were the last ones of the original Board.

The last three standards of the original Board were all issued in May 1990. The timing was very important. In June, two of the original members would be leaving. Thus, the vote on these new standards might be different with the new members. Of the three, GASB Statement No. 11, *Measurement Focus and Basis of Accounting— Governmental Fund Operating Statements,* was the most important. This statement had entered the Board's agenda in 1985, and it represented the culmination of much of the Board's work since then. Indeed, it is the only standard to ever have had two exposure drafts (EDs). The first ED looked at changing the measurement focus and basis of accounting for all governmental fund financial statements. It was considered unwieldy by many of the constituents of the Board, so a second ED was issued that scaled back the project to address only the governmental fund operating statements—or only half the reporting model. The final statement represented a

| "Old" Hierarchy 1984–1991 | "New" Hierarchy 1992–present |
|---|---|
| 1. GASB Statements and Interpretations | a. GASB Statements and Interpretations<br><br>AICPA and FASB pronouncements adopted by GASB in GASB Statements and Interpretations |
| 2. FASB Statements and Interpretations (including predecessor pronouncements still in effect) | b. GASB Technical Bulletins<br><br>AICPA Audit Guides and Accounting Guides and SOPs if (1) made applicable to SLGs by the AICPA *and* (2) cleared by the GASB |
| 3. Pronouncements of other "expert bodies" that follow due process | c. GASB Emerging Issues Task Force consensus positions [to date there is no GASB EITF]<br><br>AcSEC Practice Bulletins [none have ever applied to SLGs] |
| 4. Widely recognized practices or pronouncements that represent prevalent practice or knowledgeable application of other GAAP pronouncements to specific circumstances | d. GASB staff Implementation Guides [also known as Q&As]<br><br>Widely recognized and prevalent SLG accounting practices |
| 5. All not in levels 1–4 | e. All not in levels a–d |

**Figure 1.7 Comparison of old and new GAAP hierarchies.**

major restructuring of governmental accounting as we know it. However, it had a very interesting effective date.

All standards include an effective date. As mentioned in the discussion on GASBS 10, this date is usually soon after the issuance of the statement. GASBS 10 was the first standard to differ from this practice; GASBS 11 was the second. Paragraph 100 (the effective date paragraph) of GASBS 11 makes for interesting reading:

> The requirements of this Statement are effective for financial statements for periods *beginning after June 15, 1994*. Early application *is not permitted* because of the need for simultaneous implementation with GASB pronouncements on [1] financial reporting, [2] capital reporting, [3] pension accounting, [4] risk financing and insurance, and [5] the types of nonrecurring projects and activities that have long-term

economic benefit and for which debt meets the definition of general long-term capital debt. Transition requirements for this Statement will be established by a future Statement on financial reporting. [emphasis and [#] added]

The standard could not be implemented for 4 years after the standard was issued. Why? Because at least four other standards (#4 from the list—GASBS 10—had been issued) had to be issued before this standard could go into effect. By June 1993—one year before implementation was to have started—none of these additional standards had been issued.

The Board must have been worried, and the Board members had changed substantially. By June 1993, only Mr. Antonio and Mr. Ives remained from the original Board—Mr. Defliese and Mr. Staats had left the Board in 1990. The three part-time members were all new:

■ Dr. Robert J. Freeman had come on the Board in 1990, replacing one of the original Board members.
■ Mr. Anthony Mandolini also came on the Board in 1990. He left in June 1992, and was replaced by Mr. Edward M. Klasny.
■ Ms. Barbara A. Henderson who replaced Mr. Harmer came on the Board in 1991.

As a result of the Board's concerns, a preliminary views document was issued to examine a narrower project on balance sheet issues and other related issues that needed to be addressed prior to implementing GASBS 11. Most of the respondents to this document preferred to delay the effective date of GASBS 11 until all the issues could be addressed. From these responses came an ED proposing this delay, which resulted in GASBS 17.

GASB Statement No. 17, *Measurement Focus and Basis of Accounting—Governmental Fund Operating Statements: Amendment of the Effective Dates of GASB Statement No. 11 and Related Statements*, indefinitely delayed the implementation of GASBS 11 until all the necessary statements related to the reporting project set out in that statement could be completed. The statement also implemented the fund portion of GASBS 10 (delayed in that standard until the implementation of GASBS 11) and indefinitely delayed certain aspects of GASBS 13 that relied on GASBS 11.

The political implications of GASBS 17 are as interesting as the standard itself. Recall that three of the original Board members had left by the time GASBS 17 was issued. The vote to issue GASBS 17 was 3 to 2, with the new part-time members voting to delay and the two remaining Board members dissenting with GASBS 17. As noted earlier, whenever a Board member votes against a standard, a dissent is written as part of the document explaining the dissent. Mr. Antonio and Mr. Ives wrote just such a dissent. The dissent runs 792 words, whereas the "Standards" portion of GASBS 17 runs only 459 words, that is, the dissent is over 300 words longer than the actual document. Obviously, Mr. Antonio and Mr. Ives did not care much for the delay in implementing GASBS 11.

Compared to GASBS 11, the issues in GASB Statement No. 12, *Disclosure of Information on Postemployment Benefits Other Than Pension Benefits by State and Local Government Employers*, and GASB Statement No. 13, *Accounting for Operating Leases with Scheduled Rent Increases*, were not as contentious. GASBS 12 was an interim statement, pending completion of a larger project on accounting and reporting for other postemployment benefits.* Essentially, these benefits are accounted for on a pay-as-you-go basis. The standard requires making disclosures on a general description of the benefits provided, who is covered, the legal require-ments for providing the benefits, a description of the accounting policies for the benefits, and the dollar amount of benefits paid.

GASBS 13 was even narrower in focus. This standard examined only leases that had lower lease payments in the early years of the lease than in the later years. If the difference in lease payments reflected economic factors or a specific time pattern related to the lease, lease revenue is recognized in accordance with the lease agree-ment. However, if the difference in lease payments resulted from an inducement to get the lessee to agree to the terms, then the revenue is recognized in equal install-ments over the term of the lease.

GASBS 13 marked the end of the original board. As noted earlier in the discus-sion on GASBS 11, when Statement Nos. 11, 12, and 13 came out in 1990, they marked the last standards of the five original members of the GASB. It was defi-nitely the end of an era. Of the 13 standards published by the original Board, only on two occasions was a dissenting vote cast:

- Mr. Antonio dissented on GASBS 5
- Mr. Defliese dissented on GASBS 9

As we have already seen in the discussion on GASBS 11, that was about to change in a big way.

## 1.6 New Board, New Issues, New Standards

It would be over one year before the GASB issued another standard. By that time, only one of the original three part-time members of the Board remained: Mr. Harmer. The two new members were Dr. Freeman and Mr. Mandolini, the same two members who voted no to GASBS 14.

---

* This project has now been completed by GASBS 43 and 45. As these standards have not yet gone into effect at the time of this writing, they are excluded from this analysis of current public sector GAAP.

This statement marked a major change in the way governments reported many of their activities. Prior to GASBS 14, if there was any question about whether an activity should be included in the report of a government, it was usually omitted from the report. With the advent of GASBS 14, the position changed 180°; now if there is any doubt, the activity is usually included in the report. Also, prior to this standard, all activities were reported as funds of the government. GASBS 14 expanded the reports of governments to present discretely presented and blended component units, thus greatly expanding the concept of the reporting entity.

The concept of reporting entity came up with NCGA Statements 3 and 7, which defined the reporting entity and gave us component units, respectively. However, GASBS 14 radically changed the way we looked at these elements. But, we are, to some extent, getting ahead of ourselves. There are some terms that need to be defined:

- Primary government—state or local (county or city) governments. It also includes special purpose governments (such as an independent school district) that have a separately elected governing body, is legally separate, and is fiscally independent of other state or local governments.
- Potential component unit (PCU)—legally separate organization that may have a relationship with a primary government. The relationship may be defined by financial accountability or by its nature and significance. Excluding the potential component unit from the reporting entity would cause the financial report to be misleading or incomplete.
- Reporting entity—the primary government and its component units. However, if a component unit issues a separate report, it is the primary government of that reporting entity.

Now, imagine that a governmental entity prepares an annual report—they do that, you know. The entity takes the role of the primary government in that report. The report contains all the government's funds. About that, there should be no question—or, at least there won't be by the time you finish reading this book. However, the report needs to reflect the reporting entity—not just the primary government. Therefore, the government must examine these PCUs to determine if they should be part of the reporting entity.

The best place to start is fiscal dependency. Recall that in our definition of a primary government, entities that are fiscally independent of other SLGs are primary governments. However, if this entity—the PCU—has to go to another government to get approval (1) for the PCU's budget, or (2) for the PCU's rates or charges, or (3) for the PCU to issue debt, then the PCU is fiscally dependent on that other government. Since fiscal dependency exists, the PCU becomes a component unit.

Beyond fiscal dependency, things get a little murkier but not impossible to understand. If fiscal dependency exists, the PCU is a component unit of the primary government. However, if the fiscal dependency tests don't apply, then we must look for other indicators. The starting point is the relationship between the governing body of the primary government and the PCU. If the primary government appoints a voting majority of the PCU's governing body or the primary government established and can abolish the PCU's governing body, we have passed a major test. However, this appointment power is not enough. The primary government must also have the ability to impose its will on the PCU or could receive financial benefits or burdens from the PCU for the PCU to become a component unit.

How does the primary government determine whether it can impose its will on the PCU? There are several tests:[*]

- ■ The primary government can remove members of the PCU's governing body.
- ■ The primary government can veto, overrule, or modify decisions of the PCU's governing body.
- ■ The primary government can appoint, hire, reassign, or dismiss members of the PCU's management.

If the primary government has the appointment power and any of the powers identified here, then the PCU is a component unit.

What happens, though, if the primary government has none of these three powers? Can the PCU still be a component unit? Yes, so long as the primary government can receive a financial benefit or burden from the PCU, along with the aforementioned appointment power. If the primary government can legally access the PCU's resources, that constitutes the possibility of receiving a benefit. If the primary government is legally obligated in some manner on debt issued by the PCU, that offers the possibility of receiving a burden should the PCU default on the debt. Finally, if the primary government must finance deficits or provide financial support for the PCU, there is the possibility of receiving a burden from the PCU. If any of these three conditions exist, the PCU is a component unit of the primary government.

Once all the component units have been determined, it is necessary to include them in the financial report of the reporting entity. This presentation can be made in two ways: discrete presentation or blended presentation. Blended presentation means that the component unit appears in the annual report as if it were another fund. This method of presentation is allowed only if the governing bodies of the primary government and the component unit are substantially the same, or if the component unit provides services entirely (or almost entirely) to the primary government. If neither of these conditions are met, then discrete presentation is required.

---

[*] In this area, GASBS 14 does an odd thing. Two of the five abilities identified in the standard would make the PCU fiscally dependent on the primary government. If either of those conditions exist, having appointment authority over the PCU's governing body would not matter. Therefore, those conditions are omitted from this discussion.

The requirements of this standard were affected by GASBS 34, but not as much as some other standards.

GASB Statement No. 15, *Governmental College and University Accounting and Financial Reporting Models*, issued in October 1991, was very important when it came out, although it is much less so now. The purpose of the standard was to make resolute the accounting and reporting models that public sector colleges and universities could use. There was evidently some fear that some colleges and universities might be using the FASB model, which would not be allowed under the jurisdictional agreement. The standard clarified that either the AICPA College Guide model or the governmental model could be used. This standard was later replaced by GASB Statement No. 35, *Basic Financial Statements—and Management's Discussion and Analysis—for Colleges and Universities*. This standard is discussed later.

This last standard saw another change in the membership of the Board. Mr. Harmer, who had been the only temporary member of the Board carried forward from the original Board, left and was replaced by Barbara Henderson. Ms. Henderson had been serving as the Finance Director of Fullerton, California, up until that time. She went on to serve a total of 9 years on the Board.

Before the end of 1991, the GASB issued a totally new document. This one is popularly called a *Q&A* or an *Implementation Guide*. Whatever short title you want to use, though, the document was definitely a new type of publication from the Board. The complete title of this one was *Guide to Implementation of GASB Statement 3 on Deposits with Financial Institutions, Investments (including Repurchase Agreements), and Reverse Repurchase Agreements*; it was issued in December 1991. Also, on the title page of the document, but separated from the main title by several inches, are the words "Questions and Answers."

One of the truly strange things about this document is when it was published: 5 years, almost to the day, since the effective date of GASBS 3. That difference begs the question, really unanswered by the Q&A: "Hey guys, what took you so long?" The first question in the Q&A addresses why the Board issued GASBS 3, but not why it issued this Q&A. You must read the introductory material fairly closely to see that the Board sought to "codify" the technical questions received by the GASB staff on a regular basis. In order to have a good Q&A, the staff needs good questions to include in it. These items are not something the people who work at the GASB make up. They are actual technical inquiries received at the GASB on a daily basis. Not all inquiries are included in the Q&A, but they do provide the foundation for it. From these questions, the staff can also find other interesting items to include in the Q&A, which are usually found in the appendices. Also, by publishing the technical questions and answers in the document, it raises the responses to level "d" GAAP. Until that happens, the answers to technical questions have no standing.

This first Q&A was quite lengthy, consisting of 121 questions and 4 appendices. The questions are divided into 12 different broad sections, many with subtopics.

Some of the sections are (1) Concept of credit risk categories, (2) The meaning of the categories: Are deposits safe or unsafe, (3) Scope of Statement 3, and (4) Specific issues of deposits with financial institutions, to name just a few. In the introductory section of the document, the Board promises that this won't be the last Q&A.

True to its word, before the GASB issues another standard it issues another Q&A. This one is called *Guide to Implementation of GASB Statement 9 on Reporting Cash Flows of Proprietary and Nonexpendable Trust Funds and Governmental Entities That Use Proprietary Fund Accounting,* issued in June 1992. This one is much more timely than the last Q&A, being published only 2.5 years after the effective date of GASBS 9. This document is not quite as long as its predecessor; it contains only 75 questions. Given that the GASB requires preparing the Statement of Cash Flows using the direct method when implementing GASBS 34, this is still very much an important document and one that should be referred to often.

After this Q&A was issued, another change in the Board occurred. Mr. Mandolini, who had come on the Board in 1990, left after 2 years (the length of his appointment) and was replaced by Mr. Ed Klasny, former governmental audit partner of what was then Ernst and Whinney (now Ernst & Young). Mr. Klasny would go on to serve a total of 10 years on the Board.

The only standard issued by the Board in 1992 was No. 16, *Accounting for Compensated Absences,* issued in November of that year. This standard addresses a topic near and dear to the hearts of all employees: vacation leave and sick leave. Very few employees are ever worried about the accounting for these absences, only that they have a right to them.

Employees earn the right to vacation leave and sick leave based on a past transaction: their employment. It is up to the employer to do the accounting. For vacation leave, an accrual must be made for leave that is earned and for which the employee will receive benefits through paid time off (before retirement) or by cash payment at termination or retirement.

Unlike vacation leave, sick leave has one other requirement beyond just doing the work to earn it: to take sick leave an employee must be sick! Therefore, the accounting rules are slightly different, too. Here, an accrual must be made only if the employee will receive at the time of separation or retirement cash payments for sick leave not taken. The accruals are made at the end of the year as adjusting entries, and reflect the pay and benefits in effect at that time.

The year 1993 was a big one for the GASB. We have already mentioned GASBS 17 in our discussion of GASBS 11. That was only one of seven standards issued that year, along with another Q&A. After GASBS 17, the next standard out dealt with new rules for accounting for landfills: *Accounting for Municipal Solid Waste Landfill Closure and Postclosure Care Costs* (which came out in August). This standard was in reaction to new Environmental Protection Agency (EPA) rules on the operation of landfills and what had to be done to those landfills after they were closed. The

EPA gave many guidelines for operation of the sites, by requiring cells to be constructed in a certain way and used in certain ways during the life of the landfill. Once the landfill was closed, the EPA provided guidance on the capping of the cells (the closure costs) and the monitoring of the site to ensure there was no leakage into groundwater or the escape of methane gas into the air for 30 years after the closure of the cell (postclosure care costs).

Figure 1.8 helps to show how to account for the costs of operating a landfill, if an enterprise fund is used. If a government uses a governmental fund to account for the landfill operation, expenditures would be recorded only for the amount actually paid from current financial resources; other amounts would be recorded in the General Long-Term Liabilities list. All the actual costs incurred during the preparation of the site and the estimated costs of postclosure care are accounted for during the life of the landfill. The postclosure care costs include the equipment

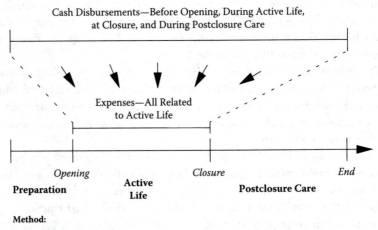

**Method:**

1. All expected costs of closure and postclosure care are estimated at the outset—the beginning of the Active Life—and are reestimated annually.

2. The useful capacity (cubic feet) of the MSWLF also is estimated initially and revised when appropriate).

3. During each year of Active Life the ratable portion of the total estimated cost of closure and postclosure care—based on the percentage (%) of total MSWLF capacity used that period—is recorded:

      Expenditure/Expense
         Liability

4. Related cash disbursements are recorded:
      Liability

         Cash

**Figure 1.8 Accounting for landfills. (Adapted with permission from Robert J. Freeman and Craig D. Shoulders, *Governmental Accounting, Reporting, and Auditing: Update*, Texas Tech University, Lubbock, 1994.)**

necessary to monitor the site during the postclosure time period, the cost of final capping, and cost of monitoring and maintaining the site during the postclosure care period. As the landfill fills up, accruals are made for estimated costs based on current cost projections. Should these projections change later, appropriate adjustments have to be made.

The third standard that came out in 1993 was a relatively minor one with a very narrow focus, although you wouldn't know it from the title: *Governmental College and University Omnibus Statement* (GASBS 19, issued in September). Usually, when the GASB uses the word "omnibus" in a standard, it tends to be a broad standard that fixes error in previous standards. This one applied to Pell grant accounting and handling risk financing activities. It has since been superceded by GASBS 35.

GASBS 20, *Accounting and Financial Reporting for Proprietary Funds and Other Governmental Entities That Use Proprietary Fund Accounting*, was also issued in September. This standard was one of the more curious standards issued by the GASB. It came about as a result of some proprietary funds—notably utilities— wanting to follow more of the FASB's pronouncements. There was a perception by these utilities that such an option would make their financial statements more comparable to those in the private sector and enable them to compete better in the bond market (this belief has never been proved).

To allow these activities to follow more FASB standards, the GASB decided to give them two options:

1. The activities could follow all pronouncements of the FASB and predecessor organizations (the Committee on Accounting Procedure [Accounting Research Bulletins] and the Accounting Principles Board [Opinions]) issued up to November 30, 1989, as long as those standards did not conflict with GASB standards.
2. The activities could follow all the pronouncements in option #1 plus those issued by the FASB after November 30, 1989, as long as those standards did not conflict with GASB standards.

The last provision in both options keeps these activities from departing from governmental GAAP. For instance, they could not implement FASBS 95, *Statement of Cash Flows*, as that would conflict with GASBS 9. Another thing to keep in mind for governments considering option #2 is that it applies to all pronouncements from the FASB, not just the standards but also interpretations, TBs, Q&As, and guidance issued by the Emerging Issues Task Force (EITF).

Another curious aspect of this standard is what it says to disclose, or more accurately, what it doesn't say about disclosure. If you examine almost any standard issued by the GASB, there will usually be a section near the end describing the disclosure requirements. This section is missing from this standard. As a result, many governments made the election between option #1 and option #2 but did not disclose it. This lack of guidance was fixed in GASBS 34.*

GASBS 21, *Accounting for Escheat Property*, issued in October, was the fifth standard of 1993. The standard defines "escheat" as the "revision of property to a governmental entity in the absence of legal claimants or heirs" (paragraph 1). In most states, escheat occurs after a certain length of time when property—usually bank deposits—is unclaimed or has no activity. Most states have a stated time period for inactivity. In Tennessee, the period is 5 years.

Once the property is claimed by the government, the government must decide what fund is going to account for the property. This fund is known as the *ultimate fund*. Once assigned to the ultimate fund, there are two options on how the property may be used:

- It may be used in the operation of the government (immediately or after the passage of a certain length of time; in some states, this period is 10 years).
- It may be held in perpetuity for a possible future claim (although the earnings from the property could be used to support government operations).

In Tennessee, the second option applies. The liability exists in perpetuity in the General Fund, but the earnings from the property can be appropriated by the State Legislature for general government operations.

GASBS 22, *Accounting for Taxpayer-Assessed Tax Revenues*, was somewhat controversial when it came out in December. The basic impact of the standard was to put revenue recognition for sales tax revenues and income tax revenues on the same footing as property tax revenues. Before this standard was issued, these revenues were almost always recognized on a cash basis, although some governments had begun to recognize them using the availability criterion used for property taxes. GASBS 22 made this process required.† The controversy caused by this standard was that governments would now recognize more revenues, but wouldn't necessarily have the cash to support them. Many finance

Two Alabama CPAs approached me about GASBS 22. Both wanted to know if they had to implement the standard. I pointed out to them that anytime a standard says this "should be done" what that really means is "you will do it." Neither liked the response, but both understood it.

Some months later I saw both of them at another meeting. I asked them how the implementation had gone. One responded that it had not gone well. I asked why not. He said it took three meetings of the city council to convince them that while revenues had gone up, they didn't have any more money to spend.

I looked at the other for his response. He said he had no trouble at all. I asked how that happened, and he responded that he decided the amount wasn't measurable. Therefore, nothing had to be accrued. I looked at him as if to say, but you know better than that. He just smiled. I then said, "Well, you are the one that signed the audit—not me!"

---

* When asked why that section was left out of the standard, a member of the GASB staff responded that everyone should know they have to disclose significant accounting policies, and this choice qualifies as one of those. The evidence of reporting between 1993 and 1999 (when GASBS 34 was published) would indicate otherwise.

† A popular expression about this standard is that it had the same impact as raising the speed limit from 55 to 65—it placed what a lot of people were already doing within the law.

directors were opposed to this recognition. However, the controversy was short-lived. The standard was superceded by GASBS 33 that came out 5 years later.

GASBS 23, *Accounting and Financial Reporting for Refundings of Debt Reported by Proprietary Activities*, issued in December, was the last standard of 1993. It was as controversial as GASBS 22 but for different reasons. This standard changed the way we had been accounting for advance refundings of debt by proprietary funds.* Prior to these new rules, an advance refunding had been accounted for in the same manner as one in the private sector. That is, the entry on an advance refunding would look something like this:

| Old debt issue | 400,000 | |
| Unamortized bond premium (old issue) | 25,000 | |
| Extraordinary loss on early retirement of debt | 95,000 | |
| Unamortized bond premium (new issue) | | 20,000 |
| New bond issue | | 500,000 |

An extraordinary loss would occur generally when the refunding was properly completed.

GASBS 23 changes this entry by eliminating the extraordinary loss and replacing it with a deferral account. This deferral is then amortized as a component of interest expense over the shorter of the remaining life of the old bonds or the life of the new bonds. The deferral is reported as a contra account to the new bond issue liability.

Many respondents to the exposure draft (ED) were opposed to the standard, because it would make refundings in proprietary funds different from their counterparts in the private sector. However, the GASB felt there were fundamental differences on why to complete a refunding in the private sector than in the public sector. Obviously, the Board believed this was a change for the better.

While we will discuss GASBS 34 shortly, one comment about it as the standard relates to advance refundings needs to be made now. Although the rules for accounting for advance refundings in governmental funds remain the same, when government-wide statements are prepared, those refundings have to be restated to match the GASBS 23 reporting requirements. This change applies to all refundings done in the year of GASBS 34 implementation and after—it is not a retroactive change.

The last document issued in 1993 was the Board's third Q&A, *Guide to Implementation of GASB Statement 10 on Accounting and Financial Reporting for Risk Financing and Related Insurance Issues*. I know what you must be thinking: GASBS 10 came out in 1989, so why did it take more than 4 years to come out with

---

* The governmental funds already have a standard on this issue—No. 7, which had been issued in 1987.

this Q&A? The answer lies in the effective date of GASBS 10. Most of the standard was to go into effect at the same time as GASBS 11. Since GASBS 17 indefinitely delayed GASBS 11, it also called for the implementation of GASBS 10.

This Q&A was the longest one up to that time, containing 110 questions and answers in 86 pages (the Q&A for #3 had 76 pages, while #9 had 58 pages). This Q&A is a little different from the other two as it has two broad sections: one for public entity risk pools (PERPs) and another for entities other than pools. Within these two sections are similar categories including (1) definition and scope, (2) recognition and measurement, and (3) disclosures.

Not as many documents were published in 1994 as in 1993, but it was still a banner year for the GASB with four major standards and another Q&A. The first standard of the year, *Accounting and Financial Reporting for Certain Grants and Other Financial Assistance* (issued in June), addressed three issues: pass-through grants, food stamps, and on-behalf payments of salaries and benefits.

First, what is a pass-through grant? It is a grant issued by a higher government (such as the state or federal government) that passes through a local government on its way to the agency or organization that will actually spend the money. Some of the terminology in this process can be a little confusing. The recipient government is known as the *primary* recipient, whereas the agency or organization that will spend the money is the *secondary* recipient. One might think that the agency for whom the money is primarily intended would be the primary recipient, but it doesn't work that way.

Prior to the issuance of this standard, most governments accounted for pass-through grants in an agency fund as the money was just coming in and going right back out. Using an agency fund made sense. However, it did limit the control over the money. To tighten this control and other internal controls over the funding, this standard requires that the funding be recognized as an intergovernmental revenue when it is received, and as an expenditure when it is disbursed. Although it is not widely used, some governments report the expenditure as an intergovernmental expenditure rather than including it as one of the other current (or operating) expenditure classifications. Most governments set up a special revenue fund (SRF) to account for these grants.

There are still certain circumstances when an SRF may not be necessary. If a government has no administrative or direct financial involvement in the program, they can still use an agency fund. Examples of administrative involvement include (these come from paragraph 5 of the standard):

- Monitoring secondary recipients for compliance with program requirements
- Determining eligibility of the secondary recipients to participate in the program, regardless of who (the primary government or the grantor) sets the eligibility requirements
- Having discretion in how the money is allocated

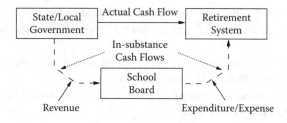

**Figure 1.9  On-behalf payments.**

Financial involvement would be having to provide financing because of matching requirements or being liable for disallowed costs.

The second issue in the standard is food stamps and applies only to state governments. An expenditure is recognized when the food stamps are distributed (or, for states using electronic benefits transfer system, when the beneficiary uses the benefit) with corresponding revenue recognized at the same time. For states still using paper food stamps, the stamps on hand at the end of the month would be reported as an asset (although not cash and cash equivalents, but as a separate account) with an offsetting deferred revenue liability.

The third issue in the standard addressed on-behalf payment of salaries and benefits. This process is summarized in Figure 1.9. The payments would typically be paid by one government for another government. For example, in some states, schools may receive a substantial amount of funding from a higher government (the state or a city or county government). Rather than transferring the money to the school and then having the school transfer the money to the retirement system, the higher government may make a direct payment to the retirement system. Prior to this standard, this payment received no accounting in the school board. Now, the school board must recognize simultaneously the revenue and expenditure or expense when the transfer is made.

GASBS 24 was the last standard on which Vice Chairman Martin Ives worked. Mr. Ives was one of the last two original members of the Board—the other being Chairman James Antonio. Both men had served since the Board was created in 1984. Under the rules that were effective at the time, Mr. Ives could have served another 5-year term but elected not to do so.* He was replaced by Mr. Tom Allen, former State Auditor of Utah.

---

* The rules on terms of both GASB and FASB members have since been changed. FASB members can serve a maximum of 14 years (the equivalent of two 7-year terms); GASB members can serve a maximum of 10 years (the equivalent of two 5-year terms). For example, when Mr. Paul Reilly was first appointed to the Board in 1995, it was for a 4-year term. He was then reappointed to a 5-year term. In 2004, at the conclusion of that last term, he was reappointed for one more year. He was replaced in the summer of 2005.

The next three standards issued by the Board came out at the same time (November), as all dealt with a similar issue: pensions. These standards were

- No. 25, *Financial Reporting for Defined Benefit Pension Plans and Note Disclosures for Defined Contribution Plans*
- No. 26, *Financial Reporting for Postemployment Healthcare Plans Administered by Defined Benefit Pension Plans*
- No. 27, *Accounting for Pensions by State and Local Governmental Employers*

As a group, these standards replaced GASBS 5 in providing the rules for accounting and reporting of pensions and pension funds. Although issued in November 1994, GASBS 25 and 26 were not effective until fiscal years ending after June 15, 1997 (GASBS 27 was effective the year after that), almost 3 years in the future. The long lead time was designed to allow governments to determine how to implement the complexities of the standards.

Obviously, GASBS 25 lays down the rules for the financial reporting—statements and disclosures—of defined benefit pension plans. Prior to this standard, pension plans followed the financial statement requirements of proprietary funds, except that they were exempt from preparing the Statement of Cash Flows. Also, pension plans didn't use the fund equity accounts found in proprietary funds. Instead, they used fund balance (similar to governmental funds), although they did report revenues and expenses.

The publishing of GASBS 25 saw the development of two new financial statements specifically designed for pensions: Statement of Plan Net Assets and Statement of Changes in Plan Net Assets. The GASB sought to get away from fund balance in the pension plans. When government officials see those two words, they usually think of money that is available for expenditure—not the case in a pension plan. Fund balance was replaced by net assets. At the same time, the Board sought to remove the concepts of revenues, expenses, and net income from pensions to eliminate the idea that these were any type of business activities. Revenues were replaced by additions, expenses by deductions, and net income by change in net assets. These new financial statements are shown later in the text. In addition to the financial statements, the Board required two schedules (reported as Required Supplementary Information) in which actuarial information about pension funds is reported. These schedules are also demonstrated later in the text.

When GASBS 25 required pension plans to mark all their investments to fair value, the effect in Alabama was most interesting. One of the largest, single investments of the Retirement System of Alabama (RSA) is in the Robert Trent Jones Golf Trail, a collection of 11 golf course complexes around the state. I had a conversation with one of their accountants on how they were going to establish a fair value on this particular investment. The accountant told me that they were going to use a discounted cash flow model. I then commented that using such a model would require (1) guessing the cash flows, (2) guessing the number of years the cash flows would last, and (3) guessing the appropriate discount rate. I will never forget his response, given in a real Alabama drawl: "Yeah, but we're real good at guessing!"

Another interesting requirement in GASBS 25 was that pension plans had to report all their investments at fair value. Although the FASB had issued a fair value requirement for investments in the private sector, the GASB had not addressed this issue until now. Of course, this requirement only applied to pension plans. The requirement would not be made applicable to SLGs until later.

GASBS 26 was an interim standard. It provided guidance on accounting for a very specific type of postemployment benefit plan. This standard has since been superceded by two new GASB standards dealing with most other postemployment benefit (OPEB) plans:

- GASBS 43, *Financial Reporting for Postemployment Benefit Plans Other Than Pension Plans*
- GASBS 45, *Accounting and Financial Reporting by Employers for Postemployment Benefits Other Than Pensions*

You will note that these two standards are similar to GASBS 25 and 27, respectively, in that one is for plans and the other is for employers. GASBS 43 and 45 replace not only GASBS 26, but also GASBS 12. As these standards will not have gone into effect at the time this chapter was written, they are not discussed here.

Finally, GASBS 27 provided guidance on the reporting of pension-related expenditures or expenses (depending on the fund type), liabilities, assets, and note disclosures for the governments participating in pension plans. Naturally, if a government ran its own pension plan, it would implement GASBS 25 and 27 at the same time. However, many governments participate in plans run by others. For example, in Alabama, there is the Retirement System of Alabama, or RSA. All state employees are required to participate in this plan. Local governments can elect to participate in the plan. Thus, GASBS 25 applies to RSA, whereas GASBS 27 applies to the state government and any local governments participating in RSA's various pension programs.

Another GASB Q&A was issued in 1994: *Guide to Implementation of GASB Statement 14 on the Financial Reporting Entity*. Recall that this standard had been issued in 1991, but it did not go into effect until fiscal years ending after December 15, 1993 (which would be in 1994 for most governments). Thus, this Q&A was probably more timely than its predecessors. As with the previous Q&As, the document is filled with technical questions posed to the GASB staff and their answers. This one contained the most questions to date, at 151. GASBS 14 continues to be a standard of great interest. The passing of over 14 years since the issuance of GASBS 14 has not lessened the interest in this standard. I regularly receive questions on whether certain entities should be a part of the reporting entity.

GASBS 28, *Accounting and Financial Reporting for Securities Lending Transactions*, was one of only two standards issued by the Board in 1995. This standard was the first one to deal specifically with an issue that arose in California a few years before. The finance and investment personnel of Orange County, California, had been very active in those years. Some of their investments proved to be quite creative—and risky—and brought the county to near financial disaster. To avoid these problems in the future, the GASB began issuing standards to avert some of the problems faced by Orange County.

This standard examined a very interesting practice in which a government loans some of its investment portfolio to a securities dealer in return for collateral. The collateral was then invested, earning interest and dividends for the government. When the securities lending transaction was complete, the collateral was returned to the broker for the government's investments. As long as all the transactions were well timed, there would be no problems. Unfortunately for Orange County, their investment personnel were a bit more creative. The investment term of the collateral didn't always match that of the lending transaction, requiring other actions on the part of the investment personnel to complete the transaction.

To avoid such problems, GASBS 28 provides several new reporting requirements. Keep in mind that the investments loaned by the government are still assets of the government. The standard requires that the collateral, usually in the form of cash but could also be securities or letters of credit, be recorded as an asset on the books of the government with a corresponding and offsetting liability. The standard also requires disclosure of whether the maturities of the investments made with the collateral generally match. Other disclosures required by the standard include the following:

- The source of legal or contractual authorization for the use of the securities lending transactions
- Violations of those provisions during the year
- General information about the transaction such as the types of securities lent and collateral received
- Whether the government has the ability to pledge or sell the collateral without the default of the borrow (broker)

GASBS 28 marked the end of an era for the Board. It was the last standard on which Mr. Antonio worked. In the summer of 1995, he left the Board, having served 11 distinguished years as its Chairman. Mr. Antonio had served longer than any other Board member. Mr. Allen, who had been earlier appointed to the Board as Mr. Ives' replacement, replaced Mr. Antonio as Chairman. At this time, Mr. Reilly was appointed to the Board to fill the remaining 4 years of Mr. Allen's appointment as a member. However, in the time line we are using for the Board's history, this does not mark a major shift in the makeup of the Board. That event will come shortly.

The mid-1990s appear to be slow years for the GASB. If one just considers the number of standards published, no other single year compares to 1993 when seven standards were issued. As has already been mentioned, only two standards were published in 1995. The next 3 years were as slow or slower in the number of standards published: one in 1996 (GASBS 30, which was discussed with GASBS 10 earlier in this chapter), two in 1997, and one again in 1998. However, this lack of new standards should not be seen as indicators of Board inactivity. These years were probably the busiest the Board has ever seen.

The other standard that came out in 1995 was No. 29, *The Use of Not-for-Profit Accounting and Financial Reporting Principles by Governmental Entities.* This standard removed some confusion as to whether certain governmental entities should be following FASBS 116, *Accounting for Contributions Received and Contributions Made,* and FASBS 117, *Financial Statements of Not-for-Profit Organizations.* Essentially, these standards apply only to the nonprofit organizations that practice in the private sector and would not apply to those that operate in the public—or governmental— sector. GASBS 29 also made clear that proprietary activities could not adopt these standards via the GASBS 20 rules as that standard applies only to FASB standards issued for business entities, not those limited to not-for-profit entities.

There was one other document published in 1995. For this, first time since 1984, the GASB issued an interpretation: No. 2, *Disclosure of Conduit Debt Obligations.* Conduit debt represents limited-obligation debt typically issued to provide financing for a third party that is not part of the government's reporting entity. This debt is often used to acquire land or construct buildings to be used as a means to attract businesses to industrial parks. The debt bears the name of the government in order to get more favorable interest rates, but the government has no obligation on the debt. Instead, it will be repaid through leases or other arrangements with the parties benefitting from land or other capital assets. The government is required to disclose a description of the transaction, the aggregate amount of debt outstanding at the balance sheet date, and the fact that the government is not obligated in any manner on the debt.

As was already noted, 1996 was a very slow year for the Board. In addition to the one standard already discussed, the Board issued another interpretation: No. 3, *Financial Reporting for Reverse Repurchase Agreements.* Clearly, this interpretation, as most do, had a very narrow focus. It looks only at this investment transaction and discusses how to report them when a government pools money from several funds for investment purposes: the investment, along with its income and costs, should be reported in the funds where the risk of loss is found and based on the equity of each fund in the pool.

In 1997, the Board had three major documents published: two standards and another Q&A. The Q&A, *Guide to Implementation of GASB Statements 25, 26, and 27 on Pension Reporting and Disclosure by State and Local Government Plans and Employers,* addressed issues related to the previously discussed pension standards. One of the two standards, GASBS 32 was already discussed earlier in this chapter.

The other standard issued in this year was GASBS 31, *Accounting and Financial Reporting for Certain Investments and for External Investment Pools.* It was, without a doubt, the most far-reaching of the two standards. As with GASBS 28 and 32, it was issued in at least partial reaction to the crises in Orange County, but it also addressed issues similar to those addressed in FASBS 115, *Accounting for Certain Investments in Debt and Equity Securities*, issued by that Board in 1993. It also applied some of the requirements from GASBS 25. However, the requirements were not as broad. Whereas GASBS 25 had required pension plans to mark all their investments to fair value, GASBS 31 was limited to some certificates of deposit and other debt and equity investments of the government. The standard requires that all applicable investments be marked to fair value and the change in fair value be reported as a component of interest (or investment) income on the operating statement of the funds with the investments.

## 1.7  A New Board—and a Whole New Ball Game

GASBS 32 was the first standard issued by a Board made up of *seven* members, not the five-member boards that had issued the first 31 standards. Increasing the Board size to seven members was a major change for the FAF and the GASB. Of course, the FASB had seven members since its founding. In the mid-1990s, it was felt that membership in the FAF needed to be broadened, with the Securities and Exchange Commission (SEC) taking a more active role and more membership from the public sector.*

### 1.7.1  Changing of the Guard

At the same time (see previous section), it was felt that membership in the GASB should be broadened. Although I doubt that it is in the GASB's charter, its members do seem to represent certain constituencies. For the GASB's first 11 years, Mr. Antonio—former State Auditor for Missouri—was its Chairman. He was replaced as Chairman in 1995 by Mr. Allen, former State Auditor for Utah. When Mr. Allen left the Board in 2004, his replacement was Mr. Robert H. Attmore, formerly the State Auditor of New York. Other members of the original Board included two representatives from local governments (Mr. Ives and Mr. Harmer), a representative from the auditor community (Mr. Defliese), and Mr. Staats, who, having served as the Comptroller of the United States, was something of the outlier of the group, having not been directly affiliated with local governments.

When the original board began to break up in 1990, Dr. Freeman became the first academic member (essentially replacing Mr. Staats). Dr. Freeman served 10 years and was replaced in 2000 by Dr. William W. Holder of the University of Southern California—the second academic to serve on the Board. Mr. Mandolini, who came on the Board with Dr. Freeman, replaced Mr. Defliese. Mr. Mandolini would be replaced 2 years later by Mr. Klasny, who was in turn replaced by

---

* Curiously, the SEC's definition of public sector and the standard definition are not the same. The standard definition is, of course, state and local governments. The SEC's definition was people with interests in publicly traded companies or in the stock markets. You should know that this is the private sector.

Mr. James M. Williams in 2002. All these men—Defliese, Mandolini, Klasny, and Williams—had been very active in the auditor community. Also, in an interesting coincidence, both Mr. Klasny (Ernst & Whinney) and Mr. Williams (Ernst & Young) had been members of the same CPA firm, albeit at different times in that firm's history.

As was noted earlier, Mr. Harmer (who was the other representative of local governments) was replaced by Ms. Henderson. She, in turn, was replaced by Mr. Richard C. Tracy (former Director of Audits for the City of Portland, Oregon) in 1999. Mr. Ives had been replaced by Mr. Allen in 1994, and when Mr. Allen was elevated to Chairman in 1995, Mr. Reilly (former finance director from Madison, Wisconsin) was appointed to fill the remaining 4 years of Mr. Allen's term as board member. When Mr. Reilly left the Board in 2005, he was replaced by Marcia Taylor, the assistant municipal manager of Mt. Lebanon, PA.

In broadening the GASB membership in 1997, two new members were added:

- Dr. Cynthia B. Green, formerly with the Citizens Budget Commission (a watchdog organization devoted to influencing constructive change in the governments of New York City and New York State). Dr. Green represented "users" of government financial statements on the GASB and is the first member not to hold a CPA license. (Dr. Green was replaced in 2007 by Girard Miller, formerly with Janus Group.)
- Mr. Edward J. Mazur, formerly the State Comptroller of Virginia. Although he has held a number of other posts, Mr. Mazur was seen as representing the comptroller community. (Mr. Mazur was replaced in 2007 by Jan I. Sylvis, the State of Tennessee Chief of Accountants.)

Now the Board had seven members who represented an ever-increasing spectrum of constituents.

## 1.7.2 The Preliminary to the Big Show

Given the new makeup of the Board, it was only natural then for the output to slacken. As mentioned before, only one standard was issued in 1998, but it was a big one: GASBS 33, *Accounting and Financial Reporting for Nonexchange Transactions.* Actually, the timing of this standard was quite interesting. It gave us recognition rules for various nonexchange transactions—rules that would really go into effect once the next standard was issued. Still, it has had some interesting impacts on financial statements.

In one sense, GASBS 33 gave us some "new names for old friends." By this I mean that income taxes and sales taxes became "derived tax revenues." Also, property taxes became "imposed nonexchange revenues," and grants became either "government-mandated nonexchange transactions" or "voluntary nonexchange transactions." But the standard brought us much more than just name changes.

Figure 1.10, which is adapted from Appendix C in the standard, nicely summarizes the new recognition rules.

The other major document issued in 1998 was another Q&A, *Guide to Implementation of GASB Statement 31 on Accounting and Financial Reporting for Certain Investments and for External Investment Pools*. This document came out in April, and did much to clarify the guidance in GASBS 31.

There was also one technical bulletin (TB) issued in 1998, *Disclosures about Year 2000 Issues*, issued in October. We haven't discussed TBs very much as they tend to be very narrow focused documents, and they are staff documents (similar to Q&As). This one is noteworthy because it was the first effort by the GASB to address the so-called Y2K problem. In this TB, the GASB called on governments to disclose in the notes to their financial statements the efforts they were undertaking to avoid a Y2K problem. Unfortunately, because the disclosure was in the notes, the AICPA threatened to issue qualified opinions on financial statements with that disclosure. So, a second TB came out in 1999 amending the first one, moving the information from the notes to required supplementary information (RSI), which require much less in the way of auditing than do notes. As we all know by now, Y2K didn't turn out to be much of an issue, and both TBs were superceded in 2000 with another TB that rescinded the disclosure requirements.

### 1.7.3 The New Reporting Model

With the aforementioned great change in Board membership occurring in the late 1990s, it would only be natural for the output of the Board to slow down some. However, that does not mean that they were inactive. Since the Board's inception in 1984, they had been working—in one form or another—on a new reporting model for state and local governments (SLGs). The development of this new model can be seen in the time line in Figure 1.11. As you can see, the first discussion memorandum (DM) on the measurement focus and basis of accounting (MFBA) was issued in the year following the establishment of the Board. This DM formed the foundation for both EDs and the subsequent issuance of GASBS 11.

After the Board issued GASBS 17 in 1993, indefinitely delaying the implementation of GASBS 11, they immediately went to work on the replacement document for it. The first document, the reporting model Invitation to Comment (ITC) was issued a year after GASBS 17. Based on what the Board learned from this document, where several different reporting models had been proposed, the Preliminary Views (PV) document was issued in the next year. The PV then served as the foundation for the ED for what became GASBS 34. Notice that it was nearly two-and-one-half years after the issuance of the ED that the final standard was issued. During this time, the membership of the Board expanded to seven members. There had to be a learning curve involved in getting the new members up to speed on what the Board had done so far. Also, the addition of two more voices to the mix increased the discussion on what the final standard would look like.

| Classes | Recognition |
|---|---|
| **Derived tax revenues**<br><br>Examples: sales taxes, personal and corporate income taxes, motor fuel taxes, and similar taxes on earnings or consumption | **Assets***<br>Period in which *underlying exchange has occurred* or when resources are received, whichever is first.<br><br>**Revenues**<br>Period when *underlying exchange has occurred.* (Report advance receipts as deferred revenues.) When modified accrual accounting is used, resources should be "available." |
| **Imposed nonexchange revenues**<br><br>Examples: property taxes, most fines and forfeitures | **Assets***<br>Period when an *enforceable legal claim has arisen* or when resources are received, whichever is first.<br><br>**Revenues**<br>Period when *resources are required to be used* or first period that use is permitted (for example, for property taxes, the *period for which levied*). When modified accrual accounting is used, resources should be "available." |
| **Government-mandated nonexchange transactions**<br><br>Examples: federal government mandates on state and local governments<br><br>**Voluntary nonexchange transactions**<br><br>Examples: certain grants and entitlements, most donations | **Assets* and liabilities**<br>Period when *all eligibility requirements have been met* or (for asset recognition) when resources are received, whichever is first.<br><br>**Revenues and expenses or expenditures**<br>Period when *all eligibility requirements have been met.* (Report advance receipts or payments for use in the following period as deferred revenues or advances, respectively. However, when a provider precludes the sale, disbursement, or consumption of resources for a specified number of years, until a specified event has occurred, or permanently [for example, permanent and term endowments], report revenues and expenses or expenditures when the resources are, respectively, received or paid and report resulting net assets, equity, or fund balance as restricted.) When modified accrual accounting is used, resources should be "available." |

* If there are purpose restrictions, report restricted net assets (or equity or fund balance) or, for governmental funds, a reservation of fund balance.

**Figure 1.10   Classes and timing of recognition of nonexchange transactions. (Used with permission of the Financial Accounting Foundation.)**

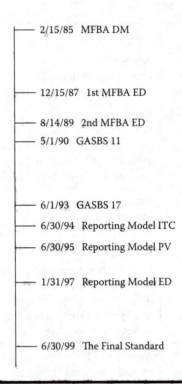

**Figure 1.11  Time line for the new reporting model.**

The year 1999 was, perhaps, the most momentous ever in the development of GAAP. It saw the publishing of the GASB's two most far-reaching standards:

- No. 34, *Basic Financial Statements—and Management's Discussion and Analysis—for State and Local Governments* (June)
- No. 35, *Basic Financial Statements—and Management's Discussion and Analysis—for Colleges and Universities* (November)

While the details of GASBS 34 are discussed later, we want to discuss some of the broader concepts here.

When you compare the length of these two standards, the difference is startling. In the *Original Pronouncements* volume published annually by the GASB, No. 34 occupies 202 pages, while No. 35 takes up only 31 pages. In CPE classes I have taught where both local government and college and university personnel have been present, the latter were always thrilled when they saw the difference in size. However, the air quickly left their balloon when I pointed out that paragraph 5 of their statement said that they had to implement No. 34. Essentially, that means they had two standards to implement, not just one.

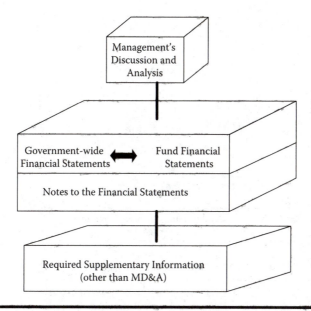

**Figure 1.12   The new reporting model: minimum requirements for general purpose external financial reporting. (Used with permission of the Financial Accounting Foundation.)**

The GASB provided a good summary of what the standards address in their diagram of the minimum requirements for general purpose external financial statements. I like to call it the new reporting model, as shown in Figure 1.12. If you compare this drawing to the Financial Reporting Pyramid in Figure 1.2, you must understand that the new model does not replace the entire pyramid. Rather, it replaces the top two layers and brings part of the third layer into the general purpose financial statements.

Still, it is a good summary of the minimum report. At the top is Management's Discussion and Analysis (MD&A). Although this is required supplementary information, it is placed at the beginning of the financial section of the report (just after the auditor's opinion). The next box represents the basic financial statements, including (1) the government-wide financial statements, (2) the fund financial statements, and (3) the notes to the financial statements. The last box is the required supplementary information other than MD&A.

Although the GASB's graphic is a good one, I have always liked the pyramid from Figure 1.2. Therefore, I combined the two into my own adaptation of the new reporting model. It is shown in Figure 1.13. I believe this graphic captures the essence of GASBS 34 in the more traditional pyramid model. As did the pyramid, it starts with the most detailed information in the accounting system. From this data, the individual fund statements and schedules are on the next level. As we shall see shortly, from these individual fund statements, the government prepares the

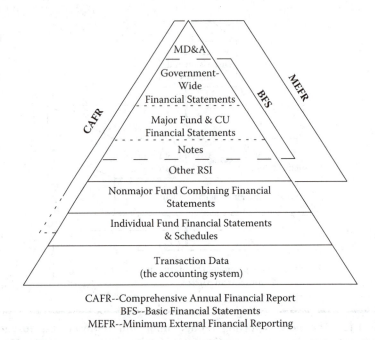

CAFR--Comprehensive Annual Financial Report
BFS--Basic Financial Statements
MEFR--Minimum External Financial Reporting

**Figure 1.13 The *new* financial reporting pyramid. (Copyright G. Robert Smith, Jr.)**

major fund statements and the nonmajor fund combining statements. The nonmajor fund statements must be prepared first as the total column then becomes a separate column in the major funds statements.

Once these statements are prepared, the government-wide financial statements can be prepared. Then, finally, the MD&A is written. Within the new pyramid, we can see the basic financial statements (described previously as part of the GASB's graphic). To the basic financial statements are added the MD&A and other RSI to form the minimum external financial reporting (MEFR) element (this element essentially replaces the old GPFS). Finally, as in the old pyramid, the CAFR contains the MEFR and as much additional information as is needed for full disclosure.

In the discussion of the new reporting requirements, GASBS 34 starts at the top of the pyramid and works down. However, as I have pointed out earlier, that is not how things work in the real world. Therefore, I prefer to discuss things from the bottom up.

Whenever I teach CPE courses, I like to point out that there are three "lies" in Figure 1.12. The first is the three-dimensional (3-D) elements that were unnecessarily added to the figure. On a piece of paper, you can't plot three dimensions—only two. I like to joke that if you want a 3-D graphic, why not make it like those on some birthday cards that when you open it the graph pops up?! The second lie is that arrow going back and forth between the government-wide financial statements and the fund financial statements. In practice, governments prepare the fund financial statements first and then prepare the government-wide statements. Therefore, this arrow should only point in one direction. The third lie is "*required* supplementary information." How can it be *required* if it is *supplementary*? I suggested that the name be changed to *additional* required information. As you can see, the GASB did not adopt this suggestion.

GASBS 34 is primarily a reporting standard—it has very little effect on the accounting system. The MFBA of all the fund types remains the same. Still, there are some important changes of which you should be aware. In accounting for long-term debt, governments formally accounted for the issuance on a net basis. For example, if a bond issue of $100,000 were issued at 99 with $15,000 in bond issue costs, the entry would look something similar to this:

| Cash | 975,000 | |
|---|---|---|
| Other financing source—bond proceeds | | 975,000 |

Now, governments must account for the details of the transaction. The discount would be reported as an Other Financing Use (OFU), while premiums would be reported as an Other Financing Source (OFS). Also, bond issue costs would be reported as an expenditure. These changes make the previous entry look similar to this:

| Cash | 975,000 | |
|---|---|---|
| Expenditures—debt service—bond issue costs | 15,000 | |
| OFU—bond discount | 10,000 | |
| Other financing source—bond principal | | 100,000 |

While all these factors are one-time events in governmental funds, they will be captured and amortized at the government-wide level. Other accounting changes include

- Easier accounting for transfers between funds. Before, governments had to distinguish between operating transfers and residual equity transfers. Now, they may be accounted and reported only as transfers (although GASBS 38 does contain a requirement to disclosure unusual or nonstandard transfers, which are similar to the old residual equity transfers).
- Capital contributions in proprietary funds. They now affect the operating statement rather than just the balance sheet.

## 1.7.4 Impact on the Funds Statements

As we already pointed out, there was no change in the MFBA for funds. There were, however, some changes in financial statements. For governmental funds, the balance sheet remained the same. As for the statement or revenues, expenditures, and changes in fund balance, all the optional methods of preparing the statement have been dropped in favor of the format known as "Format A," shown in Figure 1.14.

|   | Revenues |
|---|---|
| − | Expenditures |
| = | Excess (deficiency of revenues over (under) expenditures |
| ± | Other financing sources and uses, including transfers |
| ± | Special items |
| ± | Extraordinary items |
| = | Change in fund balance |
| + | Fund balance, beginning of year |
| = | Fund balance, end of year |

**Figure 1.14  Operating statement format.**

But, perhaps, the biggest change in financial reporting for governmental funds was saved for budget-to-actual reporting. Governments were given the choice of presenting the report as an RSI schedule or as a basic financial statement. Either way, governments now have to present the original and final budgets and the actual amounts on a budgetary basis. The variance column is optional, although most governments present it.

For proprietary funds, governments still prepare three financial statements, but not much else remains the same. The balance sheet is still there, but now it is called the *Statement of Net Assets*. A classified statement is required, using the following three categories: Assets (current and noncurrent), Liabilities (current and noncurrent), and Net Assets. That's correct: Net Assets. The fund equity accounts of contributed capital and retained earnings are gone; in their place, we classify net assets in three ways:

■ Invested in Capital Assets, Net of Related Debt. This classification is the result of a calculation: net book value of capital assets less related short-term and long-term debt.
■ Restricted Net Assets. Restrictions are externally imposed by creditors, grantors, contributors, or laws and regulations of other governments or imposed by law through constitutional provisions or enabling legislation.
■ Unrestricted Net Assets, whatever is left over. Seriously, this is a plug number if there ever was one. Net assets, naturally, are the difference between assets and liabilities. After taking out the first two classifications, unrestricted net assets is the remaining amount.*

---

* Reporting Restricted Assets as a separate category of Assets is no longer allowed. These assets must be reported as either current or noncurrent, depending on when they are expected to be expended.

|   | Operating revenues |
|---|---|
| – | Operating expenses |
| = | Operating income (loss) |
| ± | Nonoperating revenues and expenses |
| = | Income before… |
| + | Capital contributions |
| + | Additions to permanent and term endowments |
| ± | Special item |
| ± | Extraordinary items |
| ± | Transfers |
| = | Change in fund net assets |
| + | Net assets, beginning of year |
| = | Net assets, end of year |

**Figure 1.15  Proprietary fund operating statement.**

Similar to the governmental fund operating statement, the one for Proprietary Funds saw some changes as well. The name has been changed slightly to Statement of Revenues, Expenses, and Changes in Fund Net Assets. All the options for preparing this statement have been discarded in favor of a single format, summarized in Figure 1.15.

The line called "Income before … " is my own addition to the report. The GASB example calls it "Income before other revenues, expenses, gains, losses, and transfers." This is a very curious title since nonoperating revenues and expenses are frequently referred to as other revenues and expenses. I believe governments should name this line by whatever comes after it. For example, if only Capital Contributions and Transfers come between it and Changes in Fund Net Assets, the line should be called "Income Before Capital Contributions and Transfers." Seldom will all five things that could occur in this area of the statement be reported, but the title for this line could be quite long.

The single biggest change in proprietary fund reporting was perhaps left to the Statement of Cash Flows. GASBS 34 now requires that this statement be prepared using the direct method. In the Basis for Conclusions, paragraph 440, the GASB cites research that shows "that respondents from four groups—finance directors, citizens and legislators, creditors, and auditors—'clearly found the direct method to provide more and better information than the indirect method.'" The source cited for this finding is *The Use of the Statement of Cash Flows in Governmental*

*Reporting*—the PhD dissertation of G. Robert Smith, Jr. That's right: the same guy who wrote this chapter.

Perhaps the biggest change in financial reporting came with the fiduciary funds. Prior to GASBS 34, financial reporting for this fund type was somewhat segmented:

- Expendable trust funds were reported with the governmental funds
- Nonexpendable trust funds, pension trust funds, and investment trust funds (created by GASBS 31) were reported with Proprietary Funds
- Agency funds, while reported on the combined balance sheet, had their own statement: Statement of Changes in Assets and Liabilities

GASBS 34 did away with expendable and nonexpendable trust funds, at least for financial reporting. What had been reported as an expendable trust fund would now be reported as a special revenue fund. Nonexpendable trust funds were reclassified to either permanent funds (assets held for the benefit of the government), or private purpose trust funds (assets held for the benefit of others), which are reported as fiduciary funds. The financial statement formats developed for the pension trust funds in GASBS 25 have now been applied to all the fiduciary funds, including agency funds (although these funds would not appear on the Statement of Changes in Fiduciary Fund Net Assets). Also, agency funds continue to report the Statement of Changes in Assets and Liabilities, although this statement is not part of the basic financial statements.

## 1.7.5 The Change in Focus

Once all the individual fund statements are prepared in accordance with the previously mentioned guidance, nonmajor and major fund statements

One other interesting change on the operating statement for proprietary funds is that revenues are now reported as net of bad debts expense. I was not aware of this change until a government official for whom I was doing a CPE class pointed it out in my example financial statements. Naturally, I was surprised and wanted to know the source of this change. He told me it was in a footnote to Exhibit 7a in an example in the back of the Q&A for GASBS 34. To be precise, that footnote reads

> In the statement of revenues, expenses, and changes in fund net assets, the increase in the reserve for uncollectibles [bad debts expense] would be a reduction of revenue rather than an expense. See paragraph 100 (footnote 41).

I found this statement hard to believe. So, I began a series of e-mails with the GASB staff to clarify the issue. The correspondence went something similar to this:

*Me:* I believe there is an error in the footnote.
*Staff:* No, it is correct.
*Me:* What is the basis for this statement?
*Staff:* See paragraph 100, footnote 41 of the standard, as it says in the example.
*Me:* I read the reference. It says that "revenues should be reported net of discounts and allowances." It doesn't say anything about bad debts. How does that reference apply here?
*Staff:* Read paragraphs 16 and 18 of GASBS 33.
*Me:* I read the paragraphs, but they don't apply. GASBS 33 addresses nonexchange transactions. These bad debts arose from an exchange transaction. How does GASBS 33 apply?
*Staff:* We interpreted it that way.

You can't argue with that; or, if you do, you will lose. That ended the discussion.

can be prepared. The concept of a major fund is new to GASBS 34. The major fund rules apply only to governmental funds and enterprise funds. They do not apply to Internal Service Funds or Fiduciary Funds.

There are three ways for a fund to be made a major fund. First, the General Fund is always major. Second, tests are performed to see if a fund is major by calculation. Third, any other fund the government wishes to declare as major may be reported that way.

The second way to determine major funds is the most complicated. To test if a fund should be reported as major, a list of all governmental funds and enterprise funds is made. Then, four financial elements are gathered for each fund in the list: total assets, total liabilities, total revenues (which excludes extraordinary items for both governmental funds and enterprise funds), and total expenditures or expenses (again excluding extraordinary items), depending on the fund type. Subtotals for the governmental funds and enterprise funds, respectively, are determined, along with a grand total for both. Two mathematical tests are then performed. The first divides each element by its corresponding subtotal. If the result exceeds 10%, the fund may be a major fund. The second test divides each element by the grand total. If the result exceeds 5%, the fund may be a major fund. At this point, some confusion comes in to the determination. The standard implies that if one element passes the 10% test and another element for that fund passes the 5% test, then the fund is a major fund. The first Q&A stated that the same element had to pass both tests. This contradiction between the standard and the Q&A was resolved is a second statement, GASBS 37, *Basic Financial Statements—and Management's Discussion and Analysis—for State and Local Governments: Omnibus*, which adopted the method in the Q&A.

In financial reporting, the next step is to prepare the nonmajor fund combining financial statements. Combining statements would be prepared for nonmajor governmental funds (governments with many nonmajor funds of all four fund types may prepare combining statements for each fund type), nonmajor enterprise funds, internal service funds, and each fiduciary fund type. The total column from each of these statements then feeds into the major fund statements:

■ In the governmental funds, each major fund is reported in a separate column with the nonmajor funds reported in a single column. A total column is required.

■ In the proprietary funds, each major Enterprise Fund is reported in a separate column with the nonmajor Enterprise Funds reported in a single column. A total column for the Enterprise Funds is required. An aggregate column for the Internal Service Funds is reported to the right of this Enterprise Fund total column.

■ In the Fiduciary Funds, each fund type is reported in a separate column. There is a maximum of four columns on the Statement of Fiduciary Fund

Net Assets and a maximum of three columns on the Statement of Changes in Fiduciary Fund Net Assets (Agency Funds would never be reported on this statement).

## 1.7.6 The Government-Wide Financial Statements

Once all the fund financial statements have been prepared, a government is ready to prepare its government-wide financial statements. In these statements, we find one financial statement with a familiar format and another with a radically new format. In both cases, however, the MFBA is the same. For the government-wide statements, the measurement focus is on economic resources and the basis of accounting is accrual. That's right, the same MFBA we see in the proprietary funds. However, it is a different MFBA from that in the governmental funds, so some adjustments are going to be necessary to convert those statements to the MFBA for government-wide statements.

To graphically demonstrate this adjustment process, I developed "Smitty's Adaptation of the New Reporting Model," which is shown in Figure 1.16. This graphic has been compared to a wiring diagram because of the squiggly lines, but those squiggles represent the adjustments necessary to prepare the government-wide statements.

Working from the diagram, we have already prepared all the fund financial statements. From those, we will prepare the government-wide statements. As you can see, the line from the fiduciary funds (FF) goes to an "X." This "X" indicates that the fiduciary fund amounts will not be included in the government-wide statements. After all, the assets that are in the fiduciary funds are not available for general government use; therefore, these funds are left out of the government-wide statements. From the proprietary funds (PF), the line is divided. The line for the Enterprise Funds (EF) goes directly into the government-wide statements. Since both sets of statements use the same MFBA, very little (if any) adjustment should be necessary. However, the line for the Internal Service Funds (ISF) goes into the adjustment area. These adjustments are necessary because the ISFs will not be reported at the government-wide level. They are, after all, internal funds. Finally, the line from the governmental funds (GF) goes into the adjustment area because so many adjustments have to be made to convert them to government-wide statements. What kinds of adjustments? The chart in Figure 1.17 summarizes the major ones.

Other adjustments are also necessary for General Capital Assets (GCAs) and General Long-Term Liabilities (GLTL). For GCAs, governments must now capture, report, and depreciate infrastructure. The requirement to keep track of infrastructure has been around since NCGAS 1, but most governments did little, if anything, with the information. Also, all other capital assets except land, construction in progress, and other assets with infinite lives must now be depreciated. For GCAs, the depreciation expense and accumulated depreciation will be reported

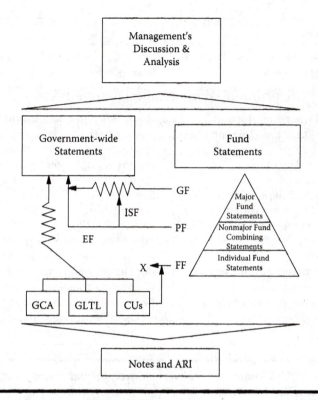

**Figure 1.16   Smitty's adaptation of the new reporting model. (Copyright G. Robert Smith, Jr.)**

only at the government-wide level; for capital assets of other fund types, these items are reported at the fund level and the government-wide level. Governments typically have very good records of their long-term liabilities. The amounts due within 1 year must now be separated for disclosure.

Hopefully, relatively few adjustments should be necessary for the component units (CUs) as they will be preparing their own government-wide financial statements. CUs that are fiduciary in nature will not be reported at the government-wide level. However, they will be integrated into the fiduciary fund statements prepared for the primary government. As for reporting the other CUs, rules from GASBS 14 still apply.

Government-wide statements include a Statement of Net Assets and a Statement of Activities. The Statement of Net Assets may be prepared in either a balance sheet format or a net asset format (which is encouraged). Governments may present assets and liabilities in the order of liquidity (which is encouraged) or use a classified format. The net asset classifications are the same as those discussed earlier for proprietary funds. Separate columns are reported for Governmental Activities (governmental funds and eliminated Internal Service Funds) and Business-Type

| Balance Sheet | Operating Statement |
|---|---|
| 1. Assimilate ISF asset, liability, and net asset amounts. | 1. Assimilate net revenues and expenses from ISFs. |
| 2. Eliminate intra-Governmental Fund receivables and payables. | 2. Eliminate intra-Governmental Fund transfers. |
| 3. Consolidate receivables and payables between Governmental Funds and Enterprise Funds into Internal Balances. | 3. Consolidate transfers to and from Enterprise Funds into a single amount. |
| 4. Pick up capital assets, net of accumulated depreciation. | 4. Eliminate expenditures that aren't expenses (capital outlay and principal payments). |
| 5. Pick up long-term liabilities. | 5. Record as revenues amounts previously deferred because of availability criterion. |
| 6. Eliminate deferred revenues that arose because of the availability criterion. | 6. Record expenses not previously recorded as expenditures (long-term debt interest and changes in other long-term liabilities). |
| 7. Accrue interest payable on long-term debt. | 7. Record depreciation on capital assets. |
| 8. Adjust other receivables and payables as necessary. | 8. Adjust other revenue and expense accounts as necessary. |

**Figure 1.17 Adjustment to convert Governmental Fund statements to Government-wide statements.**

Activities (enterprise funds). A total column for the primary government is required. The CUs are reported to the right of the total column. A total column for the reporting entity is optional. Differences between Total Net Assets on this statement and Total Fund Balance/Total Net Assets on the major fund statements must be reconciled through the use of a special schedule reported with fund statements.

The Statement of Activities is like nothing you have ever seen before. It has two sections: programs and general revenues. In the programs section, expenses and program revenues are reported on the function or activity level for governmental activities; identifiable activities for business-type activities (all or part of an enterprise fund in which the government separately accounts for revenues, expenses, gains, and losses); and by major component units (using the same option used on the Statement of Net Assets). In the general revenues section, revenues that cannot be assigned to any one function or activity are reported, as are special items, extraordinary items, and remaining transfers. The change in net assets is reported for each column (Governmental Activities, Business-Type Activities, Total, and Component Units) along with the beginning and ending net asset amounts. Differences between the Change in Net Assets on this statement and Change in Fund Balance/Change in Fund Net Assets on the major fund statements must be reconciled through the use of a special schedule reported with fund statements.

## 1.7.7 Notes to the Financial Statements

The financial statements and notes are frequently prepared simultaneously. Sometimes, the notes are needed to help prepare the financial statements, as was the case with the General Capital Assets and General Long-Term Liabilities. Other times, the statements must be done to see what needs to go in the notes. Regardless of the order of preparation, GASBS 34 added some new notes and reinforced old ones. Some of these disclosures are

- Description of the government-wide statements, including a comment that fiduciary funds and fiduciary component units are not included in the amounts
- MFBA used in the government-wide statements
- Policy for eliminating internal activity for the Statement of Activities
- Option taken in applying GASBS 20 (should have been in that statement)
- Capitalization policy for capital assets, capitalization threshold, depreciation method, and useful lives of capital assets
- Types of transactions included in program revenues on the Statement of Activities
- Policy for defining operating and nonoperating revenues in the proprietary funds
- Policy for using restricted or unrestricted resources when an expense is incurred
- Information on capital assets, including beginning balance, additions, retirements or disposals, and ending balance
- Information on long-term liabilities, including beginning balance, additions, retirements, ending balance, and amount due within 1 year
- Information on donor-restricted endowments, including net appreciation on investments, how amounts are reported in net assets, state law regarding ability to spend net appreciation, and policy for authorizing and spending investment income
- Segment information for identifiable activities where the government also separately accounts for assets, liabilities, and net assets
- If a government uses it, information on the modified approach to account for capital assets

The GASB rarely issues a statement in which new notes aren't required, so other additions to this list will be discussed with the respective standard.

## 1.7.8 MD&A and Other RSI

At some point in time, in conjunction with the financial statements and notes or after they are prepared, the other RSI and MD&A must be written.* MD&A is listed last because it is probably the last thing the government will assemble. However, that does not mean it should be left for the last minute. It is too important a document for that. Still, information is needed from other parts of the report before the MD&A can be completed.

The contents of "Other RSI" depend, in large part, on what the government has done elsewhere. Also, other RSI is placed after the notes but before the rest of the financial statements. If the government did not report budget-to-actual information in a statement, then the budget-to-actual schedule goes here. If the government elects to use the modified approach rather than depreciate their infrastructure assets, information about the assessed condition of the assets and estimated amount to maintain and actual amount spent to maintain the assets must be disclosed. Also, discussion is required for the modified approach on the basis for the condition assessment and the measurement scale used, the condition level at which the government plans to maintain the asset, and factors that affect trends in the information reported. Finally, any pension-related RSI still goes in this section.

Now, the government should have all the information it needs to complete MD&A, which is part of the minimum external financial report. As pointed out earlier, even though the GASB addresses the MD&A topic early in the standard, it is the last thing most governments will prepare. GASBS 34 laid out eight required elements that must be included in MD&A, at a minimum. The Q&A for GASBS 34 indicated that these eight things were not, in fact, the minimum but were the maximum of things to include in MD&A. GASBS 37 resolved this conflict by saying that the eight things were the only things that could be included in MD&A, but that a government could include more things than the GASB did as examples in the standard. Regardless of the rhetoric, the eight things to be included in MD&A are

1. Brief discussion of the basic financial statements, including how the government-wide statements and fund statements are related
2. Condensed summary information (14 items) derived from the government-wide statements for the current year and previous year†
3. An analysis of the government's overall financial position and results of operations

---

* Note that in Figure 1.16, I refer to RSI as ARI. ARI, or additional required information, was my suggested name change for RSI to remove one of the "lies" from the GASB drawing. Needless to say, this recommendation was not adopted by the Board.

† In the year a government implemented GASBS 34, only the current year had to be shown.

4. An analysis of balances and transactions in individual funds (with emphasis on the major funds)
5. An analysis of significant variations between the original and final budgets, and between the final budget and the actual results
6. A description of significant capital asset and long-term debt activity during the year
7. A discussion of the modified approach, if used by the government
8. A description of currently known facts that are expected to have a significant impact in the future

GASBS 34 and 35 were the first standards ever issued by the Board that went into effect at different times for different sizes of governments. Some standards have had long implementation dates (such as GASBS 11, which was also the first standard that governments were prohibited from implementing early, and GASBS 25, 26, and 27), but none had ever had staggered implementation dates. The stagger was based on total revenues of the governmental funds plus the enterprise funds for the first fiscal year ending after June 15, 1999. The dates for implementation are shown in Figure 1.18.

These standards were only the first to have staggered implementation dates. Similar staggers have also been applied to GASBI 6, GASBS 38, GASBS 43, and GASBS 45.

Without question, GASBS 34 (and 35 for colleges and universities) was the most significant standard ever issued by the GASB and implemented by state and local governments. It continues to have an impact even though all governments should have implemented the standard by now. It has been modified several times by subsequent standards and probably will be again in the future. However, the requirements of GASBS 34 are here to stay.

The only other document issued by the GASB in 1999 (as if GASBS 34 and 35 weren't enough), was GASBI 5, *Property Tax Revenue Recognition in Governmental Funds*, which came out in November. This interpretation removed the concept of "when due" from the availability criterion. However, it left in place the guidance that the availability period should not exceed 60 days.

|  | Implement in First Fiscal Year Ending After |
|---|---|
| Revenues of $100 milliion or more | June 15, 2002 |
| Revenues of $10 million or more but less than $100 million | June 15, 2003 |
| Revenues less than $10 million | June 15, 2004 |

**Figure 1.18  Implementation dates for GASBS 34 and 35.**

## 1.8 More Recent GASB Standards

Anyone who thought that GASBS 34 would be the end of the GASB was severely mistaken. Since the publications of GASBS 34 and 35, the Board has published 18 more standards. Some of these—such as GASBS 43 and 45 dealing with other postemployment benefits (OPEB)—won't be addressed here as they haven't yet gone into effect. When these later standards do go into effect, the issues will be addressed in separate chapters. In this last section, we want to touch on the standards that have gone into effect or will soon have an impact on governmental GAAP.

GASBS 36, *Recipient Reporting for Certain Shared Nonexchange Revenues*, issued in April 2000, was a very limited scope standard. It was actually an amendment to GASBS 33. The only way to amend a standard is to issue another standard; an interpretation or other GASB document just doesn't do the trick. The standard aligned reporting of shared revenues between the grantor government and the recipient government to report the revenues in the same nonexchange classification. The first Q&A for GASBS 34 was also published in 2000.

The most recent interpretation issued by the GASB also came out in 2000: *Recognition and Measurement of Certain Liabilities and Expenditures in Governmental Fund Financial Statements.* This document provided additional information about several NCGA Statements and Interpretations as well as three GASB standards. Issues addressed in GASBI 6 included the following: requiring governmental fund liabilities and expenditures that would normally be paid from current financial resources to be accrued; reporting of all forms of unmatured long-term liabilities as general long-term liabilities and not in the funds; for governments that elect to accrue interest on long-term debt that comes due "early" in the next fiscal year, "early" is defined as one to several days and not more than one month; and requiring accrual of other long-term liabilities (not debt) that mature during the period.

We have already mentioned GASBS 37 several times. This standard fixed a number of errors in GASBS 34 as well as inconsistencies between GASBS 34 and the first Q&A. Points already covered include determining major funds and what is to be included in MD&A. Other "fixes" include accounting for escheat property; removing the capitalization of interest from general capital assets; making a change to or from the modified approach, a change in estimate (as in useful life) rather than a change in principle; how to define program revenues; how to report fines and forfeitures; slightly modifying the definition of an enterprise fund to include that they charge fees to external users; defining a segment of an enterprise fund; reporting component units; and clarifying RSI reporting of the budgetary schedules where there is an excess of expenditures over appropriations.

GASBS 38, *Certain Financial Statement Note Disclosures*, was published in June 2001. This standard started out as an effort to reduce the number of notes prepared by governments. In that regard, it was a dismal failure. The end result was adding at least

11 new notes (we say "at least" because it is possible to count the number of additions different ways), while eliminating only one: the requirement to disclose the accounting policy for encumbrances. Figure 1.19 summarizes the new note requirements.

The only other major document issued in 2001 was the second Q&A on GASBS 34. Actually, the title of this version was *Guide to Implementation of GASB Statement 34 and Related Pronouncements,* as it related to more than just GASBS 34. In the foreword to the document, it states that the document addresses issues in GASBS 33, 35, 36, 37, and 38. It is interesting that both Q&As came out before the required implementation date for large governments. These were the most timely Q&As ever issued by the GASB.

GASBS 39, *Determining Whether Certain Organizations Are Component Units,* published by the GASB in May 2002, marked the first significant change to GASBS 14 since it was issued in 1991. The project for this standard actually started in the early 1990s, prior to GASBS 34, with an exposure draft on *Affiliated Organizations.* However, the Board got so involved with the new reporting model that this project was put on hold for several years. The standard addresses other organizations that were left out of GASBS 14 that should be reported in the CAFR as discretely presented component units. In most cases, the standard is concerned with foundations of colleges and universities, but can include other activities that meet the following three criteria:

1. The economic resources received or held by the separate organization are entirely or almost entirely for the direct benefit of the primary government, its component units (CUs), or its constituents.
2. The primary government, or its CUs, is entitled to, or has the ability to otherwise access, a majority of the economic resources received or held by the separate organization.
3. The economic resources received or held by an individual organization that the specific primary government, or its component units, is entitled to, or has the ability to otherwise access, are significant to that primary government.

At first, it was feared that many small organizations, such as PTAs or band booster clubs, would be included in this standard. Certainly, these types of organizations meet the first two requirements. However, they will almost always fail the third (that is not true for many booster organizations at major universities, particularly those with large athletic programs).

During the debate on GASBS 34, considerable attention was paid to the format of the budget-to-actual presentation. In some of the earlier discussions, it was felt that the format should be similar to the format of the budget document. However, this suggestion was dropped when many governments opposed it because they

Changing the definition of funds from the "boilerplate" definitions found in NCGAS 1 to describing the activities of the major funds, internal service fund type, and fiduciary fund types.

Requiring governments to disclose the amount of time used in the availability criterion.

There has always been a requirement for governments to disclose significant violations of finance-related or contractual provisions. Now, governments must address what is being done to solve the violation.

In the past, principal and interest debt service requirements on long-term debt were reported for each of the next five fiscal years and then "Thereafter" for the remaining life of the issues. Now, governments must disclose the "Thereafter" amounts in five-year increments. Several governments have elected to report *each* year until maturity, thus simplifying the disclosure even if it takes up more room.

When interest has variable rates in the above disclosure, use the rate if effect at the end of the fiscal year. Also, disclose what would cause the variable rate to change.

Obligations under capital leases are to be reported in a manner similar to the one above for long-term debt.

Governments are now required to present a schedule of short-term debt showing the amount outstanding at the beginning of the year, increases, decreases, and the amount due at the end of the year. This disclosure is required even if the amounts at the beginning of the year and/or end of the year are zero. Also, governments must disclose the purpose of the short-term debt.

Governments have always reported interfund balances by fund. That disclosure is now required for individual major funds, nonmajor Governmental Funds in the aggregate, nonmajor Enterprise Funds in the aggregate, Internal Service funds in the aggregate, and Fiduciary Fund type. Also, the purposes of the balances must be disclosed as should any amounts not expected to be repaid within one year.

If receivables and payables are aggregated in the financial statements, details about the major components must be disclosed in the notes. Also, balances not to be collected within one year must be disclosed.

Governments have always reported interfund transfers by fund. That disclosure is now required for individual major funds, nonmajor Governmental Funds in the aggregate, nonmajor Enterprise Funds in the aggregate, Internal Service Funds in the aggregate, and Fiduciary Fund type. Also, there must be a disclosure of the principal purposes of interfund transfers and separate disclosure for transfers that are unusual or contrary to the purpose of the fund [similar to the old residual equity transfers].

**Figure 1.19   New note requirements in GASBS 38.**

felt their budget format was too complicated for inclusion in the annual report.* However, after GASBS 34 came out, several governments pointed out that the requirement for reporting budget-to-actual information for the General Fund and major special revenue funds with legally adopted budgets did not match the way those governments budgeted. GASBS 41, *Budgetary Comparison Schedules—Perspective Differences*, issued in May 2003, allows governments to use functions or activities to present budget-to-actual information. However, governments using this format must report the information as an RSI schedule rather than a basic financial statement.

GASBS 42, *Accounting and Financial Reporting for Impairment of Capital Assets and for Insurance Recoveries*, issued in November 2004, is one of the stranger standards issued by the Board in its nearly 20-year history. We say it is strange because it does not require accountants or auditors to look for impairments. If they are aware that an impairment exists, then the impairment must be reported. Otherwise, there is no requirement to search out possible impairments. Also, the GASB has adopted its own rules on how to calculate and report impairments that differ significantly from those adopted by the FASB. The FASB rules tend to look at the discounted expected future cash flows from an asset compared to its book value. However, since few government capital assets generate cash flows, using that measure would have been difficult.

An impairment is defined in the standard as "a significant, unexpected decline in the service utility of a capital asset".(paragraph 5 of the standard). It is a matter of professional judgment what "significant" means, and any impairment had better be "unexpected"—otherwise, why would you have purchased the asset? The Board cites five indicators of impairment:

- Physical damage
- Change in laws and regulations or environmental factors
- Technological developments or evidence of obsolescence
- Change in duration of use
- Construction stoppage

If an asset is determined to be impaired, the standard allows three ways to calculate the amount of the impairment, including restoration cost approach, service units approach, and deflated depreciation replacement cost approach. In our opinion, the first three make the most sense, but all are doable.

Finally, we come to GASBS 44, *Economic Condition Reporting: The Statistical Section*, issued by the GASB in May 2004 but not effective until fiscal years ending after June 15, 2006. This is the first standard issued by the GASB that directly addresses the "Other Information" section of the CAFR. Most standards address what is included in minimum external financial reporting (MEFR), as defined by

---

* It makes you wonder if the budget document is too complicated for inclusion in the CAFR (given what else is included there), it might also be too complicated to be a budget.

GASBS 34. If you refer to the pyramid in Figure 1.16, it is the information below the "Other RSI" line. Everything below that point is called "Other Information." Also, in the organization of the CAFR, there are three sections:

1. Introductory Section, which the GASB rarely addresses, except to say what should go there
2. Financial Section, which contains the MEFR, combining nonmajor statement, and individual fund statements
3. Statistical Section, which, until GASBS 44, had been left largely untouched by the GASB

Instead, all we had to work with for the Statistical Section was a list of 15 tables taken from NCGAS 1 on what should be included in this section.

Now, the GASB has totally redefined the information to be presented in this section of a CAFR. It is to be divided into five categories: (a) financial trend information, (b) revenue capacity information, (c) debt capacity information, (d) demographic and economic information, and (e) operating information. To date, only a few states and some local governments have implemented this standard. It will be interesting to discover the impact these new rules have on financial reporting and other types of information included in the CAFR.

## 1.9 Conclusion

It is impossible to write any chapter like this one and be complete in the analysis of GASB standards. The last standard

This is a summary of an actual event that occurred between myself and a CPA firm in Alabama after the implementation date of GASBS 18.

It seems that one of the CPA firm's clients operated a landfill, which was an old rock quarry hole. Although the EPA rules did not apply to it (because of the type of landfill), the government still had to account for its closure and postclosure care costs. In the year of implementing GASBS 18, an accrual had to be made based on how full the hole already was. The CPA firm contacted me to get my take on how to estimate how full the hole was at that point in time.

Not being familiar with landfill operations, I tried to dismiss the question. However, the firm was in dire straits and needed an answer. Although I am not familiar with landfill operations, I am familiar with rock quarry holes. Working in one was a summer job I had for 2 years while in college. Therefore, I recommended that the CPA firm hire a well-drilling company. I then told them to park the rig in the middle of the landfill and start drilling. When the drill hit solid rock, they would know they had reached the bottom of the landfill. By then measuring the depth of the hole, they would know how full it was.

The firm immediately balked at this solution. After all, someone would have to pay the driller, and they didn't want to get involved with that. I told them I would think about it some more and get back to them, hopefully, with another solution.

After a few days I called them back to see if they knew how long it was going to take to fill up the rest of the hole. They said they did. When I asked them how, they said engineers had projected the growth in the population of the town and how much garbage they would generate. These two figures were used to project how long it would take to fill up the hole.

I said, "There is your answer." You know how long the landfill has been in operation. You know what the population was when it went into operation. Finally, the same engineers from above could estimate garbage output for the population each year (as they were going to do in the future) and come up with a reasonable amount. From these three pieces of information, it would now be possible to project how full the hole was. They liked that response and said they would use it in making their estimate.

Some months later, I saw representatives of the firm at a meeting. I asked them how they made their estimate on how full the hole was. Their response: "We guessed." I looked at them in disbelief and asked why we had gone through all the above. They had a response to that, too: "It was easier." I just smiled, shook my head, and walked away.

S tandard setting is a political process. I hope you have seen that in your study of this chapter. I thought it would be interesting to look at how the various members of the GASB have voted over time. This voting record can be seen in Figure 1.20.

From this analysis, several things stand out. First, of the 46 Standards issued in the 21-year history of the Board, there have been dissents on only 12 of them (26.1%). In 5 of those 12 cases (41.7%), there has been more than one dissenting vote. Interestingly, there has never been a dissenting vote cast on an interpretation.

Second, Mr. Antonio voted on more standards than anyone else. That is not surprising as he was the only member of the Board to serve 11 years. Since the mid-1990s, no one has been allowed to serve on the GASB or FASB for more than two full terms (10 years and 14 years, respectively). For example, had the rules not changed, Dr. Freeman could have served for 13 years: his initial 3-year appointment and two 5-year terms. In number of votes cast, Dr. Freeman and Mr. Klasny are tied for second with 28 standards, Tom Allen is fourth with 26, and Barbara Henderson and Martin Ives are tied for fifth with 25.

Third, Mr. Antonio dissented more often than any other Board member—with five "nay" votes—and has the highest percentage of nay votes among people who have served 5 years or more (Mr. Mandolini voted nay one-third of the time, but he only served 2 years and voted on 3 standards). Mr. Antonio dissented on all four pension standards that came up during his tenure and his was the only dissenting vote on any of those standards. Only once did anyone join Mr. Antonio in dissent, and that was on the highly controversial GASBS 17 that indefinitely delayed GASBS 11. No one else voted nay more than twice. Of the remaining nay votes cast, there have been only three members who have stood alone against the Board: Mr. Defliese on GASBS 9, Mr. Ives on GASBS 22, and Mr. Reilly on GASBS 45. Dr. Freeman voted nay twice and was joined by Mr. Mandolini on GASBS 14 and Mr. Klasny on GASBS 24. Mr. Klasny voted nay on GASBS 39 in which he was joined by Mr. Reilly. Mr. Allen voted nay one time, on GASBS 42, in which he was joined by Mr. Mazur in his only negative vote. Of the 17 people who have served on the Board, 8 members (Mr. Harmer, Mr. Staats, Ms. Henderson, Dr. Green, Mr. Tracy, Dr. Holder, Mr. Williams, and Mr. Attmore) have not cast a nay vote.

All things considered, that is a remarkable record of harmony on the GASB.

published by the Board while this chapter was being written was #45. Since then, seven more standards have been published:

■ No. 46, *Net Assets Restricted by Enabling Legislation* (an amendment of GASB Statement No. 34).

■ No. 47, *Accounting for Termination Benefits*.

■ No. 48, *Sales and Pledges of Receivables and Future Revenues and Intra-Entity Transfers of Assets and Future Revenues*.

■ No. 49, *Accounting and Financial Reporting for Pollution Remediation Obligations*.

■ No. 50, *Pension Disclosures* (an amendment of GASB Statements No. 25 and No. 27).

- ■ No. 51, *Accounting and Financial Reporting for Intangible Assets.*
- ■ No. 52, *Land and Other Real Estate Held as Investments by Endowments.*
- ■ No. 53, *Accounting and Financial Reporting for Derivative Instruments.*

Some of these standards have been fairly simple and straightforward; others, including No. 48, No. 49, and No. 53, have been fraught with controversy and will have long-term effects not known at this time. Standard-setting is a dynamic process, and not one that lends itself to writing a handbook like this one.

This chapter has been a rather long review of the development of governmental GAAP. After all, we have had over 70 years of activity to look at, with the most significant developments occurring in the last 20 years or so with the GASB. What will the next 20 years bring, particularly as standard-setting starts to go beyond the borders of the United States and begins to become a global process? One can only guess. But, if it is anything like the last 20 years, it will *not* be boring.

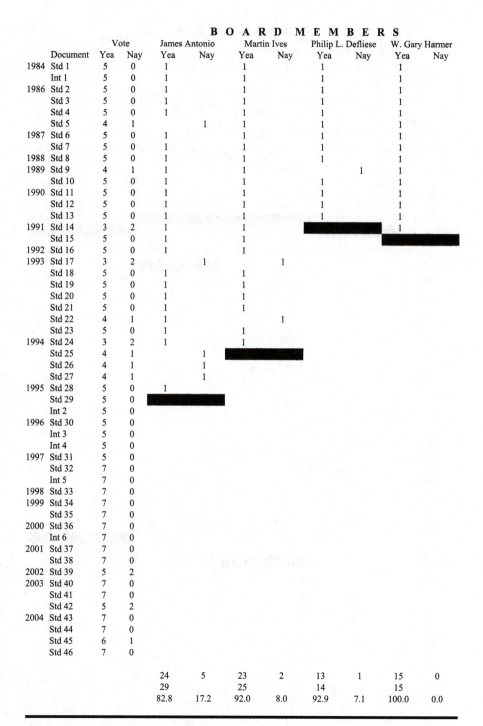

| | Document | Vote Yea | Vote Nay | James Antonio Yea | James Antonio Nay | Martin Ives Yea | Martin Ives Nay | Philip L. Defliese Yea | Philip L. Defliese Nay | W. Gary Harmer Yea | W. Gary Harmer Nay |
|---|---|---|---|---|---|---|---|---|---|---|---|
| 1984 | Std 1 | 5 | 0 | 1 | | 1 | | 1 | | 1 | |
| | Int 1 | 5 | 0 | 1 | | 1 | | 1 | | 1 | |
| 1986 | Std 2 | 5 | 0 | 1 | | 1 | | 1 | | 1 | |
| | Std 3 | 5 | 0 | 1 | | 1 | | 1 | | 1 | |
| | Std 4 | 5 | 0 | 1 | | 1 | | 1 | | 1 | |
| | Std 5 | 4 | 1 | | 1 | 1 | | 1 | | 1 | |
| 1987 | Std 6 | 5 | 0 | 1 | | 1 | | 1 | | 1 | |
| | Std 7 | 5 | 0 | 1 | | 1 | | 1 | | 1 | |
| 1988 | Std 8 | 5 | 0 | 1 | | 1 | | 1 | | 1 | |
| 1989 | Std 9 | 4 | 1 | 1 | | 1 | | | 1 | 1 | |
| | Std 10 | 5 | 0 | 1 | | 1 | | 1 | | 1 | |
| 1990 | Std 11 | 5 | 0 | 1 | | 1 | | 1 | | 1 | |
| | Std 12 | 5 | 0 | 1 | | 1 | | 1 | | 1 | |
| | Std 13 | 5 | 0 | 1 | | 1 | | 1 | | 1 | |
| 1991 | Std 14 | 3 | 2 | 1 | | 1 | | | | 1 | |
| | Std 15 | 5 | 0 | 1 | | 1 | | | | | |
| 1992 | Std 16 | 5 | 0 | 1 | | 1 | | | | | |
| 1993 | Std 17 | 3 | 2 | | 1 | | 1 | | | | |
| | Std 18 | 5 | 0 | 1 | | 1 | | | | | |
| | Std 19 | 5 | 0 | 1 | | 1 | | | | | |
| | Std 20 | 5 | 0 | 1 | | 1 | | | | | |
| | Std 21 | 5 | 0 | 1 | | 1 | | | | | |
| | Std 22 | 4 | 1 | 1 | | | 1 | | | | |
| | Std 23 | 5 | 0 | 1 | | 1 | | | | | |
| 1994 | Std 24 | 3 | 2 | 1 | | 1 | | | | | |
| | Std 25 | 4 | 1 | | 1 | | | | | | |
| | Std 26 | 4 | 1 | | 1 | | | | | | |
| | Std 27 | 4 | 1 | | 1 | | | | | | |
| 1995 | Std 28 | 5 | 0 | 1 | | | | | | | |
| | Std 29 | 5 | 0 | | | | | | | | |
| | Int 2 | 5 | 0 | | | | | | | | |
| 1996 | Std 30 | 5 | 0 | | | | | | | | |
| | Int 3 | 5 | 0 | | | | | | | | |
| | Int 4 | 5 | 0 | | | | | | | | |
| 1997 | Std 31 | 5 | 0 | | | | | | | | |
| | Std 32 | 7 | 0 | | | | | | | | |
| | Int 5 | 7 | 0 | | | | | | | | |
| 1998 | Std 33 | 7 | 0 | | | | | | | | |
| 1999 | Std 34 | 7 | 0 | | | | | | | | |
| | Std 35 | 7 | 0 | | | | | | | | |
| 2000 | Std 36 | 7 | 0 | | | | | | | | |
| | Int 6 | 7 | 0 | | | | | | | | |
| 2001 | Std 37 | 7 | 0 | | | | | | | | |
| | Std 38 | 7 | 0 | | | | | | | | |
| 2002 | Std 39 | 5 | 2 | | | | | | | | |
| 2003 | Std 40 | 7 | 0 | | | | | | | | |
| | Std 41 | 7 | 0 | | | | | | | | |
| | Std 42 | 5 | 2 | | | | | | | | |
| 2004 | Std 43 | 7 | 0 | | | | | | | | |
| | Std 44 | 7 | 0 | | | | | | | | |
| | Std 45 | 6 | 1 | | | | | | | | |
| | Std 46 | 7 | 0 | | | | | | | | |
| | | | | 24 | 5 | 23 | 2 | 13 | 1 | 15 | 0 |
| | | | | 29 | | 25 | | 14 | | 15 | |
| | | | | 82.8 | 17.2 | 92.0 | 8.0 | 92.9 | 7.1 | 100.0 | 0.0 |

**Figure 1.20   GASB voting records.**

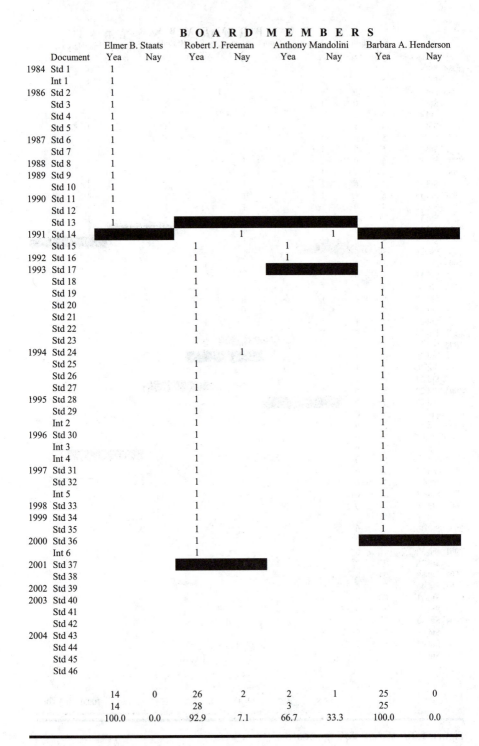

**B O A R D   M E M B E R S**

| | Elmer B. Staats | | Robert J. Freeman | | Anthony Mandolini | | Barbara A. Henderson | |
|---|---|---|---|---|---|---|---|---|
| Document | Yea | Nay | Yea | Nay | Yea | Nay | Yea | Nay |
| 1984 Std 1 | 1 | | | | | | | |
| Int 1 | 1 | | | | | | | |
| 1986 Std 2 | 1 | | | | | | | |
| Std 3 | 1 | | | | | | | |
| Std 4 | 1 | | | | | | | |
| Std 5 | 1 | | | | | | | |
| 1987 Std 6 | 1 | | | | | | | |
| Std 7 | 1 | | | | | | | |
| 1988 Std 8 | 1 | | | | | | | |
| 1989 Std 9 | 1 | | | | | | | |
| Std 10 | 1 | | | | | | | |
| 1990 Std 11 | 1 | | | | | | | |
| Std 12 | 1 | | | | | | | |
| Std 13 | 1 | | | | | | | |
| 1991 Std 14 | | | 1 | | 1 | | | |
| Std 15 | | | 1 | | 1 | | 1 | |
| 1992 Std 16 | | | 1 | | 1 | | 1 | |
| 1993 Std 17 | | | 1 | | | | 1 | |
| Std 18 | | | 1 | | | | 1 | |
| Std 19 | | | 1 | | | | 1 | |
| Std 20 | | | 1 | | | | 1 | |
| Std 21 | | | 1 | | | | 1 | |
| Std 22 | | | 1 | | | | 1 | |
| Std 23 | | | 1 | | | | 1 | |
| 1994 Std 24 | | | | 1 | | | 1 | |
| Std 25 | | | 1 | | | | 1 | |
| Std 26 | | | 1 | | | | 1 | |
| Std 27 | | | 1 | | | | 1 | |
| 1995 Std 28 | | | 1 | | | | 1 | |
| Std 29 | | | 1 | | | | 1 | |
| Int 2 | | | 1 | | | | 1 | |
| 1996 Std 30 | | | 1 | | | | 1 | |
| Int 3 | | | 1 | | | | 1 | |
| Int 4 | | | 1 | | | | 1 | |
| 1997 Std 31 | | | 1 | | | | 1 | |
| Std 32 | | | 1 | | | | 1 | |
| Int 5 | | | 1 | | | | 1 | |
| 1998 Std 33 | | | 1 | | | | 1 | |
| 1999 Std 34 | | | 1 | | | | 1 | |
| Std 35 | | | 1 | | | | 1 | |
| 2000 Std 36 | | | 1 | | | | | |
| Int 6 | | | 1 | | | | | |
| 2001 Std 37 | | | | | | | | |
| Std 38 | | | | | | | | |
| 2002 Std 39 | | | | | | | | |
| 2003 Std 40 | | | | | | | | |
| Std 41 | | | | | | | | |
| Std 42 | | | | | | | | |
| 2004 Std 43 | | | | | | | | |
| Std 44 | | | | | | | | |
| Std 45 | | | | | | | | |
| Std 46 | | | | | | | | |
| | 14 | 0 | 26 | 2 | 2 | 1 | 25 | 0 |
| | 14 | | 28 | | 3 | | 25 | |
| | 100.0 | 0.0 | 92.9 | 7.1 | 66.7 | 33.3 | 100.0 | 0.0 |

**Figure 1.20** (continued).

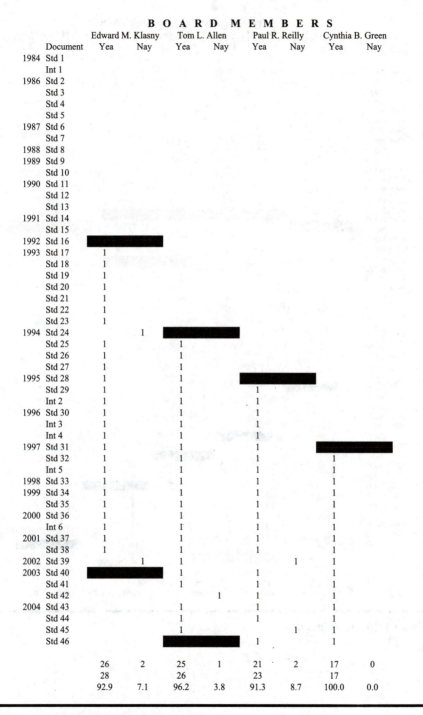

**BOARD MEMBERS**

| Document | Edward M. Klasny Yea | Nay | Tom L. Allen Yea | Nay | Paul R. Reilly Yea | Nay | Cynthia B. Green Yea | Nay |
|---|---|---|---|---|---|---|---|---|
| 1984 Std 1 | | | | | | | | |
| Int 1 | | | | | | | | |
| 1986 Std 2 | | | | | | | | |
| Std 3 | | | | | | | | |
| Std 4 | | | | | | | | |
| Std 5 | | | | | | | | |
| 1987 Std 6 | | | | | | | | |
| Std 7 | | | | | | | | |
| 1988 Std 8 | | | | | | | | |
| 1989 Std 9 | | | | | | | | |
| Std 10 | | | | | | | | |
| 1990 Std 11 | | | | | | | | |
| Std 12 | | | | | | | | |
| Std 13 | | | | | | | | |
| 1991 Std 14 | | | | | | | | |
| Std 15 | | | | | | | | |
| 1992 Std 16 | ▬▬▬ | | | | | | | |
| 1993 Std 17 | 1 | | | | | | | |
| Std 18 | 1 | | | | | | | |
| Std 19 | 1 | | | | | | | |
| Std 20 | 1 | | | | | | | |
| Std 21 | 1 | | | | | | | |
| Std 22 | 1 | | | | | | | |
| Std 23 | 1 | | | | | | | |
| 1994 Std 24 | | 1 | ▬▬▬ | | | | | |
| Std 25 | 1 | | 1 | | | | | |
| Std 26 | 1 | | 1 | | | | | |
| Std 27 | 1 | | 1 | | | | | |
| 1995 Std 28 | 1 | | 1 | | ▬▬▬ | | | |
| Std 29 | 1 | | 1 | | 1 | | | |
| Int 2 | 1 | | 1 | | 1 | | | |
| 1996 Std 30 | 1 | | 1 | | 1 | | | |
| Int 3 | 1 | | 1 | | 1 | | | |
| Int 4 | 1 | | 1 | | 1 | | | |
| 1997 Std 31 | 1 | | 1 | | 1 | | ▬▬▬ | |
| Std 32 | 1 | | 1 | | 1 | | 1 | |
| Int 5 | 1 | | 1 | | 1 | | 1 | |
| 1998 Std 33 | 1 | | 1 | | 1 | | 1 | |
| 1999 Std 34 | 1 | | 1 | | 1 | | 1 | |
| Std 35 | 1 | | 1 | | 1 | | 1 | |
| 2000 Std 36 | 1 | | 1 | | 1 | | 1 | |
| Int 6 | 1 | | 1 | | 1 | | 1 | |
| 2001 Std 37 | 1 | | 1 | | 1 | | 1 | |
| Std 38 | 1 | | 1 | | 1 | | 1 | |
| 2002 Std 39 | | 1 | 1 | | | 1 | 1 | |
| 2003 Std 40 | ▬▬▬ | | 1 | | 1 | | 1 | |
| Std 41 | | | 1 | | 1 | | 1 | |
| Std 42 | | | | 1 | 1 | | 1 | |
| 2004 Std 43 | | | 1 | | 1 | | 1 | |
| Std 44 | | | 1 | | 1 | | 1 | |
| Std 45 | | | 1 | | | 1 | 1 | |
| Std 46 | | | ▬▬▬ | | 1 | | 1 | |
| | 26 | 2 | 25 | 1 | 21 | 2 | 17 | 0 |
| | 28 | | 26 | | 23 | | 17 | |
| | 92.9 | 7.1 | 96.2 | 3.8 | 91.3 | 8.7 | 100.0 | 0.0 |

**Figure 1.20** (continued).

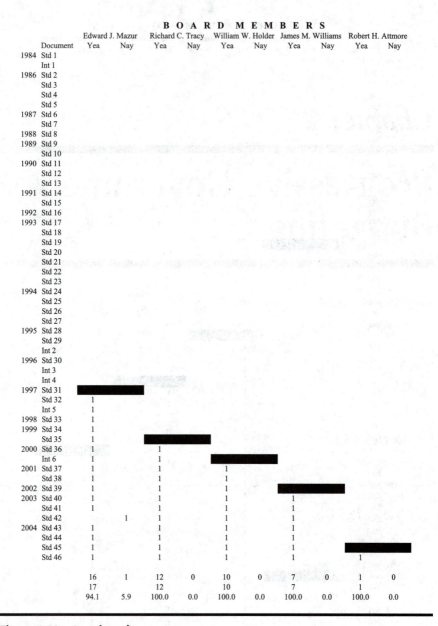

**Figure 1.20   (continued).**

# Chapter 2

# Progressive Government Budgeting

## Gerald J. Miller
*Arizona State University, School of Public Affairs*

## Donijo Robbins
*Grand Valley State University, School of Public and Nonprofit Administration*

## Contents

| | | |
|---|---|---|
| 2.1 | Introduction | 72 |
| 2.2 | Working Definitions of the Budget | 73 |
| 2.3 | Budget Process | 77 |
| 2.4 | Budget Techniques | 84 |
| | 2.4.1 Line-Item Budgeting: The Control Orientation | 87 |
| | 2.4.2 Performance Budgeting: The Management Approach and Later Developments | 89 |
| |     2.4.2.1 Level-of-Service Approach | 92 |
| |     2.4.2.2 Unit Cost Approach | 92 |
| |     2.4.2.3 Activity Costs with Goals Attached | 94 |
| |     2.4.2.4 The Full-Time Equivalent Employee (FTE) Approach | 94 |
| |     2.4.2.5 Later Developments in Performance Budgeting Found in Responsibility Center Budgeting | 101 |
| | 2.4.3 Program Budgeting | 103 |
| | 2.4.4 PPBS: The Planning Orientation | 105 |
| | 2.4.5 Zero Base Budgeting | 108 |

2.5 Revenue Analysis.................................................................................112
    2.5.1 Principles of Each Revenue Source.................................................113
    2.5.2 Principles Useful in Evaluating a Tax System..............................114
2.6 Types of Taxes..................................................................................117
    2.6.1 Income.................................................................................118
        2.6.1.1 Definition of Income .........................................118
        2.6.1.2 Methods of Taxation ..........................................118
        2.6.1.3 Evaluation..........................................................119
    2.6.2 Consumption.......................................................................120
        2.6.2.1 Methods of Taxation ........................................120
        2.6.2.2 Evaluation..........................................................121
    2.6.3 Wealth .................................................................................121
        2.6.3.1 Definition of Wealth..........................................121
        2.6.3.2 Methods of Taxation of Wealth .......................122
    2.6.4 Nontax Revenues ................................................................123
2.7 Summary .........................................................................................124
Bibliography...........................................................................................124

## 2.1 Introduction

Government leaders have a practical relationship with money through budgeting. Budget decisions on local school teacher salaries and facilities, for example, have an impact on the future economic lives of students and even the prices of their parents' houses in the community. Budget decisions on state aid to local school districts create and sustain education policy, tax policy, and even social welfare policies. Federal budgeting processes lead to judgments about measures to use and steps to take to deal with failing local school districts. Logically, the budget drives those decisions within financial management and accounting systems—how much the program will cost, where the money will come from, who will benefit, and who will pay. Through budgeting, people in government decide.

These decisions vary in magnitude. Through budgeting, everyone may propose and legislators dispose of the watershed initiatives that may shape a generation's approach to a particular problem such as education. The budget also drives everyday choices, especially those that require major or only marginal adjustment in past choices. Budget process testimony about policy and program effectiveness gives executives information about exceptional performance, both positive and negative. Also, marginal comparison gives budgeters on the front lines scorecards about how well they are doing in comparison to their peers.

Finally, the budget stabilizes expectations about decision-making processes and outcomes. A consensus may exist, for example, about good budgeting procedure because spending has achieved so much stability or substantial agreement exists among those involved. Consensus may also exist because a program or policy has a thorough hearing during budget proceedings, especially in the environment of cost control and searches for savings in some existing programs to underwrite new programs or expansions in other ones.

Budgets, therefore, drive choices that vary from those that lead to watershed change to those involving only marginal adjustment.

As a cyclical phenomenon, budgets induce change or stability, one effect following the other through time. From stability, choice may move to change of the watershed variety. After these watershed changes, budgeting may enter a period of marginal adjustment and then to stability again. This cycle may be illustrated by the transition to and from war periods in this country's budgetary history in which concerns ranged from reading (Why can't Johnny read?) to math and science (the Soviets will beat us to the moon) to overall measurement of student achievement (No Child Left Behind). Likewise, the series of choices may move in the other direction. Full stability yields to marginal adjustment and finally to watershed change.

This chapter defines and describes aspects of a budget. A budget signifies not one spending choice but rather a series of choices. "Budgets" might refer to those of one mayor's administration, those of an era of a particular party's control of a statehouse, or even those made by leaders during a particular era of government such as the New Deal or the Neoconservative Era. The stream of choices that characterize the era is referred to collectively as the budget, and at this high level of generalization, the stream of choices of whatever sequence and at whatever point in the cycle signify the budget. The stream allows us to characterize the budget as the method and substance of public policy and administration.

The forces that drive budgets along the cyclical path have an understandable dynamic and logic. Thus, we look at the forces that drive budgets, their logic, and ultimately, their dynamics as a financial management system in the following sections.

First, we need to ask what a budget is and what are the historical and cultural bases of stability and change in budgets. Then, we elaborate on the dynamics—the budget process—through which the participants formulate the budget. Finally, we characterize the budget within the context of taxes and revenues as well as financial management and accounting—the systemic expression of stability and change through the inflow, operations, and outflow of decisions about money in government.

## 2.2 Working Definitions of the Budget

What is a budget? From a theoretical perspective, the definition depends on whom you ask: the elitists, the pluralists, the executive, the legislators, the agencies or departments, or even the citizenry. A budget lists future or anticipated revenues and expenditures in a set of documents. The budget represents an estimate of revenues

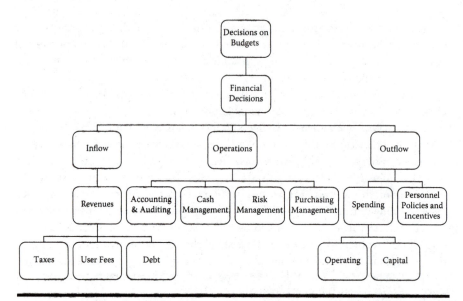

**Figure 2.1    Budgets in the hierarchy of decisions guiding inflow, operations, and outflows of funds.**

and expenditures for a future period, an estimate made by using forecasting tools that are not limited to plain and simple good guessing. The document and its purpose have changed with time. From a tool for control at first, to one for management, planning, or a combination; budgets adapt, change, and morph themselves into a tool useful to decision makers.

At their most stable, budgets are artifacts of history and culture. History and culture tend to generalize small changes to what appear to be large but infrequent turns of events. We can define a budget as a complex process in which administrators and political leaders choose to tax and spend, in the manner they believe the role of government in society dictates. Politics, power, organization, and control transform beliefs by acting as instruments that fashion budgets. We expect that beliefs transform and control budgets through the application of political action, power, and organization. If the expectation holds, there should be little doubt that budgets guide government administration and drive government financial management.

We emphasize the complex transformation of beliefs into budgets. Political and administrative actors do make decisions that create budgets, and these decisions are complex. We can elaborate the forces that tug at the choices among values, these choices being explicit amounts of taxing and spending and the target groups whose members will pay and benefit.

We see budgets as a body of choices. The dynamic of choice lies in the temporal movement of money through government as inflows, operations, and outflows (see Figure 2.1).

**Figure 2.2    The financial management cycle.**

The inflows are resource-based in that governments may tax, charge for services, or borrow. The outflows tend to be spending because spending covers plans and procedures for operations, purchase and construction of capital assets, and staffing compensation plans and procedures. Finally, the operations segment, accounting and auditing, purchasing, cash management, and risk management provide information on how well the organization is functioning and acts to detect deviation and implement budget decisions. At the center of it all stands the budget—a decision producer—that pushes the sequence of inflow and outflow.

The first budget model centers on the plan that the individuals using the process of budgeting produce. Planning is one of two ways of looking at budgeting, the other being financial management. Figure 2.2 reveals the second model, the financial management model, long advocated by the U.S. Government Accountability Office (1985). Even though the GAO characterizes federal government financial management, the process can apply to other levels of government with ease.

Figure 2.2's characterization puts budgeting in place as a part of a cycle in which information moves from the plan stage through budgeting to execution and audit stages. Driving financial management, planning and programming determine what program alternatives suit the goals and policies that departments must achieve and follow. While integration of plans, programs, and budgets has developed through use of planning, programming, budgeting systems (PPBS; discussed later), the integration of these with budget execution and accounting lags, says GAO. GAO analysts advocate the accrual basis for budgeting, accounting, and reporting to integrate the four elements of the financial management system. According to one authority, "Cash accounting records the transaction when cash is exchanged, whereas accrual indicators record a financial flow at the time economic value is created, transformed, exchanged, transferred or extinguished, whether or not cash is exchanged at the time" (Treasury, Australian Government, 1999, p. 1). Noting the poor quality of financial management information available to executives, GAO observed that "many agencies focus primarily on getting their budget approved and then do only minimum accounting and compliance-type reporting" (p. 11).

The result? GAO argues, "[A] lack of integration of budgeting and accounting systems … makes it difficult to consolidate, match, or compare financial data among agencies or different organizations within the same department or agency" (1985, p. 11). More, "budgets are frequently developed without reliable budget execution data" because budgeting done on an obligation basis—noted as the amount of money authorized by statute and encumbered for outlay within the fiscal year through contracts and other decisions—while the execution of the budget takes place on a combination basis, including obligation, cash, and even accrual of spending whenever it will form an outlay in the future. The model of Figure 2.2 pushes the integration of budgeting with other subsystems, forcing the view that the correct level at which to view budgeting is within the context of financial management.

So, what is a budget? Freeman (1972, p. 10) offers several definitions of a budget. A budget is "a plan of financial operation embodying an estimate of proposed expenditures for a given period and the proposed means of financing them, or a process for systematically relating the expenditure of funds to the accomplishment of planned objectives." He offers another more comprehensive, complementary definition: "(1) a financial expression of a [jurisdiction's] plans for a specified period of time, (2) a control device during the operating period, and (3) a vehicle by which actual results may be compared with planned results and the variances analyzed so that we may improve both our operations and budgeting in the future."

If we consider, like Sundelson (1935), what the ideal budget might be, we would find a set of generally agreed upon ideas relating the requirements of informed voters and responsible decision makers. These ideas include comprehensiveness, exclusiveness, unity, annularity, accuracy, clarity, and publicity. Comprehensiveness requires that the budget hold all authority for expenditure and revenue, which the government provides. Exclusiveness reflects the importance attached to separating fiscal matters from substantive ones; the budget should include financial matters, not other matters of substance. Unity suggests the need to relate all of the parts of the budget to one another: what revenues support what expenditures, if earmarked. Annularity forces regular review of expenditures and revenues by commanding the length of the period between them. Accuracy means that estimates of needs and resources are near the mark rather than the product of a dream or suggested by political strategy. Clarity demands that who pays what and how much as well as what is spent be unmistakable rather than confusing or simplistic. Finally, budget making must seek publicity, which essentially consists of the airing of needs, grievances, and policy positions of representative and represented.

## 2.3 Budget Process

The dollars set forth in a budget document provide a common terminology for describing the plans covering diverse governmental operations. Far from being merely a financial document, however, the budget represents the process by which government policy is made, the action program is put into effect, and policymakers establish both legislative and administrative controls. At the heart of budgeting lies the need for planning. As with most plans, there are four logical stages in which to divide the budgetary process: (1) budget preparation, (2) consideration and adoption, (3) execution, and (4) audit (see Figure 2.3). We illustrate these stages here with a typical city government organization, but, with modifications for other forms of government and for legal or constitutional provisions unique to a place, the stages would be quite similar across public organizations.

The budget process—particularly steps one and two—focuses attention, through analysis and review, on choices between programs, especially between existing and new ones. Analysis, review, and choice are a continuous process with each annual budget representing an arbitrary period over the lives of programs, the administration of a leader, the organization, and the community. To work effectively, the budget process must provide systematic and efficient "procedural devices" to reveal needs, highest and best uses of funds, and the tax prices and user fees a citizen must pay for government services.

The elements of a budget process follow generally understood norms. Many of the norms appear as "best practices" in the work of the National Advisory Council on State and Local Budgeting (e.g., Calia, Guajardo, and Metzgar, 2000). A digest of the items classified and investigated for best practices appears in Table 2.1.

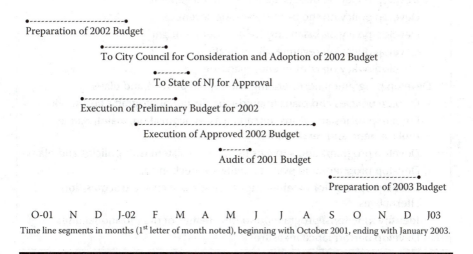

Figure 2.3  2002 budget time line for Rutherford, New Jersey.

**Table 2.1 National Advisory Council on State and Local Budgeting Recommended Practices ("Best Practices")**

| |
|---|
| *Principle* |
|   Element |
|     Recommended Practice |
| *Establish Broad Goals to Guide Government Decision Making* |
|   Assess community needs, priorities, challenges, and opportunities |
|     Identify stakeholder concerns, needs, and priorities |
|     Evaluate community condition, external factors, opportunities, and challenges |
|     Identify opportunities and challenges for government services, capital assets, and management |
|   Assess services and programs, and identify issues, opportunities, and challenges |
|     Assess capital assets, and identify issues, opportunities, and challenges |
|     Assess government management systems, and identify issues, opportunities, and challenges |
|   Develop and disseminate broad goals |
|     Identify broad goals |
|     Disseminate goals and review with stakeholders |
| *Develop Approaches to Achieve Goals* |
|   Adopt financial policies |
|     Develop policy on stabilization funds |
|     Develop policy on fees and charges |
|     Develop policy on debt issuance and management |
|     Develop policy on the use of one-time revenues |
|     Develop policy on balancing the operating budget |
|     Develop policy on revenue diversification |
|     Develop policy on contingency planning |
|   Develop programmatic, operating and capital policies and plans |
|     Prepare policies and plans to guide the design of programs and services |
|     Prepare policies and plans for capital asset acquisition, maintenance, replacement, and retirement |
|     Develop programs and services that are consistent with policies and plans |
|     Develop programs and evaluate delivery mechanisms |
|     Develop options for meeting capital needs and evaluate acquisition alternatives |
|     Identify functions, programs, and/or activities of organizational units |
|     Develop performance measures |

**Table 2.1 (continued)   National Advisory Council on State and Local Budgeting Recommended Practices ("Best Practices")**

Develop management strategies

    Develop strategies to facilitate attainment of programs and financial goals

    Develop mechanisms for budgetary compliance

    Develop the type, presentation, and time period of the budget

*Develop a Budget Consistent with Approaches to Achieve Goals*

  Develop a process for preparing and adopting a budget

    Develop a budget calendar

    Develop budget guidelines and instructions

    Develop mechanisms for coordinating budget preparation and review

    Develop procedures to facilitate budget review, discussion, modification, and adoption

    Identify opportunities for stakeholders input

  Develop and evaluate financial options

    Conduct long-range financial planning

    Prepare revenue projections

    Document revenue sources in a revenue manual

    Prepare expenditure projections

    Evaluate revenue and expenditure options

    Develop a capital improvement plan

  Make choices necessary to adopt a budget

    Prepare and present a recommended budget

    Adopt the budget

*Evaluate Performance and Make Adjustments*

  Monitor, measure, and evaluate performance

  Monitor, measure, and evaluate budgetary performance

  Monitor, measure, and evaluate financial condition

  Monitor, measure, and evaluate external factors

  Monitor, measure, and evaluate capital program implementation

  Make adjustments as needed

    Adjust the budget

    Adjust policies, plans, programs, and management strategies

    Adjust broad goals, if appropriate

*Source:* Calia et al. (2000). *Government Finance Review,* 16(2: April), 2.

The best practices in Table 2.1 comprise necessary elements of the best budget processes. Practitioners who call these elements "the best" have found them the most useful ones in formulating a budget that involves the group of locality leaders and managers as well as professional budgeters and citizens.

Common elements follow a timetable. This timetable follows in the discussion about the steps in budgeting.

First, the budget process requires planning and scheduling of each step. The chief executive can control the planning and scheduling or can delegate them to a budget director. The chief emphasis in the look ahead is allotment of time and effort to steps and people. The planning and scheduling effort produces a budget calendar. Figure 2.4 presents the fiscal year 2005 budget calendar for the City of Grand Rapids, Michigan.

Next, the executive sets policy and budget techniques through the budget instructions and statements. A budget message to staff members involved in budgeting starts the actual process of budget formulation. The message announces the start and the schedule at the very least, but the message may proclaim certain priorities among financial goals as well. Standard forms dictate how department staff members present financial estimates to those reviewing the budget requests. The forms will often follow a combination of those budget techniques discussed later: line-item detail, performance budgeting, and program-goal-driven budget requests.

Staff members who have the responsibility of formulating budget requests do so through relatively simple or complicated analyses. Simple analyses are those reflecting services mandated by other governments or by the courts. Analyses that are more complex underlie demand-driven programs and those programs to which technological development has permitted cost savings in exchange for greater investment. Efficiency and effectiveness of existing services may control analyses in other areas.

Resource estimates follow the analyses. Budget resource estimates employ a number of different techniques. Many of these techniques we present in a later section. The process of estimation only partly extrapolates from experience. The variety and diversity of revenue sources will determine the complexity of the revenue estimation process.

The budget preparation continues with individual expenditure estimates and work programs, budget requests, usually flowing to some central source such as the budget director or the chief executive. Whether or not the total of all requested resources exceeds the revenue estimate, the budget director reviews requests for the simplest of arithmetic errors, compliance with the original "Instructions and Policy Statement," or performance, service standard, and workload analysis. The budget director formulates an executive budget by revising budget requests—accepting or refusing those presented—as well as holding appeals hearings on refusals, revising estimates as greater information arrives, and formulating revenue changes for legislative action. The budget director forces a preliminary balance between expenditure requests and revenue estimates.

| Date | Action |
|------|--------|
| February 12 | • Fiscal staff met with a regional analyst for revenue estimating |
| February 24 | • Presentation to commissioners[a] with comprehensive set of recommendations and first round of appropriation requests |
| March 16 | • Delivery of general fund and internal service funds<br>• Approval of police department appropriation request |
| March 23 | • Presentation of balance of general fund and internal service funds (excluding fire department)<br>• Adoption of revised income tax exemption deduction |
| March 30 | • Review of fire department budget<br>• Approval of selected internal service fund apropriation requests<br>• Resolution to establish a public hearing on property tax administration fee |
| April 13 | • Delivery of preliminary FY2005 fiscal plan<br>• Review of enterprise, special revenue, and other funds<br>• Public hearing on property tax administration fee |
| April 20 | • Review of remaining funds<br>• Staff response to city commission question<br>• Resolution to establish a public hearing on proposed budget<br>• Approval of appropriation requests for all remaining funds (excluding general fund and internal service funds) |
| April 27 | • Adoption of property tax administration fee<br>• Approval of fire department appropriation request<br>• Approval of appropriation request for the balance of the general fund |
| May 4 | • Public hearing on proposed budget |
| May 11 | • Adoption of the FY2005 budget ordinance |
| May 18 | • Resolution to establish a public hearing on 2005 property tax levy |
| May 25 | • Public hearing on 2005 property tax levy |
| June 1 | • Resolution to establish 2005 property tax levy |

[a] City of Grand Rapids is a commission form of government.
*Source:* City of Grand Rapids Fiscal Plan 2004–2005, p. xxviii.

**Figure 2.4   Budget review calendar for the city of Grand Rapids, Michigan.**

The budget director submits the budget estimate to the chief executive. The chief executive examines decisions about expenditures and revenues. The chief executive makes the final decisions, draws up an executive budget, and proposes it to the legislative body.

The legislative body, such as a city council, reviews the executive budget. Legislators may need to consult the chief executive and budget director for explanations. The legislators hold public hearings at which citizens may testify. The legislators then formulate the final budget, adopt it, and prepare any other action to set tax rates.

The last two stages—execution and audit—complete the budgetary process. While the budget is the plan for the upcoming year, managers execute the budget for the current year at the same time that auditors examine the records for the budget of the previous year. Although accounting plays an important role in the entire process, it is most prevalent in the final stages as a way to monitor and manage expenditures. Historically, no centralized accounting process existed; for example, a century ago, ledgers were the typical way to keep track of resources. Ledgers have not disappeared, but essential accounting procedures and reporting formats have been developed to keep the budget on track. Accounting is generally viewed as a process to measure profits, but government is not in the business of making profits; therefore accounting and budgeting professionals had to develop a system to monitor, control, and measure agency productivity for budget purposes. As such, the Governmental Accounting Standards Board (GASB) defined and instituted three categories of fund accounts for state and local governments—governmental funds, proprietary funds, and fiduciary funds—which provide a mechanism to institute and maintain accountability. Each is self-balancing, and tracks revenues and appropriations. We discuss each in turn.

Governmental funds focus on the current financial resources spent to fulfill general government purposes. There are typically five types of governmental funds: a general fund, special revenue funds, capital projects funds, debt service funds, and permanent funds. All of these funds use the modified accrual basis of accounting.

Proprietary funds account for government's business-like organizations and activities, such as services that are fee-based, for example, water and sewer services. Enterprise and internal service funds constitute proprietary funds. Because these funds represent business-like activities, the accrual basis of accounting is used.

Fiduciary funds account for assets held by a government unit in a trustee or agency capacity on behalf of others, such as a pension trust fund. Generally, there are four fiduciary fund types, using accrual basis of accounting. Under GASB Statement No. 34, "Basic Financial Statements—and Managements Discussion and Analysis—for State and Local Governments" (GASB, 1999), fiduciary funds are now classified as follows: investment trust funds, private-purpose trust funds, pension (and other employee benefit) trust funds, and agency funds.

Figure 2.5 illustrates the fund structure for the city of Grand Rapids, Michigan, and Figure 2.6 explains the accounting process for the different types of funds.

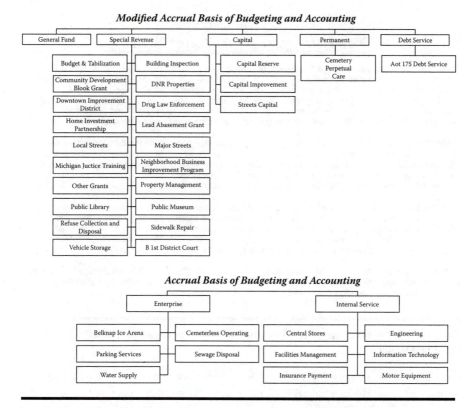

**Figure 2.5** **City of Grand Rapids fund structure for budgeted funds.**

Grand Rapids uses two of the major fund categories—governmental and proprietary—to manage its budget. Each of these categories is separated into subcategories, each with its own designated fund, with the exception of the general fund. Looking at the special revenue funds (there are 20 of them), and although most are not self-sufficient (they need not be as an enterprise fund), each is allocated earmarked revenues that have been raised via a tax of some sort, typically, a property tax at the local level. For example, the city taxes property and income; all the income tax revenue goes to the general fund whereas the property tax revenue is allocated among many funds. This is illustrated in Figure 2.7.

The fiscal plan for FY2005 estimates that $15,902,876 will be raised via property taxes and earmarks for all special revenue funds and $12,223,383 of the property taxes are nonearmarked, so they are allocated to the general fund.

Analyzing one of the special revenue funds, for example, the refuse collection and disposal fund, we see a combination of revenues, from the sale of refuse tags and bags to property taxes levied so to balance this fund (see Figure 2.8).

The refuse collection fund is not self-sufficient, resulting in the need for an earmarked property tax. In fact, prior to the FY2005 budget, the property tax, a

> ### City of Grand Rapids
> ### Fund Structure for Budgeted Funds
>
> **What are *"Budgetary Basis"* and *"Accounting Basis?"***
> Budgetary basis is the method used to determine when revenues and expenditures are recognized for budgeting purposes. Accounting basis is used to determine when revenues and expenditures are recognized for financial reporting purposes. These determinations depend on the measurement focus of the individual fund – that is, the types of transactions and events that are reported in a fund's operating statement. The City's funds use either the modified accrual or the accrual measurement focus.
>
> **Modified Accrual Basis** – Funds that focus on <u>current financial resources</u> use the modified accrual basis, which recognizes increases and decreases in financial resources only to the extent that they reflect short-term inflows or outflows of cash. Amounts are recognized as revenue when earned as long as they are collectible within the period or soon enough thereafter to be used to pay liabilities of the current period. These individual funds are known collectively as, "governmental fund types."
>
> **Accrual Basis** – Funds that focus on <u>total economic resources</u> employ the accrual basis, which recognizes increases and decreases in economic resources as soon as the underlying event or transaction occurs. Revenues are recognized as soon as they are earned and expenses are recognized as soon as a liability is incurred, regardless of the timing of related cash inflows and outflows. In the private sector, the accrual basis is often used by for-profit business enterprises and not-for-profit organizations.
>
> **Difference between the City's Budgetary Basis and Accounting Basis** – For funds that use the modified accrual basis, the portion of year-end fund balance reserved for outstanding compensated absence liabilities (for example, unused vacation) is not considered part of budgetary reserves.

**Figure 2.6 Explanation of fund accounting differences from the city of Grand Rapids, Michigan.**

millage of 1.35, was not high enough to yield sufficient revenue to balance operations; therefore, the city raised the rate to 1.55. Remember, special revenue funds do not need to be self-sufficient, and many use property tax levies to balance the fund balance.

Using these types of funds, special funds and otherwise, creates a tool of accountability such that the local government cannot use the earmarked recourses for another fund or line-item. In the end, the presence of accounting in the budget process is no mistake and its significance and role in the budgeting process must be fully understood by managers, planners, and budgeters alike. Figure 2.9 depicts the flow of decision making in the allocation of resources. At each stage and movement to the next, accounting is ever present and important.

## 2.4 Budget Techniques*

Recall Sundelson's ideas of budgeting: comprehensiveness, exclusiveness, unity, annuality, accuracy, clarity, and publicity. Yet, Sundelson's eight principles might be compressed to one, according to Burkhead (1956, p. 107; 1965, pp. 97–99):

---

* One of the best histories of the development of techniques and budget reform comes from Tyer and Willand (1997).

| | GENERAL FUND | | | SPECIAL REVENUE FUNDS | | |
|---|---|---|---|---|---|---|
| | FY2003 Actual | FY2004 Estimated | FY2005 Budget | FY2003 Actual | FY2004 Estimated | FY2005 Budget |
| FINANCIAL SOURCES: | | | | | | |
| Income Tax | 49,348,162 | 49,132,816 | 49,508,793 | - | - | - |
| State Grants/Shared Revenues | 27,006,118 | 25,062,034 | 24,129,032 | 16,695,069 | 14,805,300 | 14,894,868 |
| Property Tax | 12,806,257 | 11,064,453 | 12,223,383 | 13,940,358 | 14,534,212 | 15,902,876 |
| Services and Fees | 13,844,825 | 15,586,658 | 10,307,310 | 12,021,043 | 12,529,331 | 17,782,275 |
| Federal Grants | 1,724,994 | 2,671,200 | 495,714 | 18,987,842 | 19,836,037 | 8,169,494 |
| Contributions from Other Funds | 5,201,640 | 3,843,780 | 7,587,573 | 2,523,652 | 2,572,317 | 5,814,240 |
| Fines/Forfeitures | 3,133,378 | 3,072,500 | 566,500 | 985,824 | 566,300 | 2,136,500 |
| Interest on Investments | 767,410 | 425,052 | 400,000 | 654,144 | 453,200 | 447,147 |
| Other Local Governments | - | - | - | 200,196 | 666,666 | - |
| Miscellaneous | 3,643,075 | 3,106,261 | 2,837,840 | 2,159,390 | 615,247 | 6,915,666 |
| TOTAL SOURCES | 117,475,859 | 113,964,754 | 108,056,145 | 68,167,518 | 66,578,610 | 72,063,066 |
| | | | | | | |
| EXPENDITURES: | | | | | | |
| Public Safety Services | 75,914,256 | 74,332,063 | 60,252,274 | 699,368 | 413,463 | 8,173,067 |
| Planning & Community Dev | 13,925,225 | 13,510,123 | 12,655,080 | 15,615,347 | 14,343,859 | 13,463,974 |
| Public Works & Economic Dev | 9,748,151 | 8,667,342 | 4,875,544 | 21,367,230 | 25,763,017 | 27,458,532 |
| Cultural Services | - | - | - | 12,964,103 | 11,878,064 | 11,993,742 |
| Fiscal Services | 8,674,936 | 10,520,217 | 8,339,412 | 959,727 | 887,484 | 842,649 |
| Human Resources Services | 3,000,808 | 2,904,352 | 2,789,659 | - | - | - |
| Management Services | 3,226,565 | 3,148,043 | 3,043,299 | - | - | - |
| Capital Outlay | - | - | - | 3,402,198 | 2,717,730 | 2,768,350 |
| Debt Service | - | - | - | - | - | - |
| Contributions to Other Funds | 5,277,652 | 5,266,354 | 7,596,240 | 7,695,596 | 4,266,832 | 10,576,460 |
| Other | 2,339,355 | 3,285,827 | 7,336,043 | - | - | - |
| Estimated Appropriation Lapse | - | - | (526,938) | - | - | - |
| TOTAL USES | 122,106,948 | 121,634,321 | 106,360,613 | 62,703,569 | 60,270,449 | 75,276,774 |
| | | | | | | |
| Net Increase (Decrease) in Fund Balance | (4,631,089) | (7,669,567) | 1,695,532 | 5,463,949 | 6,308,161 | (3,213,708) |
| | | | | | | |
| General Contingencies and Reserves | - | - | - | (14,115,261) | | - |
| | | | | | | |
| Fund Balance, July 1 | 15,848,448 | 11,217,359 | 3,547,792 | 43,367,513 | 34,716,201 | 41,024,362 |
| | | | | | | |
| Fund Balance, June 30 | 11,217,359 | 3,547,792 | 5,243,324 | 34,716,201 | 41,024,362 | 37,810,654 |

**Figure 2.7 City of Grand Rapids, Michigan: Summary of estimated financial sources and uses.**

> There is probably only one principle which is likely to be useful—that of operational adequacy. The budget cycle and the budgetary process must be capable of coping with the governmental problems at hand. This means that there must be an emphasis on flexibility and adaptability, not an emphasis on an ideal that is intended to be unchanging.

Among the budget processes widely used in governments, we find much evidence that Burkhead is right. However, within these principles are contained the basic tenets for defining a management device, above all. Actual government practices are more often at the one extreme of meeting the very basic definition Freeman offered (expenditures and financial means) than at the other extreme, combining planning, control of expenditures, evaluation of actual results with planned results, and evaluation of alternative methods to achieve a desired result. We shall consider

|  | FY2003 | FY2004 | | FY2005 |
|---|---|---|---|---|
| **REVENUES:** | ACTUAL | BUDGET | ESTIMATE | BUDGET |
| Sale of Refuse Tags | 1,557,882 | 1,630,000 | 1,630,000 | 1,951,139 |
| Sale of Refuse Bags | 1,480,160 | 1,470,000 | 1,470,000 | 1,908,825 |
| Bulk Item Tags | 65,202 | 69,000 | 69,000 | 70,005 |
| Container Service | 129,780 | 99,700 | 99,700 | 134,861 |
| Sale of Yard Waste Bags | 460,090 | 400,000 | 400,000 | 600,871 |
| Sale of Yard Waste Tags | 17,400 | 17,640 | 17,640 | 68,404 |
| Sale of Appliance Stickers | 42,914 | 48,300 | 48,300 | 49,356 |
| Nuisance | 91,091 | 20,000 | 20,000 | 381,682 |
| Cart Tags | 36,178 | 76,000 | 65,000 | 65,000 |
| Recycling Stickers & Containers | 255 | 320 | 320 | 256 |
| Miscellaneous | 15,220 | 95,800 | 95,800 | 80,000 |
|  | 3,896,172 | 3,926,760 | 3,915,760 | 5,310,399 |
| **EXPENDITURES:** |  |  |  |  |
| Refuse Collection | 5,609,107 | 5,925,068 | 5,972,324 | 5,915,061 |
| Recycling | 1,129,901 | 1,223,841 | 1,349,376 | 1,124,723 |
| Yard Waste Recycling | 999,079 | 1,239,376 | 1,223,841 | 1,318,668 |
| Marketing/Distribution | 585,023 | 621,807 | 630,685 | 660,089 |
| Street Sweep/Leaf Collection | 981,309 | 1,327,884 | 1,327,884 | 1,524,264 |
| Code Enforcement | 189,166 | - | - | - |
| Butterworth Landfill | 279,683 | 283,599 | 347,154 | 259,572 |
| Trash Reduction Project | 186,449 | 357,326 | 357,326 | 532,183 |
| Capital Outlay | - | - | 236,380 | - |
|  | 9,959,717 | 10,978,901 | 11,444,970 | 11,334,560 |
| OPERATING EXCESS (DEFICIENCY) | (6,063,545) | (7,052,141) | (7,529,210) | (6,024,161) |
| Non-operating Revenues (Expenses): |  |  |  |  |
| Property Tax Levy* | 4,830,039 | 4,908,500 | 4,982,712 | 6,015,881 |
| Interest on Investments | 119,385 | 90,000 | 90,000 | 75,847 |
| Miscellaneous | 7,710 | - | - | 48,039 |
| EXCESS (DEFICIENCY) |  |  |  |  |
| OF REVENUES OVER EXPENSES | (1,106,411) | (2,053,641) | (2,456,498) | 115,606 |
| Fund Balance, beginning of year | 5,168,621 | 4,062,210 | 4,062,210 | 1,605,712 |
| Fund Balance, end of year | 4,062,210 | 2,008,569 | 1,605,712 | 1,721,318 |

*Millage rate for FY2003 and FY2004 was 1.35; for FY2005 is 1.55

**Figure 2.8  City of Grand Rapids, Michigan: Refuse Collection and Disposal Fund, Statement of Operations, Fiscal Year 2005 Budget.**

both definitions in succeeding portions of this chapter: first, the line-item budget as a rudimentary way of assessing expenditures and means; performance budgeting as a method of going one step beyond line-item budgeting by classifying items by function; and program budgeting, as a means of combining planning and budgeting for more effective use of resources.

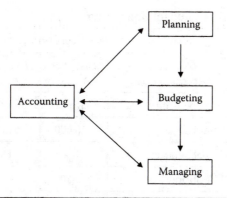

**Figure 2.9  Role of accounting in budget process.**

## 2.4.1 Line-Item Budgeting: The Control Orientation

An early approach to budgeting—a line-item or object of expenditure budget—is still the most popular approach in local government due to its simplicity and the strict accountability or control it allows. This budget, however, has limited utility as a management tool.

The line-item budget allocates funds to specific items or objects. Salaries, office supplies, and printing costs are forecasted for the next year, limiting the administrator to a certain increment per objective over the amount budgeted for that object the last fiscal year (see Table 2.2).

The Jeffersonian line-item approach was implemented again around the turn of the 20th century as a means to reform uncontrollable spending. It was devised to hold governmental units accountable for expenditures by setting an item-by-item spending schedule.

The greatest advantage of line-item budgeting is the control it exerts on financial administration. The intentions of governmental decision makers are defined as to what will be spent on what. This, in turn, provides some control over work by casting expenditures along departmental lines and character of expense.

Grossbard (n.d.) argues the insufficiency of the line-item budget. He views line-item budgeting as a result of "short-run thinking and a tendency to put off both expenditure increases and revenue measures until a later period." The problem with the traditional line-item budget format, he further argues, is that "it does not do enough." Specifically, the budget is difficult to relate to objectives. There is no relation of expenditures to accomplishment and no concept of alternatives to policy, and no integration of planning, budgeting, and control. Line-item budgeting promotes inertia in that changes are produced only as marginal changes from the previous year. Levels of service, organization structure, and methods of operation become permanent, although they may be unsatisfactory.

**Table 2.2   Line-Item Budget Illustration**

| Account Number[a] | Account Title | Fire Protection | | |
| | | Last Year Actual | This Year Estimated | Next Year Proposed |
|---|---|---|---|---|
| 01-2-2-2-9-03 | Fire Prevention-District 9-Fire Company Inspections | | | |
| -1-1-1 | Salaries | 10,000 | 11,000 | 12,000 |
| -1-1-2 | Social Security | 1,000 | 1,100 | 1,200 |
| -1-2-1 | Telephone | 100 | 150 | 200 |
| -1-2-2 | Utilities | 300 | 500 | 700 |
| -2-1-1 | Insurance | 500 | 600 | 700 |
| -2-2-1 | Office rent | 1,000 | 1,000 | 1,000 |
| -3-1-1 | Equipment | 4,000 | 5,000 | 6,000 |
| -4-1- | Expendable supplies | | | |
| -4-1-5 | Clothing supplies | 500 | 550 | 600 |
| -4-1-6 | Office supplies | 400 | 425 | 450 |
| -4-1-9 | Other supplies | 300 | 310 | 320 |
| | Total | 18,100 | 20,635 | 23,170 |

[a] See Figure 2.15 for a visual explanation of the account identifiers. This line-item budget illustration follows the model in this figure.

Anton (1964), in his study of budget practice in three Illinois cities, illustrates the marginal or incremental practices of line-item budgeting. Because the only information available to a city was the past year's budget and the marginal increases asked by each department, the budget hearing was found to provide the only clues as to what to cut and what to leave as it was. He observes (p. 16):

> Precisely because the "stakes" are inherently so political in meaning, the criteria used to decide [budget] questions are seldom relevant to departmental goals. Instead, the deciding criteria become such political factors as power and influence of the department head, the ability of the department to mobilize support for its demands, or the ability of the council to gain prestige by granting or refusing the demand.

The increases in the budget were not based on any demonstration that services from any particular department would improve or suffer as a result of increases or cuts.

In fact, all departments could have made a persuasive case for increases to improve their operations.

The departments, however, are not equal in their ability to marshal influence. Anton continues, "what is most significant here is the demonstration that in the absence of detailed information on the part of the council and in the absence of strong central control over various departments, each department is relatively free to seek improvement in its financial position by putting pressure on the council. Clearly, the advantage lies with the strong" (Anton, 1964, p. 17).

## 2.4.2 Performance Budgeting: The Management Approach and Later Developments

Due to limitations in line-item budgeting and increasing levels of expenditures, the federal government began turning to a new approach, a management approach, in the early 1930s. This change grew out of several circumstances. First, the increase in activities and expenditures under New Deal programs made some classes of activities performed more important for informational purposes than itemized objects. Second, Keynesian economics stressed more public spending to reduce economic disadvantages during the Depression; therefore, the number of expenditures increased and their performance as a group had to be measured. Third, the President's Committee on Administrative Management in 1937 advocated management of spending by the President and subsequently called for expanding the Bureau of the Budget and consolidating it in the Executive Office of the President (Schick, 1966). Fourth, the Hoover Commission in 1949 recommended "that the whole budgetary concept of the Federal Government should be refashioned by the adoption of a budget based upon functions, activities and projects" (Schick, 1966, p. 258). In fact, from the Hoover Commission came the new name, "performance budgeting."

The Hoover Commission Report also influenced local governments to introduce the concept of their budgeting systems. In a symposium held in May 1954, the Municipal Finance Officers Association (MFOA) leaders indicated that "the keen interest in [performance budgeting] was considerably stimulated by the work of the Hoover Commission and its comments regarding the federal budget" (MFOA, 1954). The symposium concerned performance budgeting and its initiation in local government. The discussion commented that "renewed interest in improved financial management of governmental units and an awakening to the possibilities inherent in the performance budget approach are causing more and more municipalities of all sizes to explore and sometimes adopt such budgets" (MFOA, 1954, p. 1).

The management approach or the idea of performance budgeting referred to by both the Hoover Commission and MFOA included several new concepts. This budget related expenditures to performance. Appropriations were made to activities—jobs to performed—rather than objects. The new concept introduced operational analysis, a method of measuring inputs—personnel services, contractual

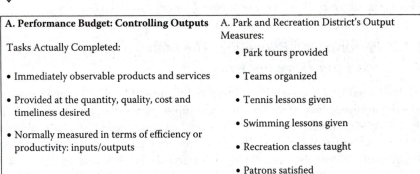

**A. Line Item Budget: Controlling Inputs**

- Dollars
- People
- Materials, supplies

A. Park and Recreation District:

- Salaries
- Maintenance
- Utilities
- Supplies

⇓

**A. Performance Budget: Controlling Outputs**

Tasks Actually Completed:

- Immediately observable products and services
- Provided at the quantity, quality, cost and timeliness desired
- Normally measured in terms of efficiency or productivity: inputs/outputs

A. Park and Recreation District's Output Measures:

- Park tours provided
- Teams organized
- Tennis lessons given
- Swimming lessons given
- Recreation classes taught
- Patrons satisfied

⇓

**A. Program Budget: Controlling Outcomes**

Goals actually achieved

- Measurable: knowing that the work group either achieved the goal or not
- Valid: knowing what difference it made whether you achieved the goal or not
- Criteria driven: judged in terms of effectiveness or cost effectiveness

A. Park and Recreation District's Outcome Checklist:

- What are the goals of the district expressed in measurable, observable terms?
- Do district managers and employees have control over the achievement of their goals?
- Of the various ways of doing the things the District is supposed to do, which is the most cost effective?

**Figure 2.10   Control and types of budgets.**

services—against outputs and how many units of activity occurred as a result. Generally, the budget called for more information on what the activity was, what the procedures used were, and what level of service could be provided for what amount. In Figure 2.10, performance lies between line-item and program budgets, concentrating attention on output control.

Necessitated by increased economic activity, the new approach was tailored to provide distinct advantages over the line-item concept. By its orientation to management, performance budgeting's principal thrust went toward helping administrators assess the work efficiency of operating units by casting budget categories in functional terms, and providing work-cost measurements to facilitate the efficient performance of prescribed activities. At the height of performance budgeting's acceptance, Simon and Ridley (1958) identified four types of measurement needs: results, costs, efforts, and performance, the last three of which were their measures of "administrative efficiency." For the first time, standards were set on the basis of the measurements made, person hour, cost accounting, and ratio of personnel (Sherwood and Best, 1975).

Many found disadvantages in performance budgeting's application in the federal government (Schick, 1966). Budget estimates were no more meaningful than those in line-item budgets. The reason for making one particular expenditure rather than another was not clear. No alternatives were presented on which to base a "best" choice. The same limitations were true in the states and cities where performance budgeting was being employed.

Work measurement presented the second difficulty for budget officers. There were inherent difficulties in measuring government output with precision. It was easy to measure government purchases, generally easy to measure government activities, but Burkhead (1956) argues that these are repetitive and discrete units. These government outputs can compare directly with private goods that may be priced based on cost and even demand. However, the ease of measurement, costing and even pricing, these government outputs are "nonsignificant as a measure of accomplishment ...," Burkhead points out (1956, p. 140).

Lastly, performance budgeting lacked the tools to deal with long-range problems. With planned expenditures set within a 1 year perspective, "almost all options [for future action] have been foreclosed by previous commitments" (Schick, 1966, p. 258).

Robert Luther, budget officer of Fairfax County, Virginia, explained the application and implementation of some performance budget concepts in a suburban county. Problems arose in several areas. Quantifying or categorizing units of work within a department met with difficulty. Collection of data on work units was not done accurately; therefore, it was unreliable. The department head questioned the concept of data collection and the need for it; there was little departmental cooperation (Luther, 1972). The difficulty was symptomatic of little or no commitment by elected officials or department heads to concepts of work measurement.

The development of a management approach to budgeting is, in retrospect, an evolutionary step toward use of the budget as a tool in both quantifying the results of a particular expenditure and in evaluating the entire budget program. The performance budget was a middle step between the traditional line-item method and the planning approach adopted by performance budgeting's successors, program budgeting and PPBS.

What they all seem to point to is a widening of the scope of budgeting from inputs via outputs to outcomes. In the traditional format, budget decision makers felt they were parsimonious when they could cut back or examine thoroughly the amount and composition of inputs. Decision makers accomplished input control through control of budget increases. The dollar control gained a powerful supplement in position control for full-time equivalent employee positions. The decision makers also provided methods for controlling spending while executing the budget. These procedures, often simply segregation of duties with substantial oversight, amount to the red tape many find in public organizations. The justification for a complicated process of control lies in prevention and punishment of fraud, waste, and abuse of the financial system.

When a budget combines input control with output control, financial managers set up a different set of controls that are far more comprehensive. The input plus the output controls give everyone in the organization a sense of a bottom line. This form of control is the real definition of performance, a bottom line that everyone seeks to reach or influence.

Efficiency and performance measures tell whether programs work to give citizens their money's worth. Obviously, there are many different ways to deal with organization, program, and individual performance through budgeting. Beyond the output control Figure 2.10 implies, modern performance budgeting (PB) can appear in several forms. Normally called a productivity budget, PB directs policymakers to follow a path and make choices in their allocation decisions. We discuss four common PB variants in the following text: level of service, unit cost, performance-to-program crosswalks, and activity base budgets.

### 2.4.2.1 Level-of-Service Approach

With the first approach, policymakers choose a level of service: Policymakers make their decisions related to how much or often a particular task will get done. Simple outputs provide the focus of control. In Figure 2.11, the focus of attention falls on the level of service connected to streetlights in San Diego (Sherwood and Best, 1958, p. 263).

Several advantages emerge in using a level-of-service approach to performance. This method focuses attention on the frequency of routine activities. The focus is not glamorous or a matter of major changes, but it emphasizes the most important aspect of routine tasks pursued by local governments. Second, the output-level approach makes employees understand service standards. Moreover, the attention to outputs can focus on how efficient services are.

Disadvantages emerge as well. Many report that in using this method, policymakers feel hamstrung by their previous commitments to maintenance and service standards. Perhaps the feeling of inflexibility arises most often in fiscal stressed times when policymakers find it hard to hide service-level reductions when dollars have to be cut from the budget.

### 2.4.2.2 Unit Cost Approach

Analysis can identify factors driving operating costs. An estimate of expenditure requirements based on this type of analysis, particularly those requirements relating

**WHAT IS THE BEST LEVEL OF SERVICE, GIVEN THE FOLLOWING?**
San Diego, 1950

| Operation | Total Unit Man-hours | Rate per Man-hour | Unit Labor Cost | Unit Material | Unit Equipment | Unit Cost |
|---|---|---|---|---|---|---|
| Washing Luminaires | 0.23 | $1.29 | $0.30 | $0.01 | $0.02 | $0.33 |
| Lamping | 0.39 | 2.11 | $0.82 | 0.96 | 0.12 | $1.90 |
| Painting Standards | 0.77 | 2.23 | $1.72 | 1.04 | 0.08 | $2.84 |

Number of Lights in Service ......................................... 5,010

| Present level of service: | |
|---|---|
| Washing luminaires | Twice per year |
| Lamping | Twice per year |
| Painting standards | Once every two years |

| | | | | | | |
|---|---|---|---|---|---|---|
| Washing luminaires | 5,010 | x | 2 | x | $0.33 | 3,273.53 |
| Lamping | 5,010 | x | 2 | x | $1.90 | 19,067.06 |
| Painting standards | 5,010 | / | 2 | x | $2.84 | 7,106.94 |

| Routine Maintenance Budget | | $29,447.53 |
|---|---|---|

**By Line Items:**

| | | |
|---|---|---|
| **Labor Cost** | | 15,519.73 |
| Washing | 2,972.93 | |
| Lamping | 8,245.46 | |
| Painting | 4,301.34 | |
| **Material** | | 12,324.60 |
| Washing | 100.20 | |
| Lamping | 9,619.20 | |
| Painting | 2,605.20 | |
| **Equipment** | | 1,603.20 |
| Washing | 200.40 | |
| Lamping | 1,202.40 | |
| Painting | 200.40 | |
| | | 29,447.53 |

**Figure 2.11    Level-of-service approach illustration.**

to programs, comprises the bulk of the budget. Fundamental conditioning factors that influence program costs include the following:

1. The scope and quality of services provided
2. The volume of work required to render the services
3. Methods, facilities, and organization for performing the work

4. Qualities and types of labor, material, equipment, and other cost elements required by the work volume
5. Price levels of the various cost elements

These conditioning factors emerge most visibly in the unit cost approach to performance budgeting, as illustrated in Figure 2.12.

With a unit cost method of performance budgeting, policymakers decide budgets on the basis of cost and number of outputs, that is, efficiency. The advantage lies in the focus. This approach through unit cost to performance focuses attention on the efficiency of traditional activities by measuring both inputs in dollars and activity costs and outputs in the amount of work done. The data, however, may not account for indirect costs or overhead in a meaningful way. Individual control may not exist either, because the unit cost approach cannot succeed in focusing employees' attention on costs that they cannot control or change.

### 2.4.2.3 Activity Costs with Goals Attached

A cousin to the unit cost approach is one we call the cross walk approach, also known as performance-program budgeting, and used in federal government efforts to comply with the Government Performance and Results Act provisions. To use this budget, policymakers decide matters based on how well activities achieve programmatic goals. The approach is a hybrid in which program managers combine efficiency and the specific policy goals provided by authorizing legislation. In the example provided in Figure 2.13, the Environmental Protection Agency, in 1999, faced Congressional scrutiny on spending for the various legislated programs members of Congress wanted to follow closely. The line-item budget EPA had submitted to Congress previously served as the basis for a cross walk to the actual program goals, such as acid rain reduction, that members of Congress wanted to follow. This form of budgeting was thought successful by the Government Accountability Office because the budget focused attention on goal achievement or the achievement of performance strategies. GAO also pointed out that the connection between performance measures and money was unclear. Analysts could see that the unclear connection could create perverse incentives to only maintain stable performance rather than achieve goals as they are commonly understood.

### 2.4.2.4 The Full-Time Equivalent Employee (FTE) Approach

The fourth approach to performance budgeting rests on the calculation of costs related to the employment of a full-time equivalent position in the work an organization does. This form is also known as Activity-Based Budgeting (ABB). Since employee compensation is the largest single category of spending in most organization budgets, the FTE approach allows policymakers to determine spending based on the number of positions required to meet demand for the organization's work.

| | Parks | | Recreation | | | | Total | Pet fairs | Holiday affairs | Personal leisure time skills | Dog obedience classes | Belly dancing classes | Knitting classes | Total |
| --- | --- | --- | --- | --- | --- | --- | --- | --- | --- | --- | --- | --- | --- | --- |
| | Rangers | Zoo | Team sports | Tennis | Pools | Other activities | | | | | | | | |
| Total FY 5 Direct services spending | 176,493 | 82,719 | 473,384 | 423,734 | 340,980 | 782,586 | 2,279,896 | 23,478 | 66,520 | 23,478 | 3,913 | 641,721 | 23,478 | 782,586 |
| Proportion of total | 8% | 4% | 21% | 19% | 15% | 34% | 100% | | | | | | | |
| Activity indicator levels FY 5 (Patrons, etc.) Narrow view -- teamsports team members; tennis lesson students | 45,900 | 8,280 | 2,250 | 700 | 53,100 | | | 1,521 | 16,200 | 280 | 23 | 19,050 | 126 | |
| Broad view -- teamsports team members, coaches, helpers, and fans; tennis patrons | | | 2,250 | 700 | | | | | | | | | | |
| | | | 22,500 | 27,810 | | | | | | | | | | |
| Quality levels FY 5 (Patron Satisfaction, etc.) Narrow view -- teams sports team members; tennis lesson students | 88% | 66% | 65% | 86% | 89% | | | 0.9 | 0.83 | 0.55 | 0.35 | 0.99 | 0.94 | |
| Broad view -- teams sports team members, coaches, helpers, and fans; tennis patrons | | | | 78% | | | | | | | | | | |
| | | | | 86% | | | | | | | | | | |
| Total FY 4 Direct services spending | 160,644 | 75,291 | 430,874 | 385,683 | 310,359 | 712,309 | 2,075,160 | 20,657 | 61,971 | 20,657 | 3,562 | 591,217 | 14,246 | 712,309 |

Figure 2.12  Unit cost approach to performance budgeting park and recreation district unit costs and customer satisfaction changes.

|  | | | | | | | | | | | |
|---|---|---|---|---|---|---|---|---|---|---|---|
| Activity indicator levels FY 4 (Patrons, etc.) | 43,655 | 8,080 | 2,020 | 550 | 41,352 | 1,216 | 12,368 | 327 | 86 | 12,495 | 110 |
| Narrow view -- teams sports team members; tennis lesson students | | | 2,020 | 550 | | | | | | | |
| Broad view -- teams sports team members, coaches, helpers, and fans; tennis patrons | | | 20,200 | 26,234 | | | | | | | |
| **Summary** | | | | | | | | | | | |
| FY5 cost/patron | 3.85 | 9.99 | 210.39 | 605.33 | 6.42 | 15.44 | 4.11 | 83.85 | 170.13 | 33.69 | 186.33 |
| FY4 cost/patron | 3.68 | 9.32 | 213.3 | 701.24 | 7.51 | 16.99 | 5.01 | 63.17 | 41.41 | 47.32 | 129.51 |
| Change FY4 - FY5 | 4.50% | 7.20% | -1.40% | -13.70% | -14.40% | -9% | -18% | 33% | 311% | -29% | 44% |
| Narrow view of patronage | | | -1.40% | -13.70% | | | | | | | |
| Broad view of patronage | | | -1.40% | 3.60% | | | | | | | |
| FY5 satisfaction | 88.00% | 66.00% | 65.00% | 86.00% | 89.00% | 90% | 83% | 55% | 35% | 99% | 94% |
| FY4 satisfaction | 88.00% | 66.00% | 62.00% | 82.00% | 86.00% | 88% | 79% | 52% | 25% | 99% | 92% |
| Change FY4 - FY5 | 0.00% | 0.00% | 4.80% | 4.90% | 3.50% | 2% | 5% | 6% | 40% | 0% | 2% |

**Figure 2.12 (continued).**

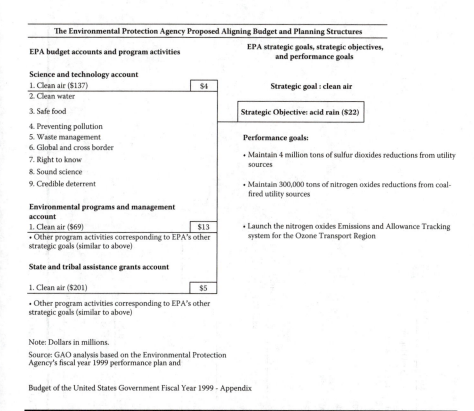

The Environmental Protection Agency Proposed Aligning Budget and Planning Structures

| EPA budget accounts and program activities | | EPA strategic goals, strategic objectives, and performance goals |
|---|---|---|
| **Science and technology account** | | |
| 1. Clean air ($137) | $4 | Strategic goal : clean air |
| 2. Clean water | | |
| 3. Safe food | | Strategic Objective: acid rain ($22) |
| 4. Preventing pollution | | |
| 5. Waste management | | **Performance goals:** |
| 6. Global and cross border | | |
| 7. Right to know | | • Maintain 4 million tons of sulfur dioxides reductions from utility sources |
| 8. Sound science | | |
| 9. Credible deterrent | | • Maintain 300,000 tons of nitrogen oxides reductions from coal-fired utility sources |
| **Environmental programs and management account** | | |
| 1. Clean air ($69) | $13 | • Launch the nitrogen oxides Emissions and Allowance Tracking system for the Ozone Transport Region |
| • Other program activities corresponding to EPA's other strategic goals (similar to above) | | |
| **State and tribal assistance grants account** | | |
| 1. Clean air ($201) | $5 | |
| • Other program activities corresponding to EPA's other strategic goals (similar to above) | | |

Note: Dollars in millions.

Source: GAO analysis based on the Environmental Protection Agency's fiscal year 1999 performance plan and

Budget of the United States Government Fiscal Year 1999 - Appendix

**Figure 2.13 Illustrations of approaches used to connect resources to results in agencies' fiscal year 1999 performance plans.**

The example in Figure 2.14 comes from a state governor's press office. In this organization, demand for service comes in the form of a need for press releases and various other bits of information. Knowing the time required to complete the average unit of activity—prepare a press release, for example, as well as knowing the level of press release activity over a fiscal year—a budget manager can forecast the total number of hours of employee time. Given existing salary and benefit levels and some basis for extending a cost estimate for supplies and materials for an employee, the budget estimate comes readily to hand.

Among the advantages of ABB, users report that it focuses attention on positions and salaries, which are the bulk of most public and nonprofit budgets. The budget estimate emerges through an estimate of the demand for services that many agencies cannot control. Demand dictates budgets.

As for disadvantages, a budget with an activity base is very hard to cut. The difficulty depends on the likelihood of a change in the nature of the work—no more press conferences in the example given earlier. Change may also proceed if the work gets reengineered to cut the number of work units; for example, the press officer

**1a. Staffing for Principal Officers (Flexible FTE Responsive to Demand)**

| Modalities | Acuity | | |
| --- | --- | --- | --- |
| | Hours Per Unit | Units Per Year | Total Employee Hours Per Modality |
| Press Release Writing or Review | 0.5 | 100 | 50 |
| Statistical Requests Reporting | 1 | 3,100 | 3,100 |
| Press Conference Organizing | 1 | 25 | 25 |
| Comment Request Reporting | 1 | 5,000 | 5,000 |
| Editorial Writing | 2 | 48 | 96 |
| Total | | 8,273 | 8,271 |
| | | 2,080 | (8 hours per day, 40 hours per week, 52 weeks per year) |
| | | 3.98 | FTE |

**1b. Flexible FTE: Support Staff**

| | | |
| --- | --- | --- |
| 1 Clerk Per Principal | 3.98 | |
| | 7.95 | FTE |

**2. Step Function FTE: Management**

| | | |
| --- | --- | --- |
| 1 Manager (Per 4 Officers and 2 Support Staff) | 1.325 | |
| 1 Support Staff Member Per Manager | 1.325 | |
| | 2.651 | FTE |
| Subtotal | 10.6 | FTE |

**Figure 2.14  An actual press office, a State of New Jersey Department, 2000.**

**Nonproductive FTE**

| | Hours | Days | |
|---|---|---|---|
| Vacation | 80 | 10 | |
| Sick Leave | 96 | 12 | |
| Administrative Leave Days | 24 | 3 | |
| Holidays | 104 | 13 | |
| Training | 40 | 5 | |
| | 344 | | Hours Per FTE (Principal Officers, Support Staff, Management) |
| Divided by | 2,080 | | Work Hours Per Year |
| | 0.17 | | |
| Times | 10.6 | | |
| | | | |
| **Total FTE** | | 1.75 | FTE |
| | | 12.36 | Estimate of Staff Needed for the Activity |

**Costing out the FTE Estimate**

**3. Average (Weighted) Salaries and Benefits**

| | Salary | Fringes at 20% | | |
|---|---|---|---|---|
| 3.98 | $60,000 | 12,000 | 286,304 | Press officers |
| 1.33 | 80,000 | 16,000 | 127,246 | Manager |
| 5.3 | 30,000 | 6,000 | 190,869 | Support staff |
| | | | $604,419 | |
| 10.6 | Divided by | | 8,271 | Units of Work Per Year |

Rate Per Employee Hour (Assuming Fixed Substitute      $73.08
for Flexible FTEs During Nonproductive Time)

**Figure 2.14 (continued).**

## 4. Variable Costs

**Material**

| Material | | |
|---|---|---|
| Paper and Pencils (@ $500 per Employee) | 5,302 | |
| Units of Work per Year | 5,302 | |
| Material Cost per Unit of Work | 0.64 | |

**Equipment**

| Equipment | Number | @ | Useful Life | Charge |
|---|---|---|---|---|
| Computers/Printers | 8 | 3,000 | 2 | 12,000 |
| Typewriters | 1 | 700 | 5 | 140 |
| Furniture | 8 | 500 | 10 | 400 |
| Xerox Lease | 1 | 500 | 1 | 500 |
| Facsimile | 1 | 1,000 | 1 | 1,000 |
| Phone Lease | 1 | 25,000 | 1 | 25,000 |
| | | | | 39,040 |
| | | | Units of Work per Year | 8,273 |
| | | | Equipment Cost per Unit of Work | 4.72 |

## 5. Budgets

| Unit Costs | Rate per Employee Hour | Cost per Unit | Unit Material | Unit Equipment | Total Unit Cost |
|---|---|---|---|---|---|
| Press Release Writing or Review | 73.08 | 36.54 | 0.64 | 4.72 | 41.9 |
| Statistical Requests Reporting | 73.08 | 73.08 | 0.64 | 4.72 | 78.44 |
| Press Conference Organizing | 73.08 | 73.08 | 0.64 | 4.72 | 78.44 |
| Comment Request Reporting | 73.08 | 73.08 | 0.64 | 4.72 | 78.44 |
| Editorial Writing | 73.08 | 146.15 | 0.64 | 4.72 | 151.51 |

**Figure 2.14 (continued).**

| Present Level of Service | Units | Unit Cost | Cost | Line-item Budget Summary | |
|---|---|---|---|---|---|
| Press Release Writing or Review | 100 | 41.9 | 4,190 | | |
| Statistical Requests Reporting | 3,100 | 78.44 | 243,154 | Salaries | 604,419 |
| Press Conference Organizing | 25 | 78.44 | 1,961 | Materials | 5,302 |
| Comment Request Reporting | 5,000 | 78.44 | 392,184 | Equipment | 39,040 |
| Editorial Writing | 48 | 151.51 | 7,273 | | |
| **Total** | | | **$648,761** | **Total** | **$648,761** |

**Figure 2.14  (continued).**

could find that more press releases might take the pressure off demand for press conferences or vice versa.

## 2.4.2.5  Later Developments in Performance Budgeting Found in Responsibility Center Budgeting

Responsibility center budgeting has grown in importance as top managers have recognized the wisdom in organizing around specific goals or tasks rather than around all-purpose functions or departments. The responsibility center idea rests on an existing and traditional map. At the top of the map lie plans: goals, programs, outcomes to achieve, and even milestones marking deadlines for achievement or progress generally. The traditional all-purpose department fits within goals, as goals may overlap traditional departments or set within departments. The fund structure may also apply organizationwide or, in the case of enterprises, in one department. Crossing department boundaries or not, functions—management, instruction for education, or gallery activities in the case of a museum—may be known and exist because these functions relate directly to outcomes desired by top managers. Below these functions lie the actual responsibilities of people with functions and within one or more departments. These activities form the basis for budgeting. Within these responsibility centers, anyone may account for traditional-line items (see Figure 2.15). The figure summarizes in fairly well-known terms—the chart of account structure—the methods for creating and using responsibility centers as presented here.

Across the organization, there may be similarities among responsibility centers. A manager may characterize these similar responsibilities as profit centers in enterprise-related activities. In almost all organizations, there are revenue centers where there may be development as grants and donations, tax collection, or simple cash collection responsibilities. Finally, there will be cost centers, investment centers, and service centers with responsibilities for providing staff and other services to the "line" centers. The important point to remember is the single responsibility dictum: profit, revenue, cost, investment, or service only.

What the responsibility center concept means is clear. There is very little top-heavy organization and management, since cost centers compete with other cost centers, and profit centers with other profit centers. These centers also work toward

**Code Group**

| 1 | 2 | 3 | 4 | 5 | 6 | 7 | 8 | 9 | Expenditure Classifications |
|---|---|---|---|---|---|---|---|---|---|
| 01- | | | | | | | | | General Fund |
| | 2- | | | | | | | | Public Safety |
| | | 2- | | | | | | | Fire Protection |
| | | | 2- | | | | | | Fire Prevention |
| | | | | 9- | | | | | District Nine |
| | | | | | 03- | | | | Fire Company Inspections |
| | | | | | | 1- | | | Variable Costs |
| | | | | | | | 1- | | Personal Services |
| | | | | | | | | 1 | Regular Payroll |

Notes on the classification and code scheme:

Two digits, 00 to 99 possibilities, providing for the identification of 100 separate

Code Group 1: funds

Code Group 2: One digit, zero to nine possibilities, providing for the identification of 10 functions, such as general government, public safety, etc.

Code Group 3: One digit, zero to nine possibilities, providing for the identification of 10 programs, departments, services, etc.

Code Group 4: One digit, zero to nine possibilities, providing for the identification of 10 programs, subprograms, divisions, services, activities, etc.

Code Group 5: One digit, zero to nine possibilities, providing for the identification of 10 cost centers, such as area, district, structure, shift, section, unit, squad, etc.

Code Group 6: Two digits, 00 to 99 possibilities, providing for the identification of performance cost centers for specific jobs, tasks, projects, etc.

Code Group 7: One digit, zero to nine possibilities, although only two numbers would be needed to record fixed and variable costs, respectively.

Code Group 8: One digit, zero to nine possibilities, for recording major object classifications, such as personal services, nonpersonal expense, etc.

Three digits, 000 to 999 possibilities, for the identification of 1,000 commodity or item cost centers, such as regular payroll,

gasoline, equipment repair

Code Group 9: etc.

**Figure 2.15  A classification and code scheme for fire protection.**

goals the center members have participated in setting. Competition and progress leave very little discretion for top managers, and the dynamics have built-in controls. The system decentralizes.

## 2.4.3 *Program Budgeting*

Program budgeting suffers from a severe identity crisis in the budgetary literature. Writers often use the name "program budgeting" synonymously with performance budgeting as well as with the Planning, Programming, Budgeting System (PPBS). Even when the Hoover Commission introduced the term "performance budget," its task force report utilized the term interchangeably with program budget. Schick reports, "Among writers there was no uniformity in usage, some preferring the 'program budgeting' label, others 'performance budgeting' to describe the same things. The level of confusion has been increased recently by the association of the term with the PPB movement." Schick (1966, p. 250) uses "program budget" interchangeably with PPBS.

Burkhead (1956, p. 139) attempts to distinguish between performance budgeting and program budgeting. A program may refer to a higher level of organization than performing organization units. Since a program may encompass several performing organizational units, the program budget has broader scope and a more integrative purpose than a performance budget. Program costs are broad summary costs that may be developed through aggregation of performing units' costs (see Table 2.3). Performance details need not be incorporated into a program budget since it is not necessarily based on performance units. Also, a department or agency may be involved in several programs simultaneously, but operating units within a department are directly responsible for performance. Therefore, in terms of organizational structure, the program budget may respond to higher-level organizational needs while the performance budget may serve lower-level operating needs better. In other words, the program budget is more centralized.

The program budget has a longer range and is forward looking. Performance budgets are based on records of past performance and accomplishments, whereas program budgets are built around estimates of what performance is reasonable to expect in the future. Program budgets are thus better prepared to project the social and economic policies of government.

According to these distinctions, different purposes are served by these two types of budgets. A program budget is more suited to the requirements of overall budgetary planning, including review by the central budget office, the chief executive, and the legislature. It is most useful for decision making at or above the department level. Performance budgets must likewise provide information for review purposes, but must also be detailed enough to serve management purposes at or below the department level.

Program budgeting involves an attempt to arrange budget expenditures around program or functional needs in order to meet broad objectives. By relating inputs

**Table 2.3   Program Budget Illustration**

| Crime Prevention Program Budget—Central Business District of a City | | |
| --- | --- | --- |
| *Subprogram* | *City* | *Business* |
| Street lighting improvements in CBD | | |
|   Public Works Department | 25,000 | |
|   Businesses | | 25,000 |
| Police street patrols | | |
|   Police Department | 10,000 | |
|   Business Security Departments | | 5,000 |
| Alarms from businesses | | |
|   Police Department hookups | 50,000 | |
|   Business store hookups | | 125,000 |
| Intensive garbage pickup | | |
|   Sanitation department | 50,000 | |
|   Business stockroom efforts | | 10,000 |
| Intensive street cleaning | | |
|   Sanitation department | 12,000 | |
|   Business effort on curbs and gutters | | 20,000 |
| Employment and training program | | |
|   Juvenile | 100,000 | |
|   Adult | 25,000 | |
| Business job potentials | | 100,000 |
| **Totals** | **272,000** | **285,000** |

Goals:  1. Increase ability to police area through patrols and better notification.
2. Increase attractiveness and pedestrian population of area.
3. Increase number of jobs and decrease number of jobless.

| Detailed Crime Prevention Program Budget—Central Business District | | |
| --- | --- | --- |
| **Total Budget** | 557,000 | |
| **City** | 272,000 | |
|   Public Works Department | | 25,000 |
|   Police Department patrols | | 10,000 |
|   Police Department hookups | | 50,000 |
|   Sanitation department garbage pickup | | 50,000 |
|   Sanitation department street cleaning | | 12,000 |
|   Employment and training program | | 125,000 |
| **Business** | 285,000 | |
|   Street lighting improvements in CBD | | 25,000 |
|   Business Security Departments street patrols | | 5,000 |
|   Business store hookups of alarms | | 125,000 |
|   Business stockroom efforts garbage | | 10,000 |
|   Business effort on curbs and gutters cleaning | | 20,000 |
|   Business job potentials | | 100,000 |

to outputs, cost-benefit analysis is facilitated, its aim being to allocate resources to the most efficient and effective means for achieving ends.

The key elements of the process include long-range planning, goal setting, program identification, quantitative analysis, including cost-benefit measurement, and performance analyses.

There are four essential steps in the construction of a program budget:

1. Definition of the ends to be achieved
2. Definitions of the methods and timetables by which they are achieved
3. Determination of the costs for each action required
4. Determination of measurements of success, whether goals are actually being achieved, through the budgeted programs

The Second Hoover Commission task force recommended that the performance budgeting concept be renamed "program budgeting" to emphasize the conceptual difference between the review of proposed new programs and the review of the performance of previously authorized programs.

Program budgeting focuses on goals and outcomes, and helps provide perspective for budget expenditures. The budget requires consideration of future implications of programs and effects of current actions. It also emphasizes the role of planning in budget decision making.

However, program budgeting may require modification of activities that have an impact on many related activities. Economic, social, and political events may not follow the anticipated pattern, which may undermine the intentions of program budgeting's long-range planning efforts. Analysis of relationships between inputs and outputs does not necessarily take into account unintended consequences or side effects of actions taken or proposed. Quantitative measurement of outputs may not be possible; even when quantitative analysis is feasible, the criteria of economy and efficiency may preclude the consideration of quality. Finally, the budget requires central coordination, since programs may cross agency lines.

## 2.4.4 PPBS: The Planning Orientation

PPBS is the product of an evolutionary process from management to planning of federal governmental expenditure allocation. Allen Schick (1966, p. 259) outlines this development:

1. Economic analysis at both micro- and macrolevels has had an increasing part in determining fiscal and budgeting policy.
2. The development of new informational and decisional technologies has enlarged the applicability of objective analysis to policy making.
3. Planning and budgeting have gradually converged.

Wider acceptance of Keynesian economic principles set the stage for PPBS in its call for governmental action in planning economic growth for the nation. Moreover, utilization of planned spending as both an impetus and a constraint on growth had been used during the underemployment economy of the depression years. Finally, a planned taxing policy has forced the implementation of a governmental economic plan.

Coupled with these developments, new methods or technologies have increased government's ability to analyze objectively the alternate policies available to it. The introduction of operations analysis during World War II and cost-benefit analysis during the 1950s both allowed the federal government more depth in optimizing the coordination of resources to attain objectives. The introduction of systems analysis, along with wider application of operations research and cost-benefit analysis by the RAND Corporation in 1961 in the Department of Defense (DoD), consolidated approaches in one package. All these techniques spurred the development of PPBS.

Based on DoD's success with PPBS, President Johnson introduced the same package in the other departments and agencies in 1965 as a means of budgeting to meet objectives. Planning and budgeting converged.

Following the example of the national government, local governments also experimented with the new system. Selma J. Mushkin (1969b) outlined the development: New York City in 1966, Philadelphia shortly afterward, and, through the 5-5-5 Intergovernmental Demonstration Project, five cities, counties, and states before the end of the year.

Most characterize PPBS as a rational means of fusing planning processes, programming efforts, and the budget system. Many found little new among the components but a revolutionary concept in the combination. Thus, planning is the determination of the basic goals of the organization and the selection of the programs best calculated to achieve these goals. Programming entails the scheduling and execution, as efficiently as possible, of the specific projects required to implement these programs. Budgeting is the process of converting the goals, programs, and projects into money estimates for review within the administrative branch and final action by the legislative branch. The basic advantage of PPBS is the emphasis on rational decision making. To improve rationality, PPBS allows policymakers to accomplish the following:

1. Establish goals and objectives after observation.
2. Assign alternative means toward accomplishing objectives.
3. Predict the consequences of each alternative.
4. Select the most beneficial alternative.
5. Program all work toward achieving objectives.

In the PBB system, internal and external disadvantages exist. First, internal difficulties concern the dynamics of the structure itself, the goal-setting procedure, and cost-benefit analysis. Within the structure of procedure of PPBS budgeting, there is a tendency to centralize decision making. The responsibility for goal setting and policy choice is centrally determined, resulting in better coordination of activities but at the cost of initiative in innovation and development of new alternatives at lower levels of policymaking (Jernberg, 1971, pp. 371–372).

PPBS's stress on the cross-structural nature of goals and objectives diminishes the importance of existing organizational boundaries. This approach disrupts present channels of communication between administrative agencies. Because there will be different cross-structural arrangements for each objective, the PPBS approach has not been found to establish a single channel to replace it.

Emphasizing the alternative results in uncertainty among all participants in the system. Uncertainty replaces the last budget system's stability.

Goal setting itself is difficult because of both the complexity of problems and the different outlooks of each goal setter. Wildavsky (1966, 1969) notes the ultimate problem with PPBS: "Budgeting, in PPBS, is intimately linked to policy; however, the basic problems in policy formulation and development stem from the fact that we do not know what it is that we are trying to accomplish."

Cost-benefit analysis itself is not sufficiently sophisticated yet to met all demands placed upon it. Harry Hatry and John Cotton (1967, p. 6), argue that there are "difficulties in considering a time stream of costs and benefits and not simply the evaluation of costs and benefits for a single point in time." The most apparent deficiency of cost-benefit analysis is that, in its present procedural form, such variables as intangible services elude measurement. Moreover, Jernberg (1971) finds two points of view on the application of cost-benefit analysis. According to one view, cost-benefit analysis should include all considerations, including political costs and benefits. The opposing view is that this leads to sole reliance on political considerations and rejection of the economic or rational considerations. In conclusion, he states (p. 372) that "cost benefit analysis [is presently viewed] as serving a more modest role of assisting and providing a more sound base for intuitive judgment." Hirsch (1966, p. 156) agrees, saying, "Policy makers want to know which groups benefit the most and where the losses are distributed as a result of their decisions."

There are other major political problems as well. In the very process of changing systems, existing programs have built up definite constituents convinced of the validity of the present approach; "members of an organization and their clients have a vested interest in the policies of the past" and fight change (Wildavsky, 1966, p. 294).

The first, and still basic, evaluation of PPBS in use comes from George Washington University's 5-5-5 Intergovernmental Demonstration Project mentioned earlier. In that project, PPBS was introduced to five cities, five counties, and five states. The project began in the spring of 1966 under the guidance of task forces from the University.

Mushkin (1969a) summarized the approaches, the problems, and the successes encountered in the process of her review of the project. The approach, she concluded, was basically incremental, "resulting in halfhearted endorsement with no real desire to implement more than one small step at a time. [The participants] were cautionary with a long timetable" (Mushkin, 1969a, p. 2). Eleven of the 15 jurisdictions chose to continue the program formally. She concluded that the project yielded the following results:

1. The beginning of a more questioning attitude toward budgeting and program planning
2. A new emphasis on the beneficiaries of public services, on the people for whom the government functions
3. A new emphasis on formulation of objectives and programs
4. A new enthusiasm about state and local government work among staff assigned to PPB work
5. A state in a few governments toward an interagency dialogue on common objectives and interrelated programs

The experiences of three of the cities bears closer scrutiny. Meiszer (1969), the assistant city manager of Dayton, Ohio, explained the development of PPBS used in Dayton in terms of four subsystems: program structure, program analysis, program budget, and program evaluation. His evaluation of the implementation of these subsystems indicated that sufficient progress had been made for the program structure to be completed. In addition, analysis had already exerted an influence on decision making. However, while program budgeting was producing good results, evaluation was lagging. He terms Dayton's implementation as still in the development stage but progressing sufficiently. Horton (1969), director of administrative analysis for Metropolitan Nashville-Davidson County, observed that "even with problems PPBS has increased awareness of administrators of need to improve the decision making process." The city, however, did experience administrative problems, lack of trained personnel at the beginning of the program, inadequate staffing, and a lack of teaching materials. In sum, there was plenty of theory, but no methods for application.

Progress in PPBS implementation in Dade County, Florida, was characterized as being slow to develop. Grizzle (1969) stated that the system had yet to be infused into the process it would replace, and that planning had not been linked to budgeting. In fact, PPBS was initially "used primarily to comply with federal planning requirements in certain federal programs."

## 2.4.5 Zero Base Budgeting

Theoretically, zero base budgeting (ZBB) requires that each previously funded program or new program proposal be justified, without regard to previous funding levels. This procedure is designed to promote objective comparisons among diverse programs requesting resources, based on their merits alone and negating the effects of historical bias.

In practice, the definition of ZBB is much less comprehensive. Peter Pyhrr (1973), an early proponent of ZBB whom many consider its inventor, recognizes the impracticality of a true zero base budget and leans toward a more practical definition, one in which evaluation has a profound effect but is not exhaustively used.

Four basic steps are required to employ ZBB. First, the jurisdiction must identify "decision units," or basically, the units of analysis, be they programs or organization units. Second, the jurisdiction defines "decision packages" or bundles of decision units, which, in reality, correspond to the organization at which the lowest-level choices will be made and priorities set. Those responsible for decision packages develop appropriations requests based on rankings of decision units within decision packages and, ultimately, across decision packages (see Figure 2.16).

A decision unit identifies a discrete activity, function, or operation. A decision package identifies and sets priorities among decision units based on each decision unit's purpose, need (expressed usually as the consequences of not performing the activity, function, or operation any longer), performance measures or methods of detecting success and failure, alternative ways of performing the activity, function, or operation, and the costs and benefits of various levels of budgetary support as they affect performance and are observed in the measures defined in the package.

The key to ZBB is the evaluation of alternatives among the decision units in the decision package. Given the information in the process, choices hinge on the different ways of performing the same function (various combinations of cutbacks and expansions among decision units to produce a department service, e.g., parks and recreation, as in Figure 2.16) and the outcomes, depending on the different levels of budgetary effort. Managers, having identified the consequences of no longer performing the activity, function or operation, estimate the differences in performance due to lower-than-current budget support, continued but stable levels of support, and greater future support. Thus, ZBB's uniqueness lies in information formatting.

The literature on the conceptual evolution of ZBB is sparse. In essence, ZBB was developed at either Texas Instruments, Inc., in 1969 (Pyhrr, 1973) or in the U.S. Department of Agriculture in 1964 (Wildavsky, 1975). In the former, Pyhrr reports success, and in the latter, Wildavsky reports failure. ZBB's greatest fame came through its introduction into public agency administration by the then governor of Georgia, Jimmy Carter.

The literature implies that ZBB has at least ten advantages. First, ZBB yields increased information from managers throughout the organization, particularly operating managers who are responsible for the actual performance of activity for which they budget. Second, it results in improved plans and budgets that themselves result from combining planning and goals setting, budgeting, and operational decision making into one process requiring detailed scrutiny of every activity. Third, ZBB encourages the use of continued evaluation of program efficiency and effectiveness throughout the budget operating year. Fourth, programs and managers who have committed themselves to certain levels of performance can be reviewed during the operating year to gauge progress. Fifth, ZBB's priority ranking system facilitates assigning cutbacks or reductions when necessary. Sixth, ZBB helps set priorities and sharpen overall objectives. Seventh, the ZBB approach shifts budget attention away

| DISCRETE ACTIVITIES | Spending Baseline* | Decision Unit | Cutback Decision Unit = 90% of Baseline** | Decision Unit | Baseline Decision Unit = 10% of Baseline | Decision Unit | Expansion Decision Unit = 10% of Baseline | Decision Unit | Total (Sum of 90%, 10%, and 10% Increments) |
|---|---|---|---|---|---|---|---|---|---|
| **Parks** | | | | | | | | | |
| Rangers Guides | 176,493 | RG1 | 158,844 | RG2 | 17,649 | RG3 | 17,649 | RG3 | 194,142 |
| Zoo | 82,719 | ZOO1 | 74,447 | ZOO2 | 8,272 | ZOO3 | 8,272 | ZOO3 | 90,991 |
| **Recreation** | | | | | | | | | |
| Team sports | 473,384 | Teams1 | 426,046 | Teams2 | 47,338 | Teams3 | 47,338 | Teams3 | 520,723 |
| Tennis | 423,734 | Tennis1 | 381,361 | Tennis2 | 42,373 | Tennis3 | 42,373 | Tennis3 | 466,108 |
| Pools | 340,980 | Pools1 | 306,882 | Pools2 | 34,098 | Pools3 | 34,098 | Pools3 | 375,078 |
| Pet fairs | 23,478 | Pets1 | 21,130 | Pets2 | 2,348 | Pets3 | 2,348 | Pets3 | 25,825 |
| Holiday affairs | 66,520 | Holidays1 | 59,868 | Holidays2 | 6,652 | Holidays3 | 6,652 | Holidays3 | 73,172 |
| Personal leisure skills | 23,478 | Leisure1 | 21,130 | Leisure2 | 2,348 | Leisure3 | 2,348 | Leisure3 | 25,825 |
| Dog obedience classes | 3,913 | Dogs1 | 3,522 | Dogs2 | 391 | Dogs3 | 391 | Dogs3 | 4,304 |
| Belly dancing classes | 641,721 | Dancing1 | 577,549 | Dancing2 | 64,172 | Dancing3 | 64,172 | Dancing3 | 705,893 |
| Knitting classes | 23,478 | Knitting1 | 21,130 | Knitting2 | 2,348 | Knitting3 | 2,348 | Knitting3 | 25,825 |
| | 2,279,896 | | 2,051,906 | | 227,990 | | | | 2,507,886 |

| Rank of Decision Unit (for example, ranking on the base of reaching the most people) | Decision Unit | | Cumulative |
|---|---|---|---|
| 1 | Pets1 | 21,130 | 21,130 |
| 2 | Holidays1 | 59,868 | 80,998 |
| 3 | Dancing1 | 577,549 | 658,547 |
| 4 | Pools1 | 306,882 | 965,429 |
| 5 | Teams1 | 426,046 | 1,391,475 |
| 6 | RG1 | 158,844 | 1,550,319 |
| 7 | Pets2 | 2,348 | 1,552,667 |
| 8 | Holidays2 | 6,652 | 1,559,319 |
| 9 | Dancing2 | 64,172 | 1,623,491 |
| 10 | Pools2 | 34,098 | 1,657,589 |
| 11 | Teams2 | 47,338 | 1,704,927 |
| 12 | RG2 | 17,649 | 1,722,576 |
| 13 | Dancing3 | 64,172 | 1,786,748 |
| 14 | Pools3 | 34,098 | 1,820,846 |
| 15 | Teams3 | 47,338 | 1,868,184 |
| 16 | Tennis1 | 381,361 | 2,249,545 |
| 17 | Holidays3 | 6,652 | 2,256,197 |

**Figure 2.16   A zero-base budget for a municipal recreation system.**

| 18 | Tennis2 | 42,373 | 2,298,570 | Spending limit equal to revenue estimate |
| 19 | RG3 | 17,649 | 2,316,219 | of ~108% of the previous year's revenue support. |
| 20+ | | | | |

Those programs cut included the zoo, dog obedience classes, and knitting classes. Budget decision makers cut back personal leisure skills classes. They expanded team sports, pools, holiday affairs, and belly dancing classes. To these decision makers, all activities were not equal, when maximizing the population served was the criteria for choice.

*Spending baseline reflects either the previous year's spending or the "baseline" budget estimate, defined as an estimate of the spending that would occur if no changes were made to current laws during the period covered by the budget. The baseline assumes that mandatory spending (e.g., retirement fund payments for employees) will continue and increase or decrease in the future as required by current law. The baseline assumes that future funding for any but mandatory spending will equal the most recently enacted appropriation, adjusted for inflation.

**Decision unit definitions (90% of the spending base, 10% and 10%) come from observations, such as the following:
90% represents the amount a budget official can reduce expenditure on an activity without making possible it's continuation as a workable or practicable endeavor
10% represents the amount that could be added to the Cutback Decision Unit to make the activity's budget equal the Baseline budget.
10% added to the Baseline budget encourages an expansion in the activity beyond it's baseline.
The definitions here — 90% and 10% increments — are arbitrary.
Variables such as number of clients, attendees, or service recipients and the cost of staff, materials, and equipment to serve Cutback, Baseline, and Expansion levels of demand would determine the size of the decision unit. A central budget office defines decision unit size by examining demand and cost patterns.

**Figure 2.16   (continued).**

from incremental approaches to last year's budget and focuses on minimum levels of operation. Eight, ZBB promotes the search for alternatives to programs, performance, and funding levels and may be most useful in reallocating funds among programs within an agency. Ninth, the ZBB approach can readily identify low-yield or low-priority programs that may be eliminated. Finally, ZBB reduces the opportunity for manipulation of budget presentation information, or "gamesmanship." If the information is present in ZBB formats, attempts at gaming become transparent.

From a theoretical perspective, the disadvantages of ZBB may include problems of implementation and compliance of users are threatened by the need to reevaluate pet projects. Also, the number of decision packages generated can overwhelm managers reviewing them; the paperwork produced can have more volume than meaning. ZBB is limited to use with only controllable elements in budgets. In the federal budget, controllables may amount to no more than 25% of the total. The ranking system remains susceptible to subjective decision, and ZBB does not aid in judging priorities among dissimilar activities such as defense, education, and energy. ZBB is difficult to apply to state and local programs whose genesis is not local but federal and whose support does not lend itself to their control. In addition, there is difficulty in identifying appropriate decision units, in gathering accurate supporting data to produce effective analysis, and in determining minimum levels of effort. ZBB requires vast improvements in agency evaluation systems necessary to make program comparisons and rankings and is expensive and time consuming to implement.

Practically, ZBB's disadvantages include its failure to fundamentally change the practice of federal budget making. Second, the Office of Management and Budget (OMB), in trying to simplify paperwork needs, drained the decision packages of their decisional utility. Third, managers decided priorities in a vacuum, without knowledge of how interrelated programs might be affected by rankings done partially by others. Thus, Program A may have been related to Program B, but A was included in a set of priorities distant from B; one's operation may have depended on the other, but one's fate could not be revealed to the other.

## 2.5 Revenue Analysis

The traditional role of public finance lies in the examination of taxes and the study of the efficiency and equity of the tax system. This section describes the major taxes in use among governments in the United States as well as their administration. Next, we inquire into the equity of a given tax system, using both normative—what is a good tax system—and analytical—incidence analysis—approaches. Why is this important to the field of public accounting? Not only do public officials need to keep track of the inflows and outflows but also important, and perhaps arguably more important, is understanding why these—in particular, the inflows—fluctuate.

Accounting for revenues upon receiving them is one thing, but properly analyzing and anticipating the inflows results in an efficient and balanced budget.

The inflow of resources to governments marks the temporal beginning of governmental financial management. Resources to governments come in three basic forms: taxes or coerced payments, charges or fees that define a trade between government and individual or organization, and transfers or the simple movement of money from one governmental level to another.

Generally, the use of each type of resource by different governments has remained fairly stable over time. The federal government relies on the income tax, states for the most part on sales taxes, and counties and cities on the property tax.*

Taxes dominate. Rather than fees or transfers, taxes have constituted about 80% of all governments' revenues, with charges making up the balance. When only state and local governments are considered, taxes make up about one-half of all revenue, charges about one-third, and intergovernmental (in this case, federal or federal and state) aid about 15%.

## 2.5.1 Principles of Each Revenue Source

Each revenue source has a basic principle with which analysts determine its effectiveness, and to some extent, its efficiency.

For taxes, the principle is called ability to pay. Thus, one can determine a fair and effective, but not always efficient, system of taxation by applying conceptually the notion that one pays according to one's means: those with more wealth or ability pay more taxes.

For charges, the principle is based on market principles or trade—the benefits the trader receives. The benefits-received principle is a more efficient approach, but perhaps less equitable. When government derives revenue from a service or good produced and priced, the customer may choose according to what the customer of the government's good or service considers the benefit received. This notion also includes an ability-to-pay concept, as one with more ability to pay may, having the same objective sense of benefit, be willing to pay more because the worth of each dollar paid is less than that of the poorer competitor.

Often the two—equity and efficiency—are at odds with each other. The debate, whether to tax or charge, is determined by the type of good. Yet a philosophical debate hangs in the background. For example, water usage used to fall under the ability-to-pay principle, according to which property taxes covered the cost—the larger the home, the more the value, and the more tax the property owner paid—the ability-to-pay principle maintained. If Jack owns a bigger house than

---

* See Advisory Commission on Intergovernmental Relations, *Significant Features of Fiscal Federalism* (Washington, DC: Advisory Commission on Intergovernmental Relations) produced annually.

Jim, it is fair to say Jack probably uses more water—more bathrooms, more sinks, more usage; also, Jack is wealthier. Even if Jim uses more water because he has a spouse and five kids, he pays less because his property is worth less than Jack's. This approach is equitable from the standpoint of wealth, but not usage. Today, city water departments charge the homeowner based on gallons used—an efficient approach to taxation. The philosophical question left hanging is, Is it fair to charge someone who has less wealth or income but uses more of a public good or service more than someone with more money and wealth but less usage?

Finally, for intergovernmental transfers, a number of principles apply. First, governments may transfer money—from federal to local, perhaps—because of the need for stabilization of local economies. In such a case, the federal government may declare the local area an economic disaster area and specify that certain services or revenues be pledged to ameliorate conditions, improving changes for economic growth, stable prices, and employment.

Second, the transfer of resources among government may stem from the need to equalize resources or even to redistribute them. Local school districts, for example, may differ markedly in local financial resources available to support education. The state government may commit resources to equalize that particular district's resource base compared to other districts. This equalization may amount to a redistribution of revenue, since the state taxes richer jurisdictions to be able to direct aid to the poorer district.

The third reason for intergovernmental transfers comes from the so-called merger of policy and budget among levels of government. That is, the federal government, desiring the cooperation of local governments in policy matters such as desegregation, may link transfers of money, for schools for example, to the promise of local governments cooperation in desegregation of schools.

## 2.5.2 Principles Useful in Evaluating a Tax System

Are tax systems created out of necessity, or is there a guide for making basic structural decisions and later marginal ones? We think the latter is true. Let us look at a good tax system and its elements for a moment. There are six elements that public finance students find meaningful in evaluating a tax system, and each is discussed in turn.

Simplicity refers to the understandability of a tax system. Whether taxpayers understand what is being taxed and how they must pay the tax depends in large part on the clarity of the base (the object taxed) and the rate of taxing it.

Resistance is a function of complexity. This explains the popularity of a flat rate income tax in which all are taxed at the same rate and the lack of popularity of the progressive income tax in which many are taxed at many different levels for different reasons.

Certainty in a tax system refers to its stability, predictability, and relative permanence. Generally, certainty is a function of the amount of "tinkering" lawmakers feel predisposed to undertake. Constant rate changes for an income tax leads to less certainty and, thus, less ability to plan spending given amounts of either disposable income or after-tax income. Certainty also reflects the nature of the underlying base and influences playing on that base. For example, the property tax for most jurisdictions remains fairly stable because the rate of property improvement—housing construction, for example—is itself rather stable. When rapid revaluation of property occurs, either through administrative means or through rapid construction or property ownership turnover, the ability to predict one's tax bill diminishes and the tax system itself becomes a volatile variable in financial planning.

Public expenditures should be financed by taxes that change little, proportionately, from year to year. Tax burdens, theory states, should not increase over time as a percentage of real, uninflated, personal income.

For selecting one tax or another, the cost of collecting a levy should have some influence. The expense of collection should remain small and should become a smaller percentage of the total as the total yield increases in order to be effective, say public finance theorists. A gasoline tax or a liquor tax collected from only a few wholesalers requires smaller administrative costs than a sales tax paid by everyone. The sales tax, in turn, is easier to collect than an income tax.

A tax system, according to most evaluators, should be neutral unless, for policy reasons, the system should have a determining effect on individuals' and businesses' behavior. Since no tax we now use has ever been found to have absolute neutrality, we refer instead to relative neutrality as a valid goal.

The measure of neutrality is usually the measure of intended incidence. Incidence measures the degree to which a tax levied on one person is actually paid by that person rather than shifted to another. Thus, the person who actually pays a tax may not be the person who bears the burden of the tax. For example, cigarette taxes are levied on the cigarette package, collected by the seller of cigarettes, but paid by the smoker.

The more inelastic the demand for a good taxed, given elastic supply, the greater the proportion of the tax that will be shifted forward. Therefore, the less the consumer is willing or able to change buying habits as a result of the imposition of a tax on a given good, the more likely the tax will be shifted forward to the consumer.

If we cause demand to become more elastic, however, and let supply become less elastic, even to a fixed supply, the more likely the tax will be shifted backward to the producer. For example, if we have no preference when choosing a soft drink, a tax levied on Pepsi-Cola but not on Coca-Cola will have the effect of forcing the makers and distributors of Pepsi-Cola to absorb the tax.

"Beggar thy neighbor" policies often lead governments to tax in such a way that nonresidents pay the bulk of the levy. Taxes on the rental of hotel rooms, to take an obvious example, tend to force the burden on visitors rather than residents.

Yet, all taxes are exported to some extent. Property taxes on the inventory of a manufacturing concern in one jurisdiction are paid by those in other jurisdictions who buy from the manufacturer because such taxes are shifted forward to the consumer. Sales taxes paid by out-of-town shoppers and income taxes paid to urban governments by workers who travel to work from suburbs illustrate the common exporting of taxes.

While neutrality may be regarded as the ultimate test of an efficient tax system, tax policy has often provided incentives or has discouraged action. While much evidence exists to the contrary, many legislators profess belief that tax exemptions alone lure industry and homeowners. Uncertainty rather than the rate itself, as we argued earlier, may have the greatest impact.

Nevertheless, considerable analytical efforts now being made testify to the fact that relieving a group of the burden of a tax is as important a resource allocation device as granting funds to the activity. Thus, Congress and what has been named "tax expenditures" comprise a lively subset of public budgeting activity.

What is a fair tax system? Often, such a system is one in which everyone who benefits by government services or goods pays in direct proportion to the benefit received. Otherwise, a fair system is one in which everyone benefits but everyone pays according to his or her ability to pay.

The benefits-received principle is the basis for fee systems and user charges for governmental goods. The ability-to-pay principle underlies the financing of most public goods.

The ability-to-pay principle may be further subdivided into two forms of equity, horizontal and vertical. Horizontal equity refers to the equity of burden among those with equal ability to pay. Thus, those with equal ability pay equally; all persons with incomes of $100,000 pay the same amount of taxes, all other things being equal as well.

Vertical equity refers to the principle of appropriate payment given unequal ability. Surrounding vertical equity we find the arguments about "the more one earns, the more one should pay" in income taxes, presumably, or "everyone should pay the same proportion of what they make"—the tithing principle. Most often we find observers of the tax system arguing that the system actually works to force more taxes on those with less ability to pay.

Each of these arguments is an observation of a condition called, respectively, progressive, proportional, or regressive taxation. A progressive tax is one that claims a greater proportion of the based taxed as the value of that base increases. Simply, as one's income increases, one's effective tax rate increases as well. Proportional taxes are those in which the relationship between taxes paid and base remain constant. Finally, a regressive tax claims more of the base, proportionately, as the base increases.

When we speak of tax rate or effective tax rate, we refer to a simple calculation. We measure the amount of taxes paid in relation to an ability measure, usually household income. This is an actual, thus effective, tax rate.

If we then divide the population paying the tax into categories along the dimension of ability to pay—household income in our example—we can determine the state of the system. Thus, dividing the effective rate paid by our wealthiest class by

**Table 2.4   Tax Equity**

| Taxpayer Income($) | Regressive System | | Proportional System | | Progressive System | |
|---|---|---|---|---|---|---|
| | Tax Paid ($) | Effective Tax Rate | Tax Paid ($) | Effective Tax Rate | Tax Paid ($) | Effective Tax Rate |
| 20,000 | 3,000 | 15.0% | 2,000 | 10.0% | 1,000 | 5.0% |
| 40,000 | 3,000 | 7.5% | 4,000 | 10.0% | 3,000 | 7.5% |
| 60,000 | 3,000 | 5.0% | 6,000 | 10.0% | 9,000 | 15.0% |

the effective rate (ER) paid by our poorest class, we get a measure of relative regressivity (ER < 1), proportionality (ER = 1), or progressivity (ER > 1).

Consider the comprehensive sales tax (illustrated in Table 2.4), the flat rate income tax, and the progressive income tax. A comprehensive sales tax is one on all items consumed by a household.

Consumption includes food and other "fixed" expenses that when taxed work to force lower-income households to pay more of their incomes in taxes than higher-income households. The effective rate (taxes paid divided by income, our ability measure) for the sales tax starts at 10% at the low end and falls to 6% at the highest income level.

In comparison to the sales tax, the flat or proportional tax neither rises nor falls, by definition. It remains a fixed proportion of income. Social security taxes work this way, up to the income ceiling provided by law.

The progressive tax structure, of course, provides that larger and larger portions of income are paid in taxes as income rises. Truly, the progressive system epitomizes the maxim "to those much is given, much is required" expressed in one form or another by both the Bible and Lenin. The progressive tax system, when combined with a transfer payment system of expenditures—veterans educational benefits, student loan interest payment subsidies, and home mortgage interest deductions—effects a redistribution of income, a Robin Hood effect, between rich and poor or relatively less rich.

# 2.6  Types of Taxes

In creating a progressive tax system, one stumbles first over what to tax, or, "what shall serve as the measure of ability to pay?" Of course, ability intuitively means some form of income. Or is it capacity to consume? Or is it wealth? Surely, it is one of the three, income, consumption, or wealth, but which one?

All three types of coerced payments, or taxes, find general use in the United States today: those based on, or the tax base of which is, income, consumption, and wealth.

## 2.6.1 Income

The income tax finds use at all three levels of government. Much of the tax reform effort at the federal level, as a matter of fact, deals with making the burden of the federal income tax fairer, considering the effect the tax may have on economic incentives.

### 2.6.1.1 Definition of Income

There are two basic views regarding defining income: the uses-of-income view and the factor-payment view. In the uses-of-income view, the amount consumed by an individual as well as that saved is the base taxed. In the factor-payment view, the salaries paid for services rendered become the base. Both views tend to underlie the federal income tax.

Income means several different things to those involved in its measurement for tax purposes. A classic definition of income is "the well-being of the person receiving it, and that depends on what the person obtains with purchasing power, not where he got it" (Bradford, 1986, p.16). Traditional definitions of income, therefore, tend to define income from a "uses" point of view, as the sum of what one consumes plus increases in wealth, the former being purchases made and the latter savings accumulated.

The federal income tax, as well as the income taxed at both state and local government levels in most areas, does not follow the "uses" definition completely. In fact, income actually taxed tends to be that earned by a worker or paid by an employer for services rendered. This "factor payment" view of income differs radically from the "consumption + savings" view in that ability is based on what comes into the household rather than on what goes out. Clearly, federal tax policy, in not taxing consumption or the accumulation of assets such as housing, encourages both. In taxing salaries, federal tax policy, in a sense, penalizes one for working for a salary and discourages it, unless, of course, one has no other choice.

### 2.6.1.2 Methods of Taxation

Income taxes differ in several ways from the better-known state and federal income taxes to those used at the local government level. First, instead of the progressive nature of some state and federal income taxes, in which taxpayers with more income generally pay a higher tax, local income taxes usually tax all incomes at the same flat rate.

Second, the administrative burden of a local tax is often higher than the broader-based state or federal tax systems owing to economies of scale. As a result, some states require local governments to "piggyback" a local income tax onto the state tax; the state then collects the local tax and remits it back to the local jurisdiction after deducting a collection fee.

A third difference is that federal and state governments tax broadly defined income, while local governments usually employ narrower income definitions. A broad-based income tax would define income to include items such as wage and salary earnings, interest and dividends, rents, capital gains, and net profits from business and professional activities.

Local governments frequently employ a simpler tax system, termed a payroll, wage, or earnings tax. The tax is levied on an individual's wage and salary earnings. By design, it discriminates against people who earn most of their income in wages and salaries as compared to those who receive their income from investments or other nonwage sources.

When a local income tax is broadly defined, tax enforcement becomes more complex since some sources of income are easily hidden. Mandatory filing of a local tax return is often imposed to seek higher levels of compliance.

As usually implemented, the tax applies to all who live or work in the city, including nonresidents. This form presents distortions when the nonresidents' home community does not also impose a similar tax. Even when there is a tax in both jurisdictions, the rate or base may differ. Often, the home community provides a full or partial credit for related local taxes paid elsewhere. Still, the nonresident worker may end up paying more for the interjurisdictional home/work pattern than a resident worker.

In those states where local income tax is allowed and imposed, the authority to levy the tax and/or the adoption of the tax source is usually restricted to a few jurisdictions within a state. Only in a few states (Ohio and Pennsylvania, for instance) is the local income tax a general grant of tax authority rather than a specific grant of authority. While most rates are set at 1%, there are isolated cases of it in the 3 to 5% range.

## 2.6.1.3 Evaluation

Is the factor-payment definition of income a fair way to tax individuals? Surely if almost everyone in the United States draws most of his paying ability from a salary, and that salary income is taxed at progressively higher rates as salary income increases, but not to the point that the tax interferes with the willingness to work, the income tax should be fair.

Some argue that the federal income tax is less fair than possible because of the deductions allowed. The deductions are prompted by tax expenditure policy that encourages and discourages spending on certain items by making that spending deductible from the gross income taxed. For example, one of the most popular deductions in federal income tax practice is that for mortgage interest paid on one's real property and improvements, such as one's home. The deduction increases horizontal inequity by discriminating among renters and homeowner mortgage holders earning the same salary. The deduction also increases vertical inequity by making the tax burden borne by the more well-to-do proportionally less than that borne by the less well off.

Likewise, economic incentives to produce, by working longer hours, diminish as the progressive rates increase the tax burden. Economic incentives to increase salaries do fail to materialize as the tax on them rises.

Finally, some investment incentives also decrease when the tax falls on salary income, however progressive. Interest on savings deposits becomes less valuable on a rate-of-return basis than other investments, such as real estate, due to their being taxed on nearly the same basis as salary income.

## 2.6.2 Consumption

Would taxing consumption be fairer? If we define consumption as the flow of funds out of a person's portfolio of assets and cash (from salary or whatever other sources there may be), we have a better definition of ability to pay. Because one can afford to pay for those things ordinarily consumed, it follows that one can afford to pay taxes. As one consumes more, one should pay more taxes. Measuring a person's well-being as a function of his spending has a compelling logic as a basis for measuring ability to pay or in determining fairness in a tax system. Because it accords with not penalizing hard work (the Protestant work ethic) and because it accords with other Biblical invocations for saving, taxes on consumption are almost holy.

### 2.6.2.1 Methods of Taxation

There are two basic methods for taxing consumption, point of retail sale and value-added taxation. The point-of-sale tax applies to only a portion of all goods consumed, namely, those bought at retail by ordinary consumers, such as sales taxes on furniture and appliances bought by homeowners. Moreover, this form of taxation must, almost always, be placed on a good as a premium rather than absorbed in the retail price of the article. For example, a $100 chair with a 5% sales tax may not, usually according to law, actually cost $95.24 with a $4.76 tax but $100 with a $5 tax. Law forces the tax to be shifted forward to the buyer. In practice, however, the law may have little effect. Between New York and New Jersey, for example, sales taxes differ in that New Jersey levies no sales tax on clothing. Wanting to remain competitive, the ordinary New York clothing retailer could absorb the difference due to New York sales tax in the retail pricing of goods. In such a case, the New York sales tax might be shifted backward to the retailer or seller.*

---

* One of the consequences of retailer and buyer reluctance to absorb the tax is effort to "play a loophole" in the sales tax law. Thus, New York retailers do not have to collect the sales tax from customers who order goods by mail from states in which the firm does not business or has no business location. New York retailers simply evade the tax by mailing goods to the New Jersey buyer's home even though the buyer may have shopped and paid for the good in the New Yorker's place of business. See Holley H. Ulbrich, "Taxing the Catalogue Buyer: Playing Fair in Interstate Commerce," *Intergovernmental Perspective* 11:4 (Fall, 1985), p. 29.

## 2.6.2.2 Evaluation

What might not be fair about this tax? Perhaps the most obvious is the tax's unfairness when the necessities of life are included in the tax base. For example, two families, each of which has the same food-buying habits but vastly different abilities to pay for food, would bear inequitable sales tax burdens. The tax would fall on the poorer family disproportionately, if we ignore all other purchases. To the extent that sales taxes tend not to punish households for purchasing essentials, the tax becomes fairer. Food and medicine exemptions commonly contribute to fairness.

Moreover, the imposition of sales taxes and income taxes with sales taxes deductible from income taxes also may contribute to fairness (Bradford, 1986).

## 2.6.3 Wealth

Finally, wealth emerges as a possible definition of ability in designing the fairest tax system. Wealth also has a compelling logic, particularly as it taps the rich versus poor dimension of progressive taxation.

### 2.6.3.1 Definition of Wealth

Wealth represents both income and consumption, but it is more. Wealth refers ultimately to accumulated ability. Wealth is the total purchasing power a person commands at a given time in the form of a stock, measured in dollars, or an asset, consisting essentially of a claim to future payments of money or future delivery of goods and services.

Two versions of the wealth definition exist. The first, book value, refers to the maximum amount of present consumption a person could finance currently by selling or otherwise committing all of the assets held (such as borrowing against them) (Bradford, 1986).

Another version, transaction value, is that actually used in measuring wealth for tax purposes. The tax value of a portfolio of assets is that realizable when a transaction actually takes place. The value for tax purposes is not computed on a daily basis but only when the transaction, realizing the asset's value, actually takes place. Local governments' property taxes may operate in either way. Some local governments use the appraised value of a new home as the basis of its tax value, computing accretion to the house's value annually based on the weighted values of other homes bought and sold during that year. Book value is tax valuation.

On the other hand, most local governments must rely on a transaction value. Only when a house is sold, or when the owner records an improvement, does the jurisdiction record a new valuation, based on the house's market value. A house may tax valuation a great deal lower than book value for many years. Obviously, the transaction approach to property tax valuation discourages housing turnover and encourages community stability.

### 2.6.3.2 Methods of Taxation of Wealth

The property tax is the most prevalent of the methods of taxing wealth. Two types of property exist for tax purposes, real property or personal property. Real property includes land and improvements such as buildings. Personal property may be further divided into tangible—touchable, seeable, physical—property and intangible—not touchable, ethereal—property. Automobiles, manufacturing inventories, and office furniture would be tangible personal property, whereas stocks, bonds, notes and the like are called intangible personal property.

A property tax is an ad valorem tax, which is a tax on wealth. Typically, a city's major source of revenue comes from property taxes, which are levied as a millage (referred to as mills) on tangible and intangible real and personal property. Property subject to taxation includes land, buildings, machinery, artwork, stocks, bonds, vehicles, among others, but it is state law that dictates what forms of wealth are taxable by local governments. As a relatively inelastic tax—unresponsive to economic changes—the property tax typically is used to balance the budget; that is, toward the end of the budgeting process, decision makers determine the amount of revenue that is necessary to match the level of expenditures not covered by nonproperty tax revenue. Cities use the following formula to calculate the property tax rate:

$$r = \frac{e - \text{NPR}}{\text{NAV}}$$

where $r$ is the tax rate, $e$ is the total expenses or expenditures, NPR is the nonproperty tax revenue, and NAV is the net assessed value of the locality. Referring to Figure 2.8, we can see how the city of Grand Rapids calculated its millage rate for the refuse collection and disposal special revenue fund for the city of Grand Rapids. The difference between revenues and expenditures ($e - \text{NPR}$) is roughly a $6 million deficit. We know from other documentation (not included in the figures) that the city has approximately $3.881 billion in assessed property (NAV). Placing these numbers into the formula, a rate of 0.0015459 calculated. This means that one dollar is taxed 0.0015459. This number is difficult to understand, so it is converted into mills, which is a tax per $1,000 in value; a 1.55 millage rate is taxed on every $1,000 worth of property. If Joe Citizen owns a parcel of property worth $100,000, he would owe the city $154.59 in property tax for the city's refuse collection and disposal. This rate for this special revenue fund balances its budget and restores a surplus.

Property tax administration requires four processes. First, discovery of the tax base may be quite easy in the case of real property and quite difficult for intangible personal property. Conventional systems for recording real property, for describing its location and physical limits, and its ownership ease its administration. At the other end of the spectrum, discovery of intangible personal property depends on the inclination of the owner to reveal it.

Second, inventory of real property essentially involves its listing by tract or plot.

Third, assessment requires appraisal of the value of the property. Market price is most often the basis for valuation, but the low number of arm's length transactions in any area makes accurate, annual valuation difficult.

Fourth, the determination of the levy requires the budget officer to subtract the estimated amounts of revenue to be received from sources other than the property tax from total estimated expenditures. The remainder is the levy or the amount to be raised by levying the property tax. The tax rate is the quotient found by dividing the levy by the jurisdiction's total value of taxable property assessments.

## 2.6.4 Nontax Revenues

Taxes comprise only a fraction of the revenues governments utilize in financing current and capital operations. Presently, user fees (priced services) and indirect cost recovery supplement traditional sources of revenue. This section deals with nontraditional revenues and discusses their sources and, particularly, their management.

The public's dissatisfaction with government tax policy in recent years has caused agencies at all levels to seek alternatives to tax revenues. In particular, this sentiment has caused these agencies to reexamine the possibility of imposing or substantially increasing user prices for services they offer.

The extent to which users should pay directly for public services has long excited controversy, however. Considerable wisdom, political, economic, and administrative, attaches to user fees, especially when examining the various ways services might be priced. Three methods illustrate the large range available for tailoring pricing systems to various needs or demands: going rate pricing, demand-oriented pricing, and cost base pricing (Crompton, 1980).

Going rate pricing applies when an agency seeks prices that reflect the average of those charged by other organizations for equivalent services. As a result, an agency charges rates comparable to those charged by other jurisdictions for the service.

Demand-oriented pricing rests on the determination of what individuals would and are willing to pay for a particular service. Prices scaled to income are common, especially when applied to senior citizens and the handicapped. Pricing may also differ by age, and the facilities charging fees in one neighborhood may differ from those in either a more affluent or less affluent one.

Pricing may also differ by time of day to encourage off-peak-time use and to ration use during peak periods. In some cases, the time basis may be used to encourage disadvantaged groups. Establishing free admission one or two days a week may remove or reduce financial barriers and enable these groups to benefit from the service.

There are three basic approaches to establishing a fee based on costs (Crompton, 1980): average cost pricing, partial overhead pricing, and variable cost pricing.

Average cost pricing covers all fixed and variable costs associated with a service. Partial overhead pricing meets all variable costs and some portion of fixed costs. Variable cost pricing covers only variable costs. Average cost pricing would be appropriate for private goods. Partial overhead pricing and variable pricing are appropriate for public goods, with variable cost pricing more appropriately applied to those services that yield more public benefit than with partial overhead pricing.

Determining what portion of fixed costs to subsidize depends on the extent that the nonusing public benefits. As the benefits accruing to nonusers increases, the portion of fixed costs met by the subsidy should increase. In practice, the appropriate portion is generally decided in some arbitrary way, frequently guided by prevailing political pressures (Pledge, 1982).

## 2.7 Summary

We set out to define a budget and determine its inner workings as they relate to accounting. A theoretical definition is difficult to pinpoint, but from a descriptive standpoint, a budget is, with no doubt, a set of documents estimating future inflows and outflows. The dollars are tracked through a set of funds accounted for on an accrual or modified accrual basis. From an accountant's point of view, it is crucial to pay attention to the funds, but also the inflow and outflows, particularly how each is analyzed, estimated, and evaluated. Accountants, being a primary set of analysts of government budget procedures and decisions, can and will take note of the economic and social impacts budget decisions have. Their educated opinion of decision consequences can provide advice to finance officials who are elected or appointed. In the end, accountants play a critical role in the information flow progressive government budgeting requires. Accountants play an imperative role in the public financial management process. Their knowledge of tools, process, frameworks, and decision consequences help keep governments on track.

## Bibliography

Advisory Commission on Intergovernmental Relations, Significant Features of Fiscal Federalism (Washington, DC: Advisory Commission on Intergovernmental Relations) produced annually.

Anton, T.J. (1964). Budgeting in Three Illinois Cities. Urbana, IL: Institute of Government and Public Affairs.

Argyris, C. (1975). What budgeting mean to people. In R.T. Golembiewski and J. Rabin (Eds.), *Public Budgeting and Finance*, 2nd ed. Itasca, IL: Peacock Publishing Company, pp. 242–250.

Auerbach, A.J. (1996). Dynamic revenue estimation. *Journal of Economic Perspectives*, 10, 141–157.

Barber, J.D. (1966). *Power in Committees.* Chicago, IL: Rand McNally.

Bradford, D.F. (1986). *Untangling the Income Tax.* Cambridge, MA: Harvard University Press.

Brown, B. and Helmer, O. (1962). *Improving the Reliability of Estimates Obtained From a Consensus of Experts.* Santa Monica, CA: Rand Corporation.

Burkhead, J. (1956). *Government Budgeting.* New York: John Wiley & Sons.

Burkhead, J. (1965). The budget and democratic government. In Roscoe C. Martin, Ed., *Public Administration and Democracy.* Syracuse, New York: Syracuse University Press, pp. 85–99.

Calia, R., Guajardo, S., and Metzgar, J. (2000). Putting the NACSLB recommended budget practices into action: Best practices in budgeting. *Government Finance Review,* 16(2: April), 1–9.

Clark, T.N. and Ferguson, L. (1983). *City Money.* New York: Columbia University Press.

Crompton, J. (1980). Pricing Park and Recreation Services. Paper presented to the National Recreation and Parks Association Congress, Phoenix, Arizona.

Dahl, R.A. (1961). *Who Governs?* New Haven, CN: Yale University Press.

Delbecq, A.L., Van de Ven, A.H., and Gustafson, D.H. (1975). *Group Techniques for Program Planning: A Guide to Nominal Group and Delphi Processes.* Glenview, IL: Scott, Foresman.

Freeman, R.J. (1972). Municipal budgeting, accounting, reporting and auditing 1972–1999. *Alabama Municipal Journal* 29 (June), 10.

GASB, Government Accounting Standards Board (1999). [Statement No. 34] Basic Financial Statements—and Management's Discussion and Analysis—for State and Local Governments. Norwalk, CT: Government Accounting Standards Board. http://www.gasb.org/repmodel/index.html. April 10, 2006.

Grizzle, G. (1969). PPBS in Dade County: Status of Development and Implementation. A Report to the Joint Economic Committee, United States Congress. Washington, DC: U.S. Government Printing Office.

Grossbard, S.I. (n.d.). PPBS for State and Local Officials. Kingston, RI: Bureau of Government Research, University of Rhode Island.

Hatry, H.P. and Cotton, J. (1967). What is PPB? In George Washington University State and Local Finances Project, Program Planning for State, City, and County Objectives, PPB Note 10, Washington, DC: George Washington University.

Hirsch, W.Z. (1966). State and Local Government Program Budgeting. Regional Science Association Papers, 18, 156.

Horton, R.A. (1969). PPBS in Metropolitan Nashville—Davidson County, Tennessee. A Report to the Joint Economic Committee, United States Congress. Washington, DC: U.S. Government Printing Office.

Jernberg, J.E. (1971). Financial administration, in James M. Banovetz, Ed., *Managing the Modern City.* Washington, DC: International City Management Association, pp. 347–376.

Jones, W.A., Jr. (1983). Historical contexts. In J. Rabin, T. Vocino, W.B. Hildreth, and G.J. Miller (Eds.), *Handbook of Public Personnel Administration and Labor Relations.* New York: Marcel Dekker, pp. 286–288

LeLoup, L.T. (1980). *Budgetary Politics,* 2nd ed. Brunswick, Ohio: King's Court Communications.

Lindblom, C.E. (2001). The science of "muddling through." In Gerald J. Miller, W. Bartley Hildreth, and Jack Rabin (Eds.), *Performance-Based Budgeting.* Boulder, CO: Westview, pp. 39–55.

Luther, R.A. (1972). PPBS in Fairfax County: A practical experience. In F.J. Lyden and E.G. Miller (Eds.), *Planning, Programming, Budgeting*, Chicago, IL: Markham Co., pp. 345–357.

Meiszer, N.M. (1969). Developing a Planning, Programming, Budgeting System in Dayton, Ohio. A Report to the Joint Economic Committee, United States Congress. Washington, DC: U.S. Government Printing Office.

Miller, G.J. (1991). *Government Financial Management Theory*. New York: Dekker.

Moak, L.L. and Hillhouse, A.M. (1975). *Concepts and Practices in Local Government Finance*. Chicago, IL: Municipal Finance Officers Association.

Municipal Finance Officers Association (1954). Performance Budgeting and Unit Cost Accounting for Governmental Units. Chicago, IL: Municipal Finance Officers Association.

Mushkin, S.J. (1969a). Innovations in Planning, Programming and Budgeting in State and Local Governments. A Report to the Joint Economic Committee, United States Congress. Washington, DC: U.S. Government Printing Office.

Mushkin, S.J. (1969b). PPB in cities. *Public Administration Review*, 29, 16–21.

Osborn, A. (1953). *Applied Imagination: Principles and Procedures of Creative Thinking*. New York: Scribner's.

Pfeffer, J. (1981). Management as symbolic action. In L.L. Cummings and B.M. Staw (Eds.), *Research in Organizational Behavior*, Vol. 3. Greenwich, CT: JAI Press, 1981, pp. 1–52.

Pledge, R.A. (1982). The Right Price: Fees and Charges in Overland Park, Kansas. Paper prepared for University of Kansas Department of Political Science Seminar in Public Financial Systems. Lawrence, KS: University of Kansas, Department of Political Science.

Pyhrr, P. (1973). *Zero-Base Budgeting*. New York: Wiley.

Ridley, C. and Simon, H.A. (1943). *Measuring Municipal Activities*. Washington, DC: International City Managers Association.

Rosenbloom, D.H. (1983). *Public Administration and Law*. New York: Marcel Dekker.

Schick, A. (1966). The road to PPB: The stages of budget reform. *Public Administration Review*, 26, 257–258.

Sherwood, F.P. and Best, W.H. (1958). Supervisory methods in municipal administration. Chicago, IL: International City Management Association.

Shirras, G.F. (1936). *The Science of Public Finance*, Vol. 1, pp. 82–83; Vol. 2, pp. 968–974. London: Macmillan & Co.

Simon, H.A. (1947). *Administrative Behavior*. New York: The Macmillan Company.

Smith, A. (1904). *The Wealth of Nations*. Edwin Cannan (Ed.). New York: G.P. Putnam's Sons.

Steinbeck, J. (1939). *The Grapes of Wrath*. New York: The Macmillan Company.

Stourm, R. (1917). *The Budget, Translated by Thaddeus Plazinski*. New York: Appleton & Company.

Sundelson, J.W. (1935). Budgetary principles. *Political Science Quarterly*, 50(2), 236–263.

Treasury, Australian Government (1999). Fiscal Policy under Accrual Budgeting. http://www.treasury.gov.au/documents/277/RTF/fpuab.rtf [Link live February 26, 2006].

Tyer, C. and Willand, J. (1997). Public Budgeting in America: A Twentieth Century Retrospective. Columbia, SC: Institute of Public Service and Policy Research, University of South Carolina. http://www.iopa.sc.edu/publication/Budgeting_in_America.htm. Accessed April 18, 2006.

U.S. General Accounting Office (1985). Managing the Cost of Government: Building an Effective Financial Management Structure, Vol. 2. 2 vols. GAO/AFMD-85-35-A. Washington, DC: U.S. General Accounting Office.

Walker, W.E. (1986). *Changing Organizational Culture*. Knoxville, TN: University of Tennessee Press.

Wildavsky, A. (1966). The political economy of efficiency. *Public Administration Review*, 26, 292–310.

Wildavsky, A. (1969). Rescuing policy analysis from PPBS. *Public Administration Review*, 29(2), 189–202.

Wildavsky, A. (1975). *Budgeting: A Comparative Theory of Budgetary Processes*. Boston, MA: Little Brown & Co.

Wildavsky, A. (1981). Budgetary reform in an age of big government. In T. Vocino and J. Rabin (Eds.), *Contemporary Public Administration*. New York: Harcourt, Brace, Jovanovich, pp. 261–291.

Wildavsky, A. (1984). *The Politics of the Budgetary Process*, 4th ed. Boston, MA: Little, Brown & Co.

*Chapter 3*

# Expenditures and Revenues in U.S. Governments

Zhirong Zhao

*University of Minnesota, Hubert H. Humphrey Institute of Public Affairs*

## Contents

3.1   Introduction ........................................................................................130
3.2   Expenditures .......................................................................................130
    3.2.1   Size and Growth of Government Expenditures in the United
        States ......................................................................................130
    3.2.2   Accounting for Growth ........................................................131
    3.2.3   Compare with the Sizes of Other Countries .......................132
    3.2.4   Expenditures of the Federal Government..............................134
    3.2.5   Expenditures of State and Local Governments ....................136
3.3   Revenues ..............................................................................................139
    3.3.1   Overview: Revenue Sources in the United States ................139
    3.3.2   Revenues of the Federal Government....................................139
    3.3.3   Revenues of State and Local Governments ..........................141
    3.3.4   Intergovernmental Grants.....................................................145
References ......................................................................................................146

## 3.1 Introduction

The United States is a federal system of government, in which each level of government has some powers, as defined by the U.S. Constitution, to levy taxes and provide certain services. A situation normally referred to as the "fiscal federalism" in the United States (Advisory Commission on Intergovernmental Relations, 1995). This chapter provides a brief overview of expenditures and revenues for all levels of U.S. governments. The first section discusses government expenditures, including the overall size and growth of government, the explanation of governmental expansion, and the breakdown of responsibilities for each level of government. The second section describes major sources of revenues for each level of government to fund their services, including revenues that are raised by a government itself as well as intergovernmental transfers.

## 3.2 Expenditures

### 3.2.1 Size and Growth of Government Expenditures in the United States

Government expenditures in the United States have been growing in the past several decades (see Table 3.1). In 1950, all levels of government combined spent about $58 billion (U.S. Bureau of the Census, 1975). In 2000, total government spending was approaching $3 trillion, an increase of more than 46 times (Office of Management and Budget, 2006). Over the past five decades, expenditures have grown dramatically at all levels of government, but the share of expenditure in different levels of government has shifted several times over the last century. In the 1900s, local governments have by far the largest share of expenditures, followed by the federal government and then the states. During the Great Depression, federal spending suddenly rose above local expenditures and has since become the leading spender (Lee, Johnson, and Joyce, 2004). The federal share of expenditure had increased to 73.6% by 1950 and stayed at about 70% in the early 1980s (Office of Management and Budget, 2006). In 2000, the federal share fell slightly to 65.9%, as the current trend is to move responsibilities of public services to levels of government closer to the people.*

One approach to measure the size of government is to compare it to the size of national economy, which has fluctuated over the past century. In the late 1920s, the total expenditures of government was only 10% of gross domestic product (GDP), but increases occurred in the 1930s due to the Great Depression, and then World War II brought expenditures to an all-time high, at about half of GDP (Office of Management and Budget, 2006). Since then, as Table 3.1 shows, the government

---

* Caution should be exercised in interpreting these numbers as they include intergovernmental transfer, that is, grants from one government to another.

**Table 3.1   Government Expenditures from 1950 to 2000**

| | 1950 | 1960 | 1970 | 1980 | 1990 | 2000 | Annual Growth Since 1950 |
|---|---|---|---|---|---|---|---|
| **Expenditures (in billions of dollars)** | | | | | | | |
| Federal | 42.6 (73.6%) | 92.2 (73.9%) | 195.6 (70.3%) | 590.9 (72.0%) | 1,253.2 (70.0%) | 1,788.8 (65.9%) | 7.76% |
| State-local | 15.4 (26.6%) | 32.5 (26.1%) | 82.7 (29.7%) | 229.3 (28.0%) | 536.3 (30.0%) | 926.0 (34.1%) | 8.54% |
| Total | 57.9 (100%) | 124.7 (100%) | 278.3 (100%) | 820.3 (100%) | 1,789.5 (100%) | 2,714.9 (100%) | 8.00% |
| **Expenditures as percentage of GDP** | | | | | | | |
| Federal | 15.6% | 17.8% | 19.3% | 21.6% | 21.8% | 18.4% | |
| State–local | 5.6% | 6.3% | 8.2% | 8.4% | 9.4% | 9.5% | |
| Total | 21.2% | 24.0% | 27.5% | 30.0% | 31.2% | 27.9% | |

*Source:* Historical Tables, Budget of the U.S. Government (FY2007), Office of Management and Budget. http://www.gpoaccess.gov/usbudget/fy07/about.html

share in GDP gradually grew from 21.2% in 1950 to 31.2% in 1990, but it then decreased a bit to 27.9% as of 2000. In general, we can say government expenditures in the United States amount to about one-third of the national economy in recent years.

## 3.2.2 Accounting for Growth

A number of analysts have explained the reasons for the growth of government expenditures, which has occurred in many counties. One major reason is that government is "responsive" to the demands of society. Wagner's law, originally proposed in the 1880s, contends that social and economic changes encourage government expansion (Abizadeli and Basilevsky, 1990). As a nation's economy shifts from subsistence agriculture to industrial production, it creates a greater need for transportation, communication, and environmental protection. As people move from rural areas to cities, they demand higher levels of law enforcement, fire protection, and sanitation services. As the technology of work becomes more complex, people need more education. Therefore, governments will be asked to do more and more to meet the increased demands, which results in budget expansion.

Another explanation for budgetary expansion contends that government has a supposed propensity to be excessive. On one hand, public bureaucrats are spending "other people's money" and want to have larger budgets that can increase their power (Buchanan and Tullock, 1977). On the other, many people underestimate the cost of many public programs and, consequently, demand more from government than they would if they knew the true costs (Buchanan, 1967). The propensity of excessive governmental growth may be particularly clear in recent decades. First, the budgetary process becomes increasingly complicated, and thus, it is harder for the public to hold government bureaucrats accountable. Second, governments increasingly rely on a variety of revenue sources that are less visible; for example, all sorts of sales taxes that tend to catch less attention from taxpayers than the property tax does. The diversified tax base creates higher level of "fiscal illusion" that can lead to overtaxing and overspending of government (Dickson and Yu, 2000).

Budgetary expansion can also be explained by the combination of incremental change and drastic growth at the time of crisis. Incrementalism, the traditional budgetary theory, holds that funding for most public programs should remain stable or increase slightly from what they received last year (Wildavsky and Caiden, 2001). Therefore, if we do not actively look for ways to cut spending, then the total budget will gradually increase over time. Moreover, governmental expenditures can be drastically increased in response to emergencies (Mosher and Poland, 1964). As Plato has observed long ago, "accidents and calamities ... are the universal legislators of the world" (Plato, 1975). Under normal conditions, people are often opposed to significant tax increases. When a major crisis strikes, however, resistance to taxation may subside, and thus governments are able to raise higher tax revenues. After the crisis passes, tax levels normally do not decline as much as they rose before the crisis. Over time, a series of wars, depressions, and other emergencies will produce much larger budgets (Dye, 2005).

The growth of governmental spending in the United States in response to the wars has provided a striking example. During the Civil War, federal expenditures jumped from $63 million in 1860 to $1.3 billion in 1865, a growth of about 20 times. Later, because of World War I, it increased from $730 million in 1916 to $18.5 billion within 3 years, and then dropped to $13.3 billion in 1920. When the United States entered into World War II, expenditures rose from $13.3 billion in 1941 to $92.7 billion in 1945, and then declined to $33.1 billion in 1948 (Lee, Johnson, and Joyce, 2004: 36).

### 3.2.3 Compare with the Sizes of Other Countries

How does the size of the American public sector compare with that of other countries? Data for some major countries of the Organization for Economic Cooperation and Development are reported in Table 3.2 (Economic and Social Data Service International, 2006).

**Table 3.2    Governments in Selected Industrialized Countries, 2000**

| Country | Government Consumption as Percentage of GDP | Total Government Tax Revenue as Percentage of GDP |
|---|---|---|
| Australia | 18.3 | 33.6 |
| Austria | 19.2 | 44.5 |
| Belgium | 21.2 | 47.1 |
| Canada | 18.7 | 36.2 |
| Denmark | 25.9 | 49.2 |
| Finland | 20.8 | 47.5 |
| France | 23.2 | 46.2 |
| Germany | 19 | 43.3 |
| Greece | 15.5 | 40.1 |
| Iceland | 23.8 | 39.1 |
| Italy | 18.3 | 42.5 |
| Luxembourg | 16.8 | 40.5 |
| Netherlands | 22.7 | 41.6 |
| Spain | 17.6 | 35.9 |
| Sweden | 26.8 | 50.3 |
| Switzerland | 14.6 | 35.6 |
| United Kingdom | 18.7 | 38.1 |
| United States | 17.8 | 29.5 |

*Source:* IMF Government Finance Statistics. http://www.esds.ac.uk/
international/support/user_guides/imf/gfs.asp

Government expenditures can be divided into two categories: government consumption and transfer payments. Government consumption covers spending on goods and services such as defense, judicial system, education, etc.; transfer payments provide income to recipients without service being required in return, such as Social Security, unemployment benefits, etc. (Mikesell, 2003: 30). Measured by government consumption expenditure, the share of government spending for these countries ranged from 14.6% of GDP in Switzerland to 26.8% in Sweden; the U.S.

value of 17.8% is relatively low. In terms of total government expenditures, the share of these countries ranges from 29.5% of GDP to 50.3%, while the U.S. falls at the low end of the table of nations. Although the United States raises and spends enormous sums of money in absolute terms, it has a smaller government component in its national economy than other industrialized nations (Mikesell, 2003: 34; Lee, Johnson, and Joyce, 2004).

### 3.2.4 Expenditures of the Federal Government

The data of federal expenditures for selected years from 1950 through 2004 are provided in Table 3.3. The single largest component of federal spending is the category of human resources. The category is fairly broad: it includes Social Security benefits, health care, public assistance for the poor, and education. Much of the expenditures in this category occur through entitlements that the federal government is obligated to pay to any individual who meets the legal criteria for eligibility. Federal expenditures for human resources have risen dramatically since World War II, as the federal government assumed more responsibility for health care and as the size of the elderly population has increased (Gruber, 2005: 394). In 2000, the share of this category accounts for about 62.3% of federal outlay (U.S. Bureau of the Census, Government Division, 2006).

Another substantial component of federal spending is national defense, although its share of the budget has declined considerably since World War II. The national defense spending exceeded 70% of total federal spending from 1942 through 1946, with a maximum of 89.5% in 1945. Since then, the defense share of federal outlay has gradually reduced to about 20% in 2004, despite some fluctuations. It had a minor upturn during 1981–1987, when the United States forced the Soviet Union to get involved in a competitive arms race that its economy could not support, which many believe caused its collapse and an end to the cold war. Another upturn of national defense budget has occurred since 2001 to combat terrorism, after the tragic events of September 11, 2001 (U.S. Bureau of the Census, Government Division, 2006; Mikesell, 2003: 31).

Interest payments for federal debts are also a major federal expense. Interest payments of total federal spending reached about 15% in 1990 because the federal government borrowed a considerable sum of money through the 1980s with the continued federal deficit (Nice, 2002: 25). The outlay of interest payments has reduced since the late 1990s because of the federal surplus during 1998–2001, but it has risen again since 2002 when the federal government again had continued budget deficits (Lee, Johnson, and Joyce, 2004: 274).

Another broad category of outlays is "physical resources," which include infrastructure, environment, commerce, housing, and community development. But the share of expenditures for this category has declined since the 1980s and accounts for only 5% total federal spending in 2004. Other functional outlays are much smaller parts of the federal total.

**Table 3.3   Federal Government Expenditures by Function (Percentage of Total)**

|  | 1950 | 1960 | 1970 | 1980 | 1990 | 2000 | 2004 |
|---|---|---|---|---|---|---|---|
| **National defense** | 32.2 | 52.2 | 41.8 | 22.7 | 23.9 | 16.5 | 19.9 |
| **Human resources** | 33.4 | 28.4 | 38.5 | 53.0 | 49.4 | 62.3 | 64.8 |
| Education, training, employ-ment, and social services | 0.6 | 1.0 | 4.4 | 5.4 | 3.0 | 3.0 | 3.8 |
| Health | 0.6 | 0.9 | 3.0 | 3.9 | 4.6 | 8.6 | 10.5 |
| Medicare | — | — | 3.2 | 5.4 | 7.8 | 11.0 | 11.8 |
| Income security | 9.6 | 8.0 | 8.0 | 14.6 | 11.9 | 14.2 | 14.5 |
| Social Security | 1.8 | 12.6 | 15.5 | 20.1 | 19.8 | 22.9 | 21.6 |
| Veterans benefits and services | 20.8 | 5.9 | 4.4 | 3.6 | 2.3 | 2.6 | 2.6 |
| **Physical resources** | 8.6 | 8.7 | 8.0 | 11.2 | 10.1 | 4.7 | 5.1 |
| Energy | 0.8 | 0.5 | 0.5 | 1.7 | 0.3 | 0.0 | 0.0 |
| Natural resources and environment | 3.1 | 1.7 | 1.6 | 2.3 | 1.4 | 1.4 | 1.3 |
| Commerce and housing credit | 2.4 | 1.8 | 1.1 | 1.6 | 5.4 | 0.2 | 0.2 |
| Transportation | 2.3 | 4.5 | 3.6 | 3.6 | 2.4 | 2.6 | 2.8 |
| Community and regional development | 0.1 | 0.2 | 1.2 | 1.9 | 0.7 | 0.6 | 0.7 |
| **Net interest** | 11.3 | 7.5 | 7.3 | 8.9 | 14.7 | 12.5 | 7.0 |
| **Other functions** | 18.7 | 8.4 | 8.8 | 7.6 | 4.8 | 6.4 | 5.8 |
| International affairs | 11.0 | 3.2 | 2.2 | 2.2 | 1.1 | 1.0 | 1.2 |
| General science, space, and technology | 0.1 | 0.6 | 2.3 | 1.0 | 1.2 | 1.0 | 1.0 |
| Agriculture | 4.8 | 2.8 | 2.6 | 1.5 | 0.9 | 2.0 | 0.7 |
| Administration of justice | 0.5 | 0.4 | 0.5 | 0.8 | 0.8 | 1.6 | 2.0 |
| General government | 2.3 | 1.3 | 1.2 | 2.2 | 0.8 | 0.7 | 1.0 |
| **Total Federal outlays** | 100.0 | 100.0 | 100.0 | 100.0 | 100.0 | 100.0 | 100.0 |

*Data source:* U.S. Census Bureau, Government Division. http://www.census.gov/
govs/www/

## 3.2.5 Expenditures of State and Local Governments

Expenditures for state and local governments in fiscal year 2003 are reported in Table 3.4 (U.S. Bureau of the Census, Government Division, 2006). Note that in recent years states transfer considerable sums of money through intergovernmental grants to their local governments. The table tallies such spending at the recipient level to make the expenditures "direct." In addition, the table follows the budget convention and separates direct general expenditures with other direct expenditures, which include government-operated utilities, liquor stores, and insurance trust systems.

As shown in Table 3.4, the largest category of state government spending is for social services and income maintenance, which includes public welfare, hospitals, health, social insurance, and veteran services. Total budget of this category accounts for about 43% of direct general expenditure. Budgets for these programs have grown rapidly since 1996 when changes of the federal welfare program have placed even greater responsibility on states and provide them a great incentive to administer carefully and move people off assistance roles. Another major expense for state governments is education, including everything from kindergartens to major universities and specialized vocational schools. The bulk of the education category, higher education, amounts to 18% of the total direct general expenditure. Bear in mind that, however, for elementary and secondary education, a great deal of state spending is distributed through grants to local school districts. These amounts are instead shown as direct expenditures at the local level. Other shares of state expenditures go to transportation (10%), public safety (7%), government administration (5%), and others (U.S. Bureau of the Census, Government Division, 2006).

Generalizing about local expenditures is a somewhat risky enterprise. In 2002, there were nearly 88,000 local governments in the United States: counties, municipalities, townships, school districts, or special districts (U.S. Bureau of the Census, Government Division, 2002). Local governments vary significantly in their service delivery. Some local governments, such as cities and counties, have a wide range of responsibilities. Others, primarily school districts and other special districts, are responsible for only one or a few types of programs (Nice, 2002: 28). Table 3.4 shows local expenditures in the United States in aggregate, but caution should be exercised in relating the overall pattern to each type of local government.

By far, the single largest share of local spending is education, which accounts for 44% of the total direct general expenditure. The bulk of this spending is aimed at elementary and secondary education, which alone amounts to 41%. Bear in mind that almost all expenditures of this category are made by independent school districts that are set up just for education although a number of large cities may operate their schools as a municipal department (Mikesell, 2003: 120). In addition, as described earlier, a considerable portion of these resources is financed by state aid, while the provision remains a critical local concern. For most cities and counties, two major traditional responsibilities are public safety (police, fire, and correction) and local transportation (public roads and highways) (Nice 2002: 28). "Social

**Table 3.4 State and Local Government Expenditures in FY 2003 (Dollars in Thousands)**

| | State Government (Thousand $) | Percentage of Direct General Expenditure | Local Government (Thousand $) | Percentage of Direct General Expenditure |
|---|---|---|---|---|
| **Total Expenditure** | **1,359,048,379** | | **1,194,931,825** | |
| **By character and object:** | | | | |
| Intergovernmental expenditure | 382,196,570 | | 12,011,356 | |
| Direct expenditure | 976,851,809 | | 1,182,920,469 | |
| **Direct expenditure by function** | **976,851,809** | | **1,182,920,469** | |
| Direct general expenditure | 781,771,632 | 100 | 1,035,741,214 | 100 |
| Education services: | 171,091,741 | 22 | 459,154,649 | 44 |
| Higher education | 137,348,890 | 18 | 26,838,042 | 3 |
| Elementary and secondary | 4,690,960 | 1 | 423,812,240 | 41 |
| Other education | 28,645,286 | 4 | — | |
| Libraries | 406,605 | 0 | 8,504,367 | 1 |

*(continued on next page)*

**Table 3.4 (continued)   State and Local Government Expenditures in FY 2003 (Dollars in Thousands)**

| | State Government (Thousand $) | Percentage of Direct General Expenditure | Local Government (Thousand $) | Percentage of Direct General Expenditure |
|---|---|---|---|---|
| Social services and income maintenance | 339,753,672 | 43 | 127,871,053 | 12 |
| Transportation | 75,344,705 | 10 | 66,909,844 | 6 |
| Public safety | 54,658,120 | 7 | 107,621,123 | 10 |
| Environment and housing | 30,048,815 | 4 | 111,522,371 | 11 |
| Government administration | 42,845,509 | 5 | 55,812,552 | 5 |
| Interest on general debt | 31,294,763 | 4 | 45,982,356 | 4 |
| Other general expenditure | 36,734,307 | 5 | 60,867,266 | 6 |
| Other direct expenditure | | | | |
| Utility expenditure | 22,404,931 | | 122,188,992 | 12 |
| Liquor store expenditure | 3,696,515 | | 705,503 | 0 |
| Insurance trust expenditure | 168,978,731 | | 24,284,760 | 2 |

*Data source:* U.S. Census Bureau, Government Division. http://www.census.gov/govs/www/

services and income maintenance" is another major item in local budgets. In recent years, local governments have spent more on welfare programs, mostly though intergovernmental grants. In addition, many local governments own hospitals or other health care facilities and administer many public health programs locally.

## 3.3 Revenues

### 3.3.1 Overview: Revenue Sources in the United States

U.S. governments collect most of their "general" revenues from taxes that are levied on income, purchases or sales, or property (ownership or transfer). In addition, they collect revenues from user charges and from miscellaneous sources, such as lotteries, interest on invested funds, royalties, etc. (Mikesell, 2003). While governments also receive revenues from business-like activities such as liquor stores, utility operations, or insurance programs, these revenue sources are traditionally categorized as "special" revenues.

Although all levels of government collect revenues from a variety of sources, generally speaking, the federal government relies primarily on income taxes, state governments on sales taxes, and local governments on property tax. In addition, the federal government relies on taxes to a greater extent, while state and local governments raised a higher portion of revenues from user charges or other sources. Of all general revenues collected in fiscal year 2003, the federal government collected 57%, the states 23%, and local governments 20% (Office of Management and Budget, 2006). In terms of direct expenditures, however, the percentage is 45 for federal government, 25 for states, and 30 for local governments (Office of Management and Budget, 2006). The difference occurs because a substantial fraction of state and local government expenditures is financed by intergovernmental grants, which will be discussed separately.

### 3.3.2 Revenues of the Federal Government

Figure 3.1 shows the percentage breakdown of all federal revenues by major sources in 2003. The total federal receipts in 2003 was about $1.8 trillion, more than all state and local governments combined (Congressional Budget Office, 2006), but the federal revenue system is not diversified among tax bases, and it relies predominantly on income or other payroll taxes (Mikesell, 2003: 280). The federal individual income tax is levied on all financial income of individuals, which includes wages and salaries, interests and dividends, and realized capital gains, etc. This tax is the single largest revenue source in recent years, accounting for almost half of total federal receipts. In a close second is the category of social insurance taxes and contributions, which include Social Security, Medicare, and federal unemployment taxes (Congressional Budget Office, 2006). These taxes, together with federal income tax, are called *federal payroll taxes* because employers are responsible for

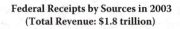

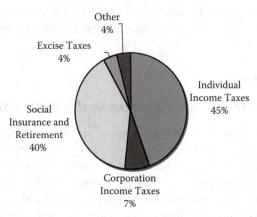

**Figure 3.1   Federal revenues by major sources in 2003. (Data source: Historical Budget Data, Congressional Budget Office. 2006.)**

withholding taxes from employees' paychecks (payrolls) and sending them to the proper government agencies. In addition, the corporate income tax, levied on the income of companies, also provides significant revenue. The three categories of income-based taxes discussed—individual income tax, social insurance, and corporate income tax—together account for more than $1.6 trillion, and make up more than 90% of federal government revenues. This represents a significant change over the course of the 20th century because federal income taxes were not introduced until 1913, and the Social Security program was established in 1936 (Tax Policy Center, 2006d; Steuerle, 2004: 35). Another category of federal revenues is excise taxes, paid when purchases are made on a specific good such as gasoline or aviation services (Tax Policy Center, 2006). Other miscellaneous revenues for the federal government are categorized in the "other" category, which includes such things as taxes on cigarettes and liquor, estate (inheritance) and gift taxes, and custom duties.

Unlike other developed countries, the U.S. federal government levies no general sales tax; in part, because general sales tax is a major revenue source for state governments, and this heavy reliance creates political resistance, each time the federal government has considered tapping the same tax base. Likewise, the federal government collects no property tax, which is the mainstay for state and local revenues. The federal government does, however, collect sales taxes on selected commodities, such as motor fuels or alcoholic beverages, and on certain imported products (customs duties), but these sources are relatively minor. In addition, the federal also borrowed significant amounts of money as additional revenue during much of the 1980s and early 1990s to meet the continued budget deficits (Mikesell, 2003: 106–111).

### 3.3.3 Revenues of State and Local Governments

Table 3.5 shows revenue sources of state and local governments in fiscal year 2003. In comparison with the federal revenue system, state and local revenue structures present much more complicated pictures. Different states and local governments rely to a different extent on a variety of sources, and not all state and local governments have the same mix.

Unlike the income-tax dominance at the federal level, state revenues come from more diversified tax bases. A substantial share of state funds comes in the form of aid from other governments, mostly from the federal government. Other than that, the most dominant source of state revenue comes from taxes on goods and services, which provide about 25% of state revenues. All but five states (Delaware, New Hampshire, Montana, Oregon, and Alaska*) levy a general sales tax, which cover all or almost all sales of products (some states exempt groceries and/or other products such as some medicines; Tax Policy Center, 2006c). In addition, all 50 states levy selective excise taxes for particular products such as motor fuel, cigarettes, and alcoholic beverages. Another major state revenue source is income taxes, but they are not levied in all states (Tax Policy Center, 2006a). Seven states—Alaska, Florida, Nevada, South Dakota, Texas, Washington, and Wyoming—have no state individual income tax. Tennessee and New Hampshire limit their tax to dividends and interest income only. Forty-four states levy corporate income taxes; exceptions are Nevada, South Dakota, Texas, Washington, Wyoming, Michigan†, and New Hampshire‡. State income taxes often mirror federal taxes. In fact, state tax returns often use information directly from the federal return in computing state liability, and state tax authorities rely heavily on the efforts of the federal government in enforcing their taxes (Brunori, 2001). In addition, a proportionally minor state revenue source that has attracted considerable attention in recent years is state lotteries, which are now found in 37 states. Lotteries have become fairly popular because it appears to be a painless, voluntary, and enjoyable approach to government finance. However, it is controversial being a regressive tax, as evidence suggests that low-income families spend a higher percentage of their income on lottery tickets than do high-income families (Brunori, 2001: 138).

Local governments obtain one-third of their money from other government, particularly state government, and the rest mainly through the property tax and other sources. Levied based on the assessed value of real estate or personal property, property tax used to be the mainstay of both state and local government finance, and it is still the single largest own-source revenue for local governments (Wallis, 2001). In 1932, property tax produced almost three quarters of all state and local tax revenue and more than 90% of local government revenue. Since the Great

---

* There is no statewide sales tax, but various municipalities and boroughs levy a local sales tax.
† Michigan has a single business tax, which is a modified value-added tax.
‡ New Hampshire has a business enterprise tax, which is a modified value-added tax.

**Table 3.5 State and Local Revenue by Major Sources in 2003 (Dollars in Thousands)**

| Description | State Governments ($1000) | Percentage of State General Revenue | Local Governments ($1000) | Percentage of Local General Revenue |
|---|---|---|---|---|
| **Total General Revenue** | 1,112,349,024 | 100.0 | 1,039,817,189 | 100.0 |
| Intergovernmental revenue | 361,617,049 | 32.5 | 416,600,971 | 40.1 |
| • From federal | 343,307,800 | 30.9 | 45,955,767 | 4.4 |
| • From state | (X) | | 370,645,204 | 35.6 |
| • From local | 18,309,249 | 1.6 | (X) | |
| General revenue from own source taxes | 750,731,975 | 67.5 | 623,216,218 | 59.9 |
| • Property tax | 10,470,510 | 0.9 | 286,212,675 | 27.5 |
| • Sales and gross receipts | 273,811,221 | 24.6 | 63,975,346 | 6.2 |
| • General sales | 184,596,707 | 16.6 | 44,625,594 | 4.3 |
| • Selective sales taxes | 89,214,514 | 8.0 | 19,349,752 | 1.9 |
| • Individual income | 181,932,513 | 16.4 | 17,474,507 | 1.7 |

| | | | | |
|---|---|---|---|---|
| • Corporate income | 28,384,474 | 2.6 | 2,984,590 | 0.3 |
| • Motor vehicle licenses | 16,009,467 | 1.4 | 1,369,575 | 0.1 |
| • Other taxes | 38,382,682 | 3.5 | 17,964,194 | 1.7 |
| • Charges and miscellaneous general revenue | 201,741,108 | 18.1 | 233,235,331 | 22.4 |
| Current charges | 106,356,917 | 9.6 | 163,203,511 | 15.7 |
| Miscellaneous general revenue | 95,384,191 | 8.6 | 70,031,820 | 6.7 |
| *Special Revenues* | 183,309,796 | | 100,815,454 | |
| Utility revenue | 12,517,945 | | 90,532,139 | |
| Liquor store revenue | 4,517,992 | | 820,199 | |
| Insurance trust revenue | 166,273,859 | | 9,463,116 | |
| **Total Revenue** | 1,295,658,820 | | 1,140,632,643 | |

*Data source:* U.S. Census Bureau, Government Division. http://www.census.gov/govs/www/

Depression, however, states have shifted their taxes on goods and services, especially retail sales taxes and motor-fuel excises, as these new taxes offered high yield and greater reliability (Brunori, 2001). However, local governments overall still rely heavily on the property tax, which amounts to about two-thirds of all local tax revenues in 2003 (U.S. Bureau of the Census, 2002). Note that the reliance on the property tax varies by type of local government (Brunori, 2003). Cities, especially large ones, rely less on the property tax. Because of their geographic size and intense commercial activities, large cities have many more opportunities to raise revenue from other sources such as levies on sales and income. By contrast, independent school districts have relied mostly on the property tax. In 1997, they raised more than $90 billion in property tax revenue, about 80% of their total revenue and about 98% of their total own-source revenue (U.S. Bureau of the Census, 1998). Somewhere in between are smaller cities and counties that have relied more on the property tax than large cities, but less than independent school districts.

The property tax produces reliable, stable, independent revenue for local governments, but it has always been unpopular (Brunori, 2003: 58). People dislike the property tax for several major reasons. For instance, the payment is very visible and so easy to evoke resistance, the assessment of property tax value is difficult to be administered fairly, and there is a mismatch between homeowner income and tax liabilities over time (Oates, 2001). For these reasons, the share of property tax in total local revenue has declined over the past several decades as a result of "property tax revolts." Since the late 1970s and early 1980s, there has been a sustained resistance to the increase of property tax, and many states enacted a variety of policies to reduce the property tax burden (O'Sullivan, Sexton, and Sheffrin, 1995; Mullins and Cox, 1995). In 1978, for instance, California voters enacted Proposition 13, which abruptly reduced local property tax revenue in the state by half; in 1980, Massachusetts voters approved Proposition 2½, which set an absolute limit on the property tax rate as well as the annual increase on tax levy (Galles and Sexton, 1998). Since these property tax revolts, local governments have increased their reliance on user charges and fees, and local option sales or income taxes. In 2003, about 15% of local general revenue is obtained from user charges and fees for a wide range of services such as water and sewer systems, trash collection, building permits, library cards for nonresidents, parking, etc. Another major nonproperty tax is local option sales tax. As of 2004, local governments in 33 states have been authorized to levy local option sales tax (Tax Policy Center, 2006c; Brunori, 2003: 71; Zhao, 2005). Of the 33 states, 23 allow both cities and counties to impose the tax, 10 states allow only cities or counties to levy the tax. The other nine states allow transit authorities or school districts to impose the tax. In aggregate, local option sales tax makes up for about 4% of total general revenue for all local governments in 2003. In addition, a number of cities levy local income taxes, but their contribution of the overall totals is limited to less than 2% (U.S. Bureau of the Census, Government Division, 2006).

## 3.3.4 *Intergovernmental Grants*

A significant amount of the money spent by state and local governments comes from assistance provided by other levels of government (Mikesell, 2003: 519). As shown in Table 3.6, state and local governments have become increasingly reliant on intergovernmental funds in the past half century. In 1955, 8.5% of state revenues were federal assistance in the form of grants; this percentage has more than doubled to over 20% in 2000. Local governments have become even more dependent on intergovernmental transfers, receiving more than one-third of their revenues from upper level governments in 2000. The expansion in the use of intergovernmental grants has not, however, been entirely continuous. As a percentage of state and local governments spending, federal aid peaked in the late 1970s at about 24% of state and local governments expenditures (Congressional Budget Office, 2006), but it then declined as the political environment became so called "fend-for-yourself federalism," in which levels of governments spending money were expected to raise that money (Shannon, 1989). Growth in the federal aid resumed nevertheless in the late 1980s and continued throughout the 1990s.

Federal transfers support a wide variety of public programs but, overall, a substantial portion of them are for income redistribution, including health programs, income security, and social services (Canada, 2003). As it is difficult for state and

**Table 3.6   Intergovernmental Grants in the United States, Selected Years**

| Year | Federal Grants as a Percentage of Federal Expenditures (%) | Federal Grants as a Percentage of State–Local Revenue (%) | Intergovernmental Revenue as a Percentage of Local General Revenue (%) |
|------|------|------|------|
| 1955 | 4.2 | 8.5 | 26.3 |
| 1960 | 7.2 | 9.5 | 27.1 |
| 1965 | 8.5 | 11.4 | 28.4 |
| 1970 | 11.2 | 16.8 | 33.1 |
| 1975 | 14.5 | 22.6 | 38.8 |
| 1980 | 14.7 | 22.8 | 39.7 |
| 1985 | 10.4 | 17.2 | 34.3 |
| 1990 | 10.6 | 16.8 | 32.9 |
| 1995 | 13.7 | 20.1 | 34.2 |
| 2000 | 16.3 | 20.1 | 34.4 |

*Data sources:* Government Division, U.S. Bureau of Census and Historical Budget Data, Office of Management and Budget.

local governments to finance aggressive redistributive programs, the federal government makes extensive use of intergovernmental transfers to assist low-income households (Gruber, 2005: 454). Much of this aid takes the form of medical expenditures such as Medicaid and Medicare. Other federal grants provide a stimulus for state–local programs that confer benefits that may "spill over" to residents of other areas, for instance, transportation, communication, education, and workforce training. These grants normally have matching requirements. By providing budgetary incentives, they enable state and local governments to address the broader interests of citizenry. In addition, in 1972, the federal government instituted a modest program of general revenue sharing with state and local governments. However, the program was discontinued in the 1980s largely because of fiscal stringency at the federal level at that time (Canada, 2003).

For local governments, the lion share of intergovernmental transfers comes from state governments (Mikesell, 2003: 529). In recent decades, state aid has risen considerably for school districts largely for the purpose of equalization. Beginning in the 1970s, a number of court rulings declared that existing systems of school financing are unconstitutional; as a result, the states have taken a more active role in financing public education, providing education grants that have somewhat equalized school spending across high- to low-income school districts (Ladd, Chalk, and Hansen, 1999). Other state aid programs are comparatively small. State governments also provide transfers to their local governments for highways, public welfare, and other programs, normally based on some type of formula. In addition, many states provide general revenue sharing for local governments without specific functional requirements.

# References

Abizadeli, S. and A. Basilevsky. 1990. Measuring the size of government. *Public Finance* 45: 359–377.

Advisory Commission on Intergovernmental Relations. 1995. *Significant Features of Fiscal Federalism*. Washington, DC: Government Printing Office.

Brunori, D. 2001. *State Tax Policy: A Political Perspective*. Washington, DC: Urban Institute Press.

———. 2003. *Local Tax Policy: A Federalist Perspective*. Washington, DC: Urban Institute Press.

Buchanan, J.M., and G. Tullock. 1977. The expanding public sector: Wagner squared. *Public Choice* (Fall): 147–150.

Buchanan, J.M. 1967. The fiscal illusion. In *Public Finance in Democratic Process: Fiscal Institutions and Individual Choice*. Chapel Hill: University of North Carolina Press.

Canada, B. 2003. Federal Grants to State and Local Government: A Brief History. In *Report for Congress: Congressional Research Service*. The Library of Congress.

Congressional Budget Office. 2006. *Historical Budget Data*. Available from http://www.cbo.gov/budget/historical.pdf [cited 03/01 2006].

Dickson, V. and W. Yu. 2000. Revenue Structures, the Perceived Price of Government Output, and Public Expenditures. *Public Finance Review* 28(1): 48–65.

Dye, T.R. 2005. *Understanding Public Policy.* 11th ed. Upper Saddle River, NJ: Pearson Prentice Hall.

Economic and Social Data Service International. 2006. *IMF Government Finance Statistics.* Available from http://www.esds.ac.uk/international/support/user_guides/imf/gfs.asp [cited 03/01 2006].

Galles, G.M. and R.L. Sexton. 1998. A tale of two tax jurisdictions: The surprising effects of California's Proposition 13 and Massachusetts' Proposition 2½. *American Journal of Economics and Sociology* 57(2): 123–132.

Gruber, J. 2005. *Public Finance and Public Policy.* New York: Worth Publishers.

Ladd, H.F., R. Chalk, and J.S. Hansen. 1999. Equity and adequacy in education finance: issues and perspectives: introduction. In *Equity and Adequacy in Education Finance: Issues and Perspectives.* Washington, DC: National Academy Press.

Lee, R.D., R.W. Johnson, and P.G. Joyce. 2004. *Public Budgeting Systems.* 7th ed. Boston, MA: Jones and Bartlett Publishers.

Mikesell, J.L. 2003. *Fiscal Administration: Analysis and Applications for the Public Sector.* 6th ed. Belmont, CA.: Wadsworth Pub. Co.

Mosher, F. and O. Poland. 1964. *The Costs of American Government.* New York: Dodd, Mead.

Mullins, D.R., and S.P. Cox. 1995. *Tax and Expenditure Limits on Local Governments.* Washington, DC: Advisory Commission on Intergovernmental Relations. Government Printing Office.

Nice, D.C. 2002. *Public Budgeting.* Belmont, CA: Wadsworth/Thomson Learning.

Oates, W.E. 2001. Property tax and local government finance: an overview and some reflections. In *Property Tax and Local Government Finance.* Cambridge, MA: Cambridge University Press.

Office of Management and Budget. 2006. *Historical Tables, Budget of the United States Government (FY 2007).* Available from http://www.gpoaccess.gov/usbudget/fy07/about.html [cited 03/01 2006].

O'Sullivan, A., T.A. Sexton, and S.M. Sheffrin. 1995. *Property Taxes and Tax Revolts: The Legacy of Proposition 13.* Cambridge, MA: Cambridge University Press.

Plato. 1975. *The Laws.* London: Penguin.

Shannon, J. 1989. The Return of Fend-for-Yourself-Federalism: The Reagan Mark. In *Readings in American Federalism: Perspectives on a Decade Change.* Washington, DC: Advisory Commission on Intergovernmental Relations.

Steuerle, C.E. 2004. *Contemporary U.S. Tax Policy.* Washington, DC: Urban Institute Press.

Tax Policy Center. 2006a. *Federal Excise Taxes.* Available from http://www.taxpolicycenter.org/TaxFacts/tfdb/TFTemplate.cfm?topic2id=80 [cited 03/01 2006].

———. 2006b. *Individual Income Tax Rates 2004.* Available from http://www.taxpolicycenter.org/TaxFacts/TFDB/TFTemplate.cfm?Docid=406&Topic2id=90 [cited 03/01 2006].

———. 2006c. *Sales Tax Rates 2004.* Available from http://www.taxpolicycenter.org/TaxFacts/TFDB/TFTemplate.cfm?Docid=411&Topic2id=90 [cited 03/01 2006].

———. 2006d. *Type of Tax as a Share of Federal Revenues, 1946–2004.* Available from http://www.taxpolicycenter.org/TaxFacts/TFDB/TFTemplate.cfm?Docid=264 [cited 03/01 2006].

U.S. Bureau of the Census. 1998. *State Tax Data.* Washington, DC: Government Printing Office.

———. 2002. *State Tax Data.* Washington, D.C.: Government Printing Office.

U.S. Bureau of the Census. Government Division. 2006. *2002 Census of Governments*. Available from http://www.census.gov/govs/www/cog2002.html[cited 03/01/2006 2006].

————. 2006. *Federal, State, and Local Governments*. Available from http://www.census.gov/govs/www/ [cited 03/01/2006 2006].

U.S. Bureau of the Census. 1975. *Historical Statistics of the United States, Colonial Times to 1970*. Bicentennial ed. Washington: U.S. Dept. of Commerce Bureau of the Census: for sale by the Supt. of Docs. U.S. Govt. Print. Off.

Wallis, J.J. 2001. A history of the property tax in America. In *Property Tax and Local Government Finance*, edited by W.E. Oates. Cambridge, Massachusetts: Lincoln Institute of Land Policy.

Wildavsky, A.B. and N. Caiden. 2001. *The New Politics of the Budgetary Process*. 4th ed. New York: Longman.

Zhao, Z. 2005. Motivations, obstacles, and resources: The adoption of the general-purpose local option sales tax in Georgia Counties. *Public Finance Review* 33(6): 721–746.

# Chapter 4

# Fund Accounting

## Frederic B. Bogui
*New Jersey Institute of Technology, School of Management*

## Contents

4.1   Introduction ................................................................................ 149
4.2   Funds Descriptions ...................................................................... 150
Endnotes ............................................................................................ 160

## 4.1 Introduction

In comparison to the financial resources of business organizations, many of the resources of state and local governments are restricted to specific activities or purposes. These restrictions on governments' revenues commonly relate to use, specific programs, time expenditures, or expenditures in compliance with legal requirements. While it is true that taxation remains the main source of government revenues, the fact is that governments derive revenues from various sources, including grants, user charges to finance certain activities, transfer payments to governments, fines or penalties for violating laws, and revenues generated from fees and permits imposed on business activities. These revenues are often confined to particular purposes or activities. A federal grant to a state government for highway maintenance can only be used for highway upkeep, and not for other purposes. Tax revenues on some consumer products may be set aside to finance particular activities, such as shelters for the homeless.

Because governments, for the most part, are not subject to marketplace competition, and budgets in state and local governments reflect public policy priorities, significant breach of legal and contractual restrictions over budgetary resources can have serious financial consequences. Understandably, governments take great care to adhere to restrictive rules on the use of public resources. To demonstrate fiscal and operational accountability and provide assurance to interested parties, such as grantors, legislators, and citizens, that resources are being used on approved purposes, most governments establish separate funds for resources earmarked to various activities. Hence, fund accounting is designed to help governments enhance control and accountability on the use of public resources.

This chapter provides an overview of the various funds used by governments for accounting and financial reporting purposes. The chapter is a prelude to the in-depth analysis of various funds discussed in later chapters.

## 4.2 Funds Descriptions

Generally Accepted Accounting Principles (GAAP) for state and local governments prescribe that "governmental accounting systems should be organized and operated on a fund basis" and define a fund as

> A fiscal and accounting entity with a self-balancing set of accounts recording cash and other financial resources, together with all related liabilities, and residual equities or balances and changes therein, which are segregated for the purpose of carrying on specific activities or attaining certain objectives in accordance with special regulations, restrictions, or limitations.[1]

A government has discretion in regard to the number of funds to establish for accounting and financial reporting of its activities. Typically, governments maintain as many funds as deemed necessary. However, the underlying principle in governmental accounting dictates that a government should make use of the least number of funds considered necessary for its operations. GAAP provide some guidelines with respect to the number of funds a government may use for its accounting and financial objectives. GAAP decree that:

> Government units should establish and maintain those funds required by law and sound financial administration. Only the minimum number of funds consistent with legal and operating requirements should be established because unnecessary funds result in inflexibility, undue complexity, and inefficient financial administration.[10]

Most governments engage in a number of activities that call for the establishment of numerous funds. Regardless of how many activities a government engages in, almost all activities can be grouped into three broad categories: governmental activities, business-type activities, and fiduciary activities.

1. Governmental activities: These activities involve resources raised and expended to carry out the general purposes of a government and are typically financed through taxes or intergovernmental grants.
2. Business-type activities: These are income-determining activities of a government and therefore financed primarily through user-charges or fees. Government business-type activities parallel those of the private sector and make use of business accounting.
3. Fiduciary activities: A government is engaged in fiduciary activities when it acts as an agent or a trustee for other parties. Fiduciary activities relate to governments acting in a trustee or agency capacity for individuals, private organizations, other governments, or outside parties.

In accordance with these three broad categories of government activities, GAAP mandate that governments categorize their funds into three categories: governmental funds, proprietary funds, and fiduciary funds.

1. Governmental funds account for government activities typically supported through tax revenues. Governmental funds are maintained to finance most governments' operating activities.
2. Proprietary funds account for a government's business-type activities typically financed through user charges or fees. These government activities mirror those of private sector entities.
3. Fiduciary funds account for resources held by a government in a trustee or agency capacity on behalf of individuals, organizations, or other entities. Fiduciary funds cannot be used to support the government's own activities. The resources in fiduciary funds are held by a government for the benefit of parties outside the government.

Each category of funds, that is, governmental funds, proprietary funds, and fiduciary funds, is a composite. Involved in each category are varieties of funds that constitute each one. GAAP established a total of eleven fund types grouped under these three categories. Table 4.1 lists fund types and their classifications.

Under the governmental funds category, five funds are characterized as governmental funds. They are the general fund, special revenue funds, debt service funds, capital project funds, and permanent funds. We shall now briefly elaborate on each of the governmental-type funds.

1. The general fund is a government primary operating fund. It accounts for all financial resources that are not required to be accounted for in other funds. In essence, the general fund is maintained to account for all unrestricted resources.

**Table 4.1  Fund Types and Classifications**

| Governmental Funds | Proprietary Funds | Fiduciary Funds |
|---|---|---|
| 1. General fund<br>2. Special revenue funds<br>3. Debt service funds<br>4. Capital projects funds<br>5. Permanent funds | 6. Enterprise funds<br>7. Internal service funds | 8. Agency funds<br>9. Investment trust funds<br>10. Private-purpose funds<br>11. Pension and other employee benefit trust funds |

The General Fund is the chief operating fund of a state or local government. GAAP prescribe that the general fund be used "to account for all financial resources except those required to be accounted for in another fund." That is, it is presumed that all government's activities are reported in the general fund unless there is a compelling reason to report an activity in some other fund type.[3]

2. Special revenue funds are maintained to account for resources legally restricted to specific purposes. Governments often maintain a number of special revenue funds to account for revenues raised for specific purposes. The use of several special revenue funds enhances control over restricted resources and may prevent the unintentional inclusion of restricted resources into the General Fund. However, the use of special revenue funds is not strictly imposed by GAAP. Interestingly, a number of local governments operate without establishing a single special revenue fund though they have funds that may fit the definition of special revenue funds. Some typical revenue sources accounted for in special revenue funds include

   ■ Fuel tax revenues mandated by a legislature to be set aside for road upkeep and construction.
   ■ A state law provides that resources generated by the lottery be used to fund education.
   ■ A state grant that must be used to train new recruits of firefighters.

   According to GAAP, special revenue funds are maintained

   > To account for the proceeds of specific revenue sources (other than trusts for individuals, private organizations, or other governments or for major capital projects) that are legally restricted to expenditure for specified purposes .... Resources that are legally limited to a particular purpose by a government cannot be used for any other purpose unless the government removes or changes the limitation by taking the same action it employed to impose the limitation initially or by taking a higher-authority action.[4]

   As a governmental-type fund, special revenue funds use accounting guidelines similar to the general fund. Nearly all accounting principles and guidelines afforded to the general fund can be applied to special revenue funds and indeed to all governmental-type funds.

3. Debt service funds account for resources accumulated for the payment of principal and interest on long-term obligations. Much like sinking funds maintained by businesses to accumulate resources to retire debts, governments maintain debt service funds for the specific purpose of servicing current and future debt service requirements. GAAP permit that debt service funds be used

> To account for the accumulation of resources for, and the payment of, general long-term debt principal and interest. Debt service funds are required if they are legally mandated and/or if financial resources are being accumulated for principal and interest payments maturing in future years.[5]

4. Capital project funds are maintained to account for financial resources to be used for acquisition and construction of major capital assets. The use of capital projects funds as a separate fund to report major capital acquisition and construction activities is a useful method to avoid commingling capital and operating funds. Capital projects resources are typically generated from the issuance of bonds, government grants, or from interfund transfers. Proceeds from issuance of bonds are restricted and maintained in capital projects funds to purchase or construct major capital assets. Based on GAAP, capital projects funds are established

> To account for financial resources to be used for the acquisition or construction of major capital facilities (other than those financed by proprietary funds, or in trust funds for individuals, private organizations, or other governments). Capital outlays financed through general obligation bond proceeds should be accounted for through a capital projects fund.[6]

5. In contrast to the government funds discussed thus far, permanent funds are comparatively new. Permanent funds were instituted as part of the governmental financial reporting model established by the GASB Statement 34, and account for resources legally restricted to the extent that only the earnings on investments, not principal, may be used to support specific programs that benefit the government itself or its citizenry.[7] The income or earnings on investments of resources in permanent funds are recognized as revenues and transferred to a special revenue fund to be expended for designated programs. In using only the earnings of the funds for expenditures, the principal is maintained. Thus, the funds are never depleted, and remain permanent.

To illustrate, suppose that a municipality receives one million dollars from a generous citizen with the stipulation that only the earnings from the investment of the one million dollars donation can be used for the purchase of new books and equipment for libraries. Upon receiving and investing the funds, the municipality would record the following journal entries:

|  | Debit | Credit |
|---|---|---|
| a. Cash | 1,000,000 | |
|     Revenues/additions to Permanent Funds | | 1,000,000 |
|     Investments | 1,000,000 | |
|       Cash | | 1,000,000 |

b. Suppose that the funds invested generated $22,000 as earnings, and these earnings were used for library expenditures as stipulated by the donor. The municipality would record the following entries:

|  | Debit | Credit |
|---|---|---|
| Cash/or interest receivable | 22,000 | |
|     Revenues from investment income | | 22,000 |
| Expenditures for books | 22,000 | |
|     Cash/or account payable | | 22,000 |

So far we discussed the various funds that constitute the governmental funds category. We are now turning our attention to another category of funds, namely, proprietary funds. They are distinctively different in nature and purpose as compared to governmental funds. The accounting of proprietary funds is similar to the accounting and financial reporting of business enterprises. In proprietary fund activities, the motive of the government is to recapture its investments through user charges. Proprietary funds are expected to be self sustaining, the focus is on income determination, and therefore public officials managing these funds intend, at a minimum, to break even. There are two proprietary-type funds: enterprise funds and internal service funds. The following is a cursory description of each of the proprietary-type funds.

1. Enterprise Funds account for government activities that provide goods or services for fees to the general public. Examples of government activities accounted for in enterprise funds include
   - Parking garages at airport facilities
   - Hospitals
   - Public service electric and gas
   - Public transportation

   Enterprise funds are established by GAAP to

   > Account for operations (a) that are financed and operated in a manner similar to private business enterprises where the intent of the governing body is that the costs (expenses, including depreciation) of providing

goods or services to the general public on a continuing basis be financed or recovered primarily through users charges; or (b) where the governing body has decided that periodic determination of revenues earned, expenses incurred, and/or net income is appropriate for capital maintenance, public policy, management control, accountability, other purposes.[8]

2. Internal Service Funds account for government activities that provide goods or services principally to other departments within the same government and at times to other governments. Some intragovernmental activities accounted for in the internal service funds include

   ■ A data-processing center that maintains financial records for other departments
   ■ A printing center that provides copy services to other departments within the same government
   ■ A repair shop that maintains and services equipments for various departments within the same government

GAAP permit that

> Internal service funds may be used to report any activities that provide goods or services to other funds, departments, or agencies of the primary government and its component units, or to other governments, on a cost-reimbursement basis. Internal service funds should be used only if the reporting entity is the predominant participant in the activity. Otherwise, the activity should be reported in an enterprise fund.[9]

In contrast to governmental and proprietary funds, fiduciary funds are maintained to account for activities benefiting parties other than the government itself. Fiduciary funds are used by a government to report assets held in trustee or agency capacity for other entities and therefore cannot be used to support the reporting government's own programs. Fiduciary funds include: agency funds, investment trust funds, private-purpose trust funds, and pension trust funds. The following is a brief description of each of the fiduciary-type funds.

1. Agency Funds are used to account for resources held by a government in purely custodial capacity. The resources deposited in agency funds are transient in nature; hence, all resources (assets) in the funds are equal to liabilities because the assets of the fund will be remitted, at some point in time, to the intended beneficiaries. Agency funds principally account for the receipt, temporary investments, and remittance of resources to individuals, private organizations, or other governments. Typical agency funds resources include, among others, taxes collected by one government for the benefit of another government entity, or refundable collateral and deposits (GASB Statement 34, paragraph 73).

2. Investment trust funds are used to account for the combined resources of separate governments in an investment portfolio for the benefit of the contributors. Governments, at times, manage investment pools, which combine other governments' funds for the benefit of the participants. Investment Trust Funds resemble the financial arrangement of mutual funds in the private sector. GAAP mandate that a government reports any external investment pool that it sponsors as an investment trust fund.

3. Private-purpose trust funds account for trust funds arrangements other than investments trust funds and pension trust funds. A private-purpose fund is used to report a trust arrangement under which the principal and income of the fund benefit individuals, private organizations, or other governments (GASB Statement 34, paragraph 72). An example of a private-purpose fund is a scholarship trust fund.

4. Pension (and other employee benefit) trust funds are used to report resources that are required to be held in trust for members and beneficiaries of defined benefit pension plans, defined contribution plans, other postemployment benefit plans, or employee benefit plans. These funds also provide income for disability and health care related insurance for retirees and their beneficiaries (GASB Statement 34, paragraph 70).

As discussed earlier, governments use different funds, namely governmental, proprietary, and fiduciary funds, to reflect different financial objectives. For instance, when a government is involved in tax-supported activities, the use of governmental funds to account for resources is appropriate. On the other hand, when the government financial objectives are business-type activities, then the use of proprietary funds is appropriate. This difference between governmental funds and proprietary funds reflects the discrepancies in measurement focus and basis of accounting.

The measurement focus characterizes the types of transactions and events that are reported in a fund's financial performance. The measurement focus determines whether a fund is to measure changes in total economic resources or changes in current financial resources. The financial performance of a proprietary fund focuses on changes in economic resources. A proprietary fund's operating statement recognizes mainly transactions or events that increase or decrease the fund's overall economic resources during the period. In contrast, the operating statement of a governmental fund aims attention at changes in current financial resources. Thus, the operating statement of a governmental fund mainly recognizes transactions or events of the period that increase or decrease the resources available for spending in the near future.

The basis of accounting relates to when transactions and events are recognized in a fund's statements. It pertains to the timing of the recognition of transactions and events. GAAP prescribe that a fund's basis of accounting is joint to its measurement focus. Proprietary funds focus on total economic resources and use the accrual basis of accounting. The accrual basis of accounting identifies increases and decreases in economic resources as a result of transactions or events. Under the accrual basis of accounting, revenues are recognized when earned, regardless of when the related cash is actually received or collected. Similarly, under the accrual basis of accounting, expenses are recognized or recorded when a liability is incurred regardless of when the related cash outflow takes place in the current or subsequent period. Thus, the accrual basis of accounting recognizes transactions that have substantive economic impact or financial consequences in the period in which those transactions occur, and focuses on events that may not involve current cash transfers but have cash consequences in the future.

Governmental funds focus on current financial resources and use the modified accrual basis of accounting. The modified accrual basis of accounting recognizes increases and decreases in current financial resources. It is, in essence, an accrual basis of accounting modified to suit governments' fund accounting orientation. Revenues are recognized when susceptible to accrual, which means that revenues are measurable and collection on receivables are made in the current period or shortly thereafter (usually 60 days of year end) to be available to finance expenditures of the current period or pay current liabilities.

The application of measurement focus and basis of accounting to fiduciary funds is similar to the one used for proprietary funds. All trust funds make use of the economic resources measurement focus and the accrual basis of accounting, in the same way as proprietary funds. Agency funds, however, are a bit atypical in that they only report assets and liabilities. Accordingly, agency funds do not report equity and do not utilize measurement focus, but do employ the accrual basis of accounting to recognize assets such as receivables and liabilities such as payables. Table 4.2 presents the basis of accounting and measurement focus of governmental, proprietary, and fiduciary funds.

Some basic sets of financial statements are required for each of the main categories of funds. The listing of the fund statements is as follows:

The governmental-fund statements are
- Balance sheet
- Statement of revenues, expenditures, and changes in fund balances

The proprietary fund statements are
- Statement of net assets
- Statement of revenues, expenses, and changes in net assets
- Statement of cash flows

The fiduciary fund statements are
- Statement of fiduciary net assets
- Statement of changes in fiduciary net assets

In summary, accounting for state and local governments make use of funds to enhance and exhibit fiscal and operational accountability on the use of public resources. Governmental accounting is essentially a fund-based reporting

**Table 4.2  Basis of Accounting and Measurement Focus of Funds**

| Funds | Basis of Accounting | Measurement Focus |
|---|---|---|
| Governmental | Modified accrual basis | Current financial resources |
| Proprietary | Full accrual basis | Economic resources |
| Fiduciary | Full accrual basis | Economic resources |

accounting system and it is referred to as fund accounting. Fund accounting segregates resources into independent fiscal and accounting entities known as funds. The use of multiple funds to account for resources enhances control over resources restricted to particular purposes or activities.

Governments maintain three categories of funds: governmental funds, proprietary funds, and fiduciary funds. Governmental funds consist of the general fund, special revenue funds, debt service funds, capital project funds, and permanent funds. Proprietary Funds account for resources resulting from government business-type activities and consist of enterprise funds and internal service funds. Fiduciary funds account for resources held by a government in a trustee or agency capacity for other entities, and consist of agency funds, investment trust funds, private-purpose funds, and pension (and other employee benefit) trust funds.

**Table 4.3  Major Distinctions between Governmental and Proprietary Funds**

| Governmental Funds | Proprietary Funds |
|---|---|
| • Appropriated budget: recording of the budget in some funds. Emphasis of stewardship of resources entrusted to public officials. | • Nonappropriated budget: recording of a budget is not required. |
| • Flow of current financial resources. | • Flow of economic resources. |
| • Events and transactions that increase or decrease spendable resources. | • Events and transactions that impact economic positions. |
| • Financial statements are reported using the current financial resources measurement focus. The aim is to measure only the current financial resources available to a governmental unit. As a result, all fixed assets and all long-term liabilities are not accounted for in the fund-based statements. | • Financial statements are reported using the economic resources measurement focus. The aim is to measure all economic resources available to a governmental unit. As a result, all assets and all current/ long-term liabilities are included in the fund financial statements. |

**Table 4.3 (continued) Major Distinctions between Governmental and Proprietary Funds**

| Governmental Funds | Proprietary Funds |
|---|---|
| • The accounting equation is stated as follows:<br><br>Assets = Liabilities + Fund Balance.<br><br>Fund balance (reserved or unreserved) is the excess of assets over liabilities or the net resources available for spending. | • The accounting equation is stated as follows:<br><br>Assets = Liabilities + Owners' Equity.<br><br>Owners' equity is the excess of assets over liabilities, or the net assets. Equity consists of capital and net assets. |
| • The basis of accounting is the modified accrual, which recognizes revenues when available and measurable to finance expenditures of the current period. Revenues are generally considered to be available when they are collectible within the current period or soon after the end of the fiscal year to pay for liabilities of the current year. | • The basis of accounting is the (full) accrual, which recognizes revenues when earned, and expenses are recognized when incurred, regardless of the timing of the related cash flows. |
| • Expenditures are recognized when the liability is incurred and the liability is expected to be extinguished using available financial resources (exceptions apply to special assessment debts, claims and judgments, pensions, compensated absences, and other expenditures that are recorded when due, rather than when incurred). | |
| • There is neither depreciation nor amortization recorded in the fund-based statements. | • Depreciation and amortization are recognized in the financial statements. |

*Source:* Adapted from the Governmental Accounting Standard Board Statements.

## Endnotes

.1. National Council on Governmental Accounting (NCGA) Statement 1, Governmental Accounting and Financial Reporting Principles, paragraph 2.
2. GASB Codification Section 1800.
3. Gauthier, J. Stephen (2005). *Governmental Accounting, Auditing, and Financial Reporting,* page 18.
4. NCGA Statement 1, paragraph 3.
5. NCGA Statement 1, paragraph 3.
6. NCGA Statement 1, paragraph 3.
7. GASB Statement 34, paragraph 65.
8. NCGA Statement 1. Governmental Accounting and Financial Reporting Principles, paragraph 18.
9. GASB Statement 34, paragraph 68.
10. NCGA Statement 1, paragraph 4.

# Chapter 5

# The General Fund

## Robert S. Kravchuk

*University of North Carolina–Charlotte, Department of Political Science*

## Contents

5.1 Introduction: The Concept of a General Fund ........................................ 162
5.2 Unique Aspects of the General Fund ..................................................... 164
    5.2.1 Number of General Funds ............................................................. 164
    5.2.2 Measurement Focus and Basis of Accounting .............................. 164
    5.2.3 Revenue Recognition .................................................................... 165
    5.2.4 Expenditure Recognition .............................................................. 165
    5.2.5 General Fund Assets ...................................................................... 165
    5.2.6 General Fund Liabilities ................................................................ 165
    5.2.7 Fund Equity and Fund Balance .................................................... 167
    5.2.8 Major Fund Focus ........................................................................ 167
    5.2.9 Budgetary Integration .................................................................. 168
    5.2.10 Encumbrances and Allotments ................................................... 168
5.3 General Fund Account Classifications .................................................... 169
    5.3.1 Estimated Revenues, Revenues, and Other Financing Sources ..... 169
    5.3.2 Appropriations, Expenditures, and Other Financing Uses ........... 170
5.4 Budgetary Integration .......................................................................... 171
5.5 Levying and Collecting General Taxes and Other Revenues ................... 172
5.6 Encumbrances and Allotments ............................................................. 173
    5.6.1 Encumbrances as an Instrument for Cash and Budget Control .... 173
    5.6.2 Allotments as a Budgetary Control Device ................................... 175

5.7 Interfund Activity ........................................................................................ 176
    5.7.1 Interfund Exchange Transactions ..................................................... 176
    5.7.2 Interfund Loans................................................................................ 177
    5.7.3 Interfund Transfers.......................................................................... 177
    5.7.4 Interfund Reimbursements .............................................................. 178
    5.7.5 Intra- and Interactivity Transactions............................................... 178
    5.7.6 Intra-Entity Transactions................................................................. 178
5.8 General Fund Financial Statements................................................................ 179
    5.8.1 General Fund Operating Statement .................................................. 179
    5.8.2 General Fund Balance Sheet ............................................................. 179
    5.8.3 Statement of Cash Flows.................................................................. 181
    5.8.4 Required Reconciliation Statements/Schedules................................ 181
    5.8.5 Required Budgetary Comparisons .................................................... 182
    5.8.6 Interim Financial Reports................................................................ 182
5.9 General Fund Accounting and Financial Reporting Issues.............................. 186
    5.9.1 Revenues Collected after the Close of the Fiscal Year ..................... 186
    5.9.2 Sales Tax Revenue............................................................................ 186
    5.9.3 Certain Tax, Revenue, or Grant Anticipation Notes....................... 186
5.10 Current and Future Developments................................................................. 186
    5.10.1 Communications Methods .............................................................. 186
    5.10.2 Elements of Financial Statements..................................................... 187
        5.10.2.1 Independent Definitions of Financial Statement
             Elements ........................................................................ 187
        5.10.2.2 Treatment of Deferrals.................................................... 188
References .......................................................................................................... 188

# 5.1 Introduction: The Concept of a General Fund

The general fund is the primary operating fund of a governmental entity. Its purpose is to account for all current financial resources except those that are required to be accounted for in another fund (GASB, 2003, §1300.104, p. 17). In its Bulletin No. 6 on *Municipal Accounting Statements*, the National Committee on Municipal Accounting (1941) described the purpose of the general fund in a way that is still relevant today:

> The General Fund is the most important fund of the municipality, being used to account for all revenues not flowing to other funds. It receives a greater variety of revenues than any other fund; for example, general property taxes, license and permits, fines and penalties, rents, charges for current services, state-shared taxes, and many other revenues flow into it. The fund also covers a wider range of activities than any other. In fact, most of the current operations of the municipality are financed by this fund. (NCMA, 1941, p. 121)

Consequently, the vast majority of the routine transactions pertaining to the operations of general government will take place in the general fund. Alternative names for the general fund include the general revenue fund, general operating fund, and current fund; however, in common usage, the term general fund is preferred.

Traditionally, the general fund has been classified as an expendable fund, insofar as the monies in the fund are available for expenditure for the purposes for which it was created (Morey, 1927). Thus, "the resources of the General Fund may be appropriated and expended to finance the general administrative departments" (NCMA, 1936, p. 101). Expendable funds, historically, were further classified according to the character of their incomes. Accordingly, the general fund has been classified as a revenue fund, which is "used by practically every branch of government in which to cover all revenues of a general character which may be used to meet the expense of any governmental activity" (Morey, 1927, p. 24). It is a long-standing principle that "all receipts which are not by law or contractual agreement applicable to specified purposes should usually be placed in the General Fund" (NCMA, 1936, p. 101).

In the modern classification scheme, the general fund is classified as a governmental-fund type, in that its operations are governmental in character (GASB, 2003, §1300.103, p. 17). Other governmental-type funds are available to account for specific activities, and their use may be required under statute, contract, or Generally Accepted Accounting Principles or GAAP (GASB, 2003, §1300.104–§1300.108, §1300.115, pp. 17–18, 20). Typically, other governmental-type funds have specific revenue sources, which may also include transfers from the General Fund. The general fund is thus distinguished from other governmental-type funds (i.e., special revenue funds, debt service funds, capital projects funds, and permanent funds) both in terms of its purpose to account for the activities of general government and its primary revenue source being general revenues.

General fund financing of governmental expenditures has been subject to some controversy in the literature on public finance. Economist and Nobel Laureate James M. Buchanan, particularly, has been highly critical of the informational asymmetries that arise when the link between revenue raising and expenditure decision making is broken (Buchanan, 1967, pp. 72–87). The gist of his argument is that separate fiscal choices for each public goods program is less desirable than earmarking revenues for specific purposes because taxpayers and voters may more clearly perceive the linkages between what is paid in taxes and what is being purchased, and what services are being provided by the governmental unit. He focuses much of his attack on the very concept of a general fund. Presumably, the links between revenues and expenditures would be more transparent, for instance, in the case of special revenue funds, which account for specific revenues dedicated to specific public purposes. From the standpoint of practical accounting, however, Buchanan's argument loses much of its force where there are clear and consistently applied rules of financial reporting, and disclosure of all material aspects of a government's revenues and program expenditures. Further, the recent implementation of GASB Statement No. 34—with its emphasis on improved operational accountability in addition to the traditional emphasis on financial accountability—has gone far toward completing and improving the quality of financial information that is reported, enabling greater overall accountability for the government's financial stewardship (Kravchuk and Voorhees, 2001).

## 5.2 Unique Aspects of the General Fund

There are several unique aspects of the general fund that help to define both its character and role in governmental accounting and finance. First and foremost is the point that the general fund is a governmental-type fund, which distinguishes its accounting rules and procedures from those employed in the cases of proprietary and fiduciary-type funds. Consequently, the accounting requirements that pertain to governmental funds will also pertain to the general fund. The following is a summary of the unique aspects and characteristics of the general fund.

### 5.2.1 Number of General Funds

GAAP require that there be one, and only one, general fund (GASB, 2003, §1300.116, p. 20). If, as a matter of law, contract, or policy, revenues need to be accounted for in a separate fund, a special revenue fund, or in the case of revenues generated from an investment portfolio that are devoted to a public purpose, a permanent fund may be established. In any event, it is entirely conceivable that a governmental entity whose operations are relatively simple and uncomplicated may have and report only a general fund.

### 5.2.2 Measurement Focus and Basis of Accounting

Since the general fund is classified as a governmental-type fund, GAAP require that the Current Financial Resources Measurement Focus and the Modified Accrual Basis of Accounting be employed (GASB, 2003, §1600, p. 51). Operationally, this means that "revenues and other governmental-fund financial resources received (for example, bond issue proceeds) are recognized in the accounting period in which they become susceptible to accrual—that is, when they become both *measurable* and *available* to finance expenditures of the fiscal period" (GASB, 2003, §1600.106, p. 54). In this connection, "available" means collectible within the fiscal current period, or shortly enough thereafter to satisfy any liabilities incurred in the current fiscal period. It is a crucial point that the general fund focus is not on *earned* revenues, as is the case with proprietary and fiduciary type funds. In general, the government's policies and criteria concerning the susceptibility to accrual of specific revenue items should be applied consistently and disclosed in the Summary of Significant Accounting Policies in the Notes to the Financial Statements (GASB, 2003, §1600.108, p. 54).

## 5.2.3 Revenue Recognition

As noted, the modified accrual basis of accounting is to be applied to general fund accounting. Consequently, revenues are to be recognized "when measurable and available." As a practical matter, this requirement pertains mainly to "property taxes, any regularly billed charges for routinely provided services, most of the grants received from other governments, interfund transfers, and sales and income taxes, where taxpayer liability is established and collectibility is assured or where losses can be reasonably estimated" (GASB, 2003, §1600.107, p. 54). In the case of revenues that are received from sources that have not been previously accrued, they are recorded on the modified accrual basis. The length of time used to define "available" for purposes of revenue recognition should be disclosed in the Summary of Significant Accounting Policies in the Notes to the Financial Statements (GASB, 2003, §1600.106, p. 54).

## 5.2.4 Expenditure Recognition

Consistent with the current financial resources measurement focus, the measurement focus of governmental-type funds is on *expenditures*, representing decreases in fund assets, as opposed to *expenses*, which include noncash items, such as depreciation of capital assets (GASB, 2003, §1600.116–117, p. 56). Expenditures are recognized in a fund when a liability is incurred that will be satisfied by the expenditure of fund assets. Expenses—including the expenses associated with governmental activities—are reported in the government-wide Statement of Activities.

## 5.2.5 General Fund Assets

In accordance with the current financial resources measurement focus, only current financial assets are to be accounted for in the general fund, and reported on general fund financial statements. This would include cash (i.e., currency, demand deposits, and deposits in cash pools, if accessible), inventories, prepaid items, and any other asset that will be converted into cash in the ordinary course of operations, such as receivables, marketable securities and other investments, and assets that have been acquired for resale in the current period, or shortly after its close (for example, foreclosure properties, gifts of land, etc.). General capital assets, intangible assets, and equity interest in joint ventures are *not* reported in the general fund but will appear on the government-wide statement of net assets (see Figure 5.1).

## 5.2.6 General Fund Liabilities

Governmental fund liabilities are claims against fund current financial resources. No governmental fund—including the general fund—may recognize longer-term liabilities in the fund, including the unmatured principal and interest on long-term

---

**Balance Sheet Accounts**

*Assets* (debit balances)
Cash
Investment in Pooled Cash
Taxes Receivable (net of uncollectibles)
Delinquent Taxes Receivable (net of uncollectibles)
Interest and Penalties Receivable on Delinquent Taxes
  (net of uncollectibles)
Marketable Securities
Supplies Inventory
Due from Other Funds

*Liabilities* (credit balances)
Vouchers Payable
Wages and Salaries Payable
Due to Federal Government (usually for payroll taxes)
Due to State Government (usually for payroll taxes)
Due to Other Funds

*Fund Balance* (credit balances)
Reserved for Supplies Inventory
Reserved for Encumbrances
Unreserved:
  Designated Fund Balance
  Undesignated Fund Balance

---

**Figure 5.1   General fund account structure (typical account names).**

debt, capital lease obligations (until due and payable), noncancellable operating lease obligations (until due and payable), claims and judgments (unless due and payable), landfill closure and postclosure costs (unless due and payable), net pension obligations, and other postemployment benefits obligations. The long-term liabilities are to be recognized in the government-wide statement of net assets. In conformity with the current financial resources measurement focus, only short-term (i.e., current) liabilities are accounted for in governmental funds (see Figure 5.1). Liabilities that will be satisfied through the expenditure of general fund assets are the subject of our present concern. If liabilities are held in another fund that will be satisfied by *that* fund's assets, they are not to be recognized as liabilities of the general fund. A pointed example would be the current interest and maturing principal of long-term debt that is to be paid by a debt service fund.

GAAP require that the government accrue in a governmental fund almost every expenditure and transfer that takes place as a *fund liability* in the period that it is incurred (GASB, 2003, §1600.118, p. 56). An important exception is the unmatured portion of long-term debt (i.e., the portion that is not yet due for payment). The same treatment is required for capital leases, compensated absences, claims and judgments, net pension obligations, special assessment debt for which the government is obligated in some manner, and a variety of other long-term commitments detailed in the pronouncements (GASB, 2003, §1500.103–104, pp. 42–43; §1600.118, p. 56). In general, it is considered sound financial management to account for expenditures of current financial resources on debt service in a debt service fund even if not legally required. However, debt service is sometimes accounted for in the general fund, where the government's debt service activities are simple and uncomplicated, and where neither the applicable laws nor sound financial management requires the use of a debt service fund. In that case, the same standards and accounting principles that are required in a debt service fund should be followed by the general fund.

## 5.2.7 Fund Equity and Fund Balance

Fund equity is the difference between fund assets and fund liabilities (Gauthier, 1991, 2005). The meaning of fund equity differs from that of private companies' equity, however. The focus of the general fund, like that of all funds classified as governmental-type funds, is on financial resources that may be expended or subject to appropriation by the appropriate legislative body. Since capital assets, capital leases, and intangibles are excluded, a large portion of fund equity may be regarded as "available for appropriation and expenditure." However, not all of the assets reported in the general fund are equally expendable or appropriable (Gauthier, 1991, p. 12). "Reserved fund balance" indicates that portion of total fund equity that is not expendable or subject to appropriation. Reservations of the general fund equity typically arise from legal restrictions, contract, unexpended encumbrances (i.e., for spending commitments made but not yet completed), prepaid items, and inventories. (See the fund balance accounts detailed in Figure 5.1.) Reservations of Fund Balance should never have negative balances.

The legislative body can also designate or "earmark" a portion of fund assets for a specific purpose, such as contingency funds and/or capital replacement. Such earmarkings are usually termed "Designated fund equity." Designations are never negative, and cannot exceed the total unreserved fund balance. Designations are self-imposed, and are therefore to be regarded as expressions of the government's preferences only. Consequently, they remain part of the expendable or appropriable fund resources. Strictly speaking, therefore, only the unreserved fund balance is available for appropriation.

## 5.2.8 Major Fund Focus

GAAP require that "the focus of governmental ... fund financial statements is on *major* funds" (GASB, 2003, §2200.149, p. 152). The general fund is always to be reported as a major fund, whether or not it meets the 5% and 10% criteria that define a fund as a major fund (GASB, 2003, §2200.150, p. 153).

---

**Debit Balances:**
Estimated Revenues [*Note:* control account; detailed revenue
    budget entries are made in the Revenues Subsidiary Ledger.]
Estimated Other Financing Sources
Encumbrances [*Note:* control account; detailed entries are made
    in the Encumbrances Subsidiary Ledger.]

**Credit Balances:**
Appropriations [*Note:* control account; detailed entries are made
    in the Encumbrances Subsidiary Ledger.]
Estimated Other Financing Uses
Reserve for Encumbrances

---

**Figure 5.2 General fund budgetary accounts.**

## 5.2.9 Budgetary Integration

GAAP require that the operating budget be integrated directly into the accounts of any fund for which there is a legally adopted budget (GASB, 2003, §1700.118–119, p. 69). In the case of the general fund, this means that the governmental entity's operating budget normally is posted directly to it, either at the beginning of the fiscal year or upon its adoption, if that occurs after the start of the fiscal year. Further changes to the budget also must be reflected in the budgetary account balances of the general fund. This is so that budgetary control may be maintained. Budgetary integration also facilitates the creation of the required budgetary comparisons at the end of the fiscal year (GASB, 2003, §2400.102–103, pp. 296–297). The budgetary accounts, like the nominal accounts, are eliminated in the year-end closing process. Figure 5.2 provides a summary of some general fund budgetary accounts that are generally employed.

## 5.2.10 Encumbrances and Allotments

It has long been recognized that an encumbrance accounting system militates against overexpending appropriations (NCMA, 1941, p. 122). Encumbrance accounting and reporting are widely regarded as essential attributes of effective cash planning and control (GASB, 2003, §1700.128, pp. 71–72). Encumbrances essentially are entries made in order to set aside, or "reserve," funds that have been committed to payment for purchase orders and/or contracts for goods and services that have not been received or performed, but which are expected within the near future. Encumbrances are reflected in the general fund balance sheet as a reservation of the fund equity.

Allotments are also a cash control device but one that allocates funds to spending units on a periodic basis, according to the policies and preferences of the legislature and/or the chief executive officer. Typically, either quarterly or monthly allotments are made, usually in times of fiscal retrenchment. Allotments may be entered in the ledger accounts or not. If they are recorded in the ledger, then allotments and unexpended allotments will be closed to fund balance at year's end, along with expenditure accounts.

## 5.3 General Fund Account Classifications

### 5.3.1 Estimated Revenues, Revenues, and Other Financing Sources

Revenues of the general fund are reported in the general fund financial statements and in those of no other fund, in order to avoid double-counting revenues. Governmental revenues are properly classified by fund and source. Classification by fund denotes which fiscal and accounting entity is affected. Revenue source classifications should be in sufficient detail to be meaningful to readers of the financial statements. The major source categories for which estimated revenues and those commonly reported include taxes, special assessments, licenses and permits, intergovernmental revenues, charges for services, fines and forfeitures, and miscellaneous revenues. The source categories may be further subcategorized according to the preferences of the government. For instance, taxes may be reported in subcategories for property taxes, income taxes, and excises. The adopted budget for the general fund should include all of the revenues sources that will finance the operations of the fund. Consequently, in order to facilitate budgetary control, the budgetary and nominal accounts of the general fund will employ precisely the same revenue classifications.

Revenues are to be carefully distinguished from other financing sources. These represent either transfers to the general fund from other funds, interfund loans, or the proceeds of long-term borrowing. Such items are not revenues, although they do have the effect of increasing the general fund's fund balance when the accounts are closed. Other financing sources are recognized on the modified accrual basis when they are measurable and available to pay current obligations (see Figure 5.3).

A brief word is in order about the classifications of governmental revenues on the government-wide financial statements and their relation to revenues recognized in the general fund. Revenues are classified on the government-wide statement of activities as either "general revenues" or, when derived from the activities connected with some specific program, as "program revenues." Three categories of program revenues are reported: charges for services, operating program revenues, and capital program revenues.

Grants, contributions, and other nonexchange revenues restricted by other governments, organizations, or individuals for the operating purposes of a particular function or program should be reported separately from those restricted for capital

---

**Credit Balances:**
Revenues [*Note:* control account; detailed revenue entries are
made in the Revenues Subsidiary Ledger.]
Proceeds of Bonds (if any)
Other Financing Sources – Transfers In

**Debit Balances:**
Expenditures [*Note:* control account; detailed expenditure entries
are made in the Expenditures Subsidiary Ledger.]
Other Financing Uses – Transfers Out

---

**Figure 5.3   General fund operating statement accounts.**

purposes. Multipurpose grants and contributions must be reported as program
revenues if the amounts restricted are identified in the grant award or grant application. Otherwise, multipurpose grants and contributions should be reported as
general revenue. Earnings from endowments, permanent funds, or other investments that are restricted for a specific purpose should be reported as program
revenue. Unrestricted earnings from such sources should be reported as general
revenue. All taxes—including those that have been earmarked by law for a specific
purpose—should be reported as general revenue.

Note that the general fund operating statement makes no explicit distinction
between general revenues and program revenues. However, to the extent that operating program revenues and capital program revenues may be derived from grants,
contributions, and other sources that are expended through the general fund, these
data must be captured when the accompanying revenues are recognized in the general fund (and other funds) for subsequent reporting in the statement of activities.
A reconciliation statement is required, detailing the differences between the totals
reported in the general fund operating statement and the totals reported in the
government-wide statement of activities.

## 5.3.2 Appropriations, Expenditures, and Other Financing Uses

In order to promote budgetary control, appropriations and expenditures generally
are classified by fund, function (or program), department or unit, activity, character,
and object. Classification by fund denotes the fiscal and accounting entity that is
affected. Classification by function or program assists in budgeting resources to carry
out the major service activities of the government and in capturing data required
to be reported on the government-wide statement of activities. Classification by
department or unit fixes responsibility for spending, and therefore serves to pinpoint accountability for resource management. Classification by activity assists in
assessing the government's efficiency of performance in major areas of activity (such
as parks and recreation—swimming pool). According to GASB, character refers

to the fiscal period that benefits from a specific expenditure. For the general fund, classification by character thus classifies appropriations and expenditures as current expenditures, capital spending or current-period debt service, and intergovernmental outlays. (Note that the capital spending classification is not typically used in the general fund, for the obvious reason that such expenditures generally are accounted for in a capital projects fund.) Classification by object assists in determining the amounts that are expended on specific items, such as personal services, travel, supplies, etc.

Other financing uses are strictly distinguished from appropriations and expenditures. In the case of the general fund, other financing uses refers to transfers to other funds. These are *not* expenditures as these transfers have not been expended and therefore have not left the government. However, like expenditures, they will decrease the general fund's fund balance when the accounts are closed. Other financing uses are recognized on the modified accrual basis when incurred if they are expected to be repaid from currently available resources of the general fund.

As with general fund revenues, a word is in order about the relation of general fund expenditures to government-wide expenses. The focus of the government-wide statement of activities is on *expenses* rather than *expenditures*. Insofar as the government-wide financial statements are prepared on the full accrual basis of accounting, expense account balances on the statement of activities will reflect accruals for noncash charges and other estimated amounts for depreciation of capital assets, amortization of prepaid items, and bond premium or discount, etc. A reconciliation statement or schedule is required, detailing the differences between the totals reported in the general fund operating statement and the totals reported in the government-wide statement of activities, and the reasons for the differences. (See the following text.) Records on certain general fund transactions and other information must be maintained in sufficient detail to enable the preparation of the government-wide financial statements in good order and the required reconciliations.

## 5.4 Budgetary Integration

The purpose of budgetary integration is to enhance financial planning, control, and performance evaluation (GASB, 2003, §1700.101, p. 65). Consequently, GASB has adopted a three-part Statement of Principle for Budgeting and Budgetary Control (GASB, 2003, §1700, p. 65; §2400.102–104, pp. 296–297):

1. Every governmental unit should adopt an annual budget.
2. The appropriate basis for budgetary control is the accounting system.
3. Budgetary comparison schedules should be included for all governmental units that have annually adopted budgets.

Consequently, the budgets of all funds for which there are legally adopted budgets must be integrated directly into the accounts of those funds.

Recording and revising the annual budget is a straightforward procedure. Budgeted revenues are debited to an estimated revenues control account, with a corresponding credit to an appropriations control account. The revenue and expenditures subsidiary ledgers would contain the necessary details, with revenue source (property taxes, licenses and permits, fines and forfeitures, etc.) and appropriations by function of government (general government, public safety, parks and recreation, etc.). If there is any planned operating surplus or deficit, this would be reflected in the entry as a debit to fund balance (where appropriations exceed estimated revenues) or a credit to fund balance (estimated revenues exceed appropriations). The following is representative of an initial budget entry for a government that plans to spend down part of its unreserved fund balance (all amounts are assumed):

| To record the original adopted budget: | Debit | Credit |
|---|---|---|
| Estimated revenues | 563,647,692 | |
| Fund balance | 30,951,698 | |
| Appropriations | | 594,599,390 |

Assuming that the government subsequently determines that it will collect less revenue and expend more than the original budget called for, the entry to revise the budget might be recorded as follows (again, the amounts are assumed):

| | Debit | Credit |
|---|---|---|
| Fund balance | 21,337,002 | |
| Estimated revenues | | 1,230,474 |
| Appropriations | | 20,106,528 |

## 5.5 Levying and Collecting General Taxes and Other Revenues

Under GASB standards, property tax revenues are classified as "Imposed Nonexchange Revenues" (GASB, 2003, §P70.106, p. 686). As such, the receivable for property taxes is to be debited when there is an enforceable claim. Under the modified accrual basis of accounting, property taxes are not subject to accrual until they are "measurable and available" (GASB, 2003, §P70.104, p. 686). As a practical matter, this will mean that property taxes are not accrued until they are levied. The levy establishes a legal obligation to pay on the part of property owners. The government levying the taxes will establish a receivable as of the levy, along with an estimate of uncollectible taxes, with the balance credited to an appropriately titled revenue account. The estimate of uncollectible taxes generally is based on the government's historical experience. The sum credited to estimate uncollectible taxes ought to approximate the amount that the government believes will remain uncollected at the end of the fiscal year. The accounting for the levy is straightforward. For example:

| To record the semiannual property tax levy: | Debit | Credit |
|---|---|---|
| Taxes receivable—current | 441,000,000 | |
| Estimated uncollectible current taxes | | 17,640,000 |
| Unalloted appropriations | | 423,360,000 |

Property tax collections are simply debited to cash, with an accompanying credit to Taxes Receivable—Current. During the year-end adjustments process, current property taxes that remain uncollected will be reclassified as Taxes Receivable—Delinquent, and Estimated Uncollectible Current Taxes reclassified as Estimated Uncollectible Delinquent Taxes. Further, interest and penalties on delinquent taxes will also be subject to accrual at the fiscal year-end. Finally, all delinquent taxes receivable that the government believes it is not reasonable to expect to be paid should be written off the books, along with any accompanying interest and penalties due on them. Note that this does not relieve the taxpayer of the obligation to pay; rather, in the interests of conservatism, it recognizes that receipt of the taxes, interest, and penalties to cover the government's current obligations is highly unlikely.

## 5.6 Encumbrances and Allotments

### 5.6.1 Encumbrances as an Instrument for Cash and Budget Control

As previously noted, an encumbrance accounting system is an essential device for the prevention of overspending general fund appropriations. In operating a system of encumbrances, it is useful to distinguish between appropriations, expenditures, encumbrances, and vouchers. When the budget is legally adopted, an "appropriation" is an authorization to incur liabilities on behalf of the governmental unit, for purposes specified in the budget. An appropriation is properly considered to be "expended" when the previously authorized liabilities have been incurred (but not necessarily paid). Encumbrances are not liabilities, but are, rather, *potential* liabilities. When a purchase order or contract is issued, for control purposes, a portion of

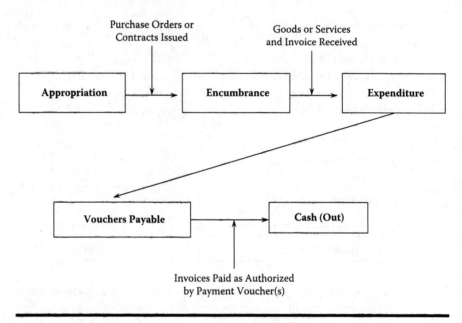

**Figure 5.4 Tracing the flow of funds through the control accounts.**

the appropriation is "set aside" (as it were) in order to remove the necessary funds from spending. Until an invoice is actually received, the encumbrance represents an *estimate* of the liability that will have to be paid. A *voucher* is a control document that provides evidence that a transaction is proper (usually, one or more authorized signatures are required). A voucher payable is a liability for goods and services that have been approved for payment on the basis of a payment voucher. Figure 5.4 presents a schematic of the flow of funds through the expenditure control accounts from appropriations through final payment.

The following are illustrative general fund journal entries (amounts are assumed):

|  | Debit | Credit |
|---|---|---|
| To record the issuance of purchase orders: |  |  |
| Encumbrances | 67,300 |  |
| Reserve for encumbrances |  | 67,300 |
| To record receipt of goods (partial shipment): |  |  |
| Reserve for encumbrances | 40,200* |  |
| Encumbrances |  | 40,200 |

|  | Debit | Credit |
|---|---|---|
| *To record liability to vendors:* | | |
| Expenditures | 41,000* | |
| Vouchers payable | | 41,000 |
| *To record payment to vendors:* | | |
| Vouchers payable | 41,000 | |
| Cash | | 41,000 |

The $800 difference* between the amount reserved and the amount payable is due to the liability being recorded at *actual cost*, whereas the reserve for encumbrances was recorded at its then *estimated cost*. No accounting difficulties are caused by this difference as long as goods or services are received in the same fiscal year as they were ordered. In the event that goods and services are received after the close of the fiscal year, they are charged against the subsequent year's appropriations. Note that this is not a problem, provided that the amount is not material in magnitude.

Any balance remaining in the reserve for encumbrances account at fiscal year-end will appear in the fund equity section of the general fund balance sheet as a reservation of fund balance.

## 5.6.2 Allotments as a Budgetary Control Device

Allotments divide an annual appropriation into portions such as quarterly or monthly portions, making the portions available to spending departments and agencies for expenditure or encumbrance during the allotment period. Accounting for allotments is straightforward. When the initial budget entry is made, the credit is made to Unalloted Appropriations, instead of Appropriations, as follows:

| To record the original adopted budget: | Debit | Credit |
|---|---|---|
| Estimated revenues | 563,647,692 | |
| Fund balance | 30,951,698 | |
| Unalloted appropriations | | 594,599,390 |

Suppose now that some $50 million is allotted for the first month of the fiscal year. The following entry reflects the allotment:

|                           | Debit      | Credit     |
|---------------------------|------------|------------|
| Unalloted appropriations  | 50,000,000 |            |
| Allotments                |            | 50,000,000 |

In the year-end closing process, all unexpended allotments and unalloted appropriations, along with expenditures and encumbrances, are closed to Fund Balance.

## 5.7 Interfund Activity

Interfund transactions involve purchases of goods and service from, and on behalf of, other funds, interfund loans, transfers, and reimbursements. See Figure 5.5 for a summary of types of interfund activity.

### 5.7.1 Interfund Exchange Transactions

It is a fairly common occurrence for departments accounted for in the general fund to make purchases on behalf of other funds, to purchase services from other funds, and/or to provide other funds with services directly. An example of an interfund purchase would be a city water utility providing water and (perhaps) sewer service to the city's offices and other facilities on a cost-reimbursement basis. GASB has termed such internal exchange transactions "Interfund Services Provided and Used" (GASB, 2003, §1800.102.a(2), p. 77). Transactions between governmental funds generally are recognized as expenditures when a liability is credited (Due to Other Funds, or some other appropriately descriptive name). The fund receiving

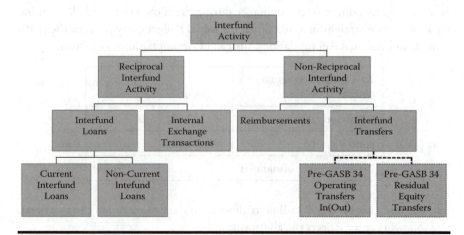

**Figure 5.5   Classification of interfund activity under current GASB standards.**

the payment may recognize it as a revenue item. It should be stressed that this is the only form of interfund transfer that will result in revenue recognition on the part of the fund providing the service. The general rule is that revenue be recognized only once, and that too on the part of the fund that initially collects the revenue (GASB, 2003, §1800.102, p. 77).

Government-owned and operated utilities customarily make some contribution to the municipal government in the form of payments "in lieu of taxes," generally in recognition of the police and fire protection that the government affords the utility. As a matter of municipal policy, the amount remitted may or may not approximate the fair value of the services provided. Nonetheless, such payments would be debited as a receivable to the general fund and credited to Revenues—Payments in Lieu of Taxes (or some other appropriately named account).

### 5.7.2 Interfund Loans

Interfund loans are those made from one fund to another with the intent that they will be repaid (GASB, 2003, §1800.102.a(1), pp. 76–77). If repayment is not expected "within a reasonable time," then the interfund loan balance should be reduced, with the amount that is not expected to be repaid reported as an interfund transfer from/to the fund that made/received the loan. Interfund loans are to be classified as Interfund Loans Receivable—Current (or Payable—Current), if the intent is to repay the loan during the current year (or shortly thereafter). Otherwise, they are to be classified as noncurrent items.

### 5.7.3 Interfund Transfers

Nonreciprocal interfund transfers of both operating transfer and equity transfers are classified as Interfund Transfers under current GASB standards (GASB, 2003, §1800.102.b(1), p. 77). Under the financial reporting model that prevailed prior to the issuance of GASB Statement No. 34, interfund transfers were reported as either Operating Transfers or Residual Equity Transfers. Interfund transfers take place without an equivalent flow of assets back to the transferring fund, neither with any expectation of repayment. They are reported on the financial statements as Other Financing Uses by the fund making the transfer, and as Other Financing Sources by the receiving fund.

A typical example of an operating transfer is the payment of debt service by a debt service fund using a portion of general tax revenues collected by the general fund. In keeping with the general rule that revenues be recognized only once (in the fund that collects them), in this instance the general fund recognizes an other financing use for the transfer to the debt service fund, which recognizes the transfer as an other financing source. A fairly common example of an equity transfer concerns the permanent transfer of "seed money" from the general fund to a new capital projects fund in order to initiate the acquisition or construction of a capital asset, or the transfer of residual balances from a capital projects fund that has completed its work to another fund. [*Note:* The rule is that the residual monies be transferred to the general fund unless the government has issued debt to finance the project, in which case the residual equity would be transferred to the debt service fund that will service the debt.]

### 5.7.4 Interfund Reimbursements

Reimbursements are "repayments from the funds responsible for particular expenditures or expenses to the funds that initially paid for them" (GASB, 2003, §1800.102.b(2), p. 77). In this instance, one fund records an expenditure for items that should have been recorded as expenditures of the fund that is responsible for those kinds of expenditures. When that happens, the fund receiving the reimbursement should record it as a reduction (credit) of its expenditures (or expenses), with a corresponding debit to cash. Reimbursements are not to be reported in the financial statements.

### 5.7.5 Intra- and Interactivity Transactions

These types of transactions concern what and how interfund transfers are reported on the government-wide financial statements. Intra-activity transactions are those that take place between two governmental-type funds (including internal service funds), or between two enterprise funds. Neither governmental activities nor business-type activities are affected at the government-wide level of reporting, so there are no requirements for additional entries or record-keeping in the general fund for these transactions. However, in the case of interactivity transactions, interfund loans or other transactions take place between a governmental fund (including internal service funds) and an enterprise fund. In this case, additional entries and record-keeping become necessary, insofar as internal balances are reported in the government-wide statement of net assets, and transfers in the statement of activities (GASB, 2003, §1800.103–105, pp. 77–78).

### 5.7.6 Intra-Entity Transactions

Intra-entity transactions are exchange or nonexchange transactions between the primary government and its component units (GASB, 2003, §1800.106, p. 78). To the extent that any such transaction involves the primary government and a blended component unit of the reporting entity, these transfers should be reclassified as internal interfund activity of the reporting entity. However, resources that flow between a fund of the primary government and its discretely reported component units should be treated as if they were transactions with an external entity and recognized as revenues or expenses on the government-wide statement of activities. In either case, if such transactions occur between the general fund and any component unit of the reporting entity, records should be kept in sufficient detail to permit accurate reporting of the transaction in the government-wide financial statements.

## 5.8 General Fund Financial Statements

In contrast to the government-wide financial statements, which report on the government's *operational* accountability, the general fund financial statements—like all governmental fund financial statements—report on the government's *fiscal* accountability (GASB, 1999). The focus of general fund reporting is therefore on the flow and use of current financial resources employed in general government operations. Therefore, the general fund statements report on cash and near-cash assets used to satisfy the current liabilities of general government (GASB, 2003, §2200.152–160, pp. 153–156).

### 5.8.1 General Fund Operating Statement

The operating statement is formally entitled the "Statement of Revenues, Expenditures and Changes in Fund Balances," and must be labeled as such when officially published (GASB, 2003, §2200.152, p. 153). The statement reports the following information, in the format and sequence indicated (GASB, 2003, §2200.156, p. 154):

Revenues (in detail)
Expenditures (in detail)
    Excess (deficiency) of revenues over expenditures
Other financing sources and uses, including transfers (in detail)
Special and extraordinary items (in detail)
    Net change in fund balances
Fund balances—beginning of period (including reserved and unreserved amounts)
Fund balances—end of period

In accordance with the emphasis on major funds, the operating statement will include columns for all major governmental funds, a single column for nonmajor funds, and a total column. Consequently, the general fund will be reported on the same set of financial statements as all governmental-type funds. As an example, Figure 5.6 provides the governmental funds operating statement for the City of San Antonio, Texas, for the year ended September 30, 2005.

### 5.8.2 General Fund Balance Sheet

The governmental funds balance sheet reports information about the current financial resources for each major governmental fund and nonmajor governmental funds

—— CITY OF SAN ANTONIO, TEXAS ——

STATEMENT OF REVENUES, EXPENDITURES, AND CHANGES IN FUND BALANCES
GOVERNMENTAL FUNDS
YEAR ENDED SEPTEMBER 30, 2005
(In Thousands)

| | GENERAL | DEBT SERVICE | CONVENTION CENTER HOTEL FINANCE CORPORATION | NONMAJOR GOVERNMENTAL FUNDS | TOTAL GOVERNMENTAL FUNDS |
|---|---|---|---|---|---|
| **Revenues** | | | | | |
| Taxes: | | | | | |
| Property Taxes | $ 171,229 | $ 98,923 | $ - | $ 1,338 | $ 271,490 |
| General Sales and Use Taxes | 162,786 | | | 4,546 | 167,332 |
| Selective Sales and Use Taxes | 4,473 | | | | 4,473 |
| Gross Receipts Business Taxes | 26,274 | | | | 26,274 |
| Occupancy Taxes | | | | 51,717 | 51,717 |
| Penalties and Interest on Delinquent Taxes | 2,268 | 1,137 | | 29 | 3,434 |
| Licenses and Permits | 20,716 | | | | 20,716 |
| Intergovernmental | 3,055 | | | 187,196 | 190,251 |
| Revenues from Utilities | 221,775 | | | | 221,775 |
| Charges for Services | 33,622 | | | 73,642 | 107,264 |
| Fines and Forfeits | 12,025 | | | | 12,025 |
| Miscellaneous | 11,841 | | 16 | 14,991 | 26,848 |
| Investment Earnings | 2,445 | 3,970 | 2,022 | 10,107 | 18,544 |
| In-Kind Contributions | | | | 24,872 | 24,872 |
| Total Revenues | 672,509 | 104,030 | 2,038 | 368,438 | 1,147,015 |
| **Expenditures** | | | | | |
| Current: | | | | | |
| General Government | 64,020 | | | 5,312 | 69,332 |
| Public Safety | 402,544 | | | 17,090 | 419,634 |
| Public Works | 10,478 | | | 75,462 | 85,940 |
| Health Services | 13,995 | | | 74,538 | 88,533 |
| Sanitation | 2,576 | | | 192 | 2,768 |
| Welfare | 19,757 | | | 111,255 | 131,012 |
| Culture and Recreation | 63,010 | | | 16,576 | 79,586 |
| Convention and Tourism | | | | 48,315 | 48,315 |
| Conservation | | | | 2 | 2 |
| Urban Redevelopment and Housing | | | | 25,557 | 25,557 |
| Economic Development and Opportunity | 4,392 | | | 11,945 | 16,337 |
| Capital Projects | | | 36,963 | 109,887 | 146,850 |
| Debt Service: | | | | | |
| Principal Retirement | | 57,581 | | | 57,581 |
| Interest | | 60,202 | | | 60,202 |
| Issuance Costs | | 1,027 | | | 1,027 |
| Total Expenditures | 580,772 | 118,810 | 36,963 | 496,131 | 1,232,676 |
| **Excess (Deficiency) of Revenues Over (Under) Expenditures** | 91,737 | (14,780) | (34,925) | (127,693) | (85,661) |
| **Other Financing Sources (Uses)** | | | | | |
| Long-Term Debt Issued | | 86,010 | | 106,319 | 192,329 |
| Payments to Refunded Bond Escrow Agent | | (93,163) | | | (93,163) |
| Amounts from Notes and Loans | | | 208,145 | 2,462 | 210,607 |
| Premium on Long-term Debt | | 6,914 | 66 | 5,924 | 12,904 |
| Transfers In | 14,122 | 16,423 | | 129,276 | 159,821 |
| Transfers Out | (85,956) | | | (74,655) | (160,611) |
| Total Other Financing Sources (Uses) | (71,834) | 16,184 | 208,211 | 169,326 | 321,887 |
| Net Change in Fund Balances | 19,903 | 1,404 | 173,286 | 41,633 | 236,226 |
| Fund Balances, October 1 | 98,510 | 83,723 | | 354,495 | 536,728 |
| Fund Balances, September 30 | $ 118,413 | $ 85,127 | $ 173,286 | $ 396,128 | $ 772,954 |

The accompanying notes are an integral part of these basic financial statements.

**Figure 5.6    Statement of revenues, expenditures, and changes in fund balances.**

in the aggregate (GASB, 2003, §2200.153, p. 153). Assets, liabilities, and fund balances are presented in a balance sheet format, as in the recent balance sheet for the City of San Antonio, Texas, detailed in Figure 5.7. Reserved and unreserved fund balances are to be reported in a segregated fashion (GASB, 2003, §2200.154, p. 154). Reserved fund balances should be reported in sufficient detail and labeled so as to disclose the purpose of the reservation.

—— CITY OF SAN ANTONIO, TEXAS ——

**BALANCE SHEET**
**GOVERNMENTAL FUNDS**
**AS OF SEPTEMBER 30, 2005**
(In Thousands)

| | | | | CONVENTION CENTER HOTEL | NONMAJOR | TOTAL |
| | | | DEBT | FINANCE | GOVERNMENTAL | GOVERNMENTAL |
| | | GENERAL | SERVICE | CORPORATION | FUNDS | FUNDS |
|---|---|---|---|---|---|---|
| **Assets** | | | | | | |
| Cash and Cash Equivalents | $ | 1,928 | $ 21,946 | $ 177,355 | $ 36,817 | $ 238,046 |
| Investments | | 26,057 | 60,080 | | 395,030 | 481,167 |
| Receivables | | 103,948 | 9,416 | 466 | 50,683 | 164,513 |
| Allowance for Uncollectibles | | (19,827) | (937) | | (19,991) | (40,755) |
| Prepaid Expenditures | | 2 | | | | 2 |
| Due from Other Funds | | 44,687 | 1,539 | | 22,149 | 68,375 |
| Due from Other Governmental Agencies | | 83 | | | 54,698 | 54,781 |
| Materials and Supplies, at Cost | | 2,712 | | | 1,190 | 3,902 |
| Deposits | | | | | 261 | 261 |
| Total Assets | $ | 159,590 | $ 92,044 | $ 177,821 | $ 540,837 | $ 970,292 |
| **Liabilities and Fund Balances** | | | | | | |
| Liabilities: | | | | | | |
| Vouchers Payable | $ | 4,000 | $ - | $ 4,535 | $ 4,901 | $ 13,436 |
| Accounts Payable - Other | | 4,620 | | | 41,466 | 46,086 |
| Accrued Payroll | | 8,974 | | | 5,056 | 14,030 |
| Accrued Leave Payable | | 5,031 | | | 1,261 | 6,292 |
| Unearned Revenues | | 16,888 | 6,917 | | 19,073 | 42,878 |
| Due To: | | | | | | |
| Other Funds | | 1,664 | | | 68,512 | 70,176 |
| Other Governmental Agencies | | | | | 4,440 | 4,440 |
| Total Liabilities | | 41,177 | 6,917 | 4,535 | 144,709 | 197,338 |
| Fund Balances: | | | | | | |
| Reserved: | | | | | | |
| Reserved for Encumbrances | | 8,209 | | 3,698 | 99,067 | 110,974 |
| Reserved for Materials and Supplies, at Cost | | 2,712 | | | 853 | 3,565 |
| Reserved for Prepaid Expenditures | | 2 | | | | 2 |
| Reserved for Debt Service | | | 85,127 | | | 85,127 |
| Unreserved: | | | | | | |
| Designated | | 31,950 | | | | 31,950 |
| Designated: Special Revenue Funds | | | | | 6,085 | 6,085 |
| Designated: Permanent Funds | | | | | 2,825 | 2,825 |
| Undesignated | | 75,540 | | | | 75,540 |
| Undesignated: Special Revenue Funds | | | | | 85,644 | 85,644 |
| Undesignated: Capital Projects Funds | | | | 169,588 | 191,532 | 361,120 |
| Undesignated: Permanent Funds | | | | | 10,122 | 10,122 |
| Total Fund Balances | | 118,413 | 85,127 | 173,286 | 396,128 | 772,954 |
| Total Liabilities and Fund Balances | $ | 159,590 | $ 92,044 | $ 177,821 | $ 540,837 | $ 970,292 |

The accompanying notes are an integral part of these basic financial statements.

**Figure 5.7   Balance sheet.**

## 5.8.3  Statement of Cash Flows

A statement of cash flows is not required for the general fund.

## 5.8.4  Required Reconciliation Statements/Schedules

In order to avoid confusion concerning financial and operating results being reported on two different bases of accounting—full accrual accounting at the government-wide level and modified accrual accounting for governmental funds—GASB standards require that reconciliations be provided either at the bottom of the fund financial statements or in accompanying schedules (GASB, 2003, §2200.160, p. 155). If presented as accompanying schedules, they are to be designated as schedules and not as statements.

The items that typically need to be reconciled are specified in the standard, including revenues reported on the accrual basis, depreciation expense versus capital expenditures, long-term debt reported as a liability instead of as an other financing source, and expenses reported at the government-wide level on the accrual basis. Figures 5.8 and 5.9 present the required reconciliations for the City of San Antonio, Texas, for both the governmental funds operating statement and balance sheet.

## 5.8.5 Required Budgetary Comparisons

Budgetary comparison information must include the original adopted budget, final appropriated budget (including the effects of all amendments that may have occurred during the fiscal year), and actual inflows, outflows, and balances on the government's budgetary basis (GASB, 2003, §2400.102, p. 296). No other comparisons are to be presented. See Figure 5.10 for a representative budgetary comparison schedule for the City of San Antonio, Texas. A separate column also may be included to report the variance between actual and final budgeted amounts, but is not required. The use of value-laden terms to label the variances (such as "favorable," "positive," "unfavorable," and "negative") is discouraged. Users of the financial statements are to make their own determinations as to the significance of reported variances. The actual amounts are reported on the basis of accounting used in executing the budget.

All governments are encouraged to present their budgetary comparison information as schedules as part of their required supplementary information (RSI); however, governments have the option of reporting budgetary comparison information in the form of a statement as part of the basic financial statements (GASB, 2003, §2400.102, n. 1, p. 296). When presented as a basic financial statement, the budgetary comparison is denoted as a "Statement." This presentation places the budgetary comparison within the scope of the independent audit. When presented as RSI, the budgetary comparison is denoted as a "Schedule," which is subject to limited test procedures by the independent auditor.

Notes to the RSI should disclose the budgetary basis of accounting for all individual funds presented in a budgetary comparison statement (GASB, 2003, §2400.103, p. 297). GASB notes that there will often be few differences between the budgetary basis of accounting and the modified accrual basis (GASB, 2003, §1700.116, p. 68). Where the legally prescribed basis for budgetary accounting differs from GAAP, then supplementary records should be kept in order to permit the preparation of financial statements on a GAAP basis (GASB, 2003, §1700.117, p. 69).

## 5.8.6 Interim Financial Reports

Interim financial statements are considered desirable cash and budget control devices. Administrators and legislators have the greatest need for interim—quarterly or monthly—reports (GASB, 2003, §2900.101–104, p. 383). Interim financial

——— CITY OF SAN ANTONIO, TEXAS ———

RECONCILIATION OF THE STATEMENT OF REVENUES, EXPENDITURES,
AND CHANGES IN FUND BALANCES OF GOVERNMENTAL FUNDS
TO THE STATEMENT OF ACTIVITIES
YEAR ENDED SEPTEMBER 30, 2005
(In Thousands)

Amounts reported for governmental activities in the Statement of Activities are different because:

| | | |
|---|---|---|
| Net change in Fund Balances - Total Governmental Funds | | $ 236,226 |

Governmental funds report capital outlays as expenditures. However, in the Statement of Activities, the cost of those assets is depreciated over their estimated useful lives and reported as depreciation expense. This is the amount by which capital outlays exceed depreciation in the current period.

| | | |
|---|---|---|
| Donated capital assets | 364 | |
| Expenditures for Capital Assets | 99,821 | |
| Less Current Year Deletions | (201) | |
| Less Current Year Depreciation | (84,483) | 15,501 |

Revenues in the Statement of Activities that do not provide current financial resources are not reported as revenues in the funds.    (11,194)

Bond proceeds provide current financial resources to governmental funds, but issuing debt increases long-term liabilities in the Statement of Net Assets. Repayment of bond principal is an expenditure in the governmental funds, but the repayment reduces long-term liabilities in the Statement of Net Assets. This is the amount by which proceeds exceeded repayments (See Footnote 14).

| | | |
|---|---|---|
| Bond and Loan Amounts | (440,525) | |
| Payments to Escrow Agent | 93,163 | |
| Amortization of Bond Premiums and Deferred Charges (Net) | 14,721 | |
| Principal Payments | 57,581 | (275,060) |

Some expenses reported in the Statement of Activities do not require the use of current financial resources and, therefore, are not reported as expenditures in governmental funds (See Footnote 14).    (9,990)

Internal service funds are used by management to charge the cost of certain activities to individual funds. The net (expense) of the internal service funds is reported with governmental activities.    13,166

| | | |
|---|---|---|
| Change in Net Assets of Governmental Activities | | $ (31,351) |

The accompanying notes are an integral part of these basic financial statements.

**Figure 5.8  Reconciliation of the statement of revenues, expenditures, and changes in fund balances.**

————— CITY OF SAN ANTONIO, TEXAS —————

**RECONCILIATION OF THE BALANCE SHEET
TO THE STATEMENT OF NET ASSETS
GOVERNMENTAL ACTIVITIES
AS OF SEPTEMBER 30, 2005**
(In Thousands)

Amounts reported for governmental activities in the Statement of Net Assets are different because:

| | | | |
|---|---|---:|---:|
| Fund Balances - Total Governmental Funds | | $ | 772,954 |
| | | | |
| Capital assets used in governmental activities are not financial resources and, therefore, are not reported in the governmental funds. | | | |
| | | | |
| Governmental capital assets: | | | |
| Land and Land Improvements | | 1,268,142 | |
| Construction In Progress | | 614,763 | |
| Buildings | | 396,373 | |
| Improvements | | 106,838 | |
| Infrastructure Assets | | 2,054,838 | |
| Machinery and Equipment | | 96,481 | |
| Less: Accumulated Depreciation | | (1,514,558) | |
| Total Capital Assets | | | 3,022,877 |
| | | | |
| Some of the City's revenues will be collected after year-end but are not available soon enough to pay for the current periods expenditures and, therefore, are not reported in the governmental funds (See Footnote 14). | | | 23,958 |
| | | | |
| Internal service funds are used by management to charge the cost of certain activities to individual funds. The assets and liabilities of the internal service funds are reported with governmental activities in the Statement of Net Assets. | | | 50,741 |
| | | | |
| Long-term liabilities, including bonds payable, are not due and payable in the current period and, therefore, are not reported in the governmental funds (See Footnote 14). | | | |
| | | | |
| Governmental Bonds Payable | | (1,438,372) | |
| Premium on Bonds | | (49,799) | |
| Deferred Amount on Refunding | | 13,839 | |
| Leases Payable | | (6,079) | |
| Amounts received from notes & loans | | (1,369) | |
| Unamortized Debt Expense | | 22,623 | |
| Accrued Interest | | (11,960) | |
| Arbitrage Rebate | | (1,688) | |
| Compensated Absences | | (121,132) | |
| | | | (1,593,937) |
| | | | |
| Net assets of Governmental Activities | | $ | 2,276,593 |

The accompanying notes are an integral part of these basic financial statements.

**Figure 5.9    Reconciliation of the balance sheet to the statement of net assets.**

statements resemble the official annual statements in most important respects but also will contain items that do not appear in the annual statements. For instance, an interim balance sheet will report both proprietary and budgetary accounts, summing to Total Assets and Resources on the left-hand side. Resources include estimated revenues less revenues collected to date. On the right-hand side, the interim balance sheet fund equity section also will report appropriations less expenditures to date, resulting in the remaining available appropriations. Further, the term *Available for Appropriation* will sometimes be used as the title for the equity section of the balance sheet instead of fund balance. There usually is no interim operating statement,

—— CITY OF SAN ANTONIO, TEXAS ——

**GENERAL FUND**
**BUDGETARY COMPARISON SCHEDULE**
**YEAR ENDED SEPTEMBER 30, 2005**

| | | 2005 | | |
|---|---|---|---|---|
| | BUDGETED AMOUNTS | | | VARIANCE WITH FINAL BUDGET POSITIVE |
| | ORIGINAL | FINAL | ACTUAL | (NEGATIVE) |
| **Resources (Inflows):** | | | | |
| Taxes | $ 350,282,729 | $ 350,282,729 | $ 367,030,243 | $ 16,747,514 |
| Licenses and Permits | 17,542,550 | 17,542,550 | 20,715,743 | 3,173,193 |
| Intergovernmental | 2,795,306 | 2,795,306 | 3,055,128 | 259,822 |
| Revenues from Utilities | 196,784,803 | 196,784,803 | 221,774,673 | 24,989,870 |
| Charges for Services | 29,101,948 | 29,101,948 | 33,622,089 | 4,520,141 |
| Fines and Forfeits | 12,315,804 | 12,315,804 | 12,025,344 | (290,460) |
| Miscellaneous | 11,668,023 | 11,668,023 | 14,286,093 | 2,618,070 |
| Transfers from Other Funds | 14,673,148 | 14,778,703 | 14,121,847 | (656,856) |
| Amounts Available for Appropriation | 635,164,311 | 635,269,866 | 686,631,160 | 51,361,294 |
| **Charges to Appropriations (Outflows):** | | | | |
| General Government | 79,512,765 | 87,405,500 | 66,746,538 | 20,658,962 |
| Public Safety | 400,696,219 | 405,154,154 | 404,491,342 | 662,812 |
| Public Works | 10,698,288 | 10,698,288 | 10,477,765 | 220,523 |
| Health Services | 13,947,697 | 14,245,069 | 14,378,887 | (133,818) |
| Sanitation | 2,886,374 | 2,886,374 | 2,582,840 | 303,534 |
| Welfare | 20,837,267 | 22,018,578 | 21,578,358 | 440,220 |
| Culture and Recreation | 66,031,937 | 66,726,827 | 63,478,741 | 3,248,086 |
| Economic Development and Opportunity | 4,054,036 | 4,525,265 | 4,552,704 | (27,439) |
| Transfers to Other Funds | 75,209,927 | 87,057,100 | 86,649,587 | 407,513 |
| Total Charges to Appropriations | 673,874,510 | 700,717,155 | 674,936,762 | 25,780,393 |
| Excess (Deficiency) of Resources Over (Under) Charges to Appropriations | (38,710,199) | (65,447,289) | 11,694,398 | 77,141,687 |
| Fund Balance Allocation | 38,710,199 | 65,447,289 | (11,694,398) | (77,141,687) |
| Excess (Deficiency) of Resources Over (Under) Charges to Appropriations | $ - | $ - | $ - | $ - |

**Explanation of Differences between Budgetary Inflows and Outflows and GAAP Revenues and Expenditures**

**Sources/Inflows of Resources:**
Actual amounts (budgetary basis) "available for appropriation" from the budgetary
comparison schedule                                                                                                                    $ 686,631,160
Differences - budget to GAAP:

   Transfers from other funds are inflows of budgetary resources but are not revenues
   for financial reporting purposes                                                                                    (14,121,847)
Total revenues as reported on the statement of revenues, expenditures, and changes
in fund balances - governmental funds                                                                                            $ 672,509,313

**Uses/Outflows of Resources:**
Actual amounts (budgetary basis) "total charges to appropriations" from the budgetary
comparison schedule                                                                                                                    $ 674,936,762
Differences - budget to GAAP:

   Encumbrances for supplies and equipment ordered but not received is reported in the
   year the order is placed for budgetary purposes, but in the year the supplies are
   received for financial reporting purposes.                                                                   (7,514,793)
   Transfers to other funds are outflows of budgetary resources but are not expenditures
   for financial reporting purposes.                                                                                   (86,649,587)
Total expenditures as reported on the statement of revenues, expenditures, and changes
in fund balances - governmental funds                                                                                            $ 580,772,382

**General Fund Budgetary Information**
The City Charter establishes requirements for the adoption of budgets and budgetary control. Under provisions of the Charter, expenditures of each City function and activity within individual funds cannot legally exceed the final budget approved by the City Council. Amendments to line items within a departmental budget may be initiated by Department Directors.

The City prepares an annual budget for the General Fund on a modified-accrual basis, which is consistent with generally accepted accounting principles. The annual budgetary data reported for the General Fund represents the original appropriation ordinance and amendments thereto as adopted by the City Council, adjusted for encumbrances outstanding at the beginning of the fiscal year. All annual appropriations lapse at fiscal year-end.

(unaudited - see accompanying accountants' report)

**Figure 5.10   General fund budgetary comparison schedule.**

but rather, schedules accompanying the interim balance sheet will disclose budgeted versus actual revenues, appropriations, expenditures, and encumbrances in sufficient detail as to be useful to executive branch officials, managers, and legislators.

## 5.9 General Fund Accounting and Financial Reporting Issues

Major general fund accounting and financial reporting issues concern the recognition of certain revenue items and the liabilities associated with certain tax, revenue, or grant anticipation notes.

### 5.9.1 Revenues Collected after the Close of the Fiscal Year

Taxes receivable at fiscal year-end must be reclassified as delinquent, and an estimate of uncollectibles made and recorded. Interest and penalties due on delinquent taxes also must be recognized at fiscal year-end. However, according to GASB Interpretation No. 5, revenues to be collected after the close of the current fiscal year, but which will be used to satisfy liabilities of the current year, may be subject to recognition in the current period.

### 5.9.2 Sales Tax Revenue

Since municipal sales tax revenue is classified as an "imposed nonexchange revenue item, it is not to be accrued when collected by merchants unless and until they are due and payable to the government" (GASB, 2003, §N50.126–127, p. 604). In general, municipal sales tax revenue is to be recognized on the modified accrual basis.

### 5.9.3 Certain Tax, Revenue, or Grant Anticipation Notes

In general, tax anticipation notes, other revenue anticipation notes, and grant anticipation notes are to be treated as liabilities of the funds that will receive the proceeds (GASB, 2003, §B50.102, p. 386). If the general fund issues such notes but subsequently transfers the proceeds to other funds, the amount transferred becomes a liability in the recipient funds.

## 5.10 Current and Future Developments

### 5.10.1 Communications Methods

In April 2005, the GASB issued Concepts Statement No. 3 concerning the proper placement of information in the general financial reports (GASB, Concepts Statement No. 3, 2005). Four possible placements of financial information are contemplated:

recognition in the financial statements, notes disclosures, RSI disclosure, and presentation as supplementary information. The statement can be expected to impact the placement of financial information for all funds, including the general fund.

That is, to be recognized in the financial statements, a particular item must first meet the definition of an element of the financial statements. If such an element can be measured with sufficient reliability, then the item must be reported in the financial statements. If an item has a relationship to information presented in the financial statements and is essential to a user's understanding of the financial statements, then the information must be disclosed in the notes to the financial statements. Required supplementary information is used when disclosure is essential—and supplementary information is employed when disclosure is useful (but not essential)—for putting the financial statements and related notes into context.

## 5.10.2 *Elements of Financial Statements*

In August 2006, the GASB released an exposure draft of a new, fourth concepts statement entitled *Elements of Financial Statements* (GASB, 2006). The statement, once formally adopted, will provide guidance concerning what items will be reported in the financial statements, and which ones will not. The statement, therefore, has potential to affect the items reported in the general fund financial statements and, in fact, in all the financial statements, both at the fund level and at the government-wide level. The proposed statement represents a departure from GASB's previous efforts in two ways.

### 5.10.2.1 *Independent Definitions of Financial Statement Elements*

First, the statement defines financial statement elements independently of one another. Currently, the elements of financial statements are defined largely in terms of one another. For instance, the GASB notes that assets are commonly conceived as increasing through revenues, or through the satisfaction of liabilities (GASB, 2006). Liabilities are incurred as expenditures are made. Consequently, understanding what assets and liabilities are requires also understanding what revenues and expenditures are. However, the GASB did not believe that any element is more important than any other element. The exposure draft therefore adopts the concept of a "resource" as a central attribute of the basic elements. Resources are defined as something "with a present capacity to provide, directly or indirectly, services" (GASB, 2006, p. 2).

Five elements definitions in the proposed statement incorporate this notion of a resource:

- *Assets* are resources that the governmental entity controls at present.
- *Liabilities* are present obligations to sacrifice resources, now or in the future, that a government has little or no discretion to avoid.

- *Net assets* are the residual of all other elements presented in a statement of financial position.
- An *outflow of resources* is a consumption of net resources that is applicable to the current reporting period.
- An *inflow of resources* is an acquisition of net resources that is applicable to the current reporting period.

Assets, liabilities, and net assets are elements of statements of financial position, and would pertain, for example, to the governmental funds balance sheet, which includes the general fund, and to the government-wide statement of net assets. Outflows and inflows of resources are elements of what the statement terms "resource flows statements," which include the governmental-fund statement of revenues, expenditures, and changes in fund balance. The overall intent of the new definitions is to enhance understanding of information presented in the financial statements by defining the basic elements in terms of their basic characteristics. The GASB hopes to arrive at a point where a common set of definitions of elements may be employed, whether the modified accrual or full accrual basis of accounting is employed.

### 5.10.2.2 Treatment of Deferrals

The second point of departure from previous efforts is the explicit definition of deferrals. Deferred items have not previously been uniquely defined, leading to some confusion over just what they are when they appear with assets and liabilities on the balance sheet. Insofar as they do not have similar characteristics as assets and liabilities, the GASB undertook to define them separately:

- A *deferred outflow of resources* is a consumption of net resources by a government that applies to a future reporting period.
- A *deferred inflow of resources* is an acquisition of net resources by a government that applies to a future reporting period.

Examples of deferred items are unearned revenues and deferred expenses.

## References

Buchanan, J.M. (1967). *Public Finance in Democratic Process: Fiscal Institutions and Individual Choice*. Chapel Hill, NC: University of North Carolina Press.

Copley, P.A. and Engstrom, J.H. (2007). *Essentials of Accounting for Governmental and Not-for-Profit Organizations*, 8th ed. New York: McGraw-Hill Irwin.

Gauthier, S.J. (1991). *An Elected Official's Guide to Fund Balance*. Chicago: Government Finance Officers Association.

Gauthier, S.J. (2005). *Governmental Accounting, Auditing, and Financial Reporting.* Chicago: Government Finance Officers Association.

GASB, Governmental Accounting Standards Board (1999). *Statement No. 34: Basic Financial Statements—and Management's Discussion and Analysis—for State and Local Governments.* Norwalk, CT: Governmental Accounting Standards Board.

GASB, Governmental Accounting Standards Board (2003). *Codification of Governmental Accounting and Financial Reporting Standards.* Norwalk, CT: Governmental Accounting Standards Board.

GASB, Governmental Accounting Standards Board (2005). *Concepts Statement No. 3, Communication Methods in General Purpose External Financial Reports That Contain Basic Financial Statements.* Norwalk, CT: Governmental Accounting Standards Board.

GASB, Governmental Accounting Standards Board (2006). *Exposure Draft: Concepts Statement No. 4, Elements of Financial Statements.* Norwalk, CT: Governmental Accounting Standards Board.

Kravchuk, R.S. and Voorhees, W.R. (2001). The New Governmental Financial Reporting Model Under GASB Statement No. 34: An Emphasis on Accountability. *Public Budgeting and Finance (21)* 3: 1–30.

Morey, L. (1927). *Introduction to Governmental Accounting.* New York: John Wiley & Sons.

NCMA, National Committee on Municipal Accounting (1936). *Bulletin No. 6: Municipal Accounting Statements.* Chicago: Municipal Finance Officers Association.

NCMA, National Committee on Municipal Accounting (1941). *Bulletin No. 12: Municipal Accounting Statements,* Revised Edition. Chicago: Municipal Finance Officers Association.

# Chapter 6

# Debt Service Funds

## Dwayne N. McSwain

*Middle Tennessee State University, Jennings A. Jones College of Business, Department of Accounting*

## Contents

6.1   Types of Debt Instruments.................................................................194
6.2   Expenditure Recognition ..................................................................195
6.3   Accounting for Debt Service Fund Transactions.....................................196
6.4   Reporting for Debt Service Funds........................................................202
6.5   Special Assessments.........................................................................203
6.6   Reporting for Special Assessment Debt Service Funds ..........................208
6.7   Extinguishment of Debt.....................................................................208
6.8   Accounting for and Reporting of Debt Refundings ...............................211
6.9   Disclosure Requirements...................................................................212
6.10 Concluding Comments.....................................................................213
Endnotes...............................................................................................213

State and local governments borrow money for many different reasons (to purchase or build capital assets, to construct or improve infrastructure, to pay claims or judgments, to finance current operations, etc.) and in many different forms (leases, loans, notes, warrants, and bonds). The fund category and duration of these governmental borrowings is most important because governments use two different models to focus on what is being measured by the accounting information. In governmental-type funds, the focus is on current financial resources and short-term fiscal accountability. For proprietary and fiduciary-type funds, the focus is on economic resources and long-term operational accountability. This means that governmental-type funds contain only short-term (current) accounts, while proprietary and fiduciary-type funds are composed of both short- and long-term (noncurrent) accounts.

The accounting for debt-related transactions differs based on the related fund type. For proprietary and fiduciary-type funds, the GASB states

> Bonds, notes, and other long-term liabilities (for example, for capital and operating leases, pensions, claims and judgments, compensated absences, special termination benefits, landfill closure and postclosure care, and similar commitments) directly related to and expected to be paid from proprietary funds and fiduciary funds should be included in the accounts of such funds. These are specific fund liabilities, even though the full faith and credit of the governmental unit may be pledged as further assurance that the liabilities will be paid. Too, such liabilities may constitute a mortgage or lien on specific fund properties or receivables.[1]

With regard to general long-term liabilities for governmental funds, the GASB maintains that

> The general long-term debt of a state or local government is secured by the general credit and revenue-raising powers of the government rather than by the assets acquired or specific fund resources. Further, just as general capital assets do not represent financial resources available for appropriation and expenditure, the unmatured principal of general long-term debt does not require current appropriation and expenditure of governmental fund financial resources. To include it as a governmental fund liability would be misleading and dysfunctional to the current period management control (for example, budgeting) and accountability functions.[2]

Short-term borrowings by governmental-type funds are recorded in the balance sheet of the fund responsible for repayment of the debt. These obligations have a maturity of 12 months or less even if the term of the obligation spans across two fiscal years. Since the measurement focus is the flow of current financial resources, the presentation of such an obligation in a governmental-type fund balance sheet indicates that it is a current liability. This observation is pointed out because governmental-type funds use an unclassified balance sheet. That is, there is no distinction between short- and long-term obligations on a governmental-type fund balance sheet because the balance sheet is comprised of only current items. Repayment of short-term debt and interest will require the use of current financial resources.

Any borrowing agreement having a maturity of more than 12 months is a long-term obligation. Long-term obligations are not recorded in the governmental-type funds, because they will not require the use of current financial resources. Long-term debt for governmental-type funds is recorded in the general long-term liabilities nonfund account (formerly known as the general long-term debt account group) and presented only in the government-wide statement of net assets. General long-term debt is not presented in the fund financial statements for governmental-type funds, but there are several associated disclosures required in the notes to the financial statements. Repayment of general long-term debt and interest requires the use of future financial resources.

To meet these future cash disbursement requirements for long-term debt, governments may choose to wait until the principal and interest are legally due (current) and then service the debt through the general fund, or they may establish a separate fund for serving the principal and interest payments. According to the GASB, debt service funds are used

> ... to account for the accumulation of resources for, and the payment of, general long-term debt principal and interest. Debt service funds are required if they are legally mandated and/or if financial resources are being accumulated for principal and interest payments maturing in future years.[3]

This means that governmental entities are not required to use debt service funds unless there is a legal or contractual obligation to do so. In other words, general long-term debt may be serviced through the general fund if there is no legal reason for establishing a debt service fund. However, using debt service funds to separate general long-term debt principal and interest payments from the general fund is a good financial management practice and probably most prudent.

Only long-term debt recorded in the general long-term debt nonfund account should be serviced through debt service funds. Furthermore, unless there is a legal reason to maintain separate debt service funds, all general long-term obligations of a government may be serviced through one debt service fund.

This chapter focuses on the use of debt service funds to account for principal and interest payments on general long-term debt obligations. The remainder of this chapter is organized as follows:

- Types of debt instruments
- Expenditure recognition
- Accounting for debt service fund transactions
- Reporting for debt service funds
- Special Assessments
- Reporting for special assessment debt service funds
- Extinguishment of debt
- Disclosure requirements

## 6.1 Types of Debt Instruments

Debt transactions take on many different forms. These different forms or "types" of debt have unique characteristics and legal implications. The following summary of debt instruments does not present a comprehensive discussion of the topic; it is simply a summary as such. For a more detailed discussion of debt instruments, see *Black's Law Dictionary* or the *Merriam-Webster Dictionary of Law.*

A *lease* is a written agreement between two parties that conveys the use of real or personal property for a specified period of time.[4] Government lease contracts are subject to the capital lease requirements adopted from FASB Statement No. 13, *Accounting for Leases*.[5] An important issue in accounting for leases is the distinction between a capital lease and an operating lease. From the lessee's standpoint, operating leases are like renting capital assets. That is, the lessee does not record a leased asset or lease liability; the lessee records an operating expense for the amount of each lease payment. The lessor keeps the leased asset on his or her books and maintains the rights and obligations of owning the leased asset. Although many leases are operating leases, a capital lease is any lease agreement that meets any one of four criteria: (1) The lease transfers title of the leased asset to the lessee. (2) The lease contains a bargain purchase option. (3) The lease term is 75% or more of the estimated useful life of the lease asset. (4) The present value of the lease payments is 90% or more of the market value of the leased asset.[6] In effect, *capital lease* contracts are a form of long-term borrowing.

*Loans* are written two-party agreements involving advances of money and a promise by the borrower to repay the principal sum with interest.[7] *Notes* are unilateral instruments whereby the borrower promises to pay a sum of money (usually at interest) to the lender.[8] These agreements may have a single maturity date, or they may mature periodically. The primary difference between loans and notes is the degree of negotiability. Loans are ordinary contracts, and notes are negotiable instruments that can be transferred (exchanged like money) to a third party free of personal defenses existing between the original contracting parties as long as the transferee is a "holder in due course." This transferability is not possible under an assignment of ordinary contracts. To qualify as a holder, one must possess bearer paper or order paper that has been properly endorsed. A holder in due course must first be a holder who "takes the instrument by negotiation, for value, in good faith, and without notice that it is overdue or has been dishonored or of any defense against or claim to it on the part of any person."[9] Another very important aspect of negotiability is instrument form. If the instrument is order paper (three-party paper), it must first be endorsed by the payee and then delivered to a subsequent party to be negotiated. However, if the instrument is bearer paper (two-party paper), only delivery of the instrument is needed for negotiation. Instruments that are neither bearer paper nor order paper are nonnegotiable.

A *warrant* is an order by the drawer authorizing the payment of a particular sum of money.[10] According to *Black's Law Dictionary*, a warrant is

A command of a council, board, or official whose duty it is to pass upon the validity and determine the amount of claim against the municipality, to the treasurer to pay money out of any funds in the municipal treasury, which are or may become available for the purpose specified, to a designated person whose claim therefor[e] has been duly adjusted and allowed.[11]

The difference between a warrant and a bond is negotiability. Warrants are not negotiable; however, *bonds* are negotiable securities that obligate the issuer to pay principal plus interest to the bondholder.[12] A formal written document, an "indenture," specifies the rights of bondholders for a particular bond issue. Governments often use bond proceeds to finance the acquisition and/or construction of major capital assets. Thus, most bond issues are for millions of dollars, and the duration of such issues is for an extended period of time (10 to 25 years). The principal on *term bonds* is repayable at a single maturity date, with interest paid periodically. The principal and interest on *serial bonds* is repayable in equal annual installments over the life of the issue. *General obligation bonds* pledge the full faith and credit of the government to repay the debt. *Revenue bonds* pledge future revenues generated by a specific activity or group of activities supported by the bond proceeds. *Refunding bonds* are issued to retire outstanding bonds. Refunding bond proceeds may be used to consummate a "current refunding" or an "advance refunding." Bond refundings are discussed further in the "Extinguishment of Debt" section of this chapter.

## 6.2 Expenditure Recognition

Although expenditures are usually recognized when incurred by the government, there is a major exception when it comes to general long-term debt. The GASB pronounces that debt service on formal debt issues (such as bonds and capital leases) generally should be recognized as a governmental-fund liability and expenditure when due (matured)—with optional additional accrual under certain conditions, as interpreted in section 1600.121 of the *Codification*.[13]

This nonaccrual of debt service expenditures at year-end is in keeping with the current financial resources measurement focus. That is, the accrual of future debt service payments could cause the fund financial statements to be misleading, since future—not current—financial resources will be used to make such payments.

However, if current financial resources accumulated in a debt service fund are to be used for payment of principal and interest due within 30 days of the fiscal year end, the total debt service payment (principal and interest) *may* be accrued in the debt service fund, and the debt principal may be removed from the general long-term liabilities nonfund account. The GASB indicates that

A government has "provided" financial resources to a debt service fund if it has deposited in or transferred to that fund financial resources that are dedicated for payment of debt service. "Early in the following year" refers to short time period—usually one to several days and not more than one month. Accrual of additional fund liability and expenditure is not permitted for (a) financial resources that are held in another governmental fund or (b) nondedicated financial resources transferred to a debt service fund at the discretion of management.[14]

# 6.3 Accounting for Debt Service Fund Transactions

When general long-term debt is issued, the proceeds from the issuance are recorded as "other financing sources" in the fund that is authorized to receive the funds, and the debt principal is recorded in the general long-term liabilities nonfund account. Any debt issue costs or discounts upon issuance are usually deducted from the issuance proceeds. Bond premiums, if any, are usually transferred to the appropriate debt service fund.

To illustrate the accounting for debt service fund transactions, assume the Anywhere Independent School District (ISD) authorizes a $21,000,000 general obligation serial bond issue to finance the construction of a new high school. The school building bonds are 20-year bonds and pay interest semiannually each May 15 and November 15. The bonds bear interest of 5% per year. The District's fiscal year end is August 31. The bonds are issued on November 15, 20X7, at 103 (no accrued interest). Bond principal of $1,050,000 is due annually, starting on November 15, 20X8. In addition, assume that the District typically transfers any premiums and any payments received for accrued interest to the appropriate debt service fund. The Board of Trustees also authorized a $525,000 transfer from the general fund to the school building debt service fund for the 20X8 fiscal year.

The governing body of Anywhere ISD adopted the following budget for the School Building Bonds Debt Service Fund for 20X8:

| Estimated Revenues and Transfers In: | |
|---|---|
| Investment Income | $60,000 |
| Transfers from General Fund | 525,000 |
| Transfers from Capital Projects Fund | 630,000 |
| | 1,215,000 |
| **Appropriations:** | |
| Bond Interest Payments | 525,000 |
| | |
| Budgeted Increase in Fund Balance | $690,000 |

### The following transactions occurred in the 20X8 fiscal year:

The GASB does not require governments to adopt a formal budget for debt service funds; however, many governments record budgets for these funds because of the importance of making debt service payments on time. Resources for paying debt service obligations often come from transfers from other funds, taxes, and interest earnings on investments. Therefore, the annual operating budget for a debt service fund normally consists of estimated revenues, other financing sources, and appropriations. The following entry records the debt service fund budget for the first year:

| | | |
|---|---|---|
| Estimated Revenues–Investment Income | $60,000 | |
| Estimated Other Financing Sources–Transfers In ($525,000 transfer from general fund + $630,000 transfer from capital projects fund) | 1,155,000 | |
| Appropriations–Debt Service–Interest | | $525,000 |
| Unreserved Fund Balance (This is the budgeted increase in fund balance.) | | 690,000 |
| To record 20X8 budget. | | |

If the bond premium is transferred from the capital projects fund, the debt service fund entry is:

| | | |
|---|---|---|
| Cash | $630,000 . | |
| Other Financing Sources–Transfers From– Capital Projects Fund ($21,000,000 × 103% selling price – $21,000,000 face value, or simply $21,000,000 × 3%) | | $630,000 |
| To record cash received from the capital projects fund. | | |

If the debt service fund receives a $525,000 transfer from the general fund on May 1 to provide for the May 15 interest payment, the debt service fund entry is:

| | | |
|---|---|---|
| Cash | $525,000 | |
| Other Financing Sources–Transfers From– General Fund | | $525,000 |
| To record cash received from the general fund. | | |

When the May 15 interest is legally due, and assuming it is paid, the required entry is:

| Expenditures–Debt Service–Interest | $525,000 | |
|---|---|---|
| Cash | | $525,000 |
| To record the first semiannual interest payment. | | |

Assume the investment interest earned for the 20X8 year was $34,800. The necessary entry is:

| Cash | $34,800 | |
|---|---|---|
| Revenues–Investment Income | | $34,800 |
| To record investment interest received. | | |

At fiscal year end, August 31, 20X8, the closing entries are:

| Appropriations–Debt Service–Interest | $525,000 | |
|---|---|---|
| Unreserved Fund Balance | 690,000 | |
| Estimated Revenues–Investment Income | | $60,000 |
| Estimated Other Financing Sources–Transfers In | | 1,155,000 |
| To reverse 20X8 budget. | | |

| Revenues–Investment Income | $34,800 | |
|---|---|---|
| Other Financing Sources–Transfers From–Capital Projects Fund | 630,000 | |
| Other Financing Sources–Transfers From–General Fund | 525,000 | |
| Expenditures–Debt Service–Interest | | $525,000 |
| Unreserved Fund Balance | | 664,800 |
| To close the accounts at the end of 20X8. | | |

**The following transactions occurred in the 20X9 fiscal year:**
The District's property tax levy for the 20X9 fiscal year contains $948,000 allocable to the debt service fund, of which 2% is estimated to be uncollectible. The Board of Trustees also authorized a $1,000,000 transfer from the general fund to the school building debt service fund.

The governing body of Anywhere ISD adopted the following budget for the School Building Bonds Debt Service Fund for 20X9:

| | |
|---|---:|
| **Estimated Revenues and Transfers In:** | |
| Property Taxes | $948,000 |
| Investment Income | 50,000 |
| Transfers from General Fund | 1,000,000 |
| | 1,998,000 |
| | |
| **Appropriations:** | |
| Bond Principal Payments | 1,050,000 |
| Bond Interest Payments | 1,023,750 |
| | 2,073,750 |
| | |
| Budgeted Decrease in Fund Balance | ($ 75,750) |

[a] ($1,023,750 = $525,000 + $498,750, where:
  $525,000 = $21,000,000 principal × 5% × 6/12 for
    11/15/20X8 Interest
  $498,750 = $19,950,000 principal × 5% × 6/12 for
    5/15/20X9 Interest)

To record the budget for the second year, the entry on September 1 is:

| | | |
|---|---|---|
| Estimated Revenues–Property Taxes | $948,000 | |
| Estimated Revenues–Investment Income | 50,000 | |
| Estimated Other Financing Sources–Transfers In | 1,000,000 | |
| Unreserved Fund Balance (This is the budgeted decrease in fund balance.) | 75,750 | |
| Appropriations–Debt Service–Principal | | $1,050,000 |
| Appropriations–Debt Service–Interest | | 1,023,750 |
| To record 20X9 budget. | | |

When the property tax is levied on October 1, 20X8, the required debt service fund entry is:

| | | |
|---|---|---|
| Property Taxes Receivable–Current | $948,000 | |
| Allowance for Uncollectible Property Taxes–Current ($948,000 property tax levy × 2% estimate for uncollectibles) | | $18,960 |
| Revenues–Property Taxes | | 929,040 |
| To record 20X9 debt service portion of the property tax levy. | | |

Assume the tax collections for October were $470,000. The necessary debt service fund entry is:

| | | |
|---|---|---|
| Cash | $470,000 | |
| Property Taxes Receivable–Current | | $470,000 |
| To record cash received from tax collections. | | |

If the debt service fund receives a $1,000,000 transfer from the general fund on November 1 to help provide for the November 15 principal and interest payment, the debt service fund entry is:

| | | |
|---|---|---|
| Cash | $1,000,000 | |
| Other Financing Sources–Transfers From–General Fund | | $1,000,000 |
| To record cash received from the general fund. | | |

If the District pays the bond principal and interest on November 15 when due, the following entry is required:

| | | |
|---|---|---|
| Expenditures–Debt Service–Principal | $1,050,000 | |
| Expenditures–Debt Service–Interest | 525,000 | |
| Cash | | $1,575,000 |
| To record annual principal payment and semiannual interest payment. | | |

On February 1, taxes levied but not collected become delinquent. If tax collections from November through January totaled $445,000, the required entry is:

| | | |
|---|---|---|
| Cash | $445,000 | |
| Property Taxes Receivable–Current | | $445,000 |
| To record cash received from tax collections. | | |

To reclassify the remainder of the property taxes, the entry is:

| | | |
|---|---|---|
| Property Taxes Receivable–Delinquent<br>($948,000 Current Property Taxes Receivable –<br>$915,000 Tax Collections, where:<br>$915,000 = $470,000 October collections +<br>$445,000 November–January collections) | $33,000 | |
| Allowance for Uncollectible Property<br>Taxes–Current | 18,960 | |
| Property Taxes Receivable–Current | | $33,000 |
| Allowance for Uncollectible Property Taxes–<br>Delinquent | | 18,960 |
| To reclassify property taxes now delinquent. | | |

When the May 15 interest is legally due, and assuming it is paid, the required entry is:

| | | |
|---|---|---|
| Expenditures–Debt Service–Interest<br>($19,950,000 principal × 5% × 6/12) | $498,750 | |
| Cash | | $498,750 |
| To record a semiannual interest payment. | | |

Assume the investment interest earned for the 20X9 year was $29,148. The necessary entry is:

| | | |
|---|---|---|
| Cash | $29,148 | |
| Revenues–Investment Income | | $29,148 |
| To record investment interest received. | | |

At fiscal year end, August 31, 20X9, the closing entries are:

| | | |
|---|---|---|
| Appropriations–Debt Service–Principal | $1,050,000 | |
| Appropriations–Debt Service–Interest | 1,023,750 | |
| Estimated Revenues–Property Taxes | | $948,000 |
| Estimated Revenues–Investment Income | | 50,000 |
| Estimated Other Financing Sources–Transfers In | | 1,000,000 |
| Unreserved Fund Balance | | 75,750 |
| To reverse 20X9 budget. | | |

| | | |
|---|---|---|
| Revenues–Property Taxes | $929,040 | |
| Revenues–Investment Income | 29,148 | |
| Other Financing Sources–Transfers From–General Fund | 1,000,000 | |
| Unreserved Fund Balance | 115,562 | |
| Expenditures–Debt Service–Principal | | $1,050,000 |
| Expenditures–Debt Service–Interest | | 1,023,750 |
| To close the accounts at the end of 20X9. | | |

# 6.4 Reporting for Debt Service Funds

There are two annual financial statements required for debt service funds:

(1) Balance Sheet
(2) Statement of Revenues, Expenditures, and Changes in Fund Balance

Although GASB suggests that

> The comprehensive annual financial report (CAFR) should include budgetary comparison schedules for individual nonmajor special revenue funds and other governmental funds of the primary government (including its blended component units).[15]

The *Codification* specifically excludes these funds from being presented in the basic financial statements or in the required supplementary information (RSI).

```
┌────────────────────────────────────────────────────────────┐
│              Anywhere Independent School District            │
│                     Debt Service Fund                        │
│                 20X8 School Building Bonds                    │
│                      Balance Sheet                           │
│                     August 31, 20X8                          │
│                                                              │
│                         Assets                               │
│                                                              │
│    Cash ................................................. $664,800 │
│                                                              │
│             Liabilities and Fund Balance                     │
│                                                              │
│    Unreserved Fund Balance................................ $664,800 │
└────────────────────────────────────────────────────────────┘
```

**Figure 6.1    Debt service fund balance sheet for year one.**

Budgetary comparisons should be presented for the general fund and for each major special revenue fund that has a legally adopted annual budget. Governments are encouraged to present such budgetary comparison information in schedules as part of RSI.[16]

Thus, any debt service fund budgetary comparison schedules presented in a CAFR would have to be included as other supplementary information (OSI).

The Anywhere ISD debt service fund balance sheets at the end of 20X8 and 20X9 are presented in Figures 6.1 and 6.3, respectively. The District's operating statements for both years are depicted in Figures 6.2 and 6.4.

# 6.5  Special Assessments

Special assessments are often levied against property owners who are expected to benefit by the acquisition or construction of capital projects, such as streets, sewers, curbs, sidewalks, lighting, recreation facilities, etc. According to GASB,

The local government then acts on behalf of those property owners by organizing a special assessment district, performing the project (often using private contractors), overseeing and approving the progress and completion of the project, providing or arranging for financing, and collecting the assessments to pay any debt incurred to finance the project.[17]

The accounting for any long-term debt incurred for such capital improvement special assessments depends on the government's financial obligation. If the government is not obligated in any manner for the special assessment debt, the related debt service payments are accounted for in an agency fund. Otherwise, the debt service

Anywhere Independent School District
Debt Service Fund
20X8 School Building Bonds
Statement of Revenues, Expenditures, and Changes in Fund Balance
For the Year Ended August 31, 20X8

Revenues:
Investment Income...................................................... $664,800

Expenditures:
Debt Service–Interest................................................. 525,000

Excess of Expenditures over Revenues.......................... (409,200)

Other Financing Sources:
Transfers From–Capital Projects Fund....................... 630,000
Transfers From–General Fund.................................... 525,000
Total Other Financing Sources.............................. 1,155,000

Net Change in Fund Balance.......................................... 664,800

Fund Balance, September 1............................................. –
Fund Balance, August 31................................................ $ 664,800

**Figure 6.2   Debt service fund operating statement for year one.**

Anywhere Independent School District
Debt Service Fund
20X8 School Building Bonds
Balance Sheet
August 31, 20X9

**Assets**

Cash ............................................................................. $535,198
Property Taxes Receivable–Delinquent, Net................ 14,040
Total Assets ............................................................. $549,238

**Liabilities and Fund Balance**

Unreserved Fund Balance.............................................. $549,238

**Figure 6.3   Debt service fund balance sheet for year two.**

Anywhere Independent School District
Debt Service Fund
20X8 School Building Bonds
Statement of Revenues, Expenditures, and Changes in Fund Balance
For the Year Ended August 31, 20X9

| Revenues: | | |
|---|---|---|
| Property Taxes | $929,040 | |
| Investment Income | 29,148 | |
| Total Revenues | | $ 958,188 |
| | | |
| Expenditures: | | |
| Debt Service–Principal | 1,050,000 | |
| Debt Service–Interest | 1,023,750 | |
| Total Expenditures | | 2,073,750 |
| | | |
| Excess of Expenditures over Revenues | | (1,115,562) |
| | | |
| Other Financing Sources: | | |
| Transfers From–General Fund | | 1,000,000 |
| | | |
| Net Change in Fund Balance | | (115,562) |
| | | |
| Fund Balance, September 1 | | 664,800 |
| Fund Balance, August 31 | | $ 549,238 |

**Figure 6.4   Debt service fund operating statement for year two.**

payments should be accounted for in a debt service fund or a proprietary fund, depending on the resulting capital asset's relationship to the proprietary funds. The GASB has provided guidance on determining the extent of a government's liability for special assessment debt by stating that

> A government is obligated in some manner for special assessment debt if (a) it is legally obligated to assume all or part of the debt in the event of default or (b) the government *may* take certain actions to assume secondary liability for all or part of the debt—*and* the government takes, or has given indications that it will take, those actions.[18]

To illustrate the accounting for special assessment debt service fund transactions, assume that Anywhere City, in accordance with all pertinent laws and regulations, authorized a special assessment project for the construction of neighborhood sidewalks and indicated that any debt incurred for this project would be secondarily secured by the full faith and credit of the city. Anywhere City also agreed to contribute $120,000 from the city's general fund to the neighborhood sidewalks debt service fund to be used for the first principal and interest payment on the special assessment bonds. The remaining debt payments are to be recovered by levying assessments against property owners within the special assessment district. The city council duly authorized a bond issue not to exceed $500,000.

Special assessment bonds of $500,000 were issued at par on August 1, 20X7. The bond proceeds were properly recorded in the capital projects fund, and the associated long-term liability was properly recorded in the general long-term liabilities nonfund account. The special assessment bonds were 4%, five-year bonds with interest and $100,000 of principal due annually, starting on August 1, 20X8. The City's fiscal year end is December 31.

The project was completed on May 31, 20X8, at the budgeted cost of $620,000, and special assessments of $500,000 were levied on benefited properties. The city council duly authorized the transfer of $120,000 from the general fund to the neighborhood sidewalks debt service fund. In an agreement reached between the city council and the citizens of the special assessment district, one-fifth of the levy is due on June 1, 20X8, without interest. Beginning with June 1, 20X9, one-fifth of the total levy and 10% interest on the beginning uncollected balance are due each of the next four years.

Omitting the required debt service fund budgetary entries, as shown earlier in this chapter, the following transactions would be made to the debt service fund during the first year. Note that there were no transactions for the special assessment debt service fund in 20X7. Thus, there would be no financial statements to be reported for the neighborhood sidewalks debt service fund prior to 20X8.

**The following transactions occurred in the 20X8 fiscal year:**

Assuming that one-fifth of the $500,000 special assessment levy meets the availability criterion when levied on June 1, 20X8, the required debt service fund entry is:

| | | |
|---|---|---|
| Assessment Receivable–Current ($500,000 × 1/5) | $100,000 | |
| Assessment Receivable–Deferred | 400,000 | |
| Revenues–Assessments | | $100,000 |
| Deferred Revenues–Assessments | | 400,000 |
| To record levy of special assessments. | | |

If the debt service fund received the $120,000 transfer from the general fund on July 1 to provide for the August 1 principal and interest payment, the debt service fund entry is:

| Cash | $120,000 | |
|---|---|---|
| Other Financing Sources–Transfers From– General Fund | | $120,000 |
| To record cash received from General Fund. | | |

If the City pays the bond principal and interest on August 1 when due, the following entry is required:

| Expenditures–Debt Service–Principal | $100,000 | |
|---|---|---|
| Expenditures–Debt Service–Interest ($500,000 × 4%) | 20,000 | |
| Cash | | $120,000 |
| To record annual principal and interest payment. | | |

Assume the special assessment collections for 20X8 were $97,500, the necessary debt service fund entry is:

| Cash | $97,500 | |
|---|---|---|
| Assessments Receivable–Current | | $97,500 |
| To record cash received from tax collections. | | |

If the City invested $90,000 of special assessment funds with an approved investment pool, the entry would be:

| Investments | $90,000 | |
|---|---|---|
| Cash | | $90,000 |
| To record cash investments. | | |

Assuming that all uncollected assessments for 20X8 will be collected within the first 60 days of 20X9, the reclassification entry at year-end is:

| Assessments Receivable–Delinquent ($100,000 Assessment Receivable–Current & $97,500 Assessment Collections) | $2,500 | |
|---|---|---|
| Assessments Receivable–Current | | $2,500 |
| To reclassify special assessments now delinquent. | | |

At fiscal year end, December 31, 20X8, the budget balances would be reversed and the actual closing entries are:

| | | |
|---|---|---|
| Revenues–Assessments | $100,000 | |
| Other Financing Sources–Transfers From–General Fund | 120,000 | |
| Expenditures–Debt Service–Principal | | $100,000 |
| Expenditures–Debt Service–Interest | | 20,000 |
| Unreserved Fund Balance | | 100,000 |
| To close the accounts at the end of 20X8. | | |

## 6.6 Reporting for Special Assessment Debt Service Funds

Special assessment debt service funds have the same two basic financial statements (the balance sheet and the operating statement) as any other debt service fund. However, there is one unique feature about the special assessment balance sheet—deferred assessments receivable. In effect, the deferred assessments account is a noncurrent asset that does not conform to the flow of current financial resources measurement focus used by governmental funds. The GASB addresses this matter and points out that "[a]t the time of the levy, special assessments receivable should be recognized and should be offset by deferred revenue; deferred revenue should be reduced as the assessments become measurable and available."[19]

Figures 6.5 and 6.6 present the special assessment debt service fund balance sheet and operating statement, respectively, for the Anywhere City at the end of 20X8.

## 6.7 Extinguishment of Debt

The extinguishment of debt occurs when the state or local government (the debtor) is relieved from obligation. Debt may be extinguished at maturity, or prior to maturity. The GASB has elected to follow FASB Statement No. 76, *Extinguishment of Debt*, criteria for determining whether debt is considered to be extinguished for financial reporting purposes. According to FASB Statement No. 76, debt is considered to be extinguished when one of the following is met:

- The debtor pays the creditor and is relieved of all its obligations with respect to the debt.
- The debtor is legally released from being the primary obligor under the debt either judicially or by the creditor, and it is probable that the debtor will not be required to make future payments with respect to the debt under the guarantees.

```
┌─────────────────────────────────────────────────────────────┐
│                    Anywhere City                            │
│        Special Assessment Debt Service Fund                 │
│              Neighborhood Sidewalks                         │
│                  Balance Sheet                              │
│                December 31, 20X8                            │
│                                                             │
│                      Assets                                 │
│                                                             │
│ Cash ..................................................  $  7,500    │
│ Investments ..........................................     90,000    │
│ Assessments Receivable–Deferred ......................    400,000    │
│ Assessments Receivable–Delinquent ....................      2,500    │
│    Total Assets ......................................            $500,000 │
│                                                             │
│             Liabilities and Fund Balance                    │
│                                                             │
│ Liabilities:                                                │
│    Deferred Revenues–Assessments .....................       $400,000 │
│                                                             │
│ Unreserved Fund Balance...............................        100,000 │
│    Total Liabilities and Fund Balance ................        $500,000 │
└─────────────────────────────────────────────────────────────┘
```

**Figure 6.5   Special assessment debt service fund balance sheet.**

■ The debtor irrevocably places cash or other assets in a trust to be used solely for satisfying scheduled payments of both interest and principal of a specific obligation and the possibility that the debtor will be required to make future payments with respect to that debt is remote. In this circumstance, debt is extinguished even though the debtor is not legally released from being the primary obligor under the debt obligation.[20]

The extinguishment of general obligation long-term debt prior to its maturity is commonly known as refunding. According to the GASB

> Refundings involve the issuance of new debt whose proceeds are used to repay previously issued ("old") debt. The new debt proceeds may be used to repay the old debt immediately (a *current refunding*); or the new debt proceeds may be placed with an escrow agent and invested until they are used to pay principal and interest on the old debt at a future time (an *advanced refunding*).[21]

The GASB indicates that debt may be advance refunded to take advantage of lower interest rates, extend maturity dates, revise payment schedules, or remove or modify restrictions on old debt agreements.[22] Perhaps the most common method of refunding is advanced refunding, which, in effect, substitutes new debt for old

Anywhere City
Special Assessment Debt Service Fund
Neighborhood Sidewalks
Statement of Revenues, Expenditures, and Changes in Fund Balance
For the Year Ended December 31, 20X8

| | | |
|---|---:|---:|
| Revenues: | | |
| Assessments ................................................................ | | $100,000 |
| | | |
| Expenditures: | | |
| Debt Service–Principal ................................................. | 100,000 | |
| Debt Service–Interest ................................................... | 20,000 | |
| Total Expenditures ..................................................... | | 120,000 |
| | | |
| Excess of Expenditures over Revenues ......................... | | (20,000) |
| | | |
| Other Financing Sources: | | |
| Transfers From–General Fund ..................................... | | 120,000 |
| | | |
| Net Change in Fund Balance ........................................... | | 100,000 |
| | | |
| Fund Balance, January 1 ................................................. | | – |
| Fund Balance, December 31 ........................................... | | $100,000 |

**Figure 6.6   Special assessment debt service fund operating statement.**

debt. If the old debt is defeased, the governmental entity should replace the old debt with the new debt in its accounts and statements. The GASB states that

> Most advance refundings result in defeasance of debt. Defeasance of debt can be either legal or in substance. A *legal defeasance* occurs when debt is legally satisfied based on certain provisions in the debt instrument even though the debt is not actually paid. An *in-substance defeasance* occurs when debt is considered defeased for accounting and financial reporting purposes … even though a legal defeasance has not occurred. When debt is defeased, it is no longer reported as a liability on the face of the financial statements; only the new debt is reported as a liability.[23]

If an advance refunding does not result in defeasance of the old debt, the state or local government is required to maintain both the new debt and the old debt in its accounts and statements. Such a nondefeasance of old debt would double the amount of general long-term liabilities, and the amount placed in escrow would be reported as investments—escrow agent in the debt service fund.

# 6.8 Accounting for and Reporting of Debt Refundings

The accounting and reporting of debt refundings depends on whether the transaction relates to a governmental fund or a proprietary fund. Since the focus of this chapter is on debt service funds, this section will illustrate the refunding of general obligation debt. For accounting and disclosure standards related to proprietary fund debt refundings, see GASB Statement No. 23: *Accounting and Financial Reporting for Refundings of Debt Reported by Proprietary Activities.*

When accounting for a refunding, the proceeds from the new bond issue are recorded as Other Financing Sources, and any payments to the escrow agent from those proceeds are recorded as Other Financing Uses. Comparatively, payments to the escrow agent from all other sources are recorded as debt service expenditures. To illustrate, assume that Anywhere City issued new bonds to finance an in-substance defeasance of an old outstanding bond issue. The new bonds were sold at par, $18,000,000 (no accrued interest), and the bond underwriter withheld $25,000 of bond issuance costs. The town paid $19,000,000 to an irrevocable trust to defease in-substance $18,750,000 (par) of the old debt.

To record the new bond issue, the debt service fund entry would be:

| | | |
|---|---|---|
| Cash<br>($18,000,000 selling price & $25,000 bond underwriter fee) | $17,975,000 | |
| Expenditures–Debt Service–Bond Issuance Costs | 25,000 | |
|    Other Financing Sources–Refunding Bond<br>   Principal | | $18,000,000 |
| To record issuance of advance refunding bonds. | | |

Defeasance of the old debt is recorded with the following entry:

| | | |
|---|---|---|
| Other Financing Uses–Payments to Escrow Agent | $17,975,000 | |
| Expenditures–Debt Service–Payments to Escrow Agent<br>($19,000,000 trust payment – $17,975,000 refunding issue proceeds) | 1,025,000 | |
|    Cash | | $19,000,000 |
| To record payment to escrow agent to defease bonds. | | |

Assuming this transaction meets the in-substance defeasance criteria, the new debt would be recorded in the general long-term liabilities nonfund account, and the old debt would be removed from the town's books. Moreover, the advance refunding should be disclosed in the notes to the financial statements as follows.

All current and advanced refundings of general long-term debt should be reported in the governmental activities column of government-wide financial statements. General long-term debt refunding transactions reported in the entitywide statements should be reported in the same manner as refundings for proprietary funds. In other words, the GASB states that

> … the difference between the reacquisition price and the net carrying amount of the old debt should be deferred and amortized as a component of interest expense … over the remaining life of the old debt or the new debt, whichever is shorter. On the statement of net assets, this deferred amount should be reported as a deduction from or an addition to the new debt liability.[24]

## 6.9 Disclosure Requirements

The necessary disclosures about advance refundings are different for the year of the refunding and for subsequent years. In the year of the advance refunding, the governmental entity should provide a general description of the advance refunding, and, at a minimum, should disclose

> … (a) the difference between the cash flows required to service the old debt and the cash flows required to service the new debt and complete the refunding, and (b) the economic gain or loss resulting from the transaction.[25]

In all periods following an in-substance defeasance, the amount of defeased debt outstanding, if any, should be disclosed. This disclosure guidance is set forth in the GASB Codification Section D20.114.

The GASB also provides guidance for disclosing debt service requirements for general long-term debt obligations. In general, the following debt service requirements to maturity should be disclosed in the notes to the financial statements:

a. Principal and interest requirements to maturity, presented separately, for each of the five subsequent fiscal years and in five-year increments thereafter. Interest requirements for variable-rate debt should be determined using the rate in effect at the financial statement date.

b. The terms by which interest rates change for variable-rate debt.[26]

Furthermore, the GASB requires certain note disclosures about long-term debt and other long-term liabilities.

> Information about long-term liabilities should include both long-term debt (such as bonds, notes, loans, and leases payable) and other long-term liabilities (such as compensated absences, and claims and judgments). Information presented about long-term liabilities should include:
>
> a. Beginning- and end-of-year balances (regardless of whether prior-year data are presented on the face of the government-wide financial statements)
> b. Increases and decreases (separately presented)
> c. The portions of each item that are due within one year of the statement date
> d. Which governmental funds typically have been used to liquidate other long-term liabilities (such as compensated absences and pension liabilities) in prior years.[27]

## 6.10 Concluding Comments

This chapter focused on the use of debt service funds. Although general long-term debt may be serviced through the general fund, most governments use debt service funds "to account for the accumulation of resources for, and the payment of, general long-term debt principal and interest."[28] Only long-term debt (such as bonds, notes, loans, and leases payable) recorded in the general long-term debt nonfund account should be serviced through debt service funds.

## Endnotes

1. Governmental Accounting Standards Board, Codification of Governmental Accounting and Financial Reporting Standards as of June 30, 2005 (Norwalk, CT: GASB, 2005), sec. 1500.102.
2. Governmental Accounting Standards Board, *Codification of Governmental Accounting and Financial Reporting Standards as of June 30, 2005* (Norwalk, CT: GASB, 2005), sec. 1500.104.
3. Ibid., sec. 1300.107.
4. Bryan A. Garner, ed., *A Handbook of Basic Law Terms* (St. Paul, MN: West, 1999), p. 121.
5. GASB *Codification*, sec. L20.109.
6. Financial Accounting Standards Board, *Current Text: Accounting Standards as of June 1, 2005* (Norwalk, CT: FASB, 2005), sec. L10.103.

7. Garner, p. 129.
8. Ibid., p. 147.
9. The American Law Institute and the National Conference of Commissioners on Uniform State Laws, *Uniform Commercial Code* (Philadelphia, PA: ALI-NCCUSL, 2001), sec. 3-302.
10. Garner, p. 229.
11. Henry C. Black, *Black's Law Dictionary*, 4th ed. (St. Paul, MN: West, 1968), p. 1756.
12. The Wikimedia Foundation, *Wikipedia: The Free Encyclopedia* (St. Petersburg, FL: Wikimedia, 2006) http://en.wikipedia.org/wiki/Bond, accessed March 24, 2006.
13. GASB *Codification*, sec. 1600.120.
14. GASB *Codification*, sec. 1600.121.
15. GASB *Codification*, sec. 2400.105.
16. Ibid., sec. 2400.102.
17. Ibid., sec. S40.102.
18. GASB *Codification*, sec. S40.115.
19. GASB *Codification*, sec. S40.118.
20. FASB *Statement of Financial Accounting Standards No. 76, Extinguishment of Debt* (Norwalk, CT: FASB, 1983).
21. GASB *Codification*, sec. D20.102.
22. Ibid., sec. D20.104.
23. Ibid., sec. D20.102.
24. GASB *Codification*, sec. D20.108.
25. GASB *Codification*, sec. D20.111.
26. Ibid., sec. 1500.118.
27. Ibid., sec. 2300.114.
28. Ibid., sec. 1300.107.

*Chapter 7*

# Capital Projects Funds

## Barbara Chaney
*University of Montana, School of Business Administration*

## Contents

7.1   Budgetary Accounting in Capital Project Funds ........................................ 216
7.2   Construction Expenditures ................................................................. 218
7.3   Issuance of Capital Debt .................................................................... 218
7.4   Investments and Arbitrage.................................................................. 219
7.5   Grants .......................................................................................... 220
7.6   Capital Contributions ....................................................................... 220
7.7   Interfund Transfers .......................................................................... 221
7.8   Special Assessments.......................................................................... 221
7.9   Fund Balance .................................................................................. 222
7.10  Financial Reporting .......................................................................... 222
7.11  Budgetary Reporting......................................................................... 224
7.12  Summary ...................................................................................... 224
Exhibit Financial Reports: The City of Raleigh, North Carolina...................... 225

Governments are often responsible for financing and managing long-term capital projects that result in ownership of general capital assets. For example, a government is usually the principal investor in local infrastructure such as roads and bridges, and a frequent builder of public projects such as county courthouses and community centers. The accounting for these immense capital projects should reflect the government's awesome stewardship responsibilities. Capital Projects Funds (CPF) should be used "to account for financial resources to be used for the acquisition or construction of major capital facilities (other than those financed by proprietary

funds or in trust funds for individuals, private organizations, or other governments). Capital outlays financed from general obligation bond proceeds should be
accounted for through a capital projects fund" [GASB Codification 1300.106].

A CPF is a type of governmental fund with a measurement focus on current
financial resources and a modified accrual basis of accounting. It is similar to a
special revenue fund in that it receives a source of financing that is dedicated for
a governmental purpose. The "special revenue" is isolated in a fund for stewardship purposes so that its expenditure can be monitored. In the case of a CPF, the
intended use of the financing is capital construction or acquisition. A government
may maintain just one CPF for all its ongoing capital projects. However, it may be
useful for operational monitoring purposes to maintain a separate fund for each
ongoing project.*

The CPF differs from other governmental fund types in that it usually has a
project orientation rather than a period orientation. The capital projects are typically
long-term, with financing achieved at the beginning of the project and expenditures following in subsequent periods. Governments typically plan and evaluate the
activity in the CPF by project, rather than by period. Therefore, the fund accounting system must capture and report financial resource and expenditure information
for the current period and in total, as well as an ongoing fund financial position
[GASB Codification 1300.124]. This would be most reasonably accomplished by
establishing a "fund" for a specific capital project at its origination and leaving it
open until the completion of the project.

## 7.1 Budgetary Accounting in Capital Project Funds

The fund accounting system need not capture the same level of budgetary detail
necessary for the general fund and special revenue funds because capital projects
are not usually controlled with appropriation budgets. Instead, capital projects are
managed within the capital budgeting process. Spending is authorized indirectly
via approval of project financings and contract authorizations to independent contractors. Therefore, there is no need to record estimated revenues and appropriations. Full or partial budgetary account integration would only be necessary in a
CPF where a government's labor force is constructing the capital project or where
numerous projects are being financed through a single capital projects fund [GASB

---

* GASB Codification 1300.117 states that some governments may need more than one fund
of a certain type, specifically naming capital projects funds. However, GASB Codification
1300.118 also states that the minimum number of separate funds necessary should be used to
avoid inflexibility and undue complexity.

Codification 1700.119]. In the former circumstance the government finances the expenditures with scarce current revenues that are normally subject to appropriation budget procedures. In the latter circumstance it becomes difficult to adequately provide stewardship over multiple projects within a single fund without using traditional budgeting techniques.

Although traditional budgetary accounting is not normally employed in CPF, encumbrance accounting is useful to monitor the progress of project contracts and open purchase orders. An encumbrance represents a commitment to a contract with an external party as opposed to commitment of a portion of an appropriation budget. Upon signing a contract or issuing a purchase order, the government would record an Encumbrance and an offsetting Fund Balance Reserved for Encumbrances. When a progress billing or goods are received, the Encumbrance and Reserve would be reversed and replaced with an Expenditure and liability for payment to the contractor or vendor.

For example, consider fictional White County. The county commissioners authorized a $9 million project to construct a bridge across the White River and established a White River Bridge CPF. At the conclusion of the bidding process, River Run Construction was awarded the project and the County signed a contract for $8.9 million. When the contract was signed, an encumbrance was likely recorded in the CPF as follows:

| | | |
|---|---|---|
| Encumbrances | $8.9 | |
| Fund Balance Reserved for Encumbrances | | $8.9 |

Subsequently, when White County receives a $3 million progress billing from River Run, it will reverse the encumbrance and replace it with a capital expenditure.

| | | |
|---|---|---|
| Fund Balance Reserved for Encumbrances | $3 | |
| Encumbrances | | $3 |
| Capital Outlay Expenditures | $3 | |
| Contracts Payable | | $3 |

Encumbrances is a temporary budgetary account that is normally closed at the end of a fiscal reporting period. Open encumbrances are then reestablished with a reversing entry at the beginning of the subsequent fiscal year. However, because CPF are not usually subject to an appropriation budget, it is not necessary to close the Encumbrances account. The CPF will be evaluated as the capital project(s) are completed, rather than periodically.

## 7.2 Construction Expenditures

The construction projects accounted for in a CPF are long-term by nature. However, contractors require interim payments for construction in progress. It is industry practice to allow a construction client to "hold out" a retained percentage of the progress billing that will not be paid until the project is completed to the client's satisfaction. Until the contractor completes the final "punch list" the total contract price is not paid. White County would likely pay only a portion of the progress, billing it as received from River Run. By isolating the Retained Percentage in a liability account separate from Contracts Payable it is clear that the liability is not currently due and payable but contingent upon a future event.

| Contracts Payable | $3 | |
| Cash | | $2.7 |
| Retained Percentage | | $.3 |

## 7.3 Issuance of Capital Debt

A capital project usually requires significant external financing. Often, a government issues long-term bonds to finance the project. As a governmental fund type, a CPF would not record a long-term liability for the bonds. Instead, the proceeds would be recognized as an Other Financing Source. The face value of the bonds must be recognized separately from any bond premiums (or bond discount) [GASB Codification 1300.108]. Thus, bonds issued at a premium would result in the recognition of two Other Financing Sources—one for the face amount and another for the premium. Typically, bond indentures require that bond premiums not be used for the capital project but instead be remitted to a bond sinking or debt service fund for the eventual repayment of bond principal and/or interest. Therefore, the CPF would record a nonreciprocal transfer out to a debt service fund for the amount of the premium.

If underwriting fees are deducted from the proceeds of a bond issuance, it should not be deducted from the amount of Other Financing Sources recognized. Instead, the underwriting fees should be recognized as an expenditure in the CPF [GASB Codification 1300.110].

An anomalous situation occurs when bonds are issued at a discount. Again, the amount of the discount should not be deducted from Other Financing Sources. Instead, it should be recognized as an Other Financing Use. A government issuing bonds at a discount may be faced with a financing shortfall for its capital project and be required to obtain additional financing from other sources, such as transfers from other funds within the government or external capital grants. For example, if

White County had issued bonds with a face value of $9 million for $8.75 million and also had underwriting fees of $.1 million, it will not have enough cash to pay its contractor.

| | | |
|---|---|---|
| Cash | $8.65 | |
| Underwriting Expenditures | $.1 | |
| Other Financing Uses—Bond Discount | $.25 | |
| Other Financing Sources—Bond Proceeds | | $9 |

Governments sometimes issue short-term bond anticipation notes (BANs) to finance initial construction of capital projects. The loans bridge the initiation of construction with the receipt of construction bond proceeds. BANs are usually secured by the proceeds from unissued long-term construction bonds. If the refinancing arrangement is legally viable and all parties are in a position to consummate the refinancing, the BANs can be treated as long-term debt for financial reporting purposes.* The result is that BANs proceeds will be presented as an Other Financing Source on the operating statement rather than as a liability on the CPF balance sheet. When the BANs are subsequently replaced with long-term bonds, the transaction should be recorded as a debt refunding.

## 7.4 Investments and Arbitrage

Governments can avoid issuing BANs if they issue long-term construction debt prior to initiation of construction. The government pays an artificially low interest cost on the debt because the interest revenue to the investor is exempt from income taxes. There may be a temptation to arbitrage the bond proceeds prior to their use for construction costs. However, governments are precluded by federal legislation from earning inappropriate investment revenue on tax-exempt debt proceeds. There are specific provisions in the Internal Revenue Code that specify what level of arbitrage is acceptable if bond proceeds are spent within a certain period of time. In general, however, governments cannot earn a higher return on invested bond proceeds than they are paying as interest costs. Violating arbitrage rules could result in a continuum of consequences from rebating the arbitrage profits to the IRS to paying interest and penalties to losing tax-exempt status of debt.

---

* GASB Codification Section B50.101 repeats the FASB Statement No. 6 criteria for determining when a short-term liability may be considered long-term for reporting purposes.

## 7.5 Grants

Grants received by a CPF would likely be considered capital as opposed to operating. In the CPF financial statements the grant would be recognized as revenue by its source—grant revenue or intergovernmental revenue. In the government-wide financial statements the grant would be considered a program revenue categorized as capital grants and contributions. GASB 33 [GASB Codification N50] prescribes the recognition criteria for revenues from nonexchange transactions, such as grants. Revenue and assets should not be recognized until the recipient has met all eligibility requirements.

The GASB makes clear that a purpose restriction is not an eligibility requirement [GASB Codification N50.111]. Only time requirements and contingencies that must be fulfilled by the recipient constitute eligibility requirements. One example of a contingency is a donor's requirement that a recipient generate matching funds prior to becoming eligible to receive grant funds. Another common eligibility requirement is inherent in reimbursement-based or expenditure-driven grants. A recipient must spend monies for the intended purpose and provide documentation to support its reimbursement request before it is eligible to receive grant dollars. Therefore, grant revenue should not be recognized until the recipient fulfills its obligation. If a recipient receives cash from the grantor prior to meeting its eligibility requirement, it must defer the revenue until the requirement is met.

For example, if White County was awarded a $250,000 reimbursement-based federal grant for paving the bridge, it would not recognize the revenue until it spent the money to pave the bridge. If the county drew down a cash advance on the grant in the amount of $50,000, it would defer revenue recognition.

| Cash | $.05 | |
|---|---|---|
| Deferred Grant Revenue | | $.05 |

In the fund financial statements there is another revenue recognition issue because the CPF uses the financial resources measurement focus and modified accrual basis of accounting. Thus, revenue must be both measurable and available to be recognized. Every government must provide a working definition of when the revenues will be available to finance current expenditures. The GASB dictates a definition of 60 days beyond fiscal year-end for property taxes but does not prescribe a specific definition of "available" for any other revenues.

## 7.6 Capital Contributions

Another financing source for capital projects is developers. Governments often charge real estate developers impact fees or other charges to offset the cost of street, sidewalk, and other improvements for new developments. The fees are a result of an imposed nonexchange transaction. Assets should be recognized in the period when an enforceable legal claim to the fees arises or when received, whichever occurs first. Revenue should be recognized at the same time, unless there is a time restriction for using the fees. With time restrictions, revenue should be recognized when the fees are required to be used or first permitted to be used [GASB Codification N50.114-.115].

## 7.7 Interfund Transfers

A CPF may receive a portion of the financing for a capital project from another fund within the government. Nonreciprocal transfers from one fund to another are accounted for as Other Financing Sources in the receiving fund and as an Other Financing Use in the disbursing fund.

At the conclusion of a project that was accounted for in a CPF established solely for the project, the CPF is dissolved. There may be resources remaining in the fund that must be disbursed appropriately. Oftentimes bond indentures stipulate that residual resources must be transferred to a debt service fund for the eventual repayment of debt principal and/or interest. In the absence of specific requirements, a CPF may transfer its residual balances to its General Fund.

For example, assume that White County completed its bridge at a cost of $8.8 million rather the contract price of $8.9 million because of construction savings. Further assume that all contracts have been paid, and the CPF is left with $.1 million in cash. White County would close all temporary accounts and transfer remaining cash and fund balance to the debt service fund.

| | | |
|---|---|---|
| Other Financing Use—Transfer to DSF | $.1 | |
| Cash | | $.1 |
| (To transfer remaining balances to DSF.) | | |

| | | |
|---|---|---|
| Other Financing Sources—Bond Proceeds | $9 | |
| Grant Revenue | $.25 | |
| Underwriting Expenditures | | $.1 |
| Other Financing Uses—Bond Discount | | $.25 |
| Other Financing Uses—Transfer to DSF | | $.1 |
| Capital Outlay Expenditures | | $8.8 |
| (To close temporary accounts in the CPF.) | | |

## 7.8 Special Assessments

Some capital projects are financed with special assessments. They are undertaken to benefit only a subset of the government's constituency. The government will likely issue debt to finance such projects. The debt might be general obligation (GO) debt backed by the full faith and credit of the government, debt for which the government has no legal liability, or debt for which the government is obligated in some manner. The property owners who directly benefit are assessed an amount to fund the debt service payments.

The accounting issues are rather straightforward for the construction phase of special assessment projects. Construction expenditures should be accounted for in a CPF, regardless of whether the government is obligated in some manner for the special assessment debt [GASB Codification S40.118-119]. The accounting for the proceeds from the debt depends upon whether the government is obligated in some manner. If there is an obligation, the proceeds should be recorded as an Other Financing Source from bond proceeds in the CPF. If there is no obligation, the proceeds should be reported as an Other Financing Source from capital contributions from property owners. The subsequent collection of special assessments and payment of debt service does not occur in the CPF. If the government is obligated in some manner, the transactions are recorded in a debt service fund. If the government is not obligated for the debt, the transactions are recorded in an agency fund.

## 7.9 Fund Balance

An issue particularly relevant to CPF is currently being addressed by the GASB. In its fund balance reporting project, the GASB has tentatively concluded that only net resources that are legally restricted for a purpose that is not clearly distinguished by the purpose of the fund itself should be reported as Reserved Fund Balance. For example, the White River Bridge CPF should report any net resources that are restricted by the bond indenture as Unreserved Fund Balance. The definition of Unreserved Fund Balance within the context of a fund created for a specific purpose is that the net resources are clearly restricted for the named purpose. If, however, the bridge construction project were accounted for in a Highway and Bridges CPF that encompasses numerous road projects, it would be appropriate to report the project's net assets as Fund Balance Reserved for Capital Construction. The context of the Highway and Bridges fund is too broad to assume all net resources are restricted for capital construction.

## 7.10 Financial Reporting

All CPF that meet the definition of a major fund should be presented in the governmental fund financial statements.* Each major governmental fund is presented in a

---

* The determination of what funds are major is largely a size issue. Assets, liabilities, revenues, and expenditures of an individual fund are evaluated in comparison to totals for all governmental funds and to totals for the entire primary government. Funds meeting the criteria must be separately disclosed on the face of the financial statements. See GASB Codification 2200.150 for specific criteria.

separate column in a Balance Sheet and a Statement of Revenues, Expenditures, and Changes in Fund Balance. For example, the City of Missoula, Montana, reports two CPF as major funds in addition to its General Fund. One of the funds presents activity for a GO bond financing aquatic facility construction. The other presents activity for a special assessment project.

In the fund financial statements, all nonmajor funds are combined and the totals are reported in a single column. Governments provide combining statements for the nonmajor funds as supplemental information in the Comprehensive Annual Financial Report (CAFR). The nonmajor funds are often grouped according to fund type in the supplemental schedules. The City of Missoula presents eight CPF in its nonmajor CPF combining statements. (See the City of Raleigh's combining statements for an example of CPF reporting.)

Cash and short-term investments will often be the only assets reported on the Balance Sheet of a CPF. The City of Raleigh's CPF include restricted cash and investments for bond proceeds and deposits. It is separately disclosed on the Balance Sheet. Other assets include various amounts receivable from other governments, interest, and sales tax revenues designated for capital projects. Liabilities include contracts payable, including retained percentages. (See **Construction Expenditures.**) If the CPF was created for a special assessment project the balance sheet is likely to include assessments receivable and deferred assessment revenue (see the Street Improvement Fund in Raleigh's combining statements). The full amount of the outstanding assessment is recognized even if it will not be collected within the coming year (and is technically not a *current* financial resource). (See **Special Assessments.**) Because fees paid by developers in the Facility Fees Fund in the City of Raleigh may be reimbursed, a liability is accrued in the Balance Sheet.

If a CPF is established for a specific purpose, its fund balance is implicitly restricted for that purpose. Therefore, there is no need to present a Reserved Fund Balance. (See **Fund Balance.**) In the City of Raleigh's Balance Sheet, none of the CPF reports a Reserved Fund Balance. All funds, however, present at least one designation of fund balance. Designating a portion of fund balance merely expresses management's intent.

On the Statement of Revenues, Expenditures, and Changes in Fund Balance it is likely that expenditures will exceed revenues. Many of the increases in Fund Balance will be reported as Other Financing Sources. The City of Raleigh reports intergovernmental revenue, probably grants, in several of its CPF. (See **Grants.**) It also relies on fees from developers for streets and parks. (See **Capital Contributions.**) The portion of special assessments that are measurable and available are recognized as revenues in Raleigh's Street Improvement and Sidewalk Funds. (See **Special Assessments.**) Another lucrative source of revenues for the City of Raleigh is investment income.

Most of Raleigh's current expenditures are capital, and most exceed revenues. The Miscellaneous Capital Improvement Fund also reports an expenditure for debt issuance costs. (See **Issuance of Capital Debt.**) Seemingly incongruous are debt service expenditures recognized in Raleigh's Park Improvement and Park Bond Funds. This is a feature unique in North Carolina. Local governments in North Carolina do not use debt service funds. Debt service expenditures are recognized in other governmental funds.

CPF often have Other Financing Sources from bond proceeds and interfund transfers in and Uses for interfund transfers out. (See *Issuance of Capital Debt and Interfund Transfers*.) The City of Raleigh's Miscellaneous Capital Improvements Fund reports separate line items for debt proceeds and premium on debt. Other funds routinely subsidize capital projects with transfers in. CPF also routinely transfer monies to other funds authorized to expend the resources.

## 7.11 Budgetary Reporting

CPF are budgeted as multi-year projects. Therefore, they fall outside the scope of the requirement to present budget-to-actual comparisons as Required Supplementary Information (RSI) for the general fund and each major special revenue fund that has a legally adopted annual budget [GASB Codification 2200.179]. The Implementation Guide for GASB 34 clarifies that a CPF budgetary presentation may not be included with other RSI budgetary comparisons [Paragraph 382 of the *Implementation of GASB Statement 34 on Basic Financial Statements—and Management's Discussion and Analysis—for State and Local Governments, and Related Pronouncements*]. An alternative for reporting budgetary information for nonmajor funds is to include the information with the combining statements. The placement of the budgetary comparisons is, therefore, outside of the basic financial statements and RSI.

Because CPF are multi-year by nature, it is useful to present budgetary information for the length of the project in addition to the current year. (See *Budgetary Accounting in Capital Project Funds*.) The City of Raleigh's Schedule of Revenues and Expenditures Compared with Budget for each of its CPF is one example of a budgetary reporting format. Raleigh aggregates all prior-year activity in a column and current year activity in another, with a total provided in comparison to the project's budget. Variances are also provided. (See the Street Improvement Fund's Schedule of Revenues and Expenditures Compared with Budget.)

## 7.12 Summary

CPF are useful tools for stewardship. Isolating monies that are legally restricted or otherwise designated for capital projects facilitates planning and monitoring. Financial reporting using the current financial resources measurement focus and modified accrual basis of accounting promotes fiscal accountability.

# Exhibit Financial Reports:
# The City of Raleigh, North Carolina

*Source:* www.raleigh-nc.org

## C. Capital Assets

Capital asset activity for the year ended June 30, 2005, was as follows (stated in thousands):

| Governmental Activities | Balance June 30, 2004 | Additions | Transfers | Deletions | Balance June 30, 2005 |
|---|---|---|---|---|---|
| **Capital assets, not being depreciated:** | | | | | |
| Land | $99,610 | $1,837 | | | $101,447 |
| Construction in progress | 14,016 | 6,444 | (11,995) | | 8,465 |
| **Total capital assets, not being depreciated** | **113,626** | **8,281** | **(11,995)** | | **109,912** |
| **Capital assets, being depreciated:** | | | | | |
| Buildings and machinery | 87,124 | 609 | 980 | 66 | 88,647 |
| Streets and sidewalks | 463,785 | 60,285 | 7,769 | | 531,839 |
| Equipment | 68,073 | 14,031 | | 7,835 | 74,269 |
| Furniture and fixtures | 1,007 | 273 | | 40 | 1,240 |
| Improvements—general and parks | 110,868 | 8,122 | 2,870 | 118 | 121,742 |
| **Total capital assets being depreciated** | **730,857** | **83,320** | **11,619** | **8,059** | **817,737** |
| **Less accumulated depreciation for:** | | | | | |
| Buildings and machinery | 30,802 | 2,130 | | 66 | 32,866 |
| Streets and sidewalks | 191,795 | 22,195 | | | 213,990 |
| Equipment | 52,988 | 6,847 | | 7,835 | 52,000 |
| Furniture and fixtures | 508 | 214 | | 40 | 682 |
| Improvements—general and parks | 41,720 | 5,550 | (113) | 118 | 47,039 |
| **Total accumulated depreciation** | **317,813** | **36,936** | **(113)** | **8,059** | **346,577** |
| **Total capital assets being depreciated, net** | **413,044** | **46,384** | **11,732** | | **471,160** |
| **Governmental activities capital assets, net** | **$526,670** | **$54,665** | **$(263)** | | **$581,072** |

Depreciation expense was charged to functions/programs of the governmental activities as follows:

| | |
|---|---|
| General government | $644 |
| Community development | 80 |
| Public works | 24,676 |
| Public safety | 1,102 |
| Solid waste services | 38 |
| Leisure services | 4,566 |
| Capital assets held by certain internal service funds are charged to the various governmental functions based on the usage of the assets | 5,830 |
| **Total depreciation expense—governmental activities** | **$36,936** |

Annexations: The amount reported above as additions for streets and sidewalks of $60,285,000 includes $36,409,891 of annexations of streets that were transferred to the City from the North Carolina Department of Transportation during 2004–05. Such transfers occur infrequently and the volume and value of the 2004–05 transfers are significantly greater than normally occurs.

| Business-Type Activities | Balance June 30, 2004 | Additions | Transfers | Deletions | Balance June 30, 2005 |
|---|---|---|---|---|---|
| Capital assets, not being depreciated: | | | | | |
| Land | $48,482 | $4,171 | — | | $52,653 |
| Construction in progress | 17,889 | 37,632 | (13,461) | | 42,060 |
| **Total capital assets, not being depreciated** | **66,371** | **41,803** | **(13,461)** | | **94,713** |
| Capital assets, being depreciated: | | | | | |
| Buildings and machinery | 97,955 | 1,795 | 2,088 | 10,166 | 91,672 |
| Water and sewer systems | 570,331 | 33,804 | 7,668 | | 611,803 |
| Parking decks | 43,803 | 14,058 | — | | 57,861 |
| Buses | 16,742 | 4,679 | | 345 | 21,076 |
| Equipment | 26,260 | 3,213 | 18 | 2,894 | 26,597 |
| Furniture and fixtures | 1,952 | 20 | | 1,521 | 451 |
| Improvements | 54,244 | 2,265 | 4,063 | 21,087 | 39,485 |
| **Total capital assets being depreciated** | **811,287** | **59,834** | **13,837** | **36,013** | **848,945** |

| Business-Type Activities | Balance June 30, 2004 | Additions | Transfers | Deletions | Balance June 30, 2005 |
|---|---|---|---|---|---|
| Less accumulated depreciation for: | | | | | |
| Buildings and machinery | 34,062 | 2,317 | | 6,920 | 29,459 |
| Water and sewer systems | 135,103 | 12,385 | | | 147,488 |
| Parking decks | 9,412 | 1,360 | | | 10,772 |
| Buses | 9,008 | 1,567 | | 345 | 10,230 |
| Equipment | 16,037 | 2,715 | | 2,887 | 15,865 |
| Furniture and fixtures | 1,809 | 58 | | 1,515 | 352 |
| Improvements | 19,801 | 2,784 | 113 | 11,845 | 10,853 |
| **Total accumulated depreciation** | **225,232** | **23,186** | **113** | **23,512** | **225,019** |
| **Total capital assets being depreciated, net** | **586,055** | **36,648** | **13,724** | **12,501** | **623,926** |
| **Business-type activities capital assets, net** | **$652,426** | **$78,451** | **$263** | **$12,501** | **$718,639** |

Depreciation expense was charged to functions/programs of the business-type activities as follows:

| | |
|---|---|
| Water/sewer | $15,105 |
| Convention center | 3,169 |
| Parking | 1,404 |
| Mass transit | 1,888 |
| Storm water | 10 |
| Capital assets held by certain internal service funds are charged to the various business-type activities based on the usage of the assets | 1,610 |
| **Total depreciation expense—business-type activities** | **$23,186** |

## Special Item: Impairment of Capital Assets

During 2005, the convention center fund (a business-type activity) recognized a special item of $12.5 million for a loss due to the impairment of capital assets, the Raleigh Convention and Civic Center and the Fayetteville Street Mall. A new convention center is currently under construction and the existing civic center is being readied for complete demolition. The Fayetteville Street Mall has been removed and construction is under way to return the mall to vehicular traffic. These assets were recorded in the convention center fund at $34.5 million and accumulated depreciation of $22 million for a net book value of $12.5 million.

## Commitments—Construction Projects

At June 30, 2005, the City has $239,469,770 in project obligations for business-type activities for construction projects in progress as follows: $37,472,464, water and sewer projects; $177,027,734, new convention center project; and $24,969,572, underground parking garage project. These obligations are fully budgeted and are being financed primarily by state loans, general obligation bond proceeds, revenue bond proceeds, and certificates of participation.

In addition, the City has $24,499,772 in general government project obligations at June 30, 2005. These obligations relate to construction in progress projects for street construction, redevelopment projects, and community center and park construction. These projects are fully budgeted and the funding for these governmental projects is indicated through designations of fund balance at June 30, 2005.

## D. Interfund Receivables, Payables, and Transfers

The composition of interfund balances as June 30, 2005, is as follows:

| | | Due from | | | | |
|---|---|---|---|---|---|---|
| | | Nonmajor Governmental Funds | Convention Center Fund | Nonmajor Enterprise Funds | Internal Service Funds | Total |
| | General fund | $1,834,210 | $22,068 | $4,877,878 | $2,215,719 | $8,949,875 |
| | Parking facilities fund | | 1,000,000 | | | 1,000,000 |
| Q | Total | $1,834,210 | $1,022,068 | $4,877,878 | $2,215,719 | $9,949,875 |

The balance of $1,000,000 due to the parking facilities fund from nonmajor governmental funds results from loans made to provide cash for the convention center and memorial auditorium capital projects fund until pledges for construction of the BTI Center are received. The balance of $8,949,875 due to the general fund includes $8,444,303 of reclasses of negative cash to due to the general fund and a corresponding reduction in general fund cash and a due from other funds. Negative cash reclassed consisted of $2,215,719 from internal service funds, $4,806,298 from nonmajor enterprise funds, and $1,422,286 from nonmajor governmental funds.

All remaining balances resulted from timing differences between the dates that (1) interfund goods and services are provided or reimbursable expenditures occur,

(2) transactions are recorded in the accounting system, and (3) payments between funds are made.

A summary of interfund transfers for the fiscal year ended June 30, 2005, is as follows:

| | | |
|---|---|---|
| Transfers to general fund from: | | |
| Nonmajor governmental funds | | $6,913,717 |
| Water and sewer fund | | 148,290 |
| Parking facilities fund | | 200,000 |
| Internal service funds | | 2,400,000 |
| **Total transfers to general fund** | | **$9,662,007** |

| | | |
|---|---|---|
| Transfers to nonmajor governmental funds from: | | |
| General fund | $5,813,466 | |
| Water and sewer fund | 462,632 | |
| Parking fund | 442,000 | |
| **Total transfers to nonmajor governmental funds** | **$6,718,098** | |
| Transfers to convention center fund from: | | |
| General fund | $2,803,447 | |
| Nonmajor governmental funds | 589,500 | |
| **Total transfers to convention center fund** | **$3,392,947** | |
| Transfers to parking fund from: | | |
| General fund | $580,000 | |
| Nonmajor governmental funds | 4,670,000 | |
| Convention center fund | 250,000 | |
| **Total transfers to parking fund** | **$5,500,000** | |
| Transfers to nonmajor enterprise funds from: | | |
| General fund | $7,679,765 | |
| Nonmajor governmental funds | 699,063 | |
| Water and sewer fund | 112,025 | |
| **Total transfers to nonmajor enterprise funds** | **$8,490,853** | |
| Transfers to internal service funds from: | | |
| General fund | $78,918 | |
| Nonmajor governmental funds | 2,600,000 | |
| Water and sewer fund | 70,000 | |
| Internal service funds | 29,258 | |
| **Total transfers to internal service funds** | **$2,778,176** | |

Transfers are used to (1) move revenues from the fund that statute or budget requires to collect them to the fund that statute or budget requires to expend them, (2) move receipts restricted to debt service from the funds collecting the receipts to the general fund as debt service payments become due, and (3) use unrestricted revenues collected in the general fund to finance various programs accounted for in other funds in accordance with budgetary authorizations.

During the fiscal year ended June 30, 2005, $1,625,000 was transferred from general capital projects funds to the general fund. These transfers were made to support specific related operating activities ($110,000) or to replenish funds advanced from the general fund to capital projects prior to debt issuance ($1,500,000). A transfer of $4,670,000 from general capital projects to the parking fund was made to replenish funds advanced to general capital projects prior to issuance of debt. The general equipment replacement fund transferred $2,400,000 to the general fund for the purchase of garbage carts for the city's automated trash pickup program.

Also, during 2004–05 certain noncash transactions were reported as transfers in the financial statements, however, they are not included in the summary of interfund transfers above. Capital assets (net) of $263,376 were transferred from the governmental activities to the parking fund (a business-type activity). Capital assets of $97,707 were transferred from the convention center (a business-type activity) to the governmental activities.

## E. Operating Leases

During 2004–05 total rental payments on noncancelable operating leases was $3,420,767. The following is a schedule by years of minimum future rentals on noncancelable operating leases as of June 30, 2005:

| Fiscal Year Ending June to— | |
|---|---|
| 2006 | $2,025,480 |
| 2007 | 1,084,206 |
| 2008 | 246,272 |
| 2009 | 36,013 |
| 2010 | 31,136 |
| | **$3,423,107** |

## F. Long-Term Obligations

### 1. General Obligation Bonds

The City issues general obligation bonds to provide funds for the acquisition and construction of major capital facilities. General obligation bonds have been issued for both the governmental and business-type activities. The bonds are direct obligations and pledge the full faith and credit of the City. The utility related issues are expected to be repaid with user charges and the remaining bonds are expected to be repaid with general fund revenues. Interest on the bonds is payable semi-annually.

General obligation bonds outstanding as of June 30, 2005, are as follows:

| Purpose | Interest Rates | Date Issued | Date Series Matures | Amount of Original Issue | Balance Outstanding June 30, 2005 |
|---|---|---|---|---|---|
| **Governmental Activities** | | | | | |
| Housing—Series 199413—Taxable | 7.75% to 8.0% | 9/1/1994 | 3/1/2011 | $2,900,000 | $1,525,000 |
| Parks—Series 1996 | 5.2% to 5.3% | 6/1/1996 | 6/1/2016 | 27,900,000 | 1,505,000 |
| Housing—Series 1996 | 5.4% to 5.75% | 6/1/1996 | 6/1/2016 | 2,280,000 | 1,265,000 |
| Fire Station—Series 1996 | 5.2% to 5.3% | 6/1/1996 | 6/1/2016 | 2,145,000 | 105,000 |
| Public Improvement Refunding—Series 1997 | 4.25% to 5.0% | 10/1/1997 | 4/1/2012 | 22,255,000 | 9,940,000 |
| Housing—Series 1997—Taxable | 6.7% | 10/1/1997 | 4/1/2016 | 3,920,000 | 2,870,000 |
| GO Refunding, Series 1998 | 4.0% to 4.2% | 12/1/1998 | 6/1/2012 | 6,740,000 | 4,440,000 |
| Street Improvement, Series 1998 | 4.3% to 4.4% | 12/1/1998 | 6/1/2017 | 22,000,000 | 16,300,000 |
| Public Improvement, Series 2002 | 4.0% to 5.0% | 6/1/2002 | 6/1/2021 | 9,700,000 | 8,800,000 |
| Public Improvement, Series 2002A | 3.0% to 4.5% | 12/1/2002 | 2/1/2021 | 2,900,000 | 2,700,000 |
| Public Improvement, Series 2002B | 3.0% to 4.5% | 12/1/2002 | 2/1/2021 | 43,000,000 | 40,550,000 |
| Public Improvement, Series 2002C | 2.0% to 4.0% | 12/1/2002 | 2/1/2013 | 14,905,000 | 9,340,000 |
| Public Improvement, Series 2004 | 2.0% to 4.0% | 3/1/2004 | 4/1/2022 | 15,000,000 | 14,550,000 |

*(continued on next page)*

| Purpose | Interest Rates | Date Issued | Date Series Matures | Amount of Original Issue | Balance Outstanding June 30, 2005 |
|---|---|---|---|---|---|
| Public Improvement Refunding—Series zoo4A | 2.0% to 4.0% | 3/1/2004 | 4/1/2016 | 17,338,150 | 17,118,236 |
| Housing—Series 2004B | 3.13% to 4.38% | 3/1/2004 | 4/1/2017 | 7,000,000 | 6,645,000 |
| Housing Refunding—Series 2004B | 3.13% to 4.0% | 3/1/2004 | 4/1/2012 | 2,355,000 | 2,060,000 |
| **Total Governmental Activities** | | | | | **$139,713,236** |
| **Business-Type Activities** | | | | | |
| *Water and Sewer:* | | | | | |
| Water—Series 1996 | 5.2% to 5.3% | 6/1/1996 | 6/1/2016 | $11,120,000 | $575,000 |
| Sanitary Sewer—Series 1996 | 5.2% to 5.3% | 6/1/1996 | 6/1/2016 | 6,880,000 | 345,000 |
| Sanitary Sewer Refunding—Series 1997 | 4.25% to 5.0% | 10/1/1997 | 4/1/2012 | 16,325,000 | 7,290,000 |
| Sanitary Sewer Refunding— Series 2002C | 2.0% to 4.0% | 12/1/2002 | 2/1/2013 | 3,055,000 | 1,915,000 |
| Water Refunding, Series 2004A | | | | | |
| Sanitary Sewer Refunding— | 2.0% to 4.0% | 3/1/2004 | 4/1/2016 | 6,187,620 | 6,109,137 |
| Series 2004A | 2.0% to 4.0% | 3/1/2004 | 4/1/2016 | 3,674,230 | 3,627,627 |
| **Water and Sewer Total** | | | | | **19,861,764** |
| *Parking Facilities:* | | | | | |
| Parking Facilities Refunding—Series 1997 | 4.25% to 5.0% | 10/1/1997 | 4/1/2012 | 3,230,000 | 1,445,000 |
| Parking Facilities—Series 1997 | 4.70% to 5.0% | 10/1/1997 | 4/1/2016 | 8,670,000 | 5,870,000 |
| **Parking Facilities Total** | | | | | **7,315,000** |
| **Total Business-Type Activities** | | | | | **$27,176,764** |
| **Total Bonded Indebtedness** | | | | | **$166,890,000** |

## Combining Balance Sheet Nonmajor Governmental Funds—June 30, 2005

| | Special Revenue Funds | Capital Projects Funds | Total Nonmajor Governmental Funds |
|---|---:|---:|---:|
| **Assets** | | | |
| Cash and cash equivalents | $26,456,692 | $78,118,687 | $104,575,379 |
| Assessments receivable, net of allowance for uncollectables of $37,750 | — | 717,241 | 717,241 |
| Due from other governmental agencies | 4,365,557 | 1,064,098 | 5,429,655 |
| Accrued interest receivable | 63,388 | 205,542 | 268,930 |
| Other receivables and assets | | 40,200 | 40,200 |
| Sales tax receivable | 41,268 | 243,679 | 284,947 |
| Loans receivable | 36,607,321 | | 36,607,321 |
| Cash and cash equivalents/investments—restricted deposits and bond proceeds | 2,618,862 | 22,788,142 | 25,407,004 |
| **Total assets** | **$70,153,088** | **$103,177,589** | **$173,330,677** |
| **Liabilities and Fund Balances** | | | |
| **Liabilities:** | | | |
| Accounts payable | $268,911 | $4,403,818 | $4,672,729 |
| Arbitrage rebate payable | 566 | | 566 |
| Accrued salaries and employee payroll taxes | 38,290 | | 38,290 |
| Loan servicing escrow | 716,029 | — | 716,029 |
| Reimbursable facility fees | — | 4,267,407 | 4,267,407 |
| Claims payable and other liabilities | 983 | 332,571 | 333,554 |
| Due to other funds | 1,834,210 | | 1,834,210 |
| Deferred revenue | 36,607,321 | 717,241 | 37,324,562 |
| Unearned revenue | 194,447 | 102,791 | 297,238 |
| **Total liabilities** | **39,660,757** | **9,823,828** | **49,484,585** |

*(continued on next page)*

| | Special Revenue Funds | Capital Projects Funds | Total Nonmajor Governmental Funds |
|---|---|---|---|
| **Fund balances:** | | | |
| Reserved for new convention center project | 19,001,204 | | 19,001,204 |
| Unreserved: | | | |
| Designated for subsequent year's appropriation | 8,069,059 | 80,885,459 | 88,954,518 |
| Designated for specific purposes | — | 12,350,869 | 12,350,869 |
| Undesignated | 3,422,068 | 117,433 | 3,539,501 |
| **Total fund balances** | **30,492,331** | **93,353,761** | **123,846,092** |
| **Total liabilities and fund balances** | **$70,153,088** | **$103,177,589** | **$173,330,677** |

## Combining Statement of Revenues, Expenditures and Changes In Fund Balances Nonmajor Governmental Funds for the Fiscal Year Ended June 30, 2005

| | Special Revenue Funds | Capital Projects Funds | Combining Eliminations | Total Nonmajor Governmental Funds |
|---|---|---|---|---|
| **Revenues** | | | | |
| Intergovernmental | $23,545,902 | $836,404 | | $24,382,306 |
| Developer participation | 138,233 | | | 138,233 |
| Assessments | | 726,414 | | 726,414 |
| Interest on investments | 559,843 | 2,189,778 | | 2,749,621 |
| Facility fees | — | 3,733,422 | | 3,733,422 |
| Rents | 311,721 | | | 311,721 |
| Program income | 2,687,858 | | | 2,687,858 |
| Miscellaneous other | 134,341 | 2,100,420 | | 2,234,761 |
| **Total revenues** | **27,239,665** | **9,724,671** | | **36,964,336** |
| **Expenditures** | | | | |
| General government | 55,104 | | | 55,104 |
| Community development services | 6,943,125 | | | 6,943,125 |
| Public works | 833,214 | | | 833,214 |
| Public safety | 888,222 | | | 888,222 |

| | Special Revenue Funds | Capital Projects Funds | Combining Eliminations | Total Nonmajor Governmental Funds |
|---|---|---|---|---|
| Solid waste services | 2,328 | | | 2,328 |
| Leisure services | 348,716 | | | 348,716 |
| Economic development programs | 2,643,467 | | | 2,643,467 |
| Other expenditures | 2,041 | — | | 2,041 |
| Capital outlay | | 26,976,298 | | 26,976,298 |
| Debt service: | | | | |
|   Principal | | 1,270,566 | | 1,270,566 |
|   Interest | | 99,302 | | 99,302 |
|   Other debt service expenditures | | 212,232 | | 212,232 |
| **Total expenditures** | **11,716,217** | **28,558,398** | | **40,274,615** |
| **Excess (deficiency) of revenues over (under) expenditures** | **15,523,448** | **(18,833,727)** | | **(3,310,279)** |
| **Other Financing Sources (Uses)** | | | | |
| Transfers in | 1,359,026 | 10,700,072 | (5,341,000) | 6,718,098 |
| Transfers out | (11,219,217) | (9,594,063) | 5,341,000 | (15,472,280) |
| Certificates of participation issued | | 19,805,000 | | 19,805,000 |
| Premium on certificates of participation | | 435,445 | | 435,445 |
| **Total other financing sources (uses)** | **(9,860,191)** | **21,346,454** | | **11,486,263** |
| Net change in fund balances | 5,663,257 | 2,512,727 | | 8,175,984 |
| **Fund balance— beginning of year** | **24,829,074** | **90,841,034** | | **115,670,108** |
| **Fund balance—ending of year** | **$30,492,331** | **$93,353,761** | | **$123,846,092** |

## Combining Balance Sheet Nonmajor Capital Projects Funds—June 30, 2005

| | Street Improvement Fund | Street Bond Fund | Sidewalk Fund | Park Improvement Fund |
|---|---|---|---|---|
| **Assets** | | | | |
| Cash and cash equivalents | $21,526,605 | $12,141,700 | $3,069,283 | $10,056,307 |
| Assessments receivable, net of allowance for uncollectables of $37,750 | 717,241 | — | | |
| Due from other governmental agencies | 487,500 | 239,020 | — | — |
| Accrued interest receivable | 58,905 | 33,167 | 8,388 | 27,531 |
| Other receivables and assets | — | — | | |
| Sales tax receivable | 63,416 | 55,511 | 2,212 | 34,306 |
| Cash and cash equivalents/ investments–restricted deposits and bond proceeds | | 10,889,893 | | |
| **Total assets** | **$22,853,667** | **$23,359,291** | **$3,079,883** | **$10,118,144** |
| **Liabilities and Fund Balances** | | | | |
| **Liabilities:** | | | | |
| Accounts payable | $722,275 | $1,587,127 | $36,716 | $534,115 |
| Reimbursable facility fees | | | | — |
| Claims payable and other liabilities | 285,182 | | | 26,887 |
| Deferred revenue | 717,241 | | | |
| Unearned revenue | — | | | |
| **Total liabilities** | **1,724,698** | **1,587,127** | **36,716** | **561,002** |
| **Fund balances:** | | | | |
| Unreserved: | | | | |
| Designated for subsequent year's appropriation | 19,824,405 | 21,531,853 | 3,017,071 | 8,849,691 |
| Designated for specific purposes | 1,304,564 | 240,311 | 26,096 | 707,451 |
| Undesignated | — | — | — | |
| **Total fund balances** | **21,128,969** | **21,772,164** | **3,043,167** | **9,557,142** |
| **Total liabilities and fund balances** | **$22,853,667** | **$23,359,291** | **$3,079,883** | **$10,118,144** |

## Combining Balance Sheet Nonmajor Capital Projects Funds (continued)

| Miscellaneous Capital Facility Fees Fund | Park Bond Fund | Improvements Fund | Walnut Creek Amphitheater Projects Fund | Storm Water Projects Fund | Technology Capital Projects Fund | Total Nonmajor Capital Projects Funds |
|---|---|---|---|---|---|---|
| $4,867,293 | $5,882,814 | $13,355,726 | $255,074 | $3,314,268 | $3,649,617 | $78,118,687 |
| | | | | | | 717,241 |
| — | 250,000 | | | 87,578 | — | 1,064,098 |
| 13,335 | 16,085 | 36,549 | 696 | 917 | 9,969 | 205,542 |
| — | | 40,200 | | — | | 40,200 |
| 16,643 | | 56,315 | 1,069 | 857 | 13,350 | 243,679 |
| | | 11,898, 249 | | | | 22,788,142 |
| **$4,880,628** | **$6,165,542** | **$25,387,039** | **256,839** | **$3,403,620** | **$3,672,936** | **$103,177,589** |
| — | $304,674 | $1,119,280 | | | $99,631 | $4,403,818 |
| $4,267,407 | | — | | | | 4,267,407 |
| 12,566 | | 7,936 | | | | 332,571 |
| — | | | | | | 717,241 |
| | 102,791 | | | | | 102,791 |
| **4,279,973** | **407,465** | **1,127,216** | | | **99,631** | **9,823,828** |
| 600,655 | | 20,683,033 | 252,581 | 3,403,620 | 2,722,550 | 80,885,459 |
| 5,758,077 | | 3,459,357 | 4,258 | | 850,755 | 12,350,869 |
| — | | 117,433 | — | | — | 117,433 |
| **600,655** | **5,758,077** | **24,259,823** | **256,839** | **3,403,620** | **3,573,305** | **93,353,761** |
| **$4,880,628** | **$6,165,542** | **$25,387,039** | **$256,839** | **$3,403,620** | **$3,672,936** | **$103,177,589** |

## Combining Statement of Revenues, Expenditures and Changes In Fund Balances Nonmajor Capital Projects Funds for the Fiscal Year Ended June 30, 2005

| | Street Improvement Fund | Street Bond Fund | Sidewalk Fund | Park Improvement Fund | Facility Fees Fund |
|---|---|---|---|---|---|
| **Revenues** | | | | | |
| Inter-governmental | $337,500 | $27,839 | | $43,450 | |
| Developer participation | 138,233 | | — | | |
| Assessments | 596,453 | | 129,961 | | |
| Interest on investments | 444,820 | 546,122 | 62,040 | 195,459 | 138,776 |
| Facility fees | — | — | — | — | 3,733,422 |
| Miscellaneous other | 513,470 | 4,000 | 159,811 | 408,713 | — |
| **Total revenues** | **2,030,476** | **577,961** | **351,812** | **647,622** | **3,872,198** |
| **Expenditures** | | | | | |
| **Current:** | | | | | |
| Public improvements: | | | | | |
| Street paving/ sidewalk projects | 3,913,519 | 7,715,737 | 135,359 | | |
| Parks and recreation projects | | | | 2,746,028 | |
| Walnut Creek Amphitheater projects | | | | | |
| Storm water and drainage projects | | | | | |
| Other public improvements | | | | | |
| Technology capital projects | | | | | |

**Combining Statement of Revenues, Expenditures and Changes
In Fund Balances Nonmajor Capital Projects Funds
for the Fiscal Year Ended June 30, 2005 (continued)**

| Park Bond Fund | Miscellaneous Capital Improvements Fund | Walnut Creek Amphitheater Projects Fund | Storm Water Projects Fund | Technology Capital | Combining Projects Fund Eliminations | Total Nonmajor Capital Projects Funds |
|---|---|---|---|---|---|---|
| $406,966 | | | $20,649 | | | $836,404 |
| | | | | | | 138,233 |
| | | — | — | — | | 726,414 |
| 140,079 | 553,680 | 4,258 | 47,492 | 57,052 | | 2,189,778 |
| | | — | — | — | | 3,733,422 |
| 27,000 | 644,223 | 304,697 | 38,506 | | | 2,100,420 |
| **574,045** | **1,197,903** | **308,955** | **106,647** | **57,052** | | **9,724,671** |
| | | | | | | 11,764,615 |
| 3,544,558 | | | | | | 6,290,586 |
| | | 52,116 | | | | 52,116 |
| | | | 635,750 | | | 635,750 |
| | 6,021,921 | | | | | 6,021,921 |
| | — | | | 2,211,310 | | 2,211,310 |

*(continued on next page)*

## Combining Statement of Revenues, Expenditures and Changes In Fund Balances Nonmajor Capital Projects Funds for the Fiscal Year Ended June 30, 2005 (continued)

| | Street Improvement Fund | Street Bond Fund | Sidewalk Fund | Park Improvement Fund | Facility Fees Fund |
|---|---|---|---|---|---|
| **Debt service:** | | | | | |
| Principal | | | | 607,900 | |
| Interest | | | | 45,592 | |
| Other debt service expenditures | | | | — | |
| **Total expenditures** | **3,913,519** | **7,715,737** | **135,359** | **3,399,520** | |
| **Excess (deficiency) of revenues over (under) expenditures** | **(1,883,043)** | **(7,137,776)** | **216,453** | **(2,751,898)** | **3,872,198** |
| **Other Financing Sources (Uses)** | | | | | |
| Transfers in | 5,995,295 | 2,890,012 | 420,000 | 3,136,800 | |
| Transfers out | (3,512,614) | | (214,053) | (566,405) | (4,157,000) |
| Certificates of participation issued | | | | | |
| Premium on certificates of participation issued | | | | | |
| **Total other financing sources and uses** | **2,482,681** | **2,890,012** | **205,947** | **2,570,395** | **(4,157,000)** |
| Net change in fund balances | 599,638 | (4,247,764) | 422,400 | (181,503) | (284,802) |
| **Fund balance— beginning of year** | **20,529,331** | **26,019,928** | **2,620,767** | **9,738,645** | **885,457** |
| **Fund balance— ending of year** | **$21,128,969** | **$21,772,164** | **$3,043,167** | **$9,557,142** | **$600,655** |

## Combining Statement of Revenues, Expenditures and Changes In Fund Balances Nonmajor Capital Projects Funds for the Fiscal Year Ended June 30, 2005 (continued)

| Park Bond Fund | Miscellaneous Capital Improvements Fund | Walnut Creek Amphitheater Projects Fund | Storm Water Projects Fund | Technology Capital | Combining Projects Fund Eliminations | Total Nonmajor Capital Projects Funds |
|---|---|---|---|---|---|---|
| 662,666 | | | | | | 1,270, 566 |
| 53,710 | | | | | | 99,302 |
| — | 212,232 | | | | | 212,232 |
| 4,260,934 | 6,234,153 | 52,116 | 635,750 | 2,211,310 | | 28,558,398 |
| (3,686,889) | (5,036,250) | 256,839 | (529,103) | (2,154,258) | | (18,833,727) |
| 1,362,590 | 3,156,200 | | | 2,472,830 | (8,733,655) | 10,700,072 |
| | (9,267,000) | | (610,646) | | 8,733,655 | (9,594,063) |
| | 19,805,000 | | — | | | 19,805,000 |
| | 435,445 | | | | | 435,445 |
| 1,362,590 | 14,129,645 | | (610,646) | 2,472,830 | | 21,346,454 |
| (2,324,299) | 9,093,395 | 256,839 | (1,139,749) | 318,572 | | 2,512,727 |
| 8,082,376 | 15,166,428 | | 4,543,369 | 3,254,733 | | 90,841,034 |
| $5,758,077 | $24,259,823 | $256,839 | $3,403,620 | $3,573,305 | | $93,353,761 |

**Schedule of Changes in Capital Assets Used in the Operation of Governmental Funds by Function and Activity for the Fiscal Year Ended June 30, 2005**

| | Balance June 30, 2004 | Additions | Transfers | Deductions | Balance June 30, 2005 |
|---|---|---|---|---|---|
| **General government:** | | | | | |
| City manager | $45,249 | $8,589 | $(34,602) | $10,647 | $8,589 |
| Personnel | 38,392 | — | (7,925) | | 30,467 |
| Administrative services | 702,203 | — | 451,908 | | 1,154,111 |
| Finance | 1,403,326 | 25,327 | | 48,655 | 1,379,998 |
| Information services | 2,243,317 | 2,444,954 | 1,330,124 | 9,223 | 6,009,172 |
| **Total general government** | 4,432,487 | 2,478,870 | 1,739,505 | 68,525 | 8,582,337 |
| **Community development services:** | | | | | |
| Community development | 12,162,392 | | | | 12,162,392 |
| Planning | 15,250 | — | | | 15,250 |
| Inspections | 851,296 | 82,142 | | 359,573 | 573,865 |
| Community services | 28,053 | — | | — | 28,053 |
| **Total community development services** | 13,056,991 | 82,142 | | 359,573 | 12,779,560 |

| | | | | |
|---|---|---|---|---|
| **Public works:** | | | | |
| Central engineering | 7,113,655 | — | — | 109,267 | 7,004,388 |
| Transportation | 552,984,457 | 62,757,218 | 8,057,159 | 27,794 | 623,771,040 |
| **Total public works** | **560,098,112** | **62,757,218** | **8,057,159** | **137,061** | **630,775,428** |
| **Public safety:** | | | | |
| Emergency communications | 2,900,754 | 575,751 | — | | 3,476,505 |
| Police | 9,330,104 | 410,339 | 111,334 | 3,960,909 | 5,890,868 |
| Fire | 23,851,149 | 846,662 | 911,247 | 558,338 | 25,050,720 |
| **Total public safety** | **36,082,007** | **1,832,752** | **1,022,581** | **4,519,247** | **34,418,093** |
| **Solid waste services** | **7,689,184** | | **(451,908)** | **999,960** | **6,237,316** |
| **Leisure services:** | | | | |
| Walnut Creek Amphitheater | 15,145,659 | — | — | | 15,145,659 |
| Parks and recreation | 160,181,021 | 6,311,784 | 1,251,436 | 298,226 | 167,446,015 |
| **Total leisure services** | **175,326,680** | **6,311,784** | **1,251,436** | **298,226** | **182,591,674** |
| **Construction in progress** | **14,015,661** | **6,444,343** | **(11,995,026)** | | **8,464,978** |
| **Total general capital assets** | **$810,701,122** | **$79,907,109** | **$(376,253)** | **$6,382,592** | **$883,849,386** |

This schedule presents only the capital asset balances related to governmental funds. Accordingly, the capital assets reported in certain internal service funds are excluded from the above amounts. Generally, the capital assets of internal service funds are included as governmental activities in the Statement of Net Assets.

## Capital Assets Used in the Operation of Governmental Funds Schedule by Function and Activity for the Fiscal Year Ended June 30, 2005

| | Land | Buildings | Streets and Sidewalks |
|---|---|---|---|
| **General government:** | | | |
| City manager | | | |
| Personnel | | | |
| Administrative services | | | |
| Finance | | | |
| Information services | | | |
| **Total general government** | | | |
| **Community development services:** | | | |
| Community development | 10,371,641 | 107,755 | 47,838 |
| Planning | | | |
| Inspections | | | |
| Community services | | | |
| **Total community development services** | **10,371,641** | **107,755** | **47,838** |
| **Public works:** | | | |
| Central engineering | 2,886,075 | | |
| Transportation | 37,514,533 | 19,396,849 | 530,976,048 |
| **Total public works** | **40,400,608** | **19,396,849** | **530,976,048** |
| **Public safety:** | | | |
| Emergency communications center | | 654,311 | |
| Police | | 911,710 | |
| Fire | 523,396 | 14,972,369 | |
| **Total public safety** | **523,396** | **16,538,390** | |
| **Solid waste services** | **2,772,456** | **15,331** | |
| **Leisure services:** | | | |
| Walnut Creek Amphitheater | 1,250,047 | 13,420,210 | |
| Parks and recreation | 46,128,738 | 38,937,587 | 815,220 |
| **Total leisure services** | **47,378,785** | **52,357,797** | **815,220** |
| **Total governmental funds capital assets** | **$101,446,886** | **$88,416,122** | **$531,839,106** |

This schedule presents only the capital asset balances related to governmental funds. Accordingly, the capital assets reported in certain internal service funds are excluded from the above amounts. Generally, the capital assets of internal service funds are included as governmental activities in the Statement of Net Assets.

**Schedule of Revenues and Expenditures Compared with Budget Street Bond Fund for the Fiscal Year Ended June 30, 2005**

| | Actual | | | | Over (Under) Budget |
|---|---|---|---|---|---|
| | Prior Years | Current Year | Total | Budget | |
| **Revenues** | | | | | |
| Inter- governmental | | | | | |
| State of North Carolina | $373,387 | $27,839 | $401,226 | $510,000 | $(108,774) |
| Interest on investments | 546,122 | 546,122 | 350,000 | 196,122 | |
| Miscellaneous other | 4,000 | 4,000 | 43,489 | (39,489) | |
| **Total revenues** | 373,387 | 577,961 | 951,348 | 903,489 | 47,859 |
| **Other Financing Sources** | | | | | |
| Transfers from: | | | | | |
| Street improvement fund | 2,886,197 | 2,886,197 | 2,886,197 | | |
| Park improvement fund | 3,815 | 3,815 | 3,815 | | |
| Bond proceeds | 48,004,007 | | 48,004,007 | 73,127,000 | (25,122,993) |
| **Total other financing sources** | 48,004,007 | 2,890,012 | 50,894,019 | 76,017,012 | (25,122,993) |
| **Total revenues and other financing sources** | $48,377,394 | $3,467,973 | $51,845,367 | 76,920,501 | $(25,075,134) |
| Fund balance appropriated | | | 30,040,539 | | |
| | | | $106,961,040 | | |
| **Expenditures** | | | | | |
| Street projects | $52,648,011 | $7,715,737 | $60,363,748 | $106,961,040 | $(46,597,292) |

## Schedule of Revenues and Expenditures Compared with Budget Street Improvement Fund for the Fiscal Year Ended June 30, 2005

| | Actual | | | | Over (Under) Budget |
|---|---|---|---|---|---|
| | Prior Years | Current Year | Total | Budget | |
| **Revenues** | | | | | |
| Inter-governmental: | | | | | |
| State of North Carolina | $150,000 | $337,500 | $487,500 | $512,500 | $(25,000) |
| Developer participation | 252,860 | 138,233 | 391,093 | 2,717,633 | (2,326,540) |
| Assessments | | 596,453 | 596,453 | 220,000 | 376,453 |
| Interest on investments | | 444,820 | 444,820 | 325,000 | 119,820 |
| Miscellaneous other | | 513,470 | 513,470 | 407,000 | 106,470 |
| **Total revenues** | 402,860 | 2,030,476 | 2,433,336 | 4,182,133 | (1,748,797) |
| **Other Financing Sources** | | | | | |
| Transfers from: | | | | | |
| General fund | | 106,610 | 106,610 | 106,610 | |
| Powell bill fund | | 3,215,000 | 3,215,000 | 3,215,000 | |
| Miscellaneous capital projects fund | | 482,000 | 482,000 | 482,000 | |
| Sidewalk fund | | 214,053 | 214,053 | 214,053 | |
| Facility fees fund | | 1,865,000 | 1,865,000 | 1,865,000 | |
| Water sewer operating fund | | 42,920 | 42,920 | 42,920 | |
| Water capital projects fund | | 69,712 | 69,712 | 69,712 | |
| **Total other financing sources** | | 5,995,295 | 5,995,295 | 5,995,295 | |
| **Total revenues and other financing sources** | $402,860 | $8,025,771 | $8,428,631 | 10,177,428 | $(1,748,797) |

**Schedule of Revenues and Expenditures Compared with Budget Street Improvement Fund for the Fiscal Year Ended June 30, 2005 (continued)**

| | Actual | | | | Over (Under) Budget |
| --- | --- | --- | --- | --- | --- |
| | Prior Years | Current Year | Total | Budget | |
| Fund balance appropriated | | | | 46,681,409 | |
| | | | | $56,858,837 | |
| **Expenditures** | | | | | |
| Street projects | $26,973,587 | $3,913,519 | $30,887,106 | $53,346,223 | $(22,459,117) |
| **Other Financing Uses** | | | | | |
| Transfers to: | | | | | |
| General fund | | 110,000 | 110,000 | 110,000 | |
| Street bond fund | | 2,886,197 | 2,886,197 | 2,886,197 | |
| Park improvement fund | | 378,000 | 378,000 | 378,000 | |
| Mass transit fund | | 138,417 | 138,417 | 138,417 | |
| **Total other financing uses** | | 3,512,614 | 3,512,614 | 3,512,614 | |
| **Total expenditures and other financing uses** | $26,973,587 | $7,426,133 | $34,399,720 | $56,858,837 | $(22,459,117) |

*Chapter 8*

# Proprietary Funds

## John D. Wong
*Wichita State University, School of Urban and Public Affairs*

## Carl D. Ekstrom
*University of Nebraska at Omaha, School of Public Administration*

## Stephen Coberley
*City of Wichita, Certified Public Finance Officer*

## Vincent Miller
*Wichita State University, Office of Institutional Research*

## Contents

8.1 Governmental Funds Compared to Proprietary Funds............................252
    8.1.1 Measurement Focus.................................................................254
    8.1.2 Basis of Accounting ...............................................................254
    8.1.3 Equity Recognition.................................................................257
    8.1.4 Pricing .....................................................................................259
    8.1.5 Transfers ................................................................................. 260
8.2 Financial Statements ..........................................................................261
    8.2.1 Balance Sheet..........................................................................262
    8.2.2 Income Statement...................................................................264
    8.2.3 Cash Flow Statement .............................................................268

8.3 Financial Ratios ................................................................................271
    8.3.1 Liquidity Indicators ...............................................................276
    8.3.2 Solvency Indicators ................................................................276
    8.3.3 Debt Indicators.......................................................................277
    8.3.4 Debt Service Indicators...........................................................278
    8.3.5 Efficiency Indicators ...............................................................278
8.4 Internal Service Funds......................................................................279
    8.4.1 Advantages of Internal Service Funds ..................................... 280
    8.4.2 Disadvantages of Internal Service Funds..................................281
    8.4.3 Pricing Policy..........................................................................282
    8.4.4 Transfers ............................................................................... 284
    8.4.5 Financial Statements.............................................................. 284
8.5 Enterprise Funds .............................................................................285
    8.5.1 Financial Statements...............................................................293
        8.5.1.1 Balance Sheet...............................................................294
        8.5.1.2 Income Statement ........................................................303
        8.5.1.3 Cash Flow Statement (adapted from GASB 34
               Manual, 2003: 42–43) ..................................................307
    8.5.2 Interfund Transfers................................................................ 311
    8.5.3 The Future of Enterprise Funds .............................................313
References ..................................................................................................314

Little known to many people is the fact that many units of government have what are essentially separate business operations embedded within their organizational structures. These units may take on a reasonably independent status and receive substantial support and patronage from the public, such as a municipal golf course or a municipal swimming pool. At the same time, many units of government may also have relatively obscure internal business-like operations such as a print shop, motor pool, or office space pool. Irrespective of how well known or unknown these business-type activities are, their financial transactions are recorded and reported as part of the government's financial accounting and reporting systems, and all of these activities have counterparts in the private sector.

This chapter presents an overview of financial accounting practices related to these business-like governmental operations, which are commonly known as proprietary funds. As discussed in earlier chapters, accounting systems are organized around and operated using funds. The Governmental Accounting Standards Board (GASB) defines a fund as follows:

> A fund is defined as a fiscal and accounting entity with a self-balancing set of accounts recording cash and other financial resources, together with all related liabilities and residual equities, or balances, and changes therein, which are segregated for the purpose of carrying on specific

activities or attaining certain objectives in accordance with special regulations, restrictions, or limitations. (GASB Statement 1)

There are three broad fund types used by state and local governments for financial reporting of specific activities: *governmental funds, proprietary funds,* and *fiduciary funds.* According to Holder (1996: 175), these proprietary funds consist of the following:

- ■ *Enterprise funds* account for business-type activities supported largely by user charges, such as local utilities, golf courses, swimming pools, and toll bridges.
- ■ *Internal service funds* are similar to enterprise funds, except that the services are not rendered to the public but to other governmental entities within the same jurisdiction.

For governmental entities to ensure the proper segregation of resources and to maintain proper accountability, an entity's accounting system should be organized and operated on a fund basis. Each fund is a separate fiscal entity and is established to conduct specific activities and objectives in accordance with statutes, laws, regulations, and restrictions, or for specific purposes. A fund is defined in GASB Codification Section 1300 as a fiscal and accounting entity with a self-balancing set of accounts recording cash and other financial resources, together with all related liabilities and residual equities or balances, and changes therein, which are segregated for the purpose of carrying on specific activities or attaining certain objectives in accordance with special regulations, restrictions, or limitations (Financial Accounting, 2003: 30). An example of these fund types is found in Exhibit 8.1, which shows the fund structure for the City of Wichita, Kansas. The city has four categories of funds: enterprise, governmental, internal service, and special revenue. The city uses enterprise funds to account for the airport, the golf course system, the sewer utility, the water utility, the storm water utility, and transit. The city employs internal service funds to account for fleet and buildings, information technology, stationary stores, and self-insurance.

For financial accounting purposes, proprietary funds are handled in a manner that is different from governmental or fiduciary funds. Proprietary funds are used to account for a government's ongoing organizations and activities that are similar to those often found in the private sector. All assets, liabilities, net assets, revenues, expenses, and transfers relating to the government's business and quasi-business activities—in which changes in net assets or cost recovery are measured—are accounted for through proprietary funds (enterprise and internal service funds). Generally accepted accounting principles for proprietary funds are similar to those applicable to businesses in the private sector; the measurement focus is on determining operating income, financial position, and cash flows (Financial Accounting, 2003: 31). Accounting for proprietary funds probably has more in common with accounting for business enterprises than with accounting for governmental operations in governmental and fiduciary funds.

FUND STRUCTURE

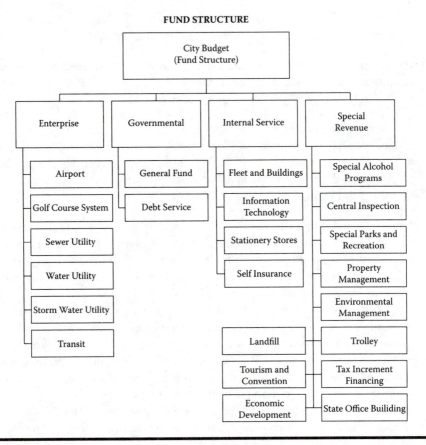

**Exhibit 8.1   Fund structure, City of Wichita, Kansas.**

## 8.1  Governmental Funds Compared to Proprietary Funds

Proprietary funds differ fundamentally from governmental funds. According to Holder (1996: 177–178):

> When a local government enterprise is run on a fully self-supporting, independent basis, the financial accounting and reporting practices parallel those found in business enterprises. Because proprietary funds must cover all operating costs through user charges, an income determination/capital maintenance accounting model is employed.

It can be argued that proprietary funds allow much more operational flexibility than governmental funds. Contrary to governmental funds, in which expenditures are explicitly limited within the context of the budgetary process, both expenditures and revenues for proprietary funds may rise or fall depending on the ultimate demand for the unit's good or service provided. According to Solano and Brams (1996: 130–131):

> Because governmental commercial entities are supposedly self-sustaining, budgetary authority is nonexpendable, or revolving—that is, authorization for collecting revenue and incurring expenses neither lapses at the end of the fiscal period nor requires renewal at the beginning of the next period.

However, some jurisdictions do choose to make proprietary fund appropriations annually. Also, capital outlays and long-term debt transactions of proprietary funds are accounted for within the fund itself as opposed to within general fixed asset and/or general long-term debt account groups used for governmental operations.

While governmental funds account for most governmental functions, proprietary funds account for a government's ongoing activities that are similar to those found in the private sector. Proprietary funds may be of two types: enterprise funds and internal service funds. Enterprise funds account for the following operations:

■ Those that are financed and operated in a manner similar to private business, where the intent of the governing body is that the cost (expenses, including depreciation) of providing goods or services to the general public on a continuing basis be financed and recovered primarily through user charges

■ Those where the governing body has decided that periodic determination of revenues earned, expenses incurred, and/or net income is appropriate for capital maintenance, public policy, management control, accountability, or other purposes

Internal service funds account for the financing of goods or services provided by one department or agency to other departments or agencies of the governmental unit, or to other governmental units, on a cost-reimbursement basis (Accounting and Reporting Manual, 2002: 5–6).

Three important differences between accounting practices for proprietary funds and those for governmental funds are differences in measurement focus, basis of accounting, and equity recognition. Measurement focus refers to what is measured and reported in a fund's operating statement; the basis of accounting determines when a transaction or event is recognized in these funds; while equity recognition involves how "ownership" of economic resources is recognized and documented. Special considerations also include transfer pricing and interfund transfers.

All of these special conditions concerning proprietary funds are explained in the following sections.

### 8.1.1 Measurement Focus

According to Governmental Accounting Standards Board Statement No. 11, "Measurement Focus and Basis of Accounting":

> Measurement focus refers to what is expressed in reporting an entity's financial performance and position. A particular measurement focus is accomplished by considering which resources are measured and when the effects of transactions and events involving those resources are recognized.

Measurement focus is the accounting convention that determines (1) which assets and which liabilities are included on a government's balance sheet and where they are reported there, and (2) whether an operating statement presents information on the flow of financial resources (revenues and expenditures) or information on the flow of economic resources (revenues and expenses) (Accounting and Reporting Manual, 2002: 193). One important distinction between governmental funds and proprietary funds is that governmental funds focus narrowly on the availability of economic resources to the entity, while proprietary funds focus broadly on the overall economic condition of the entity. Another important distinction is that governmental funds focus narrowly on the flow of financial resources, while proprietary funds focus broadly on the flow of economic resources. Finally, governmental funds also differ from proprietary funds in the exhaustion of capital assets. Governmental funds do not recognize depreciation, or the decline in the economic value of capital assets, because depreciation does not immediately have an impact on spendable financial resources. On the other hand, proprietary funds do recognize depreciation since depreciation diminishes the overall economic position of the entity, because the capital asset will eventually have to be replaced. The accounting term *debit* comes from the Latin word *debere* meaning "left." Asset and expense accounts increase in value when debited, whereas liability, capital, and revenue accounts decrease in value when debited. Debit is abbreviated DR. The opposite of a debit is a *credit*. Liability, capital, and revenue accounts increase in value when credited, while asset and expense accounts decrease in value when credited. Exhibit 8.2 presents an overview and examples of significant differences between the measurement focus for proprietary funds and governmental funds.

### 8.1.2 Basis of Accounting

An entity's basis of accounting determines when transactions and economic events are reflected in its financial statements. The basis refers to when revenues, expenditures, expenses, and transfers—and the related assets and liabilities—are recognized in the accounts and reported in the financial statements. Specifically, it relates to the timing of the measurements made, regardless of the nature of the

| Governmental Funds | Proprietary Funds |
|---|---|
| **Measurement Focus** | |
| • Are there more or less resources that can be spent in the near future as a result of events and transactions of the period?<br>• Flow of current financial resources—(modified accrual)<br>• Increase in spendable resources—revenues or other financing sources<br>• Decrease in spendable resources—expenditures and other financing uses | • Is the fund better or worse off economically as a result of events and transactions?<br>• Flow of economic resources—(accrual)<br>• Events and transactions that improve the economic positions—revenues or gains<br>• Events and transactions that diminish economic positions—expenses or losses |
| **Receipt of Long-Term Debt Proceeds** | |
| • Decrease in resources available<br>• DR Cash<br>  – CR Other Financing Sources | • No economic improvement<br>• DR Cash<br>  – CR Bonds Payable |
| **Repayment of Principal on Long-Term Debt** | |
| • Decrease in spendable resources<br>• Expenditure for interest due on the debt<br>• DR Expenditure<br>  – CR Cash | • Economic position not diminished<br>• Expense for interest due on the debt<br>• DR Bonds Payable<br>  – CR Cash |
| **Capital Acquisition** | |
| • Decrease in spendable resources<br>• DR Expenditure<br>  – CR Cash | • Economic position not diminished<br>• DR Equipment<br>  – CR Cash |
| **Exhaustion of Capital Assets** | |
| • No effect on spendable resources<br>• Depreciation is not recognized | • Economic position diminished<br>• DR Depreciation Expense<br>  – CR Accumulated Depreciation |

**Exhibit 8.2    Measurement focus.**

| Deferrals and Amortization | |
|---|---|
| • Decrease in spendable resources<br>• Entire disbursement recognized in current period<br>• DR Expenditure<br>  – CR Cash | • Economic positions diminished only by the expense for the benefited period<br>• Expense allocated over entire period of benefit<br>• DR Deferred Charge<br>  – CR Cash<br>• DR Amortization Expense<br>  – CR Deferred Charge |

Source: *Accounting and Reporting Manual*, 2002: 10-11.

**Exhibit 8.2 (continued).**

measurement, on either the cash or the accrual method (Accounting and Reporting Manual, 2002: 181). Generally, governmental fund revenues and expenditures are recognized on the modified accrual basis. As such, revenues are recognized in the accounting period in which they become available and measurable, while expenditures are recognized in the accounting period in which the fund liability is incurred, if measurable, except unmatured interest on long-term debt, which is recognized when due. On the other hand, proprietary fund revenue and expenses are generally reported on the accrual basis. On the accrual basis, the financial effects on a government of transactions and other events and circumstances that have cash consequences for the government are recorded in the periods in which those transactions, events, and circumstances occur, rather than only in the periods in which cash is received or paid by the government (Accounting and Reporting Manual, 2002: 177). Thus, revenues are recognized in the accounting period in which they are earned and become measurable; expenses should be recognized in the period incurred, if measurable (Accounting and Reporting Manual, 2002: 12).

According to Holder (1996: 177–178), "An expenditure reflects the cost of acquiring a good or service. An expense may represent, in addition, the expiration of the value of the good or service." In other words, an expenditure is recorded when financial resources are spent, while an expense would be recorded when economic resources were actually consumed. The essential point of the concept of expense is to record an expense when an asset is actually used. Very little difference occurs over an expense or an expenditure as it applies to the payment of direct labor costs, since these are consistent or regular during a fiscal period. Differences, however, occur when applied to the use of inventory or the use of equipment. In the concept of expenditure, the cost of inventory is recorded when it is obtained. In the concept of expense, inventory is carried as an asset and expensed as it is used. This does make a difference in many proprietary activities that consume significant amounts of inventory, such as a central print shop or central motor pool, sometimes at differential rates.

The more critical distinction occurs when related to the use of equipment. By expensing a depreciation cost over the lifetime of a fixed asset, one is fully expensing the cost of that asset. The result is that at the end of the life expectancy of the asset, its book value will be zero. Although GASB requires depreciation of capital assets, the Statement does not prescribe the method. As a result, depreciation methods are a management decision that should be based on the resources necessary to determine the various calculations and the capabilities of asset management systems. In addition to composite or group methods, any established depreciation method may be used (e.g., straight-line, sum-of-the-years' digits, or double-declining balance). Depreciation may be calculated for individual assets or it may be determined for the following:

- A class of assets
- A network of assets
- A subsystem of a network

The depreciation method can vary for different categories of assets. To simplify the calculations involved, the composite method may be used to calculate depreciation expense. It is applied to a group of similar assets or dissimilar assets in the same class, using the same depreciation rate, but not across classes of assets. The estimated life for the group may be based on the individual weighted average, the simple average of the useful lives of the assets in the group, or the weighted average or assessment of the life of the group as a whole. This method assumes no salvage value for assets; therefore, it simplifies the calculations and the recording of asset dispositions (Financial Accounting, 2003: 52). Exhibit 8.3 presents an overview and examples of significant differences between the basis of accounting for proprietary funds and governmental funds.

## 8.1.3 Equity Recognition

Equity recognition involves ownership of economic resources that is recognized and documented. Proprietary fund activities require some initial infusion of capital. This could result from designated transfers from other funds, typically the general fund. The equity of a proprietary fund may include contributed capital, such as financial resources, property, facilities, or equipment from another governmental entity or from a private entity. When income exceeds expenses in an accounting cycle, the equity of the unit will increase as long as the earnings remain within the entity. On the one hand, the fund balance for governmental funds is the value of financial resources available for future use. Because of the current financial resources measurement focus of governmental funds, fund balance is often

| Governmental Funds | Proprietary Funds |
|---|---|
| **Basis of Accounting** ||
| Modified Accrual—Cash flow must occur within a short-enough period to affect current spendable resources. Revenues must be both measurable and available and expenditures are generally recognized when they are expected to draw upon current spendable resources. | Full Accrual—Revenue/gain or expense/loss recognized when they occur regardless of cash flow. |
| **Billing for Services Rendered** ||
| • Only the amount available to finance liabilities of the current period would be recognized as revenues. <br> • DR Receivable <br> – CR Revenue <br> – CR Deferred Revenue | • Entire revenue recognized in period in which services were provided. The timing of collections is not relevant. <br> • DR Receivable <br> – CR Revenue |
| **Employees Earn Vacation Leave That Will Be Taken Sometime in the Future** ||
| • Leave would only be recognized as an expenditure to the extent it is expected to be liquidated with current spendable resources. <br> • No expenditure | • The liability has been incurred. <br> • DR Expense <br> – CR Accrued Liability |

Source: *Accounting and Reporting Manual,* 2002: 10–11.

**Exhibit 8.3   Basis of accounting.**

considered a measure of available expendable financial resources. This is a particularly important measure in the general fund because it reflects the primary functions of the government and includes both state aid and local tax revenues. The relative amount of unreserved fund balance reflected in the general fund is used by rating agencies as a measure of financial strength of the government. Declines in the amount of unreserved fund balance may signal deterioration in the financial condition of the entity. On the other hand, net assets or retained earnings for a proprietary fund are the residual value of economic assets generated from and available for the ongoing operation of the entity. Solana and Brams (1996: 141–142) suggest that these resources should be employed to produce services connected with the primary function of the unit. According to Ruppel (2005: 78) one of the most

| Governmental Funds | Proprietary Funds |
|---|---|
| **Equity Recognition** | |
| • Fund Balance<br> – Reserved<br> – Unreserved | • Net Assets—Invested in capital<br> assets, net of related debt<br> – Restricted<br> – Unrestricted |

*Source: Accounting and Reporting Manual, 2002: 10–11.*

**Exhibit 8.4   Equity recognition.**

significant changes brought about by Governmental Accounting Standards Board Statement No. 34 concerns accounting for capital contributed by a government into the proprietary fund. Previously, these capital contributions were recorded directly as additions to net assets. GASB Statement No. 34 now requires that these contributions pass through the income statement, where they are reported separately from operating revenues and expenses, but not directly as an addition to net assets.

Exhibit 8.4 presents an overview of significant differences between the basis of accounting for proprietary funds and governmental funds.

## 8.1.4  Pricing

The primary expectation of governmental activities reported in proprietary funds is that these activities are self-sustaining. To measure whether or not this expectation is being met requires a primary focus on operating income and what is the equivalent of profitability. In the governmental sector, the terms *surplus* and *deficit* are used instead of *profit* and *loss,* but the meanings for operational purposes are the same. This means an emphasis on generating income while holding down costs and retaining consumer satisfaction, unlike the primary expectation of a governmental fund activity such as public safety, where the activities use a predetermined amount of limited budgetary authorized (appropriated) resources to deliver the services. Because of these different expectations for different governmental activities, proprietary financial statements need to be presented using the economic resources measurement focus and the full accrual basis of accounting.

Thus, an important decision that must be made concerning proprietary funds is the determination of transfer pricing. Transfer pricing is the determination of prices to be charged for the goods and services produced. According to Solano and Brams (1996: 129): "The main purpose of these business-like organizations is to provide services to consumers at a price that will cover both the current cost of operations (expenses) and the maintenance and financing of necessary capital assets." As such, proprietary operations are the most efficient when the rates charged for services are sufficient to cover all costs of operations and necessary reinvestment. In these cases, careful attention is given to full cost recovery by ensuring that the charges made to using departments of the governmental unit at least cover the costs involved. This includes the cost of capital as well as depreciation of fixed assets that are used in production of the good or service. These operations do not need to generate a surplus, but must achieve a breakeven position. In some cases, such as a central motor pool operation, this means that the fees charged to using units may be higher than those fees charged by private providers outside the unit of government for comparable services. An example of this noncompetitive charge is in the case of a motor pool operation that must also provide specialized and expensive equipment that has limited use. The cost of such equipment is cross-subsidized by fees charged to users of personal automobiles and other standard equipment. In these cases, the governmental unit also prohibits the use of outside vendors to protect the financial position of the governmental operation. Typically, a governmental unit that maintains these internal service activities prohibits its governmental units from going outside the organization to acquire these services, effectively creating a monopoly situation. It should be kept in mind that pricing a good or service at any price other than cost will result in distorted consumption preferences. Pricing at less than cost gives consumers an incentive to overconsume, while overpricing will lead to less than optimal consumption. According to Solano and Brams (1996: 141–142):

> When rates yield excess revenues, then the rates should be reduced. If the excess retained earnings are transferred to other funds, users of the services are subsidizing other programs from which they may not benefit in direct proportion to the amount of the subsidy.

Exhibit 8.5 illustrates the basic differences between the operations of enterprise activities and internal service activities.

## 8.1.5 Transfers

An important issue involving proprietary funds is the transfer of resources to and from such entities. Financial transactions involving contributed or advanced capital are typically accomplished via interfund transfers. A quasi-external transaction is a payment by one fund for a good or service provided by another fund (Ruppel, 2005: 80). Interfund transactions that would be treated as revenues, expenditures, or expenses if they involved organizations external to the government unit (e.g., payments in lieu of taxes from an enterprise fund to the general fund; internal service fund billings to departments; and routine employer contributions to a pension trust fund and routine service charges for inspection, engineering, utilities, or similar services provided by a department financed from one fund to a department financed from another fund). These transactions should be accounted for as revenues, expenditures, or expenses in the funds involved. In some cases where

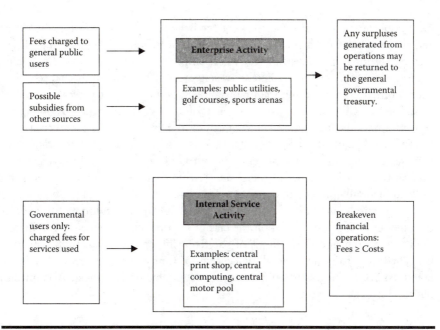

**Exhibit 8.5    Business-type operations in government.**

the proprietary fund accumulates earnings in excess of that needed to cover costs, the "excess" earnings from functions such as water or wastewater utilities may be transferred to the general fund to support other uses (Accounting and Reporting Manual, 2002: 197). In other instances, resources may be transferred from the general fund to the proprietary fund to subsidize the operation of a publicly desired function such as a swimming pool or other recreational programs. According to Bland and Rubin (1997: 161):

> Interfund transactions are one of the potential trouble spots in financial accountability. One of the purposes of the fund structure is to ensure that earmarked money has been spent appropriately, but interfund transactions can muddy the waters, making it difficult to determine what the money was actually spent for .... If revenue is transferred twice ... the switch is virtually impossible to trace ...

## 8.2  Financial Statements

Financial statements are used to convey to managers, governing bodies, citizens, and other interested parties, information regarding the operations and financial status of governmental entities (Herbert, Killough, and Steiss, 1984: 27). The three most important financial statements are the balance sheet, the income statement, and the cash flow statement. The balance sheet, or statement of financial position, presents information concerning the financial position of an entity as of a specific point in time. The income statement, or statement of revenues and expenses, presents information concerning the financial operation of an entity over a period of time. The cash flow statement, or statement of changes in financial position, presents information concerning the movement of financial resources for an entity.

The concept of major fund reporting was introduced and defined by GASB Statement 34 to simplify the presentation of fund information and to focus attention on the major activities of the entity. Rather than require each type of fund to be individually presented, Statement 34 requires the individual presentation of only major funds, with all other funds combined into a single column. This reduces the number of funds presented on the face of the financial statements, and directs the focus on the significant funds of the reporting entity. Major fund reporting is applied only to governmental and enterprise funds. Internal service funds are exempted from the major fund reporting requirements (Financial Accounting, 2003: 32).

## 8.2.1 Balance Sheet

A balance sheet, sometimes referred to as a statement of net assets or a statement of financial position, presents the entity financial position as of a specific point in time. Financial position refers to the relationship between the amount of economic resources available compared to the quantity of economic obligations owed. The major sections of a balance sheet include assets, liabilities, and net assets. The balance sheet is premised on the following relationship:

Assets = Liabilities + Fund Equity (or fund balance).

The balance sheet communicates information about the resources and obligations of the fund at a particular point in time. The balance sheets of proprietary funds differ from those of governmental funds in at least two significant ways:

- Plant assets used to render proprietary fund services are reported as assets of the fund net of an allowance for accumulated depreciation
- Long-term debt incurred by a proprietary fund is reported as a liability of that fund rather than as a liability of the local government as a whole (Holder, 1996: 178)

A balance sheet presents assets, liabilities, and net assets by fund at the specified date. It is a snapshot of a proprietary fund's financial position as of the balance sheet date. Account balances in the assets section are normally debits. Normal account balances in the liabilities and net assets or equity sections are usually credits.

Account balances that are opposite their normal balance (assets with credit balances or liabilities and/or equity with debit balances) are bracketed and reported as reductions. Financial statements are a means of conveying to managers, elected officials, citizens, and other interested outside parties such as creditors, bond buyers, and bond rating agencies, a concise representation of the financial position and operations of an entity.

Assets are the economic resources available to the entity. Assets may be current or noncurrent. Current assets are those that can be quickly converted to cash, sold, or otherwise consumed or disposed of during the normal course of an accounting cycle, typically 1 year. Current assets are usually listed in order of liquidity, or convertibility into cash, from the most to the least liquid. Examples of current assets include cash and short-term investments, receivables, balances due from other entities, inventories, and prepaid items. Noncurrent assets may include restricted assets or capital assets. Restricted assets are those that may only be legally used for specifically defined purposes. This limits the use of these resources for general purposes. Capital assets, sometimes referred to as fixed assets or property, plant, and equipment (PPE), are assets that have an extended expected life. As such, they are not assets that are typically liquidated over the short term. Examples of capital assets include land, airfields, buildings, improvements, machinery and equipment, and construction work in progress (CWIP) (Herbert, Killough, and Steiss, 1984: 39).

Liabilities are obligations owed by the entity to third parties. Liabilities are listed by order from current to long term. Liabilities may be current or noncurrent. Current liabilities are those that are expected to be paid within the normal course of an accounting cycle, typically one year. Examples of current liabilities include accounts payable and accrued expenses, accrued interest payable, temporary notes payable, deposits, amounts due to other entities, current bonds payable, current contracts payable, current claims payable, or current compensated absences. Noncurrent liabilities may include noncurrent bonds payable, unamortized deferred bond refunding, unamortized bond premiums, noncurrent contracts payable, noncurrent claims payable, and noncurrent compensated absences (Herbert, Killough, and Steiss, 1984: 39–40).

Net assets, sometimes referred to as equity, is the difference between assets and liabilities. Net assets are the residual value of the economic resources of the entity after taking into consideration obligations owed to third parties. Net assets may result from economic resources contributed by other entities or earnings derived from the operation of the entity and not otherwise transferred out of the fund.

All governmental units provide financial reports that are merged into a comprehensive annual financial report (CAFR). Such reports contain the individual statements by fund as listed in the sections following but they also contain two government-wide reports. The government-wide reports reflect a consolidation of all funds into a single statement of net assets and a statement of activities. In these reports, the financial activity for enterprise funds is listed under the column marked "business-type activities."

Exhibit 8.6 presents a balance sheet for proprietary funds for the City of Wichita, Kansas. Enterprise Funds are reported under column heading "Business-Type Activities" in the Financial Section of the Consolidated Annual Financial Report (CAFR). Golf, Transit, and Storm Water Enterprise Funds are classified as nonmajor funds (GASB 34) and reported in a separate section of the CAFR. Nonmajor funds are rolled into the "Other Enterprise Funds" column in this balance sheet. A total column is provided to show combined totals for Enterprise Funds for each classification of assets, liabilities, and net assets. A final column aggregates all internal service funds and does not add these totals to enterprise funds.

According to Governmental Accounting Standards Board Statement No. 20, "Accounting and Financial Reporting for Proprietary Funds and Other Governmental Entities That Use Proprietary Fund Accounting," proprietary funds must follow all applicable Financial Accounting Standards Board (FASB) Statements and Interpretations, Accounting Practices Board (APB) Opinions, and Committee on Accounting Procedure (CAP) Accounting Research Bulletins issued on or before November 30, 1989, unless there is a conflict or contradiction with Government Accounting Standards Board pronouncements. Subsequent to this date, proprietary funds may follow all FASB Statements and Interpretations that do not conflict with GASB pronouncements (Razek, Hosch, and Ives, 2000: 262). Once a proprietary fund elects to apply or not apply these FASB and other pronouncements, it must be consistent from year to year (Ruppel, 2005: 75).

## 8.2.2 Income Statement

The income statement, sometimes referred to as a statement of revenue and expenses or statement of activities, is a record of the governmental unit's earnings or losses for a given period. It shows the entity's revenues and expenses during this period. This is an important indicator of "profitability" over the fiscal year and should be carefully monitored. "Net income," or profit, is earned when revenues over a given time period exceed expenses. Specifically, the income statement is based on the following relationship:

$$\text{Net Income} = \text{Revenue} - \text{Expenses}$$

The major sections of an income statement include revenues, expenses, net income, capital contributions and operating transfers, and net assets.

This statement is used to identify revenue sources and types of expenses, by fund, for the selected fiscal year. Operating revenues and expenses are reported without brackets, unless the amount reported is a reduction of revenue or expense. Amounts in the nonoperating section of the statement are positive if they are additions to net assets and negative if they are reductions.

Ending net assets balance for the prior fiscal year becomes beginning net assets for the current fiscal year. Increase or (decrease) in net assets for the selected fiscal

**CITY OF WICHITA, KANSAS**

BALANCE SHEET
PROPRIETARY FUNDS
December 31, 2004

| | Business-type Activities - Enterprise Funds | | | Business-type Activities - Enterprise Funds | | Governmental Activities |
| --- | --- | --- | --- | --- | --- | --- |
| | Water Utility | Sewer Utility | Airport Authority | Other Enterprise Funds | Totals | Internal Service Funds |
| **ASSETS** | | | | | | |
| **Current assets:** | | | | | | |
| Cash and temporary investments | $ 4,141,174 | $ 2,869,996 | $ 6,617,730 | $ 3,966,978 | $ 17,595,878 | $ 40,870,040 |
| Investments | - | - | - | - | - | 244,091 |
| Receivables, net | 5,796,479 | 906,175 | 1,092,233 | 174,598 | 7,969,485 | 107,971 |
| Due from other funds | - | - | - | - | - | 3,500,000 |
| Due from other agencies | - | - | - | 455,596 | 455,596 | - |
| Inventories | 1,127,246 | - | - | 331,340 | 1,458,586 | 370,950 |
| Prepaid items | 1,054 | - | 61,880 | - | 62,934 | 14,271 |
| Restricted assets: | | | | | | |
| Cash and temporary investments | 7,703,118 | 6,176,724 | 7,537,069 | - | 21,416,911 | - |
| Receivables | - | - | 332,993 | - | 332,993 | - |
| Net investment in direct financing leases | - | - | 3,691,173 | - | 3,691,173 | - |
| Total current assets | (A) 18,769,071 | 9,952,895 | 19,333,078 | 4,928,512 | 52,983,556 | 45,107,323 |
| **Noncurrent assets:** | | | | | | |
| Restricted assets: | | | | | | |
| Cash and temporary investments | 26,263,219 | 14,588,310 | - | 4,852,932 | 40,851,529 | - |
| Receivables | - | - | - | - | - | - |
| Net investment in direct financing leases | - | - | 70,474,980 | - | 70,474,980 | - |
| Capital assets: | | | | | | |
| Land | 8,392,267 | 3,340,576 | 12,704,695 | 4,852,932 | 29,290,470 | 71,340 |
| Airfield | - | - | 107,800,053 | - | 107,800,053 | - |
| Buildings | 62,402,821 | 85,300,905 | 38,730,241 | 13,828,636 | 200,262,603 | 3,332,437 |
| Improvements other than buildings | 334,496,702 | 233,182,641 | 23,966,816 | 88,275,722 | 679,021,881 | - |
| Machinery, equipment and other assets | 34,783,056 | 23,023,814 | 17,687,560 | 20,893,391 | 96,387,821 | 39,413,047 |
| Construction in progress | 40,577,754 | 36,443,400 | 28,413,311 | 3,601,608 | 109,036,073 | - |
| Less accumulated depreciation | (122,172,334) | (87,980,153) | (127,577,655) | (23,369,046) | (341,099,188) | (32,636,681) |
| Total capital assets (net of accumulated depreciation) | 358,480,266 | 313,311,183 | 101,725,021 | 108,083,243 | 881,599,713 | 10,180,143 |
| Other assets | 1,775,953 | 1,708,318 | 27,390 | - | 3,601,661 | - |
| Total noncurrent assets | 386,519,438 | 329,697,811 | 172,227,391 | 108,083,243 | 996,527,863 | 10,180,143 |
| Total assets | (K) $ 405,288,509 | $ 339,650,706 | $ 191,560,469 | $ 113,011,755 | $ 1,049,511,439 | $ 55,287,466 |
| | | | | | | (Continued) |

**Exhibit 8.6    Balance sheet—proprietary funds, City of Wichita, Kansas.**

| | Business-type Activities – Enterprise Funds | | | Business-type Activities – Enterprise Funds | | Governmental Activities |
|---|---|---|---|---|---|---|
| | Water Utility | Sewer Utility | Airport Authority | Other Enterprise Funds | Totals | Internal Service Funds |
| **LIABILITIES** | | | | | | |
| **Current liabilities:** | | | | | | |
| Accounts payable and accrued expenses | $ 643,199 | $ 657,341 | $ 100,667 | $ 158,835 | $ 1,560,042 | $ 2,225,827 |
| Accrued interest payable | 226,019 | | 68,266 | 48,370 | 342,655 | – |
| Temporary notes payable | | | | 600,500 | 600,500 | |
| Deposits | 1,885,881 | | 18,641 | 145 | 1,905,667 | |
| Due to other funds | | | | 529,944 | 529,944 | |
| **Current portion of long-term obligations:** | | | | | | |
| General obligation bonds payable | | | 560,000 | 2,485,302 | 3,075,302 | |
| Contracts payable | 277,803 | | | | 277,803 | |
| Claims payable | | | | | | 5,686,565 |
| Compensated absences | 413,739 | 251,127 | 255,303 | 278,260 | 1,198,519 | 279,550 |
| **Current liabilities payable from restricted assets:** | | | | | | |
| Accounts payable and accrued expenses | | | 105,310 | | 105,310 | |
| Accrued interest payable | 1,527,404 | 1,415,826 | 332,903 | | 3,276,313 | |
| Revenue bonds payable | 6,175,624 | 4,780,868 | 3,691,173 | | 14,627,665 | |
| Total current liabilities | (B) 11,149,759 | 7,085,162 | 5,163,443 | 4,101,356 | 27,499,750 | 8,191,942 |
| **Noncurrent liabilities:** | | | | | | |
| General obligation bonds payable | (J) | | 3,150,000 | 9,620,542 | 12,770,542 | |
| Revenue bonds | 117,856,718 | 113,709,855 | 70,474,980 | | 302,041,553 | |
| Unamortized deferred refunding | (430,301) | (369,210) | | | (805,511) | |
| Unamortized revenue bond premium | 2,103,788 | 3,150,277 | | | 5,254,065 | |
| Contracts payable | | | | | | |
| Claims payable | | | | | | 13,398,055 |
| Compensated absences | 64,235 | 38,089 | 41,296 | 39,158 | 183,678 | 45,046 |
| Total noncurrent liabilities | 119,588,440 | 116,529,911 | 73,666,276 | 9,659,700 | 319,444,327 | 13,443,101 |
| Total liabilities | 130,738,199 | 123,615,103 | 78,829,719 | 13,761,056 | 346,944,077 | 21,635,043 |
| **NET ASSETS** | | | | | | |
| Invested in capital assets, net of related debt | 237,381,238 | 185,567,489 | 87,563,762 | 94,798,585 | 625,331,074 | 10,180,143 |
| **Restricted for:** | | | | | | |
| Capital projects | | | 7,537,090 | 22,522 | 7,559,591 | |
| Debt Service | 1,424,312 | 1,415,832 | | | 2,840,144 | |
| Revenue bond reserves | 26,187,711 | 14,425,260 | | | 40,612,961 | |
| Unrestricted | 9,557,049 | 4,627,032 | 7,600,919 | 4,429,592 | 26,223,592 | 23,472,280 |
| Total net assets | 274,550,310 | 216,035,603 | 112,730,750 | 99,250,699 | 702,567,362 | 33,652,423 |
| Total liabilities and net assets | $ 405,288,509 | $ 339,650,706 | $ 191,560,469 | $ 113,011,755 | $ 1,049,511,439 | $ 55,287,466 |

Total net assets — $ 702,567,362

Some amounts reported for business-type activities in the statement of net assets are different because certain internal service fund assets and liabilities are included with business-type activities — (658,762)

Net assets of business-type activities — $ 701,908,600

The accompanying notes to the financial statements are an integral part of this statement.

**Exhibit 8.6 (continued).**

year is added to beginning net assets balance to determine ending balance of net assets for the fiscal period reported by the statement of changes.

Revenue is the inflow of economic resources into the entity. Revenue may be operating or nonoperating. Operating revenues are the direct result of the primary function of the entity, such as charges for services and sales or fees or rentals. Nonoperating revenues are the indirect result of resources flowing into the entity for other reasons such as grants, interest on investments, gains from the sale of assets, or bond premium amortization.

Operating revenues are generated directly from operating activities of an enterprise fund. Operating income is a governmental unit's earnings from its primary operations after it has deducted the cost of goods and services and its general operating expenses. Operating Income can be calculated as follows:

Operating Income = Gross Revenue – General Operating Expenses – Depreciation Expense

Expenses are the outflow of economic resources from an entity. Expenses may also be operating or nonoperating. Operating expenses may include items such as cost of personal services, cost of contractual services materials and supplies, cost of materials used, administrative charges, payments in lieu of franchise fees, depreciation, employee benefits, or insurance claims. Nonoperating expenses may include items such as interest expense, losses from the sale of assets, or bond discount amortization.

Operating expenses are incurred in production of the goods and services provided by an enterprise fund. General operating expenses are typical expenses incurred in the day-to-day operation of the governmental unit. For a water and sewer utility, for example, this would include personal services, contractual services, material and supplies, administrative charges, and payment in lieu of franchise tax. Expenses also include depreciation, which is the gradual loss in value of equipment and other tangible assets over the course of their estimated service life. Depreciation is used to allocate the value of a long-term asset during the periods it will be used. If a water utility purchased a pump, the calculation of depreciation on this item is the cost of the pump, less any salvage value, prorated over the estimated service life of the pump. Each fiscal reporting period would be charged a portion of the cost of the pump.

Nonoperating revenues (expenses) include income and expenses generated outside the unit's primary activity. Interest on investments would be recorded in this section. Nonoperating expenses include interest expenses or other financing costs such as bond discount amortization.

Net income or loss is the final line on the statement, giving it the distinction of commonly being referred to as the "bottom line." Net income measures the amount of revenue after deducting all related expenses. The enterprise fund activity will make a determination at the end of a fiscal year as to how much of this earning should be "retained" for future use within the enterprise. Such resources comprise the working capital for future operations and possible one-time investments such as equipment. In some instances, the governmental unit may also "earmark" a portion of earnings to be shifted via an interfund transfer to the governmental fund (general fund) as support for the general activities of the governmental unit. The logic of such transfers is that these payments are made in lieu of taxes. In other words, the privately owned golf course must make property tax payments to the municipality or county based on the value of the course's property, and these revenues are used by the municipality to support governmental activity including public safety activities, some of which benefit the private golf course. Since the private golf course is required to make property tax payments, it is considered only fair that a publicly owned golf course also make comparable payments to the parent unit.

Net income is the difference between revenues and expenses. Capital contributions are economic resources contributed to begin or continue operation of the entity. Transfers are economic resources advanced from or to other funds. Net assets or retained earnings are the residual value of economic resources resulting from both current and past activities. Exhibit 8.7 is an example of a statement of revenues, expenses, and changes in fund net assets for proprietary funds in the City of Wichita, Kansas.

## 8.2.3 Cash Flow Statement

Only proprietary funds use the cash flow statement, sometimes referred to as a statement of changes in financial position, which presents information concerning the flow of economic resources into and out of an entity. A cash flow statement presents an entity's inflows and outflows of economic resources. This is important because the unit must have sufficient resources to meet its obligations when they fall due. While an income statement indicates whether or not the governmental unit had net income, a cash flow statement shows whether the unit generated cash. Cash flow statements show changes over time rather than a snapshot of a point in time. The cash flow statement uses the information from the governmental unit's balance sheet and statement of revenues, expenses, and changes in fund net assets or fund equity. The cash flow statement reports cash flows in four activities: operating activities, noncapital financing activities, capital and related investing activities, and investing activities. The major sections of a cash flow statement include cash flows from operating activities, cash flows from noncapital financing activities, cash flows from capital financing activities, and cash flows from investing activities.

Operating activities analyze a governmental unit's cash flow from net income or losses. The cash flow statement reconciles the net income (as shown on the statement of revenues, expenses, and changes in fund net assets or fund equity) to the actual cash the unit received or used in operating. Reconciliation is done by deducting from net income any noncash items (such as depreciation or an increase or decrease in inventory) and any cash that was used or provided by other operating assets and

**CITY OF WICHITA, KANSAS**

STATEMENT OF REVENUES, EXPENSES AND CHANGES IN FUND NET ASSETS

PROPRIETARY FUNDS

For the year ended December 31, 2004

| | Business-type Activities - Enterprise Funds | | | | | Governmental Activities |
| --- | --- | --- | --- | --- | --- | --- |
| | Water Utility | Sewer Utility | Airport Authority | Other Enterprise Funds | Totals | Internal Service Funds |
| **OPERATING REVENUES** | | | | | | |
| Charges for services and sales | $ 33,455,073 | $ 25,880,494 | $ 3,382,609 | $ 7,413,917 | $ 70,132,093 | $ 8,732,399 |
| Fees | | | 3,002,088 | 2,665,644 | 5,667,732 | |
| Rentals | 5,811 | | 11,864,041 | 618,102 | 12,518,854 | 9,121,874 |
| Employer contributions | | | | | | 21,729,851 |
| Employee contributions | | | | | | 8,177,412 |
| Other | 20,994 | 22,984 | 48,795 | 37,611 | 128,374 | 476,365 |
| Total operating revenues | (C) 33,481,868 | 25,903,478 | 18,326,433 | 10,735,274 | 88,447,053 | 46,237,901 |
| **OPERATING EXPENSES** | | | | | | |
| Personal services | 7,539,116 | 8,817,561 | 5,536,814 | 8,057,853 | 29,751,334 | 5,852,208 |
| Contractual services | 5,214,503 | 4,118,502 | 3,028,961 | 3,749,163 | 16,111,129 | 4,132,235 |
| Materials and supplies | 2,880,236 | 2,070,705 | 3,383,227 | 1,769,223 | 10,113,390 | 2,744,948 |
| Cost of materials used | | | | | | 2,271,630 |
| Administrative charges | 851,130 | 205,060 | 306,780 | 432,670 | 1,795,640 | 313,660 |
| Payments in lieu of franchise fees | 1,972,560 | 1,505,140 | | 150,000 | 3,627,700 | |
| Depreciation | 8,652,803 | 6,216,912 | 7,105,745 | 4,195,522 | 26,170,982 | 2,648,320 |
| Employee benefits | | | | | | 25,208,985 |
| Insurance claims | | | | | | 6,876,993 |
| Total operating expenses | (E) 27,120,347 | 22,733,870 | 19,361,527 | 18,354,431 | 87,570,175 | 50,048,979 |
| Operating income (loss) | 6,361,521 | 3,169,608 | (1,035,094) | (7,619,157) | 876,878 | (3,811,078) |

**Exhibit 8.7** Statement of revenues, expenses, and changes in fund net assets, proprietary funds, City of Wichita, Kansas.

**NONOPERATING REVENUES (EXPENSES)**

| | | | | | |
|---|---|---|---|---|---|
| Operating grants | 387,931 | 4,932,857 | 3,155,956 | | |
| Interest on investments | (261,361) | 246,156 | 47,934 | 5,614,878 | 307,917 |
| Other revenues (expenses) | (28,877) | (2,035) | 1,382 | (260,891) | |
| Interest expense | (4,670,814) | (3,796,045) | (5,000,155) | (614,274) | (14,171,088) |
| Gain (loss) from sale of assets | (15,104) | (185,048) | (562,389) | 10,714 | (751,827) | (220,237) |
| Bond premium (discount) amortization | (12,540) | 48,180 | (5,508) | | 30,132 | 87,680 |
| Total nonoperating revenues (expenses) | (4,571,888) | (3,688,792) | (723,813) | 2,571,453 | (8,412,640) | |
| Income (loss) before contributions and transfers | 1,799,833 | (519,184) | (1,756,907) | (5,047,704) | (5,535,962) | (3,723,398) |
| Capital contributions and operating transfers: | | | | | | |
| Capital contributions | 7,785,899 | 9,167,897 | 10,985,138 | 4,210,897 | 32,119,631 | 354,962 |
| Transfers from other funds | | 99,008 | | 4,275,430 | 4,374,488 | 702,810 |
| Transfers to other funds | (1,866,611) | (882,600) | (763,200) | (694,345) | (4,036,756) | (1,531,750) |
| Increase (decrease) in net assets | 7,859,121 | 7,854,971 | 8,463,031 | 2,744,278 | 26,921,401 | (4,197,376) |
| Total net assets – beginning | 266,691,189 | 208,180,632 | 104,267,719 | 90,506,421 | 675,645,961 | 37,849,799 |
| Total net assets – ending | $ 274,550,310 | $ 216,035,603 | $ 112,730,750 | $ 99,250,699 | $ 702,567,362 | $ 33,652,423 |

Increase in net assets per fund statements    $    26,921,401

Some amounts reported for business-type activities in the statement of activities are different because the net revenue (expense) of certain internal service funds is reported with business-type activities    (1,012,005)

Change in net assets of business-type activities    $    25,909,396

The accompanying notes to the financial statements are an integral part of this statement.

**Exhibit 8.7** (continued).

liabilities. Cash flows from operating activities result from the flow of economic resources into and out of an entity resulting from its primary activity. These cash flows may include cash received from customers, cash payments to suppliers, cash payments to employees, and payments in lieu of franchise fees.

The second part of a cash flow statement shows the cash flow from all financing activities. Financing activities include cash raised by the selling of bonds. Debt service on bonds, for example, would be reflected as cash outflow. Cash flows from noncapital financing activities result from the flow of economic resources into and out of any entity resulting from such sources as operating grants or transfers to or from other entities. Cash flows from capital activities may result from activities such as payment of temporary notes, additions to capital assets, debt service, proceeds from the sale of assets, or capital contributions.

Finally, the third part of a cash flow statement shows the cash flow from all investing activities. This includes purchases or sales of long-term assets. If a governmental unit purchases major equipment with cash, the cash flow statement would show this activity as a cash outflow from investing activities. Likewise, if the unit sold a major piece of equipment, the revenue from the sale would be shown as a cash inflow because it provided cash.

A proprietary statement of cash flows, as its title implies, identifies cash inflows and outflows in proprietary funds. Enterprise Funds are reported under column heading "Business-Type Activities" in the Financial Section of the Consolidated Annual Financial Report (CAFR). Golf, Transit, and Storm Water Enterprise Funds are classified as nonmajor funds (GASB 34) and reported in a separate section of the CAFR. Nonmajor funds are rolled into the "Other Enterprise Funds" column in this statement of cash flows. A total column is provided to show combined totals for Enterprise Funds for each cash flow activity.

A cash flow statement shows increases or (decreases) in cash balances, for each fund, which occurred during the fiscal period being reported. It gives a visual indication of activities generating cash and activities that are net consumers of cash. It also reports ending cash balances that agree with the cash and temporary investments balances reported on the proprietary fund balance sheet.

Internal service funds are reported as individual funds in the internal service funds section of the CAFR. The combined total is rolled up into the financial section of the CAFR and reported in one column as "Governmental Activities." Exhibit 8.8 presents a statement of cash flows for the proprietary funds in the City of Wichita, Kansas.

## 8.3  Financial Ratios

In addition to being legally required in many instances, financial statements also provide important information for managerial purposes. The purpose of financial

**CITY OF WICHITA, KANSAS**

STATEMENT OF CASH FLOWS
PROPRIETARY FUNDS
For the year ended December 31, 2004

| | Business-type Activities - Enterprise Funds | | | | | Governmental Activities |
|---|---|---|---|---|---|---|
| | Water Utility | Sewer Utility | Airport Authority | Other Enterprise Funds | Totals | Internal Service Funds |
| **CASH FLOWS FROM OPERATING ACTIVITIES** | | | | | | |
| Cash received from customers (M) | $ 33,436,497 | $ 26,196,547 | $ 19,909,461 | $ 10,856,052 | $ 90,398,557 | $ 46,046,488 |
| Cash payments to suppliers for goods and services | (9,686,460) | (6,211,561) | (7,083,852) | (6,016,434) | (28,998,316) | (39,463,374) |
| Cash payments to employees for services | (7,512,545) | (8,818,382) | (5,509,144) | (8,042,972) | (29,883,043) | (5,826,957) |
| Payment in lieu of franchise fees | (1,972,560) | (1,505,140) | - | (150,000) | (3,627,700) | - |
| Other operating revenues | 20,964 | 22,984 | 46,705 | 37,611 | 128,374 | 369,531 |
| Net cash provided by (used in) operating activities (N) | 14,285,907 | 9,884,448 | 7,363,260 | (3,315,743) | 28,317,872 | 1,666,688 |
| **CASH FLOWS FROM NONCAPITAL FINANCING ACTIVITIES** | | | | | | |
| Operating grant received | - | - | - | 3,281,702 | 3,281,702 | |
| Transfers from other funds | - | - | - | 3,783,080 | 3,783,080 | 702,810 |
| Transfers to other funds | (1,597,553) | (882,600) | (763,200) | (201,995) | (3,445,348) | (1,531,750) |
| Net cash provided by (used in) noncapital financing activities | (1,597,553) | (882,600) | (763,200) | 6,862,787 | 3,619,434 | (828,940) |
| **CASH FLOWS FROM CAPITAL AND RELATED FINANCING ACTIVITIES** | | | | | | |
| Payment of temporary notes (K) | (18,330,747) | (12,363,236) | (14,739,306) | 374,600 | 374,600 | |
| Additions to property, plant and equipment (L) | (6,152,135) | (4,528,274) | (575,000) | (3,053,844) | (48,487,133) | (2,390,709) |
| Debt service - principal | (6,207,223) | (5,675,917) | (229,285) | (1,871,368) | (13,126,777) | |
| Debt service - interest | | | | (623,500) | (12,935,925) | |
| Proceeds from sale of assets | 60,175 | 27,268 | 26,194 | 10,937 | 124,504 | 128,254 |
| Capital contributions | 4,534,675 | 2,216,488 | 10,986,520 | 1,172,358 | 18,910,041 | |
| Net cash provided by (used in) capital and related financing activities | (26,095,255) | (20,523,661) | (4,530,877) | (3,990,817) | (55,140,600) | (2,262,455) |
| **CASH FLOWS FROM INVESTING ACTIVITIES** | | | | | | |
| Proceeds from sale and maturity of investment securities | | | | | | 2,892 |
| Interest on investments | 387,931 | 246,156 | 60,595 | 47,934 | 742,616 | 307,917 |
| Net cash provided by investing activities | 387,931 | 246,156 | 60,595 | 47,934 | 742,616 | 310,809 |
| Net increase (decrease) in cash and temporary investments | (12,918,970) | (11,275,647) | 2,129,778 | (395,839) | (22,460,678) | (1,081,896) |
| Cash and temporary investments - January 1 | 51,026,481 | 34,910,677 | 12,025,021 | 4,362,817 | 102,324,996 | 41,951,936 |
| Cash and temporary investments - December 31 | $ 38,107,511 | $ 23,635,030 | $ 14,154,799 | $ 3,966,978 | $ 79,864,318 | $ 40,870,040 |

(Continued)

**Exhibit 8.8    Cash flow statement—priority funds.**

| | Business-type Activities - Enterprise Funds | | | | | Governmental Activities |
|---|---|---|---|---|---|---|
| | Water Utility | Sewer Utility | Airport Authority | Other Enterprise Funds | Totals | Internal Service Funds |
| **RECONCILIATION OF OPERATING INCOME (LOSS) TO NET CASH PROVIDED BY (USED IN) OPERATING ACTIVITIES** | | | | | | |
| Operating income (loss) | $ 8,361,521 | $ 3,169,608 | $ (1,035,094) | $ (7,619,157) | $ 876,878 | $ (3,611,078) |
| Adjustments to reconcile operating income (loss) to net cash provided by (used in) operating activities: | | | | | | |
| Depreciation | 8,662,803 | 6,216,912 | 7,105,745 | 4,195,522 | 26,170,982 | 2,648,320 |
| Changes in assets and liabilities: | | | | | | |
| (Increase) decrease in accounts receivable | (83,528) | 318,053 | 1,625,369 | 159,212 | 2,017,106 | 778,118 |
| (Increase) decrease in inventory | 90,378 | - | - | (10,203) | 86,175 | 128 |
| (Increase) decrease in prepaid items | 454 | - | (11,307) | - | (10,853) | (18,206) |
| (Increase) decrease in fixed assets due to expenditure reclass | - | - | - | 218,243 | 218,243 | |
| (Decrease) increase in accounts payable/accrued expenses | (727,433) | 182,708 | (363,578) | (273,418) | (1,171,723) | 255,535 |
| (Decrease) increase in deposits | 59,141 | - | 4,455 | (823) | 62,773 | |
| Increase in claims payable | | | | | | 1,822,620 |
| (Decrease) increase in compensated absences | 26,571 | (831) | 27,670 | 14,881 | 68,291 | 23,251 |
| Total adjustments | 8,024,386 | 6,714,940 | 8,398,354 | 4,303,414 | 27,440,904 | 5,509,766 |
| Net cash provided by (used in) operating activities | $ 14,385,907 | $ 9,884,448 | $ 7,363,260 | $ (3,315,743) | $ 28,317,872 | $ 1,898,688 |
| **Supplemental Schedule of Non-Cash Investing and Financing Activities** | | | | | | |
| Assets contributed by benefit districts | $ 2,962,045 | $ 6,041,209 | $ - | $ 3,004,947 | $ 12,008,201 | $ - |
| Change in assets contributed by other government | | | | | | |
| Capital grants received | | | | | | |
| Capital contributed by local government | | | | | | 354,962 |
| Decrease in net investment in direct financing leases | | | 3,403,698 | | 3,403,698 | |
| (Decrease) in revenue bonds payable | | | (3,403,698) | | (3,403,698) | |
| Decrease in interest receivable on direct financing leases | | | 37,821 | | 37,821 | |
| (Decrease) in accrued interest payable on revenue bonds | | | (37,821) | | (37,821) | |
| Interest income on investment in direct financing leases | | | 4,872,262 | | 4,872,262 | |
| Interest expense on revenue bonds payable | | | 4,872,262 | | 4,872,262 | |
| Contribution of capital assets | 260,179 | | | | 260,179 | |
| Transfer of assets between proprietary funds | (99,058) | 99,058 | | | | |

**Exhibit 8.8** (continued).

analysis is to provide information about an entity for decision-making purposes. However, Garrison (1979: 640) cautions that:

> No matter how carefully prepared, all financial statements are essentially historical documents. They tell what has happened during a particular year or series of years. The most valuable information to most users of financial statements ... concerns what probably will happen in the future. The purpose of financial statement analysis is to assist statement users in predicting the future by means of comparison, evaluation, and trend analysis.

The principal objective of financial analysis is to determine the entity's fiscal performance and the soundness and liquidity of its financial position. Financial analysis is typically more important for proprietary entities than governmental ones because proprietary units are usually expected to be at least somewhat self-sufficient. Two sources against which an entity's performance may be judged are past performance and the performance of "peer" entities.

Horizontal or dynamic analysis involves the comparison of data over time. Comparing information for a current period with data for previous years provides useful information for assessing whether the entity's performance is satisfactory or deteriorating. However, a weakness of horizontal analysis is that historical comparisons do not provide an adequate basis for comparison in absolute terms. For example, the fact that an entity's revenues are increasing may not necessarily be good news, if the revenues for "competing" entities are increasing twice as rapidly. In part, the limitations of horizontal analysis may be overcome by establishing a standard benchmark for comparison, such as comparing an entity's performance with a comparable entity or an average of comparable entities. For example, a municipal water system may compare its financial indicators with a comparable water system in a neighboring community or with a comparable industry average. In addition, vertical or static analysis provides a valuable supplement to horizontal analysis. Vertical analysis involves the review of a particular financial statement item to a total that includes that item (Meigs and Meigs, 1979: 644–645). A common-size statement is one that presents the financial information entirely in percentage terms instead of dollar terms (Garrison, 1979: 644). Common tools used for financial analysis include dollar changes, percentage changes, component changes, and ratios (Meigs and Meigs, 1979: 642). Dollar changes provide information about the absolute magnitude of a financial change. Percentage changes provide information about the relative magnitude of a financial change. Presenting changes in percentage terms provides a perspective for the significance of the changes over time. Component changes express the contribution of a piece of a financial item relative to the whole of which it is a part. Ratios express the relationship of one financial item to another. As business-type organizations, these activities are concerned

| **Financial Ratios** |
|---|
| **Liquidity Indicators** |
| • Current Ratio = Current Assets/Current Liabilities |
| • Quick (Acid-Test) Ratio = Quick Assets/Current Liabilities |
| • Working Capital = Current Assets – Current Liabilities |
| • Liability-Revenue Ratio = Liabilities/Revenues |
| • Liquidity Ratio = Cash/Liabilities |
| • Average Monthly Cash-Expense Ratio = Cash/Expenses/12 |
| **Solvency Indicators** |
| • Own-Source Revenue Ratio = Own Source Revenue/Total Revenue |
| • Revenue-Expense Ratio = Revenues/Expenses |
| • Net Asset-Revenue Ratio = Net Assets/Revenue |
| • Net Asset-Expense Ratio = Net Assets/Expenses |
| • Transfer Ratio = Transfers/General Fund Sources |
| **Debt Indicators** |
| • Debt Ratio = Debt/Assets |
| • Per Capita Debt = Debt/Population |
| • Debt-Income Ratio = Debt/Per Capita Personal Income |
| • Debt-Revenue Ratio = Debt/Revenue |
| **Debt Service Indicators** |
| • Debt Service-Revenue Ratio = Debt Service/Revenues |
| • Debt Service-Expense Ratio = Debt Service/Expenses |
| **Efficiency Indicators** |
| • Operating Expense Ratio = Operating Expenses/Total Expenses |
| • Per Capita Revenue = Total Revenues/Population |
| • Return on Assets = Net Income and Interest Expense/Assets |
| • Accounts Receivable Turnover = Sales/Average Accounts Receivable Balance |
| • Inventory Turnover = Cost of Goods Sold/Average Inventory |

**Exhibit 8.9  Financial ratios.**

about their liquidity position and need a reporting of how receipts and expenses are affecting this position. However, Garrison (1979: 641) notes that "ratios should be viewed as a starting point, as indicators of what to pursue in greater depth." Exhibit 8.9 presents commonly used financial ratios.

## 8.3.1 Liquidity Indicators

> **See Exhibit 8.6**
> A / B = 1.68
> 18,769,071 / 11,149,759

Liquidity indicators provide an indication of the ability of an entity to obtain cash or to convert other assets into cash to meet its short-term obligations. Liquidity or cash solvency refers to the ability to generate and maintain enough cash to pay liabilities in a timely manner. For example, if a utility has assets that cannot be converted to cash quickly, it may have difficulty making debt payments. The current ratio is computed by dividing current assets by current liabilities. Based on data from the balance sheet for proprietary funds for the City of Wichita, Kansas, the current ratio (current assets/current liabilities) for the water utility would be 1.68.

This indicates that the water utility has $1.68 in current assets for every $1.00 in current liabilities. A high current ratio indicates that current assets are sufficient to meet current liabilities. The quick ratio is similar to the current ratio, but it excludes inventories. The quick ratio is computed by subtracting inventories from current assets before dividing by current liabilities. The quick ratio excludes inventory because the governmental unit might not be able to convert its inventory quickly into cash. These ratios are only helpful if they have a comparison ratio for other similar governmental units, for example, other water and sewer utilities or reference to past practice and past ratios. It is helpful to establish a group of governmental units of similar size and structure to conduct a peer analysis to see how a particular entity compares not only on financial measures, but staffing and budgetary basis as well. Another liquidity indicator is to determine the entity's working capital. Working capital is equal to the difference between current assets and current liabilities. This indicator gives an actual dollar amount and can be used to compare against the unit's financial obligations to evaluate whether or not there is a comfortable amount of working capital. The liability-revenue ratio measures how well revenue inflows are servicing the current payables owed. A low ratio suggests that short-term obligations are being met with the normal flow of revenues. The average monthly cash-expense ratio measures the availability of cash to meet expenses on a monthly basis. A high ratio suggests that sufficient cash is available to cover expenses on a monthly basis.

## 8.3.2 Solvency Indicators

Solvency indicators provide an indication of the ability of an entity to meet its obligations when due, with existing resources. The own-source revenue ratio provides an indication of whether an entity has sufficient own-source revenues to maintain operations or whether it needs to be subsidized with outside sources. A high ratio indicates that the entity is largely self-sufficient. The revenue-expense ratio provides an indication of whether the entity is generating revenues sufficient to meet expenses. Based on data from the statement of revenues, expenses, and changes in fund net assets for the City of Wichita, Kansas, the revenue-expense ratio (operating revenues/operating expenses) for the water utility would be 1.06.

**See Exhibit 8.7**

$$C \quad + \quad D \quad / \quad E \quad + \quad F \quad + \quad G \quad + \quad H \quad + \quad I$$

$$33{,}481{,}868 + 387{,}931) / (27{,}120{,}347 + 261{,}361 + 4{,}670{,}614 + 15{,}104 + 12{,}540) = 1.06$$

This indicates the water utility receives $1.06 in revenue for every $1.00 it spends. The net asset-revenue ratio and the net asset-expenditure ratio provide an indication of the degree of coverage provided by the net assets in the event of an unexpected decrease in revenues and/or an unexpected increase in expenses. The transfer ratio provides an indication of the extent to which the entity is either subsidizing the general fund or is being subsidized by the general fund. A high ratio of transfer to the general fund suggests that the government is relying on transfers from other sources to finance operations. One possible major source of such transfers might be enterprise operations.

## 8.3.3 Debt Indicators

Debt indicators provide an assessment of an entity's ability to cover its debt obligations. Governmental units that finance assets with a high percentage of debt may not be able to meet their debt obligations and may need a cash infusion from the general fund to stay operating if the units do not perform as expected. The debt ratio indicates the percentage of assets financed through borrowing. Based on data from the balance sheet for proprietary funds for the City of Wichita, Kansas, the debt ratio (debt/assets) for the water utility would be 0.29.

**See Exhibit 8.6**

$$J \quad / \quad K$$

$$(117{,}856{,}718 \ / \ 405{,}288{,}509) = 0.29$$

This indicates that the water utility has $0.29 in debt for every $1.00 in assets. A higher debt ratio indicates that a higher proportion of operations is financed through borrowing. Per capita debt indicates the average amount of debt borne by each citizen. Since increased population denotes an increased need for capital improvements, this amount remains relatively steady. Increases in debt per capita reveal that the growth of debt is exceeding the population growth. The debt-income ratio indicates the level of debt relative to the level of per capita income. Increases in the debt-income ratio reveal that the growth of debt is exceeding the growth in income. The debt-revenue ratio indicates the level of debt relative to the level of income for the entity. Increases in the debt-revenue ratio reveal that the growth of debt is exceeding the growth in revenue.

### 8.3.4 Debt Service Indicators

Debt service indicators provide an indication of the ability of an entity to meet debt service obligations as they fall due. The debt service-revenue ratio gives an indication of the ability of the entity's revenue stream to cover debt service obligations. Based on data from the statement of cash flows for proprietary funds for the City of Wichita, Kansas, the debt service-revenue ratio (debt service/revenue) for the water utility would be 0.37.

**See Exhibit 8.8**

$$K + L / M + N$$
$$((6,152,135 + 6,207,223) / (33,426,497 + 20,984)) = 0.37$$

This indicates that the water utility has \$0.37 in debt service for every \$1.00 in revenue. If the ratio is increasing, this indicates that the ability of the entity's revenue to cover debt service obligations is decreasing. The debt service-expense ratio gives an indication of debt service payments as a proportion of expenses. If this ratio is increasing, the share of expenses going to meet debt service obligations is increasing, meaning the share of resources for expense requirements is decreasing.

### 8.3.5 Efficiency Indicators

**See Exhibit 8.7**
$$E / E + F + G + H + I$$
$$(27,120,347 / (27,120,347 + 261,361 + 4,670,614 + 15,104 + 12,540)) = 0.85$$

Efficiency indicators provide an indication of the efficiency of operation of the entity. The operating expense ratio demonstrates the ability to devote a larger share of expenses to nonoperating purposes. Based on data from the statement of revenues, expenses, and changes in fund net assets for the City of Wichita, Kansas, the operating expense ratio on an operating basis (operating expenses/total expenses) for the Water Utility would be 0.85.

This indicates the water utility spends $0.85 of every $1.00 in total expenses on operations. A high ratio suggests that operating expenses comprise a larger share of total expenses. Per capita revenue demonstrates the ability of the entity to acquire additional revenues. A high ratio suggests a lesser ability to acquire additional revenue. Return on assets measures how well assets have been employed, that is, operating performance. A higher return on assets indicates that the entity's assets are being used more efficiently. Accounts receivable turnover provides an indication of the efficiency of payments, while inventory turnover provides an indication of the efficiency of inventory management.

## 8.4 Internal Service Funds

*Internal service funds* (ISFs) are funds used by a governmental entity to account for the financing of goods and services provided by one department or agency to other departments or agencies on a cost-reimbursement basis. Internal service funds are also sometimes referred to as intragovernmental service funds, working capital funds, revolving funds, and other similar names (Engstrom and Hay, 1994: 147). The difference between an enterprise fund and an internal service fund is that enterprise funds account for services provided to the general public, while internal service funds provide services to other governmental departments. Examples of operations in which internal services funds are commonly used include motor pools, data processing, printing, warehousing, office space allocation, engineering services, self-insurance funds, loan funds, and procurement. ISFs may be used to accomplish the following:

- Take advantage of economies of scale
- Avoid duplication of effort
- Accurately identify costs of specific governmental services
- Subject the task to competitive pressures (Allred, Ball, and Walthers, 2002: 1; Ukeles, 1982)

For example, a government might establish a printing and copying unit to provide these services to other departments. The rationale used to establish the printing and copy center could be that it is more cost-effective than having each department contract with private vendors to do the work or it may be more cost-effective than having each department purchase and maintain their own equipment. Alternatively it could even be more expensive than an outsourced option, but the governmental unit wants more control over the activity (tight deadlines) or requires specialized equipment that would not typically be available with the private provider. Thus, some jurisdictions even require that internal service fund functions compete with private vendors (Davenport, 1996).

According to the AICPA (2004: 19) internal service funds are defined as follows:

> Permitted for any activity that provides goods or services to other funds, departments, or agencies of the primary government and its component units, or to other governments, on a cost-reimbursement basis when the reporting government is the predominant participant in the activity.

Generally Accepted Accounting Principles (GAAP) does not require the use of internal service funds, nor do they require that ISFs include the full cost of services that are provided. However, GAAP does mandate that the predominant activity of the fund must be internal to the reporting entity if an ISF is used (Ruppel, 2005: 79–80).

A study conducted by the Utah Office of the Legislative Fiscal Analyst for the Utah Executive Appropriations Committee identified the advantages and disadvantages of using internal service funds (Allred, Ball, and Walthers, 2002: 2–4).

## 8.4.1 Advantages of Internal Service Funds

- *More efficient use of resources.* ISFs allow equipment and staff to be fully utilized and costs to be shared across several users, rather than duplicate partially used equipment and staff within each agency. An ISF should be able to increase or decrease resources in response to demand from a broad base of users.
- *Allows more accurate accounting of the full cost of providing a particular service.* This is much more difficult to determine from information in the traditional budget, where services can seem "free" because they are appropriated. These costs then send price signals that force users to respond with purchasing decisions that maximize benefits under limited resources. Additionally, this accounting enables one governmental entity to bill another for cost reimbursement.
- *Market incentives.* When rates are set to recover the full cost of the service (including the cost of equipment through depreciation schedules), users can compare the benefit of the service to the cost. If users decide to buy less of the service, the ISF must respond by reducing costs in order to break even.
- *Long-term outlooks.* ISFs have the flexibility to carry funds over from year to year rather than operate on a yearly cycle (however, they must annually account for their acquisition authority). Therefore, they can plan for long-term breakeven with no incentive to expend the full appropriation at year-end. However, some jurisdictions do choose to make internal service fund appropriations annually. ISFs also encourage better long-range planning regarding equipment purchases and other internal services necessary for state government.

■ *Better cost comparisons.* ISFs allow users to compare the cost of buying the service against the cost of that service in the private sector or in other state agencies.

■ *Control and consistency.* ISFs enable decision makers to more easily control goods or services delivered than if each agency has its own delivery point. They provide for consistency in service and in reporting. This makes agencies accountable and results in more useful and accurate information for decision makers.

■ *Better planning for capital acquisitions.* By charging for depreciation through their rates, ISFs systematically accumulate funds to replace their equipment when its useful life expires. This allows the budgetary authority to establish a base level of appropriation to cover the full cost of services without the need for fluctuations to meet specific purchase needs each year.

## 8.4.2 Disadvantages of Internal Service Funds

■ *More complicated to understand.* ISF financial reports are presented in a more complicated format than the appropriated budget reports. Fully understanding them requires some familiarity with accounting terminology. Because they require more effort to analyze, and because they are not directly funded with general funds, they do not always receive the same level of scrutiny as other budgets.

■ *Disparate treatment.* Internal service funds typically set rates to recover costs. By definition, if costs increase, rates must increase (after approval through the budget cycle, although they are allowed to establish interim rates for new services). However, appropriated agencies do not necessarily receive funding for their cost increases, especially inflationary increases. Moreover, ISFs are able to charge agencies the full cost of their services even during times when the budgetary authority has not fully funded rate increases in the agencies' base budgets, essentially creating a de facto budget cut for the customer agencies.

■ *Customer disconnect.* Because customer agencies typically do not directly manage ISF operations, they do not feel the ability to control costs, and as a result do not see a clear incentive to do so. While agencies may have the opportunity to participate in the rate-setting process, they often perceive, whether valid or not, that ISFs are not managing costs as tightly as everyone else. Some may resent that rates are developed externally and yet the agencies must "cut a check," or cut services, trusting that the ISF is managing efficiently.

■ *Lack of choice.* Customer agencies are encouraged, and in some cases required, to use the services of ISFs and, therefore, most ISFs are not under true competitive pressure to lower costs and improve customer service. It is unreasonable to expect the ISFs to go out of business if they are outcompeted. However, the ISFs do experience pressure from their customers, the rate-setting authority, and from policymakers, and typically do use benchmarks to compare themselves to the private sector.

■ *Overhead.* There are some agencies that, individually, could provide services in-house more cheaply than the ISFs. To them, the ISFs are an overhead burden.

In addition, Gianakis (1995) concludes that the operation of internal service funds is complicated by several factors:

■ A limited customer base places an expensive premium on service to internal user agencies that often have idiosyncratic needs.
■ Overhead charges are very viable to user agencies, while the costs of avoiding the internal service agency can be hidden.
■ Costs that the internal service agency can recover through its prices are usually incomplete, and the most efficient price cannot be revealed through market mechanisms.
■ Program managers must consider management policy about the service they are delivering, and the budget may not function as an effective policy control mechanism.

Similarly, Falk and Granof (1990) argue that internal service funds

■ Are commonly established indiscriminately without authoritative guidelines,
■ Allow surpluses and shortages that would otherwise be illegal,
■ Facilitate unorthodox debt accounting practices,
■ Foster the use of arbitrary or otherwise inappropriate transfer pricing, and
■ Permit the depreciation of assets that otherwise would not be allowed.

Because of these and other problems, Falk and Granof (1990) conclude that internal service funds are the weakest component of state and local government accounting systems.

## 8.4.3 Pricing Policy

Although internal service funds can provide the data necessary for the accurate pricing of services (Gianakis, 1995), Metzger (1994) points out that the price-setting policy for internal service funds must consider several objectives that may sometimes conflict:

■ Fund sustainability
■ Performance measurement
■ Impact on user behavior
■ Equitable sharing of costs

Typically, an internal service fund sets its rates to recover the full cost of providing a particular service. The goods and services provided by an internal service fund should be priced to break even. It does not benefit the governmental unit if the internal service fund shows a large profit at the end of the fiscal year. What this reflects is that the internal service fund is overcharging other departments for their goods and services. Likewise, it does not benefit the governmental unit if the internal fund has a large deficit at the end of the fiscal year. What this reflects is that the internal service fund is not charging other departments enough for the goods and services it provides.

Other units within an organization usually have internal service fund costs built into their operating budgets, and each ISF bills the other units for goods or services provided. Chang (1987) points out that internal service funds are the only fund type available to public organizations that is cost management focused. Henke (1980) argues that the use of internal service funds tends to cause managers to be more aware of costs. According to Holder (1996: 178), "This objective places many of the profit-oriented incentives for efficiency and effectiveness into the conduct of governmental operations." For example, treating building space essentially as a "free good" provides a disincentive for efficient operation, because the user units have an incentive to request additional space since it would be essentially free. If units are charged the cost for space occupied, they have an incentive to use only as much space as is efficient for operations (Holder, 1996: 182). Davis (1991) suggests that the efficiency and responsiveness of internal service fund units could be improved by subjecting the entities to outside competition. The use of internal service funds also facilitates the establishment of an audit trail for the allocation of overhead costs to grants (Glick, 1988).

In addition, internal service funds usually operate with *flexible* budget control as opposed to *fixed* budget control. According to Razek, Hosch, and Ives (2000: 261), "A flexible budget is a budget in which the level of budgeted expenses is related to the level of operations." Thus, the budget of the ISF will be determined indirectly by the operating budgets of its "customers." This basically means that the level of expense is adjusted to the volume of service rendered, as opposed to a fixed budget that is associated with most governmental fund activities in which a specific allocation is made for the fiscal year. The activity can only make adjustments in its budget with policy board approval, often with the requirement that such funding be taken from another program. This characteristic suggests that most internal service activities have both fixed and variable costs, which along with the potential for setting transfer prices, makes this type of activity a ready candidate for periodic break-even analysis (Anthony and Young, 2003). According to Razek, Hosch, and Ives (2000: 262):

> Because flexible operating budgets are used, we usually do not find the budget recorded in the accounts of internal service funds, or do we usually find the use of encumbrance accounting for these funds. Because there is no absolute spending limit, the use of encumbrance accounting would not serve any purpose.

## 8.4.4 Transfers

Internal service funds are usually established subject to legislative approval, with the original capital typically transferred from another unit "intended as a *contribution* not to be repaid, or as a transfer that is in the nature of a long-term *advance* to be repaid by the internal service fund over a period of years" (Engstrom and May, 1994: 147). For example, a printing and copy center may receive its original allocation of capital from a transfer from the general fund or an enterprise fund. The issue of general obligation debt to fund start-up cost for an internal fund activity could also be possible. Although the underlying goal is to manage operating costs to match expenses, internal service funds may not always be self-sustaining. In many cases, unexpected fluctuations in the demand for an internal service fund's goods and/or services may lead to fund deficits or surpluses. According to Razek, Hosch, and Ives (2000: 261), "Use of an internal service fund is especially important in those instances in which the governmental unit provides an operating subsidy for an activity. By comparing the activity's full cost of operations, and comparing these costs with the revenues earned, the extent of the subsidy needed can easily be determined." Similar to enterprise funds, many transactions between internal service funds and other funds take the form of quasi-external transactions. In the case of a quasi-external transaction, the funds receiving the goods or services from the internal service fund report an expenditure or an expense, while the internal service fund reports revenue.

## 8.4.5 Financial Statements

Just as is the case with enterprise fund activities, internal service funds are required to use the same three financial statements used in an enterprise fund. These financial statements are (1) the statement of net assets or balance sheet, (2) statement of revenues, expenses, and changes in fund net assets or fund equity or income statement, and (3) statement of cash flows or changes in financial position. According to Razek, Hosch, and Ives (2000: 262):

> Use of the capital management approach results in recording of all of the costs incurred in providing the goods or services. These costs include depreciation on fixed assets, an item not found in the governmental-type funds or in the other funds that follow a spending measurement focus. In addition, fixed assets are included on the balance sheet of an internal service fund. Thus, the balance sheet and the operating statement of an internal service fund will be similar to those of a private business providing the same goods and services.

GASB Statement No. 34 requires that internal service fund information appear in the proprietary fund financial statements, but aggregated in a single column. The reason for this requirement is that reporting internal service fund activity separately in general purpose financial statements double-counts internal service fund expenses and client fund expenditures. An example of how this occurs is when a printing and copy center records an expense to provide goods and services to another department, this department also records the expenditure for the charges it receives from the printing and copy center. Elimination accounting entries should be in the financial statements to remove the double counting of internal fund activities. According to GASB Statement No. 34, for the purposes of the government-wide statement of net assets, any asset or liability not eliminated would be reported in the governmental activities column of the statement if the primary users of goods or services are predominantly governmental as opposed to proprietary in nature (Ruppel, 2005: 81). Statement No. 34 states that although internal service funds are reported as proprietary funds of the reporting entity, the activities accounted for in internal service funds are usually more governmental than business-type in nature. If enterprise funds are the predominant or only participants in an internal service fund, however, the entity should report the internal service fund's residual assets and liabilities within the business-type activities column in the Statement of Net Assets (Financial Accounting, 2003: 80).

Although the contents differ slightly, balance sheets; statements of revenues, expenses, and changes in fund net assets; and cash flow statements for internal service funds are very similar to those for enterprise funds. The following are examples of financial reports for internal service funds in the City of Wichita, Kansas. Exhibit 8.10 presents a combining balance sheet for internal service funds, while Exhibit 8.11 presents a combining statement of revenues, expenses, and changes in net fund assets for internal service funds, and Exhibit 8.12 presents a combining statement of cash flows for internal service funds.

## 8.5 Enterprise Funds

Using a nationwide sample of large cities, Bunch (2000: 15) found the following:

- The aggregate number of enterprise funds increased, with the largest increases occurring in solid waste and drainage.
- Part of the increase was offset by the elimination of some enterprise funds, particularly in the area of recreational services.
- Sixty percent of the cities experienced one or more changes in the types of enterprise funds they used.
- The revenues associated with most types of enterprise funds have increased at a faster rate than general fund revenues.
- Some cities are using alternative fiscal structures to account for services that are reported as enterprise funds in other cities.

**CITY OF WICHITA, KANSAS**

COMBINING BALANCE SHEET
INTERNAL SERVICE FUNDS
December 31, 2004
(with comparative totals for the year ended December 31, 2003)

| | Information Technology | Fleet and Buildings | Stationery Stores | Self Insurance | Totals 2004 | Totals 2003 |
|---|---|---|---|---|---|---|
| **ASSETS** | | | | | | |
| Current assets: | | | | | | |
| Cash and temporary investments | $ 2,541,843 | $ 5,875,884 | $ 334,339 | $ 32,118,174 | $ 40,870,040 | $ 41,861,938 |
| Investments | | | | 244,091 | 244,091 | 246,994 |
| Receivables, net | 8,330 | 95,990 | 3,651 | - | 107,971 | 886,088 |
| Due from other funds | | | | 3,500,000 | 3,500,000 | 3,500,000 |
| Inventories | | 366,334 | | 4,616 | 370,950 | 366,462 |
| Prepaid items | | | 14,271 | | 14,271 | 681 |
| Total current assets | 2,550,173 | 6,338,008 | 352,261 | 35,866,881 | 45,107,323 | 46,962,153 |
| Noncurrent assets: | | | | | | |
| Capital assets: | | | | | | |
| Land | | 71,340 | | | 71,340 | 71,340 |
| Buildings | 53,364 | 3,279,073 | | | 3,332,437 | 3,283,131 |
| Machinery, equipment and other assets | 9,501,459 | 28,440,154 | 109,070 | 362,384 | 39,413,047 | 39,573,935 |
| Less accumulated depreciation | (8,571,385) | (23,849,152) | (75,574) | (140,570) | (32,636,681) | (32,507,123) |
| Total capital assets (net of accumulated depreciation) | 983,438 | 8,941,415 | 33,496 | 221,794 | 10,180,143 | 10,431,283 |
| Total assets | $ 3,533,611 | $ 15,279,423 | $ 385,757 | $ 36,088,675 | $ 55,287,466 | $ 57,383,436 |

Exhibit 8.10  Combining balance sheet, internal service funds, City of Wichita, Kansas.

**LIABILITIES**

**Current liabilities:**

| | | | | | | |
|---|---|---|---|---|---|---|
| Accounts payable and accrued expenses | $ 245,963 | $ 112,988 | $ 36,039 | $ 1,830,837 | $ 2,225,827 | $ 876,092 |
| Deposits | - | - | - | - | - | 1,094,200 |
| Current portion of long-term obligations: | | | | | | |
| Claims payable | - | - | - | 5,686,565 | 5,686,565 | 5,051,000 |
| Compensated absences | 114,380 | 142,868 | - | 22,302 | 279,550 | 283,294 |
| Total current liabilities | 360,343 | 255,856 | 36,039 | 7,539,704 | 8,191,942 | 7,284,586 |
| Noncurrent liabilities: | | | | | | |
| Claims payable | - | - | - | 13,398,055 | 13,398,055 | 12,211,000 |
| Compensated absences | 19,709 | 21,494 | - | 3,843 | 45,046 | 38,051 |
| Total noncurrent liabilities | 19,709 | 21,494 | - | 13,401,898 | 13,443,101 | 12,249,051 |
| Total liabilities | 380,052 | 277,350 | 36,039 | 20,941,602 | 21,635,043 | 19,533,637 |
| **NET ASSETS** | | | | | | |
| Invested in capital assets | 983,438 | 8,941,415 | 33,496 | 221,704 | 10,180,143 | 10,431,283 |
| Unrestricted | 2,170,121 | 6,060,658 | 316,222 | 14,925,279 | 23,472,280 | 27,418,516 |
| Total net assets | 3,153,559 | 15,002,073 | 349,718 | 15,147,073 | 33,652,423 | 37,849,799 |
| Total liabilities and net assets | $ 3,533,611 | $ 15,279,423 | $ 385,757 | $ 36,088,675 | $ 55,287,466 | $ 57,383,436 |

**Exhibit 8.10   (continued).**

## CITY OF WICHITA, KANSAS

COMBINING STATEMENT OF REVENUES, EXPENSES AND CHANGES IN FUND NET ASSETS

INTERNAL SERVICE FUNDS

For the year ended December 31, 2004

(with comparative totals for the year ended December 31, 2003)

| | Information Technology | Fleet and Buildings | Stationery Stores | Self Insurance | Totals 2004 | Totals 2003 |
|---|---|---|---|---|---|---|
| **OPERATING REVENUES** | | | | | | |
| Charges for services and sales | $ 7,040,095 | $ 940,597 | $ 751,707 | $ - | $ 8,732,399 | $ 7,988,404 |
| Rentals | - | 9,121,874 | - | - | 9,121,874 | 7,652,781 |
| Employer contributions | - | - | - | 21,729,851 | 21,729,851 | 20,529,764 |
| Employee contributions | - | - | - | 6,177,412 | 6,177,412 | 5,072,708 |
| Other | - | 106,834 | - | 369,531 | 476,365 | 436,628 |
| Total operating revenues | 7,040,095 | 10,169,305 | 751,707 | 28,276,794 | 46,237,901 | 41,680,341 |
| **OPERATING EXPENSES** | | | | | | |
| Personal services | 3,002,479 | 2,795,172 | 54,557 | - | 5,852,208 | 5,798,297 |
| Contractual services | 2,499,499 | 1,575,062 | 57,674 | - | 4,132,235 | 3,151,755 |
| Materials and supplies | 241,757 | 2,502,429 | 762 | - | 2,744,948 | 2,709,855 |
| Cost of materials used | - | 1,620,676 | 650,954 | - | 2,271,630 | 2,175,227 |
| Administrative charges | 79,330 | 189,560 | 44,770 | - | 313,660 | 234,270 |
| Depreciation | 293,168 | 2,308,790 | 11,653 | 34,709 | 2,648,320 | 2,982,889 |
| Employee benefits | - | - | - | 25,208,985 | 25,208,985 | 19,504,044 |
| Insurance claims | - | - | - | 6,876,993 | 6,876,993 | 5,068,039 |
| Total operating expenses | 6,116,233 | 10,991,689 | 820,370 | 32,120,687 | 50,048,979 | 42,524,376 |
| Operating income (loss) | 923,862 | (822,384) | (68,663) | (3,843,893) | (3,811,078) | (844,035) |

**Exhibit 8.11** Combining statement of revenues, expenses, and changes in net fund assets, internal service funds, City of Wichita, Kansas.

## NONOPERATING REVENUES (EXPENSES)

|  |  |  |  |  |  |  |
|---|---|---|---|---|---|---|
| Interest earnings | (247,970) | - | - | 307,917 | 307,917 | 455,649 |
| Gain (loss) on the sale of assets | - | 28,370 | (637) | - | (220,237) | 73,030 |
| Total nonoperating revenues (expenses) | (247,970) | 28,370 | (637) | 307,917 | 87,680 | 528,679 |
| Income (loss) before contributions and transfers | 675,892 | (794,014) | (69,300) | (3,535,976) | (3,723,398) | (315,356) |
| Capital contributions and operating transfers: |  |  |  |  |  |  |
| Capital contributions | 336,832 | 18,030 | - | - | 354,982 | 490,051 |
| Transfers from other funds | 193,190 | 161,400 | 35,000 | 313,220 | 702,810 | 662,108 |
| Transfers to other funds | (562,000) | - | - | (969,750) | (1,531,760) | (2,546,763) |
| Change in net assets | 644,014 | (614,584) | (34,300) | (4,192,506) | (4,197,376) | (1,709,960) |
| Total net assets - beginning | 2,509,545 | 15,616,657 | 384,018 | 19,339,579 | 37,849,799 | 39,558,759 |
| Total net assets - ending | $ 3,153,559 | $ 15,002,073 | $ 349,718 | $ 15,147,073 | $ 33,652,423 | $ 37,848,799 |

**Exhibit 8.11** (continued).

# CITY OF WICHITA, KANSAS

## COMBINING STATEMENT OF CASH FLOWS (CONTINUED)
### INTERNAL SERVICE FUNDS
For the year ended December 31, 2004
(with comparative totals for the year ended December 31, 2003)

| | Information Technology | Fleet Buildings | Stationery Stores | Self Insurance | Totals 2004 | Totals 2003 |
|---|---|---|---|---|---|---|
| **CASH FLOWS FROM OPERATING ACTIVITIES** | | | | | | |
| Cash received from customers | $ 7,040,660 | $ 10,154,092 | $ 752,071 | 28,699,665 | $ 46,646,488 | $ 37,506,893 |
| Cash payments to suppliers for goods and services | (2,789,139) | (6,045,320) | (762,206) | (29,891,709) | (39,488,374) | (31,537,222) |
| Cash payments to employees for services | (3,005,391) | (2,780,197) | (54,557) | 11,188 | (5,828,957) | (5,753,199) |
| Other operating revenues | | | | 369,531 | 369,531 | 436,626 |
| Net cash provided by (used in) operating activities | 1,246,130 | 1,328,576 | (64,692) | (811,325) | 1,698,688 | 653,098 |
| **CASH FLOWS FROM NONCAPITAL FINANCING ACTIVITIES** | | | | | | |
| Transfers from other funds | 193,190 | 161,400 | 35,000 | 313,220 | 702,810 | 662,108 |
| Transfers to other funds | (562,000) | | | (969,750) | (1,531,750) | (2,546,763) |
| Net cash provided by (used in) noncapital financing activities | (368,810) | 161,400 | 35,000 | (656,530) | (828,940) | (1,884,655) |
| **CASH FLOWS FROM CAPITAL AND RELATED FINANCING ACTIVITIES** | | | | | | |
| Additions to property, plant and equipment | (129,765) | (2,260,944) | - | | (2,390,709) | (2,130,041) |
| Proceeds from sale of assets | | 128,264 | - | | 128,264 | 73,030 |
| Net cash used in capital and related financing activities | (129,765) | (2,132,680) | - | | (2,262,455) | (2,057,011) |
| **CASH FLOWS FROM INVESTING ACTIVITIES** | | | | | | |
| Proceeds from sale and maturity of investment securities | - | - | - | 2,892 | 2,892 | 65,000 |
| Interest on investments | | | | 307,917 | 307,917 | 480,170 |
| Net cash provided by investing activities | - | - | - | 310,809 | 310,809 | 525,170 |
| Net increase (decrease) in cash and temporary investments | 747,555 | (842,715) | (29,692) | (1,157,046) | (1,081,898) | (2,763,398) |
| Cash and temporary investments - January 1 | 1,794,288 | 6,518,399 | 364,031 | 33,275,220 | 41,951,938 | 44,715,336 |
| Cash and temporary investments - December 31 | $ 2,541,843 | $ 5,675,684 | $ 334,339 | $ 32,118,174 | $ 40,870,040 | $ 41,951,938 |
| | | | | | | (Continued) |

**Exhibit 8.12   Combining statement of cash flows, internal service funds, City of Wichita, Kansas.**

| | Information Technology | Fleet and Buildings | Stationery Stores | Self Insurance | Totals | |
|---|---|---|---|---|---|---|
| | | | | | 2004 | 2003 |
| **RECONCILIATION OF OPERATING INCOME TO NET CASH PROVIDED BY (USED IN) OPERATING ACTIVITIES** | | | | | | |
| Operating income (loss) | $ 923,862 | $ (822,384) | $ (68,663) | $ (3,843,893) | $ (3,811,078) | $ (844,035) |
| Adjustments to reconcile operating income (loss) to net cash provided by (used in) operating activities | | | | | | |
| Depreciation | 293,168 | 2,306,790 | 11,653 | 34,709 | 2,646,320 | 2,982,889 |
| Changes in assets and liabilities: | | | | | | |
| (Increase) decrease in accounts receivable | 505 | (15,213) | 384 | 792,402 | 778,118 | (3,736,822) |
| Decrease in inventory | - | 128 | - | - | 128 | 112,476 |
| (Increase) decrease in prepaid items | - | - | (13,590) | (4,610) | (18,200) | 1,986 |
| Increase (decrease) in accounts payable and accrued expenses | 31,447 | (157,721) | 5,544 | 376,266 | 255,535 | 270,593 |
| Increase in claims payable | - | - | - | 1,822,620 | 1,822,620 | 1,825,000 |
| Increase (decrease) in compensated absences | (2,912) | 14,975 | - | 11,188 | 23,251 | 41,011 |
| Total adjustments | 322,208 | 2,150,959 | 3,971 | 3,032,568 | 5,509,766 | 1,497,133 |
| Net cash provided by (used in) operating activities | $ 1,246,130 | $ 1,328,575 | $ (64,692) | $ (811,325) | $ 1,698,688 | $ 653,098 |
| **Supplemental Schedule of Non-Cash Investing and Financing Activities** | | | | | | |
| Capital contributed by local government | $ 336,932 | $ 18,030 | $ - | $ - | $ 354,962 | $ 490,051 |

**Exhibit 8.12** (continued).

*Enterprise funds* report the financial activities of a government that are "business-like" and produce goods and services that are purchased by customers outside of the governmental organization. Examples: water, wastewater, electric and natural gas utilities, toll roads, airports, public transit, docks, golf courses, public housing, hospitals, and parking facilities. Engstrom and Hay (1994: 153–154) recommend that:

> ... governmentally owned enterprises use the accounting structures developed for investor-owned enterprises of the same nature. Budgetary accounts should be used only if required by law. Debt service and construction activities of a governmental enterprise are accounted for within an enterprise fund, rather than by separate debt service and capital project funds. Thus, the reports of enterprise funds are self-contained; and creditors, legislators, or the general public can evaluate the performance of a governmental enterprise by the same criteria as they can the performance of investor-owned enterprises in the same industry.

According to the American Institute for Certified Public Accountants (AICPA, 2004: 19–20):

> Enterprise funds may be used to report any activity for which a fee is charged to external users for goods or services. However, GASB Statement No. 34, paragraph 67, states that activities are required to be reported as enterprise funds if any one of the following criteria is met in the context of the activity's principal revenue sources, focusing on fees charged to external users.
>
>   1. The activity is financed with debt that is secured solely by a pledge of the net revenues from fees and charges of the activity.
>   2. Laws or regulations require that the activity's costs of providing services, including capital costs, be recovered with fees and charges, rather than with taxes or similar revenues.
>   3. The pricing policies of the activities establish fees and charges designed to recover its costs, including capital costs.
>
> Footnote 33 in paragraph 67 of GASB Statement No. 34 states that these criteria do not require insignificant activities of governments to be reported as enterprise funds.

Furthermore, GASB Statement No. 34 continues the previous practice that an enterprise fund may be use to report any activity for which a fee is charged to external users. Activities undertaken by governmental units that satisfy the criteria for enterprise fund inclusion are essentially "profit-centered" activities. In the context of responsibility centers used by Anthony and Young (2003), these would be defined as "profit responsibility centers." Bunch and Ducker (2003) suggest that there is a growing trend toward using enterprise funds to account for public works services that are financed through user charges.

Molinari and Tyer (2003) identify three primary reasons for the use of enterprise funds:

- Enterprise funds services are generally financed through user fees and charges, which allows for a high degree of equity and fairness since those using the service often pay in proportion to usage and benefits received.
- The use of fees or charges helps to simultaneously avoid tax increases and expand service delivery.
- User fees and charges can also reduce the wasteful utilization of governmental services.

However, Molinari and Tyer (2003) also caution that there are also some significant concerns regarding the increased usage of enterprise funds:

- Enterprise funds often rely on user fees and charges that have a "regressive pattern."
- Enterprise funds may be subject to less financial scrutiny than other government services.
- Enterprise fund transfers to the general fund can be a form of "fiscal illusion" and "public avoidance."

Bland and Rubin (1997: 2003) suggest that

> Most local governments present a greater level of detail for the operating departments in the general fund than they do for enterprise funds, possibly because these funds usually pay for themselves. However, because the lack of detail provided for enterprise funds sometimes contributes to a notion that they are secret, local governments that have financial responsibility for enterprise funds would be wise to provide an amount of detail for those funds that is parallel to that provided for the general fund.

## 8.5.1 Financial Statements

According to GASB Codification Sec. 2000, the information that should be presented for enterprise funds is that which is deemed essential to make the General Purpose Financial Statements not misleading (Engstrom and Hay, 1994: 162):

- Material intergovernmental operating subsidies to an enterprise fund
- Material intragovernmental operating subsidies to or from an enterprise fund

- Material enterprise fund tax revenues
- A material enterprise fund operating income or loss
- A material enterprise fund net income or loss

As such, accounting for enterprises in separate funds makes it easier to see whether those entities are generating sufficient revenue to cover all their costs. According to Bland and Rubin (1997: 57), enterprise funds should be self-supporting if

- The benefits largely accrue to users of the service,
- Collecting a fee from users is administratively feasible, and
- Pricing the service at its full cost will not cause users to take actions that are more costly than the revenues obtained through service charges.

After making this determination, policymakers can then decide whether to set fees according to cost or to subsidize the fund from general revenues. The decision maker should establish an explicit policy documenting which enterprise funds are expected to balance—and, of those that are not expected to balance, on what basis the fund will be subsidized by the general fund.

### 8.5.1.1 Balance Sheet

### 8.5.1.1.1 Assets (adapted from Financial Accounting, 2003: 42–54)

Assets are defined as probable future economic benefits obtained or controlled by a particular entity as a result of past transactions or events. The following typically represent the major asset categories:

- Cash and Investments
- Receivables
- Prepaid Items
- Inventory
- Capital Assets

8.5.1.1.1.1 Cash and Investments — Cash and investments often represent a large portion of the assets on an enterprise fund's balance sheet. Because of the importance of these assets, proper management based on sound investment policies and strategies is vital. The investment of excess funds is often governed by statute. Many state governments have adopted legal frameworks that restrict the investment activities of local governments. These restrictions often place limitations on the types of investments allowed, regulate procedures used to manage investments, and require governing bodies to institute certain review procedures.

Certain words in common usage have more limited definitions when they are used for accounting and financial reporting. Within the context of governmental accounting, the following definitions describe the specific content of accounts used by governmental entities:

- Cash is considered to be the most liquid (readily available) asset owned by an entity and represents readily available cash held by the organization.
- Cash equivalents are short-term, highly liquid investments (readily convertible to known amounts of cash) that are so near to maturity that they present an insignificant risk of changes in value resulting from changes in interest rates. Generally, only investments with original maturities of 3 months or less qualify under this definition. Items commonly considered cash equivalents are treasury bills, commercial paper, short-term deposits in financial institutions, and money market funds. However, investments that qualify as cash equivalents are not all required to be treated as cash equivalents. Therefore, an entity should establish a policy concerning the classification of qualified investments as cash equivalents, which may be no more liberal than the authoritative definition except as discussed in the following text under pooling of cash and investments. The policy must be disclosed in the notes to the financial statements.
- Investments are defined as securities and similar assets acquired primarily to earn income or profit. A security is a transferable financial instrument that evidences ownership or creditor status. Securities that are often held by or pledged to entities generally include U.S. Treasury bills, notes, and bonds; federal agency and instrumentality obligations; direct obligations of a state or its agencies; commercial paper; negotiable and nonnegotiable certificates of deposit; fully collateralized repurchase agreements; and prime domestic bankers' acceptances.

8.5.1.1.1.2 Receivables — Receivables usually arise as a result of revenue transactions. The main sources of revenues for enterprise funds that would result in outstanding receivables are the following

- State and federal grants
- Intergovernmental revenues (due from other governmental entities)
- Interest income

The accounting for revenues and related accounts receivable in governmental entities depends on the type of fund in which the revenue is recorded. Proprietary funds use the accrual basis of accounting to determine when revenues and related receivables should be recorded. Revenues are recognized when they are earned, that is, when the earnings process is complete and an exchange has taken place.

8.5.1.1.1.3 Inventory — Not all enterprise funds will carry inventories, depending on the nature of the good or service provided. Some enterprises such as water, wastewater, storm water, electric, or natural gas utilities may report inventories for such items as piping, wiring, and meters, while enterprises such as motor pools and transit authorities may report inventories for such items as spare parts, fuel, and other consumable commodities.

8.5.1.1.1.4 Capital Assets — Governmental entities are responsible for accounting for, controlling, and reporting both current and capital assets. Capital assets have certain properties that distinguish them from other types of assets:

- Tangible or intangible in nature
- Long-lived (have a life longer than 1 year)
- Of a significant value at the time of purchase or acquisition
- Reasonably identified and controlled through a physical inventory system

Capital assets may include the following:

- Land and land improvements
- Easements
- Buildings and building improvements
- Vehicles
- Machinery and equipment
- Technological assets such as computers and network equipment
- Works of art and historical treasures
- Infrastructure
- Software

Capital assets are included in the financial records at cost. In some situations, the purchase or acquisition documents may not be available for capital assets already on hand. If reliable historical records are not available, an estimate or appraisal of the original cost based on other information, such as price index levels at time of acquisition, may be used. The intent of such valuation is to record a fair value at the date of acquisition and not expend excessive resources in ascertaining exact costs. If capital assets are acquired by gift, then the fair value on the date received is the appropriate amount to include in the capital asset records.

Capital assets may be acquired by several methods:

- Purchase
- Lease-purchase
- Construction
- Tax foreclosures
- Gifts and contributions

All capital assets acquired in some manner other than by gift are recorded at the cost necessary to place the asset in service. Capital assets arising from gifts or donations are recorded at their estimated fair value at the time of receipt.

GASB Statement No. 34 establishes reporting requirements for general government capital assets. Statement No. 34 establishes the following new reporting requirements for capital assets:

■ Depreciable capital assets should be reported in the Statement of Net Assets (a government-wide statement) at historical cost, net of accumulated depreciation.

■ The historical cost should include the ancillary charges necessary to place the asset into its intended location and condition for use, including freight and transportation charges, site preparation costs, and professional fees that directly relate to the acquisition of the asset.

■ Depreciable capital assets may be reported on the face of the Statement of Net Assets as a single item or by major class. Detailed information will be reported in the notes.

■ Significant nondepreciable capital assets that are inexhaustible, such as land, certain nondepreciable site improvements, and infrastructure assets reported using the modified approach should be reported separately from depreciable capital assets on the Statement of Net Assets. GASB has defined an inexhaustible capital asset as one whose economic benefit or service is used up so slowly that its estimated useful life is extraordinarily long. Construction in progress should be included with nondepreciable capital assets in the Statement of Net Assets.

■ Accumulated depreciation may be reported on the face of the Statement of Net Assets, parenthetically or as a separate line item reducing capital assets. However, regardless of the statement presentation in the Statement of Net Assets, the notes to the financial statements should disclose balances and changes in accumulated depreciation for the period by major asset class, as well as information regarding depreciation methods used.

Many enterprise operations may have significant infrastructure assets. Infrastructure assets are long-lived capital assets that are normally stationary in nature and that can be maintained for a significantly greater number of years than most capital assets. Infrastructure assets include the following:

■ Roads
■ Bridges
■ Drainage systems
■ Water and sewer systems
■ Lighting systems

Parking lots and related lighting systems may be defined by the entity as part of the associated building, rather than as infrastructure. Infrastructure assets are reported at historical cost or estimated historical cost. If a determination of the historical cost is not viable because of incomplete records, an estimated historical cost may be determined in the following ways.

GASB Statement No. 34 allows two distinct approaches to reporting infrastructure assets in the Statement of Net Assets. The standard approach requires governmental entities to capitalize all major infrastructure assets and depreciate them over their useful lives. This approach does not differ from the accounting and reporting treatment of other types of capital assets. Alternatively, entities may elect to use a modified approach to infrastructure asset reporting under a specific set of conditions. The modified approach allows governmental entities to capitalize assets and yet avoid the depreciation of their eligible infrastructure assets if they meet two criteria:

- The entity has a qualifying asset management system that:
  - has an up-to-date inventory of infrastructure;
  - performs consistent and complete condition assessments every 3 years, the results of which are summarized using a measurement scale; and
  - can estimate, on an annual basis, the cost to maintain and preserve the infrastructure assets at the disclosed condition level.
- The entity documents that the eligible infrastructure assets are being preserved approximately at or above a condition level established and disclosed by the government.

The modified approach is not limited to general infrastructure assets, that is, infrastructure assets associated with governmental activities. Eligible infrastructure assets of enterprise funds that were previously depreciated may also be reported using the modified approach. If entities choose the modified approach for reporting general infrastructure assets, they are required to present information on condition and on estimated versus actual maintenance as required supplementary information (RSI).

## 8.5.1.1.2 Liabilities (adapted from Financial Accounting, 2003: 54–62)

Liabilities represent financial obligations of an entity to transfer assets or provide services to other entities in the future as a result of past transactions or events. Because proprietary funds use an accrual basis of accounting for liability recognition, all obligations of the fund should be reflected as fund liabilities.

8.5.1.1.2.1 Accounts Payable — Accounts payable are those liabilities incurred in the normal course of business for which goods or services have been received but payment has not been made as of the end of the fiscal year.

**8.5.1.1.2.2 Salaries and Related Benefits Payable** — Expenditures should be recorded and reported in the period in which the liability has been incurred. Therefore, unpaid salaries and related benefits that have not yet been paid at the close of the accounting period should be accrued.

**8.5.1.1.2.3 Due to/From Other Funds** — Each fund is a separate self-balancing set of accounts. Therefore, amounts due to/from other funds generally arise from interfund loans or interfund services used/interfund services provided between funds. For instance, one fund may make an advance to another fund, or one fund may provide services to another without payment at the time the services are provided. Although interfund receivables and liabilities may be classified as current or noncurrent depending on the terms for repayment, all such transactions must be reflected as fund receivables and liabilities. The advancing fund should reserve fund balance for the noncurrent portion of amounts due from another fund.

**8.5.1.1.2.4 Compensated Absences** — Compensated absences include future vacations, sick leave, sabbatical leave, and other leave benefits. Requirements for accruing a liability for sick leave or similar compensated absences is attributed to services already rendered and it is probable that payment will be made at termination. Therefore, sick leave benefits that have been earned but will only be used as sick leave should not be accrued. Liabilities for compensated absences should be calculated at the end of each fiscal year and adjusted (and recorded) to current salary rates, unless payment will be made at rates other than the current salary rate. This liability also includes the employer's share of Social Security and Medicare taxes, as well as others. For proprietary funds, all of the liability is a fund liability.

**8.5.1.1.2.5 Deferred Compensation and Pension Plans** — A deferred compensation plan allows employees to defer the receipt of a portion of their salary and, therefore, the associated tax liability on that salary. Authorization for deferred compensation plans is established by the Internal Revenue Service (IRS) and is listed in Internal Revenue Code Chapter 457.

**8.5.1.1.2.6 Debt** — Enterprise entities may borrow money on a short-term basis either to meet operating cash needs or in anticipation of long-term borrowing at later dates:

■ *Short-term obligations* are loans, negotiable notes, time-bearing warrants, or leases with a duration of 12 months or less, regardless of whether they extend beyond the fiscal year. Using the current financial resources measurement focus, short-term debt should be reflected in the balance sheet of the governmental fund that must repay the debt. The presentation of the liability on the balance sheet of a governmental fund implies that the debt is current and will require the use of current financial resources. Bond anticipation notes may be classified as long-term debt if the criteria of FASB Statement No. 6, *Classification of Short-Term Obligations Expected to be Refinanced*, are met.

■ *Long-term obligations* are loans, negotiable notes, time-bearing warrants, bonds, or leases with a duration of more than 12 months. Noncurrent obligations that will be repaid from revenues generated by proprietary funds should be recorded in the related proprietary fund, whereas noncurrent obligations to be repaid from governmental funds should be reported only on the government-wide statement of net assets.

GASB Codification Section 1500.102 states the following:

> Bonds, notes and other long-term liabilities directly related to and expected to be repaid from proprietary funds and fiduciary funds should be included in the accounts of such funds. These are specific fund liabilities, even though the full faith and credit of the governmental unit may be pledged as further assurance that the liabilities will be paid. Too, such liabilities may constitute a mortgage or lien on specific fund properties or receivables.

The proceeds of the debt will thus be recorded as an increase in cash and long-term debt accounts; there will be no effect on operations. If the debt was issued at a discount, the discount should be recorded as a reduction from the face value of the debt and amortized over the term of the debt. All debt issue costs should also be recorded as a deferred charge and amortized over the term of the debt. Currently, the only specific accounting guidance on debt transactions in proprietary funds is Statement 23, *Accounting and Reporting for Refundings of Debt Reported by Proprietary Activities*. Therefore, generally accepted accounting principles for commercial enterprises should be followed for debt transactions in proprietary funds.

**Types of Debt Instruments.** *General obligation bonds* are issued for the construction or acquisition of major capital assets. The security pledged for the bonds is the general taxing power of the government. General obligation bonds are usually either term bonds, which are due in total on a single date, or serial bonds, which are repaid in periodic installments over the life of the issue.

*Revenue bonds* are issued to acquire, purchase, construct, or improve major capital facilities. The revenue generated by the facility or the activity supporting the facility is pledged as security for the repayment of the debt.

*Tax anticipation notes* and other *revenue anticipation notes* are often issued to pay current operating expenditures prior to the receipt of the revenues. The proceeds from the revenue sources are pledged as security for the notes.

*Installment financing* may be used for either constructing or acquiring property. The security for the financing is the property being acquired or constructed.

*Leases* are agreements between two parties that convey the use of property for a specified period of time. A lease must be classified as *capital* if it meets the criteria of FASB Statement 13, *Accounting for Leases*, or as *operating* if it does not qualify as a capital lease. Capital leases are considered to be debt financing; operating leases are not. Capital leases are in substance an acquisition of an asset. This determination is made using the following criteria:

■ The ownership of the property transfers to the lessee at the end of the lease term, or
■ The lease contains a bargain purchase option, or
■ The lease term is equal to 75% or more of the estimated useful life of the leased property, or
■ At the inception of the lease, the present value of the minimum lease payments is equal to 90% or more of the fair value of the leased property.

When a lease satisfies one of the foregoing criteria, an asset and a liability should be recorded. The initial value of the asset should be recorded as the lesser of the fair value of the leased property or the present value of the net minimum lease payments.

### 8.5.1.1.2.7 Extinguishment of Debt

GASB has established a range of accounting and reporting requirements for debt refundings. These requirements are presented primarily in GASB Codification Section D20 and GASB Statement 23, *Accounting and Financial Reporting for Refundings of Debt Reported by Proprietary Activities*.

The extinguishment of debt is the reacquisition or calling of the debt or the removal of the debt prior to or at the maturity of the debt. When debt is extinguished, the entity either has no further legal responsibilities under the original debt agreement or continues to be legally responsible for the debt, but the extinguishment is considered an in-substance defeasance (retirement). GASB Statement 23 concludes that debt is considered to be extinguished when one of the following criteria is met:

■ The debtor pays the creditor and is relieved of all its obligations with respect to the debt, or
■ The debtor is legally released as the primary obligor under the debt either judicially or by the creditor, and it is probable that the debtor will not be required to make future payments with respect to the debt under the guarantees, or
■ The debtor irrevocably places cash or other assets with an escrow agent in a trust to be used solely for satisfying scheduled payments of both interest and principal of the defeased debt, and the possibility that the debtor will be required to make future payments on that debt is remote. In this circumstance, usually referred to as "in-substance defeasance," debt is extinguished

even though the debtor is not legally released as the primary obligor under the debt obligation.

In an advance refunding transaction, new debt is issued to provide funds to pay principal and interest on old, outstanding debt as it becomes due, or at an earlier call date. An advance refunding occurs before the maturity or call date of the old debt, and the proceeds of the new debt are invested until the maturity or call date. Debt may be advance-refunded for a variety of reasons, including to accomplish the following:

■ Take advantage of lower interest rates
■ Extend maturity dates
■ Revise payment schedules
■ Remove or modify restrictions contained in the old debt agreements

Some advance refundings are intended to achieve short-term budgetary savings by extending debt service requirements further into the future. In these cases, total debt service requirements over the life of the new debt may be more or less than total service requirements over the life of the existing debt. Advance refundings undertaken for other reasons, such as to remove undesirable covenants of the old debt, may also result in higher or lower total debt service requirements. It may be necessary in an advance refunding to issue new debt in an amount greater than the old debt. In these cases, savings may still result if the total new debt service requirements (interest and principal payment) are less than the old debt service requirements. Most advance refundings result in defeasance of debt.

Defeasance of debt can be either legal or in-substance. A legal defeasance occurs when debt is legally satisfied on the basis of certain provisions in the debt instrument even though the debt is not actually paid. An in-substance defeasance occurs when debt is considered defeased for accounting and financial reporting purposes, as discussed in the following text, even though a legal defeasance has not occurred. When debt is defeased, it is no longer reported as a liability on the face of the balance sheet; only the new debt, if any, is presented in the financial statements.

Debt is considered defeased in-substance for accounting and financial reporting purposes if the entity irrevocably places cash or other assets with an escrow agent in a trust to be used solely for satisfying scheduled payments of both interest and principal of the defeased debt, and when the possibility that the debtor will be required to make future payments on that debt is considered remote. The trust that is created should be restricted to monetary assets that are essentially risk-free as to the amount, timing, and collection of interest and principal.

Certain disclosures are required on defeasance of debt. GASB Codification Section D20.111 requires that a general description of the transaction should be provided in the notes to the financial statements in the year of refunding and that the disclosure should include at a minimum the following:

- The difference between the cash flows required to service the old debt and the cash flows required to service the new debt and complete the refunding
- The economic gain or loss resulting from the transaction

### 8.5.1.1.3 Fund Balance/Net Assets (adapted from Financial Accounting, 2003: 62–65)

Within proprietary funds, equity is reported as net assets. Net assets are the difference between fund assets and liabilities reflected on the balance sheet or statement of net assets. Within proprietary and fiduciary fund statements of net assets, net asset balances are classified into three components:

- *Invested in capital assets, net of related debt* represents the net amount invested in capital assets (original cost, net of accumulated depreciation, and capital-related debt)
- *Restricted* represents the amount of net assets for which limitations have been placed by creditors, grantors, contributors, laws, and regulations
- *Unrestricted* is the amount of net assets that is not restricted or invested in capital assets, net of related debt

In addition to the major enterprise funds (Water Utility, Sewer Utility, and Airport Authority), the City of Wichita also has three nonmajor enterprise funds (Storm Water Utility, Golf Course System, and Wichita Transit). These nonmajor enterprise funds are detailed out in the Enterprise Fund of the Comprehensive Annual Financial Report, but are aggregated and listed under Other Enterprise Funds in the Proprietary Funds section of the Financial Section of the CAFR. Exhibit 8.13 presents a combining balance sheet for nonmajor enterprise funds from the City of Wichita, Kansas.

### *8.5.1.2 Income Statement*

#### 8.5.1.2.1 Revenues (adapted from Financial Accounting, 2003: 65–69)

The accounting and financial reporting for revenues within a governmental entity is determined by the economic substance of the underlying transactions. Generally accepted accounting principles have established criteria for recognition based on the classification and characteristics of the transaction. Within governmental entities, transactions may be classified as either exchange (or exchange-like) transactions or

## CITY OF WICHITA, KANSAS

### COMBINING BALANCE SHEET
### NONMAJOR ENTERPRISE FUNDS
December 31, 2004
(with comparative totals for December 31, 2003)

| | Storm Water Utility | Golf Course System | Wichita Transit | Totals 2004 | Totals 2003 |
|---|---|---|---|---|---|
| **ASSETS** | | | | | |
| **Current assets:** | | | | | |
| Cash and temporary investments | $ 2,639,137 | $ 231,423 | $ 1,096,418 | $ 3,966,978 | $ 4,362,817 |
| Receivables, net | 142,944 | - | 31,654 | 174,598 | 322,464 |
| Due from other funds | - | - | - | - | 11,346 |
| Due from other agencies | - | - | 455,596 | 455,596 | 641,724 |
| Inventories | 36,862 | - | 294,478 | 331,340 | 321,137 |
| Total current assets | 2,818,943 | 231,423 | 1,878,146 | 4,928,512 | 5,659,488 |
| **Noncurrent assets:** | | | | | |
| **Capital assets:** | | | | | |
| Land | 2,314,582 | 631,534 | 1,906,816 | 4,852,932 | 4,298,770 |
| Buildings | 2,428,303 | 2,765,591 | 8,634,742 | 13,828,636 | 13,828,636 |
| Improvements other than buildings | 73,731,457 | 14,202,084 | 342,181 | 88,275,722 | 81,687,409 |
| Machinery, equipment and other assets | 2,806,598 | 1,843,696 | 16,243,097 | 20,893,391 | 21,015,942 |
| Construction in progress | 2,431,230 | 73,434 | 1,096,944 | 3,601,608 | 5,743,960 |
| Less accumulated depreciation | (8,030,528) | (6,712,910) | (8,625,608) | (23,369,046) | (20,232,092) |
| Total capital assets (net of accumulated depreciation) | 75,681,642 | 12,803,429 | 19,598,172 | 108,083,243 | 106,342,625 |
| Total noncurrent assets | 75,681,642 | 12,803,429 | 19,598,172 | 108,083,243 | 106,342,625 |
| Total assets | $ 78,500,585 | $ 13,034,852 | $ 21,476,318 | $ 113,011,755 | $ 112,002,113 |

**Exhibit 8.13   Combining balance sheet, nonmajor enterprise funds, City of Wichita, Kansas.**

## LIABILITIES

| Current liabilities: | | | | | |
|---|---:|---:|---:|---:|---:|
| Accounts payable and accrued expenses | $ 43,685 | $ 67,767 | $ 47,383 | $ 158,835 | $ 403,376 |
| Accrued interest payable | 21,310 | 27,060 | - | 48,370 | 55,755 |
| Temporary notes payable | 600,500 | - | - | 600,500 | 225,900 |
| Deposits | - | 145 | - | 145 | 968 |
| Due to other funds | - | 529,944 | - | 529,944 | - |
| Current portion of long-term obligations: | | | | | |
| General obligation bonds payable | 1,831,320 | 653,982 | - | 2,485,302 | 2,401,312 |
| Compensated absences | 66,066 | 76,131 | 136,063 | 278,260 | 269,248 |
| Total current liabilities | 2,562,881 | 1,355,029 | 183,446 | 4,101,356 | 3,356,559 |
| Noncurrent liabilities: | | | | | |
| General obligation bonds payable | 3,894,020 | 5,726,522 | - | 9,620,542 | 12,105,844 |
| Compensated absences | 10,257 | 13,118 | 15,783 | 39,158 | 33,289 |
| Total noncurrent liabilities | 3,904,277 | 5,739,640 | 15,783 | 9,659,700 | 12,139,133 |
| Total liabilities | 6,467,158 | 7,094,669 | 199,229 | 13,761,056 | 15,495,692 |

## NET ASSETS

| | | | | | |
|---|---:|---:|---:|---:|---:|
| Invested in capital assets, net of related debt | 69,334,492 | 5,865,921 | 19,598,172 | 94,798,585 | 91,553,814 |
| Restricted for capital projects | - | - | 22,522 | 22,522 | 4,754 |
| Unrestricted | 2,698,935 | 74,262 | 1,656,395 | 4,429,592 | 4,947,853 |
| Total net assets | 72,033,427 | 5,940,183 | 21,277,089 | 99,250,699 | 96,506,421 |
| Total liabilities and net assets | $ 78,500,585 | $ 13,034,852 | $ 21,476,318 | $ 113,011,755 | $ 112,002,113 |

Exhibit 8.13   (continued).

nonexchange transactions. Exchange transactions are those in which the parties involved give up and receive essentially equal values. Within a commercial enterprise, transactions between businesses and their customers meet this definition. Within a proprietary fund of a governmental entity, fees or charges made for goods or services represent exchange transactions. Revenues in the proprietary funds are recognized using the accrual basis of accounting, (i.e., in the period in which they are earned). They are classified either as *operating* or *nonoperating revenues*. Operating revenues are generated by the primary activity of the fund. Conversely, nonoperating revenues are not generated by the primary activity of the fund, but by other means, such as through grants or interest earnings. Proprietary fund revenues include charges for services, charges to other funds for services rendered, and grant revenues.

### 8.5.1.2.2 Expenses (adapted from Financial Accounting, 2003: 71–73)

Expenses are defined as the outflows or expiration of assets or the incurrence of liabilities during a period from providing or producing goods, rendering services, or carrying out other activities that constitute the entity's primary operations. Proprietary funds recognize expenses using the accrual basis of accounting (i.e., when the related liability is incurred) without regard for the timing of the payment. This recognition criterion is consistent with the following guidelines discussed in Financial Accounting Standards Board (FASB) Concepts Statement No. 5. Although FASB Concepts Statements do not represent authoritative guidance for governments, the discussion is useful in classifying expense transactions within proprietary funds.

- *Associating cause and effect.* Some expenses are recognized on recognition of revenues that result directly and jointly from the same transactions or other events as the expenses.
- *Systematic and rational allocation.* Some expenses are allocated by systematic and rational procedures to the periods during which the related assets are expected to provide benefits.
- *Immediate recognition.* Many expenses are recognized during the period in which cash is spent or liabilities are incurred for goods or services that are used up either simultaneously with acquisition or soon after.

As examples, the major types of governmental expenditures are accounted for differently in proprietary fund expenses as follows:

- *Capital.* Capital asset acquisition in proprietary funds is accounted for using the flow of economic resources method. Amounts disbursed for the acquisition of capital assets are not recorded as an expense. Instead, the appropriate property, plant, or equipment asset account is debited on the purchase. Depreciation expense is recorded to reflect the allocation of the cost of the assets to operations over the service life of the assets.

■ *Debt service.* Principal payments on debt do not represent expenses for proprietary funds, but rather are recorded as a reduction of the obligation. Payments of interest represent expenses to be accounted for on the accrual basis of accounting. Accrual of interest at year-end is usually necessary to reflect the proper amount of expense for the period.

Exhibit 8.14 presents a combining statement of revenues, expenses, and changes in fund net assets for nonmajor enterprise funds from the City of Wichita, Kansas.

### 8.5.1.3 Cash Flow Statement (adapted from GASB 34 Manual, 2003: 42–43)

A statement of cash flows should be prepared for enterprise funds. The statement should be formatted using the direct method in computing cash flows from operating activities. The statement should also include a reconciliation of operating cash flows and operating income (GASB Statement No. 9, paragraph 31).

A statement of cash flows tracks where cash comes from and where it goes. Did the government raise enough cash to pay its bills? If a government did not raise enough money to pay its expenses, it must list the source of the cash used.

The four major sources of cash inflows are as follows:

■ Operating cash flows
■ Noncapital financing cash flows
■ Capital and related financing cash flows
■ Investing cash flows

#### 8.5.1.3.1 Operating Cash Flows

Cash flows generated by and used for basic operations are designated operating cash flows. Examples include cash received for goods and services and cash paid to employees and suppliers. The direct method requires, at a minimum, delineation of the following sources and uses:

■ Receipts from customers
■ Receipts from interfund services provided
■ Receipts from other operating activities
■ Payments to suppliers of goods and services
■ Payments of other operating activities (GASB Statement No. 34, paragraph 130)

## CITY OF WICHITA, KANSAS

### COMBINING STATEMENT OF REVENUES, EXPENSES AND CHANGES IN FUND NET ASSETS
#### NONMAJOR ENTERPRISE FUNDS
For the year ended December 31, 2004

(with comparative totals for the year ended December 31, 2003)

| | Storm Water Utility | Golf Course System | Wichita Transit | Totals 2004 | Totals 2003 |
|---|---|---|---|---|---|
| **OPERATING REVENUES** | | | | | |
| Charges for services and sales | $ 5,513,078 | $ 293,119 | $ 1,607,720 | $ 7,413,917 | $ 7,079,172 |
| Fees | - | 2,665,644 | - | 2,665,644 | 2,850,133 |
| Rentals | - | 592,690 | 25,412 | 618,102 | 494,217 |
| Other | - | 13,536 | 24,075 | 37,611 | 28,703 |
| Total operating revenues | 5,513,078 | 3,564,989 | 1,657,207 | 10,735,274 | 10,452,225 |
| **OPERATING EXPENSES** | | | | | |
| Personal services | 1,483,147 | 1,457,948 | 5,116,758 | 8,057,853 | 7,782,222 |
| Contractual services | 780,175 | 1,017,069 | 1,951,919 | 3,749,163 | 3,518,103 |
| Materials and supplies | 70,063 | 461,493 | 1,237,667 | 1,769,223 | 1,504,881 |
| Administrative charges | 61,680 | 72,600 | 298,390 | 432,670 | 376,700 |
| Payments in lieu of franchise fees | 150,000 | - | - | 150,000 | 159,020 |
| Depreciation | 1,199,367 | 981,756 | 2,014,399 | 4,195,522 | 3,981,510 |
| Total operating expenses | 3,744,432 | 3,990,866 | 10,619,133 | 18,354,431 | 17,322,436 |
| Operating income (loss) | 1,768,646 | (425,877) | (8,961,928) | (7,619,157) | (6,870,211) |

Exhibit 8.14   Combining statement of revenues, expenses, and changes in net fund assets, nonmajor enterprise funds, City of Wichita, Kansas.

**NONOPERATING REVENUES (EXPENSES)**

| | | | | | |
|---|---:|---:|---:|---:|---:|
| Operating grants | - | - | 3,155,956 | 3,155,956 | 2,547,646 |
| Interest on investments | 23,942 | 4,589 | 19,403 | 47,904 | 62,852 |
| Other revenues (expenses) | - | - | (28,877) | (28,877) | (20,000) |
| Interest expense | (255,767) | (358,154) | (353) | (614,274) | (713,562) |
| Gain (loss) from sale of assets | - | 6,876 | 3,838 | 10,714 | (77,914) |
| Total nonoperating revenues (expenses) | (231,825) | (346,689) | 3,149,967 | 2,571,453 | 1,798,822 |
| | | | | | |
| Income (loss) before contributions and transfers | 1,536,821 | (772,566) | (5,811,959) | (5,047,704) | (5,071,389) |
| | | | | | |
| Capital contributions and operating transfers: | | | | | |
| Capital contributions | 3,640,476 | - | 570,421 | 4,210,897 | 7,294,567 |
| Transfers from other funds | 308,000 | - | 3,967,430 | 4,275,430 | 3,818,080 |
| Transfers to other funds | - | (60,120) | (634,225) | (894,345) | (181,606) |
| | | | | | |
| Change in net assets | 5,485,297 | (832,686) | (1,908,333) | 2,744,278 | 5,859,652 |
| Total net assets - beginning | 66,548,130 | 6,772,869 | 23,185,422 | 96,506,421 | 80,646,768 |
| | | | | | |
| Total net assets - ending | $ 72,033,427 | $ 5,940,183 | $ 21,277,089 | $ 99,250,699 | $ 86,506,421 |

Exhibit 8.14   (continued).

## 8.5.1.3.2 Noncapital Financing Cash Flows

This type of cash flow usually is from short-term notes to finance operations. As long as the notes are not secured by long-term assets, this is the location of the proceeds or payments, inflows and outflows of the short-term unsecured notes. Some of the possible sources and uses using the direct method are the following:

- Receipts from other funds
- Pay back cash borrowed from other funds
- Receipt of money from borrowing for other than capital assets

## 8.5.1.3.3 Capital and Related Financing Cash Flows

This cash flow comes from borrowing and repaying funds for buildings and other long-term assets. Some of the possible sources and uses are the following:

- Capital contributions
- Acquisition of fixed assets
- Borrowing and repaying funds for building or reconstructing capital assets
- Cash receipts from the sale of capital assets
- Grants or other aid from other governmental units used to finance capital assets

## 8.5.1.3.4 Investing Cash Flows

Investing cash flows include cash used to buy or sell long-term investments or money collected from loans or cash investments. Examples of investing cash flows are the following:

- Cash receipts from the sale of long-term investments
- Cash receipts from investment dividends and interest from investments
- Cash payments for the purchase of investments

The net cash flows from each category should be totaled to determine the overall net increase or decrease in cash.

## 8.5.1.3.5 Reconciliation of Cash and Changes in Fund Net Assets

The last section of the statement of cash flows for enterprise funds is the reconciliation of net cash provided or used by operating activities, with the operating income or loss in the statement of revenues, expenses and changes in fund net assets. This information can be submitted in a separate schedule. Noncash transactions include the following:

**CITY OF WICHITA, KANSAS**

COMBINING STATEMENT OF CASH FLOWS
NONMAJOR ENTERPRISE FUNDS
For the year ended December 31, 2004
(with comparative totals for the year ended December 31, 2003)

| | Storm Water Utility | Golf Course System | Wichita Transit | Totals 2004 | 2003 |
|---|---|---|---|---|---|
| **CASH FLOWS FROM OPERATING ACTIVITIES** | | | | | |
| Cash received from customers | $ 5,577,271 | $ 3,550,630 | $ 1,728,151 | $ 10,856,052 | $ 10,279,406 |
| Cash payments to suppliers for goods and services | (957,416) | (1,582,785) | (3,476,233) | (6,016,434) | (5,318,553) |
| Cash payments to employees for services | (1,481,325) | (1,449,539) | (5,112,108) | (8,042,972) | (7,797,307) |
| Payment in lieu of franchise fees | (150,000) | - | - | (150,000) | (159,020) |
| Other operating revenues | - | 13,536 | 24,075 | 37,611 | 28,703 |
| Net cash provided (used) by operating activities | 2,988,530 | 531,842 | (6,836,115) | (3,315,743) | (2,966,771) |
| **CASH FLOWS FROM NONCAPITAL FINANCING ACTIVITIES** | | | | | |
| Operating grant received | - | - | 3,281,702 | 3,281,702 | 2,674,226 |
| Transfers from other funds | 308,000 | - | 3,475,080 | 3,783,080 | 3,818,080 |
| Transfers to other funds | - | (60,120) | (141,875) | (201,995) | (54,050) |
| Net cash provided (used) by noncapital financing activities | 308,000 | (60,120) | 6,614,907 | 6,862,787 | 6,438,256 |
| **CASH FLOWS FROM CAPITAL AND RELATED FINANCING ACTIVITIES** | | | | | |
| Payment of temporary notes | 374,600 | - | - | 374,600 | (2,983,800) |
| Proceeds from capital debt | - | - | - | - | 2,821,860 |
| Additions to property, plant and equipment | (2,193,990) | (279,961) | (579,893) | (3,053,844) | (3,314,703) |
| Debt service - principal | (1,751,320) | (104,038) | (16,010) | (1,871,368) | (2,138,992) |
| Debt service - interest | (261,861) | (361,215) | (424) | (623,500) | (714,824) |
| Proceeds from sale of assets | - | 6,876 | 4,061 | 10,937 | (77,914) |
| Capital contributed for capital purposes | 475,243 | - | - | 475,243 | - |
| Capital contributed by local government | 70,286 | - | (3,429) | 66,857 | 61,571 |
| Capital contributed by other government | - | - | 165,886 | 165,886 | 407,846 |
| Capital grants received | - | - | 464,372 | 464,372 | 1,565,605 |
| Net cash provided (used) by capital and related financing activities | (3,287,042) | (738,338) | 34,563 | (3,990,817) | (4,373,751) |
| **CASH FLOWS FROM INVESTING ACTIVITIES** | | | | | |
| Interest on investments | 23,942 | 4,589 | 19,403 | 47,934 | 62,652 |
| Net cash provided by investing activities | 23,942 | 4,589 | 19,403 | 47,934 | 62,652 |
| Net increase (decrease) in cash and temporary investments | 33,430 | (262,027) | (167,242) | (395,839) | (839,814) |
| Cash and temporary investments - January 1 | 2,805,707 | 493,450 | 1,263,660 | 4,362,817 | 5,202,431 |
| Cash and temporary investments - December 31 | $ 2,839,137 | $ 231,423 | $ 1,096,418 | $ 3,966,978 | $ 4,362,817 |

(Continued)

**Exhibit 8.15 Combining statement of cash flows, nonmajor enterprise funds, City of Wichita, Kansas.**

- Adding back noncash expenses such as depreciation
- Adjusting for net change in fair value of investments
- Adjusting for capital asset donations
- A change in inventory that does not involve cash uses and would have to be added back to the changes in fund net assets

Exhibit 8.15 presents a combining statement of cash flows for nonmajor enterprise funds from the City of Wichita, Kansas.

## 8.5.2 Interfund Transfers

Cox (1994) recommends that before choosing to make transfers, policymakers should examine the future implications of the transfer on both the donor and recipient funds and operations. Cox (1994) suggests that a jurisdiction with an informed, rational, well-documented transfer policy will benefit from enhanced credit quality.

**CITY OF WICHITA, KANSAS**

COMBINING STATEMENT OF CASH FLOWS (CONTINUED)
NONMAJOR ENTERPRISE FUNDS
For the year ended December 31, 2004
(with comparative totals for the year ended December 31, 2003)

| | Storm Water Utility | Golf Course System | Wichita Transit | Totals 2004 | 2003 |
|---|---|---|---|---|---|
| **RECONCILIATION OF OPERATING INCOME (LOSS) TO NET CASH PROVIDED (USED) BY OPERATING ACTIVITIES** | | | | | |
| Operating income (loss) | $ 1,768,646 | $ (425,877) | $ (8,961,926) | $ (7,619,157) | $ (6,870,211) |
| Adjustments to reconcile operating income (loss) to net cash provided (used) by operating activities: | | | | | |
| Depreciation | 1,199,367 | 981,756 | 2,014,399 | 4,195,522 | 3,981,510 |
| Changes in assets and liabilities: | | | | | |
| (Increase) decrease in accounts receivable | 64,193 | - | 95,019 | 159,212 | (144,542) |
| (Increase) decrease in inventory | (15,478) | - | 5,275 | (10,203) | 33,788 |
| (Increase) decrease in fixed assets due to expenditure reclass | - | - | 218,243 | 218,243 | - |
| Increase (decrease) in accounts payable/accrued expenses | (30,020) | (31,623) | (211,775) | (273,418) | 47,343 |
| Increase (decrease) in deposits | - | (823) | - | (823) | 426 |
| Increase in compensated absences | 1,822 | 8,409 | 4,650 | 14,881 | (15,085) |
| Total adjustments | 1,219,884 | 957,719 | 2,125,811 | 4,303,414 | 3,903,440 |
| Net cash provided (used) by operating activities | $ 2,988,530 | $ 531,842 | $ (6,836,115) | $ (3,315,743) | $ (2,966,771) |
| **Noncash, investing, capital and financing activities:** | | | | | |
| Assets contributed by benefit districts | $ 3,094,947 | $ - | $ - | $ 3,094,947 | $ 4,724,076 |
| Contribution of capital assets | - | - | - | - | 486,779 |
| Transfer of assets between proprietary funds | - | - | - | - | (127,556) |

---

**Exhibit 8.15 (continued).**

In many instances, interfund transfers from enterprise funds may not be permissible. Enterprise funds may in some cases be legally prevented from making transfers. In other instances, bond covenants may restrict transfers from enterprise funds. In addition, transfers into and out of an enterprise fund make it difficult to determine rates for publicly provided services. According to Bland and Rubin (1997: 58), the advantages of setting the price of enterprise fund goods and/or services equal to the cost of production are the following:

■ It facilitates maintaining a balanced budget within the fund
■ It protects against transfers to subsidize other funds
■ It maintains the integrity and validity of financial statements

Pricing to maintain a balanced budget will help minimize transfers both into and out of the fund. Transfers into the fund cause goods and services to be underpriced, resulting in inefficient overconsumption by consumers. Even if there is general agreement about the desirability of the transfer, it can be very difficult to come to an agreement concerning the appropriate level of the subsidy. In addition, excessive transfers into the fund limit the incentive for the unit to operate efficiently. On the other hand, transfers out of the fund cause goods and services of the enterprise to be overpriced, resulting in inefficient underconsumption by customers. The resulting transfers will also limit the incentive for the recipient fund to operate efficiently. While interfund transfers promote management flexibility, excessive or arbitrary transfers between funds may result in misleading financial statements and reduce the accountability and responsiveness of both the donor and recipient funds (Bland and Rubin, 1997: 98–100).

Another approach to setting the transfer price and, hence, the appropriate level of transfers to other funds is to include *payments in lieu of taxes* (PILOTs) and/or *payments in lieu of franchise fees* (PILOFFs) to the cost of service production. The argument is that if a private entity were delivering the service, it would have to pay taxes and/or franchise fees to the government. However, since the government is itself providing the service, it should likewise pay itself the equivalent of what the private provider would have paid in taxes and fees. According to Bland and Rubin (1997: 58): "In some jurisdictions, such transactions are justified as returns on investment or as overhead charges assessed to the enterprise activity for the indirect costs incurred by the general fund in administering the activity." If this approach is pursued, Bland and Rubin (1997: 58) suggest that decision makers should establish a standard policy concerning the percentage that should be transferred to the general fund as PILOTs and PILOFFs. Cox (1994) concludes that this type of transfer "is clearly defensible and typically has little impact on credit quality, unless it could otherwise be foregone and thus contribute to a better competitive position for the enterprise." Another alternative would be to set transfers from the enterprise fund to the general fund equal to the average return on investment made by comparable private sector entities.

According to Cox (1994) there are six questions that should be asked to help determine whether a transfer policy will positively or negatively affect credit quality:

- Does the policy balance the needs and requirements of both the giver and the receiver of the transfer by providing reasonable and defensible flexibility in times of special circumstances?
- Is the transfer policy consistently applied and does it result in predictability for both the enterprise and general fund?
- Is there long-term competitive pressure on the enterprise that can be alleviated by reduced transfers?
- Does the transfer policy result in legal or political challenges by other cities or customers served by an enterprise?
- Is the transfer policy reasonably and comfortably communicated and disclosed to customers, analysts, and investors?
- Does the transfer represent a significant concentration in expense or revenues of the enterprise and the general fund, respectively?

## 8.5.3 *The Future of Enterprise Funds*

There is some evidence that local governments have shifted to an increasing reliance on user fees to support governmental activity. This is consistent with the growing reliance on market mechanisms for the allocation of resources. Arguably, these trends point to the increasing growth and reliance on enterprise-type activities.

U.S. Census of Government data in 2002 showed that for all municipal units of government in the United States, the percentage of total municipal revenue attributed to current charges and utility revenue increased from 29.2% of total revenue in 1991–1992 to 31.6% of total revenue in 2001–2002. For state and local units of government combined, the shift was slightly greater, with charges and miscellaneous and utility and liquor store revenue rising from 25.7% of total revenue in 1986–1987 to 29.1% of total revenue in 2001–2002. On the other hand, the specialized activities typically found in internal service funds may be experiencing a decline. New technological developments that have facilitated the development of decentralized solutions and the push for competitive outsourcing have reduced the need for many internal service operations. Movements toward paperless office environments combined with different copying technology have eliminated the necessity for central print shops or central copy shops. The wireless Internet combined with decentralized computing have substantially reduced the need for centralized computing services. The consequence is that we are likely to encounter an increasing use of enterprise funds, which creates a need for more entrepreneurial management skills.

# References

*Accounting and Reporting Manual for Cities, Villages, Counties and Towns.* (2002). Albany, NY: Office of the New York State Comptroller, Division of Local Government Services and Economic Development.

Allred, S., Ball, J., and Walthers, K. (2002). *Internal Service Funds: Cost Structure and Budget Impacts.* Salt Lake City, UT: Utah Office of the Legislative Fiscal Analyst.

*AICPA Audit and Accounting Guide: State and Local Governments.* (2004). New York: American Institute of Certified Public Accountants, Inc.

Anthony, R.N. and Young, D.W. (2003). *Management Control in Nonprofit Organizations,* 7th ed. New York: McGraw-Hill.

Bland, R.L. and Rubin, I.S. (1997). *Budgeting: A Guide for Local Governments.* Washington, DC: International City/County Management Association.

Bunch, B.S. (2000). Changes in the Usage of Enterprise Funds by Large City Governments. *Public Budgeting and Finance,* 20 (Summer): 15–29.

Bunch, B.S. and Ducker, R.R. (2003). Implications of Using Enterprise Funds to Account for Public Works Services. *Public Works Management and Policy,* 7 (January): 216–225.

Chang, S.Y. (1987). *A Study of the Basic Criteria and Standards for Internal Service Funds.* Lubbock, TX: Texas Tech University Press.

Cox, W.J., Jr. (1994). Interfund Transfers: A Credit Perspective. *Government Finance Review,* 10 (June): 24–25.

Davenport, L.W. (1996). Internal Service Fund Functions: Should They Be Required to Compete with Private Vendors?, *Government Finance Review,* 12 (October): 11–13.

Falk, David L. and Granof, Michael H. (1990). Internal Service Funds Are Beyond Salvation. *Accounting Horizons,* 4 (June): 58–66.

Garrison, Ray H. (1979). *Managerial Accounting: Concepts for Planning, Control, Decision Making, Revised Edition*. Dallas: Business Publications.

*GASB 34 Manual for Texas Cities and Counties*. (2003). Austin, TX: State of Texas, Comptroller of Public Accounts.

Gianakis, Gerasimos. (1995). Productivity Issues in Internal Service Fund Agencies. *Public Productivity and Management Review*, 18 (Summer): 349–363.

Glick, P.E. (1988). Government Accounting, Auditing, and Financial Reporting. Chicago, IL: Government Finance Officers Association.

Henke, E.O. (1980). *Introduction to Nonprofit Organization Accounting*. Boston, MA: Wadsworth.

Herbert, L., Killough, L.N., and Steiss, A.W. (1984). *Governmental Accounting and Control*. Belmont, CA: Brooks/Cole.

Hildreth, W.B. et al. (2002). *Sedgwick County, Kansas: Financial and Debt Ratio Analysis*. Wichita, KS: Hugo Wall School of Urban and Public Affairs, Kansas Public Finance Center.

Holder, William W. (1996). Financial Accounting, Reporting, and Auditing. In *Management Policies in Local Government Finance*, 4th ed., J. Richard Aronson and Eli Schwartz. (Eds.). Washington, DC: International City/County Management Association.

Martin, S.W. and West, E.N. (2003). *Today's Essentials of Governmental and Not-for-Profit Accounting and Reporting*. Mason, OH: Thompson/Southwest.

Mead, D.M. (2000). *What You Should Know about Your Local Government's Finances*. Norwalk, CT: Government Accounting Standards Board.

Mead, D.M. (2001). *An Analyst's Guide to Governmental Financial Statements*. Norwalk, CT: Government Accounting Standards Board.

Mead, D.M. (2005). *What Else You Should Know About a Government's Finance*s. Norwalk, CT: Government Accounting Standards Board.

Meigs, W.B. and Meigs, R.F. (1979). *Financial Accounting*, 3rd ed. New York: McGraw-Hill.

Metzger, L.M. (1994). A Pricing Model for Internal Service Funds. *Government Finance Review*, 10 (December): 17–20.

Molinari, J. and Tyer, C. (2003). Local Government Enterprise Fund Activity: Trends and Implications. *Public Administration Quarterly*, 27 (Fall): 369–391.

Razek, J.R., Hosch, G.A., and Ives, M. (2000). *Introduction to Governmental and Nonprofit Accounting*. Upper Saddle River, NJ: Prentice Hall.

Ruppel, W. (2005). *Governmental Accounting Made Easy*. Hoboken, NJ: John Wiley and Sons.

Schaeffer, M. (2000). *Municipal Budgeting Toolkit*. Washington, DC: World Bank, Urban Division.

Solano, P.L. and Brams, M.R. (1996). Budgeting. In *Management Policies in Local Government Finance*, 4th ed., J. Richard Aronson and Eli Schwartz (Eds.). Washington, DC: International City/County Management Association.

Ukeles, J.B. (1982). *Doing More with Less: Turning Public Management Around*. New York: AMACOM.

# Chapter 9

# Fiduciary Funds

## Jun Peng

*University of Arizona, School of Public Administration and Policy*

## Contents

9.1   Fiduciary Fund Classification under GASB 34.........................................317
    9.1.1   Pension Trust Funds ..................................................................321
        9.1.1.1   Two Basic Financial Statements......................................322
        9.1.1.2   Two Required Schedules.................................................325
    9.1.2   Investment Trust Funds..............................................................330
    9.1.3   Private-Purpose Trust Funds.......................................................332
    9.1.4   Agency Funds ............................................................................335
9.2   Summary ...............................................................................................336
References ........................................................................................................338

## 9.1  Fiduciary Fund Classification under GASB 34

Of the three major government fund groups, the fiduciary fund group has seen the most changes under GASB Statement 34, *Basic Financial Statements—and Management's Discussion and Analysis—for State and Local Governments*. GASB 34 defines fiduciary funds as those that are used to report assets held in a trustee or agency capacity for others and therefore cannot be used to support the reporting government's own programs.* To understand what changes have been made and why they are made to the classification of fiduciary funds, it is therefore useful to compare the classification of fiduciary funds under GASB 34 to that prior to GASB 34.

---

* See GASB 34, paragraph 69.

Prior to GASB 34, the fiduciary fund group included the following funds: pension (and other employee benefit) trust funds, investment trust funds, expendable trust funds, nonexpendable trust funds, and agency funds. Under GASB 34, the fiduciary fund group now includes: pension (and other employee benefit) trust funds, investment trust funds, private-purpose trust funds, and agency funds. It is easy to see that three funds remain in the fiduciary fund group under GASB 34: pension trust fund, investment trust fund, and agency fund. Pension trust funds are the funds that include defined benefit pension plans, defined contribution plans, and other postemployment benefit plans where resources are held in trust for members and beneficiaries. Investment trust funds are these funds that report the external portion of investment pools reported by the sponsoring government. Agency funds account for resources for which the reporting government's role is only custodial. What these funds have in common is that the resources they hold do not belong to the reporting government and cannot be used on the programs of the reporting government.

What GASB 34 has changed then is eliminating the expendable and non-expendable trust funds from the fiduciary fund group and adding a newly created fiduciary fund called private-purpose trust fund. Expendable trust funds refer to funds of which both principal and interest may be expended for purposes designated by the donor. Nonexpendable trust funds refer to funds of which only the income may be expended for purposes specified by the donor. Private-purpose trust funds refer to trust arrangements under which principal and income benefit individuals, private organizations, or other governments.* How are private-purpose trust funds different from expendable and nonexpendable trust funds?

Prior to GASB 34, expendable and nonexpendable trust funds included resources used for both private and public purposes. They also included resources used for the reporting government's programs. Under GASB 34, expendable trust funds and nonexpendable trust funds used for the public purposes of the reporting government are no longer considered part of the fiduciary fund group. Expendable trust funds used for the public purposes of the reporting government are now classified as special revenue funds and thus moved into the governmental fund group. Nonexpendable trust funds used for the public purposes of the reporting government are now classified as permanent funds under GASB 34 and are also moved out of the fiduciary fund group into the governmental fund group. Permanent fund is also a new fund created under GASB 34 "to report resources that are legally restricted to the extent that only earnings, and not principal, may be used to support the reporting government's programs, that is, for the benefit of the government or its citizenry."† An example of a permanent fund is Arizona's Land Endowments Fund. The Land Endowments Fund holds lands granted to the state by the federal government for the benefit of public school and other public institutions. "Principal

---

* See GASB 34, paragraph 72.
† See GASB 34, paragraph 65.

**Table 9.1   Balance Sheet for Land Endowment Fund, June 30, 2003 (expressed in thousands)**

| | |
|---|---:|
| **Assets** | |
| Cash | $28 |
| Cash and pool investment with state treasurer | $60,203 |
| Receivables, net of allowances | |
|     Interest | $2,143 |
|     Loans and notes | $260,229 |
|     Other | $548 |
| Due from other funds | $291 |
| Endowment investment | $1,119,469 |
|     **Total assets** | $1,442,911 |
| **Liabilities and Fund Balances** | |
| Liabilities | |
|     Accounts payable | $7,371 |
|     Accrued liabilities | $16 |
|     Due to other funds | $24,853 |
|     Unavailable deferred revenue | $262,807 |
|     Unearned deferred revenue | $23,681 |
|     **Total liabilities** | $318,728 |
| Fund balances | |
|     Reserved for | |
|         Permanent funds | $1,123,523 |
|         Continuing appropriations | $660 |
|         **Total fund balances** | $1,124,183 |
|     **Total liabilities and fund balances** | $1,442,911 |

*Source:* State of Arizona Comprehensive Annual Financial Report for the Fiscal Year Ended June 30, 2003.

is maintained intact and investment earnings and lease revenues are distributed to beneficiaries according to state statute."* Tables 9.1 and 9.2 present two financial statements for this fund, which are similar to financial statements for other governmental funds. Table 9.1 is the fund's balance sheet. While the fund has total assets to the tune of $1.44 billion as of June 30, 2003, much of that is tied up in long-term investment and is not available for current spending. Table 9.2 is the fund's statement of revenues, expenditures, and changes in fund balances. The major beneficiaries of this fund are the state's education, health care, and public safety programs. The expenditure from the fund in 2003 was $80 million, of which $70 million was

---

* Arizona State Comprehensive Annual Financial Report for Fiscal Year 2004, page 68.

**Table 9.2 Statement of Revenues, Expenditures, and Changes in Fund Balances for the Fiscal Year Ended June 30, 2003 (expressed in thousands)**

| | |
|---|---:|
| **Revenue** | |
| Intergovernmental | $25 |
| Earnings on investment | $33,959 |
| Sales and charges for services | $9,333 |
| Other | $8,917 |
| **Total revenue** | $52,234 |
| **Expenditures** | |
| General government | $454 |
| Health and welfare | $5,300 |
| Education | $70,267 |
| Protection and safety | $2,571 |
| Natural resources | $1,387 |
| Debt service—principal | $166 |
| **Total expenditures** | $80,145 |
| Excess (deficiency) of revenue over expenditures | ($27,911) |
| **Other Financing Sources (Uses)** | |
| Transfer in | $400 |
| Transfer out | ($19,123) |
| Proceeds from sale of trust land | $88,066 |
| **Total other financing sources (uses)** | $69,343 |
| Net change in fund balance | $41,432 |
| Fund balances—beginning | $1,082,751 |
| **Fund balances—ending** | $1,124,183 |

*Source:* State of Arizona Comprehensive Annual Financial Report for the Fiscal Year Ended June 30, 2003.

spent on education. Close to half of that spending was supported by the earnings from the endowment investment.

After moving expendable and nonexpendable trust funds used for public purposes to the governmental fund group, what remain are expendable and nonexpendable trust funds used for private purposes. These funds are now classified as private-purpose trust funds under GASB 34. By now the rationale behind the change is quite clear. With expendable and nonexpendable trust funds used for the public purposes of the reporting government removed from the fiduciary fund group, GASB 34 makes the fiduciary fund group truly fiduciary in nature, holding only resources that benefit individuals, private organizations and other governments.

All types of fiduciary funds (except agency funds) under GASB 34 are required to present two financial statements, the statement of net assets and the statement of changes in net assets.* Both statements are also required to be prepared using the economic resources measurement focus and the accrual basis of accounting.† The statement of net assets lists the fund's total assets, liabilities and net assets. The value of net assets is arrived at by subtracting liabilities from assets. Net assets can also be interpreted as the equity of the fund. The statement of changes in net assets lists all the financial activities that cause the value of net assets to change from the previous fiscal year.

In the remainder of this chapter, financial statements for each fiduciary fund are discussed. As the pension trust fund is by far the largest and most complicated fiduciary fund, much of the discussion is focused on the pension trust fund. Comparisons will also be drawn between pension trust funds and other fiduciary funds.

### 9.1.1 Pension Trust Funds

Pension trust funds are used to report resources that are required to be held in trust for the members and beneficiaries of defined benefit pension plans, defined contributions plans, other postemployment benefit plans, or other employee benefit plans.‡

The financial reporting of state and local pension trust funds is governed by GASB Statement 25, Financial Reporting for Defined Benefit Pension Plans and Note Disclosures for Defined Contribution Plans. GASB 25 applies to three kinds of defined benefit plan: single-employer plan, agent multiple-employer plan, and cost-sharing multiple-employer plan.§ Public pension plans are administered by

---

* See GASB 34, paragraph 106.
† Measurement focus and basis of accounting go hand in hand. What measurement focus is used determines what basis of accounting is used. The following explanation is largely drawn from Mead (2000). Measurement focus refers to the kinds of assets, liabilities, and changes in net assets a government should concentrate on when recording transactions and the basis of accounting describes when to record the assets, liabilities, and changes in net assets. Economic resources measurement focus records all financial and capital resources that flow in and out, and all changes in net assets as long as a monetary value can be put on them. Therefore, the full accrual basis of accounting must report all transactions occurring during the year and having an impact on its finances, regardless of whether cash changes hands. In contrast, for governmental funds, the measurement focus is current financial resources and the basis of accounting is modified accrual.
‡ See GASB 34, paragraph 70.
§ Single-employer plan refers to a plan that covers the pension benefits of employees of only one employer. Agent multiple-employer plan refers to an aggregation of single-employer plans that pool together the administrative and investment activities but maintain separate accounts. Cost-sharing multiple-employer plan refers to a single plan in which all participating employers share the cost with no separate individual accounts.

public employee retirement systems (PERS), and many state governments operate statewide PERS. However, GASB 25 emphasizes that PERS is only the administrator of the pension plan and is not the pension plan itself.*

GASB 25 establishes a financial reporting framework for *defined benefit pension plans* that distinguishes between two categories of information: (1) current financial information about plan assets and financial activities and (2) actuarially determined information, from a long-term perspective, about the funded status of the plan and the progress being made in accumulating sufficient assets to pay benefits when due. Plans should include information in the first category in two financial statements: (1) a *statement of plan net assets* and (2) a *statement of changes in plan net assets*. Information in the second category includes two required schedules: (1) a *schedule of funding progress* and (2) a *schedule of employer contributions*. In this section, we will first look at the two basic financial statements. Then we will examine the two required schedules.

### 9.1.1.1 Two Basic Financial Statements

As indicated by GASB 25, the two basic financial statements contain current financial information about plan assets and financial activities. Tables 9.3 and 9.4 provide an example of these two statements. They are collected from the comprehensive annual financial report (CAFR) of South Dakota Retirement System (SDRS). The statement of net assets contains three components: assets, liabilities, and net assets. Assets are listed in the order of liquidity: cash, receivables, and investments. Since these two statements are prepared on an accrual basis, any economic resources, such as employer and employee pension contribution, earned but not yet received before the end of the fiscal year will be recorded as accounts receivable. Investments, always the most important part of the assets for pension trust funds, are valued using the fair market value of investment securities, such as bonds and stocks. The fair market value reflects the market prices at which the securities can be sold at the end of the fiscal year. The fair market value of each component of the investments also tells us something about the asset allocation of the pension plan. Asset allocation refers to the decision as to how much of the investment portfolio should be invested in different asset categories, such as bonds and stocks. In the case of South Dakota, 40% is invested in bonds, 52% in stocks, and 4% each for real estate and private equity. After subtracting liabilities from the total assets, the value of the plan's net assets is arrived at. Net assets are the funds available to pay for promised pension benefits in the future. Since the statement of net assets does not include the information on the amount of long-term pension benefits (or pension liabilities from the employer's point of view)† it can not be concluded from this

---

* See GASB 25, paragraphs 14–17.
† In this chapter, pension benefits and pension liabilities are used interchangeably.

**Table 9.3    Statement of Plan Net Assets, as of June 30, 2004**

| Assets | |
|---|---:|
| Cash and cash equivalents | $21,591,402 |
| Receivables | |
| Employer | $2,580,440 |
| Employee | $11,110,352 |
| Benefits | $64,370 |
| Unsettled investment sales | $36,197,805 |
| Accrued interest and dividends | $20,335,240 |
| **Total receivables** | $70,288,207 |
| Investments, at fair value | |
| Fixed income | $2,239,722,750 |
| Equities | $2,898,780,258 |
| Real estate | $248,409,458 |
| Private equity | $240,667,666 |
| **Total investments** | $5,627,580,132 |
| Invested securities lending collateral | $315,689,006 |
| Other assets | $97,901 |
| **Total assets** | $6,035,246,648 |
| **Liabilities** | |
| Accounts payable and accrued expenses | $2,805,170 |
| Securities sold, but not yet purchased | $164,424,053 |
| Unsetted investment purchase | $34,102,464 |
| Securities lending collateral | $315,689,006 |
| **Total liabilities** | $517,020,693 |
| **Net Asset Held in Trust For Pension Benefits** | $5,518,225,955 |

*Source:* South Dakota Retirement System Comprehensive Annual Financial Report for the Fiscal Year Ended June 30, 2004.

statement whether the plan has sufficient assets to pay for future pension liabilities. Such information is only available from the schedule of funding progress.

The statement of changes in net assets also includes three parts: additions, deductions, and net increase. Additions to assets come in two forms: pension contributions from the employers and employees, and investment income. Deductions are primarily pension benefits paid and administrative expenses. Net increase is the difference between additions and deductions, which is also the reason behind the change in the value of net assets from year to year. As seen in Table 9.4, the plan's net asset value increased by $734 million in FY2004, a 15% increase from the previous year. This increase in net assets primarily resulted from the investment

**Table 9.4  Statement of Changes in Plan Net Assets for the Fiscal Year Ended June 30, 2004**

| | |
|---|---|
| **Additions** | |
| Contributions: | |
| Employee | $104,655,550 |
| Employer | $74,854,496 |
| **Total contributions** | $179,510,046 |
| Investment income: | |
| From investing activities | |
| Net increase in investments in fair value | $636,634,223 |
| Interest | $74,660,719 |
| Dividends | $58,269,884 |
| Real estate | $15,481,311 |
| **Investment income** | $785,046,137 |
| Less investment activity income | $9,100,952 |
| **Net investment activity income** | $775,945,185 |
| From security lending activities | |
| Security lending incomes | $2,656,354 |
| Security lending expenses | ($1,710,590) |
| **Net security lending activity income** | $945,764 |
| **Total investment income** | $776,890,949 |
| **Total additions** | $956,400,995 |
| **Deductions** | |
| Benefits | $198,454,410 |
| Refunds of contributions | $21,414,639 |
| Administrative expenses | $2,493,039 |
| **Total deductions** | $222,362,088 |
| **Net Increase** | $734,038,907 |
| Net assets held in trust for pension benefits | |
| Beginning of year | $4,784,187,048 |
| End of year | $5,518,225,955 |

*Source:* South Dakota Retirement System Comprehensive Annual Financial Report for the Fiscal Year Ended June 30, 2004.

activities. The fair value of investments increased by $636 million, largely due to the significant increase in the value of stocks over this period. This case shows that the value of net assets can be quite volatile from one year to the other, as it is based on the fair value of securities that can increase or decrease by a significant amount in any given year because of the fluctuation in the financial market. In other words, the addition to the assets will not necessarily be positive every year. If the stock market drops substantially in one year, the addition can be negative, and the value of net asset can decrease from the previous year's level.

### 9.1.1.2 Two Required Schedules

In addition to the two basic financial statements, GASB 25 also requires the publication of two schedules: a schedule of funding progress that reports the actuarial value of assets, the actuarial accrued liability, and the relationship between the two over time, and a schedule of employer contributions that provides information about the annual required contributions of the employer(s) (ARC) and the percentage of the ARC recognized by the plan as contributed. These two schedules are intended to provide a long-term actuarial perspective on the pension funds. As these two schedules are important in assessing the long-term financial health of a pension fund, they usually garner more attention than the two statements. Tables 9.5 and 9.6 provide an example of these two schedules for SDRS. Understanding these two schedules involves some basic knowledge of actuarial valuation of assets and liabilities. Therefore, before examining these two schedules, we need to discuss the actuarial evaluation method first.

Pension trust funds by nature are forward-looking. One fundamental question facing any pension fund is if there are enough assets to pay for future promised pension benefits. To make this comparison, we have to know how an employee's future benefits are calculated. The size of an employee's pension benefits at the time of retirement is based on a formula like this: final salary × years of service × multiplying factor. For example, an employee's final salary is $50,000 after government service for 30 years. Suppose the multiplying factor is 2% of the salary at the end of each year of service, then the annual pension will be $30,000. The pension sponsor also needs to make an assumption about how long the pension will be paid after retirement, and the inflation rate if the pension benefits are adjusted for inflation in the future. Last, because of the time value of money, all future pension benefits are discounted to the date of evaluation to find the present value of future liabilities.* This present value of future liabilities is one of the three components in determining the funding status of a pension fund.

---

* The discount rate used for such discounting will be discussed later in this section.

**Table 9.5 Schedule of Funding Progress (expressed in millions)**

| (a) | | (b) | | | | (c) |
| --- | --- | --- | --- | --- | --- | --- |
| Actuarial Valuation Date | Actuarial Value of Assets | Actuarial Accrued Liability— Entry Age [AAL] | Unfunded Actuarial Accrued Liability [UAAL] (b–a) | Funded Ratio (a/b) | Covered Payroll | UAAL as a Percentage of Covered Payroll ([b–a]/c) |
| 6/30/1990 | $1,275.10 | $1,404.60 | $129.50 | 90.80% | $582.70 | 22.20% |
| 6/30/1992 | 1,605.50 | 1,714.50 | 109.0 | 93.6 | 694.3 | 15.7 |
| 6/30/1994 | 1,945.90 | 2,108.30 | 162.4 | 92.3 | 788.6 | 20.6 |
| 6/30/1996 | 2,390.20 | 2,539.00 | 148.8 | 94.1 | 820.1 | 18.1 |
| 6/30/1997 | 2,813.30 | 2,956.50 | 143.2 | 95.2 | 835.1 | 17.1 |
| 6/30/1998 | 3,337.30 | 3,471.90 | 134.6 | 96.1 | 875.9 | 15.4 |
| 6/30/1999 | 3,875.20 | 3,997.90 | 122.8 | 96.9 | 902.5 | 13.6 |
| 6/30/2000 | 4,427.10 | 4,611.90 | 184.8 | 96.0 | 944.6 | 19.6 |
| 6/30/2001 | 4,521.40 | 4,688.40 | 167.0 | 96.4 | 1,029.70 | 16.2 |
| 6/30/2002 | 4,425.40 | 4,576.90 | 151.5 | 96.7 | 1,080.10 | 14.0 |
| 6/30/2003 | 4,683.90 | 4,806.90 | 133.1 | 97.2 | 1,117.30 | 11.9 |
| 6/30/2004 | 4,937.50 | 5,051.70 | 114.2 | 97.7 | 1,164.00 | 9.8 |

*Source:* South Dakota Retirement System Comprehensive Annual Financial Report for the Fiscal Year Ended June 30, 2004.

Now that the present value of the pension liability of this employee is known, the next step is to figure out how to fund this pension liability over the working life of the employee. There are several actuarial cost methods to distribute the cost over time. GASB 25 allows the following methods to allocate the actuarial cost for public pension funds: entry age normal, frozen entry age normal, attained age normal, frozen attained age, projected unit credit, and aggregate cost.* Of these, the most commonly used is the entry age normal cost method. Under this method, the present value of future benefits is allocated as a level percentage of the individual's projected compensation between the time he starts working and the time he retires. The purpose of such a method is to spread evenly over time the cost of funding. The part of this total cost allocated to the year in which the service is provided is considered that year's normal cost and the part allocated to future years is considered

---

* For a definition of all these allocation methods, please see GASB 25.

**Table 9.6   Schedule of Employer Contributions**

| For the Year Ended June 30 | Annual Required Contributions | Percentage Contributed |
|---|---|---|
| 1993 | $39,319,892 | 100 |
| 1994 | 43,991,265 | 100 |
| 1995 | 46,238,393 | 100 |
| 1996 | 45,022,762 | 100 |
| 1997 | 47,664,275 | 100 |
| 1998 | 47,145,364 | 100 |
| 1999 | 50,069,614 | 100 |
| 2000 | 52,622,437 | 100 |
| 2001 | 55,697,940 | 100 |
| 2002 | 58,544,918 | 100 |
| 2003 | 71,989,308 | 100 |
| 2004 | 74,854,496 | 100 |

*Source:* South Dakota Retirement System Comprehensive Annual Financial Report for the Fiscal Year Ended June 30, 2004.

future normal cost. The present value of future normal cost is the second component in determining the funding status of a pension fund. The employer's pension contributions to pay for the normal cost become the assets of the pension funds, which will be invested to earn investment income.

Once a person has started working, then he has earned (or accrued) pension benefits that the pension plan has to pay when he retires. The present value of all his future benefits thus is divided into two parts: the present value of benefits already earned (or accrued) due to the service provided, and the present value of benefits yet to be earned. The first part should be covered by the assets already held in the pension plan and the second part should be covered by the present value of all future normal cost. To evaluate whether the pension benefits for employees have been funded sufficiently at any given time, the actuarial accrued liabilities (AAL) are compared to the actuarial value of assets (AVA). The AAL is the difference between the present value of all future liabilities and the present value of all future normal costs.

What remains to be explained in this equation is the AVA, which is also the third component in determining the funding ratio of a pension plan. In the statement of net assets, we already came across the fair market value of the assets in the pension fund. What is the difference between fair market value and the actuarial value of assets? As the previous discussion on the two basic financial statements has shown, the fair market value of the assets can fluctuate tremendously from year to year due to the fluctuation in the financial market. To reduce such volatility, a smoothing technique is adopted in valuing the asset. Such technique involves calculating a 4- to 5-year moving average of investment return when valuing the asset. For example, if using a 4-year moving average, then only 25% of the investment gains or losses each year over the past 4 years will be recognized in valuing the assets for the current evaluation year. The value of assets arrived at using such a smoothing technique is called the AVA. The AVA leads to a more stable investment return over a 4- to 5-year period. How will the AVA differ from fair market value under different financial market conditions? When the stock market is on the rise, generally the AVA should be lower than the fair market value of assets because part of the gains in value will not be recognized for several more years. If the stock market is in decline, then the AVA should be higher than the fair market value as part of the losses will not be factored in for several more years. Table 9.7 compares the Arizona state retirement system's net asset value and the AVA between 1998 and 2003. From 1998 to 2000, when the stock market boomed, the AVA was substantially lower than the fair value of net assets. However, in the following 3 years when the stock market suffered heavy losses, the actuarial value of assets was higher than the fair market value of net assets. It is obvious that while the market value of net assets experienced considerable volatilities over this period, the actuarial value of assets grew at a very steady pace.

Why is smoothing out the value of assets such an important issue? This has to do with the measurement of the funding ratio of a pension fund. When the AVA is

**Table 9.7   Arizona State Retirement System Assets (expressed in millions)**

| Year | Actuarial Value of Assets | Net Assets |
|------|---------------------------|------------|
| 1998 | $15,577 | $19,930 |
| 1999 | $18,043 | $22,427 |
| 2000 | $20,292 | $23,926 |
| 2001 | $21,888 | $21,731 |
| 2002 | $22,642 | $19,210 |
| 2003 | $22,572 | $18,730 |

*Source:* Arizona State Retirement System Comprehensive Annual Financial Report for various years.

divided by the AAL, the funding ratio of a pension fund is arrived at. If the AVA is greater than the AAL, the funding ratio is greater than 100% and the plan is overfunded. If the ratio is less than 100%, then the plan is underfunded. The difference between AAL and AVA is called the unfunded actuarial accrued liability (UAAL). When the UAAL occurs, the government pension contribution consists of two parts: the normal cost and another part to amortize the UAAL over a period of time. If the market value of assets is used in calculating the UAAL, that can lead to substantial fluctuation in the UAAL from one year to the other and also fluctuation in government pension contributions. The AVA thus reduces such volatility in the pension funding ratio, UAAL, and pension contributions. When discussing the funding status of pension funds, it is important to understand which value is being used, the actuarial value or the market value of assets. State and local governments are required by GASB to report pension funding status based on the AVA, not the market value. However, in a widely cited 2004 report on state and local retirement systems, Wilshire Associates (2004) used market value of assets to measure the funding status. As can be inferred from Table 9.7, the market value of assets was lower than the actuarial value of assets in 2004 due to the stock market decline between 2000 and 2002, thus leading to lower overall pension funding ratios in the Wilshire Associates (2004) than the ones reported by state and local governments.

To fully understand the funding ratio, it is also important to understand the assumptions underlying the calculation of AAL. These assumptions fall into two categories, economic and demographic. Economic assumptions include rate of investment return, inflation rate, and salary growth. Demographic assumptions include mortality rate and disability rate, among others.* Of all these assumptions, the assumption on the rate of investment return is the most important one by far. The rate of return determines how fast the assets are projected to grow in the future. It is also the rate used to discount the future benefits and future normal cost to the present value. This assumption on the rate of return is important because different rates can lead to very different present value of future pension liabilities. For the same amount of future pension liabilities, an assumption of a higher rate of return (or discount rate in this case) will lead to a smaller present value of pension liabilities. Since it is the present value, rather than the future value of pension liabilities that matters in evaluating the funding status of a pension plan, a smaller present value of pension liabilities would leave the plan in a better funding status than otherwise.

Other assumptions are also important in determining the value of future benefits. For example, salary growth projection will determine what a person's final salary will be. Inflation projection will determine what cost of living adjustment for current retirees will be. Mortality rate will determine how long a retiree will receive pension benefits.

---

* For a more detailed discussion of assumptions, please see Hustead (2001).

Armed with the basic understanding of actuarial valuation, we can reexamine the two schedules for the state of South Dakota in Tables 9.5 and 9.6. In both tables historical data are presented, which is required by GASB 25. While it is important to know the funding status of a pension fund at any particular time, it is more important to know whether the funding ratio is improving or deteriorating over time. The funding ratio of South Dakota's retirement system has been improving gradually over this period, even during the severe stock market crash between 2000 and 2002. At almost 98%, the plan is approaching full funding status in 2004. Another positive sign is that the UAAL, measured in both absolute amount and as a percentage of covered payroll, is also decreasing. South Dakota has also fully paid its required pension contributions over an 11-year period. Both schedules indicate that the pension system in South Dakota is in good health and well managed.

Each pension fund is also required by GASB 25 to disclose some basic information about its actuarial valuation. For example, SDRS disclosed in its 2004 CAFR that its actuarial method was entry age, asset valuation method was 5-year smoothed market, investment rate of return was 8%, and cost-of-living adjustments was 3.1%.

## 9.1.2 Investment Trust Funds

Investment trust funds are used to report the external portions of investment pools reported by the sponsoring government.* An investment trust fund is required when a government sponsors an external investment pool and the reporting government is the trustee. Investment trust funds are set up by state or county governments, which pool together the idle cash of local governments and invest the cash on a short-term basis for the local governments. This is an important treasury management tool for small local governments, which usually do not have the financial expertise and personnel to manage cash investment on their own. For a very small amount of management fee paid to the sponsor of the investment pool, local governments will have the safety of investment and more importantly, the convenience of depositing and withdrawing funds from the pool with only a short notice. For example, the Arizona State Treasurer's Office manages an investment pool for Arizona local governments. Tables 9.8 and 9.9 present the two statements for this investment pool. It is interesting to compare these two statements to those of the pension trust fund. One thing these two funds have in common is that for the statement of net assets, the vast majority of the assets are held in investments. In Arizona's case, pretty much all the assets are held in investments that are also valued at fair market value. This has to be the case for the investment pool because that is what is set up for. Like the components of the investments seen in the case of the pension fund, we also see that for the investment pool. In this case, about 30% of

---

* See GASB 34, paragraph 71.

**Table 9.8 Statement of Fiduciary Net Assets—
Local Government Investment Pool, June 30, 2003
(expressed in thousands)**

| Assets | |
|---|---|
| Receivables, net of allowances: | $2,358 |
| Accrued interest and dividends | $2,358 |
| Total receivables | |
| Investments, at fair value: | |
| United State Government securities | $435,053 |
| Corporate bonds | $991,551 |
| Total investments | $1,426,604 |
| Total assets | $1,428,962 |
| **Liabilities** | |
| Due to local governments | $2,147 |
| Total liabilities | $2,147 |
| **Net Assets** | |
| Held in trust for pool participants | $1,426,815 |

*Source:* State of Arizona Comprehensive Annual Financial Report for Fiscal Year Ended June 30, 2003.

the pool was invested in safe Treasury securities and 70% was in corporate bonds. Another similarity between the two funds comes in the statement of changes in net assets. Both funds exhibit fairly substantial changes in net assets from year to year. In Arizona's case, it decreased by 57% in 2004. The difference between these two funds, however, is that the reasoning for such volatility is quite different. For the pension fund, the volatility was largely due to the increase or decrease in the fair value of investments, resulting from the fluctuation in the stock market. For the investment pool, the change in the fair value of the investments did not play much of a role, largely because the assets were invested in short-term fixed-income securities whose values do not change much over time. The changes in net assets were mostly a result of the difference between redemption of shares and purchase of shares. In Arizona's case, more shares were redeemed than purchased by pool participants, leading to a substantial drop in net assets. In other words, more cash was withdrawn from than deposited into the trust fund by pool participants over this period. Therefore, the change in net assets for investment pools does not have any significance, whereas that for pension funds has major implication for the financial well-being of the funds.

**Table 9.9  Statement of Changes in Fiduciary Net Assets—Local Government Investment Pool, June 30, 2003 (expressed in thousands)**

| | |
|---|---:|
| **Additions** | |
| Investment income | |
| Net increase in fair value of investments | $2,581 |
| Interest income | $48,537 |
| Total investment income | $51,118 |
| Less: Investment activity expenses | $1,990 |
| Net investment incomes | $49,128 |
| Capital share and individual account transactions: | |
| Shares sold | $3,410,971 |
| Reinvested interest income | $54,286 |
| Shares redeemed | ($5,394,842) |
| Net capital share and individual account transactions | ($1,929,585) |
| **Total additions** | ($1,880,457) |
| **Deductions** | |
| Dividends to investors | $49,128 |
| **Total deductions** | $49,128 |
| Change in net assets held in trust for pool participants | ($1,929,585) |
| Net Assets—beginning | $3,356,400 |
| **Net Assets—ending** | $1,426,815 |

*Source:* State of Arizona Comprehensive Annual Financial Report for Fiscal Year Ended June 30, 2003.

## 9.1.3  Private-Purpose Trust Funds

As indicated in the beginning section, private-purpose trust funds include all trust arrangements under which the principal and income benefit other governments, private organizations, or individuals. The resources in the funds are managed by the reporting government and will be used for designated private purposes that are not related to the reporting government's programs. A very good example now of a private-purpose trust fund is a state-sponsored 529 plan. It is a savings plan for higher education expenses that allows parents to make after-tax contributions to an investment fund managed by the state government. The contributions will grow tax-free and when their children are ready to enter college, the parents will withdraw the funds to pay for their higher education expenses. Thus, the funds accumulated do not belong to the state and are used purely to finance private citizens' consumption of higher education. Another common example of a private-purpose trust fund is a fund receiving donations and contributions to be used on K–12 students in the form of scholarships.

Tables 9.10 and 9.11 present examples of private-purpose trust funds for these two purposes. They are the North Dakota Student Donations Trust Fund and North Dakota's version of 529 plan, College SAVE. Table 9.10, the statement of net assets, lists all the assets and liabilities for both funds at the end of fiscal year 2003. Both funds had an investment component, although the percentage was quite different for the two. As in the case of two previous funds, the investments were valued at the fair market value. Investment in mutual fund accounted for almost all the assets in the College SAVE fund whereas it accounted for a relatively

**Table 9.10  Statement of Fiduciary Net Assets Private-Purpose Trust Funds, June 30, 2003**

|  | Student Donations | College SAVE |
|---|---|---|
| **Assets** | | |
| Cash deposits at the Bank of ND | $97,483 | — |
| Cash and cash equivalents | $11,916 | $712,153 |
| Receivables: | | |
| Accounts receivable—net | — | $436,350 |
| Due from other funds | $22 | — |
| **Total Receivables** | $22 | $436,350 |
| Investments, at fair value: | | |
| Investments, at the Bank of ND | $18,465 | — |
| Fixed income | $27,667 | — |
| Mutual funds | — | $85,280,735 |
| **Total investments** | $46,132 | $85,280,735 |
| **Total assets** | $155,553 | $86,429,238 |
| **Liabilities** | | |
| Accounts payable | — | $1,077,518 |
| **Total liabilities** | $0 | $1,077,518 |
| **Net Assets** | $155,553 | $85,351,720 |

Source: State of North Dakota Comprehensive Annual Financial Report for the Fiscal Year Ended June 30, 2003.

**Table 9.11    Statement of Changes in Fiduciary Net Assets Private-Purpose Trust Funds for Fiscal Year Ended June 30, 2003**

|  | Student Donations | College SAVE |
|---|---|---|
| **Addition** | | |
| Contributions: | | |
| From participants | | $94,397,117 |
| Donations | $12,990 | |
| **Total contributions** | $12,990 | $94,397,117 |
| Investment income | | |
| Net increase (decrease) in fair value of investment | | ($7,723,172) |
| Interest and dividends | $2,097 | $831,660 |
| Less investment income | | |
| **Net investment income** | $2,097 | ($6,891,512) |
| **Total additions** | $15,087 | $87,505,605 |
| **Deductions** | | |
| Payment in accordance with trust agreements | | |
| Administrative expenses | $8,041 | $4,481,631 |
| **Total deductions** | $8,041 | $4,481,631 |
| Change in net assets held in trust: | $7,046 | $83,023,974 |
| Net assets—beginning of year | $148,507 | $2,327,746 |
| **Net assets—end of year** | $155,553 | $85,351,720 |

*Source:* State of North Dakota Comprehensive Annual Financial Report for the Fiscal Year Ended June 30, 2003.

small portion of the assets in the Student Donations Fund. This is understandable since College SAVE is a long-term investment plan. Such asset composition should have a different impact on the changes in net assets, which can be found in Table 9.11, the statement of changes in net assets. College SAVE lost close to $8 million in investment in fiscal year 2003, as a result of the stock market decline during this period. There was no loss in investment for the Student Donations Fund. Student Donations Fund received $12,990 in donations and paid out $8,041 in scholarships to students in FY2003. College SAVE fund received $94 million in contributions and paid $4.5 million for college-related expenses. In one sense, the

College SAVE private-purpose trust fund is very similar to a pension trust fund. Contributions are made and invested over a long period of time when the children are still young or when the employees are still working. When the children enter college or when the employees are retired, then funds are withdrawn to pay for the college-related expenses or pension benefits. There is one major difference between these two, however. The pension benefits to the retired employees are guaranteed in the future, regardless of the performance of investments in the pension trust funds. The amount of funds available to cover higher education expenses in the future, however, is not guaranteed, holding contributions constant. It depends on the performance of investment in the 529 plans.

Private-purpose trust fund, while itself a new creation under GASB 34, is also affected by the changes made to the fiduciary fund structure in another way. This has to do with the reporting of escheat property, which has been previously governed by GASB 21, *Accounting for Escheat Property*.\* GASB 21 requires that escheat property generally be reported in either an expendable trust fund or the fund to which the property ultimately escheats (the "ultimate fund"). With the elimination of expendable trust funds, GASB issued Statement 37, *Basic Financial Statements—and Management's Discussion and Analysis—for State and Local Governments: Omnibus—an Amendment of GASB Statements No. 21 and No. 34*, to address this change. GASB 37 requires that escheat property be reported as an asset in the governmental or proprietary fund to which the property escheats and that escheat property held for individuals, private organizations, or another government be reported in a private-purpose trust or agency fund, as appropriate.†

## 9.1.4 Agency Funds

Agency funds account for resources held by the reporting government in a custodial capacity. "Agency funds typically involve only the receipt, temporary investment, and remittance of fiduciary resources to individuals, private organizations, or other governments."‡

Of all the four fiduciary funds, only an agency fund does not have the two traditional financial statements: statement of net assets and statement of changes in net assets. Instead, it reports two different statements: statement of assets and liabilities and statement of changes in assets and liabilities. The difference is that the latter two statements do not have the "net assets" concept. The assets in agency funds are always equal to liabilities, because agency funds involve only the receipt,

---

\* "An escheat is the reversion of property to a governmental entity in the absence of legal claimants or heirs. Property escheats from the estate of a person who dies intestate without any known or discoverable heirs at the time the estate is settled. For GASB Statement 21, escheat property also includes abandoned and unclaimed property." (GASB 21, Note 1)

† See GASB 37, paragraph 3.

‡ See GASB 34, paragraph 73.

**Table 9.12   Statement of Fiduciary Assets and Liabilities for the Fiscal Year Ended 6/30/2003**

|  | *Child Support* |
|---|---|
| **Assets** | |
| Cash deposits at the Bank of ND | $961,987 |
| Cash and cash equivalents | $672,904 |
| Accounts receivable—net | $21,718 |
| **Total assets** | $1,656,609 |
| **Liabilities** | |
| Amounts held in custody for others | $1,656,609 |
| **Total liabilities** | $1,656,609 |

*Source:* State of North Dakota Comprehensive Annual Financial Report for the Fiscal Year Ended June 30, 2003.

temporary investment, and remittance of assets to their respective owners. In other words, agency fund is mostly a pass-through account with no permanent assets in it. Unlike the other funds, there are also no administrative expenses associated with agency funds. Because of this pass-through nature of agency funds, their two financial statements do not have accounting basis or measurement focus.

The best example of an agency fund is one for depositing local sales taxes collected by state governments on behalf of the local governments. Since state governments collect all the sales taxes, including those that belong to the local governments, this portion of the sales taxes are deposited in an agency fund temporarily before they are remitted to the local governments in a very short period of time. Another example of agency fund is a fund for depositing child support funds collected by the state. Again the state does not own these funds and keeps them in an agency fund only for a short period of time before remittance. Tables 9.12 and 9.13 present an example of the North Dakota state child support agency fund. Table 9.12 lists the assets and liabilities in this agency fund. Assets are exactly equal to liabilities. Table 9.13 shows the changes in assets and liabilities. The pass-through nature of this fund is clearly demonstrated by the fact that large additions to both the assets and liabilities were offset by larges deductions.

## 9.2 Summary

This chapter begins by analyzing the changes made to the classification of fiduciary funds under GASB 34. The key change is the elimination of resources from the fiduciary funds used for the programs of the reporting government. What remain in the fiduciary fund group are pension trust funds, investment trust funds,

**Table 9.13  Combining Statement of Changes in Assets and Liabilities for the Fiscal Year Ended June 30, 2003**

|  | *June 30, 2002* | *Additions* | *Deductions* | *June 30, 2003* |
|---|---|---|---|---|
| **Assets** | | | | |
| Cash deposits at the Bank of ND | $902,477 | $89,825,537 | $89,766,027 | $961,987 |
| Cash and equivalents | $10,255 | $662,649 | | $672,904 |
| Accounts receivable—net | $298,328 | $89,524,616 | $89,801,226 | $21,718 |
| Data from other funds | $12 | $513,874 | $513,886 | — |
| **Total assets** | $1,211,072 | $180,526,676 | 180,081,139$ | $1,656,609 |
| **Liabilities** | | | | |
| Due to other funds | | $7,096,762 | $7,096,762 | — |
| Amounts held in custody for others | $1,211,072 | $173,027,706 | $172,582,169 | $1,656,609 |
| **Total liabilities** | $1,211,072 | $180,124,468 | $179,678,931 | $1,656,609 |

*Source:* State of North Dakota Comprehensive Annual Financial Report for the Fiscal Year Ended June 30, 2003.

private-purpose trust funds, and agency funds, all of which hold resources for entities other than the reporting government. Pension trust funds hold assets to pay for government employees' retirement benefits. Investment trust funds report assets held in an investment pool for other government entities. Private-purpose trust funds report assets held in a trust agreement for individuals, private organizations, and other government entities. Agency funds account for resources held by the reporting government in a purely custodial capacity.

While it has been emphasized throughout this chapter that fiduciary funds are created to account for the resources held and used for entities other than the reporting government itself, this chapter ends with an analysis of two key differences between pension trust fund and all other fiduciary funds in this respect. First, the origin of the resources is different. Some of the resources in a pension fund come from the reporting government in the first place, in the form of pension contributions whereas the resources in other fiduciary funds come directly from private organizations, individuals, or other government units.

Second, and more important, the connection with the reporting government's programs is also different. For the pension trust funds, even if the assets can only be used for future pension benefits payment and are not available for use to the reporting government, the assets are still connected with the reporting government's programs in an indirect way. They are connected indirectly because the reporting government is responsible for the investment performance of the assets held in the pension plan. If the value of assets falls due to poor investment performance, then the pension funding ratio will drop and the reporting government's pension contribution will have to increase. Such an increase in pension contribution will make less funding available for other programs of the reporting government. The value of investments can also increase substantially due to better investment return than expected. This can lead to an increase in pension funding ratio and a decrease in pension contribution, making more funds available to be used on other government programs. The same thing can not be said about assets held in other fiduciary funds. The investment performance of assets held in investment trust funds and private-purpose trust funds do not have any impact on the reporting government's finance. The gain or loss in the value of assets due to investment performance will be born by the owners of assets, i.e., individuals, private organizations, and other government entities.

# References

Arizona State Retirement System Comprehensive Annual Financial Report, various years.

GASB Statement 21, *Accounting for Escheat Property*.

GASB Statement 25, *Financial Reporting for Defined Benefit Pension Plans and Note Disclosures for Defined Contribution Plans*.

GASB Statement 34, *Basic Financial Statements—and Management's Discussion and Analysis—for State and Local Governments*.

GASB Statement 37, *Basic Financial Statements—and Management's Discussion and Analysis—for State and Local Governments: Omnibus—an Amendment of GASB Statements No. 21 and No. 34*.

Hustead, E.C., Determining the cost of public pension plans, in *Pensions in the Public Sector*, Ed. Michel Olivia and Edwin C. Hustead, University of Pennsylvania Press, 2001.

Mead, D.M. 2000. What You Should Know about Your Local Government's Finances: A Guide to Financial Statements. Government Accounting Standards Board.

South Dakota Retirement System Comprehensive Annual Financial Report, for the Fiscal Year Ended June 30, 2004.

State of Arizona Comprehensive Annual Financial Report, for the Fiscal Year Ended June 30, 2003.

State of North Dakota Comprehensive Annual Financial Report, for the Fiscal Year Ended June 30, 2003.

Wilshire Associates. 2004. 2004 Wilshire Report on State Retirement Systems: Funding Levels and Asset Allocation.

## Chapter 10

# Governmental Financial Reporting

## Randall L. Kinnersley
*Western Kentucky University, College of Business, Department of Accounting*

## Contents

10.1 Introduction .................................................................................. 340
10.2 Defining the Governmental Reporting Entity ............................................. 341
    10.2.1 Determining a Primary Government ............................................. 341
    10.2.2 Component Units ................................................................ 341
        10.2.2.1 Identifying Component Units ..................................... 341
        10.2.2.2 Reporting Component Units ...................................... 343
    10.2.3 Related Reporting Entity Topics ................................................ 344
10.3 Comprehensive Annual Financial Report .................................................. 344
    10.3.1 Introduction ..................................................................... 344
    10.3.2 Introductory Section ............................................................ 345
    10.3.3 Financial Section ................................................................ 346
        10.3.3.1 Introduction .................................................... 346
        10.3.3.2 Management's Discussion and Analysis ........................... 346
        10.3.3.3 Basic Financial Statements ....................................... 346
        10.3.3.4 Notes to the Financial Statements ............................... 346
        10.3.3.5 Required Supplementary Information (RSI) ...................... 348
        10.3.3.6 Supplemental Information ....................................... 351
    10.3.4 Statistical Section ............................................................... 351
10.4 Basic Financial Statements ................................................................. 353

10.4.1 Introduction................................................................353
10.4.2 Determining Major Funds ............................................354
10.4.3 Governmental Fund Statements.....................................354
    10.4.3.1 Balance Sheet.................................................354
    10.4.3.2 Statement of Revenues, Expenditures, and Changes
            in Fund Balance..............................................356
    10.4.3.3 Budgetary Comparison Statement.....................356
10.4.4 Proprietary Fund Statements.........................................358
    10.4.4.1 Introduction.................................................358
    10.4.4.2 Statement of Net Assets.................................361
    10.4.4.3 Statement of Revenues, Expenses, and Changes in
            Net Assets ....................................................362
    10.4.4.4 Statement of Cash Flows ................................363
10.4.5 Fiduciary Fund Statements............................................365
    10.4.5.1 Introduction.................................................365
    10.4.5.2 Statement of Fiduciary Net Assets.................... 366
    10.4.5.3 Statement of Changes in Fiduciary Net Assets .............367
10.4.6 Government-Wide Statements.........................................367
    10.4.6.1 Introduction.................................................367
    10.4.6.2 Statement of Net Assets.................................369
    10.4.6.3 Statement of Activities...................................372
10.4.7 Component Unit Combining Statements...........................377
    10.4.7.1 Introduction.................................................377
    10.4.7.2 Component Unit Combining Statement of Net
            Assets ..........................................................377
    10.4.7.3 Component Unit Combining Statement of Activities....380
    10.4.7.4 Other Information .........................................380
10.5 Conversion from Fund Reporting to Government-Wide Reporting .........380
10.6 Summary ........................................................................387
References ................................................................................387

## 10.1 Introduction

Financial reporting for governments is based primarily on pronouncements issued by the Governmental Accounting Standards Board (GASB). The GASB recommends each government issue a comprehensive annual financial report (CAFR). A CAFR has three main sections: introductory, financial, and statistical. This chapter discusses each of these main sections.

The basic financial statements, a part of the financial section, are the main topic in this chapter. Basic financial statements report the financial activity of the government. Each basic financial statement is illustrated and discussed in section IV of this chapter. Also, the chapter introduces the process for summarizing and including fund information in the government-wide statements.

This chapter assumes that the CAFR is for a general purpose government. Many special purpose governments have unique reporting options available to them. The reporting options depend on the nature of the special purpose government and whether its program is governmental, proprietary, or fiduciary in nature. Special purpose government reporting is beyond the scope of this chapter, but more information is available in section Sp20 of the codification (Cod) (GASB 2008).

This chapter is divided into six sections. The introduction is presented above. Section 10.2 defines the reporting entity and the methods for reporting component units. The CAFR is discussed in Section 10.3. Section 10.4 illustrates and highlights the information in the basic financial statements. A summary of the conversion from fund reporting to the government-wide statements is presented in Section 10.5. Finally, a short summary concludes the chapter.

# 10.2 Defining the Governmental Reporting Entity

## 10.2.1 Determining a Primary Government

"[T]he financial reporting entity consists of (a) the primary government (b) organizations for which the primary government is financially accountable, and (c) other organizations for which … exclusion would cause the reporting entity's financial statements to be misleading or incomplete" (Cod. 2100.111). "A primary government consists of all organizations that make up its legal entity" (Cod. 2100.113). "The foundation of a primary government is a separately elected governing body …" (Cod. 2100.112). Any state, county, municipality, or other general purpose government is a primary government. Special purpose governments, such as school districts, are also considered a primary government if the government meets all of the following criteria: (1) has a separately elected governing body, (2) is legally separate, and (3) is fiscally independent of other state and local governments.

## 10.2.2 Component Units

"Component units are legally separate organizations for which the elected officials of the primary government are financially accountable" (Cod. 2100.119). The GASB defines financial accountability as "the kind of relationship warranting the inclusion of a legally separate organization in the reporting entity of another organization" (Cod. 2100.120). GASB standards provide criteria to determine if a financial accountability relationship exists.

### 10.2.2.1 Identifying Component Units

A primary government should identify governmental organizations, nonprofit corporations, and for-profit corporations that may potentially meet the financial

**Table 10.1   Criteria to Be Included in a Separate Legal Entity in a Government's Reporting Entity**

| |
|---|
| A potential component unit is included in the reporting entity of a government if any of the following three criteria are met: |
| 1) The separate legal entity must seek approval from the primary government before taking any of these actions |
|    A)  Adopt a budget |
|    B)  Change tax rates or user charges |
|    C)  Issue bonds |
| 2) The primary government appoints a majority of the separate legal entity's governing board AND one of the two following relationships exist |
|    A)  the primary government can impose its will on the separate legal entity, OR |
|    B)  a financial benefit or financial burden relationship exists between the two entities |
| 3) The financial statements would be misleading or incomplete if the potential component unit is left out |

accountability criteria. Each potential component unit (PCU) is evaluated based on three sets of criteria. Primary governments must report a PCU as a component unit if the PCU meets any of the three sets of criteria. Table 10.1 summarizes the criteria.

Some PCUs may be fiscally dependent on the primary government. An organization that is *fiscally dependent* on the primary government is also considered *financially accountable* to the primary government. A PCU is fiscally dependent on the primary government if the primary government has authority to approve or modify any of the following financial activities of the PCU: (1) the budget, (2) the tax levy or charges, or (3) bond issues. Separate legal entities are part of the reporting entity of the primary government if it meets any one of the three fiscal dependency criteria.

The second set of criteria is a two-step process. A PCU is a part of the primary government reporting entity if (step 1) the primary government appoints the voting majority of the PCU governing board, and (step 2) either (1) the primary government can impose its will on the PCU or (2) a financial benefit or financial burden relationship exists between the primary government and the PCU. A primary government must appoint the majority of the PCU board or the step 2 criteria are irrelevant. Notice that either the imposition of will or the financial benefit or burden criteria are sufficient to meet the second step criteria.

Finally, the most general test is whether the financial statements of the reporting entity would be misleading or incomplete if the PCU is left out. In practice, this test is rarely the justification for including a PCU in the reporting entity.

## 10.2.2.2 Reporting Component Units

"Financial statements of the reporting entity should provide an overview of the entity, yet allow users to distinguish between the primary government and its component units" (Cod. 2600.105). Primary governments must report component units using one of two methods. The reporting method depends on the relationship between the component unit and the primary government.

### 10.2.2.2.1 Blended Component Units

Blended component units are "so intertwined with the primary government that they are, in substance, the same as the primary government. These component units should be reported as part of the primary government in both the fund financial statements and the government-wide financial statements" (Cod. 2600.112). Blending is required if a component unit meets one of two criteria. The first criterion is if "[t]he component unit's governing body is substantively the same as the governing body of the primary government" (Cod. 2600.113a).

Substantively, the same governing body, as defined by GASB, occurs when the majority (more than half) of the primary government's governing body is also a voting majority of the component unit's governing body. The second criterion that requires blending is if "[t]he component unit provides services ... almost entirely to the primary government or ... almost exclusively benefits the primary government even though it does not provide services directly to it" (Cod. 2600.113b).

Blended component unit "balances and transactions should be reported in a manner similar to the balances and transactions of the primary government itself" (Cod. 2600.112). Governments should report each blended component unit as part of the appropriate fund statements or nonmajor combining statements of the primary government. Thus, for most users of financial statements, blended component unit funds are not distinguishable from the primary government fund information without reading the notes to the financial statements. In addition, governments should report blended component unit information within the primary government captions of the government-wide financial statements.

### 10.2.2.2.2 Discretely Presented Component Units

Discretely presented component units are separate legal entities that meet the component unit criteria but do not meet any of the blending criteria. "Discrete presentation entails reporting component unit financial data in columns and rows separate from the financial data of the primary government" (Cod. 2600.107). Governments should only report discretely presented component units in the government-wide statements, except fiduciary funds of component units that are reported as part of the fiduciary fund statements. "The discrete column(s) should be located to the right of the total column of the primary government ..." (Cod. 2600.107) on the government-wide statements. The discretely presented component units presentation format is illustrated as part of the basic financial statements later in this chapter.

### 10.2.3 Related Reporting Entity Topics

Some legally separate PCUs do not meet the criteria for reporting as component units in the financial statements, but do require disclosure in the notes to the basic financial statements. One example is a related organization. "Organizations for which a primary government is accountable because it appoints a voting majority of the board, but is not financially accountable, are related organizations" (Cod. 2600.127). Related organizations meet part of the component unit criteria, but the primary government cannot impose its will on the separate entity nor is there a financial benefit or burden relationship. The note disclosure requirements are found in codification section 2600.127.

Joint ventures and jointly governed organizations are also separate legal entities that require note disclosure. "A joint venture is a legal entity or other organization that results from a contractual arrangement and that is owned, operated, or governed by two or more participants as a separate and specific activity subject to joint control, in which the participants retain (a) an ongoing financial interest or (b) an ongoing financial responsibility" (Cod. J50.102). A jointly governed organization is similar to a joint venture except the primary government has "no ongoing financial interest or responsibility" (Cod. J50.111). Joint ventures require more financial information in the note disclosure than related organizations or jointly governed organizations. Governments must report an equity interest in a joint venture in the appropriate financial statements of the primary government. The details of the required notes disclosures for joint ventures can be found in codification section J50.106–109.

## 10.3 Comprehensive Annual Financial Report

### 10.3.1 Introduction

The GASB identifies the required and suggested content of the comprehensive annual financial report. The standards indicate that "[a] comprehensive annual financial report should be prepared and published, covering all funds and activities of the primary government (including its blended component units) and providing an overview of all discretely presented component units of the reporting entity—including introductory section, management's discussion and analysis (MD&A), basic financial statements, required supplementary information other than MD&A, appropriate combining and individual fund statements, schedules, narrative explanations, and statistical section" (Cod. 2200b). The contents of each of the three primary sections of the CAFR—introductory, financial, and statistical—are summarized next.

## 10.3.2 Introductory Section

The introductory section is unaudited information. Management can provide information to the citizenry without the limitations of the GASB standards. Codification section 2200.105a lists the content of the introductory section to include a "table of contents, letter(s) of transmittal, and other material deemed appropriate by management." The letter of transmittal is the only item in the CAFR in which management can discuss plans and anticipated problems. *Governmental Accounting, Auditing, and Financial Reporting* (GAAFR), known as the Blue Book, suggests including the following other material in the introductory section: (1) a list of principal officials, (2) an organizational chart, and (3) the GFOA Certificate of Achievement for Excellence in Financial Reporting (if earned). Table 10.2 summarizes the content of the introductory section.

**Table 10.2   Contents of the Introductory Section of the Comprehensive Annual Financial Report**

| Introductory Section |
| --- |
| **Items required by GASB (Cod. 2200.105a)** |
| 1   Table of Contents |
| 2   Letter(s) of Transmittal |
| 3   Other material deemed necessary by management |
| **Items recommended by Governmental Accounting, Auditing, and Financial Reporting (GAAFR, p. 245)** |
| 4   List of Principal Officers |
| 5   Organizational Chart |
| 6   GFOA Certificate of Achievement for Excellence in Financial Reporting (if earned) |

### 10.3.3 Financial Section

#### 10.3.3.1 Introduction

Table 10.3 summarizes the contents of the financial section in the order in which the items should be presented. The independent auditor's report informs users whether the government complied with generally accepted accounting principles (GAAP), and if not, identifies the material exceptions to GAAP in the financial statements.

#### 10.3.3.2 Management's Discussion and Analysis

Management's discussion and analysis (MD&A) is the second item presented in the financial section. MD&A is considered required supplemental information (RSI). Governments must include RSI with the financial statements, but RSI does not require the same level of audit procedures. "MD&A should discuss current-year results in comparison with the prior year, with emphasis on the current year.... The use of charts, graphs, and tables is encouraged ..." (Cod. 2200.107). MD&A should focus on the primary government and must only contain information on eight topics specified by the GASB. Table 10.4 lists the eight topics. In addition, the MD&A must report only known historical facts. The GASB prohibits speculation about future plans or events in MD&A.

#### 10.3.3.3 Basic Financial Statements

The basic financial statements are the third group of items presented in the financial section. Table 10.3 lists the order in which the statements should be presented. The next major section of this chapter, Section 10.4, will focus on the basic financial statements. A discussion of the basic financial statements is delayed until then.

#### 10.3.3.4 Notes to the Financial Statements

The notes to the financial statements are "an integral part of the basic financial statements" (Cod. 2300.102) and they should be presented immediately following the basic financial statements. "... [N]otes to the financial statements should communicate information essential for fair presentation of the basic financial statements that are not displayed on the face of the financial statements" (Cod. 2300.102). "Certain information may be presented either on the face of the financial statements or in the notes to the financial statements. Disclosure in the notes to the financial statements is needed only when the information required to be disclosed is not displayed on the face of the financial statements" (Cod. 2300.103). Similar to MD&A, the notes should focus on primary government activities. Governments should present major discretely presented component unit information only if it is significant in the circumstances. In addition, the government must clearly

**Table 10.3   Contents of the Financial Section of the Comprehensive Annual Financial Report**

| *Financial Section* |
|---|
| **Independent Auditor's Report** |
| **Management's Discussion and Analysis (part of Required Supplemental Information)** |
| **Basic Financial Statements** |
| **Government-Wide Statements**<br>Statement of Net Assets<br>Statement of Activities |
| **Fund Statements**<br><br>*Governmental Fund Statements*<br>Balance Sheet<br>Statement of Revenues, Expenditures, and Changes in Fund Balance<br>Comparative Budgetary Information (optional, may also be reported as RSI)<br><br>*Proprietary Fund Statements*<br>Statement of Net Assets (or Balance Sheet)<br>Statement of Revenues, Expenses, and Changes in Net Assets<br>Statement of Cash Flows<br><br>*Fiduciary Fund Statements*<br>Statement of Net Assets<br>Statement of Changes in Net Assets<br><br>*Component Unit Combining Statements*<br>Combining Component Unit Statement of Net Assets<br>Combining Component Unit Statement of Activities |
| **Notes to the Financial Statements** |
| **Required Supplemental Information (RSI)** |
| Supplemental Information (not required for an unqualified audit opinion) |

*Source:* Adapted from Cod. 2200.105b.

distinguish the component unit information from the primary government information in the notes. Table 10.5 presents note disclosures essential to fair presentation as listed in the codification (2300.106). The codification also provides a list of potential additional note disclosures in section 2300.107, but an itemized list is not presented in a table due to its length.

**Table 10.4  Contents of Management's Discussion and Analysis**

| *Required Elements of Management's Discussion and Analysis (if applicable)* |
|---|
| 1) A brief discussion of the basic financial statements. |
| 2) Condensed financial information derived from government-wide financial statements comparing the current year to the prior year. (The specific accounting elements normally appropriate for inclusion are identified in Cod. 2200.109b.) |
| 3) An analysis of the government's overall financial position and results of operations to assist users in assessing whether the financial position has improved or deteriorated as a result of the year's operations. |
| 4) Analysis of balances and transactions of individual funds. |
| 5) An analysis of significant variations between original and final budget amounts and between final budget amounts and actual budget results for the general fund (or its equivalent). |
| 6) A description of significant capital asset and long-term debt activity during the year. |
| 7) A discussion by governments that use the modified approach to report some or all their infrastructure assets. (Topics to discuss are listed in Cod. 2200.109g.) |
| 8) A description of currently known facts, decisions, or conditions that are expected to have a significant effect on financial position (net assets) or results of operations (revenues, expenses, and other changes in net assets). |

*Source:* Adapted from Cod. 2200.109a–h.

## 10.3.3.5 Required Supplementary Information (RSI)

"Required supplementary information consists of schedules, statistical data, and other information that the GASB has determined are an essential part of financial reporting and should be presented with, but not part of, the basic financial statements..." (Cod. 2200.181). Required supplemental information, other than MD&A, is "presented immediately following the notes to the basic financial statements" (Cod. 2200.181). Table 10.6 lists the items included in the required supplemental information (RSI), if appropriate. RSI includes information about the following major topics: (1) budgetary comparison schedules, (2) information about the modified approach for reporting infrastructure assets, and (3) pension and other postemployment benefit plans managed by the government.

"Budgetary comparisons should be presented for the general fund and for each major special revenue fund that has a legally adopted annual budget. Governments are encouraged to present such budgetary comparison information in schedules

**Table 10.5  Note Disclosures Essential to Fair Presentation**

| |
|---|
| 1) Summary of significant accounting policies (Cod. 2300.106a identifies 12 polices to include) |
| 2) Cash deposits with financial institutions |
| 3) Investments |
| 4) Significant contingent liabilities |
| 5) Encumbrances outstanding |
| 6) Significant effects of subsequent events |
| 7) Annual pension cost and net pension obligations (NPO) |
| 8) Significant violations of finance-related legal or contractual provisions and actions taken to address such violations |
| 9) Debt service requirements to maturity |
| 10) Commitments under noncapital (operating) leases |
| 11) Construction and other significant commitments |
| 12) Required disclosures about capital assets |
| 13) Required disclosures about long-term liabilities |
| 14) Deficit fund balance or net assets of individual nonmajor funds |
| 15) Interfund balances and transfers |
| 16) For each major component unit, the nature and amount of significant transactions with other discretely presented component units or with the primary government |
| 17) Disclosures about donor-restricted endowments |

*Source:* Adapted from Cod. 2300.106a–q.

as a part of RSI" (Cod. 2200.182). Governments may also "report this budgetary comparison information in a budgetary comparison statement as part of the basic financial statements, rather than RSI" (Cod. 2200.182, footnote 35) provided a budgetary perspective difference does not exist. Section 10.4 of this chapter illustrates and discusses the format and contents of the budgetary schedule (statement), since governments can include it as part of the basic financial statements.

The GASB permits two methods to allocate annual costs for infrastructure assets. The most common method is to depreciate the assets over a useful life, similar to other fixed assets. A second method, referred to as the modified approach, permits governments to charge the current year maintenance expenditures on

**Table 10.6   Required Supplemental Information (Other Than MD&A), if Applicable**

| |
|---|
| 1) Budgetary Comparison Schedules |
|    a)  General Fund |
|    b)  Major Special Revenue Funds that have a legally adopted budget |
| 2) Infrastructure Information when using the Modified Approach |
|    a)  The assessed condition of infrastructure assets (performed at least every three years) for the three most recent complete condition assessments, indicating the dates of the assessments. |
|    b)  The estimated annual amount calculated at the beginning of the fiscal year to maintain and preserve at (or above) the condition level established and disclosed by the government compared with the amounts actually expended. |
|    c)  Certain other disclosures as listed in Cod. 1400.119 |
| 3) Employee Benefit Related Information for Each Defined Benefit and Other Postemployment Benefit Plans |
|    a)  Schedule of Funding Progress |
|    b)  Schedule of Employer Contributions |

infrastructure to the current year, if the expenditures are necessary to preserve the infrastructure at a predetermined level. A complete discussion of the modified approach for reporting infrastructure costs is beyond the scope of this chapter. However, if the modified approach for reporting infrastructure cost is chosen, RSI must include: (1) the assessed condition of infrastructure assets for at least the three most recent complete condition assessments with the dates of the assessments; and (2) the estimated annual amount calculated at the beginning of the fiscal year to maintain and preserve infrastructure assets at (or above) the desired condition level established and disclosed by the government compared with the amounts actually expended. Illustrations of how to present the infrastructure information in RSI are in codification sections 2200.901–903.

Employee benefits related to defined benefit pension plans (DBPP) and other postemployment benefits (OPEB) also require RSI schedules. The GASB requires two schedules for sole and agent employers of DBPP and OPEB plans: (1) a Schedule of Funding Progress and (2) a Schedule of Employer Contributions. These schedules are prepared from actuarial analyses and other sources rather than from the financial statements. Governments should include the most recent and two preceding actuarial valuations for each plan as part of the RSI schedules.

## 10.3.3.6 Supplemental Information

Supplemental information provides schedules that are not required in the basic financial statements. Combining statements are required in a CAFR to support any column that reports more than one fund in a single column in a fund statement. Columns that may require a combining statement include: (1) internal service funds, (2) all fiduciary fund columns (pension trust funds, private-purpose trust funds, investment trust funds, and agency funds), and (3) nonmajor fund columns in governmental or proprietary fund statements. "Total columns of the combining statements of nonmajor governmental and enterprise funds and for internal service and fiduciary funds should agree with the appropriate aggregated column in the fund financial statements" (Cod. 2200.184).

The GASB requires individual statements and schedules if they are necessary to demonstrate compliance with finance-related legal and contractual provisions. "Schedules are … used to present: (1) data on a legally or contractually prescribed basis different from GAAP, and (2) other data that management wants to present that is not required by GAAP" (Cod. 2200.186). Examples of supplemental schedules are budgetary comparison schedules for legally adopted budgets of: (1) nonmajor special revenue funds, (2) capital project funds, (3) debt service funds, and (4) any other fund with a legally adopted budget.

## 10.3.4 Statistical Section

"The objectives of statistical section information are to provide financial statement users with additional historical perspective, context, and detail to assist in using the information in the financial statements, notes to financial statements, and required supplementary information to understand and assess a government's economic condition" (Cod. 2800.104). "Statistical tables present comparative data for several periods of time—often ten or more years—or contain data from sources other than the accounting records" (Cod. 2800.102). "Statistical section information should be presented in five categories—financial trends information, revenue capacity information, debt capacity information, demographic and economic information, and operating information" (Cod. 2800.105). The GASB requires disclosure of specific information in the schedules. It also provides nonauthoritative illustrations of required and optional schedules. A government must follow the GASB standards for statistical information if the statistical section accompanies the basic financial statements. Table 10.7 lists 18 statistical tables GASB illustrates, in Statement 44 *Economic Condition Reporting: The Statistical Section,* as appropriate for general purpose local governments. Governments are encouraged to provide other tables that may enhance the usefulness of the information in the CAFR. Statement 44 also illustrates optional schedules, alternative formats, and illustrations specifically for states and other governmental entities.

**Table 10.7 Statistical Tables (General Purpose Local Governments)**

| *Statistical Section* |
| --- |

**Financial Trends Information**

1) Net Assets by Component, last ten fiscal years

2) Changes in Net Assets, last ten fiscal years

3) Fund Balances, Governmental Funds, last ten fiscal years

4) Changes in Fund Balances, Governmental Funds, last ten fiscal years

**Revenue Capacity Information**

1) Assessed Value and Actual Value of Taxable Property, last ten fiscal years

2) Direct and Overlapping Property Tax Rates, last ten fiscal years

3) Principal Property Tax Payers, current year and nine years ago

4) Property Tax Levies and Collections, last ten fiscal years

**Debt Capacity Information**

1) Ratios of Outstanding Debt by Type, last ten fiscal years

2) Ratios of General Bonded Debt Outstanding, last ten fiscal years

3) Direct and Overlapping Governmental Activities Debt as of Current Year End

4) Legal Debt Margin Information, last ten fiscal years

5) Pledged-Revenue Coverage, last ten fiscal years

**Demographic and Economic Information**

1) Demographic and Economic Statistics, last ten calendar years

2) Principal Employers, current year and nine years ago

**Operating Information**

1) Full-Time Equivalent City Gov't Employees by Function/Program, last ten fiscal years

2) Operating Indicators by Function/Program, last ten fiscal years

3) Capital Asset Statistics by Function/Program, last ten fiscal years

*Source:* Adapted from Statement 44, *Economic Condition Reporting: The Statistical Section* (Append. C).

# 10.4 Basic Financial Statements

## 10.4.1 Introduction

Financial reporting for governments is frequently summarized in a reporting pyramid. Figure 10.1 provides an overview of the organization of financial information for governments. It illustrates how financial transactions are summarized into the basic financial statements. The information in Figure 10.1 flows from the bottom to the top of the figure.

Financial transactions, shown at the bottom of Figure 10.1, are first summarized into individual funds. Individual funds are then reported as part of one of the three fund categories—governmental, proprietary, or fiduciary. Major funds, discussed in Section 10.4.2, are reported individually on the appropriate governmental or proprietary fund statements. All nonmajor governmental or proprietary funds are combined into a single column on the appropriate fund statements. Fiduciary funds are summarized differently. Fiduciary funds are combined by fiduciary fund type—pension trust funds, private-purpose trust funds, investment trust funds, and agency funds. One column reports all funds of a particular fiduciary fund type. For example, all pension trust funds are reported as a single column on the two fiduciary fund basic financial statements.

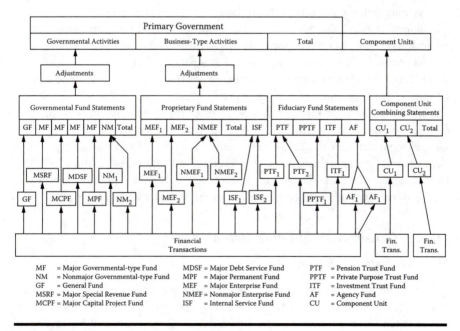

| MF | = Major Governmental-type Fund | MDSF | = Major Debt Service Fund | PTF | = Pension Trust Fund |
| NM | = Nonmajor Governmental-type Fund | MPF | = Major Permanent Fund | PPTF | = Private Purpose Trust Fund |
| GF | = General Fund | MEF | = Major Enterprise Fund | ITF | = Investment Trust Fund |
| MSRF | = Major Special Revenue Fund | NMEF | = Nonmajor Enterprise Fund | AF | = Agency Fund |
| MCPF | = Major Capital Project Fund | ISF | = Internal Service Fund | CU | = Component Unit |

**Figure 10.1   Flow of financial information.**

All governmental funds are then consolidated (as defined by GASB) into a single governmental activities column on the government-wide statements. Similarly, all enterprise funds are consolidated into a single business-type activities column on the government-wide statements. Fiduciary funds are not reported on the government-wide statements; however, discretely presented component units are reported, after a primary government total, on the government-wide statements. Figure 10.1 illustrates the flow of all this financial information.

Table 10.3, near Section 10.3.3, lists the required basic financial statements in the order in which they should be presented in the CAFR. This section discusses and illustrates the basic financial statements. Figures 10.2 to 10.13 illustrate the format and content of the various statements using financial statements adapted from a recent City of Richmond, Virginia, CAFR. The discussion focuses on the column headings and major row labels. Unique items of the fund statements are highlighted when appropriate. Each statement is covered in more detail following a discussion of major funds.

## 10.4.2 Determining Major Funds

"The focus of governmental and proprietary fund financial statements is on major funds. Fund statements should present the financial information of each major fund in a separate column. Nonmajor funds should be aggregated and displayed in a single column" (Cod. 2200.152). "The … main operating fund (the general fund or its equivalent) should always be reported as a major fund. Other individual governmental and enterprise funds should be reported in separate columns as major funds …" (Cod. 2200.153). The process to determine major funds is "based on these criteria (a) total assets, liabilities, revenues, or expenditures/expenses of that individual governmental or enterprise fund are at least 10% of the corresponding element total (assets, liabilities, and so forth) for all funds of that category or type … , and (b) the same element that met the 10% criterion in (a) is at least 5% of the corresponding element total for all governmental and enterprise funds combined" (Cod. 2200.153). Governments can report other governmental funds or enterprise funds as major funds if the government's officials believe it is important to financial statement users.

## 10.4.3 Governmental Fund Statements

### 10.4.3.1 Balance Sheet

"The balance sheet should report … each major governmental fund [individually] and … nonmajor governmental funds in aggregate. A total column should be presented. Assets, liabilities, and fund balances of governmental funds should be displayed in a balance sheet format (assets equal liabilities plus fund balances)" (Cod. 2200.156). Also, "[g]overnmental fund balances should be segregated into reserved and unreserved amounts" (Cod. 2200.157). Figure 10.2 presents the City

CITY OF RICHMOND, VIRGINIA
BALANCE SHEET
GOVERNMENTAL FUNDS
June 30, 20X8

| | General | Debt Service | Other Governmental Funds | Total |
|---|---|---|---|---|
| **Assets** | | | | |
| Cash and Cash Equivalents (Note 3) | $ 60,905,925 | $ -- | $ 7,455,298 | $ 68,361,223 |
| Receivables (Net of Allowance for Doubtful Accounts): | | | | |
| Taxes and Licenses | 45,537,175 | -- | -- | 45,537,175 |
| Accounts | 12,582,409 | 296,212 | 3,011,667 | 15,890,288 |
| Accrued Interest | -- | -- | -- | -- |
| Due From Other Funds (Note 4) | 5,410,062 | -- | -- | 5,410,062 |
| Due From Component Units | 26,858,483 | -- | -- | 26,858,483 |
| Due From Other Governments (Note 5) | 18,544,704 | -- | 18,296,220 | 36,840,924 |
| Other Assets | -- | 222,909 | -- | 222,909 |
| Restricted Assets - Cash and Investments (Note 3) | -- | 1,480,501 | 45,502,898 | 46,983,399 |
| Advances To Other Funds | 150 | -- | -- | 150 |
| Advances To Component Units | 262,800 | -- | -- | 262,800 |
| Notes Receivable (Note 6) | 5,043,100 | -- | -- | 5,043,100 |
| Total Assets | $ 175,144,808 | $ 1,999,622 | $ 74,266,083 | $ 251,410,513 |
| | | | | |
| **Liabilities and Fund Balances** | | | | |
| **Liabilities:** | | | | |
| Accounts Payable | $ 8,033,958 | $ -- | $ 4,512,960 | $ 12,546,918 |
| Accrued Liabilities | 4,696,719 | -- | 419,301 | 5,116,020 |
| Due To Other Funds (Note 4) | -- | 507,660 | 2,467,773 | 2,975,433 |
| Due To Other Governments | 3,142,727 | -- | 30,602 | 3,173,329 |
| Due To Various Agents | 784,319 | -- | -- | 784,319 |
| Due To Component Units | 39,977,148 | -- | -- | 39,977,148 |
| Deferred Revenue | 56,628,407 | -- | 708,381 | 57,336,788 |
| Total Liabilities | 113,263,278 | 507,660 | 8,139,017 | 121,909,955 |
| | | | | |
| **Fund Balances:** | | | | |
| Fund Balance - Reserved (Note 9): | | | | |
| Encumbrances | 5,139,373 | -- | -- | 5,139,373 |
| Advances to Component Units | 262,800 | -- | -- | 262,800 |
| Debt Service | -- | 1,480,501 | -- | 1,480,501 |
| Trust Corpus | -- | -- | 462,370 | 462,370 |
| Notes Receivable | 5,043,100 | -- | -- | 5,043,100 |
| Other | 10,883,528 | -- | 45,040,528 | 55,924,056 |
| Fund Balance - Unreserved: | | | | |
| Designated for Specific Projects (Note 9): | | | | |
| General Fund | 1,500,000 | -- | -- | 1,500,000 |
| Debt Service Fund | -- | -- | -- | -- |
| NonMajor Special Revenue Funds | -- | -- | 20,589,668 | 20,589,668 |
| Non-Major Capital Projects Funds | -- | -- | -- | -- |
| Non-Major Permanent Funds | -- | -- | -- | -- |
| Undesignated: | | | | |
| General Fund | 39,052,729 | -- | -- | 39,052,729 |
| Debt Service Fund | -- | 11,461 | -- | 11,461 |
| NonMajor Capital Projects Funds | -- | -- | 34,500 | 34,500 |
| Total Fund Balances | 61,881,530 | 1,491,962 | 66,127,066 | 129,500,558 |
| Total Liabilities and Fund Balances | $ 175,144,808 | $ 1,999,622 | $ 74,266,083 | $ 251,410,513 |

**Figure 10.2    Governmental Funds—Balance Sheet. (Adapted from a recent City of Richmond, Virginia, CAFR.)**

of Richmond balance sheet for Governmental Funds, which illustrates the GASB reporting requirements. It reports only two governmental funds as major. The City reports the general fund in the first column labeled "General" because it is automatically a major fund. The debt service fund is the only other governmental fund to meet the criteria for major fund reporting. Thus, the City of Richmond reports it in the second column. A single column labeled "other governmental funds" reports all nonmajor governmental funds. A total column, that is merely the sum of the amounts in the first three columns, is presented last. Any time more than one fund is reported in a single column of the basic financial statements, a combining statement is required in the supplemental information section of the CAFR.

### 10.4.3.2 Statement of Revenues, Expenditures, and Changes in Fund Balance

Figure 10.3 illustrates the statement of revenues, expenditures, and changes in fund balance for the City of Richmond Governmental Funds. The first thing to notice is that the column headings are identical to the balance sheet. The major fund criteria are the same for both required governmental fund statements.

"Governmental fund revenues should be classified … by major revenue source … Governmental fund expenditures should be classified, at a minimum, by function …" (Cod. 2200.160). Expenditures are categorized first by character—current, capital outlay, and debt service by the City of Richmond. Expenditures within the current character are then reported by function and the debt service character expenditures are reported by object.

The codification also requires that "… other financing sources and uses include the face amount of long-term debt, issuance premium or discount, certain payments to escrow agents for bond refundings, transfers, and sales of capital assets …" (Cod. 2200.161). Other financing sources (uses) are presented after determining the subtotal *Excess of Revenues over (under) Expenditures*. The subtotal *Net Change in Fund Balance* represents the amount fund balance increased or decreased because of current year activity. Ending fund balance on the statement of revenues, expenditures, and changes in fund balance must equal the total fund balance on the balance sheet for the similarly labeled column. The City of Richmond meets or exceeds the GAAP reporting requirements as illustrated in Figure 10.3.

### 10.4.3.3 Budgetary Comparison Statement

Recall that the GASB encourages presenting budgetary comparison information as part of RSI, but governments may report it as part of the basic financial statements. If the budgetary comparison statements are part of the basic financial statements, they should be placed immediately after the governmental funds statement of revenues, expenditures, and changes in fund balance.

CITY OF RICHMOND, VIRGINIA
STATEMENT OF REVENUES, EXPENDITURES, AND CHANGES IN FUND BALANCES
GOVERNMENTAL FUNDS
For the Fiscal Year Ended June 30, 20X8

| | General | Debt Service | Other Governmental Funds | Total |
|---|---|---|---|---|
| **Revenues** | | | | |
| City Taxes | $ 306,292,416 | $ -- | $ -- | $ 306,292,416 |
| Licenses, Permits and Privilege Fees | 33,259,137 | -- | -- | 33,259,137 |
| Intergovernmental | 107,442,810 | 112,558 | 46,877,964 | 154,433,332 |
| Service Charges | 17,924,528 | -- | -- | 17,924,528 |
| Fines and Forfeitures | 7,774,458 | -- | -- | 7,774,458 |
| Payment in Lieu of Taxes | 17,518,465 | -- | -- | 17,518,465 |
| Investment Income | -- | -- | 669,795 | 669,795 |
| Miscellaneous | 5,717,780 | 37,616,855 | 13,876,952 | 57,211,587 |
| Total Revenues | 495,929,594 | 37,729,413 | 61,424,711 | 595,083,718 |
| | | | | |
| **Expenditures** | | | | |
| Current: | | | | |
| General Government | 48,127,130 | -- | 17,986,219 | 66,113,349 |
| Public Safety and Judiciary | 127,096,129 | -- | 12,222,866 | 139,318,995 |
| Highways, Streets, Sanitation and Refuse | 45,549,587 | -- | 455,254 | 46,004,841 |
| Human Services | 64,105,652 | -- | 23,531,585 | 87,637,237 |
| Culture and Recreation | 20,715,896 | -- | 1,385,414 | 22,101,310 |
| Education | 128,823,925 | -- | -- | 128,823,925 |
| Non-Departmental | 23,461,527 | -- | -- | 23,461,527 |
| Capital Outlay | -- | -- | 35,347,332 | 35,347,332 |
| Debt Service: | | | | |
| Principal Retirement | -- | 37,206,080 | -- | 37,206,080 |
| Interest Payments | -- | 34,974,162 | -- | 34,974,162 |
| Issuance Costs | -- | 382,904 | -- | 382,904 |
| Total Expenditures | 457,879,846 | 72,563,146 | 90,928,670 | 621,371,662 |
| | | | | |
| Excess of Revenues Over (Under) Expenditures | 38,049,748 | (34,833,733) | (29,503,959) | (26,287,944) |
| | | | | |
| **Other Financing Sources (Uses)** | | | | |
| Proceeds from Refunding Bonds | -- | -- | 36,630,116 | 36,630,116 |
| Payment to Escrow Agent | -- | -- | (36,630,116) | (36,630,116) |
| Proceeds from Issuance of Bonds | 2,716,298 | -- | 47,381,695 | 50,097,993 |
| Transfers In-Other Funds | 1,819,000 | 34,845,194 | 10,785,617 | 47,449,811 |
| Transfers In-Component Units | -- | -- | -- | |
| Transfers Out-Other Funds | (39,946,466) | -- | (6,127,162) | (46,073,628) |
| Total Other Financing Sources (Uses), Net | (35,411,168) | 34,845,194 | 52,040,150 | 51,474,176 |
| **Special Item** | | | | |
| Gain on Sale of Land | -- | -- | 174,264 | 174,264 |
| | | | | |
| Net Change in Fund Balances | 2,638,580 | 11,461 | 22,710,455 | 25,360,496 |
| | | | | |
| Fund Balances - July 1, 20X7 | 59,242,950 | 1,480,501 | 43,416,611 | 104,140,062 |
| Fund Balances - June 30, 20X8 | $ 61,881,530 | $ 1,491,962 | $ 66,127,066 | $ 129,500,558 |

**Figure 10.3 Governmental Funds—Statement of Revenues, Expenditures, and Changes in Fund Balances. (Adapted from a recent City of Richmond, Virginia, CAFR.)**

The information contained in the budgetary comparison statement (schedule) is the same whether it is presented as part of the basic financial statements (a statement) or part of RSI (a schedule), except the title. "The budgetary comparison schedule [statement] should present both (a) the original and (b) the final appropriated budget for the reporting period as well as (c) actual inflows, outflows, and balances, stated on the government's budgetary basis. A separate column to report the variance between the final budget and actual amounts is encouraged but not required" (Cod. 2200.182).

"Governments may present the budgetary comparison schedule [statement] using the same format, terminology, and classifications as the budget document, or using the format, terminology, and classifications in a statement of revenues, expenditures, and changes in fund balances. Regardless of the format used, the schedule should be accompanied by information ... that reconciles budgetary information to GAAP information, ..." (Cod. 2200.183).

Figure 10.4 adapts the City of Richmond Budget Comparison Schedule for the General Fund. The original budgetary comparison schedule was four pages long to meet legal requirements. Figure 10.4 is adapted to report revenues by source and expenditures by function from the schedule, thus excluding the detailed accounts in the original presentation. The City of Richmond provides the budgetary comparison information as part of RSI. The only change necessary to present this information as part of the basic financial statements is to change the title from a schedule to a statement and display it after the statement of revenues, expenditures, and changes in fund balances in the basic financial statements. No other budgetary comparison schedules are presented by the City, since it does not have any major special revenue funds.

Notice that the City of Richmond budgetary comparison schedule includes the three required columns—original budget, final budget, and actual amounts—all presented using the budgetary basis. The City also includes the optional variance column. The statement of revenues, expenditures, and changes in fund balance format, terminology, and classifications are used by the City.

## 10.4.4 *Proprietary Fund Statements*

### 10.4.4.1 Introduction

The GASB requires separate reporting of enterprise funds and internal service funds in the proprietary fund statements. The codification states: "... proprietary fund statements should present the financial information for each major enterprise fund in a separate column. Nonmajor enterprise funds should be aggregated and displayed in a single column, and a combined total column should be presented for all enterprise funds. Major fund reporting requirements do not apply to internal service funds. The combined totals for all internal service funds should

CITY OF RICHMOND, VIRGINIA
BUDGETARY COMPARISON SCHEDULE
GENERAL FUND
For the Fiscal Year Ended June 30, 20X8

| | Original Budget | Final Budget | Actual | Variance with Final Budget Positive (Negative) |
|---|---|---|---|---|
| **Revenues** | | | | |
| Total City Taxes | $ 304,187,928 | $ 304,474,687 | $ 306,292,416 | $ 1,817,729 |
| Total Licenses, Permits and Privilege Fees | 33,024,020 | 33,024,020 | 33,259,137 | 235,117 |
| Total Intergovernmental | 106,001,300 | 110,242,357 | 107,442,810 | (2,799,547) |
| Total Service Charges | 18,045,144 | 18,045,144 | 17,924,528 | (120,616) |
| Total Fines and Forfeitures | 6,939,133 | 6,939,133 | 7,774,458 | 835,325 |
| Total Payment in Lieu of Taxes | 16,846,202 | 16,846,202 | 17,518,465 | 672,263 |
| Total Miscellaneous Revenues | 5,122,300 | 5,313,173 | 5,717,780 | 404,607 |
| Total General Fund Revenues | 490,166,027 | 494,884,716 | 495,929,594 | 1,044,878 |
| | | | | |
| **Expenditures** | | | | |
| **Current** | | | | |
| Total General Government | 46,353,635 | 51,909,996 | 48,127,130 | 3,782,866 |
| Total Public Safety and Judiciary | 122,378,055 | 126,828,231 | 124,091,129 | 2,737,102 |
| Total Public Works | 43,147,427 | 44,797,077 | 45,549,587 | (752,510) |
| Total Human Services | 63,933,672 | 70,350,617 | 62,525,571 | 7,825,046 |
| Total Culture and Recreation | 19,955,319 | 20,883,245 | 20,715,896 | 167,349 |
| Total Non-Departmental | 32,220,982 | 28,052,748 | 23,461,527 | 4,591,221 |
| Total General Fund Expenditures | 327,989,090 | 342,821,914 | 324,470,840 | 18,351,074 |
| | | | | |
| Excess of Revenues Over Expenditures | 162,176,937 | 152,062,802 | 171,458,754 | 19,395,952 |
| | | | | |
| **Other Financing Sources (Uses)** | | | | |
| Proceeds from Notes Payable / Capital Leases | -- | 2,934,237 | 2,716,298 | (217,939) |
| Transfers In - Other Funds | 3,000,660 | 5,251,504 | 1,819,000 | (3,432,504) |
| Transfers Out - Component Units | (128,823,925) | (128,823,925) | (133,409,006) | (4,585,081) |
| Transfers Out - Other Funds | (36,353,672) | (36,353,672) | (39,946,466) | (3,592,794) |
| Total Other Financing Uses, Net | (162,176,937) | (156,991,856) | (168,820,174) | (11,828,318) |
| | | | | |
| Excess of Revenues and Other Financing Sources Over (Under) Expenditures and Other Financing Uses | -- | (4,929,054) | 2,638,580 | 7,567,634 |
| | | | | |
| Fund Balance - Beginning of Year | 59,242,950 | 59,242,950 | 59,242,950 | -- |
| Fund Balance- End of Year | $ 59,242,950 | $ 54,313,896 | $ 61,881,530 | $ 7,567,634 |

**Figure 10.4  Budgetary Comparison Schedule—General Fund. (Adapted from a recent City of Richmond, Virginia, CAFR.)**

be reported in separate columns on the face of the proprietary fund financial statements to the right of the total enterprise funds column" (Cod. 2200.165).

Governments must display the same column headings on each of the three required proprietary fund statements. Figures 10.5 to 10.7 illustrate the City of Richmond using the same column headings on each proprietary fund statement.

CITY OF RICHMOND, VIRGINIA
STATEMENT OF NET ASSETS
PROPRIETARY FUNDS
June 30, 20X8

| | Enterprise Funds | | | | | Governmental Activities - Internal Service Funds |
|---|---|---|---|---|---|---|
| | Gas | Water | Wastewater | Other | Total | |
| **Assets** | | | | | | |
| Current Assets: | | | | | | |
| Cash and Cash Equivalents (Note 3) | $ 11,920,298 | $ 3,549,036 | $ 34,276,821 | $ 410,532 | $ 50,156,687 | $ 40,994,362 |
| Receivables (Net of Allowance for Doubtful Accounts): | | | | | | |
| Accounts | 19,261,063 | 8,391,123 | 6,751,276 | 1,441,962 | 35,845,424 | 3,178,162 |
| Estimated Unbilled Service Revenues | 466,652 | 247,874 | 452,367 | -- | 1,166,893 | -- |
| Due From Other Funds (Note 4) | 802,924 | 246,478 | 2,514,465 | -- | 3,563,867 | -- |
| Due From Component Units | -- | -- | -- | -- | -- | -- |
| Due From Other Governments | -- | -- | -- | -- | -- | 16,961 |
| Other Assets | -- | -- | -- | -- | -- | -- |
| Inventories of Materials and Supplies | 12,840,047 | 133,455 | 60,714 | 82,127 | 13,116,343 | 3,901,945 |
| Advances To Other Funds | | | | | | |
| Prepaid Expenses and Other Current Assets | 1,815,074 | 1,238,378 | 1,321,625 | 36,912 | 4,411,989 | 931,269 |
| Total Current Assets | 47,106,058 | 13,806,344 | 45,377,268 | 1,971,533 | 108,261,203 | 49,022,699 |
| Noncurrent Assets: | | | | | | |
| Restricted Assets - Cash and Investments (Note 3) | 28,745,925 | 10,591,626 | 10,171,915 | -- | 49,509,466 | -- |
| Advances To Other Funds (Notes 4) | 19,605,111 | 19,081,068 | 21,534,342 | -- | 60,220,521 | 3,294,908 |
| Deferred Expenses | 18,354,654 | 10,172,670 | 8,780,157 | -- | 37,307,481 | 145,905 |
| Capital Assets (Note 7): | | | | | | |
| Land | -- | -- | -- | 12,815,550 | 12,815,550 | 98,000 |
| Buildings and Structures | -- | -- | -- | 38,510,784 | 38,510,784 | 90,400,865 |
| Equipment | -- | -- | -- | 4,232,699 | 4,232,699 | 55,984,359 |
| Plant Held for Future Use | 25,813 | -- | 207,075 | -- | 232,888 | -- |
| Plant-in-Service | 289,057,830 | 252,865,122 | 214,044,829 | -- | 755,967,781 | -- |
| Completed Construction | 6,300,727 | 4,611,848 | 75,197,463 | -- | 86,110,038 | -- |
| Less: Accumulated Depreciation | (76,472,381) | (65,721,637) | (95,551,089) | (23,728,508) | (261,473,615) | (77,643,515) |
| Construction in Progress | 23,061,532 | 20,477,193 | 63,686,082 | -- | 107,224,807 | 7,981,752 |
| Total Capital Assets | 241,973,521 | 212,232,526 | 257,584,360 | 31,830,525 | 743,620,932 | 76,821,461 |
| Total Noncurrent Assets | 308,679,211 | 252,077,890 | 298,070,774 | 31,830,525 | 890,658,400 | 80,262,274 |
| Total Assets | $ 355,785,269 | $ 265,884,234 | $ 343,448,042 | $ 33,802,058 | $ 998,919,603 | $ 129,284,973 |

**Figure 10.5 Proprietary Funds—Statement of Net Assets. (Adapted from a recent City of Richmond, Virginia, CAFR.)**

The City of Richmond reports three major enterprise funds—gas, water, and wastewater—in individual columns. They summarize all nonmajor enterprise funds in a single column followed by a total column for all enterprise funds. Governments report internal service funds in a single column after the enterprise fund total column. The primary fund type serviced by the internal service funds—governmental activities or business-type activities—is included in the internal service fund column label. The City of Richmond internal service funds primarily serves governmental activities. Since the City of Richmond reports more than one nonmajor enterprise fund in an aggregate "other" column and more than one internal service fund in the internal service fund column, two combining statements are required in the supplemental information section of the CAFR for each proprietary fund statement.

| | | | Enterprise Funds | | | Governmental Activities - Internal Service Funds |
|---|---|---|---|---|---|---|
| | Gas | Water | Wastewater | Other | Total | |
| **Liabilities:** | | | | | | |
| Current Liabilities: | | | | | | |
| Accounts Payable | $ 11,562,567 $ | 3,563,232 $ | 2,132,058 $ | 910,556 $ | 18,168,413 $ | 1,731,695 |
| Accrued Liabilities | 1,202,029 | 1,582,168 | 3,764,295 | 596,444 | 7,144,936 | 2,097,710 |
| Due To Other Funds (Note 4) | -- | -- | -- | 2,121,750 | 2,121,750 | 3,876,746 |
| Accrued Interest on Bonds Payable | 5,457,597 | 2,954,655 | 3,915,591 | 160,886 | 12,488,729 | 1,375,606 |
| General Obligation Bonds and Capital Leases (Note 8) | 4,590,410 | 3,597,754 | 2,590,273 | 1,171,952 | 11,950,389 | 6,015,150 |
| Accreted Interest | -- | -- | -- | -- | -- | -- |
| Revenue Bonds Payable (Note 8) | 781,376 | 65,255 | 2,723,081 | -- | 3,569,712 | -- |
| Compensated Absences | 614,523 | 410,573 | 452,210 | 103,705 | 1,581,011 | 181,257 |
| Other Liabilities and Claims Payable (Note 10) | -- | -- | -- | -- | -- | 5,582,181 |
| Total Current Liabilities | 24,208,502 | 12,173,637 | 15,577,508 | 5,065,293 | 57,024,940 | 20,860,345 |
| Noncurrent Liabilities: | | | | | | |
| Liabilities to be Repaid from Restricted Assets: | | | | | | |
| Customers' Deposits | 2,624,175 | -- | -- | -- | 2,624,175 | -- |
| Accreted Interest on Bonds Payable (Note 8) | 649,475 | 1,039,070 | 424,895 | -- | 2,113,440 | 92,655 |
| Deferred Revenue | 7,612,973 | 35,641,284 | 17,207,432 | -- | 60,461,689 | 422,703 |
| General Obligation Bonds and Capital Lease Liabilities (Note 8) | 115,379,573 | 89,544,818 | 48,151,024 | 14,601,052 | 267,676,467 | 14,656,337 |
| Revenue Bonds Payable (Note 8) | 115,792,877 | 36,275,082 | 104,867,083 | -- | 256,935,042 | -- |
| Compensated Absences | 21,054 | 228,976 | 137,884 | 21,540 | 409,454 | 271,991 |
| Other Liabilities and Claims Payable (Note 10) | -- | -- | -- | -- | -- | 14,099,879 |
| Advances from Other Funds | -- | -- | -- | -- | -- | 63,515,579 |
| Total Noncurrent Liabilities | 242,080,127 | 162,729,230 | 170,788,318 | 14,622,592 | 590,220,267 | 93,059,144 |
| Total Liabilities | 266,288,629 | 174,902,867 | 186,365,826 | 19,687,885 | 647,245,207 | 113,919,489 |
| **Net Assets:** | | | | | | |
| Invested in Capital Assets, Net of Related Debt | 33,525,735 | 92,302,173 | 108,999,919 | 16,057,521 | 250,885,348 | 56,057,319 |
| Restricted for Capital Projects | 28,745,925 | 10,591,626 | 10,171,915 | -- | 49,509,466 | -- |
| Unrestricted | 27,224,980 | (11,912,432) | 37,910,382 | (1,943,348) | 51,279,582 | (40,691,835) |
| Total Net Assets | $ 89,496,640 $ | 90,981,367 $ | 157,082,216 $ | 14,114,173 $ | 351,674,396 $ | 15,365,484 |

**Figure 10.5    (continued).**

## 10.4.4.2  Statement of Net Assets

"Governments may use either a net asset format—assets less liabilities equal net assets—or a balance sheet format—assets equal liabilities plus net assets—to report their proprietary funds" (Cod. 2200.167). The net asset format is used rather than the balance sheet format in Figure 10.5. Figure 10.5 also presents the City of Richmond Statement of Net Assets in a classified format, because the codification states that "[a]ssets and liabilities of proprietary funds should be presented in a classified format to distinguish between current and long-term assets and liabilities …" (Cod. 2200.166). One item to notice is that all restricted assets, including restricted cash, are considered noncurrent. Similarly, noncurrent liabilities report all liabilities payable from restricted assets. Also, the City reports the current portion of long-term liabilities separately from the remaining noncurrent liabilities. The GASB states that "[r]estricted assets should be reported when restrictions … on asset use change the nature or normal understanding of the availability of the asset. For example, … cash and investments held in a separate account that can be used to pay debt principal and interest only … should be reported as restricted assets" (Cod 2200.168). Finally, "[n]et assets should be displayed in three broad components— invested in capital assets, net of related debt; restricted (distinguishing between

CITY OF RICHMOND, VIRGINIA
STATEMENT OF REVENUES, EXPENSES, AND CHANGES IN THE FUND NET ASSETS
PROPRIETARY FUNDS
For the Fiscal Year Ended June 30, 20X8

| | Enterprise Funds | | | | | Governmental Activities - Internal Service Funds |
| --- | --- | --- | --- | --- | --- | --- |
| | Gas | Water | Wastewater | Other | Total | |
| **Operating Revenues** | | | | | | |
| Charges for Goods and Services | $ 170,141,567 | $ 41,481,040 | $ 43,980,217 | $ 4,042,532 | $ 259,645,356 | $ 37,925,202 |
| **Operating Expenses** | | | | | | |
| Purchased Gas | 117,563,809 | -- | -- | -- | 117,563,809 | -- |
| Intragovernmental Goods and Services Sold | -- | -- | -- | -- | -- | 7,707,732 |
| Salaries and Wages | 9,090,971 | 6,507,816 | 6,687,046 | 2,725,497 | 25,011,330 | 3,577,549 |
| Data Processing | 709,131 | 232,502 | 220,877 | -- | 1,162,510 | 110,457 |
| Materials and Supplies | 746,529 | 965,746 | 566,229 | 340,010 | 2,618,514 | 684,529 |
| Rents and Utilities | 221,179 | 3,681,134 | 1,730,881 | 751,134 | 6,384,328 | 2,209,935 |
| Maintenance and Repairs | 6,811,937 | 3,304,651 | 2,288,553 | 251,140 | 12,656,281 | 585,936 |
| Depreciation and Amortization | 8,663,181 | 5,063,893 | 7,085,382 | 1,552,751 | 22,365,207 | 9,547,571 |
| Claims and Settlements | -- | -- | -- | -- | -- | 6,429,801 |
| Miscellaneous Operating Expenses | 13,373,135 | 11,620,937 | 13,643,349 | 529,196 | 39,166,617 | 4,414,945 |
| Total Operating Expenses | 157,179,872 | 31,376,679 | 32,222,317 | 6,149,728 | 226,928,596 | 35,268,455 |
| Operating Income (Loss) | 12,961,695 | 10,104,361 | 11,757,900 | (2,107,196) | 32,716,760 | 2,656,747 |
| **Non-Operating Revenues (Expenses)** | | | | | | |
| Government Subsidies | 245,035 | 1,271,803 | 5,450,413 | 81,338 | 7,048,589 | 181,163 |
| Interest on Long-Term Debt | (12,088,485) | (6,685,473) | (8,429,750) | (704,873) | (27,908,581) | (1,802,177) |
| Interest Income | 876,554 | 280,099 | 694,672 | 4,574 | 1,855,899 | -- |
| Interest Expense | (4,404) | (509,550) | -- | -- | (513,954) | -- |
| Amortization of Debt Discount and Expense | (1,369,139) | (1,003,731) | (776,422) | -- | (3,149,292) | -- |
| Miscellaneous Revenue | 402,044 | 450,731 | 1,698,203 | 220,643 | 2,771,621 | 785,180 |
| Miscellaneous Expenses | -- | -- | -- | (395,074) | (395,074) | (216,952) |
| Total Non-Operating (Expenses) | (11,938,395) | (6,196,121) | (1,362,884) | (793,392) | (20,290,792) | (1,052,786) |
| Net Income (Loss) Before Transfers | 1,023,300 | 3,908,240 | 10,395,016 | (2,900,588) | 12,425,968 | 1,603,961 |
| Transfers In-Other Funds | -- | -- | -- | 826,959 | 826,959 | -- |
| Transfers Out-Other Funds | (89,000) | (336,000) | (1,122,000) | -- | (1,547,000) | (22,000) |
| Change In Net Assets | 934,300 | 3,572,240 | 9,273,016 | (2,073,629) | 11,705,927 | 1,581,961 |
| Net Assets - Beginning of Year | 88,562,340 | 87,409,127 | 147,809,200 | 16,187,802 | 339,968,469 | 13,783,523 |
| Net Assets - End of Year | $ 89,496,640 | $ 90,981,367 | $ 157,082,216 | $ 14,114,173 | $ 351,674,396 | $ 15,365,484 |

**Figure 10.6 Proprietary Funds—Statement of Revenues, Expenses, and Changes in Net Assets. (Adapted from a recent City of Richmond, Virginia, CAFR.)**

major categories of restrictions); and unrestricted" (Cod. 2200.167). The City of Richmond illustrates these three categories of net assets in Figure 10.5.

### 10.4.4.3 Statement of Revenues, Expenses, and Changes in Net Assets

The statement of revenues, expenses, and changes in net assets is the operating statement for proprietary funds. "This statement … should distinguish between operating and nonoperating revenues and expenses … and should present a separate subtotal for *operating revenues, operating expenses, and operating income.* Nonoperating revenues and expenses should be reported after operating income" (Cod. 2200.169). "Revenues should [also] be reported by major source ..." (Cod. 2200.169). Figure 10.6 illustrates the Statement of Revenues, Expenses, and Changes in Net Assets for the City of Richmond. The major row labels include operating revenues, operating expenses, operating income, and nonoperating revenues (expenses) as required by the GASB. "Governments should establish a policy that defines operating revenues and expenses that is appropriate to the nature of the activity being reported, ..." (Cod. 2200.171).

Notice that the City of Richmond labels the subtotal after operating revenues and operating expenses *operating income.* It labels the subtotal after nonoperating revenues (expenses) *net income (loss) before transfers.* The City of Richmond uses this label because it only reports transfers in and transfers out after the subtotal. Items that might be included in this section of the statement are identified by GASB as "[r]evenues from capital contributions ... , special and extraordinary items, and transfers ..." (Cod. 2200.169). The final subtotal *change in net assets* represents the total change in the net assets for each column.

## 10.4.4.4 Statement of Cash Flows

"Governments should present a statement of cash flows for proprietary funds..." (Cod. 2200.174). "A statement of cash flows should explain the change during the period in cash and cash equivalents regardless of whether there are restrictions on their use" (Cod. 2450.105). Cash receipts and cash payments should be classified as "operating, noncapital financing, capital and related financing, or investing activities" (Cod. 2450.112). Figure 10.7 presents the City of Richmond statement of cash flows that illustrates the four categories: (1) cash flows from operating activities, (2) cash flows from noncapital financing activities, (3) cash flows from capital and related financing activities, and (4) cash flows from investing activities.

"Operating activities generally result from providing services and producing and delivering goods .... Cash flows from operating activities generally are the cash effects of transactions and other events that enter into the determination of operating income" (Cod. 2450.113). "The direct method of presenting cash flows from operating activities (including a reconciliation of operating cash flows to operating income) should be used" (Cod. 2200.174). The City of Richmond uses the direct method for operating activities in Figure 10.7. It also includes a reconciliation of operating income (from the statement of revenues, expenses, and changes in net assets) to cash flows from operating activities (on the Statement of Cash Flows) as required by GASB.

Cash flows from "[n]oncapital financing activities include borrowing money for purposes other than to acquire, construct, or improve capital assets and repaying

**CITY OF RICHMOND, VIRGINIA**
**STATEMENTS OF CASH FLOWS**
**PROPRIETARY FUNDS**
**For the Fiscal Year Ended June 30, 20X8**

| | Enterprise Funds | | | | | Governmental Activities - Internal Service Funds |
| --- | --- | --- | --- | --- | --- | --- |
| | Gas | Water | Wastewater | Other | Total | |
| **Cash Flows From Operating Activities** | | | | | | |
| Receipts from Customers | $ 164,493,634 | $ 43,363,984 | $ 44,547,719 | $ -- | $ 252,405,337 | $ -- |
| Payments to Suppliers | (132,131,454) | (16,361,973) | (11,977,487) | -- | (160,470,914) | -- |
| Payments to Employees | (8,695,360) | (6,135,793) | (6,448,469) | 4,159,193 | (17,120,429) | 37,651,138 |
| Payments to Other Funds | (5,859,961) | (5,142,698) | (6,939,047) | (2,062,617) | (20,004,323) | (16,233,790) |
| Other Receipts or (Payments) | (1,988,135) | (802,144) | 1,553,235 | (2,677,234) | (3,914,278) | (8,221,768) |
| Net Cash Provided By (Used In) Operating Activities | 15,818,724 | 14,921,376 | 20,735,951 | (580,658) | 50,895,393 | 13,195,580 |
| **Cash Flows From Noncapital Financing Activities** | | | | | | |
| Transfers In and Government Subsidies | -- | -- | -- | -- | -- | -- |
| Transfers Out - Other Funds | -- | -- | -- | -- | -- | -- |
| Net Cash Provided By Noncapital Financing Activities | -- | -- | -- | -- | -- | -- |
| **Cash Flows From Capital and Related Financing Activities** | | | | | | |
| Acquisition of Capital Assets | (21,611,162) | (11,681,031) | (20,020,114) | -- | (53,312,307) | -- |
| Capital Contributions | -- | -- | -- | -- | -- | -- |
| Proceeds From Bond Sale | 28,109,764 | 16,972,487 | -- | (164,301) | 44,917,950 | -- |
| Repayments of Capital Leases | -- | -- | -- | -- | -- | -- |
| Interest Paid on Capital Leases | -- | -- | -- | 247,820 | 247,820 | -- |
| Repayments of Revenue and General Obligation Bonds | (32,084,920) | (19,603,829) | (3,636,776) | (55,973) | (55,381,498) | (8,407,787) |
| Repayments of Notes Payables | -- | -- | -- | -- | -- | 4,942,708 |
| Interest Paid on Long-Term Debt | (10,726,007) | (6,271,401) | (7,837,700) | (32,415) | (24,867,523) | (2,508,529) |
| Net Cash (Used In) Capital and Related Financing Activities | (36,312,325) | (20,583,774) | (31,494,590) | (4,869) | (88,395,558) | (5,973,608) |
| **Cash Flows From Investing Activities** | | | | | | |
| Interest Earned on Operating Funds | 876,554 | 280,099 | 694,671 | -- | 1,851,324 | -- |
| Interest Paid on Customers' Deposits | (12,088,485) | (6,685,473) | (8,429,750) | -- | (27,203,708) | -- |
| Net Cash Provided By (Used In) Investing Activities | (11,211,931) | (6,405,374) | (7,735,079) | -- | (25,352,384) | -- |
| Net Increase (Decrease) in Cash and Cash Equivalents | (31,705,532) | (12,067,772) | (18,493,718) | (585,527) | (62,852,549) | 7,221,972 |
| Cash and Cash Equivalents at July 1, 20X7 | 25,317,697 | 14,599,862 | 26,273,630 | 30,806 | 66,221,995 | (1,898,809) |
| Cash and Cash Equivalents at June 30, 20X8 | $ (6,387,835) | $ 2,532,090 | $ 7,779,912 | $ (554,721) | $ 3,369,446 | $ 5,323,163 |
| **Adjustments to Reconcile Operating Income (Loss) To Net Cash Provided By (Used In) Operating Activities** | | | | | | |
| Operating Income (Loss) | $ 13,373,135 | $ 11,620,937 | $ 13,643,349 | $ -- | $ 38,637,421 | $ -- |
| Adjustment to Reconcile Operating to Net Cash Provided By Operating Activities: | | | | | | |
| Depreciation | 221,179 | 3,681,134 | 1,730,881 | -- | 5,633,194 | -- |
| Miscellaneous Income | 402,044 | 450,732 | 1,698,203 | -- | 2,550,979 | -- |
| (Increase) Decrease in Assets and Increase (Decrease) in Liabilities: | | | | | | |
| Accounts Receivable | 18,474,946 | 2,977,766 | 5,631,801 | (20,427) | 27,064,086 | 380,585 |
| Due From Other Funds | (6,190,389) | 1,635,464 | 593,927 | -- | (3,960,998) | -- |
| Due From Component Units | -- | -- | -- | 31,185 | 31,185 | (11,266) |
| Due From Other Governments | 526,866 | 16,132 | (560,603) | -- | (17,605) | -- |
| Estimated Unbilled Service Revenues | -- | -- | -- | -- | -- | -- |
| Inventories of Material and Supplies | -- | -- | -- | -- | -- | -- |
| Prepaid Expenses | (3,038,002) | 3,174 | -- | -- | (3,034,828) | (4,030) |
| Deferred Expenses | (2,663,535) | (1,252,876) | (144,967) | -- | (4,061,378) | 101,835 |
| Accounts Payable | -- | -- | -- | (5,201) | (5,201) | 5,049 |
| Accrued Liabilities | -- | -- | -- | (3,133) | (3,133) | (79,532) |
| Deferred Revenue | 273,247 | -- | -- | (182,803) | 90,444 | 220,274 |
| Customers' Deposits | -- | -- | -- | (6,828) | (6,828) | -- |
| Due to Other Funds | 2,038,982 | (1,207,578) | (400,730) | -- | 430,674 | 190,579 |
| Due to the City | -- | -- | -- | -- | -- | -- |
| Compensated Absences | (3,178,932) | (2,564,877) | (942,398) | 551,281 | (6,134,926) | 55,871 |
| Outstanding Liabilities and Claims | (781,376) | (65,255) | (2,723,082) | -- | (3,569,713) | (126,828) |
| Total Adjustments | 6,085,030 | 3,673,816 | 4,883,032 | 364,074 | 15,005,952 | 732,537 |
| Net Cash Provided By (Used In) Operating Activities | $ 19,458,165 | $ 15,294,753 | $ 18,526,381 | $ 364,074 | $ 53,643,373 | $ 732,537 |
| **Supplemental Cash Flow Information** | | | | | | |
| Non-cash Transactions: | | | | | | |
| Principal payments made by City Debt Service Fund on behalf of Coliseum | -- | -- | -- | -- | -- | -- |
| Interest payments made by City Debt Service Fund on behalf of Coliseum | -- | -- | -- | -- | -- | -- |
| Proceeds from Issuance of General Obligation Bonds received on behalf of Fund | -- | -- | -- | 656,425 | 656,425 | -- |
| Acquisitions of Capital Assets on behalf of Coliseum | -- | -- | -- | 335,250 | 335,250 | -- |
| Refunded General Obligation Bonds on behalf of Fund | -- | -- | -- | (3,449,410) | (3,449,410) | -- |

**Figure 10.7 Proprietary Funds—Statement of Cash Flows. (Adapted from a recent City of Richmond, Virginia, CAFR.)**

those amounts borrowed, including interest. This category includes proceeds from all borrowings … not clearly attributable to acquisition, construction, or improvement of capital assets, regardless of the form of the borrowing" (Cod. 2450.117). Cash flows from noncapital assets include all transfers out of the fund and any transfers in not specified for the purchase of capital assets. Cash flows from "[c]apital and related financing activities include (a) acquiring and disposing of capital assets used in providing services or producing goods, (b) borrowing money for acquiring, constructing, or improving capital assets and repaying the amounts borrowed, including interest, and (c) paying for capital assets obtained from vendors on credit" (Cod. 2450.120). Any cash flow related to the purchase or sale of a capital asset, including any borrowing and the repayment of capital debt, is reported in this category. Cash flows from investing activities is usually very limited in the statement of cash flows for most governments. "Investing activities include making and collecting loans … and acquiring and disposing of debt or equity instruments" (Cod. 2450.123).

Each of the four categories of cash flow are summarized into a single value by the City of Richmond as required. The city sums the four subtotals (some positive and some negative) to determine the *net increase (decrease) in cash and cash equivalents*. One final item that is part of the statement of cash flow reporting is information about significant noncash transactions. "Information about investing, capital, and financing activities of a governmental enterprise during a period that affect recognized assets or liabilities but do not result in cash receipts or cash payments in the period should be reported. This information should be presented in a separate schedule … and it should clearly describe the cash and noncash aspects of transactions involving similar items. The schedule may be presented … on the same page as the statement of cash flows" (Cod. 2450.132). The City of Richmond reports noncash transactions after the reconciliation in Figure 10.7.

## 10.4.5 Fiduciary Fund Statements

### 10.4.5.1 Introduction

"Fiduciary fund financial statements should include information about all fiduciary funds of the primary government, as well as component units that are fiduciary in nature. The statements should provide a separate column for each fund type—pension (and other employee benefit) trust funds, investment trust funds, private-purpose trusts, and agency funds" (Cod. 2200.175). If a government has more than one fund of any fiduciary fund type, a combining statement must be presented in the supplementary section of the CAFR. The City of Richmond reports only pension trust funds and agency funds, which is common for cities of its size. Many governments do not have private-purpose trust funds and most governments, with the exception of state governments, do not have investment trust funds.

## 10.4.5.2 Statement of Fiduciary Net Assets

"The statement of fiduciary net assets should include information about the assets, liabilities, and net assets for each fiduciary fund type" (Cod. 2200.176). A maximum of four columns are reported on the statement of fiduciary net assets, one column for each fiduciary fund type. A total column is not included on the statement. Figure 10.8 shows the City of Richmond statement of fiduciary net assets that reports only pension trust funds and agency funds. A unique item in the asset

**CITY OF RICHMOND, VIRGINIA**
**STATEMENT OF FIDUCIARY NET ASSETS**
**June 30, 20X8**

| | Pension Trust Funds | Agency Funds |
|---|---|---|
| Assets: | | |
| Cash and Short-term Investments | $ 26,334,491 | $ 1,541,685 |
| Receivables | 28,209,062 | -- |
| Due From Other Governments | 691,396 | -- |
| Other Assets | 3,986 | -- |
| Investments, at Fair Value: | | |
|    U.S. Government and Agency Securities | 84,836,362 | -- |
|    Corporate Bonds | 52,239,245 | -- |
|    Common Stock | 181,519,796 | -- |
|    International Stocks | 79,824,108 | -- |
|    International Bonds | 20,613,689 | -- |
|    Cash Collateral Received - Security Lending Program | 28,115,630 | -- |
|     Total Investments, at Fair Value | 447,148,830 | -- |
|      Total Assets | 502,387,765 | 1,541,685 |
| Liabilities: | | |
| Accounts Payable | 874,624 | 158,206 |
| Refundable Deposits | -- | 411,699 |
| Payable for Collateral Received - Security Lending Program | 28,115,630 | -- |
| Due to Other Governments | 2,049,753 | -- |
| Due to Various Agents for Securities Purchased | 37,366,399 | |
| Funds Held for Others | -- | 971,780 |
|     Total Liabilities | 68,406,406 | 1,541,685 |
| Net Assets Held in Trust for Pension Benefits and Other Purposes | $ 433,981,359 | $ -- |

**Figure 10.8 Fiduciary Funds—Statement of Fiduciary Net Assets. (Adapted from a recent City of Richmond, Virginia, CAFR.)**

section is the presentation of investments. Notice that the City reports investments at fair value as of the reporting date and that it reports the investments by major type of investment. The requirements for reporting investments are found in section 150 of the codification. The City of Richmond has properly titled net assets as "net assets held in trust for pension benefits and other purposes." Notice that the agency fund has no net assets, since "… agency fund assets should equal liabilities" (Cod. 2200.178).

### 10.4.5.3 Statement of Changes in Fiduciary Net Assets

"The statement of changes in fiduciary net assets should include information about the additions to, deductions from, and net increase (decrease) for the year in net assets for each fiduciary fund type" (Cod. 2200.177). Governments can include only the three types of trust funds on this statement. "Agency funds should not be reported in the statement of changes in fiduciary net assets" (Cod. 2200.178). Governments do not include agency funds because agency funds do not have net assets. Figure 10.9 shows the City of Richmond statement of changes in fiduciary net assets. It reports only a pension trust fund column, because the City does not have investment trust funds or private-purpose trust funds. Notice that the statement of changes in fiduciary net assets reports additions and deductions rather than revenue and expenses. The GASB intends the terms "additions" and "deductions" to communicate that the fiduciary responsibility of the government has changed, but the financial resources of the government have not. "The detailed display requirements of Sections Pe5 and Po50 [of the codification] apply to the statements of changes in plan net assets for pension and other employee benefit trust funds" (Cod. 2200.177).

## 10.4.6 Government-Wide Statements

### 10.4.6.1 Introduction

The fund financial statements are used to report the financial activities for each fund type category. However, a method to evaluate the government as a whole is also important. Government-wide statements provide the overall view of the government. The objectives of the government-wide statements as listed in codification section 2200.110 are to:

a. "Report information about the overall government without displaying individual funds or fund types"
b. "Exclude information about fiduciary activities, …"
c. "Distinguish between the primary government and its discretely presented component units"

**CITY OF RICHMOND, VIRGINIA**
**STATEMENT OF CHANGES IN FIDUCIARY NET ASSETS**
**For the Fiscal Year Ended June 30, 20X8**

| | Pension Trust Funds |
|---|---:|
| Additions: | |
| Contributions | $ 22,529,811 |
| Outstanding Loans | |
| Loan Repayments | -- |
| | |
| Investment Income: | |
| Net Appreciation in Fair Value of Investments | 3,843,544 |
| Interest | 2,635,250 |
| Dividends | 6,835,238 |
| Net Income Earned On Securities Lending Transactions: | |
| Securities Lending Income | 380,785 |
| Securities Lending Expense | (324,646) |
| Total Net Income Earned On Securities Lending Transactions | 56,139 |
| Investment Income | 13,370,171 |
| Less Investment Expense | 2,049,753 |
| Net Investment Income | 11,320,418 |
| Total additions | 33,850,229 |
| | |
| Deductions: | |
| Benefits | 45,210,835 |
| Loan Issuance | -- |
| Administrative Expenses | 775,424 |
| Total deductions | 45,986,259 |
| | |
| Net Decrease | (12,136,030) |
| Net Assets Held In Trust For Pension Benefits and Other Purposes - Beginning of Year | 446,117,389 |
| Net Assets Held In Trust For Pension Benefits and Other Purposes - End of Year | $ 433,981,359 |

**Figure 10.9 Fiduciary Funds—Statement of Changes in Fiduciary Net Assets. (Adapted from a recent City of Richmond, Virginia, CAFR.)**

    d. "Distinguish between governmental activities and business-type activities of the primary government"

    e. "Measure and report all assets (both financial and capital), liabilities, revenues, expenses, gains, and losses using the economic resources measurement focus and basis of accounting."

These five items are very evident in the government-wide statements.

The GASB requires two government-wide statements—a statement of net assets and a statement of activities. "The focus of the government-wide financial statements should be on the primary government …. Separate rows and columns should be used to distinguish between the primary government and its discretely presented component units" (Cod. 2200.112). "Separate rows and columns also should be used to distinguish between governmental and business-type activities of the primary government" (Cod. 2200.113).

The two types of government-wide statements are discussed next. Recall that the two government-wide statements are presented before any of the fund statements in the basic financial statements. A discussion of the government-wide statements is delayed to this point because the government-wide statements are derived from the fund financial statements. Section 10.5 of this chapter introduces the process of converting fund statement information to government-wide statements.

## 10.4.6.2  Statement of Net Assets

The statement of net assets allows users to assess the overall financial position of the government. Figure 10.10 shows the four columns on the City of Richmond statement of net assets that are most common for cities with discretely presented component units. The first three columns report information related to the primary government, while the last column provides information on the discretely presented component units. The presentation format clearly distinguishes governmental activities (in the first column) from business-type activities (in the second column). A total column summarizes the primary government activities. The discretely presented component unit information is presented in the fourth (last) column after the primary government totals to distinguish it from the primary government information.

The statement of net assets reports three major categories of account information—assets, liabilities, and net assets. "Governments are encouraged to present the statement in a format that displays *assets less liabilities equal net assets*, although the traditional balance sheet format (assets equal liabilities plus net assets) may be used. Regardless of the format used, however, the statement of net assets should report the difference between assets and liabilities as net assets, …" (Cod. 2200.115). The City of Richmond statement of net assets, in Figure 10.10, uses the assets less liabilities equal net assets display method.

"Governments are encouraged to present assets and liabilities in order of their liquidity …. Liabilities whose average maturities are greater than one year should be reported in two components—the amount due within one year and the amount due in more than one year" (Cod. 2200.116). Governments can present assets and liabilities in a classified format, but the GASB does not require it.

One asset category that is new in the governmental activities column is capital assets. Two accounts within capital assets are not common outside governments—infrastructure and works of art. Infrastructure capital assets "are stationary in

CITY OF RICHMOND, VIRGINIA
STATEMENT OF NET ASSETS
June 30, 20X8

| | Primary Government | | | |
| | Governmental Activities | Business-type Activities | Total | Component Units |
| --- | --- | --- | --- | --- |
| **Assets** | | | | |
| Cash and Cash Equivalents (Note 3) | $ 78,719,937 | $ 80,792,335 | $ 159,512,272 | $ 19,007,867 |
| Receivables (Net of Allowance for Doubtful Accounts): | | | | |
| Taxes and Licenses | 45,537,175 | -- | 45,537,175 | -- |
| Accounts | 19,065,822 | 35,848,052 | 54,913,874 | 34,627,326 |
| Estimated Unbilled Service Revenues | -- | 1,166,893 | 1,166,893 | -- |
| Internal Balances | 1,852,791 | (1,852,791) | -- | -- |
| Due From Primary Government | -- | -- | -- | 39,977,148 |
| Due From Component Units | 7,281,647 | -- | 7,281,647 | -- |
| Due From Other Governments | 36,857,885 | -- | 36,857,885 | 10,856,353 |
| Inventories of Materials and Supplies | 486,716 | 16,531,572 | 17,018,288 | 388,266 |
| Prepaid Assets | 650,958 | 4,692,300 | 5,343,258 | -- |
| Other Assets | 333,566 | -- | 333,566 | 497,665 |
| Restricted Assets - Cash and Investments (Note 3) | 46,983,399 | 49,509,466 | 96,492,865 | 44,992,925 |
| Advances To Component Units | 262,800 | -- | 262,800 | -- |
| Advances To Other Funds | -- | -- | -- | -- |
| Deferred Expenses | -- | 37,342,729 | 37,342,729 | -- |
| Notes Receivable (Note 6) | 5,043,100 | -- | 5,043,100 | -- |
| Mortgage Loans Receivable and Other Non-Current Assets | -- | -- | -- | 52,081,544 |
| Due From Component Units | 19,576,836 | -- | 19,576,836 | -- |
| Capital Assets, net (Note 7): | | | | |
| Land and Works of Art/Historical Treasures | 21,909,621 | 12,815,550 | 34,725,171 | 35,499,949 |
| Infrastructure, Net | 304,389,148 | -- | 304,389,148 | 272,597 |
| Buildings, Structures, and Equipment, Net | 193,051,801 | 647,979,464 | 841,031,265 | 147,089,115 |
| Construction in Progress | 55,697,766 | 112,839,227 | 168,536,993 | 32,040,619 |
| Total Capital Assets, net | 575,048,336 | 773,634,241 | 1,348,682,577 | 214,902,280 |
| Total Assets | 837,700,968 | 997,664,797 | 1,835,365,765 | 417,331,374 |

**Figure 10.10 Government-wide—Statement of Net Assets. (Adapted from a recent City of Richmond, Virginia, CAFR.)**

nature and normally can be preserved for a significantly greater number of years than most capital assets. Examples include … roads, bridges, tunnels, drainage systems, water and sewer systems, dams, and lighting systems" (Cod. 1400.103). Works of art and historical treasures are not depreciated if they meet certain criteria. The codification provides the criteria in section 1400.109 for collections. The City of Richmond includes works of art and historical treasures with land because both categories of capital assets are considered inexhaustible. Governments should report works of art and historical treasures as routine capital assets and depreciate them if they do not meet the GASB criteria for collections.

Governments report liabilities in two major categories—current liabilities and noncurrent liabilities. The City of Richmond reports the noncurrent liabilities due within one year as part of noncurrent assets. Many governments report similar

| | Primary Government | | | |
| --- | --- | --- | --- | --- |
| | Governmental Activities | Business-type Activities | Total | Component Units |
| **Liabilities** | | | | |
| Current Liabilities: | | | | |
| Accounts Payable | 13,594,445 | 18,852,581 | 32,447,026 | 10,686,466 |
| Accrued Liabilities | 7,084,077 | 7,274,589 | 14,358,666 | 25,729,113 |
| Internal Balances | -- | -- | -- | -- |
| Due To Primary Government | -- | -- | -- | 7,281,647 |
| Due To Other Governments | 3,173,329 | -- | 3,173,329 | 6,189,848 |
| Due To Various Agents | 784,319 | -- | 784,319 | -- |
| Due To Component Units | 39,977,148 | -- | 39,977,148 | -- |
| Accrued Interest on Bonds and Notes Payable | 11,778,919 | 12,488,729 | 24,267,648 | -- |
| Advances from Primary Government | -- | -- | -- | 262,800 |
| Non-Current Liabilities (Notes 8 and 10): | | | | |
| Liabilities to be Paid From Restricted Assets: | | | | |
| Customers' Deposits | -- | 2,624,175 | 2,624,175 | 350,177 |
| Accreted Interest on Bonds Payable | 92,655 | 2,113,440 | 2,206,095 | -- |
| Deferred Compensation | -- | -- | -- | -- |
| Non-Current Liabilities (Notes 8 and 10): | | | | |
| Due Within One Year: | | | | |
| General Obligation Bonds, Certificates of Participation, | | | | |
| Serial Notes Payable, and Capital Leases | 30,701,647 | 11,950,389 | 42,652,036 | 5,496,750 |
| Revenue Bonds Payable | -- | 3,569,712 | 3,569,712 | -- |
| Compensated Absences | 9,045,753 | 1,598,886 | 10,644,639 | 2,014,410 |
| Other Liabilities and Claims Payable | 5,582,181 | -- | 5,582,181 | 4,211,471 |
| Advances from Primary Government | -- | -- | -- | -- |
| Due In More Than One Year: | | | | |
| General Obligation Bonds, Certificates of Participation, | | | | |
| Serial Notes Payable, and Capital Leases | 390,909,491 | 267,676,467 | 658,585,958 | 140,976,514 |
| Discount on Revenue Bonds Payable | -- | -- | -- | (1,881,134) |
| Due To Primary Government | -- | -- | -- | 19,576,836 |
| Revenue Bonds Payable | -- | 256,935,042 | 256,935,042 | -- |
| Deferred Revenue | 27,954,318 | 60,496,937 | 88,451,255 | 3,262,291 |
| Compensated Absences | 4,697,997 | 409,454 | 5,107,451 | 13,187,051 |
| Other Liabilities and Claims Payable | 14,099,879 | -- | 14,099,879 | 699,398 |
| Early Retirement Plan Net Pension Obligation | -- | -- | -- | 2,697,562 |
| Total Liabilities | 559,476,158 | 645,990,401 | 1,205,466,559 | 240,741,200 |
| **Net Assets** | | | | |
| Invested In Capital Assets, Net of Related Debt | 199,865,572 | 280,898,657 | 480,764,229 | 109,677,728 |
| Restricted for: | | | | |
| Capital Projects | 45,040,528 | 49,509,466 | 94,549,994 | 8,963,113 |
| Debt Service | 1,480,501 | -- | 1,480,501 | -- |
| Permanent Funds: | | | | |
| Expendable | 425,372 | -- | 425,372 | 521,195 |
| Nonexpendable | 36,998 | -- | 36,998 | 203,472 |
| Unrestricted | 31,375,839 | 21,266,273 | 52,642,112 | 57,224,666 |
| Total Net Assets | $ 278,224,810 | $ 351,674,396 | $ 629,899,206 | $ 176,590,174 |

**Figure 10.10 (continued).**

liabilities as part of current liabilities and label them as noncurrent liabilities due within one year. Regardless, the City of Richmond has clearly met the GAAP reporting requirements.

"Net assets should be displayed in three components—*invested in capital assets, net of related debt; restricted* (distinguishing between major categories of restriction); *and unrestricted*" (Cod. 2200.117). Invested in capital assets, net of related debt "consists of capital assets ... , including *restricted* capital assets, net of accumulated depreciation and reduced by the outstanding balances of any bonds, mortgages, notes, or other borrowings that are attributable to the acquisition, construction, or improvement of those assets" (Cod. 2200.118).

Governments should report restricted net assets "when constraints placed on net asset use are either:

a. Externally imposed by creditors (such as through debt covenants), grantors, contributors, or laws or regulations of other governments
b. Imposed by law through constitutional provisions or enabling legislation

*Enabling legislation* ... authorizes the government to assess, levy, charge, or otherwise mandate payment of resources (from external resource providers) *and* includes a legally enforceable requirement that those resources be used only for the specific purposes stipulated in the legislation" (Cod. 2200.119). "When permanent endowments or permanent fund principal amounts are included, 'restricted net assets' should be displayed in two additional components—expendable and nonexpendable" (Cod. 2200.123). The City of Richmond properly displays restricted net assets in Figure 10.10, including the use of the expendable and nonexpendable categories within permanent funds.

Unrestricted net assets represent all net assets "that do not meet the definition of 'restricted' or 'invested in capital assets, net of related debt'" (Cod. 2200.124). Unrestricted net assets is the default value. Unrestricted "net assets are often *designated* to indicate that management does not consider them to be available for general operations .... [T]hese types of constraints on resources are *internal* and management can remove or modify them ... . Designations of [unrestricted] net assets should not be reported on the face of the statement of net assets" (Cod. 2200.125). The City of Richmond properly reports unrestricted net assets on a single line in the net assets section of the statement of net assets. Designations were reported on the City of Richmond governmental funds balance sheet in Figure 10.2, which is acceptable.

### 10.4.6.3 Statement of Activities

The statement of activities reports the operating performance of the government as a whole. "The operations of the reporting government should be present in a format that reports the *net (expense) revenue* of its individual functions. Net (expense) revenue is sometimes referred to as 'net cost' of a function or program and represents the total expenses of the function or program less its program revenues—that is, charges or fees and fines that derive directly from the function or program and grants and contributions that are restricted to the function or program. An objective of using the net (expense) revenue format is to report the relative financial burden of each of the reporting government's functions on its taxpayers .... General revenues, contributions..., special and extraordinary items, and transfers should be reported separately after the total net expenses of the government's functions, ultimately arriving at the 'change in net assets' for the period" (Cod. 2200.126). The City of Richmond statement of activities in Figure 10.11 illustrates the format used to accomplish these requirements.

The statement of activities should, "[a]t a minimum, present

a. Activities accounted for in governmental funds by function … to coincide with the level of detail required in the governmental fund statement of revenues, expenditures, and changes in fund balances
b. Activities accounted for in enterprise funds by different identifiable activities" (Cod. 2200.127).

Governments can report discretely presented component units individually or in total on the statement of activities. Condensed financial information in the notes or a combining component unit statement in the basic financial statements is required when a single row or column reports more than one discretely presented component unit.

The City of Richmond statement of activities in Figure 10.11 summarizes the function/program or activities labels in the top portion of the statement separately for the primary government and component units. It also summarizes the governmental activities separately from the business-type activities within the primary government rows. Notice that the governmental activities are reported by function similar to the governmental funds operating statement. Also, the business-type activities are summarized by identifiable activities. Finally, the City of Richmond lists each discretely presented component unit separately.

Three main column headings are reported on the statement of activities. Governments label the first column *expenses*. They label the next group of three columns *program revenues* with individual columns labeled: (1) *charges for services*, (2) *operating grants and contributions*, and (3) *capital grants and contributions*. *Net (expense) revenues and changes in net assets* is the main label for the final four columns. Two subheadings of the final four columns are *primary government* (three columns) and *component units* (one column). The primary government column labels mirror the row labels: (1) *governmental activities*, (2) *business-type activities*, and (3) *total* for the primary government activities.

The expense column is presented first and "as a minimum … should report direct expense for each function" (Cod. 2200.129). "Some functions, such as general government, support services, or administration, include expenses that are, in essence, *indirect* expenses of other functions" (Cod. 2200.130). An option exists to permit the allocation of indirect expenses, but it is not addressed here because few governments have applied this option. "Depreciation expense for capital assets that can specifically be identified with a function should be included in its direct expenses. Depreciation expense for 'shared' capital assets … should be ratably included in the direct expenses of the appropriate functions. Depreciation expense

CITY OF RICHMOND, VIRGINIA
STATEMENT OF ACTIVITIES
For the Fiscal Year Ended June 30, 20X8

| | | | Program Revenues | |
| --- | --- | --- | --- | --- |
| Functions/Program Activities | Expenses | Charges for Services | Operating Grants and Contributions | Capital Grants and Contributions |
| **Primary Government:** | | | | |
| **Governmental:** | | | | |
| General Government | $ 85,220,510 | $ 40,875,918 | $ 16,648,997 | $ -- |
| Public Safety and Judiciary | 141,560,046 | 8,324,242 | 26,274,033 | -- |
| Highways, Streets, Sanitation and Refuse | 76,549,273 | 10,226,487 | 18,216,124 | 10,610,426 |
| Human Services | 89,294,156 | 2,164,691 | 81,373,701 | -- |
| Culture and Recreation | 26,127,447 | 663,061 | 1,197,492 | -- |
| Education | 138,209,993 | -- | -- | -- |
| Transportation | 6,114,308 | -- | -- | -- |
| Interest and Fiscal Charges | 35,659,959 | -- | -- | -- |
| Total Governmental Activities | 598,735,692 | 62,254,399 | 143,710,347 | 10,610,426 |
| **Business-type:** | | | | |
| Gas | 167,936,098 | 173,251,482 | 245,035 | -- |
| Water | 34,294,537 | 42,239,247 | 1,271,803 | -- |
| Wastewater | 37,587,401 | 44,784,105 | 5,450,413 | -- |
| Coliseum | 4,066,451 | 2,337,854 | 81,338 | -- |
| Landmark Theater | 1,580,618 | 318,101 | -- | -- |
| Cemeteries | 1,602,606 | 1,386,577 | -- | -- |
| Total Business-type Activities | 247,067,711 | 264,317,365 | 7,048,589 | -- |
| Total Primary Government | $ 845,803,403 | $ 326,571,764 | $ 150,758,936 | $ 10,610,426 |
| **Component Units:** | | | | |
| School Board | 264,920,152 | 3,794,808 | 73,740,974 | 8,507,349 |
| Richmond Ambulance Authority | 10,696,501 | 9,328,485 | -- | -- |
| Hospital Authority of Richmond | 8,320,521 | 8,209,284 | -- | -- |
| Port of Richmond Commission | 1,589,703 | 967,975 | -- | 29,250 |
| Richmond Behavioral Health Authority | 26,136,508 | 10,488,324 | 13,095,354 | -- |
| Richmond Redevelopment and Housing Authority | 68,228,790 | 22,428,703 | 36,562,678 | 11,757,796 |
| Broad Street Community Development Authority | 529,021 | 95,833 | -- | -- |
| Total Component Units | $ 380,421,196 | $ 55,313,412 | $ 123,399,006 | $ 20,294,395 |

General Revenues:
  City Taxes
  Intergovernmental Revenue Not Restricted to Specific Programs
  Payment From Primary Government
  Investment Earnings
  Miscellaneous
Special Item - Gain on Sale of Land
Transfers
    Total General Revenues, Special Item and Transfers

Changes in Net Assets

Net Assets - Beginning of Year
Net Assets - End of Year

**Figure 10.11 Government-wide—Statement of Activities. (Adapted from a recent City of Richmond, Virginia, CAFR.)**

for capital assets such as city hall or a state office building that essentially serves all functions ... may be included as a separate line in the statement of activities or as part of 'general government' ..." (Cod. 2200.132).

| | Net (Expenses) Revenues and Changes in Net Assets | | | |
| --- | --- | --- | --- | --- |
| | Primary Government | | | |
| | Governmental Activities | Business-type Activities | Totals | Component Units |
| $ | (27,695,595) $ | -- $ | (27,695,595) $ | -- |
| | (106,961,771) | -- | (106,961,771) | -- |
| | (37,496,236) | -- | (37,496,236) | -- |
| | (5,755,764) | -- | (5,755,764) | -- |
| | (24,266,894) | -- | (24,266,894) | -- |
| | (138,209,993) | -- | (138,209,993) | -- |
| | (6,114,308) | -- | (6,114,308) | -- |
| | (35,659,959) | -- | (35,659,959) | -- |
| | (382,160,520) | -- | (382,160,520) | -- |
| | -- | 5,560,418 | 5,560,418 | -- |
| | -- | 9,216,513 | 9,216,513 | -- |
| | -- | 12,647,117 | 12,647,117 | -- |
| | -- | (1,647,259) | (1,647,259) | -- |
| | -- | (1,262,517) | (1,262,517) | -- |
| | -- | (216,029) | (216,029) | -- |
| | -- | 24,298,243 | 24,298,243 | -- |
| $ | (382,160,520) $ | 24,298,243 $ | (357,862,277) $ | -- |
| | -- | -- | -- | (178,877,021) |
| | -- | -- | -- | (1,368,016) |
| | -- | -- | -- | (111,237) |
| | -- | -- | -- | (592,478) |
| | -- | -- | -- | (2,552,830) |
| | -- | -- | -- | 2,520,387 |
| | -- | -- | -- | (433,188) |
| $ | -- $ | -- $ | -- $ | (181,414,383) |
| | 318,520,867 | -- | 318,520,867 | -- |
| | 112,628 | -- | 112,628 | 58,531,522 |
| | -- | -- | -- | 136,952,770 |
| | 669,795 | 1,855,899 | 2,525,694 | 1,152,461 |
| | 45,050,330 | 2,771,621 | 47,821,951 | 1,166,798 |
| | 174,264 | -- | 174,264 | -- |
| | 17,219,836 | (17,219,836) | -- | -- |
| | 381,747,720 | (12,592,316) | 369,155,404 | 197,803,551 |
| | (412,800) | 11,705,927 | 11,293,127 | 16,389,168 |
| | 278,637,610 | 339,968,469 | 618,606,079 | 160,201,006 |
| $ | 278,224,810 $ | 351,674,396 $ | 629,899,206 $ | 176,590,174 |

**Figure 10.11    (continued).**

"Depreciation expense for general infrastructure assets should not be allocated to various functions. It should be reported as a direct expense of the function ... that the reporting government normally associates with capital outlays for, and maintenance of, infrastructure assets ..." (Cod. 2200.133). The City of Richmond assigns infrastructure depreciation to the *Highways, Streets, Sanitation, and Refuse* function of governmental activities. In addition, "*[i]nterest on general long-term liabilities* generally should be considered an indirect expense" (Cod. 2200.134) and most interest "should be reported in the statement of activities as a separate line ..." (Cod. 2200.134). The City of Richmond reports *interest and fiscal charges* on a separate line in Figure 10.11.

The second through fourth columns report program revenues. "Program revenues derive directly from the program itself or from parties outside the reporting government's taxpayers or citizenry ...; they reduce the net cost of the function to be financed from the government's general revenues" (Cod. 2200.136). The statement of activities uses three categories (columns) to report program revenues—charges for services, operating grants and contributions, and capital grants and contributions. Each program revenue is reported on the same row as the governmental function or business-type activity that incurred the expenses associated with the program revenue.

"*Charges for services* is the term used for a broad category of program revenues that arise from charges to customers, applicants, or others who purchase, use, or directly benefit from the goods, services, or privileges provided, or are otherwise directly affected by the service" (Cod. 2200.137). Essentially, this category includes any fee paid to the government to receive a specific service from the government.

"*Program-specific grants and contributions (operating and capital)* include revenues arising from mandatory and voluntary nonexchange transactions with other governments, organizations, or individuals that are restricted for use in a particular program" (Cod. 2200.138). Capital grants and contributions "should be reported separately from grants and contributions that may be used *either* for operating expenses or for capital expenditures of the program at the discretion of the reporting government. These categories of program revenue are specifically attributable to a program and reduce the net expense of that program to the reporting government" (Cod. 2200.138). Figure 10.11 shows *operating grants and contributions* and *capital grants and contributions* reported under program revenues. Finally, "[m]ultipurpose grants that do not provide for specific identification of the programs and amounts should be reported as general revenues" (Cod. 2200.138). General revenue reporting is discussed shortly.

Governments report *Net (expense) revenue and changes in net assets* in the final four columns of the statement of activities. The "objective of using the net (expense) revenue format is to report the relative financial burden of each of the reporting government's functions on its taxpayers ..." (Cod. 2200.126). The values in the governmental activities column, the business-type activities column, and the component unit column are each calculated by subtracting the expenses from the program revenue of each function or activity. Totals are prepared for each subgroup of rows in all columns discussed to this point.

Only the four *net (expenses) revenues and changes in net assets* columns carry forward to the bottom portion of the statement of activities, which presents general revenues and other nonactivity specific revenues and expenses. "All revenues are *general revenues* unless they are required to be reported as program revenues …. All taxes, even those that are levied for a specific purpose, are general revenues and should be reported by type of tax …. All other nontax revenues … that do not meet the criteria to be reported as program revenues should also be reported as general revenues. General revenues should be reported after total net expense of the government's functions" (Cod. 2200.140). Governments report all general revenues on the bottom portion of the statement of activities. Other income not related to specific programs is also reported as part of general revenues.

"Contributions to term and permanent endowments, contributions to permanent fund principal, special and extraordinary items … and transfers … between governmental and business-type activities should each be reported separately from, but in the same manner as, general revenue. That is, these sources of financing the net cost of the government's programs should be reported at the bottom of the statement of activities to arrive at an all-inclusive change in net assets for the period" (Cod. 2200.141). The City of Richmond reports one special item and transfers after general revenues near the bottom of the statement of activities in Figure 10.11. The subtotal of *total general revenues, special items, and transfers* is added to the appropriate *net (expense) revenue and changes in net assets* subtotal in the same column. The result is *changes in net assets* for that column.

## 10.4.7 Component Unit Combining Statements

### 10.4.7.1 Introduction

Governments usually include component unit combining statements in the basic financial statements if the government reports more than one component unit in a single column of the government-wide statements. Alternatively, condensed financial information on each major component unit can be disclosed in the notes. Notice that the component unit combining statements are part of the basic financial statements and not supplemental information.

### 10.4.7.2 Component Unit Combining Statement of Net Assets

Figure 10.12 presents the City of Richmond component unit combining statement of net assets. The combining statement of net assets for the City of Richmond presents seven discretely presented component units in individual columns. The seven columns are then added across to determine the total for each asset, liability, or net asset account. The amounts in the component unit statement of net assets

**CITY OF RICHMOND, VIRGINIA**
**COMPONENT UNITS**
**COMBINING STATEMENT OF NET ASSETS**
**June 30, 20X8**

| | School Board | Richmond Ambulance Authority | Hospital Authority of Richmond | Port of Richmond Commission | Richmond Behavioral Health Authority | Richmond Redevelopment and Housing Authority | Broad Street Community Development Authority | Total |
|---|---|---|---|---|---|---|---|---|
| **Assets** | | | | | | | | |
| Cash and Cash Equivalents (Note 3) | $ 1,023,201 | $ 1,938,064 | $ 2,804,545 | $ 2,844,695 | $ 1,142,275 | $ 9,255,087 | $ -- | $ 19,007,867 |
| Due From Primary Government | 39,977,148 | -- | -- | -- | -- | -- | -- | 39,977,148 |
| Due From Other Governments (Note 5) | 10,856,353 | -- | -- | -- | -- | -- | -- | 10,856,353 |
| Accounts Receivable | 9,123,704 | 3,112,920 | 1,471,896 | 82,121 | 1,829,685 | 18,970,418 | 36,582 | 34,627,326 |
| Inventories of Materials and Supplies | 207,182 | 116,786 | 27,290 | -- | 37,008 | -- | -- | 388,266 |
| Prepaid Expenses and Other Current Assets | -- | 67,914 | 98,106 | -- | 331,645 | -- | -- | 497,665 |
| Restricted Assets | 2,502,846 | -- | 104,291 | -- | 245,886 | 891,190 | 41,248,712 | 44,992,925 |
| Mortgage Loans Receivable and Other Non-Current Assets | -- | -- | -- | -- | -- | 52,081,544 | -- | 52,081,544 |
| Capital Assets (Note 7): | | | | | | | | |
| Land | -- | -- | 111,508 | 157,337 | -- | 35,231,104 | -- | 35,499,949 |
| Infrastructure | -- | -- | -- | 272,597 | -- | -- | -- | 272,597 |
| Buildings and Structures | -- | 1,803,963 | 7,189,524 | 3,470,354 | -- | 227,751,033 | 23,896,610 | 264,111,484 |
| Plant-in-Service | -- | -- | -- | 14,623,403 | -- | -- | -- | 14,623,403 |
| Equipment | 21,649,640 | 6,197,548 | 1,406,271 | 2,706,108 | 2,949,255 | 10,499,138 | -- | 45,407,960 |
| Less Accumulated Depreciation | (15,962,246) | (4,841,772) | (5,139,810) | (9,237,651) | (1,882,870) | (139,923,004) | (66,379) | (177,053,732) |
| Construction in Progress | -- | -- | -- | 338,971 | -- | 31,701,648 | -- | 32,040,619 |
| Total Capital Assets | 5,687,394 | 3,159,739 | 3,567,493 | 12,331,119 | 1,066,385 | 165,259,919 | 23,830,231 | 214,902,280 |
| Total Assets | $ 69,377,828 | $ 8,395,423 | $ 8,073,621 | $ 15,257,935 | $ 4,652,884 | $ 246,458,158 | $ 65,115,525 | $ 417,331,374 |

**Figure 10.12  Component Unit Combining Statement of Net Assets. (Adapted from a recent City of Richmond, Virginia, CAFR.)**

| | | | | | | | | |
|---|---:|---:|---:|---:|---:|---:|---:|---:|
| **Liabilities** | | | | | | | | |
| Accounts Payable | $ 4,600,152 | $ 136,838 | $ 788,543 | $ 127,559 | $ 1,043,154 | $ 3,947,998 | $ 42,222 | $ 10,686,466 |
| Accrued Liabilities | 18,468,313 | 903,038 | 47,107 | – | – | 5,896,334 | 414,321 | 25,729,113 |
| Internal Balances | – | 108,767 | – | – | – | – | – | 108,767 |
| Due To Primary Government | – | – | – | – | – | 7,172,880 | – | 7,172,880 |
| Due To Other Governments | 1,026,039 | – | – | – | – | 5,163,809 | – | 6,189,848 |
| Deferred Revenue | 2,497,395 | 60,295 | – | – | 570,000 | – | – | 3,127,690 |
| Advances from Primary Government | 12,800 | 250,000 | – | – | – | – | – | 262,800 |
| Liabilities to be Paid From Restricted Assets: | | | | | | | | |
| Customers' Deposits | – | – | 104,291 | – | 245,886 | – | – | 350,177 |
| Non-Current Liabilities (Notes 8 and 10): | | | | | | | | |
| Due Within One Year: | | | | | | | | |
| Bonds, Notes Payable and Capital Leases | – | 27,880 | 17,473 | – | – | 5,451,397 | – | 5,496,750 |
| Compensated Absences | 692,002 | – | – | 11,964 | – | 1,310,444 | – | 2,014,410 |
| Workers' Compensation | 910,523 | – | – | – | – | – | – | 910,523 |
| Incurred But Not Reported Claims | 3,300,948 | – | – | – | – | – | – | 3,300,948 |
| Advances from Primary Government | – | – | – | – | – | – | – | – |
| Due In More Than One Year: | | | | | | | | |
| Bonds, Notes Payable and Capital Leases | – | 396,572 | 74,569 | – | – | 73,765,373 | 66,740,000 | 140,976,514 |
| Less Discount on Revenue Bonds Payable | – | – | – | – | – | – | (1,881,134) | (1,881,134) |
| Due To Primary Government | – | – | – | – | – | 19,576,836 | – | 19,576,836 |
| Compensated Absences | 11,530,201 | – | – | – | 614,324 | 1,042,526 | – | 13,187,051 |
| Deferred Revenue | – | – | – | – | – | 134,601 | – | 134,601 |
| Workers' Compensation | 291,417 | – | – | – | – | – | – | 291,417 |
| Incurred But Not Reported Claims | 407,981 | – | – | – | – | – | – | 407,981 |
| Early Retirement Plan Net Pension Obligation | 2,697,562 | – | – | – | – | – | – | 2,697,562 |
| Total Liabilities | 46,435,333 | 1,883,390 | 984,876 | 186,630 | 2,473,364 | 123,462,198 | 65,315,409 | 240,741,200 |
| | | | | | | | | |
| **Net Assets** | | | | | | | | |
| Invested In Capital Assets, Net of Related Debt | 5,687,394 | 2,735,287 | 3,475,451 | 12,331,119 | 1,066,385 | 86,043,149 | (1,661,057) | 109,677,728 |
| Restricted for: | | | | | | | | |
| Capital Projects | 8,963,113 | – | – | – | – | – | – | 8,963,113 |
| Permanent Funds | | | | | | | | |
| Expendable | 521,195 | – | – | – | – | – | – | 521,195 |
| Nonexpendable | 203,472 | – | – | – | – | – | – | 203,472 |
| Unrestricted | 7,567,321 | 3,776,746 | 3,613,294 | 2,740,186 | 1,113,135 | 36,952,811 | 1,461,173 | 57,224,666 |
| Total Net Assets | $ 22,942,495 | $ 6,512,033 | $ 7,088,745 | $ 15,071,305 | $ 2,179,520 | $ 122,995,960 | $ (199,884) | $ 176,590,174 |

**Figure 10.12  (continued).**

total column are the same as the component unit column of the government-wide statement of net assets illustrated in Figure 10.10.

### 10.4.7.3 Component Unit Combining Statement of Activities

The single component unit column on the City of Richmond statement of activities also reports information for the same seven component units. Figure 10.13 presents the combining statement of activities for the City of Richmond component units. The combining statement of activities is organized similarly to the government-wide statement of activities, except the City only reports the component unit in individual rows and individual columns for each component unit's *net (expense) revenue and changes in the net assets*. The seven component unit columns are added to arrive at the total *net (expense) revenue and changes in net assets* for all component units. The values from the *net (expense) revenue and changes in the net assets* total column on the combining component unit statement of activities are the same as in the component unit column on the City of Richmond statement of activities in Figure 10.11.

### 10.4.7.4 Other Information

Other reporting methods are available to communicate the required information contained in the combining statement discussed above. One possibility is to provide more component unit information on the face of the government-wide statements. The GASB provides the details of optional component unit presentation methods in section 2600 of the codification. Most governments provide the component unit combining statements as discussed and presented in this chapter, when required.

## 10.5 Conversion from Fund Reporting to Government-Wide Reporting

Government-wide statements summarize the governmental fund statements, the proprietary fund statements, and the combining component unit statements into two government-wide financial statements. The GASB intends the two statements to help users evaluate the financial position (condition) and the operating results of the government as a whole. Government-wide statements exclude information about fiduciary funds because they "… report assets held in a trustee or agency capacity for others and therefore cannot be used to support the government's own programs" (Cod. 1300.102c).

Essentially, the governmental activities columns and rows of the government-wide statements are an aggregation of the governmental fund statements plus other governmental activity related items. Business-type activities are mostly a combining of the enterprise funds plus consolidating internal service funds that primarily serve enterprise funds. Governments must include discretely presented component unit information in the government-wide statements by transferring the row and column totals from the component unit combining statements to the appropriate component unit row(s) and column(s) on the government-wide statements. This process was discussed at the end of Section 10.4.

"In the process of aggregating data for the statement of net assets and the statement of activities, some amounts reported as interfund activity and balances in the funds should be eliminated or reclassified" (Cod. 2200.145). "Eliminations should be made in the statement of net assets to minimize the 'grossing-up' effect on assets and liabilities within the governmental and business-type funds. As a result, amounts reported in the funds as interfund receivables and payables should be eliminated in the governmental and business-type activities, except for the net residual amounts due between governmental and business-type activities, which should be presented as internal balances" (Cod. 2200.146).

Eliminating interfund activity and balances must occur in both the conversion of governmental funds to governmental activities and the conversion of enterprise funds to business-type activities. Governments must eliminate transfers among governmental funds and among enterprise funds. Only the residual transfers between the governmental funds (activities) and the enterprise funds (business-type activities) should remain in the statement of activities. Figure 10.11 illustrates the reporting of transfers by the City of Richmond near the bottom of the statement of activities. The transfers between the governmental activities and business-type activities offset each other so that the City reports no transfers for the primary government as a whole.

Governments must follow a similar process to eliminate the interfund receivables and payables. Receivables and payables among governmental funds and among enterprise funds must be eliminated. Only the residual receivables and payables between governmental activities and enterprise (business-type) activities, labeled as "internal balances," should remain in the statement of net assets. The City of Richmond statement of net assets, illustrated in Figure 10.10, shows internal balances as part of assets. Notice that the amount for governmental activities offsets the internal balance amount in business-type activities. As a result, the City reports no internal balance for the primary government as a whole.

In addition, "[e]liminations should be made in the statement of activities to remove the 'doubling-up' effect of internal service fund activity" (Cod. 2200.147). However, "[t]he effect of interfund services provided and used ... between functions ... should not be eliminated in the statement of activities" (Cod. 2200.148). "Internal service fund asset and liability balances that are not eliminated in the statement of net assets should normally be reported in the *governmental* activities column. Although internal service funds are reported as proprietary funds, the activities accounted for in them ... are usually more governmental than business-type in nature" (Cod. 2200.150).

**CITY OF RICHMOND, VIRGINIA**
**COMPONENT UNIT**
**COMBINING STATEMENT OF ACTIVITIES**
**For the Fiscal Year Ended June 30, 20X8**

| Functions/Program Activities | Expenses | Program Revenues | | |
| --- | --- | --- | --- | --- |
| | | Charges for Services | Operating Grants and Contributions | Capital Grants and Contributions |
| School Board | $ 264,920,152 | $ 3,794,808 | $ 73,740,974 | $ 8,507,349 |
| Richmond Ambulance Authority | 10,696,501 | 9,328,485 | -- | -- |
| Hospital Authority of Richmond | 8,320,521 | 8,209,284 | -- | -- |
| Port of Richmond Commission | 1,589,703 | 967,975 | -- | 29,250 |
| Richmond Behavioral Health Authority | 26,136,508 | 10,488,324 | 13,095,354 | -- |
| Richmond Redevelopment and Housing Authority | 68,228,790 | 22,428,703 | 36,562,678 | 11,757,796 |
| Broad Street Community Development Authority | 529,021 | 95,833 | -- | -- |
| Total Component Units | $ 380,421,196 | $ 55,313,412 | $ 123,399,006 | $ 20,294,395 |

General Revenues:
Payment From Primary Government
Intergovernmental Revenue Not Restricted to Specific Programs
Investment Earnings
Miscellaneous
    Total General Revenues

        Changes in Net Assets

Net Assets - Beginning of Year
Net Assets - End of Year

**Figure 10.13   Component Unit Combining Statement of Activities. (Adapted from a recent City of Richmond, Virginia, CAFR.)**

Net (Expenses) Revenues and Changes in Net Assets

| | School Board | Richmond Ambulance Authority | Hospital Authority of Richmond | Port of Richmond Commission | Richmond Behavioral Health Authority | Richmond Redevelopment and Housing Authority | Broad Street Community Development Authority | Total |
|---|---|---|---|---|---|---|---|---|
| | $ (178,877,021) | $ — | $ — | $ — | $ — | $ — | $ — | $ (178,877,021) |
| | — | (1,368,016) | — | — | — | — | — | (1,368,016) |
| | — | — | (111,237) | — | — | — | — | (111,237) |
| | — | — | — | (592,478) | — | — | — | (592,478) |
| | — | — | — | — | (2,552,830) | — | — | (2,552,830) |
| | — | — | — | — | — | 2,520,387 | — | 2,520,387 |
| | — | — | — | — | — | — | (433,188) | (433,188) |
| | $ (178,877,021) | $ (1,368,016) | $ (111,237) | $ (592,478) | $ (2,552,830) | $ 2,520,387 | $ (433,188) | $ (181,414,383) |
| | 128,823,925 | 3,005,000 | — | — | 1,580,081 | 3,543,764 | — | 136,952,770 |
| | 57,909,782 | — | 237,285 | — | — | 384,455 | — | 58,531,522 |
| | — | 23,332 | 31,428 | 45,360 | 24,585 | 831,034 | 196,722 | 1,152,461 |
| | 841,491 | 24,943 | 316 | 2,403 | 261,063 | — | 36,582 | 1,166,798 |
| | 187,575,198 | 3,053,275 | 269,029 | 47,763 | 1,865,729 | 4,759,253 | 233,304 | 197,803,551 |
| | 8,698,177 | 1,685,259 | 157,792 | (544,715) | (687,101) | 7,279,640 | (199,884) | 16,389,168 |
| | 14,244,318 | 4,826,774 | 6,930,953 | 15,616,020 | 2,866,621 | 115,716,320 | — | 160,201,006 |
| | $ 22,942,495 | $ 6,512,033 | $ 7,088,745 | $ 15,071,305 | $ 2,179,520 | $ 122,995,960 | $ (199,884) | $ 176,590,174 |

**Figure 10.13** (continued).

Internal service funds are usually "consolidated" with the governmental activities for the reason stated above. All internal service fund assets and liabilities that are not receivable from or payable to a governmental fund should be added to the governmental activities in the government-wide statement of net assets. Governments must also eliminate the receivables and payables among the internal service funds and all governmental funds. Similarly, a government must eliminate any transfer between all governmental funds and all internal service funds for the government-wide statement of activities. Also, any net income derived from transactions between a governmental fund and an internal service fund must be eliminated. Governments would follow a similar process if an internal service fund primarily served enterprise funds.

The process of converting the enterprise fund totals from the proprietary funds statements to the business-type activities rows and columns of the government-wide statements is straightforward. The primary reason is that both the enterprise funds and the business-type activities in the government-wide statements are reported on the economic resources measurement focus and accrual basis of accounting. "Generally, the amounts reported as net assets and changes in net assets in the proprietary fund financial statements for total enterprise funds will be the same as net assets and changes in net assets of the business-type activities in the government-wide statement of activities. However, if there are differences …, they should be explained on the face of the fund financial statement (or in an accompanying schedule) …" (Cod. 2200.173).

The previously discussed eliminations of interfund receivables, payables, and transfers are the only adjustments necessary for most governments when converting enterprise funds to business-type activities. Notice that these eliminations do not change total net assets for the combined enterprise funds. A few governments must also consolidate the internal service funds into business-type activities. The financial information in the enterprise total column is carried forward to the business-type activities column of the government-wide statement of net assets for most items. Even for the City of Richmond, which consolidated some internal service funds into the business-type activities column, it is easy to trace most numbers from the enterprise fund total column to the business-type activities rows and columns on government-wide statements.

The conversion from governmental funds to the governmental activities column of the government-wide statements is the most challenging process. The primary reason for the difficulty is that governmental funds use the flow of current financial resources measurement focus and modified accrual accounting, while the government-wide statements use an economic resources measurement focus and an accrual basis of accounting. Table 10.8 provides a list of common adjusting entries that are necessary to convert governmental fund totals to governmental activities in the government-wide statements. The first step in the conversion process is to eliminate the receivable, payables, and transfers as discussed above. Also, governments should consolidate the internal service funds if they primarily serve governmental

| Table 10.8 Converting Governmental Funds Statements to Governmental Activities in the Government-Wide Statements | |
|---|---|
| *Governmental Funds Balance Sheet* | *Governmental Funds Statement of Revenues, Expenditure, and Changes in Fund Balance* |
| **Adjustments** | |
| Eliminate all interfund payable/ receivable balances except those from/to enterprise funds. Label net receivable/payable from enterprise funds as "internal balances" | Eliminate transfers among governmental funds and report only the residual transfers between governmental type funds and enterprise funds |
| Add the assets and liabilities of internal service fund that primarily serve governmental funds | Eliminate any internal service fund "income" derived from governmental funds |
| Adjust deferred revenues when eliminating the available criteria | Convert revenue recognition from modified accrual basis to an accrual basis of accounting |
| Add governmental capital assets and the related accumulated depreciation | Eliminate capital outlay expenditures and record depreciation expense |
| Add general long-term liabilities (bonds, compensated absences) including adjustments for current year activity | Eliminate other financing sources related to bond issues and expenditures for bond principal |
| Remove the capital assets, and the related accumulated depreciation, for capital assets sold | Convert and adjust the other financing sources (uses) for the sale of a fixed assets to a gain or loss |
| Report net assets rather than fund balance | Convert all expense recognition to the accrual basis (interest expense) |
| **Governmental Activities in the Govern- mentwide Statement of Net Assets** | **Governmental Activities in the Govern- mentwide Statement of Activities** |

activities. The adjustments in Table 10.8 list only major adjustments and is not exhaustive.

Governments must also convert the governmental funds balance sheet totals to governmental activities in the government-wide statement of net assets. The GASB requires governments "to present a summary reconciliation at the bottom of the fund financial statements or in an accompanying schedule. Items that typi- cally will be required to reconcile total governmental fund balances to net assets of governmental activities in the statement of net assets include, but are not limited to, the effects of:

- Reporting capital assets at their historical cost and depreciating them instead of reporting capital acquisitions as expenditures when incurred
- Adding general long-term liabilities not due and payable in the current period
- Reducing deferred revenue for those amounts that were not available to pay current-period expenditures
- Adding internal service fund net asset balances" (Cod. 2200.158).

Also, the government must convert governmental fund balance, as adjusted, to the three categories of net assets. The left column of Table 10.8 summarizes the major adjusting entries to convert from the governmental funds balance sheet to the governmental activities column of the government-wide statement of net assets.

The process of converting the statement of revenues, expenditures, and changes in fund balances total column to the governmental activities columns and rows on the statement of activities requires adjustments related to those listed in the previous paragraph. Governments must present a "summary reconciliation at the bottom of the fund statements or in an accompanying schedule. Items that typically will be required to reconcile the total change in governmental fund balances to the change in net assets of governmental activities in the statement of activities include, but are not limited to, the effects of:

- Reporting revenues on the accrual basis
- Reporting annual depreciation expense instead of expenditures for capital outlays
- Reporting long-term debt proceeds in the statement of net assets as liabilities instead of other financing sources; also, reporting debt principal payments in the statement of net assets as reductions of liabilities instead of expenditures
- Reporting other expenses on the accrual basis
- Adding net revenue (expense) of internal service funds ..." (Cod. 2200.163).

The right column of Table 10.8 presents a summary of the major adjustments necessary to convert the statement of revenues, expenditures, and changes in fund balances total column to governmental activities on the statement of activities.

As discussed above, "Governments should present a summary reconciliation to the government-wide financial statements at the bottom of the fund financial statements or in an accompanying schedule. In many cases, brief explanations presented on the face of the financial statement will be sufficient to assess the relationship between the statements" (Cod. 2200.154). The City of Richmond provides an accompanying schedule for each of the four fund statements that require adjustments to meet the government-wide reporting requirements. Sample reconciliations are not presented in illustrations due to space constraints. The Codification provides illustrations in Section 2200.915, 2200.920, and other locations. Section 10.5 is a brief overview of the complex nature of the conversion process. Preparers and users should refer to authoritative sources when converting from the fund statements to the government-wide statements.

## 10.6 Summary

An overview of governmental financial reporting was presented in this chapter. Section 10.2 covered the method for determining the governmental reporting entity and the requirements for reporting component units in the financial statements. Section III introduced the three major sections of a Comprehensive Annual Financial Report (CAFR). The itemized contents of each section of the CAFR were also presented. Discussion and illustrations of each potential basic financial statement were presented in Section 10.4, including the method for determining major funds. Section 10.5 introduced the process for converting from fund statements to government-wide statements. This chapter only highlights major factors in financial reporting. A more comprehensive understanding of financial reporting is available from other sources.

## References

City of Richmond, VA (2003). *Comprehensive Annual Financial Report for the Year Ended June 30, 2003.* Richmond, VA: City of Richmond, Virginia.

Gauthier, S.J. (2001). *Governmental Accounting, Auditing, and Financial Reporting Using the GASB 34 Model.* Chicago, IL: Government Finance Officers Association.

Governmental Accounting Standards Board (2008). *Codification of Governmental Accounting and Financial Reporting.* Norwalk, CT: Governmental Accounting Standards Board.

Governmental Accounting Standards Board (2003). *Comprehensive Implementation Guide—2003.* Norwalk, CT: Governmental Accounting Standards Board.

Governmental Accounting Standards Board (2005). Statement 44, *Economic Condition Reporting: The Statistical Section.* Norwalk, CT: Governmental Accounting Standards Board.

## Chapter 11

# Government-Wide Financial Benchmarks for State Governments

Craig L. Johnson

*Indiana University, School of Public and Environmental Affairs*

## Contents

11.1 Introduction ...................................................................................390
11.2 Statement No. 34 of the Governmental Accounting Standards Board:
 the Statement of Net Assets and the Statement of Activities .....................391
11.3 Understanding Financial Condition ..........................................................392
11.4 Financial Condition Factors and Indicators ...............................................394
11.5 Budgetary Balance ...............................................................................395
 11.5.1 Operating Position ......................................................................395
 11.5.2 Liquidity ..................................................................................397
 11.5.3 Financial Position ......................................................................398
11.6 Revenue Measures ...............................................................................402
11.7 Service-Level Solvency .........................................................................404
11.8 Conclusion ........................................................................................407
Acknowledgment ........................................................................................408
References .................................................................................................408

## 11.1 Introduction

Financial reporting is one of government's most important responsibilities. Governments have an ethical obligation to produce financial reports that stakeholders—taxpayers, citizens, creditors, vendors, among others—can read and understand and provide the most accurate, transparent, comprehensive, and complete picture of their government. Financial reports must enhance, not hinder, the stakeholders' ability to understand, monitor, and evaluate how government finances are being managed. An outcome of the many managerial, accounting, and auditing activities undertaken by government and outside firms should be annually audited financial statements that inform stakeholders.

State and local financial reporting received a major facelift with the new government-wide financial statement requirements established by Statement No. 34 of the Governmental Accounting Standards Board (GASB, 1999). The new standards are intended to help users better understand the overall financial condition of each state and local government in the United States. Statement No. 34 requires two new government-wide financial statements, the Statement of Net Assets and the Statement of Activities, which consolidate and reconcile individual funds and fund types into an overall governmental balance sheet and operating statement using the same measurement focus and basis of accounting. This provides for the first time in governmental accounting and reporting a consistent and comprehensive basis of financial information so that users of governmental financial reports can view the government as a whole, discrete fiscal entity. External users of the new government-wide statements should be able to better monitor, understand, and evaluate overall financial condition.

Using a 3-year sample of government-wide financial statements published in comprehensive annual financial reports (CAFRs) from 50 states, this chapter presents a comprehensive set of financial condition indicators with comparative benchmarks. State governments were required to implement Statement No. 34 for the fiscal year ending in June 2002. Most states have complied with the requirement so we now have 3 years of comprehensive data to calculate state government financial benchmarks. Since our benchmarks are generated from a national sample over a 3-year period, they provide the first set of financial condition indicators based on a comprehensive, panel (crosssection of states over a 3-year time series) data set. Our benchmarks can be used as a reference to compare the financial situation in an individual state to another state and the state sector as a whole.

The chapter continues with a background discussion on Statement No. 34 from the perspective of the new information provided by government-wide financial statements to the users of state government financial reports. We then develop a series of financial indicators and benchmark data covering government revenues and expenses, assets, and liabilities, for the general purpose of helping external users of government financial reports analyze government's financial condition and, most specifically, operating and financial position.

## 11.2 Statement No. 34 of the Governmental Accounting Standards Board: the Statement of Net Assets and the Statement of Activities

The new government-wide financial statements required by Statement No. 34 of the GASB are intended to help users better understand the overall financial condition of each state and local government. According to the GASB (GASB, 1999), the new reporting requirements are explicitly intended to help users:

- Assess the finances of the government in its entirety
- Determine whether the government's overall financial position improved or deteriorated
- Evaluate whether the government's current-year revenues were sufficient to pay for current-year services
- Make better comparisons between governments

There are several features that make GASB Statement No. 34 unique. First, it requires governments to report two new government-wide financial statements, the Statement of Net Assets and the Statement of Activities, which are designed to present for the first time information about the overall government. The new government-wide statements are a major departure from the traditional governmental financial reporting model because they attempt to consolidate and present in two financial reports the financial information of the government across several different individual funds and fund types with different measurement foci and bases of accounting. In this sense, the new government-wide financial statements do not merely modify traditional government fund accounting; they disclose new information to external stakeholders and fundamentally change how overall government finances may be viewed.

The new Statement of Net Assets is presented first in the Basic Financial Statements section of the CAFR, and it reports all financial and capital resources of the government. It is intended to be a traditional balance sheet in which total assets minus total liabilities equals net assets. Governments are encouraged, but not required, to separate assets and liabilities into current (short-term) and noncurrent (long-term) groups, and present them in the order of their liability from most liquid to least liquid (GASB, 1999). This is an important distinction for analyzing financial condition because it distinguishes between short-term operating position, the ability to pay annual bills with annual revenues, and longer-term financial condition, the ability of the current and future resource base of the government to meet current and incurred obligations as they come due.

The Statement of Activities reports the annual operations of the government in a net (expense) revenue format. Individual functional program revenues are subtracted from expenses to produce a net (expense) revenue column. Then, total general revenues, contributions, special items, and transfers are added to net (expense) revenue to produce the change in net assets (for the fiscal period). Change in net assets for the fiscal year provides a measure of the change in the financial performance of the government from fiscal year operations plus any reserves on hand at the beginning of the year. The final two lines of the Statement of Activities are the net assets-beginning and net assets-ending. Therefore, the last line on the Statement of Activities, net assets-ending, now becomes, literally, the *bottom line* of the governmental operating statement.

A second aspect of Statement No. 34 that makes it different from prior reporting formats is the explicit designation of a "total primary government" (TPG). Within the TPG function, activities are separated into governmental activities (GAs) and business-type activities (BTAs). GAs and BTAs are separated largely by how their operations are financed. GAs are generally financed through taxes, intergovernmental revenues, and other nonexchange or nonmarket transaction-based revenue sources. BTAs are financed primarily by revenue from prices (user fees, user charges, license fees, etc.) charged to parties in exchange for goods or services. The summation of the total columns for GAs and BTAs is presented as the totals' column for the TPG.

In addition, component units of the primary government, such as university systems, are discretely (individually) presented, but their figures are not consolidated into primary government figures. Component unit net (expense) revenue and changes in net assets figures are reported only after primary government total figures.

All of the functions presented in the financial statements, GAs, BTAs, and the component units are reported using the economic resources measurement focus and accrual basis of accounting. This is the first time all government resources, stock resources (assets and liabilities), and flow resources (revenues and expenses) are reported on the same basis. It should be noted that different bases of accounting and measurement focus still exist in different fund types, but they are reconciled into the economic resources measurement focus and accrual basis of accounting for reporting on the government-wide financial statements.

## 11.3 Understanding Financial Condition

Financial condition analysis is used to unearth and convey the basic structural well-being of a government. The theoretical concept of financial condition is intuitive, but to be useful it must be given concrete meaning by operationalizing specific latent constructs (sometimes referred to as factors) with indicator variables. (This basic structural framework is used by Berne and Schramm, 1986; Johnson and Mikesell, 2003; and Nollenberger, Groves, and Valente, 2003.) For example, operating position is a latent construct; it has no real substantive meaning in and of itself. Operating position derives its meaning from the concrete or indicator variables associated with the flow of revenues and expenses from operations. An indicator of operating position is the ratio: revenues divided by expenses. This indicator conveys information on whether the government ran a budget surplus or deficit over the fiscal period, which provides quantitative information on the government's operating position, its ability to operate from day to day in the black.*

The government-wide financial reports provide new information that can be used to develop new and better financial indicator variables, which should lead to improved financial condition analysis. This will not, however, happen overnight. It will require the development and dissemination of new indicators that will have to be tested by several different stakeholder groups, and inevitably revised based on feedback from their actual use in the field. In addition, in order for a financial condition analysis to be insightful, it must be conducted over several years so that conclusions can be based on trends over an entire economic cycle or cycles, not just on one or a few annual data points.

We continue this section with the development of a series of financial condition indicator variables that can be taken directly from the Statement of Net Assets and the Statement of Activities. These indicators are not exhaustive, but cover several critical financial condition constructs, including operating and financial position, liquidity, revenue and service-level measures. It should be noted that a comprehensive financial condition analysis must include many other sources of information that enable the analysis of many indicator variables whose raw data are not in the new government-wide financial reports (nor the old financial reports).

For example, the government-wide financial statements add very little new information on debt burden. This is due both to design and implementation factors. For example, by design the amount of annual debt principal paid is not a line item. In addition, on the Statement of Activities, a line item for interest expense is reported for GAs, but not BTAs. Even for GAs, however, it is not clear that the total amount of interest expense is being itemized. Some states report an "unallocated" interest expense line, indicating that some interest expense has been allocated to and reported in program expenses (e.g., health expenses). Therefore, total annual debt service, a fundamentally important measure of annual debt burden, cannot be calculated with government-wide statement information.

In addition, our analysis indicates that thus far, states are not consistently categorizing debts payable on their Statement of Net Assets. Some states separate short-term debt payable from the current portion of long-term debt, others do not. Some states include a separate line for (capital) lease rental debt payable, others do not. As a result of the aforementioned problems, the new government-wide financial

---

* In order to thoroughly understand a government's operating position, a financial analyst would also have to analyze other quantitative indicators from several data sources, such as the Census Bureau. Sources of qualitative information also need to be reviewed, such as the discussion of economic and financial matters provided in the Management Discussion and Analysis (MD&A) section of the CAFR. The MD&A covers general information on the overall financial and economic condition of government, along with management's explanation of changes in financial condition over the last fiscal year.

**Table 11.1    States in Sample (N = 50)**

| Alabama | Indiana | Nebraska | Rhode Island |
|---|---|---|---|
| Alaska | Iowa | Nevada | South Carolina |
| Arizona | Kansas | New Hampshire | South Dakota |
| Arkansas | Kentucky | New Jersey | Tennessee |
| California | Louisiana | New Mexico[a] | Texas |
| Colorado | Maine | New York[b] | Utah |
| Connecticut | Maryland | North Carolina | Vermont |
| Delaware | Massachusetts | North Dakota | Virginia |
| Florida | Michigan | Ohio | Washington |
| Georgia | Minnesota | Oklahoma | West Virginia |
| Hawaii | Mississippi | Oregon | Wisconsin |
| Idaho | Missouri | Pennsylvania | Wyoming |
| Illinois | Montana | | |

[a]  CAFR not completed for 2004.
[b]  CAFR in 2002 does not reflect GASB 34 reporting changes.
*Source:* Comprehensive Annual Financial Reports (CAFRs), 2002 through 2004,
         for all 50 states.

statements do not currently provide better financial information to analyze debt burden.

The focus of this chapter is only on the variables that can be taken directly and completely from the new government-wide financial reports. The ratio benchmarks are derived from the government-wide financial statements of 50 states between 2002 and 2004. They represent state sector benchmarks. The states are listed in Table 11.1.

## 11.4 Financial Condition Factors and Indicators

Governments in sound financial condition are able to meet their current and future service demands and fulfill their financial obligations while maintaining a stable or growing resource base. We organize our financial indicators drawing on the framework developed by the International City/County Management Association (ICMA) in the *Evaluating Financial Condition* handbook (Nollenberger, Groves and Valente, 2003). The handbook defines financial condition in terms of solvency, including cash, budgetary, and service level. Governments in good financial condition have the short-term resources to meet their monthly cash flow and annual budgetary needs; they are able to meet current and expected future service-level demands placed on them by multiple stakeholder groups; and they will likely be able to meet their financial obligations incurred today but paid in the future. Most financial indicators involve using line-item financial information to calculate ratios. A ratio is one number divided by another number. Ratios are preferred over absolute numbers in analyzing financial condition because they provide a relative context to interpret financial information, and they control variation across entity size, wealth, income, etc.

Our study uses means, standard deviations, and medians to summarize data. We prefer means and standard deviations provided there are no outliers (extreme observations in the data). The mean provides a useful summary number for the group of states, and the standard deviation summarizes the variation around the mean. When using a large sample of state government financial information, however, there are inevitably outliers, which can produce nonsensical results when viewed simply with means and standard deviations. Therefore, we also summarize our data with medians, which are less vulnerable to outlier problems, lend stability to summary figures viewed over time, and provide a useful comparison to means, furthering our understanding of the data.

# 11.5 Budgetary Balance

Governments that are able to balance their operating budgets or consistently run moderate surpluses are considered solvent. Such governments regularly maintain a balance between their revenues and expenses during fiscal year operations. If over the economic cycle balance usually occurs between recurring (projected) revenues and (expected) expenses, then the budget is said to be "structurally" balanced. Two measures of structural budget balance or solvency are operating position and financial position.

## 11.5.1 Operating Position

Operating position refers to the net difference between revenues and expenses resulting from annual operations. The operating position ratio is Operating Revenues/ Expenses. The operating position indicator in Table 11.2 shows whether the government ran a surplus, deficit, or balanced budget from fiscal year operations. Total operating revenues include general and other revenues, charges for services, operating grants, and contributions. It does not include capital grants and contributions.

The reader will notice that the denominator in the previously mentioned equation is expenses rather than expenditures. This is a new feature of the Statement

**Table 11.2**

### Indicator:
### Operating Position

### Ratio:
### Operating Revenues/Expenses

*Governmental Activities (GA)*

|  | *2002 (n = 49)* | *2003 (n = 50)* | *2004 (n = 48)* |
|---|---|---|---|
| Mean | 0.9570 | 0.9810 | 1.0179 |
| Standard deviation | 0.0788 | 0.0643 | 0.1011 |
| Median | 0.9567 | 0.9841 | 1.0030 |

*Total Primary Government (TPG)*

|  | *2002 (n = 49)* | *2003 (n = 50)* | *2004 (n = 48)* |
|---|---|---|---|
| Mean | 0.9528 | 0.9748 | 1.0161 |
| Standard deviation | 0.0752 | 0.0560 | 0.0925 |
| Median | 0.9635 | 0.9787 | 1.0039 |

*Source:* State Comprehensive Annual Financial Reports (CAFRs), 2002–2004, and author's calculations.

of Activities report. Traditionally, general government financial statements were reported using expenditures reported on a modified accrual basis (except for proprietary funds). The modified accrual basis of accounting measures liabilities incurred and actual cash disbursements. In the new financial reporting model, several funds still use expenditures, but they are converted or reconciled into expenses on an accrual basis for reporting on the Statement of Activities. Expenses measure charges incurred, whether paid or unpaid, over the fiscal period. Expenses measure the cost of resources consumed to deliver services over the fiscal period, and therefore, provide a measure of the full cost of operating the government. As a result, the operating position indicator now has a denominator that is more reflective of the true cost of annually operating government.

Table 11.2 shows the operating position indicator with the standard deviation, mean and median ratio benchmarks. The table separates ratios into governmental activities (GA) only and total primary government (TPG). State operating position was stronger in 2004 than 2002. In 2004, both median and mean ratios were the highest over the 3-year period. Both mean and median ratios for GA were greater than 1 for the first time in 2004. However, the standard deviations of 0.10 for GA and 0.09 for TPG indicate that not all state governments operated in the black.

## 11.5.2 Liquidity

Another shorter-term financial indicator is the current ratio: Current Assets/ Current Liabilities. The current ratio in Table 11.3 is a measure of the amount of money owed over the fiscal year compared to the liquid resources available to meet obligations. The concept of liquidity is based on the length of time it takes to monetize an asset into its cash equivalent. In general, assets and liabilities are classified as either liquid or long term. Current assets are short-term assets and are considered liquid because they can be converted into cash quickly at the stated or expected amount (without losing substantial value in the transaction) and can be used to pay bills in the current fiscal year. Cash is the most liquid asset. One dollar can be converted immediately into one dollar of value. Noncurrent or long-term assets are less liquid because they may not be converted to cash immediately at the expected amount. For example, a long-term bond may have a face value of $5,000

**Table 11.3**

### Indicator:
### Liquidity

### Ratio:
### Current Assets/Current Liabilities

*Governmental Activities (GA)*

|  | 2002 (n = 25) | 2003 (n = 27) | 2004 (n = 25) |
|---|---|---|---|
| Mean | 2.1009 | 1.8775 | 1.8909 |
| Standard deviation | 0.8172 | 0.8263 | 0.7002 |
| Median | 1.9989 | 1.6675 | 1.6994 |

*Business-Type Activities (BTA)*

|  |  |  |  |
|---|---|---|---|
| Mean | 7.9303 | 6.3239 | 8.4040 |
| Standard deviation | 8.8259 | 7.5120 | 12.2478 |
| Median | 4.0960 | 3.5451 | 3.0911 |

*Total Primary Government (TPG)*

|  |  |  |  |
|---|---|---|---|
| Mean | 2.4361 | 2.1189 | 2.0730 |
| Standard deviation | 0.7511 | 0.7228 | 0.6471 |
| Median | 2.3378 | 1.9770 | 1.9841 |

*Source:* State Comprehensive Annual Financial Reports (CAFRs), 2002–2004, and author's calculations.

but may be worth much less if sold before final maturity. Short-term liabilities are those that are due within a year, and long-term liabilities are the ones that are due in more than 1 year.

Governments are encouraged, but not required, to separate assets and liabilities into current and long-term groups and present them in the order of their liability from most liquid to least liquid (GASB, 1999). All governments are not reporting assets and liabilities separately in current and noncurrent categories. Therefore, as shown in Table 11.3, the sample size for the current ratio indicator is only 25 or 27.

The current ratio is well above 1.00 each year. It decreased from 2002 to 2003, but stabilized in 2004 for GA and BTA. But for TPG, the growth in current liabilities outpaced that in current assets from 2002 to 2004, indicating a weaker short-term operating position for the sector. The current ratio for TPG is higher than GA because the short-term operating position of BTA is substantially stronger than GA. The BTA section of the TPG is the (current) asset rich part of government—it holds substantially more current assets than current obligations.

### 11.5.3 Financial Position

Another budgetary factor is financial position. Financial position refers to the government's ability to continue providing its basic services and fulfill its financial commitments from current year revenues and prior year savings. It indicates the cumulative extent to which all available resources have exceeded costs during the fiscal year. As shown in Table 11.4, an indicator of financial position is the ratio Unrestricted Net Assets/Expenses. Data on unrestricted assets was unavailable prior to the new Statement of Net Assets report.

Unrestricted net assets are assets available for general purposes, but not necessarily available for cash expenditures. In contrast, restricted net assets are those restricted by externally imposed constraints such as by legal agreements with creditors or grantors, or internally imposed restrictions from constitutional provisions or statutes. Also, line item "unrestricted net assets" does not include funds invested in capital assets (net of related debt).

The unrestricted net assets figure is based on the accumulation of resources over time and represents intraperiod equity or savings along with financial changes from fiscal year operations. Therefore, the financial position indicator, Unrestricted Net Assets/Expenses, measures the ability of government to cover the full cost of its past and current services with past and current resources available for general use. A negative ratio may indicate that the government may be shifting part of the burden for current services to future taxpayers.

For GA, dividing unrestricted net assets by expenses produces a deteriorating mean (and median) ratio from 2002 to 2004, dropping from 0.02 to –0.01. While BTA and TPG mean ratios are positive in 2004, the figures indicate that residual balances in the sector have not consistently kept pace with expenses. Overall, the sector is in a weaker financial position in 2004 than 2002, but 2004 saw improvement.

**Table 11.4**

### Indicator:
### Financial Position

### Ratio:
### Unrestricted Net Assets/Expenses

*Governmental Activities (GA)*

|  | 2002 (n = 49) | 2003 (n = 50) | 2004 (n = 48) |
|---|---|---|---|
| Mean | 0.0207 | −0.0161 | −0.0109 |
| Standard deviation | 0.2353 | 0.2104 | 0.2223 |
| Median | 0.0267 | −0.0025 | −0.0053 |

*Business-Type Activities (BTA)*

|  |  |  |  |
|---|---|---|---|
| Mean | 0.1752 | 0.1518 | 0.1683 |
| Standard deviation | 0.4992 | 0.4766 | 0.5372 |
| Median | 0.0630 | 0.0585 | 0.0686 |

*Total Primary Government (TPG)*

|  |  |  |  |
|---|---|---|---|
| Mean | 0.0312 | −0.0030 | 0.0022 |
| Standard deviation | 0.2287 | 0.2012 | 0.2155 |
| Median | 0.0497 | 0.0104 | 0.0090 |

*Source:* State Comprehensive Annual Financial Reports (CAFRs), 2002–2004, and author's calculations.

Tables 11.5a and 11.5b show another financial position indicator, Unrestricted Net Assets/Total Net Assets, with and without outliers. The reader will notice that in Table 11.5a the means and standard deviations are very high for GA in 2002 and 2004. This is because New Jersey (in 2002) and Rhode Island (in 2004) are outliers. In Table 11.5b, the outliers are excluded, which provides a more representative picture of the sector.

Unrestricted Net Assets/Total Net Assets measures the amount of unrestricted assets remaining at the end of the fiscal year relative to the total asset base at the end of the year. For GA, the median ratio dipped sharply from 2002 to 2004. The standard deviation, however, was much lower in 2004 than in 2003 or 2002. This shows that while unrestricted net assets were lower in 2004, there was less variation across states, resulting in a stronger sector than suggested by looking at only the mean. After improving from 2002 to 2003, the BTA mean ratio softened in

**Table 11.5a**

**Indicator:**
**Financial Position**

**Ratio:**
**Unrestricted Net Assets/Total Net Assets**

*Governmental Activities (GA)*

|  | 2002 (n = 49) | 2003 (n = 50) | 2004 (n = 48) |
|---|---|---|---|
| Mean | 4.9602[a] | 0.1356 | 4.5615[b] |
| Standard deviation | 31.9284[a] | 1.7025 | 31.0467[b] |
| Median | 0.0619 | 0.0270 | 0.0302 |

*Business-Type Activities (BTA)*

| Mean | 0.2282 | 0.3426 | 0.2789 |
|---|---|---|---|
| Standard deviation | 0.6299 | 1.8563 | 1.4058 |
| Median | 0.0796 | 0.0990 | 0.1480 |

*Total Primary Government (TPG)*

| Mean | 0.2613 | −0.0087 | 0.0384 |
|---|---|---|---|
| Standard deviation | 1.6924 | 1.8903 | 1.4058 |
| Median | 0.0758 | 0.0454 | 0.0325 |

[a] The mean and standard deviation numbers are very high because the ratio 223.59 for New Jersey is an outlier.
[b] The mean and standard deviation numbers are very high because the ratio 215.12 for Rhode Island is an outlier.
*Source:* State Comprehensive Annual Financial Reports (CAFRs), 2002–2004, and author's calculations.

2004, and the standard deviation remained well above 1.00. For TPG, the sector improved from 2003 to 2004. The mean ratio is now positive, and the standard deviation is lower. On the other hand, the median ratio is lower, even though the rate of decrease has slowed. Though the state sector ended up in generally better shape in 2004 than in 2003, it was still underperforming 2002 levels, indicating that the sector had more reserves in 2002 than it did in 2004.

The relative amount of unrestricted net assets can be viewed as a reserve or hedge against adverse financial events, such as new, unexpected liabilities or a downturn in revenues. If the amount of unrestricted net assets is decreasing, it is

**Table 11.5b**

<u>Indicator:</u>
**Financial Position**

<u>Ratio:</u>
**Unrestricted Net Assets/Total Net Assets**
(Outliers excluded)

*Governmental Activities (GA)*

|  | *2002 (n = 48)* | *2003 (n = 50)* | *2004 (n = 47)* |
|---|---|---|---|
| Mean | 0.4053 | 0.1356 | 0.0814 |
| Standard deviation | 1.6933 | 1.7025 | 0.7189 |
| Median | 0.0569 | 0.0270 | 0.0281 |

*Business-Type Activities (BTA)*

| | | | |
|---|---|---|---|
| Mean | 0.2334 | 0.3426 | 0.2869 |
| Standard deviation | 0.6355 | 1.8563 | 1.4199 |
| Median | 0.0850 | 0.0990 | 0.1503 |

*Total Primary Government (TPG)*

| | | | |
|---|---|---|---|
| Mean | 0.3270 | −0.0087 | 0.1826 |
| Standard deviation | 1.6459 | 1.8903 | 0.9997 |
| Median | 0.0787 | 0.0454 | 0.0377 |

*Source:* State Comprehensive Annual Financial Reports (CAFRs), 2002–2004, and author's calculations.

an indication that the cushion against future adverse financial events is becoming weaker. When the amount is negative, it indicates that there are no (unaccounted for) funds providing reserve protection and the government is fully exposed to all financial risks. On the other hand, when it is improving, it indicates that the state is better protected or hedged against unexpected adverse events.

Table 11.6 displays another financial position ratio, Change in Net Assets/Total Net Assets. The median ratios across GA, BTA, and TPG show a stronger sector in 2004 than in 2002. This is indicative of a sector with a growing asset base that can be used to support future operations. For TPG, the change in net assets was positive in 2003, despite the negative results in the change in BTA net assets. Moreover, the TPG mean is higher and the standard deviation is lower in 2004 than in 2003 or 2002, indicating a positive change in the asset base since 2003.

**Table 11.6**

<u>Indicator:</u>
**Financial Position**

<u>Ratio:</u>
**Change in Net Assets/Total Net Assets**

| Governmental Activities (GA) | | | |
|---|---|---|---|
| | *2002 (n = 49)* | *2003 (n = 50)* | *2004 (n = 48)* |
| Mean | 1.1795[a] | 0.0475 | −0.4785[b] |
| Standard deviation | 6.9922[a] | 0.1932 | 3.5758[b] |
| Median | 0.0131 | 0.0162 | 0.0500 |

| Business-Type Activities (BTA) | | | |
|---|---|---|---|
| Mean | −0.0437 | −0.2632 | 0.0112 |
| Standard deviation | 0.2538 | 0.7185 | 0.3605 |
| Median | −0.0013 | −0.0486 | 0.0162 |

| Total Primary Government (TPG) | | | |
|---|---|---|---|
| Mean | 0.0175 | 0.0266 | 0.0592 |
| Standard deviation | 0.4635 | 0.2482 | 0.2471 |
| Median | −0.0090 | 0.0019 | 0.0469 |

[a] New Jersey is an outlier with a high ratio of 48.61, driving up the mean and the standard deviation.
[b] Rhode Island is an outlier with a low ratio of −24.72, contributing to a negative mean and a high standard deviation.
*Source:* State Comprehensive Annual Financial Reports (CAFRs), 2002–2004, and author's calculations.

## 11.6 Revenue Measures

Revenues are additions to financial resources and are used to finance programs and activities. Statement No. 34 focuses on the sources of revenue used to finance general government and particular programs. General revenues and other sources (contributions, special items, and transfers) are shown separately at the bottom of the Statement of Activities. General revenues include all revenues unless they are required to be reported as program revenues. All taxes are reported as general revenues and are reported by the type of tax. Also, all nontax revenues that are not required to be reported as program revenues are considered general revenues.

**Table 11.7**

**Indicator:**
**Revenue**

**Ratio:**
**General Revenues + Transfers/Operating Revenues**

| Governmental Activities (GA) | | | |
|---|---|---|---|
| | *2002 (n = 49)* | *2003 (n = 50)* | *2004 (n = 48)* |
| Mean | 0.5655 | 0.5629 | 0.5614 |
| Standard deviation | 0.0761 | 0.0686 | 0.0690 |
| Median | 0.5718 | 0.5708 | 0.5667 |

| Total Primary Government (TPG) | | | |
|---|---|---|---|
| Mean | 0.5045 | 0.4963 | 0.4948 |
| Standard deviation | 0.0706 | 0.0675 | 0.0717 |
| Median | 0.4998 | 0.4914 | 0.4883 |

*Source:* State Comprehensive Annual Financial Reports (CAFRs), 2002–2004, and author's calculations.

Table 11.7 shows the ratio of General Revenues and Transfers/Operating Revenues. This measure indicates the level of annual operations dependent on general revenue sources, not revenues generated on behalf of a particular program. General revenues constitute most GA and TPG revenue in the states. In 2004, general revenues constituted 56% of all GA revenue, and it has been stable since 2002 with only a small standard deviation. The mean ratio for the TPG is slightly lower, but with a similarly small and stable standard deviation.

The revenue indicator Program Revenues/Operating Revenues, shown in Table 11.8, measures the reliance of governmental operations on program revenues. Program revenues are itemized and displayed with the program with which they are associated (e.g., health care). Program revenues are distinguished by whether funds flow directly from the program itself, such as user charges, or from external entities such as operating grants, capital grants, and other contributions. The notion is that program revenues "reduce the net cost of the function (program) to be financed from the government's general revenues" (GASB, 1999; p. 20, para. 48). Revenue from charges for services is derived from exchange-based or marketlike transactions. Such revenues are generated from the prices charged to the consumers who directly benefit from the good, service, or privilege provided by government. Program-specific operating grants, capital grants, and contributions are nonexchange-based revenues from other entities that are restricted for use in a particular program.

**Table 11.8**

**Indicator:**
**Revenue**

**Ratio:**
**Program Revenues/Operating Revenues**

*Governmental Activities (GA)*

|  | 2002 (n = 49) | 2003 (n = 50) | 2004 (n = 48) |
|---|---|---|---|
| Mean | 0.4642 | 0.4640 | 0.4624 |
| Standard deviation | 0.0923 | 0.0781 | 0.0757 |
| Median | 0.4513 | 0.4590 | 0.4520 |

*Total Primary Government (TPG)*

| Mean | 0.5229 | 0.5283 | 0.5274 |
|---|---|---|---|
| Standard deviation | 0.0857 | 0.0759 | 0.0764 |
| Median | 0.5071 | 0.5270 | 0.5299 |

*Source:* State Comprehensive Annual Financial Reports (CAFRs), 2002–2004, and author's calculations.

Program revenues reduce the net cost of the program to general taxpayers. In relation to total operating revenues (reminder: total operating revenues do not include capital grants and contributions), program revenues range in 2004 from 46% for GA and 52% for TPG.

The next revenue indicator in Table 11.9 compares charges for services to total program revenues: Charges for Services/Program Revenues. (Program revenues are capital and operating grants and contributions, and charges for services.) BTA charges for services constitute over 80% of total program revenues. Therefore, most BTA program revenues are charges, not operating or capital grants and contributions. In contrast, only a small amount of GA and TPG program revenues are charges for services, 20% and 34%, respectively. Therefore, most GA and TPG program revenues are grants and contributions, not charges for services.

## 11.7 Service-Level Solvency

Service-level solvency covers an intermediate period of time and refers to the ability of a government to deliver services over a 1- to 5-year period at the level and quality demanded by its stakeholders. This requires sustaining the delivery of essential services across several broad functional areas, including health, welfare, safety, and

**Table 11.9**

---

### Indicator:
### Revenue

### Ratio:
### Charges for Services/Program Revenues

*Governmental Activities (GA)*

|  | 2002 (n = 49) | 2003 (n = 50) | 2004 (n = 48) |
|---|---|---|---|
| Mean | 0.2221 | 0.2027 | 0.2031 |
| Standard deviation | 0.0941 | 0.0841 | 0.0789 |
| Median | 0.1956 | 0.1766 | 0.1825 |

*Business-Type Activities (BTA)*

|  |  |  |  |
|---|---|---|---|
| Mean | 0.7999 | 0.7986 | 0.8243 |
| Standard deviation | 0.1698 | 0.1611 | 0.1485 |
| Median | 0.8323 | 0.8301 | 0.8614 |

*Total Primary Government (TPG)*

|  |  |  |  |
|---|---|---|---|
| Mean | 0.3599 | 0.3483 | 0.3491 |
| Standard deviation | 0.1047 | 0.1027 | 0.1017 |
| Median | 0.3575 | 0.3280 | 0.3358 |

*Source:* State Comprehensive Annual Financial Reports (CAFRs), 2002–2004, and author's calculations.

education. Governments that are able to meet the service-level demands and community needs of its constituents over an extended period of time are considered to be service-level solvent.

An important aspect of service-level solvency is the extent to which government services are paid for with revenues other than taxes. A nontax coverage ratio measures the level of operations and funding burden that are not dependent on tax revenues. The ratio, Program Revenues/Operating Expenses, shown in Table 11.10 is a measure of operating self-sufficiency and indicates the ability of nontax revenues to fund operating expenses.

The new financial reports provide a new perspective on service-level solvency because BTAs are separated from general governmental activities, but they are reported on the same basis on a single financial statement. Therefore, operating self-sufficiency can be analyzed for the primary government and for governmental and business-type activities as well. BTAs are expected to be, but may not always be

**Table 11.10**

### Indicator:
### Service Level

### Ratio:
### Program Revenues/Expenses

*Governmental Activities (GA)*

|  | *2002 (n = 49)* | *2003 (n = 50)* | *2004 (n = 48)* |
|---|---|---|---|
| Mean | 0.4408 | 0.4549 | 0.4705 |
| Standard deviation | 0.0723 | 0.0803 | 0.0882 |
| Median | 0.4325 | 0.4525 | 0.4643 |

*Business-Type Activities (BTA)*

|  |  |  |  |
|---|---|---|---|
| Mean | 0.9294 | 0.9146 | 1.0138 |
| Standard deviation | 0.3431 | 0.2793 | 0.2843 |
| Median | 0.9401 | 0.8814 | 0.9829 |

*Total Primary Government (TPG)*

|  |  |  |  |
|---|---|---|---|
| Mean | 0.4960 | 0.5148 | 0.5354 |
| Standard deviation | 0.0736 | 0.0780 | 0.0868 |
| Median | 0.4899 | 0.5134 | 0.5258 |

*Source:* State Comprehensive Annual Financial Reports (CAFRs), 2002–2004, and author's calculations.

self-supporting. Though GAs are not expected to be self-supporting, it is useful to compare governments to see if there are major differences in the level of self-support across governments.

Table 11.10 shows that BTA functions are, on average, almost completely self-supporting, with 23 states covering over 100% of their expenses with program revenues and only 5 states covering less than 75% of total expenses. GA program revenues cover 47% of operating expenses, with only a small standard deviation. For the TPG, over half of all expenses are covered by program revenues.

Another measure of service-level solvency is shown in Table 11.11, BTA Program Revenues/TPG Expenses, which illustrates the amount of TPG expenses financed from the revenues of activities intended to be self-supporting. BTA program revenues cover only a small portion of TPG expenses, that is, 12% in 2004. Moreover, the standard deviation is small, indicating only a small variation across the sector.

**Table 11.11**

**Indicator:**
**Revenue and Service-Level Solvency**

**Ratio:**
**BTA Program Revenues/TPG Expenses**

|  | 2002 (n = 49) | 2003 (n = 50) | 2004 (n = 48) |
|---|---|---|---|
| Mean | 0.1194 | 0.1260 | 0.1268 |
| Standard deviation | 0.0641 | 0.0689 | 0.0740 |
| Median | 0.1060 | 0.1120 | 0.1098 |

*Source:* State Comprehensive Annual Financial Reports (CAFRs), 2002–2004, and author's calculations.

Most state governments are only financing a small portion of their total expenses with revenues from self-supporting activities.

# 11.8 Conclusion

The new government-wide financial statements largely fulfill their intended purpose by providing new and useful financial information, especially on operating position, financial position, and self-supporting service levels. The challenge now becomes one of mining the most useful pieces of information and communicating it in ways that are useful and informative to multiple stakeholder groups. This chapter has begun that endeavor.

In this chapter, we have developed several financial condition indicators and analyzed them using data collected from a sample of state governments. While it is clear that states are attempting to comply with Statement No. 34 government-wide statements' requirements, it is also clear that some states have a way to go before their efforts produce financial statements that give researchers and analysts the ability to easily and efficiently compare data across states and over a time series.

When the data has been collected, organized, analyzed, and is ready to be presented, we have shown that it is important to use median and mean ratios (along with standard deviations) to analyze financial information for an entire sector. When using means solely, the researcher must be careful to detect and control for outliers; when using medians solely, some measure of variation around the median must be provided in order for the data to convey important information about variation within the group or sector as a whole.

Finally, we now have new and, we believe, better information on the financial condition of governments with government-wide financial statements. Now, it is up to the academic and practitioner communities to analyze and report the raw data in a way that provides decision makers with better information on which to base their policy and administrative decisions.

## Acknowledgment

I would like to thank Nyankor Matthew and Neal Buckwalter for their exceptional research assistance.

## References

Berne, R. and R. Schramm (1986). *The Financial Analysis of Governments*. Englewood Cliffs, NJ: Prentice-Hall.

Governmental Accounting Standards Board (GASB). Statement No. 34 of the Governmental Accounting Standards Board, Basic Financial Statements—and Management's Discussion and Analysis—for State and Local Governments. (June 1999) (No. 171-A).

Johnson, C. and J. Mikesell. (2003, 2nd edition). The collapse of federal fiscal home rule in the District of Columbia: an analysis of municipal financial conditions, in *Case Studies in Public Budgeting and Financial Management*, A. Khan and W. B. Hildreth (Eds.).

Mead, D.M. (2001). *An Analyst's Guide to Government Financial Statements*. Government Accounting Standards Board.

Nollenberger, K., S. Groves, and M. Valente (2003). *Evaluating Financial Condition: A Handbook for Local Government*. International City/County Management Association.

*Various States*. Comprehensive Annual Financial Reports (CAFRs). For Fiscal Years Ended, 2002, 2003, and 2004.

# Chapter 12

# Auditing Governmental Entities

## Suzanne Lowensohn and Kristen Reilly
*Colorado State University, College of Business*

## Contents

12.1 Introduction—A Historical Perspective ................................................... 410
12.2 Governmental Accounting and Auditing ................................................ 411
    12.2.1 Governmental GAAP ................................................................... 412
    12.2.2 Governmental Audits .................................................................. 414
    12.2.3 Generally Accepted Auditing Standards ..................................... 415
    12.2.4 GAGAS General Standards ......................................................... 416
    12.2.5 GAGAS Field Work Standards .................................................... 417
    12.2.6 GAGAS Reporting Standards ..................................................... 419
12.3 Various Other Auditing Issues ............................................................... 420
    12.3.1 Financial Reporting Entity ......................................................... 420
    12.3.2 The Single Audit ........................................................................ 421
    12.3.3 Audit Reports ............................................................................. 423
    12.3.4 Auditor Selection and the Request for Proposal Process .............. 424
    12.3.5 Nonaudit Services ...................................................................... 426
12.4 Summary .............................................................................................. 428
References ...................................................................................................... 428
Appendices .................................................................................................... 430

Many of the nearly 75,000 local governmental units across the United States require external audits due to state-mandated regulation, the receipt of funding from other governments or governmental agencies, and requests from taxpayers, creditors, or political interests. An audit is a methodical examination or review performed by an independent, professional party as a means of forming an opinion about assertions made by management. Financial statement audits, which focus on an entity's management-prepared financial data, are most widely recognized; however, governmental audits may also include examination of governmental units' operations, practices, and/or policies to ascertain adherence to other predetermined requirements. Following a brief historical perspective, this chapter introduces the unique aspects of government auditing and provides an overview of governmental generally accepted accounting principles (GAAP), governmental auditing standards and guidelines, the financial reporting entity, the single audit, governmental audit reporting, auditor selection, and acceptable (non)audit services for governmental organizations.

## 12.1 Introduction—A Historical Perspective

There is evidence that municipal accounts in the United States were prepared and audited as early as the 1600s (Previts and Merino, 1979); however, until recent decades few guidelines for governmental financial statement preparation existed, and governmental statements were not routinely subject to formal audit. In the mid-1970s, highly publicized financial collapses of large city governments, as well as apparent bureaucratic corruption within government, prompted calls for governmental accountability and an emphasis on public sector efficiency. Public resources committed to governmental agencies were increased, and federal laws were passed to add audit provisions within federal grant contracts. There was an increased demand for more uniform professional accounting and attestation services in the public sector.

Periodic audits of governmental entities had historically been performed by government auditors employed by state government or federal agencies. Given the surge in governmental audit demand in the 1980s, state and governmental auditors could no longer perform timely individual audits of all governmental entities. Thus, many states and federal agencies were forced to rely on independent public accountants (i.e., nongovernmental auditors) to meet the increased governmental audit demand, and independent certified public accounting (CPA) firms (i.e., audit firms) became the principal suppliers of external audit services.

Initially, this practice resulted in substandard audits performed by inexperienced independent CPAs. In fact, a 1986 General Accounting Office (GAO) study revealed that 34% of the 120 governmental audits examined were substandard or problematic; however, subsequent professional guidance and educational requirements have helped to improve governmental audit quality. For example, in 1987, an American Institute of Certified Public Accountants (AICPA) task force published a list of 25 recommendations for the public accounting profession, classified into the following five categories: education, engagement, evaluation, enforcement, and exchange information (AICPA, 1987). Dubbed the "five Es," the recommendations called for mandatory governmental accounting and auditing training for auditors performing governmental audits, improved audit procurement processes, positive enforcement and peer review activities for audit firms conducting governmental audits, sanctions against substandard audit performance, and better communication between the profession and professional organizations. In the same year, a GAO report recommended the establishment of an audit procurement system within governmental entities that included four critical attributes (competition, solicitation, technical evaluation, and written agreement) associated with the receipt of a quality audit. Governmental accounting and auditing standards (discussed later in the chapter) were also amended.

While governmental audit quality is believed to have improved dramatically since the late 1980s, over 20% of federal quality control reviews conducted in recent years noted audit quality problems (Broadus, 2004). These results recently prompted a group of federal agencies, in conjunction with the GAO, the Office of Management and Budget (OMB), the AICPA, the President's Council on Integrity and Efficiency, and the National State Auditors Association, to institute the National Project to Statistically Measure the Quality of Single Audits. The current collaborative effort will statistically measure the quality of single audits of federal program fund recipients and make recommendations for improving audit work being performed under the OMB Circular A-133.

The auditing profession, via the AICPA, is also currently active in governmental audit activities. Since CPAs are faced with many challenges while performing governmental audits, the AICPA has created a Governmental Audit Quality Center on their Web site at www.gaqc.aicpa.org. The Center's primary purpose is to promote the importance of quality governmental audits and the value of such audits to purchasers of governmental audit services. This is an important contribution, given the unique nature of governmental entities.

## 12.2 Governmental Accounting and Auditing

Governmental entities differ from commercial audit organizations in a number of ways. Foremost among these differences is the nature of entity operations as well as their accounting and financial reporting. Governmental units are distinguished from commercial organizations by the political processes governing policy decision making, the absence of a profit-making motive, and the fact that no direct wealth effect links elected officials and taxpayers in the public sector (i.e., taxpayers typically do not receive government-provided services proportionate to the amount of taxes paid). In addition, budgeting is a legal control device, which is an integral part of public sector administration. As discussed in Chapter 10, governmental financial statements differ in form and content from their commercial counterparts. Reporting differences stem from governmental GAAP, which are unique to the public sector.

## 12.2.1 Governmental GAAP

Since 1984, the primary source of accounting principles for states, cities, counties, towns, villages, school districts, special districts and authorities, and other local government entities has been the statements and interpretations of the Governmental Accounting Standards Board (GASB). Before 1984, the most important continuous source of accounting principles for state and local governmental units had been the Municipal Finance Officers Association (MFOA) and its committees on governmental accounting. The MFOA's National Committee on Governmental Accounting (NCGA) issued *Municipal Accounting and Auditing* in 1951 and *Governmental Accounting, Auditing, and Financial Reporting* (GAAFR) or the "Blue Book" in 1968. These resources comprised the most complete frameworks of accounting principles specific to governmental units, and they provided standards for preparing and evaluating the financial reports of governmental units. In 1974, the AICPA issued its Industry Audit Guide, *Audits of State and Local Governmental Units*, in which it noted that GAAFR's accounting and reporting principles constituted GAAP except where they were modified by the *Audit Guide*. The AICPA's endorsement was important to the GAAFR's authority and general acceptance by preparers, auditors, and users of governmental financial statements. Following a 1979 GAAFR restatement, the AICPA issued Statement of Position 80–2, which amended *Audits of State and Local Governmental Units* to recognize the principles of NCGA1 as generally accepted accounting principles.

While the NCGA was successful in developing and documenting governmental accounting principles, it was criticized for its lack of independence (due to its MFOA sponsorship) and slow progress. Thus, in 1984, the Financial Accounting Foundation (which also oversees the Financial Accounting Standards Board [FASB]) formed the GASB to establish and improve standards for governmental accounting and financial reporting. Financial Accounting Foundation trustees appoint one full-time chair and six part-time members to serve on the board.

In 1985, the GASB integrated all effective accounting and reporting standards into one publication called *Codification of Governmental Accounting and Financial Reporting Standards*. The *Codification* is revised annually to reflect all current GASB official pronouncements. In 1986, the AICPA Council declared that Rule 203 of its Rules of Conduct applies to GASB's pronouncements. Therefore, the pronouncements constitute GAAP for governments. At this writing, the GASB has issued 53 statements of standards and 6 interpretations setting forth government accounting and reporting requirements. The GASB issues concepts statements, technical bulletins, implementation guides, and user guides as well.

During the first five years of GASB's existence, discussions arose about the jurisdiction of GASB and FASB. In 1990 the Financial Accounting Foundation and constituents of the two boards agreed on a jurisdictional formula. The resulting agreement, which is reflected in the AICPA's 1992 Statement on Auditing Standards (SAS) No. 69, *The Meaning of "Fairly Presents" in the Auditor's Report,* addressed the potential overlap between the two bodies by identifying the following relative authoritative strength of available resources for general purpose governmental entities:*

1. GASB Statements and GASB Interpretations. This category also includes AICPA and FASB pronouncements made applicable to state and local governments by a GASB Statement or Interpretation.
2. GASB Technical Bulletins. This category also includes AICPA Industry Audit and Accounting Guides and Statements of Position if specifically made applicable to state and local governments by the AICPA and cleared by the GASB.
3. Consensus positions of GASB's Emerging Issues Task Force (EITF) and AICPA Practice Bulletins if specifically made applicable to state and local governments by the AICPA and cleared by the GASB. (No GASB EITF currently exists.)
4. Implementation Guides published by the GASB staff and industry practices that are widely recognized and prevalent in state and local government.
5. Other accounting literature (including FASB standards not made applicable to governments by a GASB standard).

Although organizations such as the Municipal and Government Finance Officers Associations (MFOA, GFOA) had previously provided governmental entities and their auditors with guidelines, they had no formal authority to enforce compliance with their suggestions, due in part to state sovereignty, whereby each state determines reporting requirements, if any. Thus, SAS 69 helped raise the status of GASB and its issuances.

Following SAS 69, when addressing an accounting issue, governmental financial statement preparers should first look to GASB statements and interpretations, followed by GASB technical bulletins, etc. From a practical standpoint, SAS 69 requires independent auditors who audit governmental entities to express an opinion as to whether the auditee has complied with GASB pronouncements. When performing a governmental audit, auditors must be mindful of generally accepted auditing standards (GAAS), as well as generally accepted governmental auditing standards (GAGAS). Both are described in the following sections.

---

* American Institute of Certified Public Accountants. (1992). Statement on Auditing Standards No. 69. The Meaning of "Fairly Presents" in the Auditor's Report. New York: AICPA.

## 12.2.2 Governmental Audits

In a governmental setting, auditing procedures must be enhanced or altered to address issues unique to governmental accounting: budgeting, compliance with laws and regulations, fund accounting, encumbrances, comparison of budget to actual statements, specific audit reports, basis of accounting, the adequacy of internal control structures, and compliance with federal grant specifications. Governmental audits may fall into a number of categories—financial audits, attestation engagements, performance audits, and compliance audits.

Financial audits primarily focus on whether an entity's financial statements are presented fairly in all material respects in conformity with generally accepted accounting principles (GAAP). They may also include an examination of special reports, the review of interim financial information, or an audit of compliance with specified regulations. Financial audits may pertain to a full Comprehensive Annual Financial Report (CAFR), or parts thereof. The output of a financial audit consists of a written report that provides an objective assessment of the fairness of the entity's reported financial information and is conducted annually or biennially.

Financial audits are performed under the American Institute of Certified Public Accountants' (AICPA) generally accepted auditing standards (GAAS),* as well as the related AICPA Statements on Auditing Standards (SAS). Additionally, auditors of governmental entities may be required to follow the General Accounting Office (GAO) "Yellow Book" standards issued by the Comptroller General of the United States and referred to as GAGAS.† State and local laws often specify the use of GAGAS within the audit engagement letter, while entities receiving federal assistance, and their auditors, are also subject to GAGAS. GAGAS prescribe additional general, field work, and reporting standards beyond those provided by the AICPA when performing governmental financial audits (discussed later in the chapter). Financial audits performed in accordance with GAGAS also provide information about internal control, compliance with laws and regulations, and provisions of contracts and grant agreements as they relate to financial transactions, systems, and processes.

Attestation engagements involve an examination, a review, or agreed-upon procedures by the auditor. The examination, review, or agreed-upon procedure focuses on a subject matter or on an assertion about a subject matter, based on or in conformity with criteria set forth by another party. Examples of attestation engagements include reporting on an entity's internal control over financial reporting; an entity's compliance with requirements of specified laws, regulations, rules, contracts, or

---

* While the AICPA initially developed the ten generally accepted auditing standards, these standards were adopted by the Public Company Accounting Oversight Board (PCAOB) that was created with the passing of the Sarbanes–Oxley Act of 2002. The PCAOB issues standards for audits of public companies.

† Some auditors refer to GAGAS simply as "GAS" (versus "GAAS"), based on the publication *Government Auditing Standards*.

grants; the effectiveness of an entity's internal control over compliance with specified requirements; management's discussion and analysis (MD&A) presentation; prospective financial statements or pro-forma financial information; the reliability of performance measures; or specific procedures performed on a subject matter (agreed-upon procedures).

Attestation engagements are performed under the AICPA's attestation standards, as well as the related AICPA Statements on Standards for Attestation Engagements (SSAE). GAGAS prescribe additional general, field work, and reporting standards beyond those provided by the AICPA for attestation engagements as well.

Performance audits involve assessment of the performance and management of government programs in terms of objective criteria or specified information. Performance audits are also referred to as program evaluations, program effectiveness and results audits, economy and efficiency audits, operational audits, and value-for-money audits. They tend to focus on the efficiency and effectiveness of operations and provide information to improve program operations, facilitate decision making by parties with responsibility to oversee or initiate corrective action, and contribute to public accountability. Performance audits will depend upon the specifics of the engagement contract; however, auditors must comply with applicable AICPA standards and GAGAS.

Compliance audits involve the assessment of compliance with criteria established by laws, regulations, contract provisions, grant agreements, and other requirements that could affect the acquisition, protection, and use of the entity's resources and the quantity, quality, timeliness, and cost of services the entity produces and delivers. The most common compliance audits fall under the Single Audit Act of 1984, which requires an audit under GAGAS.

The following sections review GAAS and GAGAS.

## 12.2.3 Generally Accepted Auditing Standards

An approved set of standards of quality for the performance of an audit have been established by the AICPA in AU Section 150. The following ten standards are applicable to all audits—whether private sector or public sector:*

- General Standards
  1. The auditor must have adequate technical training and proficiency to perform the audit.
  2. The auditor must maintain independence in mental attitude in all matters relating to the audit.
  3. The auditor must exercise due professional care in the performance of the audit and the preparation of the report.

---

* American Institute of Certified Public Accountants. (2007). *Codification of Statements on Auditing Standards*. New York: AICPA.

- Standards of Field Work
  1. The auditor must adequately plan the work and must properly supervise any assistants.
  2. The auditor must obtain a sufficient understanding of the entity and its environment, including its internal control, to assess the risk of material misstatement of the financial statements whether due to error or fraud, and to design the nature, timing, and extent of further audit procedures.
  3. The auditor must obtain sufficient appropriate audit evidence by performing audit procedures to afford a reasonable basis for an opinion regarding the financial statements under audit.
- Standards of Reporting
  1. The auditor must state in the auditor's report whether the financial statements are presented in accordance with generally accepted accounting principles (GAAP).
  2. The auditor must identify in the auditor's report those circumstances in which such principles have not been consistently observed in the current period in relation to the preceding period.
  3. When the auditor determines that informative disclosures are not reasonably adequate, the auditor must so state in the auditor's report.
  4. The auditor must either express an opinion regarding the financial statements, taken as a whole, or state that an opinion cannot be expressed, in the auditor's report. When the auditor cannot express an overall opinion, the auditor should state the reasons therefor in the auditor's report. In all cases where an auditor's name is associated with financial statements, the auditor should clearly indicate the character of the auditor's work, if any, and the degree of responsibility the auditor is taking, in the auditor's report.

As noted earlier in the chapter, auditors are required to follow the GAO generally accepted governmental auditing standards (GAGAS) on engagements that include a Single Audit or specify GAGAS in the audit contract. The GAO GAGAS are available electronically on the GAO's Web site, where they are described as follows: "The professional standards presented in this document provide a framework for performing high-quality audit work with competence, integrity, objectivity, and independence." (GAO, 2007, p. 1). GAGAS pertain to auditors' professional qualifications and the quality of their work, the performance of field work, and the characteristics of meaningful reporting. The following sections describe the unique features of GAGAS general, field work, and reporting standards.

## 12.2.4 GAGAS General Standards

GAGAS contain four general standards in addition to the three AICPA general standards. Auditors must comply with these additional standards when citing GAGAS in their audit reports. The GAGAS general standards that relate to independence, professional judgment, competence, and quality control and assurance are:*

1. In all matters related to the audit work, the audit organization and the individual auditor, whether government or public, must be free from personal, external, and organizational impairments to independence, and must avoid the appearance of such impairments of independence.
2. Auditors must use professional judgment in planning and performing audits and attestation engagements and in reporting the results.
3. The staff assigned to perform the audit or attestation engagement must collectively possess adequate professional competence for the tasks required.
4. Each audit organization performing audits and/or attestation engagements in accordance with GAGAS must:
   a. establish a system of quality control that is designed to provide the audit organization with reasonable assurance that the organization and its personnel comply with professional standards and applicable legal and regulatory requirements, and
   b. have an external peer review at least once every three years.

Under GAGAS, auditors must demonstrate professional competence by completing at least 80 hours of continuing professional education (CPE) every 2 years. CPE that would satisfy the 80-hour requirement under GAGAS should be in subjects and topics that directly enhance the auditors' professional proficiency to perform audits or attestation engagements. At least 24 of the 80 hours of CPE should be directly related to standards used in government auditing, the government environment, or the specific or unique environment in which the audited entity operates. Those who plan, direct, or report on GAGAS assignments or charge over 20% of their time to GAGAS engagements require more.

## 12.2.5 GAGAS Field Work Standards

In addition to the general standards, GAGAS also include the following field work standards related to auditor communication, considering the results of previous audits and attestation engagements, violations of contract provisions or grant agreements from abuse, and audit documentation:†

---

* United States General Accounting Office (U.S. GAO). (2007). *Government Auditing Standards.* Washington, DC: Government Printing Office, viewed September 3, 2008, <http://www.gao.gov/govaud/ybk01.htm>.
† Ibid.

1. Under AICPA standards and GAGAS, auditors should communicate with the audited entity their understanding of the services to be performed for each engagement and document that understanding through a written communication. GAGAS broaden the parties included in the communication and the items for the auditors to communicate.

2. Auditors should evaluate whether the audited entity has taken appropriate corrective action to address findings and recommendations from previous engagements that could have a material effect on the financial statements.

3. a) Auditors should design the audit to provide reasonable assurance of detecting misstatements that result from violations of provisions of contracts or grant agreements and could have a direct and material effect on the determination of financial statement amounts or other financial data significant to the audit objectives.

   b) If during the course of the audit, auditors become aware of abuse that could be quantitatively or qualitatively material to the financial statements, auditors should apply audit procedures specifically directed to ascertain the potential effect on the financial statements or other financial data significant to the audit objectives.

4. Audit findings may involve deficiencies in internal control, fraud, illegal acts, violations of provisions of contracts or grant agreements, and abuse. The elements needed for a finding depend entirely on the objectives of the audit. Thus, a finding or set of findings is complete to the extent that the audit objectives are satisfied. When auditors identify deficiencies, auditors should plan and perform procedures to develop the elements of the findings that are relevant and necessary to achieve the audit objectives.

5. Under AICPA standards and GAGAS, auditors must prepare audit documentation in connection with each audit in sufficient detail to provide a clear understanding of the work performed (including the nature, timing, extent, and results of audit procedures performed), the audit evidence obtained and its source, and the conclusions reached. Under GAGAS, auditors also should document, before the audit report is issued, evidence of supervisory review of the work performed that supports findings, conclusions, and recommendations contained in the audit report.

AICPA standards and GAGAS require auditors to establish an understanding with the client and to communicate such understanding. GAGAS broaden the parties with whom auditors must communicate and require the communication to be written. Specific information includes the nature of planned work and reliance on internal controls, as well as any potential restriction of the auditors' reports, to reduce the risk that the needs or expectations of the parties involved might be misinterpreted.

During the planning stages, auditors must recognize that laws and regulations sometimes prescribe supplemental testing and reporting on internal control over financial reporting and compliance with laws and regulations. As part of the planning process, they should ask audited entity officials to identify previous financial audits, attestation engagements, performance audits, or other studies related to the objectives of the audit being undertaken and to use such information in assessing risk and scheduling audit tests.

AICPA standards and GAGAS require auditors to assess the risk of material misstatements of financial statement amounts or other financial data. GAGAS expressly address contracts and grant agreements. If violations come to the auditors' attention, audit procedures might need to be enhanced, especially if the violations affect financial statement balances. Furthermore, GAGAS define abuse as "behavior that is deficient or improper when compared with behavior that a prudent person would consider reasonable and necessary business practice given the facts and circumstances." Auditors who note abusive behavior should assess the potential for fraud or illegal acts. Section 4.14 – 4.18 discusses "findings" related to fraud, illegal acts, or other deficiencies and violations.

## 12.2.6 GAGAS Reporting Standards

GAGAS prescribe additional reporting standards for financial audits that go beyond the requirements contained in GAAS. Auditors must comply with these additional standards when citing GAGAS in their audit reports. The additional GAGAS reporting standards relate to:*

1. Reporting auditors' compliance with GAGAS
2. Reporting on internal control and on compliance with laws, regulations, and provisions of contracts or grant agreements
3. Reporting deficiencies in internal control, fraud, illegal acts, violations of provisions of contracts or grant agreements, and abuse
4. Communicating significant matters in the auditors' report
5. Reporting on the restatement of previously issued financial statements
6. Reporting views of responsible officials
7. Reporting confidential or sensitive information
8. Reporting distribution

While the majority of these GAGAS reporting standards have a minor effect on the report, the reporting on internal control and on compliance, as well as reporting on deficiencies, are both integral parts of governmental reporting. Auditors should include in their financial statement report either a (1) description of the scope of the

---

* United States General Accounting Office (U.S. GAO). (2007). *Government Auditing Standards*. Washington, DC: Government Printing Office, viewed September 3, 2008, <http://www.gao.gov/govaud/ybk01.htm>.

auditors' testing of internal control over financial reporting and compliance with laws, regulations, and provisions of contracts or grant agreements and the results of those tests or an opinion, if sufficient work was performed, or (2) reference to the separate report(s) containing that information. If auditors report separately, the opinion or disclaimer should contain a reference to the separate report containing this information and state that the separate report is an integral part of the audit and should be considered in assessing the results of the audit.

GAGAS also require auditors to report internal control deficiencies considered to be significant as defined in AICPA standards. In addition to significant internal control deficiencies and material weaknesses, governmental auditors are also required to report all instances of fraud and illegal acts unless clearly inconsequential, as well as significant violations of provisions of contracts, or grant agreements and abuse. In addition to the adherence of GAGAS standards, auditors also have other issues that are unique to governmental audits such as the financial reporting entity, the single audit, audit reporting, the selection of an auditor, and consideration of nonaudit services. These issues are described in the following sections.

## 12.3 Various Other Auditing Issues

### 12.3.1 Financial Reporting Entity

When performing a governmental audit, auditors must clearly define the entity under audit. Organizations that are closely related to, or financially integrated with, the primary government should be evaluated as potential component units. According to GASB-14, a legally separate potential component unit should be included in the financial reporting entity if the primary government can appoint a voting majority of the potential unit's governing board and either impose its will on the potential component unit or have a financial benefit or burden imposed upon it by the potential component unit. Whether a potential component unit warrants inclusion in the reporting entity is a matter of professional judgment. To determine if a potential component unit should be treated as a component unit, an auditor will answer a number of questions (provided in GASB-14) regarding the appointment process, imposition of will, and financial benefit or burden.

According to GASB-14, the potential component units may be presented in the financial reporting entity's financial statements in two ways: (1) blended into the appropriate fund structure of the primary government or (2) reported in a discrete presentation within the financial reporting entity's financial statements. To determine which method to use, answer the following questions: Is the component unit's governing board substantially the same as the primary government's governing board? Does the component unit provide services entirely, or almost entirely, to the primary government or otherwise exclusively, or almost exclusively, benefit the primary government even though it does not provide services directly to it? If the answer to either of these questions is yes, then the blending method should be used to include a component unit in the reporting entity's financial statements.

According to GASB-39, an amendment of GASB Statement No. 14, the legally separate, tax-exempt organization should be discretely presented as a component unit of a financial reporting entity if *all* of the following criteria are met: (1) the economic resources received or held by the separate organization are entirely or almost entirely for the direct benefit of the primary government, its component units, or its constituents; (2) the primary government, or its component units, is entitled to, or has the ability to otherwise access, a majority of the economic resources received or held by the separate organization; (3) the economic resources received or held by an *individual organization* that the specific primary government, or its component units, is entitled to, or has the ability to otherwise access, are significant to that primary government.

## 12.3.2 The Single Audit

The aforementioned single audit replaced the numerous grant-by-grant audits that state and local governments were previously subjected to by various federal and state audit agencies as well as independent public accountants. In addition to providing users of state and local government financial statements with assurance that the financial statements are fairly presented, the single audit also provides these users with important information regarding the internal control structure of governments and their compliance with applicable laws and regulations. Single audits are mandated for state and local governments expending more than $500,000 in federal financial assistance by the Single Audit Act of 1984—as amended in 1996 and implemented by OMB Circular A-133. A single audit is optional for governments expending less than $500,000 in federal financial assistance; however, records must be available for review or audit by appropriate officials of the federal agency, pass-through entity, and General Accounting Office (GAO).

The objectives of the Single Audit Act, as amended, are to:*

- Promote sound financial management, including effective internal controls, with respect to federal awards administered by nonfederal entities
- Establish uniform requirements for audits of federal awards administered by nonfederal entities
- Promote the efficient and effective use of audit resources
- Reduce burdens on state and local governments, Indian tribes, and non-profit organizations
- Ensure that federal departments and agencies, to the maximum extent practicable, rely on and use audit work done pursuant to the act

---

* United States General Accounting Office (U.S. GAO). (2000). *Single Audit—Update on the Implementation of the Single Audit Act Amendments of 1996*. Washington, DC: Government Printing Office, viewed June 6, 2005, <http://www.gao.gov/archive/2000/ai00293.pdf>.

Entities that fall under the Single Audit Act are required to submit audit reports issued by an independent auditor to the federal government agency designated as their oversight or cognizant agency.* The Single Audit Act shifted the audit responsibility from the federal funding agencies to the governmental entities, thus increasing the demand for audits by independent auditors. Guidance for federal grantees and auditors involved with Single Audit Act compliance may be found in a comprehensive guide known as the Compliance Supplement, published by the U.S. Office of Management and Budget. When determining the compliance requirements that could have a direct and material effect on various programs, use of this supplement is mandatory, and adherence to the supplement satisfies the requirements of OMB Circular A-133. Therefore, this Compliance Supplement eliminates the need for auditors to research individually many laws and regulations for each program under audit and provides a more efficient and effective approach to performing this research. The following seven parts are contained in the supplement: (1) Background, Purpose, and Applicability; (2) Matrix of Compliance Requirements; (3) Compliance Requirements; (4) Agency Program Requirements; (5) Clusters of Programs; (6) Internal Control; and (7) Guidance for Auditing Programs Not Included in This Compliance Supplement.

The audit focus of the act is on major federal financial assistance programs (MFAP). In order to determine the MFAPs, the auditor employs a risk-based approach that contains four steps. Step 1 requires identification of the larger federal programs known as Type A programs. The OMB A-133 defines these as federal programs with federal awards expended during the audit period of the larger of: (1) $300,000 or 3% (0.03) of total federal awards expended in the case of an auditee for which total federal awards expended equal or exceed $300,000 but are less than or equal to $100 million; (2) $3 million or 0.3% (0.003) of total federal awards expended in the case of an auditee for which total federal awards expended exceed $100 million but are less than or equal to $10 billion; (3) $30 million or 0.15% (0.0015) of total federal awards expended in the case of an auditee for which total federal awards expended exceed $10 billion. If a program is smaller and does not meet the criteria to be qualified as a Type A program, then it is known as a Type B program.

In the second step of the risk-based approach, it is necessary for the auditor to identify low-risk Type A programs. In order to potentially reduce audit coverage and be considered a low-risk auditee under OMB Circular A-133, all of the following criteria must apply for each of the preceding two years: (1) the performance of single audits on an annual basis; (2) unqualified opinions of the financial statements and the schedule of expenditures of federal awards; (3) no material weaknesses in

---

* According to OMB Circular A-133, an oversight agency is assigned to an organization that expends $50 million or less in federal awards, or includes no direct awards. A cognizant agency is assigned to organizations that expend more than $50 million in federal awards and includes direct awards.

internal control under GAGAS requirements; and (4) no material weakness, material noncompliance, or questioned cost (known or likely that exceed 5% of the total federal awards expended) audit findings from Type A federal programs. The exception to these basic requirements is that the cognizant or oversight agency may provide a waiver for the first three requirements. The third step involves the identification of high-risk Type B programs by using professional judgment and the federal program risk criteria in section 525 of the OMB A-133.

Finally, the auditor is required to audit, at a minimum, all of the following as major programs: (1) all Type A programs, except the auditor may exclude any Type A programs identified as low-risk under Step 2; (2) high-risk Type B programs as identified under either of the following two options: (A) Option 1—at least one half of the Type B programs identified as high-risk under Step 3, except the auditor is not required to audit more high-risk Type B programs than the number of low-risk Type A programs identified under Step 2 and (B) Option 2—one high-risk Type B program for each Type A program identified as low-risk under Step 2; and (3) such additional programs as may be necessary to comply with the percentage of coverage rule. This may require the auditor to audit more programs as major than the number of Type A programs. Under the percentage of coverage rule, the auditor is required to audit as major programs any federal programs with federal awards expended that, in the aggregate, encompass at least 50% of total federal awards expended. If the auditee meets the criteria for a low-risk auditee, the major programs audited must, in the aggregate, encompass at least 25% of total federal awards expended (OMB A-133, 2003).

Reporting on the compliance of OMB Circular A-133 can be quite burdensome. The Federal Audit Clearinghouse is in place to help minimize this burden for auditors and auditees and can be located on the Web at harvester.census.gov/sac/. Federal cognizant and oversight agencies can obtain OMB Circular A-133 data and reporting packages through this clearinghouse, which is in place to function on behalf of the U.S. Office of Management and Budget. In addition to these primary purposes, the clearinghouse disseminates audit information to federal agencies and the public, as well as supports the OMB with oversight and assessment of federal award audit requirements.

### 12.3.3 Audit Reports

Generally accepted auditing standards require auditors to express an opinion on the basic financial statements, which in the governmental setting include government-wide financial statements, fund financial statements, and notes to the financial statements as well as required supplementary information (RSI) and management's discussion and analysis (MD&A). The audit report addresses the fairness of the financial statements presented in conformity with GAAP. Government Auditing Standards (GAS) also require the auditor to issue written reports on the auditee's compliance with laws and regulations and internal controls associated with the basic financial statements and a report on fraud, mismanagement, abuse, or illegal acts. While these reports are not opinion reports, they can offer important information to third parties trying to evaluate the auditee's management style and abilities.

In the case of a single audit, audit report(s) may be presented in combination or separately and are required to state that the audit was conducted in accordance with OMB Circular A-133. In addition, the audit reports must include the following: (a) an opinion on the financial statements and the schedule of expenditures of federal awards; (b) report(s) on internal control; (c) report(s) on compliance; and (d) a schedule of findings and questioned costs (if applicable).

The AICPA Audit and Accounting Guide, *State and Local Governments*, provides several examples of the form and content of various audit reports. Sample standard audit reports from a city and county are provided in the Appendices to this chapter. Appendix A illustrates a standard unqualified opinion on basic financial statements accompanied by supplementary information. Note that the report references GAGAS (if appropriate) and refers to a report on internal controls. Two such reports are illustrated in Appendices B and C. One of the reports addresses compliance and controls over financial reporting, while the other focuses on compliance and controls applicable to major programs under a single audit.

## 12.3.4 Auditor Selection and the Request for Proposal Process

Auditor selection processes can serve a vital role in ensuring a quality governmental audit. Given prior problems with governmental audit quality and their apparent link to the audit procurement process, a formal request for proposal (RFP) is recommended for local governments that have adequate resources. Requests for proposals should describe accounting-related characteristics of the governmental entity and detail the scope of audit services being requested, as well as the specific qualifications desired of audit firms responding to the RFP. An RFP should be widely dispersed to qualified audit firms and advertised in local business and professional periodicals. An outline of the contents of a RFP appears in Exhibit 12.1.

The introductory section typically includes information about the governmental entity and the audit. Some governments, primarily those with large, complex audits, require that a local or minority audit firm be subcontracted for portions of the audit. A section outlining the details of the audit should also be included. It will cover the scope of services contained in the proposal (financial audit, single audit, and any additional compliance auditing), the auditing standards to be followed (GAAS, GAGAS, or state-mandated standards), reports to be issued, assistance to be provided to the auditor, and other considerations, such as working paper retention and access to working papers.

The government seeking an audit should also be described in the RFP. Summary financial data (e.g., total revenues, number of funds, component units) and accounting function staff characteristics should be disclosed. Prospective auditors will also be interested in the availability of prior financial reports and records, including

**Exhibit 12.1—Sample Outline for Governmental Audit RFP**

**I. INTRODUCTION**
A. General Information
B. Term of the Engagement
C. Subcontracting to Local or Minority Firms

**II. NATURE OF SERVICES REQUIRED**
A. Scope of Services
B. Auditing Standards to Be Followed
C. Reports to Be Issued
D. Assistance to Be Provided to the Auditor
E. Special Considerations
F. Component Unit(s)
G. Working Paper Retention and Access to Working Papers

**III. DESCRIPTION OF GOVERNMENT**
A. City Contact Information
B. Background Information
C. Fund Structure and Account Groups
D. Pension Plans
E. Availability of Prior Reports

**IV. TIME REQUIREMENTS**
A. Proposal Calendar
B. Schedule for Annual Audit
   1) Interim Work
   2) Detail Audit Plan and Programs
   3) Field work
   4) Draft Reports
C. Entrance Conferences, Progress Reporting, and Exit Conferences

**V. PROPOSAL REQUIREMENTS**
A. Submission of Proposals
B. Technical Proposals
   1) General Requirements Format
   2) Independence
   3) License to Practice in the State
   4) Insurance Requirements
   5) Firm Qualifications and Experience
   6) Partners, Supervisory, and Staff Qualifications and Experience
   7) Similar Engagements with Other Governmental Entities
   8) Participation in Peer Review Program
   9) Workload
   10) Audit Approach
   11) Identification of Potential Audit Problems
   12) Manner of Payment
   13) Audit Fees

**VI. EVALUATION PROCEDURES**
A. Selection Committee
B. Evaluation Criteria
   1) Mandatory Elements
   2) Technical Qualifications
   3) Responses of References
   4) Cost
C. Oral Presentations
D. Final Selection
E. Right to Reject Proposals

journal entries, as well as management letters issued and pension plan information. Engagement specifics, such as the timing of the audit, work schedules, estimated hours, prior year audit fees, and due date are also important.

The governmental entity should also specify the required qualifications of the auditing firm, in terms of experience, staff size, licensing and training, and independence. Entity officials may require both a written and an oral presentation of proposed audit services. If available, evaluation criteria should be provided within the RFP. The Government Finance Officers Association (GFOA) has made the following recommendations regarding the selection of auditing services:*

- ◼ The scope of the independent audit should encompass not only the fair presentation of the basic financial statements, but also the fair presentation of the financial statements of individual funds and component units.
- ◼ Governmental entities should require in their audit contracts that the auditors of their financial statements conform to the independence standard promulgated in the GAO's *Government Auditing Standards* even for audit engagements that are not otherwise subject to generally accepted government auditing standards.
- ◼ Governmental entities should enter into multiyear agreements of at least five years in duration when obtaining the services of independent auditors. Such multiyear agreements can take a variety of different forms (e.g., a series of single-year contracts), consistent with applicable legal requirements.
- ◼ Governmental entities should undertake a full-scale competitive process for the selection of independent auditors at the end of the term of each audit contract, consistent with applicable legal requirements.
- ◼ Professional standards allow independent auditors to perform certain types of nonaudit services for their audit clients. Any significant nonaudit services should always be approved in advance by a governmental entity's audit committee.
- ◼ The audit procurement process should be structured so that the principal factor in the selection of an independent auditor is the auditor's ability to perform a quality audit. In no case should price be allowed to serve as the sole criterion for the selection of an independent auditor.

Mandatory audit rotation is a controversial topic in government, as well as in the private sector. The complexity of governmental engagements requires knowledge of governmental GAAP and any state or local rules with which an audit must comply. With this in mind, the GFOA suggests multiyear agreements of five years or more to allow for continuity, reduce disruption, and reduce audit costs. There is also the school of thought that audit quality is increased with rotation; however, when considering this debate, it is important to recognize the apparent lack of adequate competition among audit firms qualified to perform public-sector audits.

## 12.3.5 Nonaudit Services

Many audit organizations offer professional services (nonaudit services) in addition to financial audits, attestation engagements, and performance audits. Audit organizations that provide nonaudit services must be especially mindful of maintaining

---

* Gauthier, S.J. (1992). *An Elected Official's Guide to Auditing*. Chicago: Government Finance Officers Association.

independence in fact and appearance. As defined in GAGAS, nonaudit services may include providing information or data to a requesting party without auditor evaluation or verification of the information or data, providing assistance and technical expertise to legislative bodies or independent external organizations, or providing oversight assistance in reviewing budget submissions.

Since nonaudit services could potentially impact the independence of an audit firm conducting a financial statement audit, GAGAS provide guidance regarding nonaudit services for a governmental client in the form of two overarching principles and four safeguards. The overarching principles state that audit firms should not (1) provide nonaudit services that involve performing management functions or making management decisions, or (2) audit their own work or provide nonaudit services in situations where the nonaudit services are significant/material to the subject matter of audits. If the audit firm determines that these principles have not been violated, personnel must then comply with the following safeguards:*

1. The audit organization should document its consideration of the nonaudit services, including its conclusions about the impact on independence.
2. Before performing nonaudit services, the audit organization should establish in writing an understanding with the audited entity regarding the objectives, scope of work, and product or deliverables of the nonaudit service. The audit organization should also establish and document an understanding with management that management is responsible for (1) the subject matter of the nonaudit services, (2) the substantive outcomes of the work, and (3) making any decisions that involve management functions related to the nonaudit service and accepting full responsibility for such decisions.
3. The audit organization should exclude personnel who provided the nonaudit services from planning, conducting, or reviewing audit work of subject matter involving the nonaudit service.
4. The audit organization is precluded from reducing the scope and extent of the audit work below the level that would be appropriate if the nonaudit work were performed by an unrelated party.

Audit firms are advised to document their assessment of independence issues surrounding nonaudit services and to review the status of their independence periodically. Additional guidance regarding independence and quality control is included in the Yellow Book's appendix. Examples of acceptable and unacceptable audit firm services appear in Appendix D.

---

* United States General Accounting Office (U.S. GAO). (2007). *Government Auditing Standards.* Washington, DC: Government Printing Office, viewed September 4, 2008, <http://www.gao.gov/govaud/ybk01.htm>.

## 12.4 Summary

Financial statement, attestation, and compliance audits of governmental entities are mandated by state and/or federal regulations. Inconsistent financial reporting and unacceptable audit quality warranted the establishment of specialized accounting principles and auditing to handle the unique nature of governmental entities. This chapter has provided an overview of current governmental accounting principles and auditing standards, as well as a historical perspective of their development. Generally accepted auditing standards were compared to generally accepted governmental auditing standards, and the chapter concluded with a discussion of the following auditing issues—the financial reporting entity, the single audit, audit reporting, auditor selection, and acceptable (non)audit services for governmental organizations.

## References

American Institute of Certified Public Accountants (AICPA). (1987). *Report of the Task Force on the Quality of Audits of Governmental Units*. New York: AICPA.

_____. (1992). *Statement on Auditing Standards No. 69. The Meaning of "Fairly Presents" in the Auditor's Report*. New York: AICPA.

_____. (2007). *State and Local Governments*, Audit and Accounting Guide. New York: AICPA.

_____. (2007). *Codification of Statements on Auditing Standards*. New York: AICPA.

_____. (2008). Governmental Audit Quality Center, viewed September 4, 2008, <http://gaqc.aicpa.org/>.

Broadus, W.A. Jr. (2004). *Governmental Accounting and Auditing Update*. Lewisville, TX: AICPA Publications.

Federal Audit Clearinghouse Home Page 2004, U.S. Census Bureau, Governments Division, Federal Programs Branch, viewed May 12, 2005, <http://harvester.census.gov/sac/>.

Gauthier, S.J. (1992). *An Elected Official's Guide to Auditing*. Chicago: Government Finance Officers Association.

_____. (1980). *Audit Management Guide*. Chicago: Government Finance Officers Association.

Governmental Accounting Standards Board (GASB). *Statement No. 14, The Financial Reporting Entity*. (1991). Norwalk, CT: Governmental Accounting Standards Board.

_____. (1999). *Statement No. 34, Basic Financial Statements—and Management's Discussion and Analysis—for State and Local Governments*. (1999). Norwalk, CT: Governmental Accounting Standards Board.

_____. *Statement No. 39, Basic Determining Whether Certain Organizations Are Component Units—An Amendment of GASB Statement No. 14*. (2002). Norwalk, CT: Governmental Accounting Standards Board.

Government Finance Officers Association of the United States and Canada. *Governmental Accounting, Auditing, and Financial Reporting*. (2005). Chicago: Municipal Finance Officers Association of the United States and Canada.

National Council on Government Accounting. *Governmental Accounting and Financial Reporting Principles, Statement 1*. (1979). Chicago: Municipal Finance Officers Association of the United States and Canada.

Previts, G.J. and B.D. Merino. (1979). *A History of Accounting in America, An Historical Interpretation of the Cultural Significance of Accounting*. New York: John Wiley & Sons.

U.S. Office of Management and Budget. OMB Circular A-133 Compliance Supplement March 2003, viewed May 10, 2005, <http://www.whitehouse.gov/omb/circulars/ a133_compliance/ 03/03toc.Html>.

_____. (June 2003) OMB Circular A-133, Office of Management and Budget, viewed May 24, 2005, <http://www.whitehouse.gov/omb/circulars/a133/a133.pdf>.

United States General Accounting Office (U.S. GAO). (1986). *CPA Quality: Many Governmental Audits Do Not Comply with Professional Standards. AFMD 86-33*. Washington, DC: Government Printing Office.

_____. (1987). *CPA Audit Quality: A Framework for Procuring Audit Services*. Washington, DC: Government Printing Office.

_____. (2000). *Single Audit—Update on the Implementation of the Single Audit Act Amendments of 1996*. Washington, DC: Government Printing Office, viewed June 6, 2005, <http://www.gao.gov/archive/2000/ai00293.pdf>.

_____. (2003). *Government Auditing Standards*. Washington, DC: Government Printing Office, viewed May 12, 2005, <http://www.gao.gov/ govaud/ybk01.htm>.

## Appendix A

*Unqualified Independent Auditor's Report on Basic Financial Statements Accompanied by Required Supplementary Information and Supplementary Information\**

[*Addressee*]

We have audited the accompanying financial statements of the governmental activities, the business-type activities, the aggregate discretely presented component units, each major fund, and the aggregate remaining fund information of the City of Example, Any State, as of and for the year ended [financial statement date], which collectively comprise the City's basic financial statements as listed in the table of contents. These financial statements are the responsibility of the City of Example's management. Our responsibility is to express opinions on these financial statements based on our audit.

We conducted our audit in accordance with auditing standards generally accepted in the United States and the standards applicable to financial audits contained in Government Auditing Standards, issued by the Comptroller General of the United States. Those standards require that we plan and perform the audit to obtain reasonable assurance about whether the financial statements are free of material misstatement. We were not engaged to perform an audit of the City's internal control over financial reporting. Our audit included consideration of internal control over financial reporting as a basis for designing audit procedures that are appropriate in the circumstances, but not for the purpose of expressing an opinion on the effectiveness of the City's internal control over financial reporting. Accordingly, we express no such opinion. An audit includes examining, on a test basis, evidence supporting the amounts and disclosures in the financial statements, assessing the accounting principles used and the significant estimates made by management, and evaluating the overall financial statement presentation. We believe that our audit provides a reasonable basis for our opinions.

In our opinion, the financial statements referred to above present fairly, in all material respects, the respective financial position of the governmental activities, the business-type activities, the aggregate discretely presented component units, each major fund, and the aggregate remaining fund information of the City as of [financial statement date], and the respective changes in financial position, and, where applicable, cash flows thereof for the year then ended in conformity with accounting principles generally accepted in the United States.

---

\* This sample audit report was found within the City of Orlando's September 30, 2007, Comprehensive Annual Financial Report, viewed September 4, 2008, <http://www.cityoforlando.net/admin/accounting/PDFs/2007CAFR.pdf>. The City and Auditor names were removed.

In accordance with Government Auditing Standards, we have also issued our report dated [date of report] on our consideration of the City's internal control over financial reporting and on our tests of its compliance with certain provisions of laws, regulations, contracts, and grant agreements and other matters. The purpose of that report is to describe the scope of our testing of internal control over financial reporting and compliance and the results of that testing, and not to provide an opinion on the internal control over financial reporting or on compliance. That report is an integral part of an audit performed in accordance with Government Auditing Standards and should be considered in assessing the results of our audit.

Management's discussion and analysis, the budget to actual comparison–major funds (general and special revenue), and the schedules of funding progress and employer contributions listed under required supplemental information in the table of contents are not a required part of the basic financial statements but are supplementary information required by the Governmental Accounting Standards Board. We have applied certain limited procedures, which consisted principally of inquiries of management regarding the methods of measurement and presentation of the required supplementary information. However, we did not audit the information and express no opinion on it.

Our audit was conducted for the purpose of forming opinions on the financial statements that collectively comprise the City's basic financial statements. The introductory section, combining financial statements, supplementary information, and statistical section listed in the table of contents are presented for purposes of additional analysis and are not a required part of the basic financial statements. The combining financial statements have been subjected to the auditing procedures applied in the audit of the basic financial statements and, in our opinion, are fairly stated in all material respects in relation to the basic financial statements taken as a whole. The information presented in the introductory, supplementary, and statistical sections have not been subjected to the auditing procedures applied in the audit of the basic financial statements and, accordingly, we express no opinion on them.

---

[Audit Firm Signature]

---

[Audit Firm Location]

---

[Date]

# Appendix B

*Independent Auditors' Report on Internal Control over Financial Reporting and on Compliance and Other Matters Based on an Audit of Financial Statements Performed in Accordance With Government Auditing Standards\**

[*Addressee*]

We have audited the financial statements of the governmental activities, the business-type activities, the aggregate discretely presented component units, each major fund, and the aggregate remaining fund information of the City, as of and for the year ended [financial statement date], which collectively comprise the City's basic financial statements, and have issued our report thereon dated [audit report date]. We conducted our audit in accordance with auditing standards generally accepted in the United States and the standards applicable to financial audits contained in Government Auditing Standards, issued by the Comptroller General of the United States.

## Internal Control over Financial Reporting

In planning and performing our audit, we considered the City's internal control over financial reporting as a basis for designing our auditing procedures for the purpose of expressing our opinion on the financial statements but not for the purpose of expressing an opinion on the effectiveness of the City's internal control over financial reporting. Accordingly, we do not express an opinion on the effectiveness of the City's internal control over financial reporting.

A control deficiency exists when the design or operation of a control does not allow management or employees, in the normal course of performing their assigned functions, to prevent or detect misstatements on a timely basis. A significant deficiency is a control deficiency, or combination of control deficiencies, that adversely affects the entity's ability to initiate, authorize, record, process, or report financial data reliably in accordance with generally accepted accounting principles such that there is more than a remote likelihood that a misstatement of the entity's financial statements that is more than inconsequential will not be prevented or detected by the entity's internal control.

---

\* This sample audit report was found within the City of Orlando's September 30, 2007, Comprehensive Annual Financial Report, viewed September 4, 2008, <http://www.city-oforlando.net/admin/accounting/PDFs/2007CAFR.pdf>. The City and Auditor names were removed.

A material weakness is a significant deficiency, or combination of significant deficiencies, that results in more than a remote likelihood that a material misstatement of the financial statements will not be prevented or detected by the entity's internal control.

Our consideration of internal control over financial reporting was for the limited purpose described in the first paragraph of this section and would not necessarily identify all deficiencies in internal control that might be significant deficiencies or material weaknesses. We did not identify any deficiencies in internal control over financial reporting that we consider to be material weaknesses, as defined above.

## Compliance and Other Matters

As part of obtaining reasonable assurance about whether the City's financial statements are free of material misstatement, we performed tests of its compliance with certain provisions of laws, regulations, contracts, and grant agreements, noncompliance with which could have a direct and material effect on the determination of financial statement amounts. However, providing an opinion on compliance with those provisions was not an objective of our audit and, accordingly, we do not express such an opinion. The results of our tests disclosed no instances of noncompliance or other matters that are required to be reported under Government Auditing Standards.

We noted certain matters that we reported to management of the City in a separate letter dated January 24, 2008.

This report is intended solely for the information and use of the Mayor and Members of the City Council, management, applicable federal and state grantor and pass-through agencies, and the Auditor General, State of Florida, and is not intended to be and should not be used by anyone other than these specified parties.

---

[Audit Firm Signature]

---

[Audit Firm Location]

---

[Date]

## Appendix C

*Independent Auditors' Report on Compliance with Requirements Applicable to Each Major Program and Internal Control over Compliance in Accordance with OMB Circular A-133\**

[*Addressee*]

### Compliance

We have audited the compliance of the County with the types of compliance requirements described in the *U.S. Office of Management and Budget (OMB) Circular A-133 Compliance Supplement* that are applicable to its major federal programs for the year ended [financial statement date]. The County's major federal programs are identified in the summary of audit results section of the accompanying schedule of findings and questioned costs. Compliance with the requirements of laws, regulations, contracts and grants applicable to its major federal program is the responsibility of the County's management. Our responsibility is to express an opinion on the compliance of the County based on our audit.

We conducted our audit of compliance in accordance with auditing standards generally accepted in the United States of America; the standards applicable to financial audits contained in *Government Auditing Standards*, issued by the Comptroller General of the United States; and OMB Circular A-133, *Audits of States, Local Governments, and Non-Profit Organizations*. Those standards and OMB Circular A-133 require that we plan and perform the audit to obtain reasonable assurance about whether noncompliance with the types of compliance requirements referred to above that could have a direct and material effect on a major federal program occurred. An audit includes examining, on a test basis, evidence about the County's compliance with those requirements and performing such other procedures as we considered necessary in the circumstances. We believe that our audit provides a reasonable basis for our opinion. Our audit does not provide a legal determination on the County's compliance with those requirements.

In our opinion, the County complied, in all material respects, with the requirements referred to above that are applicable to its major federal programs for the year ended [financial statement date].

---

[*] This sample audit report was found within the Salt Lake County, Utah Supplemental Report in Compliance with Government Reporting Standards and OMB Circular A-133 for December 31, 2007, viewed September 4, 2008, <http://www.slcoaud.org/pdf/mgtbudget/SingleAudit/2007SingleAudit.pdf>. The County and Auditor names were removed.

## Internal Control over Compliance

The management of the County is responsible for establishing and maintaining effective internal control over compliance with the requirements of laws, regulations, contracts, and grants applicable to federal programs. In planning and performing our audit, we considered the County's internal control over compliance with requirements that could have a direct and material effect on a major federal program in order to determine our auditing procedures for the purpose of expressing our opinion on compliance, but not for the purpose of expressing an opinion on the effectiveness of internal control over compliance.

Accordingly, we do not express an opinion on the effectiveness of the County's internal control over compliance.

A control deficiency in an entity's internal control over compliance exists when the design or operation of a control does not allow management or employees, in the normal course of performing their assigned functions, to prevent or detect noncompliance with a type of compliance requirement of a federal program on a timely basis. A significant deficiency is a control deficiency, or combination of control deficiencies, that adversely affects the County's ability to administer a federal program such that there is more than a remote likelihood that noncompliance with a type of compliance requirement of a federal program that is more than inconsequential will not be prevented or detected by the County's internal control.

A material weakness is a significant deficiency, or combination of significant deficiencies, that results in more than a remote likelihood that material noncompliance with a type of compliance requirement of a federal program will not be prevented or detected by the entity's internal control.

Our consideration of internal control over compliance was for the limited purpose described in the preceding paragraph and would not necessarily identify all deficiencies in internal control that might be deficiencies or material weaknesses. We did not identify any deficiencies in internal control over compliance that we consider to be material weaknesses, as defined above.

## Schedule of Expenditures of Federal Awards

We have audited the financial statements of the governmental activities, the business-type activities, the aggregate discretely presented component units, each major fund, and the aggregate remaining fund information of the County as of and for the year ended December 31, 200X. Our audit was performed for the purpose of forming opinions on the financial statements that collectively comprise the basic financial statements of the County. The accompanying schedule of expenditures of federal awards is presented for purposes of additional analysis as required by OMB Circular A-133 and is not a required part of the basic financial statements. Such information has been subjected to the auditing procedures applied in the audit of the basic financial statements and, in our opinion, is fairly stated, in all material respects, in relation to the basic financial statements taken as a whole.

This report is intended solely for the information and use of County management, federal awarding agencies, state funding agencies, and pass-through entities and is not intended to be and should not be used by anyone other than these specified parties.

---

[Audit Firm Signature]

---

[Audit Firm Location]

---

[Date]

# Appendix D

## *Examples of Acceptable and Unacceptable Nonaudit Services (GAGAS Section 3)*

### Acceptable Nonaudit Services Examples

Auditors may provide basic accounting assistance limited to services such as preparing draft financial statements that are based on management's chart of accounts and trial balance and any adjusting, correcting, and closing entries that have been approved by management; preparing draft notes to the financial statements based on information determined and approved by management; preparing a trial balance based on management's chart of accounts; maintaining depreciation schedules for which management has determined the method of depreciation, rate of depreciation, and salvage value of the asset.

Auditors may provide payroll services when payroll is not material to the subject matter of the audit or to the audit objectives. Such services are limited to using records and data that have been approved by entity management.

Auditors may provide appraisal or valuation services limited to services such as reviewing the work of the entity or a specialist employed by the entity where the entity or specialist provides the primary evidence for the balances recorded in financial statements or other information that will be audited; valuing an entity's pension, other postemployment benefit, or similar liabilities provided management has determined and taken responsibility for all significant assumptions and data.

Auditors may prepare an entity's indirect cost proposal or cost allocation plan provided the amounts are not material and management assumes responsibility for all significant assumptions and data.

Auditors may provide advisory services on information technology limited to services such as advising on system design, system installation, and system security if management acknowledges responsibility for the design, installation, and internal control over the entity's system and does not rely on the auditors' work as the primary basis for determining (1) whether to implement a new system, (2) the adequacy of the new system design, (3) the adequacy of major design changes to an existing system, and (4) the adequacy of the system to comply with regulatory or other requirements.

Auditors may provide human resource services to assist management in its evaluation of potential candidates when the services are limited to activities such as serving on an evaluation panel of at least three individuals to review applications or interviewing candidates to provide input to management in arriving at a listing of best qualified applicants to be provided to management.

Auditors may prepare routine tax filings in accordance with federal tax laws, rules, and regulations of the Internal Revenue Service, and state and local tax based on information provided by the audited entity.

## Unacceptable Nonaudit Services Examples

Auditors may not maintain or prepare the audited entity's basic accounting records or maintain or take responsibility for basic financial or other records that the audit organization will audit.

Auditors cannot determine account balances, determine capitalization criteria or provide payroll services that (1) are material to the subject matter of the audit or the audit objectives, and/or (2) involve making management decisions.

Auditors cannot recommend a single individual for a specific position that is key to the entity or program under audit, otherwise ranking or influencing management's selection of the candidate, or conducting an executive search or a recruiting program for the audited entity.

An audit organization cannot develop an entity's policies, procedures, and internal controls or perform management's assessment of internal controls when those controls are significant to the subject matter of the audit.

Auditors may not provide services that are intended to be used as management's primary basis for making decisions that are significant to the subject matter under audit.

An audit organization cannot be responsible for designing, developing, installing, or operating the entity's accounting system or other information systems that are material or significant to the subject matter of the audit.

An audit organization cannot develop an entity's performance measurement system when that system is material or significant to the subject matter of the audit.

The audit organization cannot maintain or prepare the audited entity's basic accounting records or maintain or take responsibility for basic financial or other records that the audit organization will audit.

Auditors should not post transactions (whether coded or not coded) to the entity's financial records or to other records that subsequently provide data to the entity's financial records.

Auditors should not serve as voting members of an entity's management committee or board of directors, make policy decisions that affect future direction and operation of an entity's programs, supervise entity employees, develop programmatic policy, authorize an entity's transactions, or maintain custody of an entity's assets.

# Chapter 13

# Federal Accounting and Financial Reporting

## Richard Fontenrose
*Federal Accounting Standards Advisory Board, Washington D.C.*

## Contents

13.1 Historical Background ................................................................. 440
    13.1.1 Government Corporation Control Act of 1945 ........................ 444
    13.1.2 The Budget and Accounting Procedures Act of 1950 ................ 445
    13.1.3 Report of the President's Commission on Budget Concepts
        of 1967 ........................................................................ 446
    13.1.4 Chief Financial Officers Act of 1990 (CFO Act) ...................... 446
    13.1.5 Federal Accounting Standards Advisory Board ........................ 447
    13.1.6 Final Note on JFMIP ....................................................... 448
13.2 Key Objectives of Federal Financial Reporting .............................. 448
    13.2.1 Objectives of Federal Accounting ....................................... 452
    13.2.2 Objectives of the Federal Accounting Standards Advisory
        Board ........................................................................... 453
    13.2.3 Other FASAB Concepts Statements ..................................... 455
    13.2.4 Statements of Federal Financial Accounting Standards ............. 456
13.3 Agencies Responsible for Federal Accounting and Reporting ............. 457
    13.3.1 Federal Accounting Standards Advisory Board (FASAB) ........... 457
        13.3.1.1 Mission .......................................................... 457
        13.3.1.2 AICPA Rule 203 Designation .............................. 458
        13.3.1.3 Due Process .................................................... 459
        13.3.1.4 Accounting and Auditing Policy Committee ............. 459

     13.3.2  Office of Management and Budget ............................................459
         13.3.2.1  Mission ..................................................................459
         13.3.2.2  The Budget of the United States................................. 460
         13.3.2.3  Budget Accounting—Appropriations, Apportionments,
                    Allotments, Obligations, and Outlays ..........................461
         13.3.2.4  On- and Off-Budget Totals.........................................461
         13.3.2.5  Audited Financial Statements Required ......................462
     13.3.3  Treasury Department—The Fiscal Service and the Financial
         Management Service......................................................................463
         13.3.3.1  Mission ..................................................................463
         13.3.3.2  Issuing Government-Wide Financial Reports...............463
         13.3.3.3  Government-Wide Accounting.................................... 464
     13.3.4  Government Accountability Office ........................................ 464
         13.3.4.1  Mission ................................................................. 464
         13.3.4.2  GAO Guidance....................................................... 464
     13.3.5  Other Fiscal Agencies..................................................................465
         13.3.5.1  Congressional Budget Office....................................465
         13.3.5.2  Bureau of Economic Analysis....................................465
13.4  Types of Accounts Maintained by Federal Entities............................... 466
     13.4.1  Budget Accounts........................................................................ 466
         13.4.1.1  Federal Funds..........................................................467
         13.4.1.2  "Trust Funds" ........................................................467
     13.4.2  Treasury Accounts ..................................................................... 468
     13.4.3  United States Government Standard General Ledger...................469
     13.4.4  Final Note Regarding Accounts .................................................470
13.5  Financial Statements Required of Federal Agencies...............................470
     13.5.1  Balance Sheet.............................................................................470
     13.5.2  Statement of Net Cost.................................................................472
     13.5.3  Statement of Changes in Net Position.........................................472
     13.5.4  Statement of Custodial Activities ................................................475
     13.5.5  Statement of Budgetary Resources ..............................................475
     13.5.6  Statement of Social Insurance .....................................................476
     13.5.7  Statement of Financing ...............................................................476
         13.5.7.1  Required Supplementary Information..........................478
Appendices...........................................................................................................479
Endnotes...............................................................................................................488

# 13.1 Historical Background

Article 1, Section 9, paragraph 7 of the U.S. Constitution states that "no money shall be drawn from the Treasury, but in consequence of appropriation made by law, and regular statement and account of the receipts and expenditures of all public money shall be published from time to time." Congress created the Treasury Department on September 2, 1789, one of the first three federal government departments, to provide accounting and reporting services, and to collect, safeguard, and disburse public money.

For the next century, the federal financial infrastructure remained modest by modern standards, and the Treasury kept the accounts. The basic functions and organizations remained essentially unchanged from 1817 to 1894. Although Alexander Hamilton had envisioned the Treasury Department as a finance ministry where appropriation estimates and funds were controlled, very early Treasury became a reviewer of departmental estimates and accounting records. The program departments themselves were the main players in the system. Individual departments and independent agencies conducted most disbursing functions without Treasury oversight. The administration of federal finances was extremely loose. Other than during time of war, the volume of government collecting and spending was relatively modest. There was little need to centralize or modernize its accounting systems.[1]

By 1893, however, the administrative system needed reform. The Treasury Auditor and his staff were not settling accounts uniformly. Controls were weak and settlement delays were a major problem. The Treasury auditors were ineffective, and the government necessarily came to rely on the individual departments' control over the process.

The Act of July 31, 1894, the Dockery Act,[2] provided reform. It reduced the number of accounting officers and placed greater responsibility on the Treasury Auditor. Final settlement was to take place in the Auditor's office, with final appeal to the Treasury Comptroller.

The period from approximately 1890 to 1920, known as the Progressive Era, experienced many civic initiatives, and municipal and federal accounting were no exceptions. The idea of creating a regular process for federal budgeting dates to the Taft Administration (1909–1913). In 1911, the Commission on Economy and Efficiency studied the matter and recommended the adoption of a national budget system in its *Report of the Taft Commission on Economy and Efficiency: The Need for a National Budget,* in 1912. However, Congress was slow to warm to the proposal; individual legislators liked the idea of budgetary restraints on others but wanted free rein for their own pet projects.

Congress began to view the issue more seriously during World War I when vast governmental expenditures raised concerns about efficiency. A bill was introduced during the Wilson Administration (1913–1921). President Woodrow Wilson, a leading proponent of government reform, wanted a stronger role for the executive branch in the budget process, as had President Theodore Roosevelt before him. However, Wilson's relationship with the Republican Congress was not good. A bill that would have required the president to prepare annual budgets for final disposition by the House and Senate was vetoed by Wilson. He objected to a provision that prevented the president from removing the comptroller general, who would be the chief government auditor, from office.

The first major post–World War I federal financial management reform took place in 1919. Treasury Secretary Carter Glass created the forerunners of Treasury's current fiscal operations bureaus, the Financial Management Service (FMS) and the Bureau of Public Debt (BPD), by approving the positions of the Commissioner of Accounts and Deposits and the Commissioner of Public Debt.

In the postwar period, Republicans regained control of the White House and Congress, and pursued their goal of reducing the cost of government and increasing its efficiency. President Warren Harding called a special session of Congress and urged, among other things, the passage of the budget bill.

The **Budget and Accounting Act of 1921**[*3] was approved in June 1921. It retained the provision opposed by Wilson and provided for the following:

- Created the Bureau of the Budget (renamed the Office of Management and Budget [OMB] in 1970) within the Treasury Department; its director was to be a presidential appointee. The bureau was originally part of the Treasury Department, but in 1939 it was transferred to the executive branch. General Charles G. Dawes, vice president during Coolidge's second term, was the first director of the Bureau of the Budget, under President Harding.
- Required that the director of the budget examine all budget requests from Congress, seek economies, and remove duplicates.
- Required the president to submit a budget proposal and a statement of the government's financial condition to Congress annually.
- Established the General Accounting Office (renamed the Government Accountability Office in 2006) (GAO) under the control of the comptroller general.

The overall aim of this legislation was to centralize the budget process. In the past, budget matters had been assigned to a variety of Congressional committees, and no central control existed.

The GAO took over the Treasury comptroller's powers and duties. The accounts of Treasury accountable officers as well as the responsibility for audit and settlement of all receipts and expenditures were transferred to the GAO. Congress gave the GAO the broad role of investigating "all matters relating to the receipt, disbursement, and application of public funds" and to "make recommendations looking to greater economy or efficiency in public expenditures."

The Budget and Accounting Act of 1921 also created a new comptroller general with the authority to prescribe forms, systems, and procedures for administrative appropriation and fund accounts, and for administrative examination of the accounts of fiscal officers. The comptroller general was assigned a term of 15 years.

---

[*] Terms defined in the glossary at Appendix 3 first appear in **boldface type**.

The Budget and Accounting Act of 1921 required the President to submit a single proposed budget to Congress, as recommended by the *Taft Commission on Economy and Efficiency*. The duty of the heads of each executive agency to prepare budget requests for submission to the Bureau of the Budget (now OMB) originated with this Act.

The government's long-standing effort to reconcile **financial accounting** and **budgetary accounting** and to institute cost accounting also originated with the Budget and Accounting Act of 1921. The heads of agencies were now required to synchronize financial and budgetary accounting and to submit cost-based budgets.

To comply with the Budget and Accounting Act of 1921, the Treasury Department began maintaining more detailed budgetary accounts for apportionments and obligations.[4] The departments now had to submit financial reports to the Treasury showing the status of available funds for the Treasury to subsequently report to the Bureau of the Budget. For this purpose, the Treasury was authorized to prescribe the agencies' reporting procedures.[5]

The Bureau of the Budget moved to the Executive Office of the President in 1939, while the Treasury retained its other financial operations. The Bureau of the Budget and later OMB assists the President in the development and implementation of the budget, program management, and regulatory policies. (For more on OMB, see "Office of Management and Budget" in the following text.)

Although it improved in the years following the passage of the Budget and Accounting Act of 1921, federal accounting was still cumbersome and duplicative. Three sets of accounts were being kept: one by the administrative office and/or the disbursing officer at the agency, another by the Treasury disbursing officer to verify the agency's spending authority, and yet another set each of central accounts kept by the Treasury and GAO. The GAO required agencies to submit original documents for examination, bookkeeping, and permanent filing, although the GAO did not "audit" the data except during a voucher examination.[6]

During the 1920s and 1930s, the executive and legislative branches were at odds over jurisdiction, among other matters. The GAO, for example, wanted to audit the Tennessee Valley Authority (TVA) as if it were just another executive branch agency, pursuant to the Budget and Accounting Act of 1921. The TVA controller, Eric Kohler, objected and claimed to be exempt, citing TVA's corporate status and the TVA Act. Congress amended the TVA Act in 1941 to clarify that TVA was subject to the GAO's authority. (For more on GAO, see "Government Accountability Office" in the following text).

In 1940, the Treasury established the Fiscal Service, which consisted of the Bureau of Accounts, the Bureau of Public Debt, and the Office of the Treasurer. A 1974 reorganization of the Fiscal Service created the Bureau of Government Financial Operations, which was formed from a merger of the Bureau of Accounts and most functions of the Office of the Treasurer. In 1984, the Bureau of Government Financial Operations was renamed the Financial Management Service.[7] (For more on the Treasury Department, see "Treasury Department" in the following text.)

## 13.1.1 Government Corporation Control Act of 1945

The **Government Corporation Control Act of 1945**[8] helped to revitalize and professionalize the GAO.[9] **Government corporations** are now commonplace and the rules applicable to them are well known, but before 1945, accountants debated the use of the corporate structure for federal activities. Congress had used the corporate structure in the 1920s and even more in the 1930s as organizations were created in response to the Great Depression. Perhaps the most controversial, the Reconstruction Finance Corporation (RFC), had enormous power. It could spend public money and obligate the taxpayers to long-term commitments.

The early corporations had been created before the GAO's audit function developed. When the GAO finally audited the RFC in 1945, the comprehensiveness of its audit set a precedent. The audit report discussed accounting deficiencies, management problems, effectiveness, internal control, and program operations.

The ascendancy of Comptroller General Lindsay Warren in 1939 marked the beginning of a new era for GAO. Before 1945, GAO audits were voucher examinations and bookkeeping chores. Accounting officers would ship original documents to the GAO. Many accountants objected to shipping vouchers to Washington from all over the world for this purpose.

In 1940, the GAO drew a distinction between governmental and "commercial" audits. In 1943, Comptroller General Lindsay stated that regular governmental audits were not suitable to the "capital fund operations" of a corporation.

The GCCA legitimized the corporate structure as a tool for federal program execution. In addition, the Act asserted Congress' control over its creations. The Act required a GAO audit of both the financial statements and the operations of the corporation and the program for which it was created.

Thus, the GCCA put the GAO on notice that Congress expected it to be a professional-class audit organization, and the GAO subsequently reorganized accordingly. In the ensuing years, the GAO would publish auditing standards and generally provide governmental auditing leadership.

By the late 1940s, it was generally agreed that federal accounting needed an overhaul. The first Hoover Commission (1947–1949) analyzed financial management and was highly critical of the GAO's voucher examining and bookkeeping approach.

Comptroller General Warren initiated discussions in 1947 with the Treasury Department and the Bureau of the Budget (now OMB) that led to the establishment of the Joint Financial Management Improvement Program (JFMIP). To a certain extent, the JFMIP agreement settled accounting jurisdictional issues. The agreement had three main thrusts:

1. Accounting and reporting would be executive branch functions, and accounting systems prescribed by the GAO should recognize this fact.
2. The GAO's proper function is auditing, and good systems are essential to auditing.
3. Developing accounting systems ought to be a cooperative effort.

These agencies signed a formal JFMIP agreement on January 6, 1949, setting up the goals of the program to provide better management for the President, better financial information to Congress, and a clearer picture of federal operations to the public. These agencies were known as the "principals" of the JFMIP, along with the Offices of Personnel Management and the General Services Administration, which were added later, and they provided leadership and program guidance as the JFMIP promoted strategies and sound financial management across government. The JFMIP worked on interagency projects that developed a financial systems framework and financial systems requirements.

The JFMIP was given statutory authorization in the **Budget and Accounting Procedures Act of 1950**.[10]

## 13.1.2 *The Budget and Accounting Procedures Act of 1950*

The Budget and Accounting Procedures Act of 1950[11] realigned and defined financial management responsibilities. The objectives of the Act were full disclosure, management information, control over assets, budgetary control, and system integration.

The Budget and Accounting Procedures Act of 1950 requires the head of each agency to establish and maintain systems of accounting and internal control designed to provide effective control over and accountability for all funds, property, and other assets. Central and agency accounting systems are to conform to GAO standards. Like the Act of 1921, the Budget and Accounting Procedures Act of 1950 called for cost-based budgets.[12]

During the Hoover Commission's deliberations and congressional consideration of bills responding to the Commission's proposals, the Comptroller General had raised concerns over potential weakening of congressional oversight and the GAO's ability to perform its responsibilities should all accounting functions be vested exclusively in the executive branch. The Budget and Accounting Procedures Act of 1950 reflected those concerns. The Act authorized the Comptroller General to discontinue maintaining agencies' accounts when the Comptroller General determined that their accounting systems and controls were sufficient to allow the Comptroller General to perform his responsibilities related to the accounts.[13] Among other things, the Act gave the GAO authority to set accounting standards for the federal government[14] and indicated that GAO audits should include consideration of the extent to which adequate internal financial control is exercised. The Comptroller General was to consult with the Treasury and OMB.

The GAO began publishing accounting standards in the 1950s under the heading "Accounting Principles Memorandum." Pursuant to section 3511(a) of the Budget and Accounting Act of 1950, the Comptroller General prescribed accounting principles, first in memorandums called *Statement of Accounting Principles and Standards for the Guidance of Executive Agencies of the Federal Government*, and later as Title 2, Appendix I, of the *Policy and Procedures Manual for Guidance of Federal Agencies* (Title 2).

Subsequent developments increasingly emphasized the concept of **accrual accounting**.[15] The Accounting Act of 1956 required executive agencies to maintain accounts on an accrual basis to show resources, liabilities, and costs of operations to help prepare cost-based budgets.

### 13.1.3 Report of the President's Commission on Budget Concepts of 1967

The budget of the United States had evolved over time and, by the mid-1960s, there was a growing concern over its complexity and lack of unity. In 1967, the President appointed a Commission to study budget concepts and make recommendations. The Report of the President's Commission on Budget Concepts made the following recommendations:

1. One unified budget.
2. Use of the budget as a broad financial plan.
3. Highlight actions requested of Congress.
4. Include all programs in the budget.
5. Budget expenditures and receipts are reported on an accrual basis.
6. Distinguish between loans and other expenditures and exclude loans for the deficit calculation.
7. Separately identify and budget for subsidies.
8. Continue to show federal insurance and guarantees outside the budget.
9. Treat sales of "participation certificates" in loans that the government continues to own as a "means of financing," that is, not a budget receipt affecting the deficit or surplus.
10. Include a means of financing section in the budget.
11. Treat proprietary receipts as offsets to expenditures to which they relate.
12. Budget information should be more frequent, more detailed, and extend further into the future.
13. The Commission strongly recommended against a capital budget.

The Report of the Commission was a seminal moment. Many of the recommendations were adopted, not the least of which was the recommendation regarding a unified budget.

### 13.1.4 Chief Financial Officers Act of 1990 (CFO Act)

The **Chief Financial Officers Act of 1990** (CFO Act)[16] was signed into law by President George H. W. Bush on November 15, 1990. Some argued that this was the most comprehensive and far-reaching financial management improvement legislation since the Budget and Accounting Procedures Act of 1950.[17] The CFO Act laid a foundation for comprehensive reform of federal financial management. The

Act established a leadership structure, provided for long-range planning, required audited financial statements, and strengthened accountability reporting. The purposes of the Act were to ensure improvement in agency systems of accounting, financial management, and internal control; to ensure the issuance of reliable financial information; and to deter fraud, waste, and abuse of government resources. The Act required preparation of annual audited financial statements in conformity with "applicable standards." Initially, this requirement applied only to trust funds, revolving funds, commercial-type activities, and 10 pilot agencies.

The Act requires that agency CFOs develop and maintain integrated agency accounting and financial management systems, including financial reporting and internal control. It requires agency CFOs to prepare and transmit an annual report to the agency head and the Director of OMB, including a summary of the reports on internal accounting and administrative control systems submitted to the President under the **Federal Managers' Financial Improvement Act of 1996**.

The **Government Management Reform Act of 1994** (GMRA) required all the CFO Act agencies to have annual audited financial statements covering the entire agency.

The **Accountability of Tax Dollars Act of 2002** extended this requirement to virtually all agencies in the executive branch.[18]

## 13.1.5 Federal Accounting Standards Advisory Board

The establishment of the Federal Accounting Standards Advisory Board (FASAB) in 1990 reflected an agreement among the GAO, OMB, and Treasury on a process for establishing financial accounting standards pursuant to the CFO Act. The CFO Act provided that the OMB Director "shall prescribe the form and content of the financial statements of executive agencies under this section, consistent with *applicable accounting principles, standards, and requirements*." The CFO Act's reference to "applicable" principles reflected both the expectation of FASAB's emergence and the sponsors' reservation of their respective authorities.

Over the last 15 years, the FASAB's work has become the basis for accounting principles for federal government financial statements. As early as 1994, Congress recognized the FASAB's work. For example, in its report on the bill that became the GMRA, the Senate Committee on Governmental Affairs noted "with approval the accepted objectives of federal financial reporting adopted by [OMB, Treasury, and GAO]" and expected "that accounting and financial principles, standards, and requirements will be prescribed to satisfy these objectives."[19]

As standards have been issued pursuant to the FASAB process, the GAO has increasingly replaced its Title 2 standards with FASAB standards, retaining Title 2 standards only to the extent FASAB standards have not superseded them.[20] In addition, the OMB has recognized FASAB statements and interpretations as the highest level of generally accepted accounting principles for the federal government.[21]

### 13.1.6 Final Note on JFMIP

On December 7, 2004, the OMB announced a "Realignment of Financial Management Policy Setting and Oversight." The principals of the JFMIP voted to realign JFMIP's responsibilities for financial management policy and oversight. This realignment was to ensure "that the federal government carries out its financial management policy and oversight responsibilities in accordance with statutory requirements." Under the new structure, the JFMIP Program Management Office (PMO), which certified financial management software, was to report to a new Chief Financial Officers Council (CFOC) committee to be chaired by the Chief of the OMB's Office of Federal Financial Management (OFFM), Federal Financial Systems Branch. Other JFMIP functions were assumed by OFFM, the Office of Personnel Management, and the CFOC. The principals continue to meet at their discretion, although the JFMIP ceased to exist as a standalone organization.

The December 7, 2004, notice explained that the "JFMIP was formed as a voluntary effort by the heads of those entities required to conduct a program for improving the government's accounting and financial reporting under the Budget and Accounting Procedures Act of 1950. The subsequent Chief Financial Officers (CFO) Act of 1990, however, created both OFFM and the CFOC, providing the broader mandate for improving financial management within the Federal Government. ..."

## 13.2 Key Objectives of Federal Financial Reporting

The federal government is unique. The U.S. Constitution separates power among three branches: the legislative branch, the executive branch, and the judicial branch.

The legislative branch, Congress, passes laws to define and initiate federal programs and activities. The programs and activities are carried out by the executive branch. The judicial branch interprets the laws and the way they are implemented in the executive branch. Most of the federal government's accounting and financial reporting is performed by the branch that conducts the programs and activities, that is, the executive branch. This chapter focuses on the executive branch. Accounting and financial reporting in the legislative and judicial branches are generally consistent with the executive branch.

Federal agencies are required to report their financial activity to the central financial agencies, the OMB and the Treasury Department, and, through them, to Congress. Financial reporting provides information for formulating policy, planning actions, evaluating performance, and other purposes. In addition, the processes of preparing and auditing financial reports can enhance the government's overall accountability structure by providing greater assurance that transactions are recorded and reported accurately, that consistent definitions are used to describe the transactions, etc. Thus, federal financial reporting helps to fulfill the government's duty to manage programs economically, efficiently, and effectively and to be publicly accountable.[22]

Financial reporting is supported and made possible by accounting and accounting systems. *Financial reporting* may be defined as the process of recording, reporting, and interpreting, in terms of money, an entity's financial transactions and events with economic consequences for the entity. Reporting in the federal government also deals with nonfinancial information about service efforts and accomplishments of the government.[23]

"Federal financial reporting" or federal accounting may mean different things to different people. An economist is likely to see reports about the national society as a whole. Among the most important of such financial reports are the national income and product accounts (NIPA) that measure the nation's aggregate expenditures on currently produced output. Federal government expenditures constitute a significant fraction of the total expenditures in the economy. The NIPAs, as a system, emerged in the 1940s based on work done by the U.S. Department of Commerce beginning in the 1930s and earlier by private organizations.[24]

The NIPAs provide a picture of the economic transactions that occur in an accounting period, such as a year. The approach is to provide such a picture through a set of accounts that aggregate the accounts belonging to the individual transactors in the economy—workers, businesses, and consumers, among others—whether or not formal accounting statements exist explicitly for all of them.[25]

The NIPAs provide vital information to policymakers and others who are planning future actions and to individuals who would like to assess the effects of past actions. The NIPAs are recognized as an essential part of economic reporting by national governments. For this reason, the United Nations has developed the System of National Accounts (SNA). The SNA is a comprehensive, integrated, and internationally comparable statistical base for analysis in key policymaking areas, such as economic growth, inflation, and productivity.[26]

The NIPAs are similar to the SNA. It is a conceptual framework that sets the international statistical standard for the measurement of the market economy consisting of an integrated set of macroeconomic accounts, balance sheets and tables based on internationally agreed concepts, definitions, classifications, and accounting rules. These principles provide a comprehensive accounting framework within which economic data can be compiled and presented in a format designed for purposes of economic analysis and policy-making. However, the United States and other national governments have tailored SNA concepts for their own purposes, and there is inconsistency among them. For example, some countries consider borrowing by a government's general fund entity from a social insurance entity to finance current expenditures to be external debt, while others see it as internal debt that would be eliminated for the purposes of consolidated financial reporting. A national government might consider such debt to be part of the government sector (or "collective sector"), while other national governments may consider such debt to be an integral part of the central government and, therefore, technically, a debt government has to itself. The latter is the position of the SNA, although supplementary accounts are under consideration for the SNA in this regard.

Federal accounting and reporting by federal agencies and other entities does not directly involve such accounts of the economic activity of the national society. The focus is on accounting systems and financial reports that deal with the budgetary integrity, operating performance, and stewardship of the government as such; that is, of the government as a legal and organizational entity within the national society. However, to report on some aspects of the government's performance and stewardship, economic and other information about the national society is essential. Thus, such economic information may be considered for certain financial reports, such as general-purpose financial reports for the U.S. government as a whole. [27]

A financial analyst on Wall Street, when asked about federal financial reporting, is likely to think of the "Daily Treasury Statement" and the "Monthly Treasury Statement of Receipts and Outlays of the United States Government." Some financial analysts study these Treasury reports regularly to assess the effect of cash flows on bank reserves and the size of the government's borrowing requirements.[28]

Someone concerned with formulating or executing the U.S. budget, when asked about the "federal accounting model," is likely to think of the budgetary accounting system. This is the system used to keep track of spending authority at various stages of budget execution from appropriation through apportionment and allotment to obligation and eventual outlay. This system is used by Congress and the executive branch for such purposes as "scoring" the budget and for assessing the economic implications of federal financial activity at an aggregate level. It also is used for planning and controlling government operations at more detailed, disaggregated levels. Of course, people involved with the budget also are informed by, and rely on, sources of information other than the budgetary accounting system, for example, program evaluation and performance measures.[29]

Accountants working for the federal government, individuals auditing government programs, or students in a governmental accounting course are likely to think first of what are known within the federal government as the "proprietary" accounts and the reports prepared, in part, from information in them. "Proprietary accounting" is often used synonymously with "accrual accounting" and "financial accounting." It is so used in this chapter.

Proprietary accounts are used to record assets and liabilities that are not accounted for in the budgetary accounts. These reports are said to present "financial position" and "results of operations" in accordance with some set of accounting standards. The federal accounting standard-setter, FASAB, and those charged with preparing and auditing federal financial statements prepared in accordance with generally accepted accounting principles (GAAP), are most directly concerned with these accounts and with the reports that are prepared, in large part, with information from them.[30]

Financial reporting is an important, basic tool in the management and oversight of most organizations. It is particularly important for the federal government because of the government's fundamental nature and responsibilities and because the federal government operates with fewer external restraints than other entities. Federal accounting and financial reporting are shaped by, and need to respond to, the unique characteristics and environment of the federal government, as discussed in the following text.[31]

The federal government is unique when compared with any other entity in the country. The citizens of the United States exercise their sovereign power through the federal government. It has the power through law, regulation, and taxation to exercise ultimate control over many facets of the national economy and society. All other entities within the nation, both public and private, operate within the context of laws, oversight, and accountability established by the national government. The federal government is accountable only to its citizens. It is politically accountable to the electorate, but no higher agency has the power to demand an accounting from the government.[32]

Because of their concern about potential abuse of the national government's power, the founders designed a government characterized by the separation of powers. Each branch of government—legislative, executive, and judicial—is checked and constrained by the others. Paradoxically, this same separation of power can obscure responsibility and reduce accountability. The interrelated responsibilities of the legislative and executive branches, for example, can make it difficult to assign responsibility for the policies that are adopted.[33]

The federal system of government—comprising federal, state, and local levels of government—also makes it difficult to pinpoint accountability for many programs. The federal government's responsibility relative to that of the states has gradually expanded. The federal government has undertaken responsibilities in areas such as income redistribution, education, and health care. Often, however, the expansion has come without direct federal control over related operations. Responsibilities and financial resources of the three levels of government have become intermingled. Citizens are not clear about who is in charge, where to press for performance, and whom they should blame for bad results.[34]

The federal government is unique in that it has continuing responsibility for the nation's common defense and general welfare. As a result, the government's financial condition is necessarily a secondary consideration in many cases. For example, the nation would enter into military conflict to protect its vital national interests despite the fact that doing so would worsen an already large deficit. (Similarly, the government's greatest resource, the national economy, is one that it does not own but can tax.)[35]

Further, providing for the nation's general welfare is a broad responsibility that involves multiple goals. There is no single measure of success (like "return on investment" or "earnings per share"). Goals often are not explicitly defined in quantifiable terms, and sometimes conflict with each other. Relevant measures of performance are usually nonfinancial. For example, many federal loan programs are charged with two conflicting goals: (1) to operate as a fiscally prudent lender, and (2) to provide high-risk lenders with credit.[36]

As noted, the federal government is unique. It has unique access to financial resources and financing. It has the power to tax, to borrow, and to create money. These powers give the government a call on the underlying wealth of the United States—a vast but finite pool of resources.[37] There is no constitutional requirement to provide sufficient revenues to fund expenditures of the federal government. There is a statutory limit on the amount of U.S. debt. This limit is routinely increased by Congress and the President.[38] The federal government—through the Federal Reserve—also has the power to create money and to control its supply. This ensures that creditors will be repaid, at least in nominal terms.[39]

The federal government is not subject to the discipline of competitive markets for private goods, services, and capital. Generally, transactions between citizens and the government are not individual exchanges between willing buyers and willing sellers. Taxpayers provide resources involuntarily, based on their consumption, wealth, or income rather than on their desire for particular government services. Even when user fees are charged, they often are not intended to represent market-clearing prices—prices that would, in markets for private goods, balance supply and demand.[40]

Thus, citizens as individuals have little say in selecting the public services they pay for. Decisions on what public services will be provided are collective decisions made through the political process. Politically influential recipients of benefits can force less influential nonrecipients to bear the cost of the benefits.[41]

Further, because most governmental revenues are not earned in individual, voluntary, exchange transactions, no private market directly measures the value of output. Consequently, the value added to society's well-being by government programs cannot be gauged by conventional measures of net income, nor is there much competitive market constraint on the quantity or quality of services provided. Instead, decisions about the quantity, quality, and value of public services are collective decisions made by the political process.[42]

### 13.2.1 Objectives of Federal Accounting

The accounting process begins with recording information about transactions between the government (or one of its component entities) and other entities, that is, inflows and outflows of resources or promises to provide them. These may involve flows of economic goods, cash, or promises. These comprise the "core" data of the accounting discipline. To enhance the usefulness of this core set of data about transactions with other entities, accountants make various accruals, classifications, interpretations, etc.[43]

In the branch of accounting called financial accounting, the most noteworthy interpretations or classifications pertain to current resources and obligations arising from past transactions and events. Financial accounting is largely concerned with assigning the value of past transactions to appropriate periods.[44]

In government, the data on transactions with other entities include information on the budget authority, obligations, outlays, receipts, and offsetting collections for the transactions. This information is maintained in what are called budgetary accounts to distinguish them from the "proprietary" accounts that record other information on transactions. The budgetary and proprietary accounts at this level are said to be "integrated." In effect, they maintain information about different stages of a transaction.[45]

"The budget" is a broad term that may include, among other things, a projection of spending authorities and means of financing them for a future period and a report of the actual spending and associated financing for a past period.

The FASAB's accounting concepts and standards may influence the reporting of actual budgetary data.[46]

## 13.2.2 Objectives of the Federal Accounting Standards Advisory Board

The FASAB classified users of financial information about the federal government in four major groups: citizens, Congress, executives, and program managers.[47] The FASAB also classified the financial information needs of these groups under four broad headings: budgetary integrity, operating performance, stewardship, and systems and controls. Federal financial information users want answers to questions such as the following:

- **Budgetary Integrity:** What legal authority was provided for financing government activities and for spending the monies? Were the financing and spending in accordance with these authorities? How much was left?
- **Operating Performance:** How much do various programs cost, and how were they financed? What outputs and outcomes were achieved? What and where are the important assets, and how effectively are they managed? What liabilities arose from operating the program, and how will they be provided for or liquidated?
- **Stewardship:** Did the government's financial condition improve or deteriorate? What provision was made for the future?
- **Systems and Control:** Does the government have cost-effective systems and controls to safeguard its assets? Is it able to detect likely problems? Is it correcting deficiencies when detected?[48]

Questions like these lead the FASAB to define four objectives of federal financial reporting in each of these areas in Statements of Federal Financial Accounting

Concepts (SFFAC) 1, *Objectives of Federal Financing Reporting*. The objectives reflect the federal environment; they also consider many of the needs expressed by current and potential users of federal financial information. They provide a framework for assessing the existing financial reporting systems of the federal government and for considering how new accounting standards might help to enhance accountability and decision making in a cost-effective manner. The four objectives of federal financial reporting are:

1. Budgetary Integrity—Federal financial reporting should assist in fulfilling the government's duty to be publicly accountable for monies raised through taxes and other means, and for their expenditure in accordance with the appropriations laws that establish the government's budget for a particular fiscal year and related laws and regulations. Federal financial reporting should provide information that helps the reader to determine
   - How budgetary resources have been obtained and used and whether their acquisition and use were in accordance with the legal authorization
   - The status of budgetary resources
   - How information on the use of budgetary resources relates to information on the costs of program operations and whether information on the status of budgetary resources is consistent with other accounting information on assets and liabilities
2. Operating Performance—Federal financial reporting should assist report users in evaluating the service efforts, costs, and accomplishments of the reporting entity; the manner in which these efforts and accomplishments have been financed; and the management of the entity's assets and liabilities. Federal financial reporting should provide information that helps the reader to determine
   - The costs of providing specific programs and activities and the composition of, and changes in, these costs
   - The efforts and accomplishments associated with federal programs and the changes over time and in relation to costs
   - The efficiency and effectiveness of the government's management of its assets and liabilities
3. Stewardship—Federal financial reporting should assist report users in assessing the impact on the country of the government's operations and investments for the period and how, as a result, the government's and the nation's financial condition has changed and may change in the future. Federal financial reporting should provide information that helps the reader to determine whether
   - The government's financial position improved or deteriorated over the period
   - Future budgetary resources will likely be sufficient to sustain public services and to meet obligations as they come due
   - Government operations have contributed to the nation's current and future well-being

4. Systems and Control—Federal financial reporting should assist report users in understanding whether financial management systems and internal accounting and administrative controls are adequate to ensure that

- Transactions are executed in accordance with budgetary and financial laws and other requirements, consistent with the purposes authorized, and are recorded in accordance with federal accounting standards
- Assets are properly safeguarded to deter fraud, waste, and abuse
- Performance measurement information is adequately supported

As of 2007, the Board has completed five Statements of Federal Financial Accounting Concepts. Concept statements set forth objectives and fundamentals on which financial accounting and reporting standards are based. The objectives identify the goals and purposes of financial reporting, and the fundamentals are the underlying concepts of financial accounting—concepts that guide the selection of transactions, events, and circumstances to be accounted for; their recognition and measurement; and the means of summarizing and communicating them to interested parties.

The FASAB's conceptual framework enhances consistency of standards and serves the public interest by providing structure and direction to federal financial accounting and reporting. The most direct beneficiaries of the FASAB's concepts statements are the Board itself, preparers, and auditors of federal financial reports. They guide the Board's development of accounting and reporting standards by providing the Board with a common foundation and basic reasoning on which to consider the merits of alternatives.

## 13.2.3 *Other FASAB Concepts Statements*

SFFAC 2, *Entity and Display*, specifies criteria for determining the federal reporting entities and the information to be displayed. Determining which entities to include was a troublesome issue because the federal government is one economic entity with undefined boundaries.

Unlike state and local governments and the private sector, federal financial entities issue financial statements for dependent subunits of that economic entity. Because there are many quasi-federal and federally funded organizations, it was necessary to establish guidelines on which subunits are parts of the federal reporting entities.

SFFAC 2 provided that meeting the four objectives of federal financial reporting could be accomplished via a financial report that included the following:

- MD&A
- Balance sheet
- Statement of net cost
- Statement of changes in net position

- Statement of custodial activities, when appropriate
- Statement of budgetary resources
- Statement of financing
- Statement of performance measures
- Accompanying notes
- Required supplemental information
- Other information

SFFAC 3, *Management's Discussion and Analysis*, describes the concepts on which the Board relied in recommending standards for management's discussion and analysis.

SFFAC 4, *Intended Audience and Qualitative Characteristics for the Consolidated Financial Report of the United States Government*, identifies the intended or primary audience for the FR and described the characteristics of the audience and the qualitative characteristics the Board believes will aid in meeting financial reporting objectives.

SFFAC 5, *Definitions of Elements and Basic Recognition Criteria for Accrual-Basis Financial Statements*, defines[49] five elements of accrual-basis financial statements of the federal government as follows:

- *Assets*—An asset is a resource that embodies economic benefits or services that the federal government controls.
- *Liabilities*—A liability is a present obligation of the federal government to provide assets or services to another entity at a determinable date, when a specified event occurs, or on demand.
- *Net position*—Net position or its equivalent, net assets, is the arithmetic difference between the total assets and total liabilities recognized in the federal government's or component entity's balance sheet. Net position may be positive (assets greater than liabilities) or negative (assets less than liabilities).
- *Revenue*—Revenue is an inflow of or other increase in assets, a decrease in liabilities, or a combination of both that results in an increase in the government's net position during the reporting period.
- *Expense*—An expense is an outflow of or other decrease in assets, an increase in liabilities, or a combination of both that results in a decrease in the government's net position during the reporting period.

SFFAC 5 also provides the two basic recognition criteria that an item must meet to be a candidate for recognition in the body of a financial statement: (1) meet the definition of an element, and (2) be measurable, meaning a monetary amount can be determined with reasonable certainty or is reasonably estimable.

### 13.2.4 Statements of Federal Financial Accounting Standards

As of 2007, the FASAB had issued 33 standards. (See Appendix 1.)

# 13.3 Agencies Responsible for Federal Accounting and Reporting

The OMB, the GAO, and the Treasury Department are primarily responsible for federal accounting and reporting. These agencies established the Federal Accounting Standards Advisory Board in 1990 pursuant to the CFO Act of 1990. The Treasury secretary, the OMB director, and the comptroller general are referred to as the FASAB "principals" because they possess legal authority under various laws to establish accounting and financial reporting standards for the federal government. These three agencies and the Congressional Budget Office (CBO) fund the FASAB.

The federal government's agencies, like most entities, provide financial reports to two broad groups of users: internal and external. Internal users are agency managers responsible for implementing and managing the programs and controlling operations on a day-to-day basis. They can and do specify the content and form of information they need to run their programs.

The major external users of agencies' financial information are:

1. OMB, which monitors the agencies' budget execution on behalf of the President and which needs information to formulate the subsequent year's budget; and which is responsible for receiving the accrual-basis financial statements required by the CFO Act and other federal laws the accounting standards for which are provided by the FASAB.
2. Treasury, which must
   a. Reconcile agency financial data with its own records to properly record receipts and deposits and avoid unauthorized disbursements
   b. Aggregate the agencies' financial information to fulfill its government-wide reporting responsibilities
   c. Review actual and projected cash flow to manage the governments cash position
3. Other federal agencies needing information for analytical purposes such as the Congressional Budget Office (CBO) and the Commerce Department's Bureau of Economic Analysis.

## 13.3.1 Federal Accounting Standards Advisory Board (FASAB)

### 13.3.1.1 Mission

The mission of the FASAB is to develop accounting standards for the federal government after considering the financial and budgetary information needs of congressional oversight groups, executive agencies, and the needs of other users of federal financial information.

Accounting and financial reporting standards are essential for public accountability and for an efficient and effective functioning of government. Thus, federal accounting standards and financial reporting play a major role in fulfilling the government's duty to be publicly accountable and can be used to (1) assess the government's accountability and its efficiency and effectiveness, and (2) contribute to the understanding of the economic, political, and social consequences of the allocation and various uses of federal resources.[50]

The Board is made up of six nonfederal and four federal members and is chaired by a nonfederal member. Members work on a part-time basis.

### 13.3.1.2 AICPA Rule 203 Designation

In October 1999 the AICPA designated the FASAB the board that promulgates GAAP for federal entities. The AICPA's Auditing Standards Board has published

---

**BOX 13.1—THE HIERARCHY OF ACCOUNTING STANDARDS**

The federal GAAP hierarchy is as follows:

A. Category (A) officially established accounting principles, consists of Federal Accounting Standards Advisory Board (FASAB) Statements and Interpretations, as well as AICPA and FASB pronouncements specifically made applicable to federal governmental entities by FASAB Statements and Interpretations. FASAB Statements and Interpretations will be periodically incorporated in a publication by the FASAB.
B. Category (B) consists of FASAB Technical Bulletins and, if specifically made applicable to federal governmental entities by the AICPA and cleared by the FASAB, AICP Industry Audit and Accounting Guides and AICPA Statements of Position.
C. Category (C) consists of AICPA AcSEC Practice Bulletins if specifically made applicable to federal governmental entities and cleared by the FASAB, as well as Technical Releases of the Accounting and Auditing Committee of the FASAB.
D. Category (D) includes implementation guides published by the FASAB staff, as well as practices that are widely recognized and prevalent in the federal government.

In the absence of a pronouncement covered by rule 203 or another source of established accounting principles, the auditor of financial statements of a federal governmental entity may consider other accounting literature, depending on its relevance in the circumstances.

---

the Statement on Auditing Standards 91, *Amendment to Statement on Auditing Standards No. 69, The Meaning of Present Fairly in Conformity with Generally Accepted Accounting Principles in the Independent Auditor's Report*, which was codified in AICPA's Professional Standards, vol. 1, AU sec. 411. This establishes the GAAP hierarchy for federal entities. (See Box 13.1.)

### 13.3.1.3 Due Process

The FASAB follows due process procedures modeled after those used by Financial Accounting Standards Board and Government Accounting Standards Board.

The FASAB develops accounting concepts and standards after considering the results of due-process procedures. To meet its unique mission, the FASAB considers the information needs of the public, Congress, managers, and other users of federal financial information. The Board considers comments from the public on its proposed statements, which are widely distributed as "exposure drafts." The Board has also issued "preliminary views" documents. The Board publishes Statements of Federal Financial Accounting Concepts and Statements of Federal Financial Accounting Standards. After the Board deliberates a proposed statement and submits it to the principals, they have 90 days to review the Statement. If OMB and GAO do not object, the Statement is published by the FASAB and becomes GAAP for federal financial reporting entities.

### 13.3.1.4 Accounting and Auditing Policy Committee

The Accounting and Auditing Policy Committee (AAPC) is a standing task force of the FASAB. The AAPC provides guidance, in the form of "Technical Releases," regarding the application of existing principles. The AAPC includes representatives from the FASAB's three sponsoring agencies, three representatives from the Chief Financial Officers community (federal financial statement preparers), three representatives from the Inspector General community (federal auditors), a non-voting member from FASAB staff, and one member at large.

Technical releases must be approved by a majority of each of the three voting blocks and reviewed by the Board prior to issuance. They are published by the FASAB and announced in the Federal Register. As in the case of FASAB meetings, AAPC meetings are open to the public.

## 13.3.2 Office of Management and Budget

### 13.3.2.1 Mission

The OMB's predominant mission is to prepare the President's annual budget, which entails requesting, adjusting, and compiling submissions from the agencies, submitting a proposed budget to Congress, and supervising the administration of the enacted budget in executive branch agencies. In helping to formulate the President's spending plans, the OMB evaluates the effectiveness of agency programs, policies, and procedures, assesses competing funding demands among agencies, and sets funding priorities. The OMB ensures that agency reports, rules, testimony, and proposed legislation are consistent with the President's budget and with Administration policies.

In addition, the OMB oversees and coordinates the Administration's procurement, financial management, information, and regulatory policies. In each of these areas, the OMB's role is to help improve administrative management, develop better performance measures and coordinating mechanisms, and reduce any unnecessary burdens on the public.

To fulfill its budget execution oversight function, the OMB prescribes certain reporting requirements and the manner in which agencies account for and report transactions affecting the budget.

## 13.3.2.2 The Budget of the United States

The Budget of the United States Government is the most widely recognized and used financial report of the federal government. The budget process is the government's principal mechanism for reaching agreement on goals, allocating resources among competing uses, and assessing the government's fiscal effects on economic stability and growth. Most attention is paid to these future-oriented roles of the budget.[51]

The budget is a vehicle for the political process to reach agreement on goals and to allocate resources among competing priorities. It provides a system for controlling expenditures. In addition, it supplies information necessary for assessing the effect of the government's fiscal policies on the economy.[52]

Accounting and financial reporting also play a role as a control mechanism. Budgetary obligation accounting is used to control activities, primarily at the budget account level. Audited financial reports can provide users with assurance that accounting systems are providing consistent and reliable data.[53] Those who formulate, select, and implement government policies and programs need information useful for planning, controlling, and conducting government functions.[54]

Budget execution is designed to control and track tax receipts and the use of resources according to the purposes for which budget authority was approved. Actual receipts, obligations, and outlays are recorded by account, as is the status of budgetary resources at the end of each fiscal year.[55]

Conversely, the FASAB focuses on developing GAAP for reporting on the financial operations, financial position, and financial condition of the federal government and its component entities and other useful financial information. This implies a variety of measures of costs and other information that complements the information available in the budget. Together with budgetary reports, these reports provide a more comprehensive and insightful understanding of the government's financial position, results of operations, and financial condition than either set of reports alone.[56]

### 13.3.2.3 Budget Accounting—Appropriations, Apportionments, Allotments, Obligations, and Outlays

Prior to 1933, apportionments of appropriated funds were the responsibility of the program agency. In 1933, President Roosevelt made the Bureau of the Budget (now OMB) responsible for apportioning appropriated funds pursuant to the **Anti-deficiency Act**, and the OMB still has that responsibility today. OMB apportions total dollars only, not individual line items, on either a monthly or a quarterly basis.

The program agencies are responsible for the budget line items, that is, for making sure the obligations and outlays are consistent with legislative intent. They report the transactions to Treasury classified by Treasury account number. The program agencies may establish internal allotment systems to allocate apportioned funds. The allotted amounts are then available to program managers for obligation and expenditure.

### 13.3.2.4 On- and Off-Budget Totals

The budget documents provide information on all federal agencies and programs. However, because the laws governing Social Security (the Federal Old-Age and Survivors Insurance and the Federal Disability Insurance trust funds) and the Postal Service Fund exclude the receipts and outlays for those activities from the budget totals and from the calculation of the deficit or surplus, the budget presents on-budget and off-budget totals. The off-budget totals include the transactions excluded by law from the budget totals. The on-budget and off-budget amounts are added together to derive the totals for the federal government. These are sometimes referred to as the unified or consolidated budget totals.

It is not always obvious whether a transaction or activity should be included in the budget. Where there is a question, OMB normally follows the recommendation of the 1967 President's Commission on Budget Concepts to be comprehensive of the full range of federal agencies, programs, and activities. In recent years, for example, the budget has included the transactions of the Universal Service Fund, the Public Company Accounting Oversight Board, Guaranty Agencies Reserves, the National Railroad Retirement Investment Trust, the United Mine Workers Combined Benefits Fund, the Telecommunications Development Fund, and the transactions of Electric Reliability Organizations (EROs) established pursuant to the Energy Policy Act of 2005.

## 13.3.2.5 Audited Financial Statements Required

Most federal entities are required to prepare and submit audited financial statements. The CFO Act, as amended by the GMRA, requires the major 24 agencies of the federal government to prepare and submit audited financial statements. In addition, the Accountability of Tax Dollars Act of 2002 (ATDA) requires those federal entities not covered by the CFO Act to prepare and submit audited financial statements to the OMB and the Congress. Finally, the **Government Corporations Control Act** requires Government Corporations to submit Annual Management Reports to the OMB and the Congress.

The **OMB Circular A-136, "Financial Reporting Requirements,"** establishes a central point of reference for all federal financial reporting guidance for executive branch departments, agencies, and entities required to submit audited financial statements and interim financial statements under the CFO Act,[57] GMRA, and ATDA,[58] and Annual Management Reports under the Government Corporations Control Act of 1945.[59]

Under the **Reports Consolidation Act of 2000,**[60] agencies are permitted to submit combined reports in implementing statutory requirements for financial and performance management reporting to improve the efficiency of executive branch performance. These reports are combined in the Performance and Accountability Report (PAR).

A PAR must include a section entitled Management's Discussion and Analysis (MD&A). The MD&A is an overview of the financial and performance results. Management assurances required under the Federal Managers Financial Integrity Act (FMFIA)[61] and **OMB Circular A-123, "Management's Responsibility for Internal Control,"** must be separately identified within the MD&A as part of the information provided.

The annual program performance information submitted per GPRA should contain all of the required elements for the Annual Performance Report as specified in OMB Circular No. A-11, as amended.

The financial section (PAR Section 3) contains

A. CFO Letter—A signed letter from the CFO briefly summarizing
   ■ Planned periods for correcting audit weaknesses and noncompliance
   ■ Major impediments to correcting audit weaknesses and noncompliance
   ■ Progress made in correcting previously reported problems
B. Auditor's Report—Reporting guidance for the Auditor's Report is located in OMB Bulletin 07-04, Audit Requirements for Federal Financial Statements. The final Report must be signed by the auditor. The report can be located either before or after the financial statements and notes.
C. Financial statements and notes:
   ■ Balance sheet
   ■ Statement of net cost

- Statement of changes in net position
- Statement of budgetary resources
- Statement of custodial activity
- Statement of social insurance
- Notes to the financial statements
- Required supplementary information
- Other accompanying information

Interim unaudited financial statements, without notes, are required on a quarterly basis from most federal entities.

## 13.3.3 Treasury Department—The Fiscal Service and the Financial Management Service

### 13.3.3.1 Mission

The Treasury Department prepares government-wide financial reports as well as functioning as the government's primary fiscal agent. Among other things, the Treasury collects money, makes payments, manages borrowings, and performs central accounting functions, as well as producing coins and currency. The Treasury provides guidance to agencies on certain accounting matters though various vehicles, including the Treasury Financial Manual and the United States Standard General Ledger (see http://www.fms.treas.gov/).

The mission of the Treasury's Financial Management Service (FMS) is to provide (1) central payment services to federal program agencies, (2) operate the federal government's collections and deposit systems, (3) provide government-wide accounting and reporting services, and (4) manage the collection of delinquent debt. FMS also supports federal agencies' financial management improvement efforts in the areas of education, consulting, and accounting operations. FMS's express and explicit mission strategically supports the overarching Treasury goal of managing the government's finances effectively, as well as two of the government-wide initiatives under the President's Management Agenda—Improved Financial Performance and Expanded Electronic Government.

### 13.3.3.2 Issuing Government-Wide Financial Reports

FMS has the critical responsibility of maintaining the federal government's accounts. It closely monitors the government's monetary assets and liabilities at all times through its oversight of central accounting and reporting systems. FMS's oversight responsibilities include assisting federal agencies with adopting uniform accounting and reporting standards and systems and assuring the continuous exchange of financial information among federal agencies, the OMB, and financial institutions.

The FMS also gathers and publishes government-wide financial information for use in establishing fiscal and debt management policies. The public and private sectors are able to monitor the government's financial status using this financial data.

FMS publications include

- The Combined Statement of Receipts, Outlays, and Balances of the United States Government (the official publication of receipts and outlays)
- The Monthly Treasury Statement (a report of the government receipts and outlays and the budget surplus or deficit that is based on agency reporting)
- The Daily Treasury Statement (a report summarizing data on the cash and debt operations of the Treasury, which is based on reporting of the Treasury account balances of the Federal Reserve Banks)
- The Financial Report of the United States Government (the consolidated audited financial statements, based on FASAB standards, for the preceding fiscal year that cover the executive branch, as well as parts of the legislative and judicial branches).

### 13.3.3.3 Government-Wide Accounting

The Financial Report is the federal government's set of audited financial statements, a requirement of the Government Management and Reform Act of 1994. Starting in 2004, the Financial Report has been published by December 15 of each year. This is 75 days after the end of the fiscal year and more than two months earlier than in fiscal year 2003. This accelerated timing allows time for the information in the financial statements to be considered in the budget process. Decision makers are able to use the financial information in this report to improve the management and programs of the federal government.

## 13.3.4 Government Accountability Office

### 13.3.4.1 Mission

The GAO is an independent, nonpartisan, professional services agency in the legislative branch of the federal government. Commonly known as the "audit and investigative arm of the Congress" or the "congressional watchdog," the GAO examines how taxpayer dollars are spent, and advises Congress and agency heads on ways to improve the operation of the government. The GAO provides reliable information and informed analysis to Congress, federal agencies, and the public. It emphasizes three core values—accountability, integrity, and reliability—as the basis for its work.

### 13.3.4.2 GAO Guidance

A substantial portion of the general guidance issued by the GAO to executive agencies was first codified into its Policy and Procedures Manual for Guidance of

Federal Agencies in 1957. The accounting standards issued by the GAO were published as "Title 2" of that manual. Some people described those standards as similar to business-type accounting; others that they were accrual-basis standards tailored for the federal environment. For example, depreciation of capital assets was recommended but not required. In addition, Title 2 described the federal fund types, and internal control standards were included as an appendix.

Over the years, the manual was updated to incorporate current changes in laws, regulations, and practices. However, changes in certain laws, especially the creation of the FASAB, have led to changes. For details on those changes and for other GAO guidance on financial management, see "Other Publications," then "Accounting and Financial Management," and "Government Policy and Guidance" at www.gao.gov.

## 13.3.5 Other Fiscal Agencies

### 13.3.5.1 Congressional Budget Office

The **Congressional Budget and Impoundment Control Act of 1974** created the Congressional Budget Office (CBO) as well as a new budget process. The CBO's mission is to provide Congress with objective, timely, nonpartisan analyses needed for economic and budget decisions, and with the information and estimates required for the Congressional budget process.

The CBO's services can be grouped in four categories:

1. Helping Congress formulate a budget plan
2. Helping it stay within that plan
3. Helping it assess the impact of federal mandates
4. Helping it consider issues related to the budget and to economic policy

Among other duties, the CBO is required to develop cost estimates for virtually every bill reported by a Congressional committee to show how it would affect spending or revenues over the next five years or more.

Both the CBO and the Administration construct baseline budget projections according to rules set forth in law, primarily the Balanced Budget and Emergency Deficit Control Act of 1985 and the Congressional Budget and Impoundment Control Act of 1974. In general, those laws instruct the CBO and the OMB to project federal spending and revenues under current laws and policies. As a result, baselines are not intended to be predictions of future outcomes; rather, they serve as neutral benchmarks that lawmakers can use to gauge the effects of spending or revenue proposals, such as those in the President's budget.

### 13.3.5.2 Bureau of Economic Analysis

The Bureau of Economic Analysis (BEA) is an agency of the Department of Commerce. Along with the Census Bureau and STAT-USA, the BEA is part of the Department's Economics and Statistics Administration. The BEA promotes a better understanding of the U.S. economy by providing timely, relevant, and accurate economic accounts data in an objective and cost-effective manner. It produces economic accounts statistics that enable government and business decision makers, researchers, and the American public to follow and understand the performance of the U.S. economy. To do this, the BEA collects source data, conducts research and analysis, develops and implements estimation methodologies, and disseminates statistics to the public.

The BEA is one of the world's leading statistical agencies. Although it is a relatively small agency, the BEA produces some of the most closely watched economic statistics that influence the decisions made by government officials, business people, households, and individuals. The BEA's economic statistics, which are intended to provide a comprehensive, up-to-date picture of the U.S. economy, are key ingredients in critical decisions affecting monetary policy, tax and budget projections, and business investment plans. The cornerstone of the BEA's statistics is the national income and product accounts (NIPAs), which feature the estimates of gross domestic product (GDP) and related measures.

The Commerce Department recognizes the GDP as its greatest achievement of the 20th century. The GDP statistics has been ranked as one of the three most influential measures that affect U.S. financial markets. Since the NIPAs were first developed in the aftermath of the Great Depression, the BEA has developed and extended its estimates to cover a wide range of economic activities. Today, the BEA prepares national, regional, industry, and international accounts that present essential information on such key issues as economic growth, regional economic development, interindustry relationships, and the United States' position in the world economy.

## 13.4 Types of Accounts Maintained by Federal Entities

### 13.4.1 Budget Accounts

The OMB assigns budget accounts to programs authorized by law. A "budget account" generally covers an organized set of activities, programs, or services directed toward a common purpose or goal.

The size and scope of budget accounts varies according to Congressional preference. They can vary from very small accounts, which are useful for constraining management, to very large accounts, which can be used to finance many activities.[62] A budget account may coincide with an organization or one or more of its suborganizations. Other times, several budget accounts need to be aggregated to constitute an organization or suborganization.[63]

Budget accounts are grouped by fund type. The term "fund" can be confusing; it can have more than one meaning for federal accounting. Depending on the context, it may mean merely a resource, as in "funds" available to pay an obligation.

For budgetary accounting, it may mean "federal funds" or "trust funds" in the sense of major groupings of accounts.

There are two major groups of funds in the budget: federal funds and trust funds.

## 13.4.1.1 Federal Funds

The federal funds include all transactions not classified by law as being in trust funds. Federal fund accounts include general fund accounts, revolving funds accounts, and special funds accounts. The main financing component of the federal funds group is referred to as the "general fund." General fund accounts carry out the general purposes of government, rather than being restricted by law to a specific program. General fund accounts consists of all collections not earmarked by law to finance other funds. [64]

The general fund group of accounts, which constitutes the greater part of the budget, includes receipt and expenditure (or appropriation) accounts. Receipts not earmarked by law for a specific purpose, such as income tax receipts, are recorded in general fund accounts, which also include the proceeds of general borrowing. Governmental receipts and "offsetting receipts," which are not available for incurring obligations or making outlays, are deposited into general fund receipt accounts.

General fund expenditure accounts are provided with budget authority (e.g., appropriations or "offsetting collections") and are used to incur obligations and record general fund expenditures. General fund appropriations draw from general fund receipts and borrowing collectively and, therefore, are not specifically linked to receipt accounts.

The revolving fund group of accounts consists of public enterprise fund and intragovernmental revolving fund accounts. Public enterprise funds are revolving funds used for programs authorized by law to conduct a cycle of business-type operations, primarily with the public, in which outlays generate collections. Intragovernmental funds are revolving funds that conduct business-type operations primarily within and between government agencies. The collections and the outlays of revolving funds are recorded in the same budget account.

Special funds consist of receipt accounts for federal fund receipts that laws have earmarked for specific purposes and the associated appropriation accounts for the expenditure of those receipts.

## 13.4.1.2 "Trust Funds"

Federal "trust funds" include receipt and expenditure of monies by the government for specific purposes. Trust funds may carry out specific purposes and programs in accordance with the terms of a statute that designates the fund as a trust fund (such as the Highway Trust Fund); or they may carry out the stipulations of a trust where the government itself is the beneficiary (such as any of several trust funds for gifts and donations for specific purposes). Trust revolving funds are trust funds credited with collections earmarked by law to carry out a cycle of business-type operations.

The federal budget meaning of the term "trust," as applied to trust fund accounts, differs significantly from its private sector usage. In the private sector, the beneficiary of a trust usually owns the trust's assets, which are managed by a trustee who must follow the stipulations of the trust. In contrast, the federal government owns the assets of most federal trust funds, and it can raise or lower future trust fund collections and payments, or change the purposes for which the collections are used, by changing existing laws. There is no substantive difference between a trust fund and a special fund, or between a trust revolving fund and a public enterprise revolving fund.

For example, in 2007 the House of Representatives HR 2895 entitled the "National Affordable Housing Trust Fund Act." The purpose of the trust fund is to expand federal housing programs, with a goal of producing, rehabilitating, and preserving 1.5 million housing units over 10 years. The press release for the bill states that it will "initially allocate between $800 million and $1 billion annually directly to states and local communities, *without increasing government spending or the federal deficit*." (emphasis added) The trust fund would be funded by assessments on newly regulated housing and finance entities. This "trust fund" is in fact a revolving fund and not what is commonly understood to be a trust fund in the private sector.

However, in some instances, the government does act as a true trustee of assets that are owned or held for the benefit of others. For example, it maintains accounts on behalf of individual federal employees in the Thrift Savings Fund, investing them as directed by the individual employee. The government accounts for such funds in deposit funds, which are not included in the budget.[65]

## 13.4.2 Treasury Accounts

The Treasury Department assigns Treasury account numbers and titles for central reporting purposes. When Congress provides budget authority for a particular purpose or under a particular title, it also provides a specific period of time for which the budget authority is available for obligation. This time of availability may be annual, multiyear, or indefinite (sometimes referred to as "no-year"). The Treasury establishes expenditure accounts based on the time of availability of the resources in the account. That is, the Treasury establishes separate accounts with separate Treasury account numbers for each period of availability, that is, annual, multiyear, or no-year amount. For budget execution, the agencies must report data for each of the expenditure accounts established by the Treasury.

Treasury accounts are not the same as budget accounts. The former are accounts established in the Treasury to, among other purposes, record the appropriations and other budgetary resources provided by statutes and the transactions affecting those accounts. For the most part, budget accounts are aggregations of Treasury accounts.[66] For budget formulation, the appropriations and other budget authority provided to the Treasury accounts with the same appropriation title for the years covered by the budget are combined and presented as a single account under a single title, e.g., "Salaries and expenses." For receipt accounts, the budget and Treasury accounts are usually the same.[67]

## 13.4.3 *United States Government Standard General Ledger*

The United States Standard General Ledger (USSGL) provides a uniform chart of accounts and technical guidance to be used in standardizing federal agency accounting.[68] The USSGL was developed by an interagency work group headed by the Transportation Department, issued and mandated by the OMB in 1986, and subsequently maintained by the Treasury Department.

The USSGL accounts are not budget accounts. They record specific homogeneous types of transactions and balances that aggregate to specific classifications and line items on the federal financial statements. They have been established so that agencies can control their financial transactions and balances, meet the basic financial reporting requirements, and integrate budgetary and financial accounting in the same general ledger.[69]

The USSGL chart of accounts provides the basic structure for the USSGL. It includes two independent sets of self-balancing (total debits equal total credits) general ledger accounts: (1) proprietary (or financial) accounts and (2) budgetary accounts. Proprietary accounts primarily are based on the FASAB standards, while budgetary accounts are based on the OMB reporting requirements.

Reporting to the Treasury Department and OMB requires a lower level of aggregation than the 4-digit USSGL account numbers provide. The USSGL accounts include attributes containing various domain values that, when added to a basic 4-digit USSGL account, provide the appropriate level of aggregation needed for central agency reporting and, in effect, create new USSGL accounts. It is this lower level of aggregation—the basic 4-digit USSGL account plus applicable attribute domain values—that agencies must capture at the transaction level to (1) comply with USSGL policy, and (2) achieve the desired result for proper Treasury and OMB reporting.[70]

The **Federal Financial Management Improvement Act (FFMIA) of 1996** requires federal agencies to use the USSGL. Section 802 of FFMIA contains congressional findings that criticize the status of federal financial management, recognize the FASAB's efforts since 1990, and state the need for federal accounting systems and practices to incorporate accepted accounting standards and reporting objectives. Section 803(a) requires that each agency have financial management systems[71] that comply substantially with (1) federal financial systems requirements, (2) applicable federal accounting standards, and (3) the United States Government Standard General Ledger at the transaction level.

The USSGL Supplement (released annually) is composed of five major sections:

1. Chart of Accounts
2. Account Descriptions
3. Accounting Transactions
4. USSGL Attributes
5. Report Crosswalks

Since each agency's programs and activities are different and therefore require unique management information, each agency is expected to establish and maintain its own accounting systems. However, the agency's chart of accounts must comply with the chart of accounts in the USSGL or otherwise be convertible to SGL accounts at the transaction level. This helps to ensure that agencies account for similar activities and record similar transactions in the same manner and increase the comparability of information. In addition, it helps to ensure that agencies fully account for all transactions and rely less on estimates and unofficial records.

### 13.4.4 Final Note Regarding Accounts

As noted, budget and Treasury accounts are used for budget formulation and execution as well as for reporting collections, disbursement, and other accounting activity to the Treasury.

The USSGL accounts are used internally by federal entities and are required for quarterly and annual reporting to the Treasury's Central Accounting System.

Most federal entities are required by law to prepare audited financial reports according to GAAP. Also, a federal entity may voluntarily or otherwise want to publish an audited financial report prepared in accordance with GAAP. The FASAB is the AICPA-designed federal GAAP standard-setter.

## 13.5 Financial Statements Required of Federal Agencies

The FASAB discussed the statements it believed constitute a full set of financial statements and described the statements themselves in SFFAC 2, Entity and Display. These statements are incorporated in the OMB Circular A-136, and the USSGL provides "crosswalk" guidance from USSGL accounts to pro forma line items for these statements. They are described in the following text.

### 13.5.1 Balance Sheet

Federal agency balance sheets (see Exhibit 13.1) display the stocks of assets and liabilities of the entity. Net position is the difference between assets and liabilities. SFFAC 2 provides guidance regarding how to display certain types of assets and liabilities.

## CONSOLIDATED BALANCE SHEET
### As of September 30, 2006 and 2005
### (in millions)

| | 2006 | 2005 |
|---|---|---|
| **Assets:** | | |
| Intragovernmental: | | |
| Fund Balance with Treasury (Note 3) | $ 42,191 | $ 42,327 |
| Investments (Note 5) | 81 | 69 |
| Accounts Receivable, Net (Note 6) | 246 | 712 |
| Other (Note 11) | - | 1 |
| Total Intragovernmental | 42,518 | 43,109 |
| | | |
| Cash and Other Monetary Assets (Note 4) | 224 | 242 |
| Investments (Note 5) | 3 | 15 |
| Accounts Receivable, Net (Note 6) | 8,635 | 9,442 |
| Loans Receivable and Related Foreclosed Property, Net (Note 7) | 77,791 | 75,176 |
| Inventory and Related Property, Net (Note 8) | 55 | 29 |
| General Property, Plant, and Equipment, Net (Note 9) | 4,905 | 4,885 |
| Other (Note 11) | 98 | 86 |
| | | |
| **Total Assets (Note 2)** | 134,229 | 132,984 |
| | | |
| Stewardship PP&E (Note 10) | | |
| | | |
| **Liabilities:** | | |
| Intragovernmental: | | |
| Accounts Payable | 7 | 821 |
| Debt (Note 13) | 83,447 | 83,515 |
| Other (Note 15) | 14,080 | 18,591 |
| Total Intragovernmental | 97,534 | 102,927 |
| | | |
| Accounts Payable | 4,170 | 4,292 |
| Loan Guarantee Liability (Note 7) | 1,296 | 1,214 |
| Debt Held by the Public (Note 13) | - | 1 |
| Federal Employee and Veterans Benefits | 808 | 834 |
| Environmental and Disposal Liabilities (Note 14) | 63 | 28 |
| Other (Notes 15 & 16) | 20,082 | 21,710 |
| **Total Liabilities (Note 12)** | 123,953 | 131,006 |
| | | |
| Commitments and Contingencies (Note 17) | | |
| | | |
| **Net Position:** | | |
| Unexpended Appropriations | - | 21,490 |
| Unexpended Appropriations - earmarked funds | 976 | - |
| Unexpended Appropriations - other funds | 25,409 | - |
| Cumulative Results of Operations | - | (19,512) |
| Cumulative Results of Operations - earmarked funds | 518 | - |
| Cumulative Results of Operations - other funds | (16,627) | - |
| **Total Net Position** | 10,276 | 1,978 |
| | | |
| **Total Liabilities and Net Position** | $ 134,229 | $ 132,984 |

The accompanying notes are an integral part of these statements.

---

**Exhibit 13.1    Balance Sheet, U.S. Department of Agriculture.**

A federal entity's assets include normal balance sheet items plus a few items unique to government. One example is the fund balance with the Treasury, which is the aggregate amount in accounts with the Treasury that the entity can use. In addition, some assets are unique to the government, for example, national parks and historical buildings, and often cannot be valued for balance sheet purposes. They are reported in nonmonetary units and described in the report's narrative.

Entities classify liabilities based on whether or not they are covered by budgetary resources. For example, environmental liabilities often involve long-term obligations for which Congress provides budget authority in annual appropriations.

The balance sheet further classifies assets and liabilities as intragovernmental or governmental.

Total assets minus total liabilities are equal to net position. Net position is further subdivided into unexpended appropriations and the cumulative results of operations. Unexpended appropriations are those appropriations not yet obligated or expended, including undelivered orders.

### 13.5.2 Statement of Net Cost

The statement of net cost (see Exhibit 13.2) displays gross and net cost of goods and services provided during the reporting period. It reports all costs less any associated exchange revenue. With some exceptions (related to intragovernmental sales), the bottom line is the amount that, over time, must be financed by nonexchange revenue and other financing sources. Appropriations and other financing sources are reported in the statement of changes in net position.

Recognition of the full cost of federal programs is necessary to improve decision making. The statement of net cost helps to achieve this goal. Costs can be classified by suborganization, program or object class, or any combination thereof.

The statement of net cost is a significant departure from traditional government accounting and financial reporting. For decades, the practice in government had been to restrict the use of accrual-basis, full cost accounting to "businesslike" activities of government. The statement of net cost is predicated on the assumption that decision makers need to know the full cost of programs to make informed policy decisions, and that meaningful performance measurement must relate results—that is, outputs and outcomes—to resources consumed to produce those results. Full costing is necessary to fulfill the intent of the **Government Performance and Results Act of 1993**, and federal financial accounting and reporting systems should place due emphasis on full costing as well as on budget execution.

### 13.5.3 Statement of Changes in Net Position

The statement of changes in net position (see Exhibit 13.3) focuses on how the net cost of operations is financed. It identifies common financing sources, including money provided to and used by an agency through appropriations, taxes, donations, and transfer to and from other federal agencies. It includes "imputed financing," which is described in SFFAC 2 as costs incurred by the reporting entity, but financed by another entity or costs attributable to the reporting entity's activities that do not

**CONSOLIDATED STATEMENT OF NET COST**
**For the Years Ended September 30, 2006 and 2005**
**(in millions)**

|  | *2006* | *2005* |
|---|---|---|
| *Enhance International Competitiveness and the Sustainability of Rural and Farm Economies:* | | |
| Cross Cost | $31,841 | $41,909 |
| Less: Earned Revenue | 6,979 | 15,136 |
| Net Cost | 24,862 | 26,773 |
| *Support Increased Economic Opportunities and Improved Quality of Life in Rural America:* | | |
| Cross Cost | 7,048 | 5,358 |
| Less: Earned Revenue | 3,960 | 4,344 |
| Net Cost | 3,068 | 1,014 |
| *Enhance Protection and Safety of the Nation's Agriculture and Food Supply:* | | |
| Cross Cost | 3,629 | 3,071 |
| Less: Earned Revenue | 649 | 630 |
| Net Cost | 2,980 | 2,441 |
| *Improve the Nation's Nutrition ahd Health:* | | |
| Cross Cost | 53,064 | 51,033 |
| Less: Earned Revenue | 36 | 46 |
| Net Cost | 53,028 | 50,987 |
| *Protect and Enhance the Nation's Natural Resource Base and Environment:* | | |
| Cross Cost | 12,592 | 10,686 |
| Less: Earned Revenue | 1,104 | 888 |
| Net Cost | 11,488 | 9,798 |
| Total Gross Costs | 108,174 | 112,057 |
| Less: Total Earned Revenues | 12,748 | 21,044 |
| **Net Cost of Operations** | **$95,426** | **$91,013** |

**Exhibit 13.2   Statement of Net Cost, U.S. Department of Agriculture.**

require a direct, out-of-pocket payment. Imputed financing reflects the fact that federal agencies are not independent economic entities. For example, the Office of Personnel Management pays certain pension benefits to civilian retirees of federal agencies. These unreimbursed employee benefits are out-of-pocket costs to OPM but would be considered expenses and imputed financing to the employer agency.

## CONSOLIDATED STATEMENT OF CHANGES IN NET POSITION
### For the Years Ended September 30, 2006 and 2005
#### (in millions)

| | 2006 Earmarked Funds | 2006 All Other Funds | 2006 Eliminations | 2006 Consolidated Total | 2005 Consolidated Total |
|---|---|---|---|---|---|
| **Cumulative Results of Operations:** | | | | | |
| Beginning Balances | $ 964 | $ (20,476) | $ - | $ (19,512) | $ (7,174) |
| **Budgetary Financing Sources:** | | | | | |
| Appropriations Used | 3,184 | 91,765 | - | 94,949 | 77,921 |
| Non-exchange Revenue | 1 | 2 | - | 2 | 8 |
| Donations and Forfeitures of Cash and Equivalents | - | - | - | 1 | 2 |
| Transfers In (Out) without Reimbursement | 915 | 2,694 | - | 3,609 | 686 |
| Other | - | - | - | - | (1) |
| **Other Financing Sources (Non-Exchange):** | | | | | |
| Donations and Forfeitures of Property | - | - | - | - | 31 |
| Transfers In (Out) without Reimbursement | - | (544) | - | (544) | (1,001) |
| Imputed Financing | 43 | 3,113 | (2,349) | 807 | 833 |
| Other | 5 | - | - | 5 | 196 |
| Total Financing Sources | 4,148 | 97,030 | (2,349) | 98,829 | 78,675 |
| Net Cost of Operations | (4,594) | (93,181) | 2,349 | (95,426) | (91,013) |
| Net Change | (446) | 3,849 | - | 3,403 | (12,338) |
| Cumulative Results of Operations, Ending | 518 | (16,627) | - | (16,109) | (19,512) |
| **Unexpended Appropriations:** | | | | | |
| Beginning Balances | 923 | 20,567 | - | 21,490 | 22,158 |
| **Budgetary Financing Sources:** | | | | | |
| Appropriations Received | 3,308 | 97,832 | - | 101,140 | 80,697 |
| Appropriations transferred in/out | (5) | 103 | - | 98 | (507) |
| Other Adjustments | (66) | (1,328) | - | (1,394) | (2,937) |
| Appropriations Used | (3,184) | (91,765) | - | (94,949) | (77,921) |
| Total Budgetary Financing Sources | 53 | 4,842 | - | 4,895 | (668) |
| Unexpended Appropriations, Ending | 976 | 25,409 | - | 26,385 | 21,490 |
| **Net Position** | $ 1,494 | $ 8,782 | $ - | $ 10,276 | $ 1,978 |

**Exhibit 13.3  Statement of Changes in Net Position, U.S. Department of Agriculture.**

### 13.5.4 Statement of Custodial Activities

The statement of custodial activities is required for federal entities whose primary mission is collecting nonexchange revenue, such as taxes and duties that finance the operations of the entire federal government, or at least programs of other federal entities. Examples of "collecting entities" are the Bureau of the Customs and the IRS.

### 13.5.5 Statement of Budgetary Resources

The statement of budgetary resources (see Exhibit 13.4) provides information on budgetary resources available and outlays for the fiscal year, as well as the status of budgetary resources at the fiscal year end. It includes a reconciliation of obligations incurred with cash outlays during the fiscal year. It is prepared using budgetary accounting rules (see the following text), which are a modified cash basis of accounting.

This statement is especially significant because it subjects federal budget execution to audit at the level of the reporting entity for the first time. Entities must make disclosures if the information in this statement differs from that shown in the "actual" column of the President's budget.

**COMBINED STATEMENT OF BUDGETARY RESOURCES**
**For the Years Ended September 30, 2006 and 2005**
**(in millions)**

| | 2006 | | 2005 | |
|---|---|---|---|---|
| | Budgetary | Non-Budgetary Credit Reform Financing Accounts | Budgetary | Non-Budgetary Credit Reform Financing Accounts |
| **Budgetary Resources:** | | | | |
| Unobligated balance, brought forward, October 1 (Note 24) | $ 19,170 | $ 6,828 | $ 18,756 | $ 6,325 |
| Recoveries of prior year unpaid obligations | 9,071 | 941 | 6,243 | 559 |
| Budget Authority - | | | | |
| Appropriation | 109,856 | - | 88,940 | - |
| Borrowing Authority (Notes 22 & 23) | 44,465 | 12,608 | 45,357 | 10,886 |
| Earned - | | | | |
| Collected | 23,265 | 7,864 | 27,460 | 8,576 |
| Change in receivables from Federal Sources | (129) | (29) | - | (113) |
| Change in unfilled customer orders - | | | | |
| Advances received | 299 | - | (1,383) | - |
| Without advance from Federal Sources | 70 | 11 | 15 | 2 |
| Expenditure transfers from trust funds | 1,050 | - | 899 | - |
| Nonexpenditure transfers, net, anticipated and actual | (342) | - | (907) | - |
| Permanently not available | (55,745) | (8,798) | (39,871) | (4,911) |
| Total Budgetary Resources | 151,030 | 19,425 | 145,509 | 21,324 |
| **Status of Budgetary Resources:** | | | | |
| Obligations Incurred (Note 21) - | | | | |
| Direct | 87,185 | 15,710 | 82,879 | 14,496 |
| Reimbursable | 42,563 | - | 43,460 | - |
| Unobligated Balance - | | | | |
| Apportioned | 7,818 | 1,625 | 5,919 | 5,672 |
| Exempt from Apportionment | 771 | - | 1,262 | 5 |
| Unobligated balance not available | 12,693 | 2,090 | 11,989 | 1,151 |
| Total status of budgetary resources | 151,030 | 19,425 | 145,509 | 21,324 |
| **Change in Obligated Balances:** | | | | |
| Obligated balance, net, brought forward October 1 (Note 24) | 26,555 | 18,202 | 21,010 | 17,136 |
| Obligations incurred | 129,748 | 15,710 | 126,339 | 14,496 |
| Gross outlays | (120,756) | (14,089) | (114,536) | (12,982) |
| Recoveries of prior year unpaid | (9,071) | (941) | (6,243) | (559) |
| Change in uncollected payments from Federal Sources | 59 | 18 | (15) | 111 |
| Obligated balance, net, end of period - | | | | |
| Unpaid obligations (Note 28) | 28,881 | 19,722 | 28,961 | 19,042 |
| Uncollected customer payments from Federal Sources | (2,344) | (822) | (2,406) | (840) |
| Obligated balance, net, end of period | 26,537 | 18,900 | 26,555 | 18,202 |
| **Net Outlays:** | | | | |
| Gross outlays | 120,756 | 14,089 | 114,536 | 12,982 |
| Offsetting collections | (24,612) | (7,864) | (26,976) | (8,576) |
| Distributed offsetting receipts | (1,708) | (987) | (1,445) | (722) |
| Net Outlays | $ 94,436 | $ 5,238 | $ 86,115 | $ 3,684 |

**Exhibit 13.4    Statement of Budget Resources, U.S. Department of Agriculture.**

## 13.5.6 *Statement of Social Insurance*

Paragraphs 27(3) and 32(3) of SFFAS 17, Accounting for Social Insurance, required a statement of social insurance (SOSI) (see Exhibit 13.5). The SOSI is to present actuarial present values for all future contributions and tax income and all future expenditures from or to or on behalf of three groups of participants:

1. Current participants who have not yet attained retirement age (e.g., the Social Security Administration has assumed an entry age of 15 years for new participants, and an age of 62 for retirement)
2. Current participants who have attained retirement age
3. Future participants expected to become participants during a projection period encompassing substantially all the present value attributed to (1) and (2) just mentioned

In addition, the SOSI displays the net present value of cash flow during the projection period. Notes to the statement present the Trust Fund balance at the valuation date. Also the notes describe how the obligation to the "closed group" of participants is calculated.

SFFAS 26[72] made some significant changes in SOSI. It requires the SOSI to be a "basic" financial statement, and hence subject to full audit procedures, rather than "required supplementary stewardship information" (RSSI). In addition, it requires the significant underlying SOSI assumptions in the notes that are an integral part of the basic financial statement. SFFAS 26 designated the other information required by SFFAS 17—including the sensitivity analysis required in para. 27(4) and 32(4)—as required supplementary information, except to the extent that the preparer elects to include some or all of that information in notes that are presented as an integral part of the basic financial statements.

## 13.5.7 *Statement of Financing*

SFFAC 2 provides concepts for reconciling budgetary and financial accounting information. It contains a category of information addressing users' need to understand "how information on the use of budgetary resources relates to information on the cost of program operations ..."[73] The objective of this information is to explain and reconcile the differences between budgetary and financial (proprietary) accounting information.

SFFAS 7, Accounting for Revenue and Other Financing Sources and Concepts for Reconciling Budgetary and Financial Accounting, requires a reconciliation of proprietary and budgetary information in a way that helps users relate the two.[74] In the concepts section of SFFAS 7, the Board illustrated a "statement of financing" (see Exhibit 13.6) to display the information. The statement of financing

**United States Government**
**Statements of Social Insurance**
**Present Value of Long-Range (75 Years, except Black Lung) Actuarial Projections**

************UNAUDITED***********

| (In billions of dollars) | 2006 | 2005 | 2004 | 2003 | 2002 |
|---|---|---|---|---|---|
| **Federal Old-Age, Survivors and Disability Insurance (Social Security): (Note 23)** | | | | | |
| *Contributions and Earmarked Taxes from:* | | | | | |
| Participants who have attained age 62 | 533 | 464 | 411 | 359 | 348 |
| Participants ages 15-61 | 16,568 | 15,290 | 14,388 | 13,576 | 13,048 |
| Future participants (under age 15 and births during period) | 15,006 | 13,696 | 12,900 | 12,213 | 11,893 |
| All current and future participants | 32,107 | 29,450 | 27,699 | 26,147 | 25,289 |
| | | | | | |
| *Expenditures for Scheduled Future Benefits for:* | | | | | |
| Participants who have attained age 62 | 5,866 | 5,395 | 4,933 | 4,662 | 4,402 |
| Participants ages 15-61 | 26,211 | 23,942 | 22,418 | 21,015 | 20,210 |
| Future participants (under age 15 and births during period) | 6,480 | 5,816 | 5,578 | 5,398 | 5,240 |
| All current and future participants | 38,557 | 35,154 | 32,928 | 31,075 | 29,851 |
| | | | | | |
| *Present value of future expenditures less future revenue* | 6,449[1] | 5,704[2] | 5,229[3] | 4,927[4] | 4,562[5] |
| **Federal Hospital Insurance (Medicare Part A): (Note 23)** | | | | | |
| *Contributions and Earmarked Taxes from:* | | | | | |
| Participants who have attained eligibility age 65 | 192 | 162 | 148 | 128 | 125 |
| Participants who have not attained eligibility age 15-64 | 5,685 | 5,064 | 4,820 | 4,510 | 4,408 |
| Future participants (under age 15 and births during period)) | 4,767 | 4,209 | 4,009 | 3,773 | 3,753 |
| All current and future participants | 10,644 | 9,435 | 8,976 | 8,411 | 8,286 |
| | | | | | |
| *Expenditures for Scheduled Future Benefits for:* | | | | | |
| Participants who have attained eligibility age 65 | 2,397 | 2,179 | 2,168 | 1,897 | 1,747 |
| Participants who have not attained eligibility age 15-64 | 15,633 | 12,668 | 12,054 | 10,028 | 9,195 |
| Future participants (under age 15 and births during period)) | 3,904 | 3,417 | 3,246 | 2,653 | 2,470 |
| All current and future participants | 21,934 | 18,264 | 17,468 | 14,577 | 13,412 |
| | | | | | |
| *Present value of future expenditures less future revenue* | 11,290[1] | 8,829[2] | 8,492[3] | 6,166[4] | 5,126[5] |
| **Federal Supplementary Medical Insurance (Medicare Part B): (Note 23)** | | | | | |
| *Premiums from:* | | | | | |
| Participants who have attained eligibility age 65 | 409 | 363 | 332 | 283 | 252 |
| Participants who have not attained eligibility age 15-64 | 3,167 | 2,900 | 2,665 | 2,148 | 1,856 |
| Future participants (under age 15 and births during period)) | 906 | 924 | 891 | 688 | 600 |
| All current and future participants | 4,481 | 4,187 | 3,889 | 3,119 | 2,708 |
| | | | | | |
| *Expenditures for Scheduled Future Benefits for:* | | | | | |
| Participants who have attained eligibility age 65 | 1,773 | 1,622 | 1,475 | 1,306 | 1,132 |
| Participants who have not attained eligibility age 15-64 | 12,433 | 11,541 | 10,577 | 8,845 | 7,463 |
| Future participants (under age 15 and births during period)) | 3,407 | 3,408 | 3,277 | 2,622 | 2,238 |
| All current and future participants | 17,613 | 16,571 | 15,329 | 12,773 | 10,833 |
| | | | | | |
| *Present value of future expenditures less future revenue*[6] | 13,131[1] | 12,384[2] | 11,440[3] | 9,653[4] | 8,125[5] |
| **Federal Supplementary Medical Insurance (Medicare Part D): (Note 23)** | | | | | |
| *Premiums and State Transfers from:* | | | | | |
| Participants who have attained eligibility age 65 | 173 | 185 | 176 | | |
| Participants who have not attained eligibility age 15-64 | 1,700 | 1,790 | 1,857 | | |
| Future participants (under age 15 and births during period)) | 492 | 572 | 618 | | |
| All current and future participants | 2,366 | 2,547 | 2,651 | | |
| | | | | | |
| *Expenditures for Scheduled Future Benefits for:* | | | | | |
| Participants who have attained eligibility age 65 | 792 | 880 | 773 | | |
| Participants who have not attained eligibility age 15-64 | 7,338 | 7,913 | 7,566 | | |
| Future participants (under age 15 and births during period)) | 2,121 | 2,440 | 2,431 | | |
| All current and future participants | 10,250 | 11,233 | 10,770 | | |
| | | | | | |
| *Present value of future expenditures less future revenue*[6] | 7,884[1] | 8,686[2] | 8,119[3] | | |

**Exhibit 13.5   Statement of Social Insurance, Financial Report of the United States Government.**

subsequently developed into a basic statement. However, the Board was uncertain at that early juncture whether this information should be displayed as a statement or in the notes to the financial statements.

The concepts section of SFFAS 7 stated that the OMB would provide guidance regarding details of the display for the statement of financing, including whether it should be presented as a basic financial statement or as a schedule in the notes to the basic financial statements.[75] Problems encountered by preparers in the construction of the statement led to the OMB changing the Circulate A-136 instructions, effective for FY 2007, to allow the reconciliation information to be presented in a note rather than a statement of financing. The information is now referred to as

**CONSOLIDATED STATEMENT OF FINANCING**
**For the Years Ended September 30, 2006 and 2005**
**(in millions)**

| | 2006 | 2005 |
|---|---|---|
| **Resources Used to Finance Activities:** | | |
| Budgetary Resources Obligated - | | |
| Obligations Incurred | $ 145,458 | $ 140,835 |
| Less: Spending authority from offsetting collections and recoveries | 42,413 | 42,258 |
| Obligations net of offsetting collections and recoveries | 103,045 | 98,577 |
| Less: Offsetting receipts | 2,695 | 2,167 |
| Net Obligations | 100,350 | 96,410 |
| | | |
| Other Resources - | | |
| Donations and forfeitures of property | - | 31 |
| Transfers in(out) without reimbursement | (544) | (1,001) |
| Imputed financing from costs absorbed by others | 807 | 833 |
| Other | 5 | 196 |
| Net other resources used to finance activities | 268 | 59 |
| | | |
| Total resources used to finance activities | 100,618 | 96,469 |
| | | |
| **Resources Used to Finance Items not Part of the Net Cost of Operations:** | | |
| Change in undelivered orders | (840) | (2,192) |
| Resources that fund expenses recognized in prior periods | (812) | (432) |
| Budgetary offsetting collections and receipts that do not affect net cost of operations - | | |
| Credit program collections which increase liabilities for loan guarantees or allowances for subsidy | 12,067 | 14,921 |
| Other | 7,811 | 10,968 |
| Resources that finance the acquisition of assets | (28,444) | (31,208) |
| Other resources or adjustments to net obligated resources that do not affect net cost of operations | (1,860) | (932) |
| | | |
| Total resources used to finance items not part of the net cost of operations | (12,078) | (8,875) |
| | | |
| Total resources used to finance the net cost of operations | 88,540 | 87,594 |
| | | |
| **Components of the Net Cost of Operations that will not Require or Generate** | | |
| **Resources in the Current Period:** | | |
| Components Requiring or Generating Resources in Future Periods - | | |
| Increase in annual leave liability | 43 | - |
| Increase in environmental and disposal liability | 35 | - |
| Upward/Downward reestimates of credit subsidy expense | 650 | (1,853) |
| Increase in exchange revenue receivable from the public | (377) | (7,791) |
| Other | 95 | 7,456 |
| Total components of Net Cost of Operations that will require or generate | | |
| resources in future periods (Note 29) | 446 | (2,188) |
| | | |
| Components not Requiring or Generating Resources - | | |
| Depreciation and amortization | 375 | 524 |
| Revaluation of assets or liabilities | (53) | (525) |
| Other | 6,118 | 5,608 |
| Total components of Net Cost of Operations that will not require or generate resources | 6,440 | 5,607 |
| | | |
| Total components of Net Cost of Operations that will not require or generate | | |
| resources in the current period | 6,886 | 3,419 |
| | | |
| Net Cost of Operations | $ 95,426 | $ 91,013 |

**Exhibit 13.6    Statement of Financing, U.S. Department of Agriculture.**

"Reconciliation of Net Cost of Operations to Budget." The OMB and the Chief Financial Officers' Council (CFOC) decided that this reconciliation would be better understood as a note rather than as a basic statement.

## 13.5.7.1 Required Supplementary Information

Some FASAB standards required supplementary information (RSI) in addition to the basic information in the financial statements and notes thereto. RSI differs from other types of information that is presented outside the basic financial statements because the FASAB considers it an essential part of the financial reporting and because guidelines for measurement and presentation have been established. Accordingly, auditors apply certain limited procedures to required supplementary information and should report deficiencies in, or the omission of, such information.[76]

# Appendix 1—Documents Resulting from FASAB and AAPC Processes

**Documents Resulting from the**
**Federal Accounting Standards Advisory Board (FASAB) and the**
**Accounting and Auditing Policy Committee (AAPC) Processes**

| 1 | 2 | Number | Title | Date Issued | FY to Implement |
|---|---|---|---|---|---|
| F | C | SFFAC 1 | Objectives of Federal Financial Reporting | Sep-93 | N/A |
| F | C | SFFAC 2 | Entity and Display | Jun-95 | N/A |
| F | C | SFFAC3 | Management's Discussion & Analysis | Apr-99 | N/A |
| F | C | SFFAC 4 | Intended Audience and Qualitative Characteristics for the Consolidated Financial Report of the United States Government | Mar-03 | N/A |
| F | S | SFFAS 1 | Accounting for Selected Assets and Liabilities | Mar-93 | 1994 |
| F | S | SFFAS 2 | Accounting for Direct Loans and Loan Guarantees | Aug-93 | 1994 |
| F | S | SFFAS 3 | Accounting for Inventory and Related Property | Oct-93 | 1994 |
| F | S | SFFAS 4 | Managerial Cost Accounting Standards & Concepts | Jul-95 | 1998 |
| F | S | SFFAS 5 | Accounting for Liabilities of the Federal Government | Dec-95 | 1997 |
| F | S | SFFAS 6 | Accounting for Property, Plant & Equipment (PP&E) | Nov-95 | 1998 |
| F | S | SFFAS 7 | Accounting for Revenue and Other Financing Sources and Concepts for Reconciling Budgetary and Financial Accounting | May-96 | 1998 |
| F | S | SFFAS 8 | Supplementary Stewardship Reporting | Jun-96 | 1998 |
| F | S | SFFAS 9 | Deferral of the Effective Date of Managerial Cost Accounting Standards for the Federal Government in SFFAS 4 | Oct-97 | 1998 |
| F | S | SFFAS 10 | Accounting for Internal Use Software | Oct-98 | 2001 |
| F | S | SFFAS 11 | Amendments to Accounting for Property, Plant, and Equipment - Definitional Changes - Amending SFFAS No. 6 and SFFAS No. 8 Accounting for Property, Plant, and Equipment and Supplementary Stewardship Reporting | Dec-98 | 1999 |
| F | S | SFFAS 12 | Recognition of Contingent Liabilities Arising from Litigation: An Amendment to SFFAS No. 5, Accounting for Liabilities of the Federal Government | Feb-99 | 1998 |
| F | S | SFFAS 13 | Deferral of Paragraph 65.2 Material Revenue-Related Transactions Disclosures | Feb-99 | 1999 |
| F | S | SFFAS 14 | Amendments to Deferred Maintenance Reporting Amending SFFAS No. 6, Accounting for Property, Plant and Equipment and SFFAS No. 8, Supplementary Stewardship Reporting | Apr-99 | 1999 |
| F | S | SFFAS 15 | Management's Discussion & Analysis | Apr-99 | 2000 |
| F | S | SFFAS 16 | Amendments to Accounting for PP&E - Multi-Use Heritage Assets | Jul-99 | 2000 |
| F | S | SFFAS 17 | Accounting for Social Insurance | Aug-99 | 2000 |
| F | S | SFFAS 18 | Amendments to Accounting Standards for Direct & Guaranteed Loans | May-00 | 2001 |
| F | S | SFFAS 19 | Technical Amendments to Accounting Standards for Direct & Guaranteed Loans | Mar-01 | 2003 |
| F | S | SFFAS 20 | Elimination of Certain Disclosures Related to Tax Revenue Transactions by the Internal Revenue Service, Customs and Others | Sep-01 | 2001 |
| F | S | SFFAS 21 | Reporting Corrections of Errors and Changes in Accounting Principles | Oct-01 | 2002 |
| F | S | SFFAS 22 | Change in Certain Requirements for Reconciling Obligations and Net Cost of Operations (amends SFFAS 7) | Oct-01 | 2001 |
| F | S | SFFAS 23 | Eliminating the Category National Defense Property, Plant, and Equipment | May-03 | 2003 |
| F | S | SFFAS 24 | Selected Standards For The Consolidated Report of the United States Government | Mar-03 | 2002 |
| F | S | SFFAS 25 | Reclassification of Stewardship Responsibilities and Eliminating the Current Services Assessment | Jul-03 | Amended 2006 |
| F | S | SFFAS 26 | Presentation of Significant Assumptions for the Statement of Social Insurance: Amending SFFAS 25 | Nov-04 | Amended 2006 |
| F | S | SFFAS 27 | Identifying and Reporting Earmarked Funds | Dec-04 | 2006 |
| F | S | SFFAS 28 | Deferral of the Effective Date of Reclassification of the Statement of Social Insurance: Amending SFFAS 25 and 26 | Jan-05 | 2006 |
| F | S | SFFAS 29 | Heritage Assets and Stewardship Land | Jul-05 | Phased-see SFFAS 29 for details |
| F | S | SFFAS 30 | Inter-Entity Cost Implementation: Amending SFFAS 4 | Aug-05 | 2009 |
| F | S | SFFAS 31 | Accounting for Fiduciary Activities | Oct-06 | 2009 |
| F | S | SFFAS 32 | CFR of the U.S. Government Requirements | Sep-06 | 2006 |
| F | ED | N/A | Definition and Recognition of Elements of Accrual-Basis Financial Statements | Jun-06 | |
| | PV | | Accounting for Social Insurance, Revised | Oct-06 | |
| F | | N/A | Implementaion Guide to Statement of Financing in Statement of Federal Financial Accounting Standards 7, Accounting for Revenue and Other Financing Sources: Detailed Information on the Statement of Financing | Apr-02 | |
| F | | N/A | Implementation Guide - Accounting for Revenue and Other Financing Sources | Jun-96 | |
| F | SIG | N/A | Guidance for Implementation of SFFAS 23, Eliminating the Category National Defense Property, Plant, and Equipment | Jan-05 | Effective upon Issuance |

Documents available at http://www.fasab.gov. Updated: 5/15/2007. Doc #759364v3.

**Documents Resulting from the
Federal Accounting Standards Advisory Board (FASAB) and the
Accounting and Auditing Policy Committee (AAPC) Processes**

| | | | | | |
|---|---|---|---|---|---|
| F | I | I-1 | Reporting on Indian Trust Funds | Mar-97 | |
| F | I | I-2 | Accounting for Treasury Judgment Fund Transactions | Mar-97 | |
| F | I | I-3 | Measurement Date for Pension and Retirement Health Care Liabilities | Aug-97 | |
| F | I | I-4 | Accounting for Pension Payments in Excess of Pension Expense | | |
| F | I | I-5 | Recognition by Recipient Entities of Receivable Nonexchange Revenue | | |
| F | I | I-6 | Accounting for Imputed Intra-departmental Costs: An Interpretation of SFFAS No. 4 | Apr-03 | FY2005 |
| F | I | I-7 | Interpretation: Items Held for Remanufacture | Jul-07 | |
| F | TB | TB 2000-1 | Purpose and Scope of FASAB Technical Bulletins and Procedures for Issuance | Jun-00 | |
| F | TB | TB 2002-1 | Assigning to Component Entities Costs and Liabilities That Result From Legal Claims Against the Federal Government | Jul-02 | |
| F | TB | TB 2002-2 | Disclosures Required by Paragraph 79(g) of SFFAS 7 | Sep-02 | |
| F | TB | TB 2003-1 | Certain Questions and Answers Related to the Homeland Security Act of 2002 | Jun-03 | |
| F | TB | TB 2006-1 | Recognition and Measurement of Asbestos-Related Cleanup Costs | Sep-06 | 2010 |
| F | Cod | Volume 1 | FASAB Volume 1, Original Statements | | |
| F | Cod | Volume 2 | Current Text | | |
| A | TR | TR 1 | Audit Legal Letter Guidance | Mar-98 | |
| A | TR | TR 2 | Environmental Liabilities Guidance | Mar-98 | |
| A | TR | TR 3 | Auditing Estimates for Direct Loan and Loan Guarantee Subsidies Under the Federal Credit Reform Act | Jan-04 | |
| A | TR | TR 4 | Reporting on Non-valued Seized and Forfeited Property | Jul-99 | |
| A | TR | TR 5 | Implementation Guidance on SFFAS 10: Accounting for Internal Use Software | May-01 | |
| A | TR | TR 6 | Preparing Estimates for Direct Loan and Loan Guarantee Subsidies Under the Federal Credit Reform Act | Jan-04 | |
| F | R | Report 1 | Overview of Federal Financial Accounting Concepts and Standards | Dec-96 | |
| F | R | Discussion Paper | Accounting for the Natural Resources of the Federal Government | Jun-00 | |
| F | R | Report 2 | Strategic Directions Report | Nov-06 | |

Key:
Column 1: F = FASAB; A = AAPC
Column 2: C = Concept; S = Standard; ED = Exposure Draft; IFV = Invitation for Views; I = Interpretation;R = Report;
            Cod. = Codification; TR = Technical Release, PV = Preliminary Views, ITC = Invitation to Comment, TB = Technical Bulletin,
            SIG = Staff Implementation Guidance
    "Under Hill Review" - Signed recommended capital accounting standard undergoing 45 day Hill review period. When released by Hill, will be
available for implementation - Web version will be updated, list will be updated, and print version will be issued.
    "UR" and "SFFAS Under Review" - "UR" means "Under review." Document approved by FASAB and sent to principals for 90-days. At the
end of the 90-day period, the document will be posted to the Web, this list will be updated, and the print version will be issued.

# Appendix 2—List of Statutes Cited in Chapter

## Budget and Accounting Act of 1921, 31 USC Ch. 11

Government Corporation Control Act of 1945, Act of Dec. 6, 1945, ch. 557, 59 Stat. 599 (codified as amended at 31 U.S.C. §§ 9101–9110).

The Budget and Accounting Procedures Act of 1950, Act of Sept. 12, 1950, §§ 110–118, 64 Stat. 834 (codified as amended in scattered sections of title 31 U.S.C.).

**Federal Managers' Financial Integrity Act of 1982**, Pub. L. No. 97–255, 96 Stat. 814 (Sept. 8, 1982) (codified at 31 U.S.C. § 3512 (c), (d)).

Chief Financial Officers Act of 1990, Pub. L. No. 101-576, 104 Stat. 2838 (Nov. 15, 1990) (codified as amended at 31 U.S.C. §§ 901–903, 3515, 3521, 9105–9106, and in other scattered sections of 31 U.S.C.).

Government Performance and Results Act of 1993, Pub. L. No. 103–62, 107 Stat. 287 (Aug. 3, 1993) (codified primarily at 5 U.S.C § 306, 31 U.S.C. §§ 1115, 1116, 9703).

Government Management Reform Act of 1994, Pub. L. No. 103–356, title IV, § 405, 108 Stat. 3410, 3415 (Oct. 13, 1994) (codified as amended at 31 U.S.C. §§ 331(c), 3515, 3521).

Federal Reports Elimination and Sunset Act of 1995, Pub. L. No. 104–66, § 3003, 109 Stat. 707 (Dec. 21, 1995) (codified at 31 U.S.C. § 1113 note).

**Federal Financial Management Improvement Act of 1996**, Pub. L. No. 104–208, Div. A,

§ 101(f), title VIII, 110 Stat. 3009–389 (Sept. 30, 1996) (codified as a note to 31 U.S.C. § 3512).

Reports Consolidation Act of 2000, Pub. L. No. 106–531, § 3, 114 Stat. 2537 (Nov. 22, 2000) (codified at 31 U.S.C. § 3516).

Accountability of Tax Dollars Act of 2002, Pub. L. No. 107–289, 116 Stat. 2049 (Nov. 7, 2002) (primarily amending 31 U.S.C. § 3515).

# Appendix 3—Glossary of Terms

## *Accountability of Tax Dollars Act of 2002*

This Act requires annual audited financial statements from most executive branch entities not previously required to prepare and submit such reports. OMB may exempt agencies with budgets under $25 million in a given year. The newly covered agencies are subject to OMB Circular A-136 Financial Reporting Requirements. This bulletin requires agencies to consolidate their audited financial statements and other financial and performance reports into combined Performance and Accountability Reports and accelerates the deadline for submission.

## *Accrual Accounting*

Accrual accounting (also see "Financial Accounting") records the effects on a reporting entity of transactions and other events and circumstances in the periods in which those transactions, events, and circumstances occur rather than only in the periods in which cash is received or paid by the entity. It recognizes that the buying, producing, selling, distributing, and other operations of an entity during a period, as well as other events that affect entity performance, often do not coincide with the cash receipts and payments of the period.[77]

## *Antideficiency Act*

The Antideficiency Act is the basic federal fiscal law controlling the obligation and expenditure of federal funds. The original Act has been amended several times. The law implements Section 9, Article 1, of the U.S. Constitution, which states: "… no money shall be drawn from the treasury but in consequence of an appropriation made by law…."

The Act prohibits

a. Making or authorizing expenditure from, or creating, or authorizing an obligation under, any appropriation or fund in excess of the amount available in the appropriation or fund unless authorized by law.

b. Involving the government in any contract or other obligation for the payment of money for any purpose in advance of appropriations made for such purpose unless law authorizes the contract or obligation.

c. Accepting voluntary services for the United States, or employing personal services in excess of that authorized by law except in cases of emergency involving the safety of human life or the protection of property.

d. Making obligations or expenditures in excess of an apportionment or reapportionment, or in excess of the amount permitted by agency regulations.

For additional information, see OMB Circular No. A–11 (2002) Section 145 at www.whitehouse.gov/omb/circulars/a11/02toc.html, and GAO's detailed guidance on appropriation law.

## Budget and Accounting Act of 1921

This Act established the foundation for the present approach to accounting in the federal government. It established the GAO as a legislative branch agency and assigned to it the power to audit and settle all public accounts as well as to prescribe the procedures for administrative and fund accounting. The Act also established the Bureau of the Budget, the forerunner of OMB, as a mechanism for bringing together the separate budget requests of the many departments and agencies. Many of the provisions of this Act have been superceded by subsequent legislation.

## Budget and Accounting Procedures Act of 1950

This Act superceded parts of the Budget and Accounting Act of 1921. It established a framework for the executive branch's accounting and financial reporting. The Act made the comptroller general, who is the head of GAO, responsible for prescribing the principles, standards, and related requirements for accounting to be observed by each executive branch agency. The agencies are responsible for establishing and maintaining their own systems of accounting and internal control, which must provide the financial information necessary for management, budget formulation, and execution, plus meet Treasury's central accounting and reporting requirements.

## Budgetary Accounting

Budgetary accounting is the system that measures and controls the use of resources according to the purposes for which budget authority was enacted, and that records receipts and other collections by source. It tracks the use of each appropriation for specified purposes in separate budget accounts through the various stages of budget execution from appropriation to apportionment, and allotment to obligation and eventual outlay. This system is used by the Congress and the Executive Branch to set priorities, to allocate resources among alternative uses, to finance these resources, and to assess the economic implications of federal financial activity at an aggregate level. Budgetary accounting is used to comply with the Constitutional requirement that "No Money shall be drawn from the Treasury, but in Consequence of Appropriations Made by Law; and a regular Statement and Account of the Receipts and Expenditures of all public money shall be published from time to time."[78]

## Congressional Budget and Impoundment Control Act of 1974

This Act established a new process by which Congress enacts the budget. It also established a requirement and process for congressional review of any decisions by the executive branch to defer or rescind, that is, impound, an appropriation or other budget authority enacted by Congress.

## Chief Financial Officers Act of 1990

The purposes of the Chief Financial Officers Act of 1990 (CFO Act) are to ensure improvement in agency systems of accounting, financial management, and internal control; to ensure the issuance of reliable financial information; and to deter fraud, waste, and abuse of government resources. The Act requires preparation of annual audited financial statements in conformity with "applicable standards." Initially, this requirement applied only to trust funds, revolving funds, commercial-type activities, and 10 pilot agencies.

The Act requires that agency CFOs develop and maintain integrated agency accounting and financial management systems, including financial reporting and internal control. It requires agency CFOs to prepare and transmit an annual report to the agency head and the Director of OMB, including a summary of the reports on internal accounting and administrative control systems submitted to the President under the FMFIA.

## Corporations, Government

Congress has created various types of government corporations since the earliest days of the Republic. The Government Corporation Control Act of 1945 (GCCA), as amended, lists those that are currently operating. The Act classifies them as either "wholly owned" (e.g., the Pension Benefit Guaranty Corporation) or "mixed ownership" (e.g., the Federal Deposit Insurance Corporation). For the full list, see http://www4.law.cornell.edu/uscode/31/9101.html. The law calls for these government corporations to publish a "management report" with statements of financial position, operations, and cash flows, and reconciliation to the budget, if applicable. A statement on internal accounting and administrative control is required from the corporation's head manager, as is an audit of the financial statements by the entity's Inspector General, an independent public accountant, or GAO. There are similar government business-type entities (e.g., Postal Service) that are not subject to the GCCA but are part of the federal government and are governed by charters or other statutes enacted by Congress.

Some other business-type entities created by the federal government, such as the Federal National Mortgage Association, are referred to as "government-sponsored enterprises." Such entities carry out programs that directly support federal policy and, to some extent, may be associated with the federal government, but they are not part of it and therefore are not considered part of the federal financial reporting entity. (See SFFAC 2 paragraphs 48–50.)[79]

Still other entities with federal charters are even less closely associated with the federal government. Though these federally chartered corporations are recognized or chartered in statute, they are private entities, not part of the federal government. Therefore, they, too, are not considered part of the federal financial reporting entity. Examples of such federally chartered corporations include the American Red Cross, the Boy Scouts of America, the Civil Air Patrol, the National Academy of Public Administration, the Disabled American Veterans, and the Jewish War Veterans, corporations, et al.

## Federal Financial Management Improvement Act of 1996 (FFMIA)

The Act requires each agency to implement and maintain financial management systems that can comply substantially with

1. System requirements
2. Applicable federal accounting standards
3. The Standard General Ledger

For the SGL and the Treasury Financial Manual, see http://www.fms.treas.gov/.

For each agency required to have audited financial statements under the provisions enacted by the GMRA, the FFMIA requires that each agency's annual audit report state whether its financial management systems comply with the requirements just listed. For related OMB guidance, see **OMB Circular A-127** and "Revised Implementation Guidance for the Federal Financial Management Improvement Act" (January 4, 2001). See also JFMIP system requirements documents at http://www.jfmip.gov/jfmip/docs.htm.

## Federal Managers' Financial Integrity Act of 1982 (FMFIA)

The Act requires GAO to prescribe standards of internal accounting and administrative control, and agencies to comply with them. Internal control is to provide reasonable assurance that (1) obligations and costs comply with applicable law, (2) assets are safeguarded against waste, loss, unauthorized use, or misappropriation, and (3) revenues and expenditures are recorded and accounted for properly so that accounts and financial and statistical reports may be prepared and the accountability of assets may be maintained.

The Act requires that the internal control standards include standards to ensure the prompt resolution of all audit findings. It also requires the OMB to establish guidelines for agency evaluation of internal control to determine compliance with the internal control standards.

The Act requires agency heads (1) annually to evaluate their internal control using the OMB guidelines, and (2) annually to report to the President[80] on whether the agency's internal controls comply with the standards and objectives set forth in the Act. If they do not fully comply, the report must identify the weaknesses and describe plans for correction. The report is to be signed by the head of the agency. The Inspector General is to report on the Agency Head's report.

## Financial Accounting

Financial accounting (also see "Accrual Accounting") is largely concerned with assigning the value of past transactions to appropriate time periods. Transaction data assigned to a period that has elapsed are said to be "recognized" as an expense or a revenue of that period. Transaction data pertaining to the future are recognized as assets and liabilities.[81]

At the initial stage of the accounting process, the information about assets and liabilities is merely the result of assigning all or part of the value of certain transactions to the future. "Assets" and "liabilities" at this stage are not statements about future benefits or sacrifices that can be proved or disproved. They are allocations of the cost of past transactions based on assumptions about future benefit and sacrifice.[82]

## Government Corporation Control Act of 1945 (GCCA)

The Enactment of the GCCA, which incorporated audit requirements in legislation enacted earlier in the year, established a consistent, consolidated approach to budgeting, financial auditing, and reporting for over 20 government corporations. The legislation provided that GAO audit the financial transactions of government corporations in accordance with the principles and procedures applicable to commercial corporate transactions. The legislation further required that the annual report of each audit include a statement of assets and liabilities, capital and surplus, or deficit; a statement of income and expenses; and other information necessary to inform Congress of the operations and financial condition of the corporation. Over the years, new government corporations generally were subject to the GCCA's financial statement audit requirement either by being listed in the GCCA, as in the case of the Pennsylvania Avenue Development Corporation,[83] or by having the GCCA or its audit provisions incorporated by reference in the corporation's authorizing legislation, as in the case of the Inter-American Foundation.

## Government Management Reform Act of 1994 (GMRA)

The GMRA[84] requires an audited annual financial statement "covering all accounts and associated activities of the executive branch of the United States Government." It requires that the first audited statement for the executive branch cover fiscal year 1997 and be issued by March 31, 1998. The 1994 enactment of a statutory requirement for a consolidated financial statement for the executive branch grew out of recent experience with limited annual audits of executive branch agency financial statements required by the CFO Act of 1990.[85]

## Government Performance and Results Act of 1993 (GPRA)

The GPRA requires agencies to prepare strategic plans, annual performance plans, and annual performance reports. As noted in the following text, the Reports Consolidation Act of 2000 allows an agency to combine its audited financial statement as required by the CFO Act, and its performance reports as required by the GPRA, to provide a more comprehensive and useful picture of the services provided. The OMB Circular A-136 now requires agencies to consolidate their audited financial statements and other financial and performance reports into combined Performance and Accountability Reports. Bulletin 01-09 is at http://www.whitehouse.gov/omb/circulars/a136/a136_revised_2008.pdf. For related OMB guidance, see http://www.whitehouse.gov/omb/financial/2003_fin-perf-reporting.html.

## OMB Circular A-123—Management Accountability and Control

This circular provides guidance to executive agencies on establishing, assessing, correcting, and reporting on internal control. Essentially this is the OMB's guidance to agencies pursuant to FMFIA. See "OMB Circular A-123, Management Accountability and Control" (revised December 2004), at http://www.whitehouse.gov/omb/financial/offm_circulars.html. For related OMB guidance, see the memo on FY 2002 Financial and Performance Reporting dated October 18, 2002, at http://www.whitehouse.gov/omb/financial/final_yr_end_memo2002.html, and more generally see http://www.whitehouse.gov/omb/financial/index.html.

## OMB Circular A-127—Financial Management Systems

This circular prescribes policies and standards to follow in developing, operating, evaluating, and reporting on financial management systems. See "OMB Circular A-127, Financial Management Systems" (July 23, 1993).

## OMB Circular A-136—Financial Reporting Requirements

This circular establishes a central point of reference for all federal financial reporting guidance for executive branch departments, agencies, and entities required to submit audited financial statements, interim financial statements, and Performance and Accountability Reports (PARs) under the CFO Act of 1990 and the Accountability of Tax Dollars Act (ATDA) of 2002. See "OMB Circular A-136," December 2004.

## Reports Consolidation Act of 2000

This Act builds on a pilot program authorized in 1994. It allows an agency to combine its audited financial statement, as required by GMRA, and its performance reports, as required by GPRA, to provide a more comprehensive and useful picture of the services provided. More specifically, the Act authorizes the head of an agency to (1) adjust the frequency and due dates of, and consolidate into an annual report to the President, Director of OMB, and Congress, certain statutorily required reports (including financial and performance management reports), and (2) submit such a consolidated report not later than 150 days after the end of the agency's fiscal year.

The law requires such a consolidated report

1. That incorporates the agency's program performance report to be referred to as a Performance and Accountability Report
2. [Or, for a report] that does not incorporate the agency's program performance report, to contain a summary of the most significant portions [of its program performance report], including the agency's success in achieving key performance goals
3. To include a statement by the agency's inspector general that summarizes the agency's most serious management and performance challenges
4. To include a transmittal letter from the agency head containing an assessment of the completeness and reliability of the performance and financial data used in the report.

# Endnotes

1. See the Treasury Department Web site for more at http://fms.treas.gov/aboutfms/background.html.

2. 28 Stat. 208.

3. See 31 USC Chap. 11.

4. Apportionment, obligation, and other terms have a specific meaning in budgetary accounting. See OMB's Circular A-11, *Preparing, Submitting, and Executing the Budget*, Section 20, "Terms and Concepts" (www.whitehouse.gov/omb/circulars/a11/current_year/s20.pdf); and *The Budget Systems and Concepts* (www.whitehouse.gov/omb/budget/fy2008/pdf/concepts.pdf) for more.

5. Treasury Department Circular No. 494, Office of the Secretary, dated August 5, 1933; also see Executive Order No. 6266 dated July 27, 1933. For future developments along these lines, see Circular No. 494 as amended at various dates throughout the period 1933–1950.

6. See the *Proceedings: The Conference of Federal Government Accounting*, sponsored by the American Institute of Accounting in cooperation with the Treasury Department, GAO, and the Bureau of the Budget, 1943, for more, for example, p. 6.

7. www.fms.treas.gov/aboutfms/welcometofms.html

8. 59 Stat. 597.

9. Pois, Joseph, "Impact of the Corporation Audit Division upon the U.S. General Accounting Office," in Cooper, William, and Yuji Ijiri, eds., *Eric Louis Kohler: Accounting's Man of Principles*, pp. 114–126.

10. 1950 Act, § 111(f), 64 Stat. at 835 (codified as revised at 31 U.S.C. § 3511(d) (authorizing GAO, Treasury, and OMB to conduct a continuous program for improving accounting and financial reporting in the government).

11. 64 Stat. 835, 31 USC 3512.

12. As did the Accounting Act of 1956, which also required accrual accounting. Conforming with the Acts of 1950 and 1956, the Interior Department's Bureau of Reclamation (BoR) submitted an accrual budget in 1957, only to have it rejected by the House Appropriations Committee, which told the BoR to resubmit the cash-based, standard budget; that was the end of cost-based budgeting even though the budget and accounting acts are still on the books.

13. 1950 Act, § 116, 64 Stat. at 837 (codified as revised at 31 U.S.C. § 3514).

14. Some people have asserted that this provision is unconstitutional.

15. The Act of 1956, Pub. L. No. 84-863, § 106(b), 70 Stat. 782 (Aug. 1, 1956) codified as revised at 31 U.S.C. § 3512(e).

16. Pub. L. 101-576).

17. See *The Chief Financial Officers' Act: A Mandate for Federal Financial Management Reform*, GAO, September 1991 GAO/AFMD-12.19.4.

18. For related OMB guidance see OMB Circular A-136, *Financial Reporting Requirements*, (www.whitehouse.gov/omb/circulars/a136/a136_revised_2007.pdf), and OMB Bulletin No.07-04, *Audit Requirements for Federal Financial Statements* (September 4, 2007) (www.whitehouse.gov/omb/bulletins/fy2007/b07-04.pdf).

19. S. Rep. No. 103-281, at 12 (1994).

20. For example, GAO, *Accounting Principles, Standards, and Requirements: Title 2 Standards Not Superseded by FASAB*, GAO-02-248G (Nov. 2001).

21. For example, OMB A-136, *Form and Content of Agency Financial Statements*, June 29, 2007.
22. SFFAC 1, para. 21.
23. SFFAC 1, para. 22.
24. SFFAC 1, para. 39.
25. SFFAC 1, para. 40.
26. SFFAS 1, para. 41.
27. SFFAC 1, 42.
28. SFFAC 1, 43.
29. SFFAC 1, 45.
30. SFFAC 1, 47.
31. SFFAC 1, 49.
32. SFFAC 1, para. 50.
33. SFFAC 1, para. 51.
34. SFFAC 1, para. 52.
35. SFFAC 1, para. 53.
36. SFFAC 1, para. 54.
37. SFFAC 1, para. 55.
38. SFFAC 1, para. 56.
39. SFFAC 1, para. 57.
40. SFFAC 1, para. 60.
41. SFFAC 1, para. 61.
42. SFFAC 1, para. 62.
43. SFFAC 1, para. 166.
44. SFFAC 1, para. 168.
45. SFFAC 1, para. 176.
46. SFFAC 1, para. 186.
47. SFFAC 1, para. 75.
48. SFFAC 1, para. 110.
49. SFFAC 5 was approved by the FASAB in September 2007 and released on December 26, 2007.
50. A detailed discussion regarding the FASAB's mission can be found in the "FASAB Facts" on the Web at http://www.fasab.gov/aboutfasab.html.
51. SFFAC 1, para. 187.
52. SFFAC 1, para. 67.
53. SFFAC 1, para. 69.
54. SFFAC 1, para. 71.
55. SFFAC 1, para. 188.
56. SFFAC 1, para. 191.
57. Pub. L. No. 101-576.
58. Pub. L. No. 107-289.
59. 31 U.S.C. § 9101 et seq.
60. Pub. L. No. 106-531.
61. Pub. L. No. 97-255.
62. SFFAC 1, *Entity and Display*, para. 13.
63. SFFAC 2, para. 16.
64. SFFAS 27, *Identifying and Reporting Earmarked Funds*, Appendix 3: Glossary.

65. *The Budget System and Concepts*, OMB, p. 395–6; see also SFFAS 31, *Accounting for Fiduciary Activities*.

66. SFFAC 1, *Entity and Display*, para. 14.

67. OMB Circular A-11 (2007) section 20.12.

68. www.fms.treas.gov/ussgl/about.html.

69. SFFAC 2, para. 15.

70. www.fms.treas.gov/ussgl/tfm_releases/07-02/2007/part1_current.html, Section I: Chart of Accounts.

71. Section 806(4) defines "financial management systems" as including financial systems and the financial portions of mixed systems necessary to support financial management. The FFMIA's use of financial management systems, rather than "accounting systems" as used in the 1950 Act and FMFIA, is not legally significant.

72. SFFAS 26, *Presentation of Significant Assumptions for the Statement of Social Insurance: Amending SFFAS 25*, para. 5.

73. SFFAS 2, paras. 64A-B; SFFAS 7, para. 15; and also see SFFAC 1, subjective 1C.

74. SFFAS 7, paras. 80–82.

75. SFFAS 7, para. 93.

76. AICPA Auditing Standards (AU) Section 558.06.

77. FASAB Consolidated Glossary. Also see Financial Accounting Standards Board Statement of Financial Accounting Concepts (SFAC) 4, *Objectives of Financial Reporting by Nonbusiness Organizations*, para. 50, SFAC 6, *Elements of Financial Statements*, paras. 139–141, 144–5; and CBO, Glossary of Budgetary and Economic Terms, "Accrual Accounting."

78. FASAB Consolidated Glossary. Also see Statement of Federal Financial Accounting Concepts No. 1, *Objectives of Federal Financial Reporting*, September 1993, Paragraphs 45–46, 112–114, and 186–191.

79. See also: Government-Sponsored Enterprises: A Framework for Strengthening GSE Governance and Oversight, by David M. Walker, Comptroller General of the United States, before the Senate Committee on Banking, Housing and Urban Affairs. GAO-04-269T, February 10. http://www.gao.gov/cgi-bin/getrpt?GAO-04-269T

80. Annual reports to Congress, which also were originally required, were eliminated by the Federal Reports Elimination and Sunset Act of 1995.

81. SFFAC 1, paras 168–9; also see SFFAS 4, paras 15 and 48.

82. SFFAC 1, para 171.

83. 31 U.S.C. § 9101(3)(I).

84. Pub. L. No. 103-356, title IV, § 405(c), 108 Stat. 3410, 3416 (Oct. 13, 1994)(codified at 31 U.S.C. § 331(e)(1)). Interestingly, while the provision's language only addresses the executive branch, its title is "Governmentwide Financial Statement."

85. Pub. L. No. 101-576, 104 Stat. 2838, 2849–2853 (Nov. 15, 1990).

## Chapter 14

# International Public Sector Accounting Standards

Jesse Hughes

*Old Dominion University, Professor Emeritus of Accounting*

## Contents

14.1 Introduction ................................................................................493
    14.1.1 International Public Sector Accounting Standards ......................494
    14.1.2 Cash Basis Standard................................................................495
    14.1.3 Budgetary Reporting................................................................497
    14.1.4 Accrual Basis Standards ..........................................................498
        14.1.4.1 IPSAS 1 and 2. Presentation of Financial Statements
                (Based on IAS 1 and IAS 7, Respectively) ......................498
        14.1.4.2 IPSAS 3. Accounting Policies, Changes in
                Accounting Estimates and Errors (Based on IAS 8) ......499
        14.1.4.3 IPSAS 4. The Effects of Changes in Foreign
                Exchange Rates (Based on IAS 21)................................499
        14.1.4.4 IPSAS 5. Borrowing Costs (Based on IAS 23)............. 500

14.1.4.5 IPSAS 6. Consolidated and Separate Financial Statements (Based on IAS 27) .................................. 500

14.1.4.6 IPSAS 7. Investments in Associates (Based on IAS 28).......................................................................... 500

14.1.4.7 IPSAS 8. Interests in Joint Ventures (Based on IAS 31) ............................................................................ 500

14.1.4.8 IPSAS 9. Revenue from Exchange Transactions (Based on IAS 18)...................................................... 500

14.1.4.9 IPSAS 10. Financial Reporting in Hyperinflationary Economies (Based on IAS 29) .......501

14.1.4.10 IPSAS 11. Construction Contracts (Based on IAS 11) ................................................................................501

14.1.4.11 IPSAS 12. Inventories (Based on IAS 2) .....................501

14.1.4.12 IPSAS 13. Leases (Based on IAS 17)...........................501

14.1.4.13 IPSAS 14. Events after the Reporting Date (Based on IAS 10) ..............................................................501

14.1.4.14 IPSAS 15. Financial Instruments: Disclosure and Presentation (Based on IAS 32) ..................................502

14.1.4.15 IPSAS 16. Investment Property (Based on IAS 40) ....502

14.1.4.16 IPSAS 17. Property, Plant, and Equipment (Based on IAS 16)..............................................................502

14.1.4.17 IPSAS 18. Segment Reporting (Based on IAS 14) ......502

14.1.4.18 IPSAS 19. Provisions, Contingent Liabilities, and Contingent Assets (Based on IAS 37) ..........................503

14.1.4.19 IPSAS 20. Related Party Disclosures (Based on IAS 24)..............................................................................503

14.1.4.20 IPSAS 21. Impairment of Non-Cash Generating Assets and IPSAS 26. Impairment of Cash Generating Assets (Based on IAS 36) ..........................503

14.1.4.21 IPSAS 22. Disclosure of Information about the General Government Sector (no comparable IAS) ......503

14.1.4.22 IPSAS 23. Revenue from Non-Exchange Transactions (Taxes and Transfers) (no comparable IAS)................................................................................. 504

14.1.4.23 IPSAS 24. Presentation of Budget Information in Financial Statements (no comparable IAS) ................ 504

14.1.4.24 IPSAS 25. Employee Benefits (Based on IAS 19) ....... 504

14.1.5 Steps for Implementation of IPSASs............................................505

14.2 Conclusion ....................................................................................... 506

Attachments ................................................................................................507

## 14.1 Introduction

In many countries, the method of budgeting used in the public sector has determined which accounting basis (cash or accrual) to use. Budgets may be prepared on the cash, obligation/commitment, or the accrual basis. Most governments in developing countries or economies in transition will prepare their budgets on the cash basis since such budgetary information is more easily comprehended by users. In addition, it is simple to implement, and costs are low due to the lower level of accounting skills required. These fixed budgets are approved by legislative bodies within governments in order to prioritize their revenue and spending plans. As governments transition to the accrual basis of accounting, many prepare their budgets on the modified accrual basis of accounting (which includes current assets and liabilities) in order to plan for the use of financial resources. As the full accrual basis of accounting (which includes total assets and liabilities) is achieved, some governments are moving to the accrual basis of budgeting so that they can plan for the use of total resources.

In the private sector, the International Accounting Standards Committee (IASC) previously accepted the challenge of establishing accrual-based International Accounting Standards (IASs) for application to commercial enterprises throughout the world. The International Accounting Standards Board (IASB) has replaced the IASC and is in the process of replacing the IASs with International Financial Reporting Standards (IFRSs). However, like the IASC, their charge does not apply to the public sector. To fill the void, the Public Sector Committee (PSC) of the International Federation of Accountants was given the responsibility to develop programs aimed at improving public sector financial management and accountability including developing accounting standards and promoting their acceptance. In order to achieve its objectives, the PSC is developing a set of accounting standards for public sector entities worldwide. The PSC was replaced by the International Public Sector Accounting Standards Board (IPSASB) in 2003. Initially, these International Public Sector Accounting Standards (IPSASs) are being developed by adapting IASs issued by the IASB to a public sector context. In undertaking that process, the IPSASB attempts, wherever possible, to maintain the accounting treatment and original text of the IASs/IFRSs unless there is a significant public sector issue that warrants a departure. In its ongoing work program, the IPSASB also intends to develop IPSASs to deal with public sector financial reporting issues that are either not comprehensively dealt with in existing IASs or for which IFRSs have not been developed or are not planned to be developed by the IASB. Examples of these issues include the nature of the governmental reporting entity and recognition principles for tax revenue.

The IPSASs apply to all public sector entities other than Government Business Enterprises (GBEs). GBEs include both trading enterprises, such as utilities, and financial enterprises, such as financial institutions. GBEs are, in substance, no different from entities conducting similar activities in the private sector, and they are expected to comply with the IASs and IFRSs. A GBE means an entity that has all the following characteristics:

1. Is an entity with the power to contract in its own name;
2. Has been assigned the financial and operational authority to carry on a business;
3. Sells goods and services, in the normal course of its business, to other entities at a profit or full-cost recovery;
4. Is not reliant on continuing government funding to be a going concern (other than purchases of outputs at arm's length); and
5. Is controlled by a public sector entity.

## 14.1.1 International Public Sector Accounting Standards

IPSASs deal with issues related to the presentation of annual general purpose financial statements. General purpose financial statements are those intended to meet the needs of users who are not in a position to demand reports tailored to meet their specific information needs. Users of general purpose financial statements include taxpayers and ratepayers, members of the legislature, creditors, suppliers, the media, and employees. In democracies, political accountability of government to the electorate should take precedence. Their elected representatives act on their behalf and use the financial statements to hold the government and the civil service to account for the resources that they were allocated to provide the agreed level of goods and services. General purpose financial statements include those that are presented separately or within another public document such as an annual report. The objectives of general purpose financial statements are to provide information useful for decision making, and to demonstrate the accountability of the entity for the resources entrusted to it.

In addition, general purpose financial statements can have a predictive or prospective role since they provide information useful to predict the level of resources required for continued operations. Further, these statements provide users with information indicating whether resources were obtained and used in accordance with the legally adopted budget. To assist users in this area, governments are encouraged to include in the financial statements a comparison of the actual results of operations with the approved budget for the reporting period.

IPSASs permit the presentation of annual general purpose financial statements on the cash or the accrual basis of accounting. The accrual basis is preferred for the following reasons: improved resource allocation, strengthened accountability over all resources, enhanced transparency on total resource costs of government activities, and more comprehensive view of government's impact on the economy. The cash basis is permitted in those instances where the countries have not yet developed the capability among their accounting staff to prepare their financial statements on the accrual basis or the costs are prohibitive. If their statements are prepared on the cash basis, the countries are encouraged to transition to the accrual basis as soon as their accounting staff is adequately trained on the requirements of an accrual accounting system and funding can be arranged. The balance of this article discusses the IPSASs and suggests a plan for implementation of these IPSASs in developing countries and economies in transition.

## 14.1.2 Cash Basis Standard

This is a comprehensive IPSAS on financial reporting under the cash basis. It establishes requirements for the preparation and presentation of a Statement of Cash Receipts and Payments, as well as notes to support accounting policy. It also encourages disclosures to enhance the cash basis report. According to the IPSASB, the application of this standard is an important step toward financial reporting improvement in terms of consistency and comparability, as well as serving as a basis for enhancement and shift to the accrual basis of accounting.

The IPSAS on Cash Basis Financial Reporting identifies the requirements applicable in all entities that prepare cash basis general purpose financial statements. It has been under development since an initial draft was issued in November 2000, and was finally issued in January 2003. The effective date of this standard was January 1, 2004, though earlier implementation was recommended. For those entities that should present consolidated financial statements for the reporting period, this standard will be applicable 3 years following the date of its initial enactment.

In April 2002, the PSC published Study 14 entitled "Transition to the Accrual Basis of Accounting: Guidance for Government and Government Entities" for entities intending to adopt the accrual basis. The aim of this IPSAS is to describe the way in which cash basis general purpose financial statements should be presented. This standard comprises two parts. The first part is mandatory and contains requirements for cash basis financial statement presentation. The second part is not obligatory and contains additional requests and explanations about the accounting policies, disclosures, and alternative methods of information presentation. The objective of this IPSAS is to promote and enhance financial accountability and financial statement transparency.

Within the first part, the requirements in connection with financial statement structure and content and the reporting entity identification are explained, as well as requirements for disclosing movements of cash and cash equivalents generated from business, investment and financial activities. In addition, the cash basis of accounting is defined, as well as all terms associated with it, such as cash, monetary resources equivalents, reporting entities, and cash controlled by the reporting entity.

Financial reporting means that entities should prepare and present general purpose financial statements that include a statement of cash receipts and payments along with accounting policies and explanatory notes. All cash receipts and payments are recognized in the statement of cash receipts and payments, as well as cash balances controlled by the entity and payments by third parties on behalf of the entity. Notes to financial statements include narratives, more detailed tables and analyses, as well as additional information on the purpose of fair presentation necessary to such information users. An illustration of the required statement of cash receipts and payments is an appendix to the cash basis IPSAS and is included as Attachment 14.1.

The information presented in the general purpose financial statements should be understandable, relevant, and truthful. Their quality will affect the report usefulness for the users. In that sense, in the second part of Annex 4 of this standard, certain qualitative features of information are presented aimed at better financial reporting. The accounting policies and remarks offer an explanation for better understanding of financial reports.

General considerations explain the treatment of the reporting period for preparation and presentation of financial statements, date of authorization, entity-related information, information in connection with the monetary balances constraints and access to loans, consistency in presenting, disclosing comparative information, identifying financial reports, error correction, consolidated financial reports, and foreign currency (i.e., treatment of foreign exchange cash flows). Within the consolidated financial statements, the standard gives an explanation about the entities, the range of the consolidated financial reports, all related to the goals, reporting entity, as well as procedures and ways of preparing consolidated financial reports on public sector entities. The section on foreign currency explains the treatment of cash inflows, outflows, and balances in foreign currencies resulting from foreign currency transactions. The first part of this standard is expanded by particular annexes in order to help explain the meaning of the standard through illustrations for its easier application in preparing and presenting general financial reports on cash basis using examples of government consolidated financial statements, additional financial reports, as well as examples of remarks in the financial reports.

The second part of the IPSAS on cash basis financial reporting refers to additional disclosures encouraged, as well as to a treatment of public sector entities intending to shift toward the accrual accounting. The following additional disclosures are encouraged:

- Reservations about Going Concerns
- Identification of Extraordinary Items
- Extent of Administered Transactions (i.e., "pass-through" cash flows and transfers)
- Major Classes of Cash Flows
- Related Parties
- Assets and Liabilities
- Comparison with Budgets
- Consolidated Financial Statements
- Joint Ventures
- Financial Reporting in Hyperinflationary Economies

Cash basis government financial reporting is characteristic of the budget in developing countries and economies in transition. Including a budgetary column in the financial reports allows for direct comparisons between the planned and actual amounts. This information is useful for external users interested in government accountability in view of approved budgets, as well as for internal users who monitor the current spending against actual expenditures.

The second part of this standard contains guidelines for those public sector entities that wish to switch to the accrual basis in terms of presenting a statement of cash receipts and payments using the same form (see Attachment 14.2) required by IPSAS 2 on the cash flow statement. Certain appendices are provided containing illustrations that should help explain how to present cash flow reports classified by operating, investing, and financing activities, as well as how to disclose cash flows generated from interests and dividends. Also, there are appendices that describe the qualitative characteristics of financial reporting (comprehensibility, relevance, truthfulness, and comparability), certain constraints for relevant and truthful information, as well as the treatment of the issues with regard to establishment of control over another entity for the purposes of financial reporting.

## 14.1.3  Budgetary Reporting

Most governments prepare budget to actual comparative statements during the fiscal period in order to maintain budgetary control. However, these comparative statements are not presently a part of the prescribed end of year general purpose financial statements. Guidance in the present IPSASs* is as follows:

> "Public sector entities are typically subject to budgetary limits in the form of appropriations or budget authorizations (or equivalent), which may be given effect through authorizing legislation. General purpose financial reporting by public sector entities may provide information on whether resources were obtained and used in accordance with the legally adopted budget. Where the financial statements and the budget are on the same basis of accounting, this standard encourages the inclusion in the financial statements of a comparison with the budgeted amounts for the reporting period. Reporting against budgets may be presented in various different ways, including:
>
> (a) the use of a columnar format for the financial statements, with separate columns for budgeted amounts and actual amounts. A column showing any variances from the budget or appropriation may also be presented, for completeness; and

---

* Paragraph 22, IPSAS 1, Presentation of Financial Statements (May 2000).

(b) a statement by the individual(s) responsible for the preparation of the financial statements that the budgeted amounts have not been exceeded. If any budgeted amounts or appropriations have been exceeded, or expenses incurred without appropriation or other form of authority, then details may be disclosed by way of footnote to the relevant item in the financial statements."

IPSAS 24, Presentation of Budget Information in Financial Statements, was issued in December 2006 to replace the aforementioned option. IPSAS 24 requires a Budget to Actual Comparative Statement and applies to all public sector entities that make their budgets publicly available. It requires that the original and final budgets be reflected in the Statement along with the actual revenues and expenses on the budgetary basis. An example of the optional Budget to Actual Comparative Statement is an Appendix to the Cash Basis IPSAS and is included as Attachment 14.3.*

## 14.1.4 Accrual Basis Standards

In addition to the Cash Basis IPSAS, there are 26 accrual IPSASs and these are summarized in this section (with the corresponding IASs shown in parenthesis).† The accrual basis means a basis of accounting under which transactions and other events are recognized when they occur (and not only when cash or its equivalent is received or paid). Therefore, the transactions and events are recorded in the accounting records and recognized in the financial statements of the periods to which they relate. The elements recognized under accrual accounting are assets, liabilities, net assets/equity, revenue, and expenses.

### 14.1.4.1 IPSAS 1 and 2. Presentation of Financial Statements (Based on IAS 1 and IAS 7, Respectively)

These IPSASs set out the overall considerations for the presentation of financial statements, guidance for the structure of those statements, and minimum requirements for their content. A complete set of financial statements includes the following components (comparable statements in the private sector are identified in parenthesis):

1. Cash flow statements (same title)—see Attachment 14.2;
2. Statement of financial position (balance sheet)—see Attachment 14.4;

---

* Appendix 2, Cash Basis IPSAS, p. 78.
† For detailed information on each standard, the reader should obtain the *Handbook of International Public Sector Accounting Pronouncements* from the International Federation of Accountants (New York) or they can be downloaded at no charge from the www.ifac.org Web site.

3. Statement of financial performance (income statement)—see Attachment 14.5;
4. Statement of changes in net assets/equity (statement of changes in equity)—see Attachment 14.6; and
5. Accounting policies and notes to the financial statements.

## 14.1.4.2 IPSAS 3. Accounting Policies, Changes in Accounting Estimates and Errors (Based on IAS 8)

All items of revenue and expense recognized in a period are included in the determination of the net surplus or deficit for the period. If fundamental errors occur, the benchmark treatment requires that the amount of the correction that relates to prior periods should be reported by adjusting the opening balance of accumulated surpluses or deficits. Further, if there has been a change in accounting policies, it should be applied retrospectively with the resulting adjustment reported as an adjustment to the opening balance of accumulated surpluses or deficits. If the amount of any resulting adjustment that relates to prior periods is not reasonably determined, the change should be applied prospectively.

## 14.1.4.3 IPSAS 4. The Effects of Changes in Foreign Exchange Rates (Based on IAS 21)

A foreign currency transaction should be recorded, on initial recognition in the reporting currency, by applying to the foreign currency amount the exchange rate between the reporting currency and the foreign currency at the date of the transaction. At each subsequent reporting date:

1. Foreign currency monetary items should be reported using the closing rate;
2. Nonmonetary items that are carried in terms of historical cost denominated in a foreign currency should be reported using the exchange rate at the date of the transaction; and
3. Nonmonetary items that are carried at fair value denominated in a foreign currency should be reported using the exchange rates that existed when the values were determined.

Exchange differences should be recognized as revenue or as expenses in the period in which they arise, with the exception of exchange differences as a result of net investment in a foreign entity. For these exceptions, exchange differences arising on a monetary item that forms part of an entity's net investment in a foreign entity should be classified as net assets/equity in the entity's financial statements until the disposal of the net investment, at which time they should be recognized as revenue or as expenses.

### 14.1.4.4 IPSAS 5. Borrowing Costs (Based on IAS 23)

This IPSAS prescribes the accounting treatment for borrowing costs and requires either the immediate expensing of borrowing costs or, as an allowed alternative treatment, the capitalization of borrowing costs that are directly attributable to the acquisition, construction, or production of a qualifying asset.

### 14.1.4.5 IPSAS 6. Consolidated and Separate Financial Statements (Based on IAS 27)

A controlling entity should present consolidated financial statements for controlled entities (foreign and domestic). Control is presumed to exist when at least one specified power condition and one specified benefit condition exists. Minority interests should be presented in the consolidated statement of financial position separately from liabilities and the controlling entity's net assets/equity. Minority interests in the net surplus or deficit of the economic entity should also be separately presented.

### 14.1.4.6 IPSAS 7. Investments in Associates (Based on IAS 28)

An associate is defined as an entity in which the investor has significant influence (generally 20% or more) and which is neither a controlled entity nor a joint venture of the investor. The investment in an associate should be accounted for in consolidated financial statements under the equity method, except when the investment is acquired and held exclusively with a view to its disposal in the near future. In this case, the cost method is required.

### 14.1.4.7 IPSAS 8. Interests in Joint Ventures (Based on IAS 31)

A joint venture is defined as a binding arrangement whereby two or more parties are committed to undertake an activity that is subject to joint control. In its consolidated financial statements, a venturer should generally report its interest in a jointly controlled entity using the reporting format for proportionate consolidation.

### 14.1.4.8 IPSAS 9. Revenue from Exchange Transactions (Based on IAS 18)

This standard distinguishes between exchange and nonexchange transactions. An exchange transaction (i.e., sale of goods or services) is one in which the entity receives assets or services, or has liabilities extinguished, and directly gives approximately equal value to the other party in exchange. Revenue from exchange transactions is measured at the fair value of the consideration received or receivable and is recognized when earned. (Nonexchange transactions, such as taxes, are not included in this standard and are being addressed in a separate standard to be published at a later date.)

### 14.1.4.9  IPSAS 10. Financial Reporting in Hyperinflationary Economies (Based on IAS 29)

This IPSAS describes the characteristics of a hyperinflationary economy and requires financial statements of entities that operate in such economies to be restated. In general, the restatement of financial statements is considered if the cumulative inflation rate over three years is approaching, or exceeds, 100%.

### 14.1.4.10  IPSAS 11. Construction Contracts (Based on IAS 11)

Since many construction contracts may exceed one or more fiscal periods, revenue and expenses should be recognized in the period incurred by reference to the stage of completion of the contract activity at the reporting date.

### 14.1.4.11  IPSAS 12. Inventories (Based on IAS 2)

Inventories should be measured at the lower of cost and net realizable value or, under specific circumstances, current replacement cost. The cost of inventories should be assigned by using the first-in, first-out or weighted average cost formulas. (Note: The last-in, first-out method previously used in the private sector is not permitted for use in the public sector.)

### 14.1.4.12  IPSAS 13. Leases (Based on IAS 17)

Each lease should be classified as a finance lease or an operating lease. A finance lease is a lease that transfers substantially all risks and rewards incident to ownership of an asset. Title may or may not eventually be transferred. Lessees should recognize assets acquired under finance leases as assets and the associated lease obligations as liabilities. Lessors should recognize lease payments receivable (at an amount equal to the net investment in the lease) under a finance lease as assets in their statements of financial position. The recognition of finance revenue should be based on a pattern reflecting a constant periodic rate of return on the lessor's net investment outstanding in respect of the finance lease. An operating lease is a lease other than a finance lease and should be recognized as revenue to the lessor or expense to the lessee in the period to which it applies.

### 14.1.4.13  IPSAS 14. Events after the Reporting Date (Based on IAS 10)

The reporting date is the date of the last day of the reporting period to which the financial statements relate. Events after the reporting date are those events that occur between the reporting date and the date when the financial statements (including the audit opinion) are authorized for issue. An entity should adjust the amounts recognized in its financial statements to reflect adjusting events after the reporting date depending on the government's intention in relation to certain matters. In most cases, the announcement of government intentions will not lead to the recognition of adjusting events but would qualify for disclosure as nonadjusting events.

### 14.1.4.14 IPSAS 15. Financial Instruments: Disclosure and Presentation (Based on IAS 32)

The issuer of a financial instrument should classify the instrument as a liability or as net assets/equity in accordance with the substance of the contractual arrangement on initial recognition and the definitions of a financial liability and an equity instrument.

### 14.1.4.15 IPSAS 16. Investment Property (Based on IAS 40)

Investment property is defined as property (land or building) held to earn rentals or for capital appreciation rather than use in the production or supply of goods or services, or for sale in the ordinary course of operations. It should be recognized as an asset when it has future economic benefit and the cost or fair value can be reliably measured.

### 14.1.4.16 IPSAS 17. Property, Plant, and Equipment (Based on IAS 16)

This standard applies to property, plant, and equipment including specialist military equipment and infrastructure assets. It does not apply to forests or minerals. Subsequent to initial recognition as an asset, the benchmark treatment permits an item of property, plant, and equipment to be carried at its cost less any accumulated depreciation and any accumulated impairment losses. The depreciable amount should be allocated on a systematic basis over its useful life and recognized as an expense. It does not require or prohibit the recognition of heritage assets.

### 14.1.4.17 IPSAS 18. Segment Reporting (Based on IAS 14)

A segment is a distinguishable activity of an entity for which it is appropriate to separately report financial information for the purpose of evaluating the entity's past performance in achieving its objectives and for making decisions about the future allocation of resources. In most cases, separate reporting will reflect the segments for which information is reported to the governing body and the most senior manager of the entity.

## 14.1.4.18 IPSAS 19. Provisions, Contingent Liabilities, and Contingent Assets (Based on IAS 37)

A provision is a liability of uncertain timing or amount. It should be recognized when an entity has a present obligation as a result of a past event, it is probably that an outflow of resources embodying economic benefits or service potential will be required to settle the obligation, and a reliable estimate can be made of the amount of the obligation. Contingent liabilities and contingent assets may be disclosed in the financial statements, if considered beneficial.

## 14.1.4.19 IPSAS 20. Related Party Disclosures (Based on IAS 24)

Parties are considered to be related if one party has the ability to control the other party or exercise significant influence over the other party in making financial and operating decisions or if the related party entity and another entity are subject to common control. Related party relationships where control exists should be disclosed irrespective of whether there have been transactions between the related parties.

## 14.1.4.20 IPSAS 21. Impairment of Non-Cash Generating Assets and IPSAS 26. Impairment of Cash Generating Assets (Based on IAS 36)

Cash generating assets are assets held with the primary objective of generating a commercial return while non-cash generating assets are all assets other than cash generating assets. An impairment is a loss in the future economic benefits or service potential of an asset, over and above the systematic recognition of the loss of the asset's future economic benefits or service potential through depreciation. If the recoverable service amount of an asset is less than its carrying amount, the carrying amount shall be reduced to its recoverable service amount. That reduction is an impairment loss and it shall be recognized immediately in surplus or deficit.

## 14.1.4.21 IPSAS 22. Disclosure of Information about the General Government Sector (no comparable IAS)

The General Government Sector (GGS) comprises all organizational entities of the general government as defined in statistical bases of financial reporting. A public sector entity may elect to disclose financial information about the GGS. If they elect to make such disclosures, the GGS shall recognize its investment in the Public Financial Corporations and Non-Financial Corporations sectors as an asset and shall account for that asset at the carrying amount of the net assets of its investees. The GGS disclosures shall be reconciled to the consolidated financial statements of the government showing separately the amount of the adjustment to each equivalent item in those financial statements.

### 14.1.4.22 IPSAS 23. Revenue from Non-Exchange Transactions (Taxes and Transfers) (no comparable IAS)

Non-exchange transactions are any transactions that are not exchange transactions. In a non-exchange transaction, an entity either receives value from another entity without directly giving approximately equal value in exchange, or gives value to another entity without directly receiving approximately equal value in exchange. In respect to taxes, an entity shall recognize an asset when the taxable event occurs and the asset recognition criteria are met. In respect to transfers, an entity shall recognize an asset when the transferred resources meet the definition of an asset and satisfy the criteria for recognition as an asset. An entity may, but is not required to, recognize services in-kind as revenue and as an asset. Stipulations relating to a transferred asset may be either conditions or restrictions. If it has conditions associated with the transfer, the recipient initially recognizes an asset and also incurs a liability. If there are restrictions on the transfer, the asset is recognized but no liability is incurred.

### 14.1.4.23 IPSAS 24. Presentation of Budget Information in Financial Statements (no comparable IAS)

This IPSAS was discussed briefly in the Budgetary Reporting section earlier.

### 14.1.4.24 IPSAS 25. Employee Benefits (Based on IAS 19)

Employee benefits are all forms of consideration given by an entity in exchange for service rendered by employees. If the benefits are short-term (due wholly within twelve months after the end of the period in which the employees render the related service), the entity recognizes the undiscounted amount of benefits expected to be paid in exchange for that service during the period in which the service is performed. If long-term, the benefits may be post-employment benefits (i.e. retirement programs or medical coverage) or other long-term benefits (i.e. sabbatical leave, disability benefits, deferred compensation, etc.). If the post-employment benefits pertain to retirement programs, it may be a defined contribution plan (recognize liability after deducting any contributions already paid) or a defined benefit plan (recognize liability on an actuarial basis). The amount recognized as a liability for other long-term employee benefits shall be the net total of the present value of the defined benefit obligations at the reporting date minus the fair value at the reporting date of plan assets out of which the obligations are to be settled directly.

## 14.1.5 Steps for Implementation of IPSASs

IFAC proposes step-by-step implementation in the transition from the cash basis to the accrual basis of accounting.* The following steps suggest an approach to implementing the IPSASs in developing countries and economies in transition:

Step 1. Identify all government-owned enterprises that operate to make a profit or to break even. These enterprises should be on the accrual basis of accounting and should comply with the IASs and IFRSs.

Step 2. Identify all other government activities (including off-budget government activities) and prepare a statement of cash receipts and payments for each entity that has a separate bank account. These governments will generally be on the cash basis (or a modified cash basis) of accounting and should comply with the IPSASs. For greater efficiency in overall cash management for the whole-of-government, a Treasury Single Account† should be established if that has not already been accomplished.

Step 3. Prepare a Consolidated Statement of Cash Receipts and Payments (Attachment 14.1) as specified in the Part 1 requirements of the Cash Basis IPSAS. This would include collecting pertinent receipt and payment data from third parties for reflection in the Consolidated Statement. This statement (with the appropriate audit opinion) should be issued within six months of the end of the reporting period.

Step 4. As encouraged by IPSAS 1 and illustrated in the Cash Basis IPSAS, a Budget to Actual Comparative Statement (Attachment 14.3) should be prepared on the same basis as the budget and issued at the same time as the Consolidated Statement of Cash Receipts and Payments. Where possible, it should be broken out by the segments used for authorizing the budget (IPSAS 18).

Step 5. Start migrating to the Part 2 disclosures in the Cash Basis IPSAS as time and capacity permits:

a. Prepare Cash Flow Statement (Attachment 14.2) in the format prescribed by IPSAS 2.

b. Disclose the value of all financial assets in the notes to the Statement of Cash Receipts and Payments. Cash is included in the body of the Statement and would not need to be included in the notes. Financial assets would include all receivables generated as a result of exchange transactions (IPSAS 9) and nonexchange transactions, as well as all other financial assets including financial instruments (IPSAS 15).

---

* See para. 2.22, Study 14—Transition to the Accrual Basis of Accounting: Guidance for Governments and Government Entities (IFAC Public Sector Committee), April 2003.

† For more information, see Treasury Reference Model by Ali Hashim (World Bank) and Bill Allan (IMF), http://www1.worldbank.org/public sector/pe/trmodel.htm (3/14/2001).

    c. Disclose the value of all financial liabilities in the notes to the Statement of Cash Receipts and Payments. This would include borrowings identified in IPSAS 5, as well as other financial liabilities identified in IPSASs 13 (finance leases), 15 (financial instruments), and 19 (provisions).

    d. Disclose the value of all nonfinancial assets in the notes to the Statement of Cash Receipts and Payments. The following priority order of disclosure is suggested: inventories (IPSAS 12); investments (including IPSASs 7, 8, and 16); finance leases (IPSAS 13); and property, plant, and equipment (IPSAS 17).

Step 6. Implement all remaining IPSASs (1, 3, 4, 6, 10, 11, 14, 20, and all other newly released IPSASs) when sufficient Part 2 options have been met. The complete set (Attachments 14.3–14.6) of the general purpose financial statements, along with the audit opinion, should be issued within six months of the end of the reporting period.

## 14.2 Conclusion

A specific time period for accomplishing the above steps has not been identified since much will be contingent on the automated system in effect and the degree of top-level management support, as well as the support of the legislative body. In any event, it will probably take most developing countries and economies in transition at least five years (and, in some cases, much longer) to implement the full set of IPSASs and move from a cash or modified cash basis of accounting to an accrual basis. In addition, a specific chart of accounts has not been proposed since it will be dependent on the financial structure adopted. Further, statistical data will need to be extracted from the financial system to meet the needs of the International Monetary Fund as specified in the Government Finance Statistics Manual.* Although it is recommended that the steps be accomplished in the order prescribed, local conditions may dictate a different sequence than that identified above.

When the transition to the accrual basis has been completed, the governmental agency will know how much it owns and how much it owes (not just where cash came from, where cash went, and the remaining cash balance). Consequently, government will be in a much better position to manage total resources rather than just the cash available to them.

---

\* Government Finance Statistics Manual, International Monetary Fund, 2001.

# Attachment 14.1—Illustrative Required Consolidated Statement of Cash Receipts and Payments

(pp. 38–39, Appendix 1a, Cash Basis IPSAS).

| (in thousands of currency units) | Note | 200X Receipts/ (Payments) Controlled by Entity | 200X Payments by Third Parties | 200X-1 Receipts/ (Payments) Controlled by Entity | 200X-1 Payments by Third Parties |
|---|---|---|---|---|---|
| **Receipts** | | | | | |
| *Taxation* | | | | | |
| Income tax | | X | — | X | — |
| Value-added tax | | X | — | X | — |
| Property tax | | X | — | X | — |
| Other taxes | | X | — | X | — |
| | | X | — | X | — |
| *Grants and Aid* | | | | | |
| International agencies | | X | X | X | X |
| Other grants and aid | | X | X | X | X |
| | | X | X | X | X |
| *Borrowings* | | | | | |
| Proceeds from borrowings | 3 | X | X | X | X |
| *Capital Receipts* | | | | | |
| Proceeds from disposal of plant and equipment | | X | — | X | — |
| *Trading Activities* | | | | | |
| Receipts from trading activities | | X | — | X | — |
| *Other receipts* | 4 | X | X | X | X |
| **Total receipts** | | X | X | X | X |

(continued on next page)

| (in thousands of currency units) | Note | 200X | | 200X-1 | |
|---|---|---|---|---|---|
| | | Receipts/ (Payments) Controlled by Entity | Payments by Third Parties | Receipts/ (Payments) Controlled by Entity | Payments by Third Parties |
| **Payments** | | | | | |
| *Operations* | | | | | |
| Wages, salaries, and employee benefits | | (X) | (X) | (X) | (X) |
| Supplies and consumables | | (X) | (X) | (X) | (X) |
| | | (X) | (X) | (X) | (X) |
| *Transfers* | | | | | |
| Grants | | (X) | — | (X) | — |
| Other transfer payments | | (X) | — | (X) | — |
| | | (X) | — | (X) | — |
| *Capital Expenditures* | | | | | |
| Purchase/ construction of plant and equipment | | (X) | (X) | (X) | (X) |
| Purchase of financial instruments | | (X) | — | (X) | — |
| | | (X) | (X) | (X) | (X) |
| *Loans and Interest Repayments* | | | | | |
| Repayment of borrowings | | (X) | — | (X) | — |
| Interest payments | | (X) | — | (X) | — |
| | | (X) | — | (X) | — |
| *Other payments* | 5 | (X) | (X) | (X) | (X) |
| **Total payments** | | (X) | (X) | (X) | (X) |
| **Increase/(Decrease) in Cash** | | X | — | X | — |

| (in thousands of currency units) | Note | 200X | | 200X-1 | |
|---|---|---|---|---|---|
| | | *Receipts/ (Payments) Controlled by Entity* | *Payments by Third Parties* | *Receipts/ (Payments) Controlled by Entity* | *Payments by Third Parties* |
| **Cash at beginning of year** | 2 | X | N/A[a] | X | N/A |
| **Increase/(Decrease) in Cash** | | X | N/A | X | N/A |
| **Cash at end of year** | 2 | X | N/A | X | N/A |

[a] N/A = Not applicable

# Attachment 14.2—Statement of Cash Flows

(pp. 111–112, Appendix, IPSAS 2).

**Public Sector Entity—Consolidated Cash Flow Statement for Year Ended 31 December 20X2 (in Thousands of Currency Units) (Direct Method)**

| | 20X2 | 20X1 |
|---|---|---|
| **Cash Flows from Operating Activities** | | |
| Receipts | | |
| Taxation | X | X |
| Sales of goods and services | X | X |
| Grants | X | X |
| Interest received | X | X |
| Other receipts | X | X |
| Payments | | |
| Employee costs | (X) | (X) |
| Superannuation | (X) | (X) |
| Suppliers | (X) | (X) |
| Interest paid | (X) | (X) |
| Other payments | (X) | (X) |
| **Net cash flows from operating activities** | **X** | **X** |

*(continued on next page)*

| | 20X2 | 20X1 |
|---|---|---|
| **Cash Flows from Investing Activities** | | |
| Purchase of plant and equipment | (X) | (X) |
| Proceeds from sale of plant and equipment | X | X |
| Proceeds from sale of investments | X | X |
| Purchase of foreign currency securities | (X) | (X) |
| **Net cash flows from investing activities** | (X) | (X) |
| **Cash Flows from Financing Activities** | | |
| Proceeds from borrowings | X | X |
| Repayment of borrowings | (X) | (X) |
| Distribution/dividend to government | (X) | (X) |
| **Net cash flows from financing activities** | X | X |
| **Net increase/(decrease) in cash and cash equivalents** | X | X |
| **Cash and cash equivalents at beginning of period** | X | X |
| **Cash and cash equivalents at end of period** | X | X |

# Attachment 14.3—Illustrative Optional Budget to Actual Comparative Statement

Appendix 2, p. 78, Comparison with budgets (paragraph 2.1.33(b)), Cash Basis IPSAS.

| *(in thousands of currency units)* | Actual | | Budgeted | | Variance | |
|---|---|---|---|---|---|---|
| **Receipts** | | | | | | |
| *Taxation* | | | | | | |
| Income tax | X | | X | | X | |
| Value-added tax | X | | X | | (X) | |
| Property tax | X | | X | | X | |
| Other taxes | X | | X | | (X) | |
| | | X | | X | | X |
| *Aid Agreements* | | | | | | |
| International agencies | X | | X | | — | |
| Other grants and aid | X | | X | | — | |
| | | X | | X | | — |

|  | Actual | Budgeted | Variance |
|---|---|---|---|
| *Borrowings* |  |  |  |
| Proceeds from borrowings | X | X | (X) |
| *Capital Receipts* |  |  |  |
| Proceeds from disposal of plant and equipment | X | X | X |
| *Trading Activities* |  |  |  |
| Receipts from trading activities | X | X | X |
| *Other receipts* | X | X | X |
| **Total receipts** | **X** | **X** | **X** |
| **Payments** |  |  |  |
| *Operations* |  |  |  |
| Wages, salaries, and employee benefits | (X) | (X) | (X) |
| Supplies and consumables | (X) | (X) | X |
|  | (X) | (X) | (X) |
| *Transfers* |  |  |  |
| Grants | (X) | (X) | — |
| Other transfers | (X) | (X) | — |
|  | (X) | (X) | — |
| *Capital Expenditures* |  |  |  |
| Purchase/construction of plant and equipment | (X) | (X) | (X) |
| Purchase of financial instruments | (X) | (X) | — |
|  | (X) | (X) | (X) |
| *Loans and Interest Repayments* |  |  |  |
| Repayment of borrowings | (X) | (X) | — |
| Interest payments | (X) | (X) | — |
|  | (X) | (X) | — |
| *Other payments* | (X) | (X) | (X) |
| **Total payments** | **(X)** | **(X)** | **(X)** |
| **Net Receipts/(Payments)** | **X** | **X** | **X** |

# Attachment 14.4—Statement of Financial Position

(pp. 75–76, Appendix 1, IPSAS 1).

**Public Sector Entity—Statement of Financial Position as of 31 December 20X2 (In Thousands of Currency Units)**

|  | 20X2 | 20X2 | 20X1 | 20X1 |
|---|---|---|---|---|
| **Assets** | | | | |
| *Current assets* | | | | |
| Cash and cash equivalents | X | | X | |
| Receivables | X | | X | |
| Inventories | X | | X | |
| Prepayments | X | | X | |
| Investments | X | | X | |
|  | | X | | X |
| *Noncurrent assets* | | | | |
| Receivables | X | | X | |
| Investments | X | | X | |
| Other financial assets | X | | X | |
| Infrastructure, plant and equipment | X | | X | |
| Land and buildings | X | | X | |
| Intangible assets | X | | X | |
| Other nonfinancial assets | X | | X | |
|  | | X | | X |
| **Total assets** | | X | | X |
| **Liabilities** | | | | |
| *Current liabilities* | | | | |
| Payables | X | | X | |
| Short-term borrowings | X | | X | |
| Current portion of borrowings | X | | X | |
| Provisions | X | | X | |
| Employee benefits | X | | X | |
| Superannuation | X | | X | |
|  | | X | | X |
| *Noncurrent liabilities* | | | | |
| Payables | X | | X | |
| Borrowings | X | | X | |
| Provisions | X | | X | |

| | 20X2 | 20X2 | 20X1 | 20X1 |
|---|---|---|---|---|
| Employee benefits | X | | X | |
| Superannuation | X | | X | |
| | | X | | X |
| **Total liabilities** | | X | | X |
| **Net assets** | | X | | X |
| **Net Assets/Equity** | | | | |
| Capital contributed by other government entities | X | | X | |
| Reserves | X | | X | |
| Accumulated surpluses/(deficits) | X | | X | |
| | | X | | X |
| Minority interest | | X | | X |
| **Total net assets/equity** | | X | | X |

# Attachment 14.5—Statement of Financial Performance

(pp. 77–79, Appendix 1, IPSAS 1).

**Public Sector Entity—Statement of Financial Performance for the Year Ended 31 December 20x2 (*Illustrating the Classification of Expenses by Function*) (In Thousands of Currency Units)**

|  | *20X2* | *20X1* |
|---|---|---|
| **Operating Revenue** | | |
| Taxes | X | X |
| Fees, fines, penalties, and licenses | X | X |
| Revenue from exchange transactions | X | X |
| Transfers from other government entities | X | X |
| Other operating revenue | X | X |
| **Total operating revenue** | X | X |
| **Operating Expenses** | | |
| General public services | X | X |
| Defense | X | X |
| Public order and safety | X | X |
| Education | X | X |
| Health | X | X |
| Social protection | X | X |
| Housing and community amenities | X | X |
| Recreational, cultural, and religion | X | X |
| Economic Affairs | X | X |
| Environmental protection | X | X |
| **Total operating expenses** | X | X |
| **Surplus/(deficit) from operating activities** | X | X |
| Finance costs | (X) | (X) |
| Gains on sale of property, plant, and equipment | X | X |
| **Total nonoperating revenue (expenses)** | (X) | (X) |
| **Surplus/(deficit) from ordinary activities** | X | X |
| Minority interest share of surplus/(deficit)[a] | (X) | (X) |
| **Net surplus/(deficit) before extraordinary items** | X | X |
| Extraordinary items | (X) | (X) |
| **Net surplus/(deficit) for the period** | X | X |

[a] The minority interest share of the surplus/(deficit) from ordinary activities includes the minority interest share of extraordinary items. The presentation of extraordinary items net of minority interest is permitted by paragraph 57(c) of IPSAS 1 "Presentation of Financial Statements." Disclosure of the minority interest share of extraordinary items is shown in the notes to the financial statements.

**Public Sector Entity—Statement of Financial Performance for the Year Ended 31 December 20x2 (*Illustrating the Classification of Expenses by Nature*) (In Thousands of Currency Units)**

|  | 20X2 | 20X1 |
|---|---|---|
| **Operating Revenue** | | |
| Taxes | X | X |
| Fees, fines, penalties and licenses | X | X |
| Revenue from exchange transactions | X | X |
| Transfers from other government entities | X | X |
| Other operating revenue | X | X |
| **Total operating revenue** | X | X |
| **Operating Expenses** | | |
| Wages, salaries and employee benefits | X | X |
| Grants and other transfer payments | X | X |
| Supplies and consumables used | X | X |
| Depreciation and amortization expense | X | X |
| Other operating expenses | X | X |
| **Total operating expenses** | X | X |
| **Surplus/(deficit) from operating activities** | X | X |
| Finance costs | (X) | (X) |
| Gains on sale of property, plant and equipment | X | X |
| **Total nonoperating revenue (expenses)** | (X) | (X) |
| **Surplus/(deficit) from ordinary activities** | X | X |
| Minority interest share of surplus/(deficit)[a] | (X) | (X) |
| **Net surplus/(deficit) before extraordinary items** | X | X |
| Extraordinary items | (X) | (X) |
| **Net surplus/(deficit) for the period** | X | X |

[a] The minority interest share of the surplus/(deficit) from ordinary activities includes the minority interest share of extraordinary items. The presentation of extraordinary items net of minority interest is permitted by paragraph 57(c) of IPSAS 1 "Presentation of Financial Statements." Disclosure of the minority interest share of extraordinary items is shown in the notes to the financial statements.

## Attachment 14.6—Statement of Changes in Net Assets/Equity

(pp. 80, Appendix 1, IPSAS 1).

**Public Sector Entity—Statement of Changes in Net Assets/Equity for the Year Ended 31 December 20x2 (In Thousands of Currency Units)**

|  | Contributed Capital | Revaluation Reserve | Translation Reserve | Accumulated Surpluses/ (Deficits) | Total |
|---|---|---|---|---|---|
| Balance at 31 December 20X0 | X | X | (X) | X | X |
| Changes in accounting policy | (X) |  |  | (X) | (X) |
| Restated balance | X | X | X | X | X |
| Surplus on revaluation of property |  | X |  |  | X |
| Deficit on revaluation of investments |  | (X) |  |  | (X) |
| Currency translation differences |  |  | (X) |  | (X) |
| Net gains and losses not recognized in the statement of financial performance |  | X | (X) |  | X |
| Net surplus for the period |  |  |  | X | X |
| Balance at 31 December 20X1 | X | X | (X) | X | X |

| | Contributed Capital | Revaluation Reserve | Translation Reserve | Accumulated Surpluses/ (Deficits) | Total |
|---|---|---|---|---|---|
| Deficit on revaluation of property | | (X) | | | (X) |
| Surplus on revaluation of investments | X | | | X | |
| Currency translation differences | | | (X) | | X |
| Net gains and losses not recognized in the statement of financial performance | | (X) | (X) | | (X) |
| Net deficit for the period | | | | (X) | (X) |
| Balance at 31 December 20X2 | X | X | (X) | X | X |

This article was originally published in the Public Fund Digest (Volume IV, No. 1, 2004, pp. 32–51). It is reprinted with permission from the International Consortium on Governmental Financial Management. Other articles of interest published in the Public Fund Digest and authored or coauthored by Dr. Hughes are as follows:

1. "Building a Common Database for International Governmental Financial Statements," Volume II, No. 1, 2002, pp. 46–53 (Coauthor Issam M. Abu-Izz).
2. "Which Financial Reports in the Public Sector Should Be Subject To External Attestation?," Volume IV, No. 2, 2004, pp. 50–59 (Coauthor Wayne Cameron).
3. "Developing a Chart of Accounts to Meet IPSAS and GFS Requirements for Financial Reporting by Governmental Entities," Volume V, No. 2, 2005, pp. 68–80.
4. "Laying the Foundation for the Internal Audit Function in Governments Throughout the World," Volume VI, No. 1, 2006, pp. 67–83.
5. "Transition to Accrual Accounting: A Suggested Work Plan," Volume VI, No. 1, 2006, pp. 99–100.
6. "A Stepwise Approach to Transition from a Cash, Modified Cash, Or Modified Accrual Basis of Accounting to a Full Accrual Basis for Developing Countries," Vol. VI, No. 2, 2007, pp. 53-62.

All of the above articles are available on the www.icgfm.org Web site.

# Index

## A

AAA. *See* American Accounting Association
  (AAA)
Accountability
  defined, 341
  fiscal, 179
  operational, 179
  reports, 486, 487
Accountability of Tax Dollars Act (2002), 447,
  462, 481
Accounting, 84
  accrual, 446, 450, 456, 481, 517
  basis, 254, 256–257, 258
  budgetary, 482–483
  for controlled entities, 500
  government-wide, 464
  for investments in associates, 500
  public sector, 493–506
    accounting for investments in associates,
      500
    accrual basis standards, 498–504
    borrowing costs, 500
    budgetary reporting, 497–498
    cash basis standard, 495–497
    cash flows, 509–510
    cash or non-cash generating assets, 503
    cash receipts and payments, 507–509
    changes in net assets/equity, 516–517
    consolidated financial statements, 500
    construction contracts, 501
    deficits, 499
    employee benefits, 504
    events after reporting date, 501–502
    exchange transactions, revenue from,
      500–501
    financial performance, 514–515
    financial position, 512–513
    financial statements, 498–499, 500, 502
    foreign exchange rates, 499
    hyperinflationary economies, financial
      reporting of, 501
    inventories, 501
    investment property, 502
    joint ventures, reporting of interests in,
      500
    leases, 501
    net surplus, 499
    optional budget to actual comparative
      statement, 511
    property, plant, and equipment, 502
    provisions, contingent liabilities and
      contingent assets, 503
    related party disclosures, 503
    revenue from non-exchange transaction,
      504
    steps for implementation, 504–506
  research bulletins, 3, 4, 33, 264
  role in budget processing, 87
Accounting research bulletins (ARBs), 3, 4,
  33, 264
Accrual accounting, 446, 450, 456, 481, 517
Actual cost, 175
Advance refunding, 35, 195, 209, 212, 302
Agency fund, 335–336
AICPA. *See* American Institute of Certified
  Public Accountants (AICPA)
Allotments, 168–169
  as budgeting control device, 175–176, 461
American Accounting Association (AAA), 9–10
American Institute of Certified Public Account-
  ants (AICPA), 3, 9, 11, 280, 292
Anticipation notes, 186, 219, 300
Antideficiency Act, 481–482

Antonio, James F., 10, 15, 37, 42

ARBs. *See* Accounting research bulletins (ARBs)

ASB. *See* Auditing Standards Boards (ASB)

Assets, 165, 187, 294–298, 456, 503
    capital, 50, 54, 63, 242, 244, 263
    current, 263, 397
    defined, 294
    net, 347, 391–392
        changes in, 367, 516
        fiduciary, 366–367
        pension trust fund, 323
        unrestricted, 399, 400, 401
    proprietary, 360, 362

Audit(s)
    compliance, 415
    governmental, 414–420
    guide, 4
    performance, 415
    reports, 423–424, 430–436
    single, 421–423

Auditing, 409–438
    issues, 420–427
        audit reports, 423–424
        audit selection and request for proposal process, 424–426
        financial reporting entry, 420–421
        nonaudit services, 426–427
        single audit, 421–423

Auditing Standards Boards (ASB), 9

Auditor's report, 423–424, 430–436
    on compliance, 434–436
    on internal control over financial reporting, 432–433
    unqualified independent, 430–431

**B**

Balance sheet(s), 202
    combining, 286–287
    combining nonmajor governmental fund, 233, 236, 237
    debt service fund, 203, 204
    enterprise funds, 294–303
    federal agency, 470–472
    general fund, 166, 179–180
    governmental-fund, 157, 347, 354, 356, 385
    proprietary funds, 262–264, 265–266, 347
    reconciliation to statement of net assets, 184

BAN. *See* Bonds, anticipation notes

Basic financial statements, 353–387

component unit combining, 377–387
    fiduciary fund, 365–367, 368
    government-wide, 367–377, 385
    governmental fund, 354–358
    proprietary fund, 358–365

Bond(s), 17, 195, 300
    anticipation notes, 219
    callable, 12
    demand, 11
    refunding, 263, 356 (*See also* Refunding)
    treasury, 14

Borrowing costs, 500

Budget(s)
    deficits, 134
    definitions, 73–76
    expenditure estimates, 80
    in hierarchy of decisions, 74
    preparation, 80
    process, 77–84
        planning and scheduling for, 80
    resource estimates, 80
    review, 80
    techniques, 84–112
    time line, 77
    working definitions, 73–76

Budget accounts, 466–468

Budget and Accounting Act (1921), 442, 480–481, 482

Budget and Accounting Procedures Act (1950), 445–446, 482

Budgetary accounting, 216–217, 445–446, 482

Budgetary balance, 395–402

Budgetary integration, 171–172

Budgetary resources, 475

Bureau of Economic Analysis, 465–466

**C**

CAFR. *See* Comprehensive annual financial report (CAFR)

CAP. *See* Committee on Accounting Procedures (CAP)

Capital assets, 296–298
    acquisition, 296
    reporting requirements, 297

Capital lease, 194

Capital project funds, 153, 215–247
    budgetary accounting, 216–217
    budgetary reporting, 224
    capital contributions, 220–221
    case study, 225–247
    construction expenditures, 218

defined, 216
financial reporting, 222–224
fund balance, 222
governmental funds *vs.,* 216
grants, 219–220
interfund transfers, 221
investments and arbitrage, 219
issuance of capital debt, 218–219
special assessments, 221–222
unreserved balance, 222
Cash disbursements, 32
Cash flow, 181
    formats, 19
    statement
        enterprise fund, 307–311
        general fund, 181
        proprietary fund, 268, 271, 272–273
Certain tax, 186
Changes in net position, 472–474
Chief Financial Officers Act (1990), 446–447,
        483
Codification, 202
Collecting general taxes, 172–173
Committee on Accounting Procedures (CAP),
        2, 3
Compliance, 422
    auditor's report on, 434–436
    internal control over, 435
Comprehensive annual financial report (CAFR),
        6, 202, 344–352, 390, 392, 393
    financial section, 346–351
    introductory section, 345
    statistical section, 351–352
Congressional Budget and Impoundment
        Control Act (1974), 465, 483
Congressional Budget Office, 465
Consumption, 120–121
Corporations, government, 483–484
Cost(s), 175, 472, 500
    unit, approach to budgeting and, 92, 94,
        95–96
Credit, 254
    balances, 179
Current refunding, 209
Custodial activities, 475

**D**

Debt, 254
Debt service funds, 153, 194–213
    accounting and reporting for, 211–212
    accounting for transactions, 196–202

balance sheet, 203, 204
CAFR, 202
codification, 202
disclosure requirement, 212–213
extinguishment, 208–210
operating statement, 204, 205
special assessments, 203
    reporting for, 208
Debt service indicators, 278
Defeasance, 210
Deferrals, 188
Deficits, 134, 499
Defliese, Philip L., 10, 42, 43
Discussion memorandum, 8, 12
Dockery Act (1894), 441

**E**

Earmarks, 83, 167, 268, 467–468, 469
Efficiency indicators, 278–279
EITF. *See* Emerging Issues Task Force (EITF)
Emerging Issues Task Force (EITF), 32
Encumbrances, 173–176
Enterprise funds, 154–155, 251
    financial statements, 293–311
        balance sheets, 294–303, 304–305
        cash flow, 307–311
        income, 303, 306
        material for, 293–294
    fund balance, 303
    future of, 313–314
    interfund transfer, 311–313
Equity recognition, 257–259
Estimated cost, 175
Exchange transactions, revenue from, 500–501
Expenditure(s), 130–139
    accounting for growth of, 131–132
    federal, 134–135
    recognition, 195–196
    size and growth of U. S., 130–131
    state and local, 136–139
    U. S. *vs.* other countries, 132–134

**F**

FAF. *See* Financial Accounting Foundation
        (FAF)
FASAB. *See* Federal Accounting Standards
        Advisory (FASAB)
FASB. *See* Financial Accounting Standards
        Board (FASB)

Federal, awards schedule of expenditures of, 435–436
Federal accounting, historical backgrounds, 440–448
Federal accounting and reporting, agencies responsible for, 457–466
Federal Accounting Standards Advisory Board (FASAB), 447
   accounting and auditing policy committee (AAPC), 459
   AICPA rule 203 designation, 458–459
   concept statements, 455–456
   documents resulting from AAPC and, 479–480
   due process, 459
   objectives, 453–455
      budgetary integrity, 454
      operating performance, 454
      stewardship, 454
      systems and control, 455
Federal Financial Accounting Standards, 456
Federal Financial Management Improvement Act (1996), 469, 481, 484
Federal funds, 467
Federal Managers' Financial Improvement Act (1996), 447
Federal Managers' Financial Integrity Act (1982), 480–481, 485
Federal payroll taxes, 139
Federal Reports Elimination and Sunset Act (1995), 481, 490
Federal Trade Commission, 2
Fees, regressive pattern of, 293
Fiduciary funds, 150, 155–157, 158, 251, 317–336
   classification, 317
   financial statements, 157, 365–367, 368
   statements, 157
Financial accounting, 485
Financial Accounting Foundation (FAF), 7, 11
Financial Accounting Standards Board (FASB), 17–18, 264, 300, 301, 306
   GASB *vs.,* 7, 8
Financial condition, 392–402
   analysis, 392–394
   factors and indicators, 394–402
      financial position as, 398–402
      liquidity as, 276, 397–398
      operating position as, 395, 396
Financial management cycle, 75
Financial position, 398–402
Financial ratios, 271, 274–279

Financial reporting pyramid, 6
Financial statement(s), 54–57
   accrual basis, 456
   basic, 353–387
      component unit combining, 377–387
      fiduciary fund, 157, 365–367, 368
      government-wide, 367–377, 385
      governmental fund, 354–358
      proprietary fund, 358–365
   communication methods, 186–187
   elements of, 187–188
   general fund, 179–186
   proprietary funds, 261–271, 358–365
   required of federal agencies, 470–478
Financial statements
   internal service fund, 284–285
Financing statement, 476–478
Fiscal federalism, 130
Foreign exchange rates, 499
Fuel tax revenues, 152
Fund(s). *See also specific types*
   accounting, 149–160
   agency, 335–336
   balance, 222
   capital project, 153, 215–247
      budgetary accounting, 216–217
      budgetary reporting, 224
      capital contributions, 220–221
      case study, 225–247
      construction expenditures, 218
      defined, 216
      financial reporting, 222–224
      fund balance, 222
      governmental funds *vs.,* 216
      grants, 219–220
      interfund transfers, 221
      investments and arbitrage, 219
      issuance of capital debt, 218–219
      special assessments, 221–222
      unreserved balance, 222
   categories, 82, 152
   debt service, 153, 194–213
      accounting and reporting for, 211–212
      accounting for transactions, 196–202
      balance sheet, 203, 204
      CAFR, 202
      codification, 202
      disclosure requirement, 212–213
      extinguishment, 208–210
      operating statement, 204, 205
      special assessments, 203
         reporting for, 208

defined, 250
descriptions, 150–160
enterprise, 154–155, 251
    financial statements, 293–311
        balance sheets, 294–303, 304–305
        cash flow, 307–311
        income, 303, 306
        material for, 293–294
    fund balance, 303
    future of, 313–314
    interfund transfer, 311–313
fiduciary, 150, 155–157, 158, 251, 317–336
    classification, 317
    financial statements, 157, 365–367, 368
    statements, 157
general, 151–152
    account classification, 169–171
    account structure, 166
    accounting and financial issues, 186
    assets, 165
    balance sheet, 179–180
    budgetary comparisons, 185
    budgetary integration, 168
    communication methods, 186–187
    concept, 162–164
    encumbrances and allotments, 173–176
    equity and balance, 167
    expenditure recognition, 165
    financial statements, 179–186
    interim financial reports, 182, 184, 186
    journal entries, 174
    liabilities, 165
    major focus, 167
    measurement focus and basis of
        accounting, 164
    number, 164
    operating statements, 179
    reconciliation statements and schedules,
        181–182
    revenue recognition, 165
    revenues collected after close of fiscal
        year, 186
    schedules, 181–182
    statement of cash flow, 181
    unique aspects, 164–169
governmental, 150–154, 251
    basis of accounting, 158
    proprietary funds *vs.*, 159, 252–261
        basis of accounting, 254, 256–257,
            258
        equity recognition, 257–259
        measurement focus, 158

    pricing, 259–260
    transfers, 260–261
    statements, 56, 157
    types of, 150
internal service, 21, 155, 251, 279–285
    advantages, 280–281
    combining financial statements,
        286–291
    disadvantages, 281–282
    financial statements, 284–285
    pricing policy, 282–283
    transfers, 284
land endowment, 319
pension trust, 321–330
permanent, 153
pricing, 259–260
proprietary, 150, 152, 154–155, 158,
    250–314
    debt indicators, 277–278
    debt service indicators, 278
    efficiency indicators, 278–279
    financial ratios, 271, 274–279
    financial statements, 157, 261–273
        balance sheet, 262–264, 265–266
        cash flow, 268, 271, 272–273
        income, 264, 267–268
    governmental funds *vs.*, 252–261
        basis of accounting, 254, 256–257,
            258
        equity recognition, 257–259
        measurement focus, 254, 255
        pricing, 259–260
        transfers, 260–261
    liquidity indicators, 276
    solvency indicators, 276–277
special revenue, 36, 152–153
structure, 252, 283
transfers, 260–261
trust, 467–468
ultimate, 34

**G**

GAAFR. *See Governmental Accounting,
    Auditing, and Financial Reporting
    (GAAFR)*
GAAP. *See Generally accepted accounting
    principles (GAAP)*
GAAS. *See Generally accepted auditing
    standards (GAAS)*
GAGAS. *See Generally accepted governmental
    auditing standards (GAGAS)*

GASB. *See* Governmental Accounting
    Standards Board (GASB)
General fund, 151–152
  account classification, 169–171
  account structure, 166
  accounting and financial issues, 186
  assets, 165
  balance sheet, 179–180
  budgetary comparisons, 185
  budgetary integration, 168
  communication methods, 186–187
  concept, 162–164
  encumbrances and allotments, 173–176
  equity and balance, 167
  expenditure recognition, 165
  financial statements, 179–186
  interim financial reports, 182, 184, 186
  journal entries, 174
  liabilities, 165
  major focus, 167
  measurement focus and basis of accounting,
    164
  number, 164
  operating statements, 179
  reconciliation statements and schedules,
    181–182
  revenue recognition, 165
  revenues collected after close of fiscal year,
    186
  schedules, 181–182
  statement of cash flow, 181
  unique aspects, 164–169
General Long-term Debt Account Group, 21
General long-term liability, 17, 21
General obligation bonds, 195, 300
General purpose financial statements (GPFS), 6
Generally accepted accounting principles
    (GAAP), 280
  ARBs, 4
  guidelines, 150
  historical perspectives, 2–11
Generally accepted auditing standards (GAAS),
    413
Generally accepted governmental auditing
    standards (GAGAS), 413, 414, 415
  field work, 417–419
  general, 416–417
  reporting, 419–420
GFOA. *See* Governmental Finance Officers
    Association (GFOA)
Government accountability office, 464–465
Government activities, 150

Government Corporation Control Act (1945),
    444–445, 483–484, 485–486
Government corporations, 444, 483–484
Government Management Reform Act (1994),
    447, 486
Government Performance and Results Act
    (1993), 486
Government-wide reporting, 367–377, 385
Government-wide statements, converting
    governmental fund statements to, 56
*Governmental Accounting, Auditing, and
    Financial Reporting* (GAAFR), 3
Governmental accounting and auditing (GAA),
    410–420
  historical perspectives, 410–411
Governmental Accounting Standards Board
    (GASB), 7–22
  categories of deposits and investments, 14
  categories of funds, 82
  FASB *vs.,* 7, 8
  financial reporting pyramid, 48
  financial statements, 54–57
    notes to, 57
  first board, 10–11
  five-year review, 22–24
  focus, 52–54
  funds statements, 49–52
  government-wide financial statement, 54–57
  new board, 27–60
  nonexchange transactions, 45
  old *vs.* new hierarchies, 25
  original's board last stand, 24–27
  predecessor organizations, 9
  Q and A reports, 9
  recent standards, 60–64
  reporting model, 44–49, 55
    timeline for, 46
  statements, 34, 391–392
    of governmental accounting standards,
      8–9
  supporting organizations, 9
  technical bulletins, 9
  website, 7–8
Governmental Finance Officers Association
    (GFOA), 7, 9
Governmental funds, 150–154, 251
  basis of accounting, 158
  proprietary funds *vs.,* 159, 252–261
    basis of accounting, 254, 256–257, 258
    equity recognition, 257–259
    measurement focus, 158

pricing, 259–260
transfers, 260–261
statements, 56, 157
types of, 150
Governmental reporting
component units, 341–344
defined, 341–344
related reporting entity topics, 344
GPFS. *See* General purpose financial statements (GPFS)
Grant anticipation notes, 186

**H**

Hoover Commission, 89, 103, 105, 444–445, 483–484, 485–486
Hyperinflationary economies, financial reporting of, 501

**I**

IASC. *See* International Accounting Standards Committee (IASC)
In-subsubstance defeasance, 210
Income, 118–120
defined, 118
evaluation, 119–120
methods of taxation, 118–119
statement
enterprise funds, 303, 306
proprietary funds, 264, 267–268
Inflow of resources, 188
Infrastructure assets, 297–298
Interfund activity, 176–179. *See also* Interfund transfer(s)
classification, 176
exchange transactions, 176–177
intra-and interactivity transactions, 178
intra-entity transactions, 178–179
loans, 177
reimbursements, 178
transfers, 177–178
Interfund transfer(s), 284
capital project funds, 221
enterprise funds, 311–313
Intergovernmental grants, 145–146
Internal Revenue Service (IRS), 10
Internal service funds (ISF), 21, 155, 251, 279–285
advantages, 280–281
combining financial statements, 286–291

disadvantages, 281–282
financial statements, 284–285
pricing policy, 282–283
transfers, 284
International Accounting Standards Committee (IASC), 493
International Public Sector Accounting Standards Board (IPSASB), 493
International Public Sector Accounting Standards (IPSAS), 493–506
accounting for investments in associates, 500
accrual basis standards, 498–504
borrowing costs, 500
budgetary reporting, 497–498
cash basis standard, 495–497
cash flows, 509–510
cash or non-cash generating assets, 503
cash receipts and payments, 507–509
changes in net assets/equity, 516–517
consolidated financial statements, 500
construction contracts, 501
deficits, 499
employee benefits, 504
events after reporting date, 501–502
exchange transactions, revenue from, 500–501
financial performance, 514–515
financial position, 512–513
financial statements, 498–499, 500, 502
foreign exchange rates, 499
hyperinflationary economies, financial reporting of, 501
inventories, 501
investment property, 502
joint ventures, reporting of interests in, 500
leases, 501
net surplus, 499
optional budget to actual comparative statement, 511
property, plant, and equipment, 502
provisions, contingent liabilities and contingent assets, 503
related party disclosures, 503
revenue from non-exchange transaction, 504
steps for implementation, 504–506
Investment property, 502
Investment trust funds, 330–331
Invitation to comment, 8
IPSAS. *See* International Public Sector Accounting Standards (IPSAS)

IPSASB. *See* International Public Sector
    Accounting Standards Board
    (IPSASB)
IRS. *See* Internal Revenue Service (IRS)
Ives, Martin, 10, 37, 43

**J**

Joint Financial Management Improvement
    Program (JFMIP), 444, 448, 484
Joint ventures, reporting of interests in, 500

**K**

Klasny, Edward M., 26, 31, 42, 43, 65

**L**

Land endowment fund, 319
Landfills, 31, 32, 64, 166, 252
Leases, 194, 301
Legal defeasance, 210
Levying taxes, 172–173
Liabilities, 165, 187, 275, 293–303, 326, 503
Line-item budgeting, 87–89
Liquidity, 397–398
    indicators, 276
Loans, 194
Long-term liability, 17
Loss, 259

**M**

Mandolini, Anthony, 26, 27, 43
Mazur, Edward J., 43
Measurement focus, 158, 164, 254, 255
MFOA. *See* Municipal Finance Officers
    Association (MFOA)
Municipal Finance Officers Association
    (MFOA), 2, 3, 89

**N**

NACUBO. *See* National Association of College
    and University Business Officers
    (NACUBO)
NASACT. *See* National Association of State
    Auditors, Controllers, and Treasurers
    (NASACT)
National Advisory Council on State and Local
    Budgeting, 78–79

National Affordable Housing Trust Fund Act
    (2007), 468
National Association of College and University
    Business Officers (NACUBO), 9
National Association of State Auditors,
    Controllers, and Treasurers
    (NASACT), 9
National Committee on Governmental
    Accounting (NCGA), 4–7, 11, 28
    governmental accounting and financial
        reporting principles, 160
National Committee on Municipal Accounting
    (NCMA), 2, 3
NCGA. *See* National Committee on
    Governmental Accounting (NCGA)
NCMA. *See* National Committee on Municipal
    Accounting (NCMA)
Net assets, 188
Net cost, 472
Net surplus, 499
Nonaudit services
    acceptable and nonacceptable, 426–427
Nonoperating revenues, 306
Nontax revenues, 123–124
Notes, 194

**O**

Office of Management and Budget (OMB)
    Antideficiency Act, 461
    budget accounting, 461
    budget of the U. S., 460–461
    circular A-123, 486–487
    circular A-127, 487
    circular A-136, 487
    mission, 459–460
    on-and off- budget totals, 461
    required audited financial statements,
        462–463
On-behalf payments, 37
Operating position indicator, 395, 396
Operating revenues, 306
Operational accountability, 179
Outflow of resources, 188

**P**

Pension trust funds, 321–330
Performance budgeting, 89–103
    full-time equivalent employee approach, 94,
        97–101
    later developments, 101, 103

level-of-service approach, 92, 93
unit cost approach, 92, 94, 95–96
Permanent fund, 153
PERP. *See* Public entity risk pool (PERP)
Planning, Programming, Budgeting System
(PPBS), 103, 105–108
Postemployment benefits, 60
PPBS. *See* Planning, Programming, Budgeting
System (PPBS)
President's Commission on Budget Concepts
(1967), 446
Pricing, 259–260
Private-purpose trust fund, 332–335
Profit, 259
Program budgeting, 103–108
Property, 502
Property tax, 122
Proprietary funds, 150, 152, 154–155, 158,
250–314
debt indicators, 277–278
debt service indicators, 278
efficiency indicators, 278–279
financial ratios, 271, 274–279
financial statements, 157, 261–273
balance sheet, 262–264, 265–266
cash flow, 268, 271, 272–273
income, 264, 267–268
governmental funds *vs.,* 252–261
basis of accounting, 254, 256–257, 258
equity recognition, 257–259
measurement focus, 254, 255
pricing, 259–260
transfers, 260–261
liquidity indicators, 276
solvency indicators, 276–277
Public entity risk pool (PERP), 36
Public sector accounting, 493–506
accounting for investments in associates,
500
accrual basis standards, 498–504
borrowing costs, 500
budgetary reporting, 497–498
cash basis standard, 495–497
cash flows, 509–510
cash or non-cash generating assets, 503
cash receipts and payments, 507–509
changes in net assets/equity, 516–517
consolidated financial statements, 500
construction contracts, 501
deficits, 499
employee benefits, 504
events after reporting date, 501–502

exchange transactions, revenue from,
500–501
financial performance, 514–515
financial position, 512–513
financial statements, 498–499, 500, 502
foreign exchange rates, 499
hyperinflationary economies, financial
reporting of, 501
inventories, 501
investment property, 502
joint ventures, reporting of interests in, 500
leases, 501
net surplus, 499
optional budget to actual comparative
statement, 511
property, plant, and equipment, 502
provisions, contingent liabilities and
contingent assets, 503
related party disclosures, 503
revenue from non-exchange transaction, 504
steps for implementation, 504–506
Public Sector Committee, 493

**R**

Refunding, 16–17, 231, 232
advanced, 35, 195, 209, 212, 302
bonds, 195, 356
current, 195, 209
deferred bond, 263
defined, 209
disclosure requirements for advanced,
212–213
report, 35, 211–212
Reports Consolidation Act (2000), 462, 487
Revenue(s), 139–146
analysis, 112–117
anticipation notes, 186
bonds, 195, 300
combining statement, 308–309
federal, 139–140
intergovernmental grants as source of,
145–146
measures, 402–404
from non-exchange transaction, 504
nonoperating, 306
nontax, 123–124
operating, 306
sources, 139
state and local government, 141–144
Roosevelt, Franklin Delano, 2

**S**

Sales tax revenue, 186
Schedule of expenditures, 435–436
SEC. *See* Securities and Exchange Commission (SEC)
Securities Act (1933), 2
Securities Act (1934), 2
Securities and Exchange Commission (SEC), 2, 42
Self-insurance, 21
Serial bonds, 195
Service-level solvency, 404–407
Single Audit Act (1984), 422
Social insurance statement, 476
Solvency indicators, 276–277
Special revenue fund (SRF), 36, 152–153
SRF. *See* Special revenue fund (SRF)
Staats, Elmer B., 10, 42
State grant, 152
State law, 152

**T**

Tax(es)
    anticipation notes, 300
    collecting general, 172–173
    system evaluation, 114–117
    types of, 117–123
Taxation, methods of, 118–119, 122–123
Term bonds, 195
Term liability, 17, 32, 54

Transfers, 260–261
Treasury accounts, 468–469
Treasury Department
    government-wide accounting, 464
    government-wide financial reports, 463–464
    mission, 463
Trust funds, 467–468

**U**

U. S. government issue bonds, 17
Ultimate fund, 34
United States Government Standard General Ledger, 469–470

**V**

Voucher, 174

**W**

Warrant, 194–195
Wealth, 121–123
    defined, 121
    methods of taxation, 122–123
Williams, James M., 43

**Z**

Zero base budgeting, 108–112